Principles of Computer Security: CompTIA Security+™ and Beyond

Second Edition

■ About the Authors

Dr. Wm. Arthur Conklin is an assistant professor in the College of Technology at the University of Houston. Dr. Conklin has terminal degrees from the Naval Postgraduate School in electrical engineering and The University of Texas at San Antonio in business administration. Dr. Conklin's research interests lie in the areas of software assurance and the application of systems theory to security issues associated with critical infrastructures. His dissertation was on the motivating factors for home users in adopting security on their own PCs. He has coauthored four books on information security and has written and presented numerous conference and academic journal papers. He has over ten years of teaching experience at the college level and has assisted in building two information security programs that have been recognized by the NSA and DHS as Centers of Academic Excellence in Information Assurance Education. A former U.S. Navy officer, he was also previously the Technical Director at the Center for Infrastructure Assurance and Security at The University of Texas at San Antonio.

Dr. Gregory White has been involved in computer and network security since 1986. He spent 19 years on active duty with the U.S. Air Force and is currently in the Air Force Reserves assigned to the Pentagon. He obtained his Ph.D. in computer science from Texas A&M University in 1995. His dissertation topic was in the area of computer network intrusion detection, and he continues to conduct research in this area today. He is currently the Director for the Center for Infrastructure Assurance and Security (CIAS) and is an associate professor of computer science at The University of Texas at San Antonio (UTSA). Dr. White has written and presented numerous articles and conference papers on security. He is also the coauthor for five textbooks on computer and network security and has written chapters for two other security books. Dr. White continues to be active in security research. His current research initiatives include efforts in high-speed intrusion detection, community infrastructure protection, and visualization of community and organization security postures.

Dwayne Williams is Associate Director, Special Projects for the Center for Infrastructure Assurance and Security at the University of Texas at San Antonio and has over 18 years of experience in information systems and network security. Mr. Williams's experience includes six years of commissioned military service as a Communications-Computer Information Systems Officer in the U.S. Air Force, specializing in network security, corporate information protection, intrusion detection systems, incident response, and VPN technology. Prior to joining the CIAS, he served as Director of Consulting for SecureLogix Corporation, where he directed and provided security assessment and integration services to Fortune 100, government, public utility, oil and gas, financial, and technology clients. Mr. Williams graduated in 1993 from Baylor University with a Bachelor of Arts in Computer Science. Mr. Williams is a Certified Information Systems Security Professional (CISSP) and coauthor of McGraw-Hill's *Voice and Data Security* and *CompTIA Security+ All-in-One Exam Guide*.

Roger L. Davis, CISSP, CISM, CISA, is Program Manager of ERP systems at the Church of Jesus Christ of Latter-day Saints, managing the Church's global financial system in over 140 countries. He has served as president of the Utah chapter of the Information Systems Security Association (ISSA) and various board positions for the Utah chapter of the Information Systems Audit and Control Association (ISACA). He is a retired Air Force lieutenant colonel with 30 years of military and information systems/security experience. Mr. Davis served on the faculty of Brigham Young University and the Air Force Institute of Technology. He coauthored McGraw-Hill's *CompTIA Security+ All-in-One Exam Guide* and *Voice and Data Security*. He holds a master's degree in computer science from George Washington University, a bachelor's degree in computer science from Brigham Young University, and performed post-graduate studies in electrical engineering and computer science at the University of Colorado.

Chuck Cothren, CISSP, is the president of Globex Security, Inc., and applies a wide array of network security experience to consulting and training. This includes performing controlled penetration testing, network security policies, network intrusion detection systems, firewall configuration and management, and wireless security assessments. He has analyzed security methodologies for voice over IP (VoIP) systems and supervisory control and data acquisition (SCADA) systems. Mr. Cothren was previously employed at the University of Texas Center for Infrastructure Assurance and Security. He is coauthor of *Voice and Data Security* and *CompTIA Security+ All-in-One Exam Guide*. Mr. Cothren holds a B.S. in Industrial Distribution from Texas A&M University.

About the Technical Editor

Glen E. Clarke, MCSE, MCSD, MCDBA, MCT, CEH, SCNP, CCENT, A+, Security+, is an independent trainer and consultant, focusing on network security assessments and educating IT professionals on hacking countermeasures. Mr. Clark spends most of his time delivering certified courses on Windows Server, SQL Server, Exchange Server, Visual Basic .NET, ASP.NET, Ethical Hacking, Security Analysis, and Cisco devices. He has authored and technical edited a number of certification titles, including *Network+ Certification Study Guide, 4th Edition*. You can visit Mr. Clark online at www.gleneclarke.com or contact him at glenclarke@accesswave.ca.

Second Edition

Wm. Arthur Conklin
Gregory White
Dwayne Williams
Roger Davis
Chuck Cothren

New York Chicago San Francisco
Lisbon London Madrid Mexico City Milan
New Delhi San Juan Seoul Singapore Sydney Toronto

Cataloging-in-Publication Data is on file with the Library of Congress

Sponsoring Editor
TIMOTHY GREEN

Editorial Supervisor
JANET WALDEN

Project Editor
LeeAnn PICKRELL

Acquisitions Coordinator
MEGHAN RILEY

Technical Editor
GLEN CLARKE

Copy Editor
WILLIAM McMANUS

Proofreader
PAUL TYLER

Indexer
KARIN ARRIGONI

Production Supervisor
JEAN BODEAUX

Composition
GLYPH INTERNATIONAL

Illustration
GLYPH INTERNATIONAL

Art Director, Cover
JEFF WEEKS

McGraw-Hill books are available at special quantity discounts to use as premiums and sales promotions, or for use in corporate training programs. To contact a representative, please e-mail us at bulksales@mcgraw-hill.com.

Principles of Computer Security: CompTIA Security+™ and Beyond, Second Edition

1 2 3 4 5 6 7 8 9 0   WDQ WDQ   0 1 9

ISBN: Book p/n 978-0-07-163377-2 and CD p/n 978-0-07-163378-9 of set 978-0-07-163375-8

MHID: Book p/n 0-07-163377-4 and CD p/n 0-07-163378-2 of set 0-07-163375-8

This book is dedicated to the many security professionals who daily work to ensure the safety of our nation's critical infrastructures. We want to recognize the thousands of dedicated individuals who strive to protect our national assets but who seldom receive praise and often are only noticed when an incident occurs. To you, we say thank you for a job well done!

■ Acknowledgments

We, the authors of *Principles of Computer Security: CompTIA Security+™ and Beyond, Second Edition*, have many individuals who we need to acknowledge—individuals without whom this effort would not have been successful. This second edition would not have been possible without Tim Green, who navigated a myriad of problems and made life easier for the author team. He brought together an all-star production team that made this book more than just a new edition, but a complete learning system.

The list needs to start with those folks at McGraw-Hill who worked tirelessly with the project's multiple authors and contributors and lead us successfully through the minefield that is a book schedule and who took our rough chapters and drawings and turned them into a final, professional product we can be proud of. We thank all the good people from the Acquisitions team, Tim Green and Meghan Riley; from the Editorial Services team, Janet Walden and LeeAnn Pickrell; from the Illustration and Production teams, Jean Bodeaux and Amarjeet Kumar and the composition team at Glyph International. We also thank the technical editor, Glen Clarke; the copyeditor, Bill McManus; the proofreader, Paul Tyler; and the indexer, Karin Arrigoni, for all their attention to detail that made this a finer work after they finished with it.

We also need to acknowledge our current employers who, to our great delight, have seen fit to pay us to work in a career field that we all find exciting and rewarding. There is never a dull moment in security, because it is constantly changing.

We would like to thank Art Conklin for herding the cats on this one.

Finally, we would each like to individually thank those people who—on a personal basis—have provided the core support for us individually. Without these special people in our lives, none of us could have put this work together.

I would like to thank my wife, best friend, muse, and love, Susan, for all the sacrifices she has made as I changed schools, moved, and stole family time to play cat herder one more time. Without her support, I could not accomplish half of what I do.

—*Art Conklin, Ph.D.*

I would like to thank my wife, Charlan, for the tremendous support she has always given me. It doesn't matter how many times I have sworn that I'll never get involved with another book project only to return within months to yet another one; through it all, she has remained supportive.

I would also like to publicly thank the United States Air Force, which provided me numerous opportunities since 1986 to learn more about security than I ever knew existed.

To whoever it was who decided to send me as a young captain—fresh from completing my master's degree in artificial intelligence—to my first assignment in computer security: thank you, it has been a great adventure!

—*Gregory B. White, Ph.D.*

For Macon.

—*Chuck Cothren*

Geena, thanks for being my best friend and my greatest support. Anything I am is because of you. Love to my kids and grandkids!

—*Roger L. Davis*

To my wife and best friend Leah for your love, energy, and support—thank you for always being there. Here's to many more years together.

—*Dwayne Williams*

ABOUT THIS BOOK

■ Important Technology Skills

Information technology (IT) offers many career paths and information security is one of the fastest-growing tracks for IT professionals. This book provides coverage of the materials you need to begin your exploration of information security.

In addition to covering all of the CompTIA Security+ exam objectives, additional material is included to help you build a solid introductory knowledge of information security.

Key Terms, identified in red, point out important vocabulary and definitions that you need to know.

Tech Tip sidebars provide inside information from experienced information security professionals.

Cross Check questions develop reasoning skills: ask, compare, contrast, and explain.

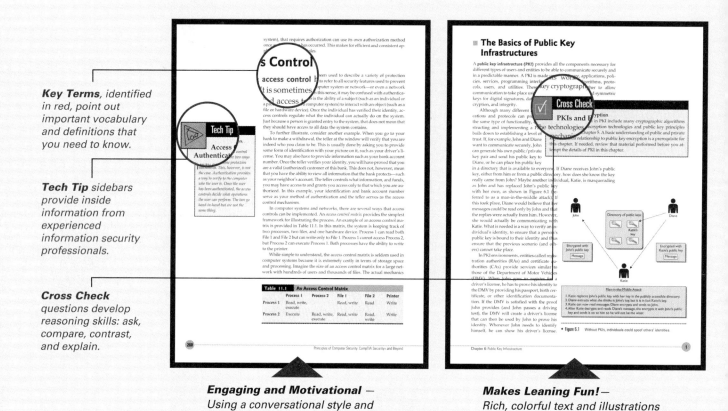

Engaging and Motivational — Using a conversational style and proven instructional approach, the authors explain technical subjects in a clear, interesting way using real-world examples.

Makes Leaning Fun! — Rich, colorful text and illustrations bring technical concepts to life.

Proven Learning Method Keeps You on Track

Designed for classroom use and written by instructors for use in their own classes, Principles of Computer Security: CompTIA Security+ and Beyond is structured to give you comprehensive knowledge of information security. The textbook's active learning methodology guides you beyond mere recall and—through thought-provoking activities, labs, and sidebars—helps you develop critical-thinking, diagnostic, and communication skills.

Effective Learning Tools

This feature-rich textbook is designed to make learning easy and enjoyable and to help you develop the skills and critical thinking abilities that will enable you to adapt to different job situations and to troubleshoot problems. Written by instructors with decades of combined information security experience, this book conveys even the most complex issues in an accessible, easy-to-understand format.

Offers Practical Experience—
Tutorials and lab assignments develop essential hands-on skills and put concepts in real-world contexts.

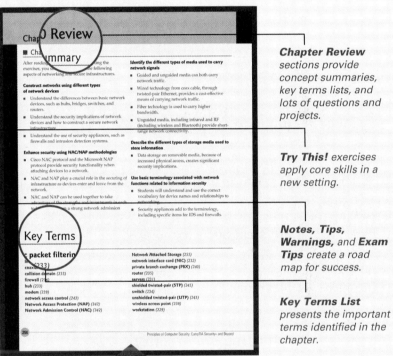

Robust Learning Tools—
Summaries, key term lists, quizzes, essay questions, and lab projects help you practice skills and measure progress.

Chapter Review sections provide concept summaries, key terms lists, and lots of questions and projects.

Try This! exercises apply core skills in a new setting.

Notes, Tips, Warnings, and **Exam Tips** create a road map for success.

Key Terms List presents the important terms identified in the chapter.

Each chapter includes:

- **Learning Objectives** that set measurable goals for chapter-by-chapter progress
- **Illustrations** that give you a clear picture of the concepts and technologies
- **Try This!**, **Cross Check**, and **Tech Tip** sidebars that encourage you to practice and apply concepts in real-world settings
- **Notes**, **Tips**, and **Warnings** that guide you, and **Exam Tips** that give you advice or provide information specifically related to preparing for the exam

- **Chapter Summaries** and **Key Terms Lists** that provide you with an easy way to review important concepts and vocabulary
- **Challenging End-of-Chapter Tests** that include vocabulary-building exercises, multiple-choice questions, essay questions, and on-the-job lab projects

CONTENTS AT A GLANCE

CONTENTS

Chapter 13
■ Intrusion Detection Systems and Network Security 318

Chapter 14
■ Baselines 358

Chapter 15
■ Types of Attacks and Malicious Software 388

PREFACE

Information and computer security has moved from the confines of academia to mainstream America in the last decade. The Code Red, Nimda, and Slammer attacks were heavily covered in the media and broadcast into the average American's home. Today, the Internet has turned 40, and with its maturing, the threats are increasing. Botnets and cyber-criminals are making news regularly. It has become increasingly obvious to everybody that something needs to be done to secure not only our nation's critical infrastructure but also the businesses we deal with on a daily basis. The question is, "Where do we begin?" What can the average information technology professional do to secure the systems that he or she is hired to maintain? One immediate answer is education and training. If we want to secure our computer systems and networks, we need to know how to do this and what security entails.

Complacency is not an option in today's hostile network environment. While we once considered the insider to be the major threat to corporate networks, and the "script kiddie" to be the standard external threat (often thought of as only a nuisance), the highly interconnected network world of today is a much different place. The U.S. government identified eight critical infrastructures a few years ago that were thought to be so critical to the nation's daily operation that if one were to be lost, it would have a catastrophic impact on the nation. To this original set of eight sectors, more have recently been added. A common thread throughout all of these, however, is technology—especially technology related to computers and communication. Thus, an individual, organization, or nation who wanted to cause damage to this nation could attack it not just with traditional weapons but with computers through the Internet. It is not surprising to hear that among the other information seized in raids on terrorist organizations, computers and Internet information are usually seized as well. While the insider can certainly still do tremendous damage to an organization, the external threat is again becoming the chief concern among many.

So, where do you, the IT professional seeking more knowledge on security, start your studies? The IT world is overflowing with certifications that can be obtained by those attempting to learn more about their chosen profession. The security sector is no different, and the CompTIA Security+ exam offers a basic level of certification for security. In the pages of this book you will find not only material that can help you prepare for taking the CompTIA Security+ exam but also the basic information that you will need in order to understand the issues involved in securing your computer systems and networks today. In no way is this book the final source for learning all about protecting your organization's systems, but it serves as a point from which to launch your security studies and career.

One thing is certainly true about this field of study—it never gets boring. It constantly changes as technology itself advances. Something else you will find as you progress in your security studies is that no matter how much technology advances and no matter how many new security devices are developed, at its most basic level, the human is still the weak link in the security chain. If you are looking for an exciting area to delve into, then you have certainly chosen wisely. Security offers a challenging blend of technology and people issues. We, the authors of this book, wish you luck as you embark on an exciting and challenging career path.

Wm. Arthur Conklin, Ph.D.
Gregory B. White, Ph.D.

INTRODUCTION

Computer security is becoming increasingly important today as the number of security incidents steadily climbs. Many corporations are now spending significant portions of their budget on security hardware, software, services, and personnel. They are spending this money not because it increases sales or enhances the product they provide, but because of the possible consequences should they not take protective actions.

Why Focus on Security?

Security is not something that we want to have to pay for; it would be nice if we didn't have to worry about protecting our data from disclosure, modification, or destruction from unauthorized individuals, but that is not the environment we find ourselves in today. Instead, we have seen the cost of recovering from security incidents steadily rise along with the rise in the number of incidents themselves. Since September 11, 2001, this has taken on an even greater sense of urgency as we now face securing our systems not just from attack by disgruntled employees, juvenile hackers, organized crime, or competitors; we now also have to consider the possibility of attacks on our systems from terrorist organizations. If nothing else, the events of September 11, 2001, showed that anybody is a potential target. You do not have to be part of the government or a government contractor; being an American is sufficient reason to make you a target to some, and with the global nature of the Internet, collateral damage from cyber attacks on one organization could have a worldwide impact.

A Growing Need for Security Specialists

To protect our computer systems and networks, we will need a significant number of new security professionals trained in the many aspects of computer and network security. This is not an easy task as the systems connected to the Internet become increasingly complex, with software whose lines of code number in the millions. Understanding why this is such a difficult problem to solve is not hard if you consider how many errors might be present in a piece of software that is several million lines long. When you add the additional factor of how fast software is being developed—from necessity as the market is constantly moving—understanding how errors occur is easy.

Not every "bug" in the software will result in a security hole, but it doesn't take many to affect the Internet community drastically. We can't just blame the vendors for this situation, because they are reacting to the demands of government and industry. Most vendors are fairly adept at developing patches for flaws found in their software, and patches are constantly issued to protect systems from bugs that may introduce security problems. This introduces a whole new problem for managers and administrators—patch management. How important this has become is easily illustrated by how many of the most recent security events have occurred as a result of a security bug for which a patch was available months prior to the security incident; members of the community had not correctly installed the patch, however, thus making the incident possible. One of the reasons this happens is that many of the individuals responsible for installing the patches are not trained to understand the security implications surrounding the hole or the ramifications of not installing the patch. Many of these individuals simply lack the necessary training.

Because of the need for an increasing number of security professionals who are trained to some minimum level of understanding, certifications such as the Security+ have been developed. Prospective employers want to know that the individual they are considering hiring knows what to do in terms of security. The prospective employee, in turn, wants to have a way to demonstrate his or her level of understanding, which can enhance the candidate's chances of being hired. The community as a whole simply wants more trained security professionals.

Preparing Yourself for the Security+ Exam

Principles of Computer Security: CompTIA Security+ and Beyond, Second Edition is designed to help prepare you to take the Security+ certification exam. When you pass it, you will demonstrate you have that basic understanding of security that employers are looking for. Passing this certification exam will not be an easy task, for you will need to learn many things to acquire that basic understanding of computer and network security.

How This Book Is Organized

The book is divided into chapters to correspond with the objectives of the exam itself. Some of the chapters are more technical than others—reflecting the nature of the security environment where you will be forced to deal with not only technical details but also other issues such as security policies and procedures as well as training and education. Although many individuals involved in computer and network security have advanced degrees in math, computer science, information systems, or computer or electrical engineering, you do not need this technical background to address security effectively in your organization. You do not need to develop your own cryptographic algorithm, for example; you simply need to be able to understand how cryptography is used, along with its strengths and weaknesses.

As you progress in your studies, you will learn that many security problems are caused by the human element. The best technology in the world still ends up being placed in an environment where humans have the opportunity to foul things up—and all too often do.

Onward and Upward

At this point, we hope that you are now excited about the topic of security, even if you weren't in the first place. We wish you luck in your endeavors and welcome you to the exciting field of computer and network security.

The logo of the CompTIA Authorized Quality Curriculum (CAQC) program and the status of this or other training material as "Authorized" under the CompTIA Authorized Quality Curriculum program signifies that, in CompTIA's opinion, such training material covers the content of CompTIA's related certification exam.

The contents of this training material were created for the CompTIA Security+™ exam covering CompTIA certification objectives that were current as of late 2008.

CompTIA has not reviewed or approved the accuracy of the contents of this training material and specifically disclaims any warranties of merchantability or fitness for a particular purpose.

CompTIA makes no guarantee concerning the success of persons using any such "Authorized" or other training material in order to prepare for any CompTIA certification exam.

■ How to Become CompTIA Certified

This training material can help you prepare for and pass a related CompTIA certification exam or exams. In order to achieve CompTIA certification, you must register for and pass a CompTIA certification exam or exams.

In order to become CompTIA certified, you must:

1. Select a certification exam provider. For more information please visit http://www.comptia.org/certifications/testprep/testingcenters.aspx.

2. Register for and schedule a time to take the CompTIA certification exam(s) at a convenient location.

3. Read and sign the Candidate Agreement, which will be presented at the time of the exam(s). The text of the Candidate Agreement can be found at http://www.comptia.org/certifications/testprep/policies/agreement.aspx.

4. Take and pass the CompTIA certification exam(s).

For more information about CompTIA's certifications, such as its industry acceptance, benefits, or program news, please visit www.comptia.org/certification.

CompTIA is a not-for-profit information technology (IT) trade association. CompTIA's certifications are designed by subject matter experts from across the IT industry. Each CompTIA certification is vendor-neutral, covers multiple technologies and requires demonstration of skills and knowledge widely sought after by the IT industry.

To contact CompTIA with any questions or comments, please call (1) (630) 678-8300 or email questions@comptia.org.

For instructor and student resources, check out www.securityplusOLC .com. Students will find chapter quizzes that will help them learn more about troubleshooting and fixing networks, and teachers can access support materials.

Additional Resources for Teachers

Resources for teachers are provided via an Online Learning Center that maps to the organization of the textbook. This site includes the following:

- Answer keys to the end-of-chapter activities in the textbook
- Answer keys to the lab manual activities
- Access to testbank files and software that allows you to generate a wide array of paper- or network-based tests, and that features automatic grading
- Hundreds of practice questions and a wide variety of question types and difficulty levels, enabling you to customize each test to maximize student progress
- Blackboard cartridges and other formats may also be available upon request; contact your sales representative
- Engaging PowerPoint slides on the lecture topics (include full-color artwork from the book)

Introduction and Security Trends

Security is mostly a superstition. It does not exist in nature, nor do the children of men as a whole experience it. Avoiding danger is no safer in the long run than outright exposure. Life is either a daring adventure or nothing.

—HELEN KELLER

In this chapter, you will learn how to

■ **List and discuss recent trends in computer security**

■ **Describe simple steps to take to minimize the possibility of an attack on a system**

■ **Describe various types of threats that exist for computers and networks**

■ **Discuss recent computer crimes that have been committed**

Why should we be concerned about computer and network security? All you have to do is turn on the television or read the newspaper to find out about a variety of security problems that affect our nation and the world today. The danger to computers and networks may seem to pale in comparison to the threat of terrorist strikes, but in fact the average citizen is much more likely to be the target of an attack on their own personal computer, or a computer they use at their place of work, than they are to be the direct victim of a terrorist attack. This chapter will introduce you to a number of issues involved in securing your computers and networks from a variety of threats that may utilize any of a number of different attacks.

The Security Problem

Fifty years ago, few people had access to a computer system or network, so securing them was a relatively easy matter. If you could secure the building that these early, very large systems were housed in, you could secure the data and information they stored and processed. Now, personal computers are ubiquitous and portable, making them much more difficult to secure physically, and are often connected to the Internet, putting the data they contain at much greater risk of attack or theft. Similarly, the typical computer user today is not as technically sophisticated as the typical computer user 50 years ago. No longer are computers reserved for use by scientists and engineers; now, even children who are barely able to read can be taught to boot a computer and gain access to their own favorite games or educational software.

Fifty years ago companies did not conduct business across the Internet. Online banking and shopping were only dreams in science fiction stories. Today, however, millions of people perform online transactions every day. Companies rely on the Internet to operate and conduct business. Vast amounts of money are transferred via networks, in the form of either bank transactions or simple credit card purchases. Wherever there are vast amounts of money, there are those who will try to take advantage of the environment to conduct fraud or theft. There are many different ways to attack computers and networks to take advantage of what has made shopping, banking, investment, and leisure pursuits a simple matter of "dragging and clicking" for many people. Identity theft is so common today that most everyone knows somebody who's been a victim of such a crime, if they haven't been a victim themselves. This is just one type of criminal activity that can be conducted using the Internet. There are many others and all are on the rise.

Tech Tip

Historical Security
Computer security is an ever-changing issue. Fifty years ago, computer security was mainly concerned with the physical devices that made up the computer. At the time, these were the high-value items that organizations could not afford to lose. Today, computer equipment is inexpensive compared to the value of the data processed by the computer. Now the high-value item is not the machine, but the information that it stores and processes. This has fundamentally changed the focus of computer security from what it was in the early years. Today the data stored and processed by computers is almost always more valuable than the hardware.

Security Incidents

By examining some of the computer-related crimes that have been committed over the last 20 or so years, we can better understand the threats and security issues that surround our computer systems and networks. Electronic crime can take a number of different forms but the ones we will examine here fall into two basic categories: crimes in which the computer was the target, and incidents in which a computer was used to perpetrate the act (for example, there are many different ways to conduct bank fraud, one of which uses computers to access the records that banks process and maintain).

We will start our tour of computer crimes with the 1988 Internet worm (Morris worm), one of the first real Internet crime cases. Prior to 1988 criminal activity was chiefly centered on unauthorized access to computer systems and networks owned by the telephone company and companies which provided dial-up access for authorized users. Virus activity also existed prior to 1988, having started in the early 1980s.

The Morris Worm (November 1988)

Robert Morris, then a graduate student at Cornell University, released what has become known as the Internet worm (or the Morris worm). This was the first large-scale attack on the Internet, though it appears doubtful that

Morris actually intended that his creation cause the impact that it did at the time. The worm infected roughly 10 percent of the machines then connected to the Internet (which amounted to approximately 6000 infected machines) and caused an estimated $100 million in damage, though this number has been the subject of wide debate. The worm carried no malicious payload, the program being obviously a "work in progress," but it did wreak havoc because it continually reinfected computer systems until they could no longer run any programs. The worm took advantage of known vulnerabilities in several programs to gain access to new hosts and then copied itself over. Morris was eventually convicted under Title 10 United States Code Section 1030 for releasing the worm and was sentenced to three years' probation, a $10,000 fine, and 400 hours of community service.

Citibank and Vladimir Levin (June–October 1994)

Starting about June of 1994 and continuing until at least October of the same year, a number of bank transfers were made by Vladimir Levin of St. Petersburg, Russia. By the time he and his accomplices were caught, they had transferred an estimated $10 million. Eventually all but about $400,000 was recovered. Levin reportedly accomplished the break-ins by dialing into Citibank's cash management system. This system allowed clients to initiate their own fund transfers to other banks. An estimated $500 billion was transferred daily during this period, so the amounts transferred by Levin were very small in comparison to the overall total on any given day. To avoid detection, he also conducted the transactions at night in Russia so that they coincided with normal business hours in New York. Levin was arrested in London in 1995 and, after fighting extradition for 30 months, eventually was turned over to U.S. authorities, was tried, and was sentenced to three years in jail. Four accomplices of Levin plead guilty to conspiracy to commit bank fraud and received lesser sentences.

Kevin Mitnick (February 1995)

Kevin Mitnick's computer activities occurred over a number of years during the 1980s and 1990s. He was arrested in February 1995 (not his first arrest on computer criminal charges) for federal offenses related to what the FBI described as a 2½-year computer hacking spree. He eventually pled guilty to four counts of wire fraud, two counts of computer fraud, and one count of illegally intercepting a wire communication and was sentenced to 46 months in jail. In the plea agreement, Mitnick admitted to having gained unauthorized access to a number of different computer systems belonging to companies such as Motorola, Novell, Fujitsu, and Sun Microsystems. He described using a number of different "tools" and techniques, including social engineering, sniffers, and cloned cellular telephones. Mitnick also admitted to having used stolen accounts at the University of Southern California to store proprietary software he had taken from various companies. He also admitted to stealing e-mails and impersonating employees of targeted companies in order to gain access to the software he was seeking.

Omega Engineering and Timothy Lloyd (July 1996)

On July 30, 1996, a software "time bomb" went off at Omega Engineering, a New Jersey–based manufacturer of high-tech measurement and control instruments. Twenty days earlier, Timothy Lloyd, a computer network program designer, had been dismissed from the company after a period of growing tension between Lloyd and management at Omega. The program that ran on July 30 deleted all of the design and production programs for the company, severely damaging the small firm and forcing the layoff of 80 employees. The program was eventually traced back to Lloyd, who had left it in retaliation for his dismissal. In May of 2000, a federal judge sentenced Lloyd to 41 months in prison and ordered him to pay more than $2 million in restitution.

Worcester Airport and "Jester" (March 1997)

In March of 1997, airport services to the FAA control tower as well as the emergency services at the Worcester Airport and the community of Rutland, Massachusetts, were cut off for a period of six hours. This disruption occurred as a result of a series of commands sent by a teenage computer "hacker" who went by the name "Jester." The individual had gained unauthorized access to the "loop carrier system" operated by NYNEX, a New England telephone company. Loop carrier systems are programmable remote computer systems used to integrate voice and data communications. Jester was eventually caught and ordered to pay restitution to the telephone company, as well as complete 250 hours of community service.

Solar Sunrise (February 1998)

In January of 1998, relations between Iraq and the United States again took a turn for the worse and it appeared as if the United States might take military action against Iraq. During this period of increased tension and military preparation, a series of computer intrusions occurred at a number of U.S. military installations. At first the military thought that this might be the start of an information warfare attack—a possibility the military had been discussing since the early 1990s. Over 500 domain name servers were compromised during the course of the attacks. Making it harder to track the actual origin of the attacks was the fact that the attackers made a number of "hops" between different systems, averaging eight different systems before arriving at the target. The attackers eventually turned out to be two teenagers from California and their mentor in Israel. The attacks, as it turned out, had nothing to do with the potential conflict in Iraq.

The Melissa Virus (March 1999)

Melissa is the best known of the early macro-type viruses that attach themselves to documents for programs that have limited macro programming capability. The virus, written and released by David Smith, infected about a million computers and caused an estimated $80 million in damages. Melissa, which clogged networks with the traffic it generated and caused problems for e-mail servers worldwide, was attached to Microsoft Word 97 and Word 2000 documents. If the user opened the file, the macro ran, infecting the current host and also sending itself to the first 50 addresses in the individual's e-mail address book. The e-mail sent contained a subject line stating "Important Message From" and then included the name of the individual who was infected. The body of the e-mail message contained the text "Here is that document you asked for … don't show anyone else ;-)." The nature of both the subject line and

Tech Tip

Intellectual Curiosity

In the early days of computer crime, much of the criminal activity centered on gaining unauthorized access to computer systems. In many early cases, the perpetrator of the crime did not intend to cause any damage to the computer but was instead on a quest of "intellectual curiosity"— trying to learn more about computers and networks. Today the ubiquitous nature of computers and networks has eliminated the perceived need for individuals to break into computers to learn more about them. While there are still those who dabble in hacking for the intellectual challenge, it is more common today for the intellectual curiosity to be replaced by malicious intent. Whatever the reason, today it is considered unacceptable (and illegal) to gain unauthorized access to computer systems and networks.

the body of the message usually generated enough user curiosity that many people opened the document and thus infected their system, which in turn sent the same message to 50 of their acquaintances. As a final action, if the minute of the current hour when the macro was run matched the day of the month, the macro inserted "Twenty-two points, plus triple-word-score, plus fifty points for using all my letters. Game's over. I'm outta here." into the current document. Smith, who plead guilty, was ultimately fined $5000 and sentenced to 20 months in jail for the incident. Because the macro code is easy to modify, there have been many variations of the Melissa virus. Recipients could avoid infection by Melissa simply by not opening the attached file.

The Love Letter Virus (May 2000)

Also known as the "ILOVEYOU" worm and the "Love Bug," the Love Letter virus was written and released by a Philippine student named Onel de Guzman. The virus was spread via e-mail with the subject line of "ILOVEYOU." Estimates of the number of infected machines worldwide have been as high as 45 million, accompanied by a possible $10 billion in damages (it should be noted that figures like these are extremely hard to verify or calculate). Similar to the Melissa virus, the Love Letter virus spread via an e-mail attachment, but in this case, instead of utilizing macros, the attachments were VBScript programs. When the receiver ran the attachment, it searched the system for files with specific extensions in order to replace them with copies of itself. It also sent itself to everyone in the user's address book. Again, since the receiver generally knew the sender, most individuals opened the attachment without questioning it. de Guzman ultimately was not convicted for releasing the worm because the Philippines, at the time, did not have any laws denoting the activity as a crime. Again, recipients avoided infection from the virus simply by not opening the attachments.

The Code Red Worm (2001)

On July 19, 2001, over 350,000 computers connected to the Internet were infected by the Code Red worm. This infection took only 14 hours to occur. The cost estimate for how much damage the worm caused (including variations of the worm released on later dates) exceeded $2.5 billion. The vulnerability exploited by the Code Red worm had been known for a month. The worm took advantage of a buffer-overflow condition in Microsoft's IIS web servers. Microsoft released a patch for this vulnerability and made an official announcement of the problem on June 18, 2001. The worm itself was "memory resident," so simply turning off an infected machine eliminated it. Unfortunately, unless the system was patched before being reconnected to the Internet, chances were good that it would soon become reinfected. Though the worm didn't carry a malicious payload designed to destroy data on the infected system, on some systems, the message "Hacked by Chinese" was added to the top-level page for the infected host's web site. If the date on the infected system was between the 1st and the 19th of the month, the worm would attempt to infect a random list of IP addresses it generated. If the date was between the 20th and the 28th of the month, the worm stopped trying to infect other systems and instead attempted to launch a denial-of-service (DoS) attack against a web site owned by the White House. After the 28th, the worm would lay dormant until the 1st of the next month. This date scheme actually ended up helping to eliminate the worm, because soon after it was released on the 19th, the worm stopped trying to infect systems. This provided a period of time when systems could be rebooted and patched before they were infected again.

Adil Yahya Zakaria Shakour (August 2001–May 2002)

On March 13, 2003, 19-year-old Adil Yahya Zakaria Shakour plead guilty to a variety of crimes, including unauthorized access to computer systems and credit card fraud. Shakour admitted to having accessed several computers without authorization, including a server at Eglin Air Force Base (where he defaced the web site), computers at Accenture (a Chicago-based management consulting and technology services company), a computer system at Sandia National Laboratories (a Department of Energy facility), and a computer at Cheaptaxforms.com. Shakour admitted to having obtained credit card and personal information during the break-in of Cheaptaxforms.com and having used it to purchase items worth over $7000 for his own use. Shakour was sentenced to one year and one day in federal prison and a three-year term of supervised release, and was ordered to pay $88,000 in restitution.

The Slammer Worm (2003)

On Saturday, January 25, 2003, the Slammer worm (also sometimes referred to as the Slammer virus) was released. It exploited a buffer-overflow vulnerability in computers running Microsoft's SQL Server or Microsoft SQL Server Desktop Engine. Like the vulnerability in Code Red, this weakness was not new and, in fact, had been discovered in July of 2002; Microsoft issued a patch for the vulnerability before it was even announced. Within the first 24 hours of Slammer's release, the worm had infected at least 120,000 hosts and caused network outages and the disruption of airline flights, elections, and ATMs. At its peak, Slammer-infected hosts were generating a reported 1TB of worm-related traffic *every second*. The worm doubled its number of infected hosts every 8 seconds. It is estimated that it took less than ten minutes to reach global proportions and infect 90 percent of the possible hosts it could infect. Once a machine was infected, the host would start randomly selecting targets and sending packets to them to attempt infection at a rate of 25,000 packets per second. Slammer did not contain a malicious payload. The problems it caused were a result of the massively overloaded networks, which could not sustain the traffic being generated by the thousands of infected hosts. The worm sent its single packet to a specific UDP port, 1434, which provided an immediate fix to prevent further network access. Thus, the response of administrators was to quickly block all traffic to UDP port 1434, effectively curbing the spread of the worm to new machines.

Tech Tip

Speed of Virus Proliferation
The speed at which the Slammer virus spread served as a wakeup call to security professionals. It drove home the point that the Internet could be adversely impacted in a matter of minutes. This in turn caused a number of professionals to rethink how prepared they needed to be in order to respond to virus outbreaks in the future. A good first step is to apply patches to systems and software as soon as possible. This will often eliminate the vulnerabilities that the worms and viruses are designed to target.

U.S. Electric Power Grid (1997–2009)

In April 2009, Homeland Security Secretary Janet Napolitano told reporters that the United States was aware of attempts by both Russia and China to break into the U.S. electric power grid, map it out, and plant destructive programs that could be activated at a later date. She indicated that these attacks were not new and had in fact been going on for years. One article in the *Kansas City Star*, for example, reported that in 1997 the local power company, Kansas City

Try This

Software Patches

One of the most effective measures security professionals can take to address attacks on their computer systems and networks is to ensure that all software is up-to-date in terms of vendor-released patches. Many of the outbreaks of viruses and worms would have been much less severe if everybody had applied security updates and patches when they were released. For the operating system that you use, use your favorite web browser to find what patches exist for the operating system and what vulnerabilities or issues they were created to address.

Power and Light, saw perhaps 10,000 attacks for the entire year. In contrast, in 2009 the company has been experiencing 10 to 20 attacks every second. While none of these attacks is credited with causing any significant loss of power, the attacks nonetheless highlight the fact that the nation's critical infrastructures are viewed as potential targets by other nations. In the event of some future conflict, the United States could expect to experience a cyber attack on the cyber infrastructures that operate its critical systems.

Conficker (2008–2009)

In late 2008 and early 2009, security experts became alarmed when it was discovered that millions of systems attached to the Internet were infected with the Downadup worm. Also known as Conficker, the worm was first detected in November 2008 and was believed to have originated in Ukraine. Infected systems were not initially damaged beyond having their antivirus solution updates blocked. What alarmed experts was the fact that infected systems could be used in a secondary attack on other systems or networks. Each of these infected systems was part of what is known as a *bot network* and could be used to cause a DoS attack on a target or be used for the forwarding of spam e-mail to millions of users. It was widely believed that this network of subverted systems would be activated on April 1, 2009, and would result in the widespread loss of data and system connectivity. As it turned out, very little damage was done on that date, though millions of dollars were spent in responding to the millions of infected systems.

Fiber Cable Cut (2009)

On April 9, 2009, a widespread phone and Internet outage hit the San Jose area in California. This outage was not the result of a group of determined hackers gaining unauthorized access to the computers that operate these networks, but instead occurred as a result of several cuts in the physical cables that carry the signals. A cable being cut is not an unusual occurrence; backhoes have been responsible for many temporary interruptions in telephone service in the past decade. What was unusual, and significant, about this incident was that the cuts were deliberate. A manhole cover had been removed to allow the attacker(s) to gain access to the cables underground. The cuts resulted in a loss of all telephone, cell phone, and Internet service for thousands of users in the San Jose area. Emergency services such as 911 were also affected, which could have had severe consequences. What is important to take away from this incident is the fact that the infrastructures that our communities, states, and the nation rely on can also be easily attacked using fairly simple physical techniques and without a lot of technical expertise.

Threats to Security

The incidents described in the previous section provide a glimpse into the many different threats that face administrators as they attempt to protect their computer systems and networks. There are, of course, the normal natural disasters that organizations have faced for years. In today's highly networked world, however, new threats have developed that we did not have to worry about 50 years ago.

There are a number of ways that we can break down the various threats. One way to categorize them is to separate threats that come from outside of the organization from those that are internal. Another is to look at the various levels of sophistication of the attacks, from those by "script kiddies" to those by "elite hackers." A third is to examine the level of organization of the various threats, from unstructured threats to highly structured threats. All of these are valid approaches, and they in fact overlap each other. The following sections examine threats from the perspective of where the attack comes from.

Viruses and Worms

While your organization may be exposed to viruses and worms as a result of employees not following certain practices or procedures, generally you will not have to worry about your employees writing or releasing viruses and worms. It is important to draw a distinction between the writers of malware and those who release them. Debates over the ethics of writing viruses permeate the industry, but currently, simply writing them is not considered a criminal activity. A virus is like a baseball bat; the bat itself is not evil, but the inappropriate use of the bat (such as to smash a car's window) falls into the category of criminal activity. (Some may argue that this is not a very good analogy since a baseball bat has a useful purpose—to play ball—but viruses *have* no useful purpose. In general, this is true but in some limited environments, such as in specialized computer science courses, the study and creation of viruses can be considered a useful learning experience.)

By far, viruses and worms are the most common problem that an organization faces because literally thousands of them have been created and released. Fortunately, antivirus software and system patching can eliminate the largest portion of this threat. Viruses and worms generally are also nondiscriminating threats; they are released on the Internet in a general fashion and aren't targeted at a specific organization. They typically are also highly visible once released, so they aren't the best tool to use in highly structured attacks where secrecy is vital. This is not to say that the technology used in virus and worm propagation won't be used by highly organized criminal groups, but its use for what these individuals are normally interested in accomplishing is limited. The same cannot be said for terrorist organizations, which generally want to create a large impact and have it be highly visible.

Tech Tip

Malware
Viruses and worms are just two types of threats that fall under the general heading of malware. *The term malware comes from "malicious software," which describes the overall purpose of code that falls into this category of threat. Malware is software that has a nefarious purpose, designed to cause problems to you as an individual (for example, identity theft) or your system. More information on the different types of malware is provided in Chapter 15.*

Intruders

The act of deliberately accessing computer systems and networks without authorization is generally referred to as **hacking**, with individuals who conduct this activity being referred to as **hackers**. The term hacking also applies to the act of exceeding one's authority in a system. This would include authorized users who attempt to gain access to files they aren't permitted to access or who attempt to obtain permissions that they have not been granted. While the act of breaking into computer systems and networks has been glorified in the media and movies, the physical act does not live up to the Hollywood hype. Intruders are, if nothing else, extremely patient, since the process to gain access to a system takes persistence and dogged determination. The attacker will conduct many preattack activities in order to obtain the information needed to determine which attack will most likely be successful. Generally, by the time an attack is launched, the attacker will have gathered enough information to be very confident that the attack will succeed. If it doesn't, the attacker will gather additional information and take a different approach (though launching the first attack may alert security personnel). Generally, attacks by an individual or even a small group of attackers fall into the **unstructured threat** category. Attacks at this level generally are conducted over short periods of time (lasting at most a few months), do not involve a large number of individuals, have little financial backing, and are accomplished by insiders or outsiders who do not seek collusion with insiders.

Intruders, or those who are attempting to conduct an intrusion, definitely come in many different varieties and have varying degrees of sophistication (see Figure 1.1). At the low end technically are what are generally referred to as **script kiddies**, individuals who do not have the technical expertise to develop scripts or discover new vulnerabilities in software but who have just enough understanding of computer systems to be able to download and run scripts that others have developed. These individuals generally are not interested in attacking specific targets, but instead simply want to find any organization that may not have patched a newly discovered vulnerability for which the script kiddie has located a script to exploit the vulnerability. It is hard to estimate how many of the individuals performing activities such as probing networks or scanning individual systems are part of this group, but it is undoubtedly the fastest growing group and the vast majority of the "unfriendly" activity occurring on the Internet is probably carried out by these individuals.

At the next level are those people who are capable of writing scripts to exploit known vulnerabilities. These individuals are much more technically competent than script kiddies and account for an estimated 8 to 12 percent of malicious Internet activity. At the top end of this spectrum are those highly technical individuals, often referred to as **elite hackers**, who not only have the ability to write scripts that exploit vulnerabilities but also are capable of discovering new vulnerabilities. This group is the smallest of the lot, however, and is responsible for, at most, only 1 to 2 percent of intrusive activity.

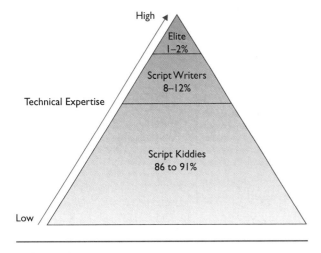

● **Figure 1.1**   Distribution of attacker skill levels

Insiders

It is generally acknowledged by security professionals that insiders are more dangerous in many respects than outside intruders. The reason for this is simple—insiders have the access and knowledge necessary to cause immediate damage to an organization. Most security is designed to protect against outside intruders and thus lies at the boundary between the organization and the rest of the world. Insiders may actually already have all the access they need to perpetrate criminal activity such as fraud. In addition to unprecedented access, insiders also frequently have knowledge of the security systems in place and are better able to avoid detection. Attacks by insiders are often the result of employees who have become disgruntled with their organization and are looking for ways to disrupt operations. It is also possible that an "attack" by an insider may be an accident and not intended as an attack at all. An example of this might be an employee who deletes a critical file without understanding its critical nature.

Employees are not the only insiders that organizations need to be concerned about. Often, numerous other individuals have physical access to company facilities. Custodial crews frequently have unescorted access throughout the facility, often when nobody else is around. Other individuals, such as contractors or partners, may have not only physical access to the organization's facilities but also access to computer systems and networks.

Criminal Organizations

As businesses became increasingly reliant upon computer systems and networks, and as the amount of financial transactions conducted via the Internet increased, it was inevitable that criminal organizations would eventually turn to the electronic world as a new target to exploit. Criminal activity on the Internet at its most basic is no different from criminal activity in the physical world. Fraud, extortion, theft, embezzlement, and forgery all take place in the electronic environment.

One difference between criminal groups and the "average" hacker is the level of organization that criminal elements employ in their attack. Criminal groups typically have more money to spend on accomplishing the criminal activity and are willing to spend extra time accomplishing the task provided the level of reward at the conclusion is great enough. With the tremendous amount of money that is exchanged via the Internet on a daily basis, the level of reward for a successful attack is high enough to interest criminal elements. Attacks by criminal organizations usually fall into the **structured threat** category, which is characterized by a greater amount of planning, a longer period of time to conduct the activity, more financial backing to accomplish it, and possibly corruption of, or collusion with, insiders.

Terrorists and Information Warfare

As nations have increasingly become dependent on computer systems and networks, the possibility that these essential elements of society might be targeted by organizations or nations determined to adversely affect another nation has become a reality. Many nations today have developed to some extent the capability to conduct **information warfare**. There are several definitions for information warfare, but a simple one is that it is warfare conducted against the information and information processing equipment used by an adversary. In practice, this is a much more complicated subject, because information not only may be the target of an adversary, but also may be used as a weapon. Whatever definition you use, information warfare falls into the **highly structured threat** category. This type of threat is characterized by a much longer period of preparation (years is not uncommon),

The Inside Threat
One of the hardest threats that security professionals will have to address is that of the insider. Since employees already have access to the organization and its assets, additional mechanisms need to be in place to detect attacks by insiders and to lessen the ability of these attacks to succeed.

tremendous financial backing, and a large and organized group of attackers. The threat may include attempts not only to subvert insiders but also to plant individuals inside of a potential target in advance of a planned attack.

An interesting aspect of information warfare is the list of possible targets available. We have grown accustomed to the idea that, during war, military forces will target opposing military forces but will generally attempt to destroy as little civilian infrastructure as possible. In information warfare, military forces are certainly still a key target, but much has been written about other targets, such as the various infrastructures that a nation relies on for its daily existence. Water, electricity, oil and gas refineries and distribution, banking and finance, telecommunications—all fall into the category of **critical infrastructures** for a nation. Critical infrastructures are those whose loss would have severe repercussions on the nation. With countries relying so heavily on these infrastructures, it is inevitable that they will be viewed as valid targets during conflict. Given how dependent these infrastructures are on computer systems and networks, it is also inevitable that these same computer systems and networks will be targeted for a cyber attack in an information war.

Another interesting aspect of information warfare is the potential list of attackers. As mentioned, several countries are currently capable of conducting this type of warfare. Nations, however, are not the only ones that can conduct information, or cyber, warfare. Terrorist organizations can also accomplish this. Such groups fall into the category of highly structured threats since they too are willing to conduct long-term operations, have (in some cases) tremendous financial support, and often have a large following. Reports out of Afghanistan related stories of soldiers and intelligence officers finding laptop computers formerly owned by members of al-Qaeda that contained information about various critical infrastructures in the United States. This showed that terrorist organizations not only were targeting such infrastructures, but were doing so at an unexpected level of sophistication.

Security Trends

The biggest change that has occurred in security over the last 30 years has been the change in the computing environment from large mainframes to a highly interconnected network of much smaller systems (smaller is a relative term here because the computing power of desktop computers exceeds the power of many large mainframes of 30 years ago). What this has meant for security is a switch from an environment in which everything was fairly contained and people operated in a closed environment to one in which access to a computer can occur from almost anywhere on the planet. This has, for obvious reasons, greatly complicated the job of the security professional.

The type of individual who attacks a computer system or network has also evolved over the last 30 years. There was, of course, the traditional intelligence service operator paid by a particular country to obtain secrets from other government computer systems. These people still exist. What has increased dramatically is the number of nonaffiliated intruders. As discussed earlier, the rise of the "script kiddie" has greatly multiplied the number of individuals who probe organizations looking for vulnerabilities to exploit. This is actually the result of another recent trend: as the level of sophistication of attacks has increased, the level of knowledge necessary to

Tech Tip

Information Warfare
Once only the concern of governments and the military, information warfare today can involve many other individuals. With the potential to attack the various civilian-controlled critical infrastructures, security professionals in nongovernmental sectors today must also be concerned about defending their systems against attacks by agents of foreign governments.

exploit vulnerabilities has decreased. This is due to the number of automated tools that have been created that allow even novice attackers to exploit highly technical and complex vulnerabilities. The resulting increase in network attacks has been reflected in a number of different studies conducted by various organizations in the industry.

One of the best-known security surveys is the joint survey conducted annually by the Computer Security Institute (CSI) and the FBI (this survey, *CSI Computer Crime and Security Survey*, can be obtained from www.gocsi.com). The respondents, who normally number over 500 individuals, come from all walks of life: government, academia, and industry. Over the last several years, the percentage of organizations that have experienced security incidents has slowly declined (from 46 percent in 2007 to 43 percent in 2008). This decline has been seen in the most frequent type of incidents experienced (viruses, insider abuse, laptop theft, and unauthorized access) which have remained the same for the last four years. Only four types of attacks showed any increase from 2007 to 2008 (unauthorized access, theft/loss of proprietary information, misuse of web applications, and DNS attacks).

One of the most interesting and oft-repeated statistics from the survey is the average loss experienced by organizations due to specific types of security incidents. The average loss as a result of theft of proprietary information, for example, hit a high of $6.57 million in 2002 but was only $2.70 million in 2003 before rising to $6.03 million in 2006 and then dropping again to $5.69 million in 2007. Financial fraud plunged from $4.63 million in 2002 to $328,000 in 2003 before rising to $2.56 million in 2006 and then sky-rocketing to $21.12 million in 2007. While it is tempting to assume that this means we, as a community, are becoming more secure (and there is indeed some indication that organizations are doing a better job of securing their systems), the reality is that these figures reflect the difficulty in quantifying the actual state of Internet security and of producing accurate results. While we all like to use figures such as those from the CSI/FBI survey, the truth of the matter is that these numbers likely don't accurately portray the state of current security. They are, however, the most reliable ones we have.

■ Avenues of Attack

There are two general reasons a particular computer system is attacked: either it is specifically targeted by the attacker, or it is an opportunistic target. In the first case, the attacker has chosen the target not because of the hardware or software the organization is running but for another reason, perhaps a political reason. An example of this type of attack would be an individual in one country attacking a government system in another. Alternatively, the attacker may be targeting the organization as part of a **hacktivist** attack. An example, in this case, might be an attacker who defaces the web site of a company that sells fur coats because the attacker feels that using animals in this way is unethical. Perpetrating some sort of electronic fraud is another reason a specific system might be targeted. Whatever the reason, an attack of this nature is decided upon before the attacker knows what hardware and software the organization has.

The second type of attack, an attack against a target of opportunity, is conducted against a site that has software that is vulnerable to a specific exploit. The attackers, in this case, are not targeting the organization; instead, they have learned of a vulnerability and are simply looking for an organization with this vulnerability that they can exploit. This is not to say that an attacker might not be targeting a given sector and looking for a target of opportunity in that sector, however. For example, an attacker may desire to obtain credit card or other personal information and may search for any exploitable company with credit card information in order to carry out the attack.

Targeted attacks are more difficult and take more time than attacks on a target of opportunity. The latter simply relies on the fact that with any piece of widely distributed software, there will almost always be somebody who has not patched the system (or has not patched it properly) as they should have.

The Steps in an Attack

The steps an attacker takes in attempting to penetrate a targeted network are similar to the ones that a security consultant performing a penetration test would take.

First, the attacker gathers as much information about the organization as possible. There are numerous ways to do this, including studying the organization's own web site, looking for postings on newsgroups, or consulting resources such as the U.S. Securities and Exchange Commission's (SEC) EDGAR web site (www.sec.gov/edgar.shtml). A number of different financial reports are available through the EDGAR web site that can provide information about an organization that is useful for an attack—particularly a social engineering attack. The type of information that the attacker wants includes IP addresses, phone numbers, names of individuals, and what networks the organization maintains. This step is known as "profiling" or "reconnaissance." Commands such as *whois* are useful in this step for obtaining information on IP blocks and DNS server addresses. An even more common tool that is useful in gathering data is a traditional web search engine such as Google.

Typically, the next step, which is the first step in the technical part of an attack, is to determine what target systems are available and active. This step moves us from profiling to actual scanning and is accomplished with methods such as a **ping sweep**, which simply sends a "ping" (an ICMP echo request) to the target machine. If the machine responds, it is reachable. The next step is often to perform a **port scan**. This will help identify which ports are open, thus giving an indication of which services may be running on the target machine. Determining the operating system (known as *OS fingerprinting*) that is running on the target machine, as well as specific application programs, follows, along with determining the

Try This

Security Tools

Numerous tools are available on the Internet to conduct the initial reconnaissance activity described in this chapter. Examples include *Nmap* and *superscan*. Most security professionals recommend that security administrators run these tools against their own systems in order to see what attackers will see when they inevitably run the same, or similar, tools against the network. Using your favorite search engine, see what open source security tools you can find. Do the same for commercial security tools. If you have access to a closed network that you can play with, you may want to download some of the tools and try them to see how they work and what information they supply.

Principles of Computer Security: CompTIA Security+ and Beyond

services that are available (which can be accomplished by *banner grabbing*). Various techniques can be used to send specifically formatted packets to the ports on a target system to view the response. Often this response provides clues as to which operating system and specific applications are running on the target system. Once this is done, the attacker would have a list of possible target machines, the operating system running on them, and some specific applications or services to target.

Up until this point, the attacker has simply been gathering the information needed to discover potential vulnerabilities that may be exploited. Further research is conducted to find possible vulnerabilities and once a list of these is developed, the attacker is ready to take the next step: an actual attack on the target. Knowing the operating system and services on the target helps the attacker decide which tools to use in the attack.

Numerous web sites provide information on the vulnerabilities of specific application programs and operating systems. This information is valuable to administrators, since they need to know what problems exist and how to patch them. In addition to information about specific vulnerabilities, some sites may also provide tools that can be used to exploit the vulnerabilities. An attacker can search for known vulnerabilities and tools that exploit them, download the information and tools, and then use them against a site. If the administrator for the targeted system has not installed the correct patch, the attack may be successful; if the patch has been installed, the attacker will move on to the next possible vulnerability. If the administrator has installed all of the appropriate patches so that all known vulnerabilities have been addressed, the attacker may have to resort to a brute-force attack, which involves guessing a user ID and password combination. Unfortunately, this type of attack, which could be easily prevented, sometimes proves successful.

This discussion of the steps in an attack is by no means complete. There are many different ways a system can be attacked. This, however, is the general process: gathering as much information about the target as possible (using both electronic and nonelectronic means), gathering information about possible exploits based on the information about the system, and then systematically attempting to use each exploit. If the exploits don't work, other, less system-specific attacks may be attempted.

Minimizing Possible Avenues of Attack

Understanding the steps an attacker will take enables you to limit the exposure of your system and minimize those avenues an attacker might possibly exploit.

The first step an administrator can take to reduce possible attacks is to ensure that all patches for the operating system and applications are installed. Many security problems that we read about, such as viruses and worms, exploit known vulnerabilities for which patches exist. The reason such malware caused so much damage in the past was that administrators did not take the appropriate actions to protect their systems.

The second step an administrator can take is system hardening, which involves limiting the services that are running on the system. Only using those services that are absolutely needed does two things: it limits the possible avenues of attack (those services with vulnerabilities that can be exploited), and it reduces the number of services the administrator has to worry about patching in the first place. This is one of the important first steps any administrator should take to secure a computer system.

Another strategy to minimize possible avenues of attack is to provide as little information as possible about your organization and its computing resources on publicly available places (such as web sites). Since the attacker is after information, don't make it easy to obtain. For example, at one time it was not uncommon for organizations to list the type of OS or browser used on login banners but, as has been discussed, this gives a potential attacker information that can be used to select possible attacks. In addition, consider what contact information is absolutely necessary to have displayed on publicly available sites.

Types of Attacks

There are a number of ways that a computer system or network can be attacked (this topic will be covered in greater detail in Chapter 15). If successful, the attack may produce one of the following: a loss of confidentiality, if information is disclosed to individuals not authorized to see it; a loss of integrity, if information is modified by individuals not authorized to change it; or a loss of availability, if information or the systems processing it are not available for use by authorized users when they need the information.

Chapter 1 Review

■ Chapter Summary

After reading this chapter and completing the quizzes, you should understand the following regarding security trends.

List and Discuss Recent Trends in Computer Security

■ Fifty years ago, few people had access to a computer system or network, so securing them was a relatively easy matter.

■ There are many different ways to attack computers and networks to take advantage of what has made shopping, banking, investment, and leisure pursuits a simple matter of "dragging and clicking" for many people.

■ The biggest change that has occurred in security over the last 30 years has been the change in the computing environment from large mainframes to a highly interconnected network of much smaller systems.

Describe Simple Steps to Take to Minimize the Possibility of an Attack on a System

■ The steps an attacker takes in attempting to penetrate a targeted network are similar to the ones that a security consultant performing a penetration test would take.

■ A ping sweep simply sends a "ping" (an ICMP echo request) to the target machine.

■ A port scan will help identify which ports are open, thus giving an indication of which services may be running on the targeted machine.

■ Numerous web sites exist that provide information on vulnerabilities in specific application programs and operating systems.

■ The first step an administrator can take to minimize possible attacks is to ensure that all patches for the operating system and applications are installed.

Describe Various Types of Threats That Exist for Computers and Networks

■ There are a number of different threats to security, including viruses and worms, intruders, insiders, criminal organizations, terrorists, and information warfare conducted by foreign countries.

■ There are two general reasons a particular computer system is attacked: it is specifically targeted by the attacker, or it is a target of opportunity.

■ Targeted attacks are more difficult and take more time than attacks on a target of opportunity

Discuss Recent Computer Crimes That Have Been Committed

■ The different types of electronic crime fall into two main categories: crimes in which the computer was the target of the attack, and incidents in which the computer was a means of perpetrating a criminal act.

■ One significant trend observed over the last several years has been the increase in the number of computer attacks.

Key Terms

critical infrastructures *(10)*
elite hackers *(8)*
hacker *(7)*
hacking *(7)*
hacktivist *(11)*
highly structured threat *(9)*

information warfare *(9)*
ping sweep *(12)*
port scan *(12)*
script kiddies *(8)*
structured threat *(9)*
unstructured threat *(8)*

Key Terms Quiz

Use terms from the Key Terms list to complete the sentences that follow. Don't use the same term more than once. Not all terms will be used.

1. A(n) _____ is a threat characterized by a greater amount of planning, a longer period of time to conduct the activity, more financial backing to accomplish it, and the possible corruption of, or collusion with, insiders.

2. A hacker whose activities are motivated by a personal cause or position is known as a _____.

3. Infrastructures whose loss would have a severe detrimental impact on the nation are called _____.

4. _____ is warfare conducted against the information and information processing equipment used by an adversary.

5. A _____ simply sends a "ping" (an ICMP echo request) to the target machine.

6. A(n) _____ is a threat that generally is short-term in nature, does not involve a large group of individuals, does not have large financial backing, and does not include collusion with insiders.

7. _____ are the most technically competent individuals conducting intrusive activity on the Internet. They not only can exploit known vulnerabilities but are usually the ones responsible for finding those vulnerabilities.

8. A _____ helps identify which ports are open, thus giving an indication of which services may be running on the targeted machine.

9. _____ are individuals who do not have the technical expertise to develop scripts or discover new vulnerabilities in software but who have just enough understanding of computer systems to be able to download and run scripts that others have developed.

10. A(n) _____ is a threat characterized by attacks that are conducted over short periods of time (lasting at most a few months), that do not involve a large number of individuals, that have little financial backing, and are accomplished by insiders or outsiders who do not seek collusion with insiders.

■ Multiple-Choice Quiz

1. Which threats are characterized by possibly long periods of preparation (years is not uncommon), tremendous financial backing, a large and organized group of attackers, and attempts to subvert insiders or to plant individuals inside a potential target in advance of a planned attack?

    A. Unstructured threats

    B. Structured threats

    C. Highly structured threats

    D. Nation-state information warfare threats

2. Which of the following is an attempt to find and attack a site that has hardware or software that is vulnerable to a specific exploit?

    A. Target of opportunity attack

    B. Targeted attack

    C. Vulnerability scan attack

    D. Information warfare attack

3. Which of the following threats has not grown over the last decade as a result of increasing numbers of Internet users?

    A. Viruses

    B. Hackers

    C. Denial-of-service attacks

    D. All of these have seen an increase over the last decade.

4. The rise of which of the following has greatly increased the number of individuals who probe organizations looking for vulnerabilities to exploit?

    A. Virus writers

    B. Script kiddies

    C. Hackers

    D. Elite hackers

5. Which of the following is generally viewed as the first Internet worm to have caused significant damage and to have "brought the Internet down"?

    A. Melissa

    B. The "Love Bug"

    C. The Morris worm

    D. Code Red

6. Which of the following individuals was convicted of various computer crimes and was known for his ability to conduct successful social engineering attacks?

    A. Kevin Mitnick

    B. Vladimir Levin

    C. Timothy Lloyd

    D. David Smith

7. According to the CSI/FBI survey, which of the following statistics decreased in 2003?

    A. The number of organizations reporting the Internet as a point of attack

    B. The number of organizations that have reported unauthorized use of their systems

    C. The average loss as a result of theft of proprietary information

    D. Both B and C

8. Which virus/worm was credited with reaching global proportions in less than ten minutes?

    A. Code Red

    B. The Morris worm

    C. Melissa

    D. Slammer

9. The act of deliberately accessing computer systems and networks without authorization is generally known as:

   A. Computer intrusions

   B. Hacking

   C. Cracking

   D. Probing

10. What is the most common problem/threat an organization faces?

    A. Viruses/worms

    B. Script kiddies

    C. Hackers

    D. Hacktivists

11. Warfare conducted against the information and information processing equipment used by an adversary is known as:

    A. Hacking

    B. Cyber terrorism

    C. Information warfare

    D. Network warfare

12. An attacker who feels that using animals to make fur coats is unethical and thus defaces the web site of a company that sells fur coats is an example of:

    A. Information warfare

    B. Hacktivisim

    C. Cyber crusading

    D. Elite hacking

13. Which of the following is not described as a critical infrastructure?

    A. Electricity (power)

    B. Banking and finance

    C. Telecommunications

    D. Retail stores

14. Criminal organizations would normally be classified as what type of threat?

    A. Unstructured

    B. Unstructured but hostile

    C. Structured

    D. Highly structured

15. Elite hackers don't account for more than what percentage of the total number of individuals conducting intrusive activity on the Internet?

    A. 1–2 percent

    B. 3–5 percent

    C. 7–10 percent

    D. 15–20 percent

■ Essay Quiz

1. Reread the various examples of computer crimes at the beginning of this chapter. Categorize each as either a crime where the computer was the target of the criminal activity or a crime in which the computer was a tool in accomplishing the criminal activity.

2. Your boss has just heard about some "nefarious computer activities" called ping sweeps and port scans. He wants to know more about them and what the impact might be of these activities on your company. Write a brief description of what they are and include your assessment of whether this activity is something to worry about or not.

3. A friend of yours has just been hired by an organization as their computer security officer. Your friend is a bit nervous about this new job and has come to you, knowing that you are taking a computer security class, to ask your advice on measures that can be taken that might help prevent an intrusion. What three things can you suggest that are simple but can tremendously help limit the possibility of an attack?

4. Discuss why insiders are considered such a threat to organizations?

5. Write a brief essay outlining what you learned from the *CSI Computer Crime and Security Survey* mentioned in the chapter.

Lab Projects

• Lab Project 1.1

A number of different examples of computer crimes were discussed in this chapter. Similar activities seem to happen daily. Do a search on the Internet to see what other examples you can find. Try and obtain the most recent examples possible.

• Lab Project 1.2

References to "script kiddies" were made frequently in this chapter. The implication was that it is easy today to perform certain types of activities because it is easy to find tools that allow you to perform them. *If* allowed at your school or by your ISP, perform a search of the Internet to see how easy it is to locate programs that will perform activities such as ping sweeps and port scans. What other types of security-related tools can you find?

General Security Concepts

chapter
2

"The only real security that a man can have in this world is a reserve of knowledge, experience and ability."

—Henry Ford

In this chapter, you will learn how to

- Define basic terms associated with computer and information security
- Identify the basic approaches to computer and information security
- Distinguish among various methods to implement access controls
- Describe methods used to verify the identity and authenticity of an individual
- Describe methods used to conduct social engineering
- Recognize some of the basic models used to implement security in operating systems

In Chapter 1, you learned about some of the various threats that we, as security professionals, face on a daily basis. In this chapter, you start exploring the field of computer security.

Basic Security Terminology

The term **hacking** has been used frequently in the media. A *hacker* was once considered an individual who understood the technical aspects of computer operating systems and networks. Hackers were individuals you turned to when you had a problem and needed extreme technical expertise. Today, primarily as a result of the media, the term is used more often to refer to individuals who attempt to gain unauthorized access to computer systems or networks. While some would prefer to use the terms *cracker* and *cracking* when referring to this nefarious type of activity, the terminology generally accepted by the public is that of hacker and hacking. A related term that may sometimes be seen is **phreaking**, which refers to the "hacking" of the systems and computers used by a telephone company to operate its telephone network.

Exam Tip: The field of computer security constantly evolves, introducing new terms frequently, which are often coined by the media. Make sure to learn the meaning of terms such as *hacking, phreaking, vishing, phishing, pharming,* and *spear phishing.* Some of these have been around for many years, such as hacking, whereas others have appeared only in the last few years, such as spear phishing.

Security Basics

Computer security itself is a term that has many meanings and related terms. Computer security entails the methods used to ensure that a system is secure. Subjects such as authentication and access controls must be addressed in broad terms of computer security. Seldom in today's world are computers not connected to other computers in networks. This then introduces the term *network security* to refer to the protection of the multiple computers and other devices that are connected together. Related to these two terms are two others: *information security* and *information assurance*, which place the focus of the security process not on the hardware and software being used but on the data that is processed by them. Assurance also introduces another concept, that of the availability of the systems and information when we want them. Still another term that may be heard in the security world is COMSEC, which stands for *communications security* and deals with the security of telecommunication systems.

Since the late 1990s, much has been reported in the media concerning computer and network security. Often the news is about a specific lapse in security that has resulted in the penetration of a network or in the denial of service for a network. Over the last few years, the general public has become increasingly aware of its dependence on computers and networks and consequently has also become interested in the security of these same computers and networks.

As a result of this increased attention by the public, several new terms have become commonplace in conversations and print. Terms such as *hacking, virus, TCP/IP, encryption,* and *firewalls* are now frequently encountered in mainstream news media and have found their way into casual conversations. What was once the purview of scientists and engineers is now part of our everyday life.

With our increased daily dependence on computers and networks to conduct everything from making purchases at our local grocery store to driving our children to school (that new car you just bought is probably using a small computer to obtain peak engine performance), ensuring that computers and networks are secure has become of paramount importance. Medical information about each of us is probably stored in a computer somewhere.

So is financial information and data relating to the types of purchases we make and store preferences (assuming you have and use a credit card to make purchases). Making sure that this information remains private is a growing concern to the general public, and it is one of the jobs of security to help with the protection of our privacy. Simply stated, computer and network security is now essential for us to function effectively and safely in today's highly automated environment.

The "CIA" of Security

Almost from its inception, the goal of computer security has been threefold: confidentiality, integrity, and availability—the "CIA" of security. The purpose of **confidentiality** is to ensure that only those individuals who have the authority to view a piece of information may do so. No unauthorized individual should ever be able to view data they are not entitled to access. **Integrity** is a related concept but deals with the generation and modification of data. Only authorized individuals should ever be able to create or change (or delete) information. The goal of **availability** is to ensure that the data, or the system itself, is available for use when the authorized user wants it.

As a result of the increased use of networks for commerce, two additional security goals have been added to the original three in the CIA of security. **Authentication** attempts to ensure that an individual is who they claim to be. The need for this in an online transaction is obvious. Related to this is **nonrepudiation**, which deals with the ability to verify that a message has been sent and received and that the sender can be identified and verified. The requirement for this capability in online transactions should also be readily apparent. Recent emphasis on systems assurance has raised the potential inclusion of the term **auditability**, which refers to whether a control can be verified to be functioning properly. In security, it is imperative that we can track actions to ensure what has or has not been done.

Tech Tip

CIA of Security

While there is no universal agreement on authentication, auditability, and nonrepudiation as additions to the original CIA of security, there is little debate over whether confidentiality, integrity, and availability are basic security principles. Understand these principles, because one or more of them are the reason for most security hardware, software, policies, and procedures.

The Operational Model of Computer Security

For many years, the focus of security was on prevention. If we could prevent somebody from gaining access to our computer systems and networks, then we assumed that we had achieved security. Protection was thus equated with prevention. While the basic premise of this is true, it fails to acknowledge the realities of the networked environment our systems are part of. No matter how well we seem to do in prevention technology, somebody always seems to find a way around our safeguards. When this happens, our system is left unprotected. Thus, we need multiple prevention techniques and also technology to alert us when prevention has failed and to provide ways to address the problem. This results in a modification to our original security equation with the addition of two new elements—detection and response. Our security equation thus becomes:

Protection = Prevention + (Detection + Response)

This is known as the **operational model of computer security**. Every security technique and technology falls into at least one of the three elements of the equation. Examples of the types of technology and techniques that represent each are depicted in Figure 2.1.

Security Principles

There are three approaches an organization can take to address the protection of its networks: ignore security issues, provide host security, or provide network-level security. The last two, host and network security, have prevention as well as detection and response components.

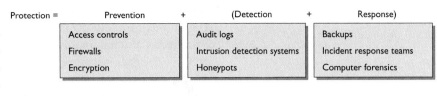

Protection =	Prevention	+	(Detection	+	Response)
	Access controls		Audit logs		Backups
	Firewalls		Intrusion detection systems		Incident response teams
	Encryption		Honeypots		Computer forensics

• **Figure 2.1**   Sample technologies in the operational model of computer security

If an organization decides to ignore security, it has chosen to utilize the minimal amount of security that is provided with its workstations, servers, and devices. No additional security measures will be implemented. Each "out of the box" system has certain security settings that can be configured, and they should be. To actually protect an entire network, however, requires work in addition to the few protection mechanisms that come with systems by default.

Host Security   **Host security** takes a granular view of security by focusing on protecting each computer and device individually instead of addressing protection of the network as a whole. When host security is used, each computer is relied upon to protect itself. If an organization decides to implement only host security and does not include network security, there is a high probability of introducing or overlooking vulnerabilities. Most environments are filled with different operating systems (Windows, UNIX, Linux, Mac), different versions of those operating systems, and different types of installed applications. Each operating system has security configurations that differ from other systems, and different versions of the same operating system may in fact have variations between them. Ensuring that every computer is "locked down" to the same degree as every other system in the environment can be overwhelming and often results in an unsuccessful and frustrating effort.

Host security is important and should always be addressed. Security, however, should not stop there, as host security is a complementary process to be combined with network security. If individual host computers have vulnerabilities embodied within them, then network security can provide another layer of protection that will, hopefully, stop any intruders who have gotten that far into the environment. Topics covered in this book dealing with host security include: bastion hosts, host-based intrusion detection systems (HIDS), antivirus software, and hardening of operating systems.

Network Security   In some smaller environments, host security by itself may be an option, but as systems become connected into networks, security should include the actual network itself. In **network security**, an emphasis is placed on controlling access to internal computers from external entities. This control can be through devices such as routers, firewalls, authentication hardware and software, encryption, and intrusion detection systems (IDSs).

Network environments tend to be unique entities because usually no two networks have exactly the same number of computers, the same applications installed, the same number of users, the exact same configurations, or the same available servers. They will not perform the same functions or

A longtime discussion has centered on whether host- or network-based security is more important. Most security experts now generally agree that a combination of both is needed to adequately address the wide range of possible security threats. Certain attacks are more easily spotted and some attacks are more easily prevented using tools designed for one or the other of these approaches.

have the same overall architecture. Since networks have so many differences, there are many different ways in which they can be protected and configured. This chapter covers some foundational approaches to network and host security. Each approach may be implemented in a myriad of ways but both network and host security need to be addressed for an effective total security program.

Least Privilege

One of the most fundamental approaches to security is **least privilege**. This concept is applicable to many physical environments as well as network and host security. Least privilege means that a subject (which may be a user, application, or process) should have only the necessary rights and privileges to perform its task with no additional permissions. Limiting an object's privileges limits the amount of harm that can be caused, thus limiting an organization's exposure to damage. Users may have access to the files on their workstations and a select set of files on a file server, but no access to critical data that is held within the database. This rule helps an organization protect its most sensitive resources and helps ensure that whoever is interacting with these resources has a valid reason to do so.

Different operating systems and applications have different ways of implementing rights, permissions, and privileges. Before an operating system is actually configured, an overall plan should be devised and standardized methods should be developed to ensure that a solid security baseline is actually implemented. For example, a company may want all of the Accounting employees, but no one else, to be able to access employee payroll and profit margin spreadsheets held on a server. The easiest way to implement this is to develop an Accounting *group*, put all Accounting employees in this group, and assign rights to the group instead of each individual person.

As another example, there may be a requirement to implement a hierarchy of administrators that perform different functions and require specific types of rights. Two administrators may be tasked with performing backups of individual workstations and servers; thus they do not need administrative permissions with full access to all resources. Three other administrators may be in charge of setting up new user accounts and password management, which means they do not need full, or perhaps any, access to the company's routers and switches. Once these lines are delineated, indicating what subjects require which rights and permissions, then it is much easier to configure settings to provide the least privileges for different subjects.

The concept of least privilege applies to more network security issues than just providing users with specific rights and permissions. When trust relationships are created, they should not be implemented in such a way that everyone trusts each other simply because it is easier. One domain should trust another for very specific reasons, and the implementers should have a full understanding of what the trust relationship allows

Try This

Examples of the Least Privilege Principle

The security concept of least privilege is not unique to computer security. It has been practiced by organizations such as financial institutions and governments for centuries. Basically it simply means that individuals are given only the absolute minimum of privileges that are required to accomplish their assigned job. Examine the security policies that your organization has in place and see if you can identify examples of where the principle of least privilege has been used.

between two domains. If one domain trusts another, do all of the users automatically become trusted, and can they thus easily access any and all resources on the other domain? Is this a good idea? Is there a more secure way of providing the same functionality? If a trusted relationship is implemented such that users in one group can access a plotter or printer that is available on only one domain, it might make sense to simply purchase another plotter so that other, more valuable or sensitive resources are not accessible by the entire group.

Another issue that falls under the least privilege concept is the security context in which an application runs. All applications, scripts, and batch files run in the security context of a specific user on an operating system. They execute with specific permissions as if they were a user. The application may be Microsoft Word and run in the space of a regular user, or it may be a diagnostic program that needs access to more sensitive system files and so must run under an administrative user account, or it may be a program that performs backups and so should operate within the security context of a backup operator. The crux of this issue is that programs should execute only in the security context that is needed for that program to perform its duties successfully. In many environments, people do not really understand how to make programs run under different security contexts, or it may just seem easier to have them all run under the administrator account. If attackers can compromise a program or service running under the administrator account, they have effectively elevated their access level and have much more control over the system and many more ways to cause damage.

 Try This

Control of Resources

Being able to apply the appropriate security control to file and print resources is an important aspect of the least privilege security principle. How this is implemented varies depending on the operating system that the computer runs. Check how the operating system that you use provides for the ability to control file and print resources.

Separation of Duties

Another fundamental approach to security is **separation of duties**. This concept is applicable to physical environments as well as network and host security. Separation of duties ensures that for any given task, more than one individual needs to be involved. The task is broken into different duties, each of which is accomplished by a separate individual. By implementing a task in this manner, no single individual can abuse the system for his or her own gain. This principle has been implemented in the business world, especially financial institutions, for many years. A simple example is a system in which one individual is required to place an order and a separate person is needed to authorize the purchase.

While separation of duties provides a certain level of checks and balances, it is not without its own drawbacks. Chief among these is the cost required to accomplish the task. This cost is manifested in both time and money. More than one individual is required when a single person could accomplish the task, thus potentially increasing the cost of the task. In addition, with more than one individual involved, a certain delay can be expected because the task must proceed through its various steps.

Implicit Deny

What has become the Internet was originally designed as a friendly environment where everybody agreed to abide by the rules implemented in the various protocols. Today, the Internet is no longer the friendly playground of researchers that it once was. This has resulted in different approaches that might at first seem less than friendly but that are required for security purposes. One of these approaches is **implicit deny**.

Frequently in the network world, administrators make many decisions concerning network access. Often a series of rules will be used to determine whether or not to allow access (which is the purpose of a network firewall). If a particular situation is not covered by any of the other rules, the implicit deny approach states that access should not be granted. In other words, if no rule would allow access, then access should not be granted. Implicit deny applies to situations involving both authorization and access.

The alternative to implicit deny is to allow access unless a specific rule forbids it. Another example of these two approaches is in programs that monitor and block access to certain web sites. One approach is to provide a list of specific sites that a user is *not* allowed to access. Access to any site not on the list would be implicitly allowed. The opposite approach (the implicit deny approach) would block all access to sites that are not specifically identified as authorized. As you can imagine, depending on the specific application, one or the other approach will be more appropriate. Which approach you choose depends on the security objectives and policies of your organization.

Exam Tip: Implicit deny is another fundamental principle of security and students need to be sure that they understand this principle. Similar to least privilege, this principle states that if you haven't specifically been allowed access, then it should be denied.

Job Rotation

An interesting approach to enhance security that is gaining increasing attention is *job rotation*. Organizations often discuss the benefits of rotating individuals through various jobs in an organization's IT department. By rotating through jobs, individuals gain a better perspective on how the various parts of IT can enhance (or hinder) the business. Since security is often a misunderstood aspect of IT, rotating individuals through security positions can result in a much wider understanding throughout the organization about potential security problems. It also can have the side benefit of a company not having to rely on any one individual too heavily for security expertise. If all security tasks are the domain of one employee, and that individual leaves suddenly, security at the organization could suffer. On the other hand, if security tasks are understood by many different individuals, the loss of any one individual has less of an impact on the organization.

One significant drawback to job rotation is relying on it too heavily. The IT world is very technical, and expertise in any single aspect often takes years to develop. This is especially true in the security environment. In addition, the rapidly changing threat environment, with new vulnerabilities and exploits routinely being discovered, requires a level of understanding that takes considerable time to acquire and maintain.

Layered Security

A bank does not protect the money that it stores only by using a vault. It has one or more security guards as a first defense to watch for suspicious activities and to secure the facility when the bank is closed. It may have monitoring systems that watch various activities that take place in the bank, whether involving customers or employees. The vault is usually located in the center of the facility, and thus there are layers of rooms or walls before arriving at the vault. There is access control, which ensures that the people entering the vault have to be given the authorization beforehand. And the systems, including manual switches, are connected directly to the police station in case a determined bank robber successfully penetrates any one of these layers of protection.

Networks should utilize the same type of **layered security** architecture. There is no 100 percent secure system, and there is nothing that is foolproof, so a single specific protection mechanism should never be solely relied upon. Every piece of software and every device can be compromised in some way, and every encryption algorithm can be broken, given enough time and resources. The goal of security is to make the effort of actually accomplishing a compromise more costly in time and effort than it is worth to a potential attacker.

As an example, consider the steps an intruder might have to take to access critical data held within a company's back-end database. The intruder first has to penetrate the firewall and use packets and methods that will not be identified and detected by the IDS (more information on these devices can be found in Chapter 13). The attacker next has to circumvent an internal router performing packet filtering, and then possibly penetrate another firewall used to separate one internal network from another (see Figure 2.2). From there, the intruder must break the access controls that are on the database, which means having to do a dictionary or brute-force attack to be able to authenticate to the database software. Once the intruder has gotten this far, the data still needs to be located within the database. This may in turn be complicated by the use of access control lists outlining who can actually view or modify the data. That is a lot of work.

This example illustrates the different layers of security many environments employ. It is important to implement several different layers because if intruders succeed at one layer, you want to be able to stop them at the next. The redundancy of different protection layers assures that there is no one single point of failure pertaining to security. If a network used only a

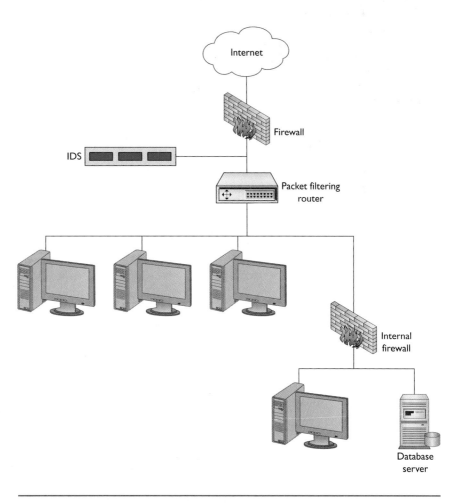

• **Figure 2.2** Layered security

firewall to protect its assets, an attacker successfully able to penetrate this device would find the rest of the network open and vulnerable.

It is important that every environment have multiple layers of security. These layers may employ a variety of methods, such as routers, firewalls, network segments, IDSs, encryption, authentication software, physical security, and traffic control. The layers need to work together in a coordinated manner so that one does not impede another's functionality and introduce a security hole. Security at each layer can be very complex, and putting different layers together can increase the complexity exponentially. Although having layers of protection in place is very important, it is also important to understand how these different layers interact either by working together or, in some cases, by working against each other.

One case of how different security methods can work against each other is exemplified when firewalls encounter encrypted network traffic. An organization may utilize encryption so that an outside customer communicating with a specific web server is assured that sensitive data being exchanged is protected. If this encrypted data is encapsulated within Secure Sockets Layer (SSL) packets and then sent through a firewall, the firewall will not be able to read the payload information in the individual packets. This may enable the customer, or an outside attacker, to send malicious code or instructions through the SSL connection undetected. There are other mechanisms that can be introduced in these situations, such as designing web pages to accept information only in certain formats and having the web server parse

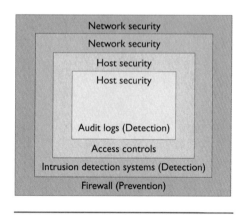

through the data for malicious activity. The important point is to understand the level of protection that each layer provides and how each level of protection can be affected by things that take place in other layers.

The layers usually are depicted starting at the top, with more general types of protection, and progressing downward through each layer, with increasing granularity at each layer as you get closer to the actual resource, as you can see in Figure 2.3. This is because the top-layer protection mechanism is responsible for looking at an enormous amount of traffic, and it would be overwhelming and cause too much of a performance degradation if each aspect of the packet were inspected. Instead, each layer usually digs deeper into the packet and looks for specific items. Layers that are closer to the resource have to deal with only a fraction of the traffic that the top-layer security mechanism does, and thus looking deeper and at more granular aspects of the traffic will not cause as much of a performance hit.

• **Figure 2.3** Various layers of security

Diversity of Defense

Diversity of defense is a concept that complements the idea of various layers of security. It involves making different layers of security dissimilar so that even if attackers know how to get through a system that comprises one layer, they may not know how to get through a different type of layer that employs a different system for security.

If an environment has two firewalls that form a demilitarized zone (DMZ), for example, one firewall may be placed at the perimeter of the Internet and the DMZ. This firewall analyzes the traffic that is entering through that specific access point and enforces certain types of restrictions.

The other firewall may then be placed between the DMZ and the internal network. When applying the diversity of defense concept, you should set up these two firewalls to filter for different types of traffic and provide different types of restrictions. The first firewall, for example, may make sure that no FTP, SNMP, or Telnet traffic enters the network but allow SMTP, SSH, HTTP, and SSL traffic through. The second firewall may not allow SSL or SSH through and may interrogate SMTP and HTTP traffic to make sure that certain types of attacks are not part of that traffic.

Another type of diversity of defense is to use products from different vendors. Every product has its own security vulnerabilities that are usually known to experienced attackers in the community. A Check Point firewall has different security issues and settings than the open source Sentry firewall; thus different exploits can be used against them to crash them or compromise them in some fashion. Combining this type of diversity with the preceding example, you might utilize the Check Point firewall as the first line of defense. If attackers are able to penetrate it, they are less likely to get through the next firewall if it is one from another vendor, such as a Cisco PIX firewall or a Sentry firewall.

There is an obvious trade-off that must be considered before implementing diversity of security using different vendor products. Doing so usually also increases operational complexity, and security and complexity are seldom a good mix. When implementing products from more than one vendor, the staff has to know how to configure two different systems, the configuration settings will be totally different, the upgrades and patches will come out at different times and contain different changes, and the overall complexity of maintaining these systems may cause more headaches than security itself. This does not mean that you should not implement diversity of defense by installing products from different vendors; it just means that you should know the implications of this type of decision.

Security Through Obscurity

Another concept in security that should be discussed is the idea of **security through obscurity**. In this case, security is considered effective if the environment and protection mechanisms are confusing or thought to be not generally known. Security through obscurity uses the approach of protecting something by hiding it. Noncomputer examples of this concept include hiding your briefcase or purse if you leave it in the car so that it is not in plain view, hiding a house key under a doormat or in a planter, or pushing your favorite ice cream to the back of the freezer so that everyone else thinks it is all gone. The idea is that if something is out of sight, it is out of mind. This approach, however, does not provide actual protection of the object. Someone can still steal the purse by breaking into the car, lift the doormat and find the key, or dig through the items in the freezer to find your favorite ice cream. Security through obscurity may make someone work a little harder to accomplish a task, but it does not prevent anyone from eventually succeeding.

Similar approaches are seen in computer and network security when attempting to hide certain objects. A network administrator may, for instance, move a service from its default port to a different port so that others will not know how to access it as easily, or a firewall may be configured to hide

It often amazes security professionals how frequently individuals rely on security through obscurity as their main line of defense. Relying on some piece of information remaining secret is generally not a good idea. This is especially true in this age of reverse-engineering, where individuals analyze the binaries for programs to discover embedded passwords or cryptographic keys. The biggest problem with relying on security through obscurity is that if it fails and the secret becomes known, there often is no easy way to modify the secret to re-secure it.

specific information about the internal network in the hope that potential attackers will not obtain the information for use in an attack on the network.

In most security circles, security through obscurity is considered a poor approach, especially if it is the only approach to security. Security through obscurity simply attempts to hide an object; it doesn't implement a security control to protect it. An organization can use security through obscurity measures to try to hide critical assets, but other security measures should also be employed to provide a higher level of protection. For example, if an administrator moves a service from its default port to a more obscure port, an attacker can still actually find this service; thus a firewall should be used to restrict access to the service. Most people know that even if you do shove your ice cream to the back of the freezer, someone may eventually find it.

Keep It Simple

The terms security and complexity are often at odds with each other, because the more complex something is, the harder it is to understand, and you cannot truly secure something if you do not understand it. Another reason complexity is a problem within security is that it usually allows too many opportunities for something to go wrong. If an application has 4000 lines of code, there are a lot fewer places for buffer overflows, for example, than in an application of two million lines of code.

As with any other type of technology or problem in life, when something goes wrong with security mechanisms, a troubleshooting process is used to identify the actual issue. If the mechanism is overly complex, identifying the root of the problem can be overwhelming if not nearly impossible. Security is already a very complex issue because there are so many variables involved, so many types of attacks and vulnerabilities, so many different types of resources to secure, and so many different ways of securing them. You want your security processes and tools to be as simple and elegant as possible. They should be simple to troubleshoot, simple to use, and simple to administer.

Another application of the principle of keeping things simple concerns the number of services that you allow your system to run. Default installations of computer operating systems often leave many services running. The keep-it-simple principle tells us to eliminate those services that we don't need. This is also a good idea from a security standpoint because it results in fewer applications that can be exploited and fewer services that the administrator is responsible for securing. The general rule of thumb should be to always eliminate all nonessential services and protocols. This of course leads to the question, how do you determine whether a service or protocol is essential or not? Ideally, you should know what your computer system or network is being used for, and thus you should be able to identify and activate only those elements that are essential. For a variety of reasons, this is not as easy as it sounds. Alternatively, a stringent security approach that one can take is to assume that no service is necessary (which is obviously absurd) and activate services and ports only as they are requested. Whatever approach is taken, there is a never-ending struggle to try to strike a balance between providing functionality and maintaining security.

Access Control

The term *access control* has been used to describe a variety of protection schemes. It sometimes refers to all security features used to prevent unauthorized access to a computer system or network. In this sense, it may be confused with authentication. More properly, **access control** is the ability to control whether a subject (such as an individual or a process running on a computer system) can interact with an object (such as a file or hardware device). Authentication, on the other hand, deals with verifying the identity of a subject. To help understand the difference, consider the example of an individual attempting to log into a computer system or network. *Authentication* is the process used to verify to the computer system or network that the individual is who they claim to be. The most common method to do this is through the use of a user ID and password. Once the individual has verified their identity, access controls regulate what the individual can actually do on the system. Just because a person is granted entry to the system does not mean that they should have access to all data the system contains.

Authentication

Access controls define what actions a user can perform or what objects a user can have access to. These controls assume that the identity of the user has been verified. It is the job of authentication mechanisms to ensure that only valid users are admitted. Described another way, authentication is using some mechanism to prove that you are who you claim to be. There are three general methods used in authentication. In order to verify your identity, you can provide

- Something you know
- Something you have
- Something about you (something that you are)

   The most common authentication mechanism is to provide something that only you, the valid user, should know. The most frequently used example of this is the common user ID (or username) and password. In theory, since you are not supposed to share your password with anybody else, only you should know your password, and thus by providing it, you are proving to the system that you are who you claim to be. Another mechanism for authentication is to provide something that you have in your possession, such as a magnetic stripe card that contains identifying information. The third mechanism is to use something about you for identification purposes, such as your fingerprint or the geometry of your hand. Obviously, for the second and third mechanisms to work, additional hardware devices need to be used (to read the card, fingerprint, or hand geometry).

Access Control vs. Authentication

It may seem that access control and authentication are two ways to describe the same protection mechanism. This, however, is not the case. Authentication provides a way to verify to the computer who the user is. Once the user has been authenticated, the access controls decide what operations the user can perform. The two go hand-in-hand but they are not the same thing. An access control list (ACL) is a mechanism that is used to define whether a user has certain access privileges for a system. For example, an ACL might be used to provide a list of individuals and what access they have for a computer system or network device.

No matter what specific mechanism is used to implement access controls in a computer system or network, the controls should be based on a specific model of access. Several different models are discussed in security literature, including discretionary access control (DAC), mandatory access control (MAC), role-based access control (RBAC), and rule-based access control (also RBAC). Access control is covered in detail in Chapter 11.

Certificates

Certificates are a method to establish authenticity of specific objects such as an individual's public key (more on this specific subject in Chapter 6) or downloaded software. A *digital certificate* is generally an attachment to a message and is used to verify that the message did indeed come from the entity it claims to have come from. The digital certificate can also contain a key that can be used to encrypt further communication. For more information on this subject, refer to Chapter 11.

Authentication and Access Control Policies

Policies are statements of what the organization wants to accomplish. The organization needs to identify goals and intentions for many different aspects of security. Each aspect will have associated policies and procedures.

Group Policy

Operating systems such as Windows and Linux allow administrators to organize users into groups, to create categories of users for which similar access policies can be established. Using groups saves the administrator time, as adding a new user will not require the administrator to create a completely new user profile; instead, the administrator can determine to which group the new user belongs and then add the user to that group.

A group policy defines for the group things such as the applicable operating system and application settings and permissions. Examples of groups commonly found include administrator, user, and guest. Take care when creating groups and assigning users to them so that you do not provide more access than is absolutely required for members of that group. It would be simple to make everybody an administrator—it would cut down on the number of requests users make of beleaguered administrators—but this is not a wise choice, as it also enables users to modify the system in ways that could impact security. Establishing the rights levels of access for the various groups up front will save you time and eliminate potential problems that might be encountered later on. More on this subject will be covered in Chapter 14.

Password Policy

Since passwords are the most common authentication mechanism, it is imperative that organizations have a policy that addresses them. The list of authorized users forms the basis of the ACL for the computer system or network that the passwords will help control. The *password policy* should address the procedures used for selecting user passwords (specifying what is considered an acceptable password in the organization in terms of the character set and length, its complexity), the frequency with which they must be changed, and how they will be distributed. Procedures for creating new passwords should an employee forget her old password also need to be addressed, as well as the acceptable handling of passwords (for example, they should not be shared with anybody else, they should not be written down, and so on). It might also be useful to have the policy address the issue of password cracking by administrators, in order to discover weak passwords selected by employees.

Note that the developer of the password policy and associated procedures can go overboard and create an environment that negatively impacts employee productivity and leads to poorer security, not better. If, for example, the frequency with which passwords are changed is too great, users might write them down or forget them. Neither of these is a desirable outcome, as the former makes it possible for an intruder to find a password and gain access to the system, and the latter leads to too many people losing productivity as they wait for a new password to be created to allow them access again. More information on password policies can be found in Chapter 22.

Exam Tip: A password policy is one of the most basic policies that an organization can have. Make sure you understand the basics of what constitutes a good password along with the other issues that surround password creation, expiration, sharing, and use.

■ Social Engineering

Social engineering is the process of convincing an authorized individual to provide confidential information or access to an unauthorized individual. Social engineering takes advantage of what continually turns out to be the weakest point in our security perimeter—the humans. Kevin Mitnick, a convicted cybercriminal turned security consultant, once stated, "Don't rely on network safeguards and firewalls to protect your information. Look to your most vulnerable spot. You'll usually find that vulnerability lies in your people." In 2000, after being released from jail, Mitnick testified before Congress and spoke on several other occasions about social engineering and how effective it is. He stated that he "rarely had to resort to a technical attack" because of how easily information and access could be obtained through social engineering.

Individuals who are attempting to social engineer some piece of information generally rely on two aspects of human nature. First, most people generally want to help somebody who is requesting help. Second, people generally want to avoid confrontation. To exploit people's natural inclination to provide help, the knowledgeable social engineer might call a help desk and pretend to be a new employee who needs help to log onto the organization's network. By doing so, the social engineer can obtain valuable information as to the type of system or network that is being employed. After making this call, the social engineer might make a second call and use the information obtained from the first call to provide background so that the next individual the attacker attempts to obtain information from will not suspect it is an unauthorized individual asking the questions. This works because people generally assume that somebody is who they claim to be, especially if they have information that would be known by the individual they claim to be.

Social engineering has for many years been one of the most successful methods that attackers have used to gain unauthorized access to computer systems and networks. The technique relies on the inherent desire in most people to be helpful. With a plausible background and a good story, a good social engineer can frequently talk individuals into divulging information that they normally would never have. Social engineering can also take the form of something simple such as striking up a conversation with a person as you approach a locked door so that when the individual opens it, you walk in with them. For many people, if the individual seems friendly and doesn't look suspicious, they will give them the benefit of the doubt and assume that they belong to the organization and are authorized access.

If the pleasant approach doesn't work, a more aggressive approach can be attempted. People will normally want to avoid unpleasant confrontations and will also not want to get into trouble with their superiors. An attacker, knowing this, may attempt to obtain information by threatening to go to the individual's supervisor or by claiming that he is working for somebody who is high up in the organization's management structure. Because employees want to avoid both a confrontation and a possible reprimand, they might provide the information requested even though they realize that doing so is against the organization's policies or procedures.

The goal of social engineering is to gradually obtain the pieces of information necessary to take the next step. This is done repeatedly until the ultimate goal is reached. If social engineering is such an effective means of gaining unauthorized access to data and information, how can it be stopped? The most effective means is through the *training and education* of users, administrators, and security personnel. All employees should be instructed in the techniques that attackers might use and trained to recognize when a social engineering attack is being attempted. One important aspect of this training is for employees to recognize the type of information that should be protected and also how seemingly unimportant information can be combined with other pieces of information to potentially divulge sensitive information. This is known as **data aggregation**.

In addition to the direct approach to social engineering, attackers can use other, indirect means to obtain the information they are seeking. These include phishing, vishing, shoulder surfing, and dumpster diving and are discussed in Chapter 4. Again, the first defense against any of these methods to gather information to be used in later attacks is a strong user education and awareness training program.

 Cross Check

Social Engineering Attacks

In Chapter 1, the topic of social engineering was mentioned several times. Social engineering attacks can come in many different forms. Taken as a whole, they are the most common attack that most users will be faced with. Be sure to understand the difference between the various types of social engineering attacks and how each can be used as part of an overall plan to attack an organization.

■ Security Policies

Policies are high-level statements created by management that lay out the organization's positions on particular issues. Policies describe mandatory activities but are not specific in their details. Policies are focused on the result, not the methods for achieving that result. *Procedures* are generally step-by-step instructions that prescribe exactly how employees are expected to act in a given situation or to accomplish a specific task. Although standard policies can be described in general terms that will be applicable to all organizations, *standards* (which define a subject's specific requirements) and procedures are often organization-specific and driven by specific organizational policies.

Regarding security, every organization should have several common policies in place (in addition to those already discussed relative to access control methods). These include security policies regarding change management, classification of information, acceptable use, due care and due diligence, due process, need to know, disposal and destruction of data, service level agreements, human resources issues, codes of ethics, and policies governing incident response.

In keeping with the high-level nature of policies, the *security policy* is a high-level statement produced by senior management that outlines both what security means to the organization and the organization's goals for security. The main security policy can then be broken down into additional policies that cover specific topics. Statements such as "this organization will exercise the principle of least access in its handling of client information" would be an example of a security policy. The security policy can also describe how security is to be handled from an organizational point of view (such as describing which office and corporate officer or manager oversees the organization's security program).

In addition to policies related to access control, the organization's security policy should include the specific policies described in the next sections. All policies should be reviewed on a regular basis and updated as needed. Generally, policies should be updated less frequently than the procedures that implement them, since the high-level goals will not change as often as the environment in which they must be implemented. All policies should be reviewed by the organization's legal counsel, and a plan should be outlined that describes how the organization will ensure that employees will be made aware of the policies. Policies can also be made stronger by including references to the authority who made the policy (whether this policy comes from the CEO or is a department-level policy, for example) and references to any laws or regulations that are applicable to the specific policy and environment.

Change Management Policy

The purpose of *change management* is to ensure proper procedures are followed when modifications to the IT infrastructure are made. These modifications can be prompted by a number of different events, including new legislation, updated versions of software or hardware, implementation of new software or hardware, or improvements to the infrastructure. The term "management" implies that this process should be controlled in some systematic way, and that is indeed the purpose. Changes to the infrastructure might have a detrimental impact on operations. New versions of operating systems or application software might be incompatible with other software or hardware the organization is using. Without a process to manage the change, an organization might suddenly find itself unable to conduct business. A change management process should include various stages, including a method to request a change to the infrastructure, a review and approval process for the request, an examination of the consequences of the change, resolution (or mitigation) of any detrimental effects the change might incur, implementation of the change, and documentation of the process as it related to the change.

Classification of Information

A key component of IT security is the protection of the information processed and stored on the computer systems and network. Organizations deal with many different types of information, and they need to recognize that not all information is of equal importance or sensitivity. This requires classification of information into various categories, each with its own requirements for its handling. Factors that affect the classification of specific information include its value to the organization (what will be the impact to the organization if it loses this information?), its age, and laws or regulations that govern its protection. The most widely known system of classification of information is that implemented by the U.S. government (including the military), which classifies information into categories such as *Confidential*, *Secret*, and *Top Secret*. Businesses have similar desires to protect information and often use categories such as *Publicly Releasable*, *Proprietary*, *Company Confidential*, and *For Internal Use Only*. Each policy for the classification of information should describe how it should be protected, who may have access to it, who has the authority to release it and how, and how it should be destroyed. All employees of the organization should be trained in the procedures for handling the information that they are authorized to access. Discretionary and mandatory access control techniques use classifications as a method to identify who may have access to what resources.

Acceptable Use Policy

An *acceptable use policy (AUP)* outlines what the organization considers to be the appropriate use of company resources, such as computer systems, e-mail, Internet access, and networks. Organizations should be concerned about personal use of organizational assets that does not benefit the company.

The goal of the AUP is to ensure employee productivity while limiting organizational liability through inappropriate use of the organization's assets. The AUP should clearly delineate what activities are not allowed. It should address issues such as the use of resources to conduct personal business, installation of hardware or software, remote access to systems and networks, the copying of company-owned software, and the responsibility of users to protect company assets, including data, software, and hardware. Statements regarding possible penalties for ignoring any of the policies (such as termination) should also be included.

Related to appropriate use of the organization's computer systems and networks by employees is the appropriate use by the organization. The most important of such issues is whether the organization considers it appropriate to monitor the employee's use of the systems and network. If monitoring is considered appropriate, the organization should include a statement to this effect in the banner that appears at login. This repeatedly warns employees, and possible intruders, that their actions are subject to monitoring and that any misuse of the system will not be tolerated. Should the organization need to use in a civil or criminal case any information gathered during monitoring, the issue of whether the employee had an expectation of privacy, or whether it was even legal for the organization to be monitoring, is simplified if the organization can point to a statement that is always displayed that instructs users that use of the system constitutes consent to monitoring. Before any monitoring is conducted, or the actual wording on the warning message is created, the organization's legal counsel should be consulted to determine the appropriate way to address this issue in the particular location.

Try This

Examples of Common Policies

A very common and also very important policy is the acceptable use policy. Make sure you understand that this policy outlines what is considered acceptable behavior for users of a computer system. This policy often goes hand-in-hand with an organization's Internet usage policy. Obtain a copy of the acceptable use policy for your organization. Compare it with samples of others that you can find on the Internet. How does yours compare with the others you found?

Internet Usage Policy

In today's highly connected environment, employee use of access to the Internet is of particular concern. The goal of the *Internet usage policy* is to ensure maximum employee productivity and to limit potential liability to the organization from inappropriate use of the Internet in a workplace. The Internet provides a tremendous temptation for employees to waste hours as they surf the Web for the scores of games from the previous night, conduct quick online stock transactions, or read the review of the latest blockbuster movie everyone is talking about. Obviously, every minute they spend conducting this sort of activity is time they are not productively engaged in the organization's business and their jobs. In addition, allowing employees to visit sites that may be considered offensive to others (such as pornographic or hate sites) can open the company to accusations of condoning a hostile work environment and result in legal liability.

The Internet usage policy needs to address what sites employees are allowed to visit and what sites they are not allowed to visit. If the company allows them to surf the Web during nonwork hours, the policy needs to clearly spell out the acceptable parameters, in terms of when they are allowed to do this and what sites they are still prohibited from visiting (such as potentially offensive sites). The policy should also describe under what circumstances an employee would be allowed to post something from the organization's network on the Web (on a blog, for example). A necessary addition to this policy would be the procedure for an employee to follow to obtain permission to post the object or message.

E-Mail Usage Policy

Related to the Internet usage policy is the *e-mail usage policy*, which deals with what the company will allow employees to send in, or as attachments to, e-mail messages. This policy should spell out whether nonwork e-mail traffic is allowed at all or is at least severely restricted. It needs to cover the type of message that would be considered inappropriate to send to other employees (for example, no offensive language, no sex-related or ethnic jokes, no harassment, and so on). The policy should also specify any disclaimers that must be attached to an employee's message sent to an individual outside the company.

Due Care and Due Diligence

Due care and *due diligence* are terms used in the legal and business community to define reasonable behavior. Basically, the law recognizes the responsibility of an individual or organization to act reasonably relative to another party. If party A alleges that the actions of party B have caused it loss or injury, party A must prove that party B failed to exercise due care or due diligence and that this failure resulted in the loss or injury. These terms often are used synonymously, but *due care* generally refers to the standard of care a reasonable person is expected to exercise in all situations, whereas *due diligence* generally refers to the standard of care a business is expected to exercise in preparation for a business transaction. An organization must take reasonable precautions before entering a business transaction or it might be found to have acted irresponsibly. In terms of security, organizations are expected to take reasonable precautions to protect the information that they maintain on individuals. Should a person suffer a loss as a result of negligence on the part of an organization in terms of its security, that person typically can bring a legal suit against the organization.

The standard applied—reasonableness—is extremely subjective and often is determined by a jury. The organization will need to show that it had taken reasonable precautions to protect the information, and that, despite these precautions, an unforeseen security event occurred that caused the injury to the other party. Since this is so subjective, it is hard to describe what would be considered reasonable, but many sectors have a set of "security best practices" for their industry, which provides a basis for organizations in that sector to start from. If the organization decides not to follow any of the best practices accepted by the industry, it needs to be prepared to justify its reasons in court should an incident occur. If the sector the organization is in has regulatory requirements, justifying why the mandated security practices were not followed will be much more difficult (and possibly impossible).

Another element that can help establish due care from a security standpoint is developing and implementing the security policies discussed in this chapter. As the policies outlined become more generally accepted, the effort required to satisfy the level of diligence and care that an organization will be expected to maintain will increase.

Due Process

Due process is concerned with guaranteeing fundamental fairness, justice, and liberty in relation to an individual's legal rights. In the United States, due process is concerned with the guarantee of an individual's rights as outlined by the Constitution and Bill of Rights. Procedural due process is based on the concept of what is "fair." Also of interest is the recognition by courts of a series of rights that are not explicitly specified by the Constitution but that the courts have decided are implicit in the concepts embodied by the Constitution. An example of this is an individual's right to privacy. From an organization's point of view, due process may come into play during an administrative action that adversely affects an employee. Before an employee is terminated, for example, were all of the employee's rights protected? An actual example pertains to the rights of privacy regarding employees' e-mail messages. As the number of cases involving employers examining employee e-mails grows, case law continues to be established and the courts eventually will settle on what rights an employee can expect. The best thing an employer can do if faced with this sort of situation is to work closely with HR staff to ensure that appropriate policies are followed and that those policies are in keeping with current laws and regulations.

Need to Know

Another common security principle is that of *need to know,* which goes hand-in-hand with *least privilege.* The guiding factor here is that each individual in the organization is supplied with only the absolute minimum amount of information and privileges he or she needs to perform their work tasks. To obtain access to any piece of information, the individual must have a justified need to know. In addition, the individual will be granted only the bare minimum number of privileges that are needed to perform their job.

A policy spelling out these two principles as guiding philosophies for the organization should be created. The policy should also address who in the organization can grant access to information and who can assign privileges to employees.

Disposal and Destruction Policy

Many potential intruders have learned the value of dumpster diving. An organization must be concerned about not only paper trash and discarded objects, but also the information stored on discarded objects such as computers. Several government organizations have been embarrassed when old computers sold to salvagers proved to contain sensitive documents on their hard drives. It is critical for every organization to have a strong *disposal and destruction policy* and related procedures.

Important papers should be shredded, and *important* in this case means anything that might be useful to a potential intruder. It is amazing what intruders can do with what appears to be innocent pieces of information.

Magnetic storage media discarded in the trash (such as disks or tapes) or sold for salvage should have all files deleted, and then the media should be overwritten at least three times with all 1's, all 0's, and then random characters. Commercial products are available to destroy files using this process. It is not sufficient simply to delete all files and leave it at that, since the deletion process affects only the pointers to where the files are stored and doesn't actually get rid of all the bits in the file. This is why it is possible to "undelete" files and recover them after they have been deleted.

A safer method for destroying files from a storage device is to destroy the data magnetically, using a strong magnetic field to *degauss* the media. This effectively destroys all data on the media. Several commercial degaussers are available for this purpose. Another method that can be used on hard drives is to use a file on them (the sort of file you'd find in a hardware store) and actually file off the magnetic material from the surface of the platter. Shredding floppy media is normally sufficient, but simply cutting a floppy into a few pieces is not enough—data has been successfully recovered from floppies that were cut into only a couple of pieces. CDs and DVDs also need to be disposed of appropriately. Many paper shredders now have the ability to shred these forms of storage media. In some highly secure environments, the only acceptable method of disposing of hard drives and other storage devices is the actual physical destruction of the devices. The importance of matching the security action to the level of risk is important to recognize in this instance. Destroying hard drives that do not have sensitive information is wasteful; proper file scrubbing is probably appropriate. For drives with ultra-sensitive information, physical destruction makes sense. There is no single answer, but as in most things associated with information security, the best practice is to match the action to the level of risk.

Service Level Agreements

Service level agreements (SLAs) are contractual agreements between entities that describe specified levels of service that the servicing entity agrees to guarantee for the customer. These agreements clearly lay out expectations in terms of the service provided and support expected, and they also generally include penalties should the described level of service or support not be provided. An organization contracting with a service provider should remember to include in the agreement a section describing the service provider's responsibility in terms of business continuity and disaster recovery. The provider's backup plans and processes for restoring lost data should also be clearly described.

Human Resources Policies

It has been said that the weakest links in the security chain are the humans. Consequently, it is important for organizations to have policies in place relative to their employees. Policies that relate to the hiring of individuals are primarily important. The organization needs to make sure that it hires individuals who can be trusted with the organization's data and that of its clients. Once employees are hired, they should be kept from slipping into the category of "disgruntled employee." Finally, policies must be developed to address the inevitable point in the future when an employee leaves the organization—either on his or her own or with the "encouragement" of the organization itself. Security issues must be considered at each of these points.

Employee Hiring and Promotions

It is becoming common for organizations to run background checks on prospective employees and to check the references prospective employees supply. Frequently, organizations require drug testing, check for any past criminal activity, verify claimed educational credentials, and confirm reported work history. For highly sensitive environments, special security background investigations can also be required. Make sure that your organization hires the most capable and trustworthy employees, and that your policies are designed to ensure this.

After an individual has been hired, your organization needs to minimize the risk that the employee will ignore company rules and affect security. Periodic reviews by supervisory personnel, additional drug checks, and monitoring of activity during work may all be considered by the organization. If the organization chooses to implement any of these reviews, this must be specified in the organization's policies, and prospective employees should be made aware of these policies before being hired. What an organization can do in terms of monitoring and requiring drug tests, for example, can be severely restricted if not spelled out in advance as terms of employment. New hires should be made aware of all pertinent policies, especially those applying to security, and should be asked to sign documents indicating that they have read and understood them.

Occasionally an employee's status will change within the company. If the change can be construed as a negative personnel action (such as a demotion), supervisors should be alerted to watch for changes in behavior that might indicate the employee is contemplating or conducting unauthorized activity. It is likely that the employee will be upset, and whether he acts on this to the detriment of the company is something that needs to be guarded against. In the case of a demotion, the individual may also lose certain privileges or access rights, and these changes should be made quickly so as to lessen the likelihood that the employee will destroy previously accessible data if he becomes disgruntled and decides to take revenge on the organization. On the other hand, if the employee is promoted, privileges may still change, but the need to make the change to access privileges may not be as urgent, though it should still be accomplished as quickly as possible. If the move is a lateral one, changes may also need to take place, and again they should be accomplished as quickly as possible. The organization's goals in terms of making changes to access privileges should be clearly spelled out in its policies.

Tech Tip

Accounts of Ex-employees

When conducting security assessments of organizations, security professionals frequently find active accounts for individuals who no longer work for the company. This is especially true for larger organizations, which may lack a clear process for the personnel office to communicate with the network administrators when an employee leaves the organization. These old accounts, however, are a weak point in the security perimeter for the organization and should be eliminated.

Retirement, Separation, or Termination of an Employee

An employee leaving an organization can be either a positive or a negative action. Employees who are retiring by their own choice may announce their planned retirement weeks or even months in advance. Limiting their access to sensitive documents the moment they announce their intention may be the safest thing to do, but it might not be necessary. Each situation should be evaluated individually. If the situation is a forced retirement, the organization must determine the risk to its data if the employee becomes disgruntled as a result of the action. In this situation, the wisest choice might be to cut off their access quickly and provide them with some additional vacation time. This might seem like an expensive proposition, but the danger to the company of having a disgruntled employee may justify it. Again, each case should be evaluated individually.

When an employee decides to leave a company, generally as a result of a new job offer, continued access to sensitive information should be carefully considered. If the employee is leaving as a result of hard feelings toward the company, it might be wise to quickly revoke her access privileges. If she is leaving as a result of a better job offer, you may decide to allow her to gracefully transfer her projects to other employees, but the decision should be considered very carefully, especially if the new company is a competitor.

If the employee is leaving the organization because he is being terminated, you should plan on him becoming disgruntled. While it may not seem the friendliest thing to do, an employee in this situation should immediately have his access privileges to sensitive information and facilities revoked.

It is better to give a potentially disgruntled employee several weeks of paid vacation than to have them trash sensitive files to which they have access. Because employees typically know the pattern of management behavior with respect to termination, doing the right thing will pay dividends in the future for a firm.

Combinations should also be quickly changed once an employee has been informed of their termination. Access cards, keys, and badges should be collected; the employee should be escorted to her desk and watched as she packs personal belongings; and then she should be escorted from the building.

No matter what the situation, the organization should have policies that describe the intended goals, and procedures should detail the process to be followed for each of the described situations.

Mandatory Vacations

Organizations have provided vacation time to their employees for many years. Few, however, force employees to take this time if they don't want to. At some companies, employees are given the choice to either "use or lose" their vacation time; if they do not take all of their vacation time, they lose at least a portion of it. From a security standpoint, an employee who never takes time off might be involved in nefarious activity, such as fraud or embezzlement, and might be afraid that if they leave on vacation, the organization will discover their illicit activities. As a result, requiring employees to use their vacation time through a policy of mandatory vacations can be a security protection mechanism.

■ Security Models

An important issue when designing the software that will operate and control secure computer systems and networks is the security model that the system or network will be based upon. The security model will implement the security policy that has been chosen and enforce those characteristics deemed most important by the system designers. For example, if confidentiality is considered paramount, the model should make certain no data is disclosed to unauthorized individuals. A model enforcing confidentiality may allow unauthorized individuals to modify or delete data, as this would not violate the tenets of the model because the true values for the data would still remain confidential. Of course, this model may not be appropriate for all environments. In some instances, the unauthorized modification of data may be considered a more serious issue than its unauthorized disclosure. In such cases, the model would be responsible for enforcing the integrity of the data instead of its confidentiality. Choosing the model to base the design on is critical if you want to ensure that the resulting system accurately enforces the security policy desired. This, however, is only the starting point, and it does not imply that you have to make a choice between confidentiality and data integrity, as both are important.

Confidentiality Models

Data confidentiality has generally been the chief concern of the military. For instance, the U.S. military encouraged the development of the **Bell-LaPadula security model** to address data confidentiality in computer operating systems. This model is especially useful in designing multilevel security systems that implement the military's hierarchical security scheme, which includes levels of classification such as *Unclassified, Confidential, Secret,* and *Top Secret.* Similar classification schemes can be used in industry, where classifications might include *Publicly Releasable, Proprietary,* and *Company Confidential.*

The Bell-LaPadula security model employs both mandatory and discretionary access control mechanisms when implementing its two basic security principles. The first of these principles is called the **Simple Security Rule**, which states that no subject (such as a user or a program) can read information from an object (such as a file) with a security classification higher than that possessed by the subject itself. This means that the system must prevent a user with only a Secret clearance, for example, from reading a document labeled Top Secret. This rule is often referred to as the "no-read-up" rule.

The second security principle enforced by the Bell-LaPadula security model is known as the ***-property** (pronounced "star property"). This principle states that a subject can write to an object only if its security classification is less than or equal to the object's security classification. This means that a user with a Secret clearance can write to a file with a Secret or Top Secret classification but cannot write to a file with only an Unclassified classification. This at first may appear to be a bit confusing, since this principle allows users to write to files that they are not allowed to view, thus enabling them to actually destroy files that they don't have the classification to see. This is true, but keep in mind that the Bell-LaPadula model is designed to enforce confidentiality, not integrity. Writing to a file that you don't have the clearance to view is not considered a confidentiality issue; it is an integrity issue.

Whereas the *-property allows a user to write to a file of equal or greater security classification, it doesn't allow a user to write to a file with a lower security classification. This, too, may be confusing at first—after all, shouldn't a user with a Secret clearance, who can view a file marked Unclassified, be allowed to write to that file? The answer to this, from a security perspective, is "no." The reason again relates to wanting to avoid either accidental or deliberate security disclosures. The system is designed to make it impossible (hopefully) for data to be disclosed to those without the appropriate level to view it. If it were possible for a user with a Top Secret clearance to either deliberately or accidentally write Top Secret information and place it in a file marked Secret, a user with only a Secret security clearance could then access this file and view the Top Secret information. Thus, data would have been disclosed to an individual not authorized to view it. This is what the system should protect against and is the reason for what is known as the "no-write-down" rule.

Not all environments are more concerned with confidentiality than integrity. In a financial institution, for example, viewing somebody's bank balance is an issue, but a greater issue would be the ability to actually modify that balance. In environments where integrity is more important, a different model than the Bell-LaPadula security model is needed.

 The Simple Security Rule is just that: the most basic of security rules. It basically states that in order for you to see something, you have to be authorized to see it.

Integrity Models

The Bell-LaPadula model was developed in the early 1970s but was found to be insufficient for all environments. As an alternative, Kenneth Biba studied the integrity issue and developed what is called the **Biba security model** in the late 1970s. Additional work was performed in the 1980s that led to the

Clark-Wilson security model, which also places its emphasis on integrity rather than confidentiality.

The Biba Security Model

In the Biba model, instead of security classifications, *integrity levels* are used. A principle of integrity levels is that data with a higher integrity level is believed to be more accurate or reliable than data with a lower integrity level. Integrity levels indicate the level of "trust" that can be placed in information at the different levels. Integrity levels differ from security levels in another way—they limit the modification of information as opposed to the flow of information.

An initial attempt at implementing an integrity-based model was captured in what is referred to as the **Low-Water-Mark policy**. This policy in many ways is the opposite of the *-property in that it prevents subjects from writing to objects of a higher integrity level. The policy also contains a second rule that states the integrity level of a subject will be lowered if it reads an object of a lower integrity level. The reason for this is that if the subject then uses data from that object, the highest the integrity level can be for a new object created from it is the same level of integrity of the original object. In other words, the level of trust you can place in data formed from data at a specific integrity level cannot be higher than the level of trust you have in the subject creating the new data object, and the level of trust you have in the subject can only be as high as the level of trust you had in the original data. The final rule contained in the Low-Water-Mark policy states that a subject can execute a program only if the program's integrity level is equal to or less than the integrity level of the subject. This ensures that data modified by a program only has the level of trust (integrity level) that can be placed in the individual who executed the program.

While the Low-Water-Mark policy certainly prevents unauthorized modification of data, it has the unfortunate side effect of eventually lowering the integrity levels of all subjects to the lowest level on the system (unless the subject always views files with the same level of integrity). This is because of the second rule, which lowers the integrity level of the subject after accessing an object of a lower integrity level. There is no way specified in the policy to ever raise the subject's integrity level back to its original value. A second policy, known as the **Ring policy**, addresses this issue by allowing any subject to read any object without regard to the object's level of integrity and without lowering the subject's integrity level. This, unfortunately, can lead to a situation where data created by a subject after reading data of a lower integrity level could end up having a higher level of trust placed upon it than it should.

The Biba security model implements a hybrid of the Ring and Low-Water-Mark policies. Biba's model in many respects is the opposite of the Bell-LaPadula model in that what it enforces are "no-read-down" and "no-write-up" policies. It also implements a third rule that prevents subjects from executing programs of a higher level. The Biba security model thus addresses the problems mentioned with both the Ring and Low-Water-Mark policies.

The Clark-Wilson Security Model

The **Clark-Wilson security model** takes an entirely different approach than the Biba and Bell-LaPadula models, using transactions as the basis for its rules. It defines two levels of integrity only: constrained data items (CDI) and unconstrained data items (UDI). CDI data is subject to integrity controls while UDI data is not. The model then defines two types of processes: integrity verification processes (IVPs), which ensure that CDI data meets integrity constraints (to ensure the system is in a valid state), and transformation processes (TPs), which change the state of data from one valid state to another. Data in this model cannot be modified directly by a user; it must be changed by trusted TPs, access to which can be restricted (thus restricting the ability of a user to perform certain activities).

It is useful to return to the prior example of the banking account balance to describe the need for integrity-based models. In the Clark-Wilson model, the account balance would be a CDI because its integrity is a critical function for the bank. A client's color preference for their checkbook is not a critical function and would be considered a UDI. Since the integrity of account balances is of extreme importance, changes to a person's balance must be accomplished through the use of a TP. Ensuring that the balance is correct would be the duty of an IVP. Only certain employees of the bank should have the ability to modify an individual's account, which can be controlled by limiting the number of individuals who have the authority to execute TPs that result in account modification. Certain very critical functions may actually be split into multiple TPs to enforce another important principle, *separation of duties*. This limits the authority any one individual has so that multiple individuals will be required to execute certain critical functions.

Chapter 2 Review

■ Chapter Summary

After reading this chapter and completing the exercises, you should understand the following regarding the basics of security, security terminology, and security models.

Define basic terms associated with computer and information security

■ Information assurance and information security place the security focus on the information and not on the hardware or software used to process it.

■ The original goal of computer and network security was to provide confidentiality, integrity, and availability—the "CIA" of security.

■ As a result of the increased reliance on networks for commerce, authentication and nonrepudiation have been added to the original CIA of security.

Identify the basic approaches to computer and information security

■ The operational model of computer security tells us that protection is provided by prevention, detection, and response.

■ Host security focuses on protecting each computer and device individually instead of addressing protection of the network as a whole.

■ Least privilege means that an object should have only the necessary rights and privileges to perform its task, with no additional permissions.

■ Diversity of defense is a concept that complements the idea of various layers of security. It means to make the layers dissimilar so that if one layer is penetrated, the next layer can't also be penetrated using the same method.

Distinguish among various methods to implement access controls

■ Access is the ability of a subject to interact with an object. Access controls are those devices and methods used to limit which subjects may interact with specific objects.

■ An access control list (ACL) is a mechanism that is used to define whether a user has certain access privileges for a system. Others methods include discretionary access control (DAC), mandatory access control (MAC), role-based access control (RBAC), and rule-based access control (also RBAC).

Describe methods used to verify the identity and authenticity of an individual

■ Authentication mechanisms ensure that only valid users are provided access to the computer system or network.

■ The three general methods used in authentication involve users providing either something they know, something they have, or something unique about them (something they are).

Describe methods used to conduct social engineering

■ Social engineering is the process of convincing an authorized individual to provide confidential information or access to an unauthorized individual.

■ With a plausible background and a good story, a good social engineer can frequently talk individuals into divulging information that they normally would never give out.

■ In addition to the direct approach to social engineering, attackers can use other, indirect means to obtain the information they are seeking, including phishing, vishing, shoulder surfing, and dumpster diving.

Recognize some of the basic models used to implement security in operating systems

■ Security models enforce the chosen security policy.

■ There are two basic categories of models: those that ensure confidentiality and those that ensure integrity.

■ Bell-LaPadula is a confidentiality security model whose development was prompted by the demands of the U.S. military and its security clearance scheme.

■ The Bell-LaPadula security model enforces "no-read-up" and "no-write-down" rules to avoid the deliberate or accidental disclosure of information to individuals not authorized to receive it.

- The Biba security model is an integrity-based model that, in many respects, implements the opposite of what the Bell-LaPadula model does—that is, "no-read-down" and "no-write-up" rules.

- The Clark-Wilson security model is an integrity-based model designed to limit the processes an individual may perform as well as require that critical data be modified only through specific transformation processes.

■ Key Terms

*-property *(43)*
access control *(31)*
auditability *(22)*
authentication *(22)*
availability *(22)*
Bell-LaPadula security model *(42)*
Biba security model *(43)*
certificates *(32)*
Clark-Wilson security model *(45)*
confidentiality *(22)*
data aggregation *(34)*
diversity of defense *(28)*
hacking *(21)*
host security *(23)*

implicit deny *(26)*
integrity *(22)*
layered security *(27)*
least privilege *(24)*
Low-Water-Mark policy *(44)*
network security *(23)*
nonrepudiation *(22)*
operational model of computer security *(22)*
phreaking *(21)*
Ring policy *(44)*
security through obscurity *(29)*
separation of duties *(25)*
Simple Security Rule *(43)*
social engineering *(33)*

■ Key Terms Quiz

Use terms from the Key Terms list to complete the sentences that follow. Don't use the same term more than once. Not all terms will be used.

1. _____ is a term used to describe the condition where a user cannot deny that an event has occurred.

2. The _____ is an integrity-based security model that bases its security on control of the processes that are allowed to modify critical data, referred to as constrained data items.

3. The security principle used in the Bell-LaPadula security model that states that no subject can read from an object with a higher security classification is called the _____.

4. The principle that states a subject has only the necessary rights and privileges to perform its task, with no additional permissions, is called _____.

5. _____ is the principle in security whose goal it is to ensure that data is modified only by individuals who are authorized to change it.

6. _____ is the term used to refer to the _____ of computers and systems used by the telephone company.

7. _____ is the process used to ensure that an individual is who they claim to be.

8. The architecture in which multiple methods of security defense are applied to prevent realization of threat-based risks is called _____.

9. _____ is the process of combining seemingly unimportant information with other pieces of information to divulge potentially sensitive information.

10. Using _____ is a method to establish authenticity of specific objects such as an individual's public key or downloaded software.

■ Multiple-Choice Quiz

1. What is the most common form of authentication used?

   A. Smart card

   B. Tokens

   C. Username/password

   D. Retinal scan

2. The CIA of security includes:

   A. Confidentiality, integrity, authentication

   B. Confidentiality, integrity, availability

   C. Certificates, integrity, availability

   D. Confidentiality, inspection, authentication

3. The security principle used in the Bell-LaPadula security model that states that no subject can read from an object with a higher security classification is the:

   A. Simple Security Rule

   B. Ring policy

   C. Mandatory access control

   D. *-property

4. Which of the following concepts requires users and system processes to use the minimal amount of permission necessary to function?

   A. Layer defense

   B. Diversified defense

   C. Simple Security Rule

   D. Least privilege

5. Which of the following is an access control method based on changes at preset intervals?

   A. Simple Security Rule

   B. Job rotation

   C. Two-man rule

   D. Separation of duties

6. The Bell-LaPadula security model is an example of a security model that is based on:

   A. The integrity of the data

   B. The availability of the data

   C. The confidentiality of the data

   D. The authenticity of the data

7. The term used to describe the requirement that different portions of a critical process must be performed by different people is:

   A. Least privilege

   B. Defense in depth

   C. Separation of duties

   D. Job rotation

8. Hiding information to prevent disclosure is an example of:

   A. Security through obscurity

   B. Certificate-based security

   C. Discretionary data security

   D. Defense in depth

9. The problem with the Low-Water-Mark policy is that it:

   A. Is aimed at ensuring confidentiality and not integrity

   B. Could ultimately result in all subjects having the integrity level of the least-trusted object on the system

   C. Could result in the unauthorized modification of data

   D. Does not adequately prevent users from viewing files they are not entitled to

10. The concept of blocking an action unless it is specifically authorized is:

    A. Implicit deny

    B. Least privilege

    C. Simple Security Rule

    D. Hierarchical defense model

■ Essay Quiz

1. Your boss mentions that recently a number of employees have received calls from individuals who didn't identify themselves and asked a lot of questions about the company and its computer infrastructure. At first, he thought this was a just a computer vendor who was trying to sell your company some new product, but no vendor has approached the company. He also says several strange e-mails requesting personal information have been sent to employees, and quite a few people have been seen searching your company's trash dumpsters for recyclable containers. Your boss asks what you think about all of these strange incidents. Respond and be sure to provide a recommendation on what should be done about the various incidents.

2. Your company has decided to increase the authentication security by requiring remote employees to use a security token as well as a password to log onto the network. The employees are grumbling about the new requirements because they don't want to have to carry around the token with them and don't understand why it's necessary. Write a brief memo to the staff to educate them on the general ways that authentication can be performed. Then explain why your company has decided to use security tokens in addition to passwords.

3. The new CEO for your company just retired from the military and wants to use some of the same computer systems and security software she used while with the military. Explain to her the reasons that confidentiality-based security models are not adequate for all environments. Provide at least two examples of environments where a confidentiality-based security model is not sufficient.

4. Describe why the concept of "security through obscurity" is generally considered a bad principle to rely on. Provide some real-world examples of where you have seen this principle used.

5. Write a brief essay describing the principle of least privilege and how it can be employed to enhance security. Provide at least two examples of environments in which it can be used for security purposes.

Lab Projects

• Lab Project 2.1

In an environment familiar to you (your school or where you work, for example), determine what different layers of security are employed. Discuss whether you think they are sufficient and whether the principle of diversity of defense has also been used.

• Lab Project 2.2

Pick an operating system that enforces some form of access controls and determine how it is implemented in that system.

Operational and Organizational Security

We will bankrupt ourselves in the vain search for absolute security.

—Dwight David Eisenhower

In this chapter, you will learn how to

- **Identify various operational aspects to security in your organization**
- **Describe the physical security components that can protect your computers and network**
- **Identify environmental factors that can affect security**
- **Identify factors that affect the security of the growing number of wireless technologies used for data transmission**
- **Prevent disclosure through electronic emanations**

Recall from Chapter 2 the operational model of computer security. The model describes the various components in computer and network security. Specifically, the operational model of computer security states that:

Protection = Prevention + (Detection + Response)

Security Operations in Your Organization

Prevention technologies are designed to keep individuals from being able to gain access to systems or data they are not authorized to use. Originally, this was the sole approach to security. Eventually we learned that in an operational environment, prevention is extremely difficult and relying on prevention technologies alone is not sufficient. This led to the rise of technologies to detect and respond to events that occur when prevention fails. Together, the prevention technologies and the detection and response technologies form the operational model for computer security.

Prevention technologies are static in the sense that they are put in place and generally left alone. This is not to say that they are not periodically evaluated and updated as needed, but they are generally designed to serve in some way as a static barrier to intruders. Detection and response technologies, on the other hand, are dynamic in the sense that they acknowledge that security is an ongoing process that needs constant monitoring. Systems and networks are constantly changing and therefore need to be continually monitored. Monitoring the operation of the various components that make up your security perimeter is an essential part of any organization's security program.

> The operational model of security is a recognition that prevention technologies alone will never be adequate. No matter how secure we attempt to make our systems, some way will always be found to circumvent the safeguards we have in place. The operational model accepts this and states that when we implement our solutions in a real, operational environment, we need to have additional mechanisms in place to detect and respond to threats the prevention technologies failed to intercept.

Policies, Procedures, Standards, and Guidelines

An important part of any organization's approach to implementing security are the policies, procedures, standards, and guidelines that are established to detail what users and administrators should be doing to maintain the security of the systems and network. Collectively, these documents provide the guidance needed to determine how security will be implemented in the organization. Given this guidance, the specific technology and security mechanisms required can be planned for.

Policies are high-level, broad statements of what the organization wants to accomplish. They are made by management when laying out the organization's position on some issue. **Procedures** are the step-by-step instructions on how to implement policies in the organization. They describe exactly how employees are expected to act in a given situation or to accomplish a specific task. **Standards** are mandatory elements regarding the implementation of a policy. They are accepted specifications that provide specific details on how a policy is to be enforced. Some standards are externally driven. Regulations for banking and financial institutions, for example, require certain security measures be taken by law. Other standards may be set by the organization to meet its own security goals. **Guidelines** are recommendations relating to a policy. The key term in this case is *recommendation*—guidelines are not mandatory steps.

> **Policies:** High-level, broad statements of what the organization wants to accomplish
> **Procedures:** Step-by-step instructions on how to implement the policies
> **Standards:** Mandatory elements regarding the implementation of a policy
> **Guidelines:** Recommendations relating to a policy

Just as the network itself constantly changes, the policies, procedures, standards, and guidelines should be included in living documents that are periodically evaluated and changed as necessary. The constant monitoring of the network and the periodic review of the relevant documents are part of the process that is the operational model. When applied to policies, this process results in what is known as the *policy lifecycle.* This operational process and policy lifecycle roughly consist of four steps in relation to your security policies and solutions:

1. Plan (adjust) for security in your organization.
2. Implement the plans.
3. Monitor the implementation.
4. Evaluate the effectiveness.

In the first step, you develop the policies, procedures, and guidelines that will be implemented and design the security components that will protect your network. Once these are designed and developed, you can implement the plans. Part of the implementation of any policy, procedure, or guideline is an instruction period during which those who will be affected by the change or introduction of this new document learn about its contents. Next, you monitor to ensure that both the hardware and the software as well as the policies, procedures, and guidelines are effective in securing your systems. Finally, you evaluate the effectiveness of the security measures you have in place. This step may include a *vulnerability assessment* (an attempt to identify and prioritize the list of vulnerabilities within a system or network) and a *penetration test* (a method to check the security of a system by simulating an attack by a malicious individual) of your system to ensure the security is adequate. After evaluating your security posture, you begin again with step one, this time adjusting the security mechanisms you have in place, and then continue with this cyclical process.

The Security Perimeter

The discussion to this point has not included any mention of the specific technology used to enforce operational and organizational security or a description of the various components that constitute the organization's security perimeter. If the average administrator were asked to draw a diagram depicting the various components of their network, the diagram would probably look something like Figure 3.1.

This diagram includes the major components typically found in a network. The connection to the Internet generally has some sort of protection attached to it such as a firewall. An intrusion detection system (IDS), also often part of the security perimeter for the organization, may be either on the inside or the outside of the firewall, or it may in fact be on both sides. The specific location depends on the company and what it is more concerned about preventing (that is, insider threats or external threats). The router can also be thought of as a security device, as it can be used to enhance security such as in the case of wireless routers that can be used to enforce encryption settings. Beyond this security perimeter is the corporate network. Figure 3.1 is obviously a very simple depiction—an actual network can have numerous subnets and extranets as well as wireless access points—but the basic components are present. Unfortunately, if

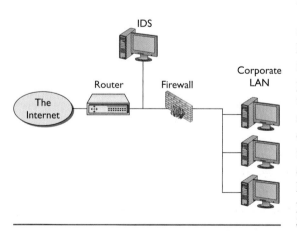

• **Figure 3.1**   Basic diagram of an organization's network

this were the diagram provided by the administrator to show the organization's basic network structure, the administrator would have missed a very important component. A more astute administrator would provide a diagram more like Figure 3.2.

This diagram includes other possible access points into the network, including the public switched telephone network (PSTN) and wireless access points. The organization may or may not have any authorized modems or wireless networks, but the savvy administrator would realize that the potential exists for unauthorized versions of both. When considering the policies, procedures, and guidelines needed to implement security for the organization, both networks need to be considered. Another development that has brought the telephone and computer networks together is the implementation of *voice over IP (VoIP)*, which eliminates the traditional land lines in an organization and replaces them with special telephones that connect to the IP data network.

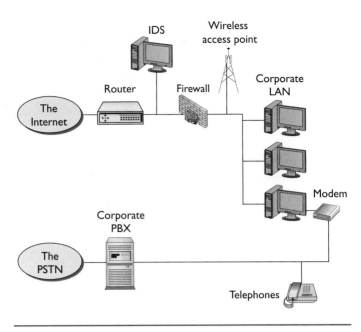

• **Figure 3.2**   A more complete diagram of an organization's network

While Figure 3.2 provides a more comprehensive view of the various components that need to be protected, it is still incomplete. Most experts will agree that the biggest danger to any organization does not come from external attacks but rather from the insider—a disgruntled employee or somebody else who has physical access to the facility. Given physical access to an office, the knowledgeable attacker will quickly find the information needed to gain access to the organization's computer systems and network. Consequently, every organization also needs security policies, procedures, and guidelines that cover physical security, and every security administrator should be concerned with these as well. While physical security (which can include such things as locks, cameras, guards and entry points, alarm systems, and physical barriers) will probably not fall under the purview of the security administrator, the operational state of the organization's physical security measures is just as important as many of the other network-centric measures.

The security perimeter, with its several layers of security, along with additional security mechanisms that may be implemented on each system (such as user IDs/passwords) create what is sometimes known as *defense-in-depth*. This implies that security is enhanced when there are multiple layers of security (the depth) through which an attacker would have to penetrate to reach the desired goal.

Physical Security

Physical security consists of all mechanisms used to ensure that physical access to the computer systems and networks is restricted to only authorized users. Additional physical security mechanisms may be used to provide increased security for especially sensitive systems such as servers and devices such as routers, firewalls, and intrusion detection systems. When considering physical security, access from all six sides should be considered—not only should the security of obvious points of entry be examined, such as doors and windows, but the walls themselves as well as the floor and ceiling should also be considered. Questions such as the following should be addressed:

- Is there a false ceiling with tiles that can be easily removed?
- Do the walls extend to the actual ceiling or only to a false ceiling?
- Is there a raised floor?
- Do the walls extend to the actual floor, or do they stop at a raised floor?
- How are important systems situated?
- Do the monitors face away from windows, or could the activity of somebody at a system be monitored?
- Who has access to the facility?
- What type of access control is there, and are there any guards?
- Who is allowed unsupervised access to the facility?
- Is there an alarm system or security camera that covers the area?
- What procedures govern the monitoring of the alarm system or security camera and the response should unauthorized activity be detected?

These are just some of the numerous questions that need to be asked when examining the physical security surrounding a system.

Access Controls

The purpose of physical access controls is the same as that of computer and network access controls—you want to restrict access to only those who are authorized to have it. Physical access is restricted by requiring the individual to somehow authenticate that they have the right or authority to have the desired access. As in computer authentication, access in the physical world can be based on something the individual has, something they know, or something they are. Frequently, when dealing with the physical world, the terms "authentication" and "access control" are used interchangeably.

The most common physical access control device, which has been around in some form for centuries, is a lock. Combination locks represent an access control device that depends on something the individual knows (the combination). Locks with keys depend on something the individual has (the key). Each of these has certain advantages and disadvantages. Combinations don't require any extra hardware, but they must be remembered (which means individuals may write them down—a security vulnerability in itself) and are hard to control. Anybody who knows the combination may provide it to somebody else. Key locks are simple and easy to use, but the key may be lost, which means another key has to be made or the lock has to be rekeyed. Keys may also be copied, and their dissemination can be hard to control. Key "bumping" is also a subject that has received considerable attention on the Internet. It involves making a special key that, when inserted into a lock, can be used to open the lock after tapping (bumping) the lock to set the pins. Newer locks replace the traditional key with a card that must be passed through a reader or placed against it. The individual may also have to provide a personal access code, thus making this form of access both a something-you-know and something-you-have method.

In addition to locks on doors, other common physical security devices include video surveillance and even simple access control logs (sign-in logs). While sign-in logs don't provide an actual barrier, they do provide a record of access and, when used in conjunction with a guard who verifies an individual's identity, can dissuade potential adversaries from attempting to gain access to a facility. As mentioned, another common access control mechanism is a human security guard. Many organizations employ a guard to provide an extra level of examination of individuals who want to gain access to a facility. Other devices are limited to their designed function. A human guard can apply common sense to situations that might have been unexpected. Having security guards also addresses the common practice of piggybacking, where an individual follows another person closely to avoid having to go through the access control procedures. For example, if one employee enters the combination to a door and then opens it, another individual might follow quickly behind before the door closes to avoid having to enter the combination. A security guard checking each individual's identification would eliminate this problem.

Biometrics

Access controls that utilize something you know (for example, combinations) or something you have (such as keys) are not the only methods to limit facility access to authorized individuals. A third approach is to utilize something unique about the individual—their fingerprints, for example—to identify them. Unlike the other two methods, the something-you-are method, known as **biometrics**, does not rely on the individual to either remember something or to have something in their possession. Biometrics is a more sophisticated access control approach and is also more expensive. Other methods to accomplish biometrics include handwriting analysis, retinal scans, iris scans, voiceprints, hand geometry, and facial geometry.

Biometrics can be used both to control access to computer systems and networks and to control physical access to restricted areas, but when used for physical access control, methods can be used that are not generally used in biometric access control for computer systems and networks. Hand geometry, for example, requires a fairly large device. This can easily be placed outside of a door to control access to the room but would not be as convenient to control access to a computer system, since a reader would need to be placed with each computer or at least with groups of computers. In a mobile environment where laptops are being used, a device such as a hand geometry reader would be unrealistic.

To add an additional layer of security, biometric devices are normally used in conjunction with another access control method. An individual might, for example, be required to also provide a personal access code (something they know) or to pass a card through a reader (something they have). While it may seem at first that nothing else should be needed besides a biometric access control, the biometric devices currently in use are not 100 percent accurate and have been known to allow access to individuals who were not authorized. This is the reason for the additional something-you-know or something-you-have method to supplement the biometric device.

Tech Tip

Physical and Information Security Convergence
In high-security sites, physical access controls and electronic access controls to information are interlocked. This means that before data can be accessed from a particular machine, the physical access control system must agree with the finding that the authorized party is present. For example, if you are in your office because you used an electronic key to open your door, your login credentials will not function from another office or from a location offsite.

Exam Tip: There are many similarities between authentication and access controls in computers and in the physical world. Remember the three common techniques for verifying a person's identity and access privileges: something you know, something you have, and something about you.

Tech Tip

Biometric Devices

Once only seen in spy or science fiction movies, biometrics such as hand and fingerprint readers, eye-scanning technology, and voiceprint devices are now becoming more common in the real world. The accuracy of these devices has improved and the costs have dropped, making them realistic solutions to many access control situations.

All forms of authentication have weaknesses that can be exploited. It is for this reason that "strong authentication" or "two-factor authentication" is often used. These methods use two of the three different types of authentication (something you have, know, or are) to provide two levels of security, as in the previous example of a biometric device and a swipe card. Which two are used in combination depends on a number of factors, including user acceptance, budget, and the exact level of security the organization is trying to obtain.

Physical Barriers

An even more common security feature (using "device" to describe them is unusual) than locks is a physical barrier. Physical barriers help implement the physical-world equivalent of layered security. The outermost layer of physical security should contain the more publicly visible activities. A guard at a gate in a fence, for example, would be visible by all who happen to pass by. As you progress through the layers, the barriers and security mechanisms should become less publicly visible to make determining what mechanisms are in place more difficult for observers. Signs are also an important element in security, as they announce to the public what areas are public and which are private. A *man trap* can also be used in this layered approach. It generally consists of a small space that is large enough for only one person at a time, with two locking doors. An individual has to enter the first door, close the first door, then attempt to open the second door. If unsuccessful, perhaps because they do not have the proper access code, the person can be caught inside this small location until security personnel show up.

In addition to walls and fences, open space can also serve as a barrier. While this may at first seem to be an odd statement, consider the use of large areas of open space around a facility. For an intruder to cross this open space takes time—time in which they are vulnerable and their presence may be discovered. In today's environment in which terrorist attacks have become more common, additional precautions should be taken for areas that may be considered a possible target for terrorist activity. In addition to open space, which is necessary to lessen the effect of explosions, concrete barriers that stop vehicles from getting too close to facilities should also be used. It is not necessary for these to be unsightly concrete walls; many facilities have placed large, round concrete circles, filled them with dirt, and then planted flowers and other plants to construct a large, immovable planter.

■ Environmental Issues

Environmental issues may not at first seem to be of a security concern, but when considering the availability of a computer system or network, they must be taken into consideration. Environmental issues include items such as **heating, ventilation, and air conditioning (HVAC)** systems, electrical power, and the "environments of nature." HVAC systems are used to maintain the comfort of an office environment. A few years back, they were also critical for the smooth operation of computer systems that had low tolerances for humidity and heat. Today's desktop systems are much more tolerant, and the limiting factor is now often the human user. The exception to this HVAC limitation is when large quantities of equipment are co-located, in server rooms and network equipment closets. In these heat-dense areas, HVAC is needed to keep equipment temperatures within reasonable ranges. Often certain security devices such as firewalls and intrusion detection systems are located in these same equipment closets and the loss of HVAC systems can cause these critical systems to fail. One interesting aspect of HVAC systems is that they themselves are often computer controlled and frequently provide remote access via telephone or network connections. These connections should be protected in a similar manner to computer modems, or else attackers may locate them and change the HVAC settings for an office or building.

HVAC systems for server rooms and network equipment closets are important because the dense equipment environment can generate significant amounts of heat. HVAC outages can result in temperatures that are outside equipment operating ranges, forcing shutdowns.

Electrical power is obviously an essential requirement for computer systems and networks. Electrical power is subject to momentary surges and disruption. Surge protectors are needed to protect sensitive electronic equipment from fluctuations in voltage. An **uninterruptible power supply (UPS)** should be considered for critical systems so that a loss of power will not halt processing. The size of the batteries associated with a UPS will determine the amount of time that it can operate before it too loses power. Many sites ensure sufficient power to provide administrators the opportunity to cleanly bring the system or network down. For installations that require continual operations, even in the event of a power outage, electric generators that automatically start when a loss of power is detected can be installed. These systems may take a few seconds to start before they reach full operation, so a UPS should also be considered to smooth the transition between normal and backup power.

The frequency of natural disasters is a contributing factor that must be considered when making contingency processing plans for an installation. In an area that experiences frequent electric storms, for example, power surge protectors and UPSs are an absolute must. In an area that experiences frequent storms and floods, devices that can sense water building up in a facility are required to warn of pending problems. In an area with frequent hurricanes, earthquakes, and tornadoes, reinforced facilities are required to protect important processing equipment. All of these natural disasters provide reasons for having not only an active program to ensure frequent backup of critical data, but offsite storage as well. Offsite storage limits the chance that a natural disaster affecting one area will result in the total loss of the organization's critical data. When considering backup and contingency plans, it is also important to consider a backup processing location in case a disaster not only destroys the data at the organization's primary site but all processing equipment as well.

Fire Suppression

Fires are a common disaster that can affect organizations and their computing equipment. Fire detection and fire suppression devices are two approaches to addressing this threat. Detectors can be useful because some may be able to detect a fire in its very early stages before a fire suppression system is activated, and they can potentially sound a warning. This warning could provide employees with the opportunity to deal with the fire before it becomes serious enough for the fire suppression equipment to kick in. There are several different types of fire detectors. The first type is activated by smoke. The second is activated by heat. Fire suppression systems are designed to discharge automatically when a fire has reached a serious enough point that if immediate action isn't taken there is a potential to lose the facility. Suppression systems come in several varieties, including sprinkler-based systems and gas-based systems. Standard sprinkler-based systems are not optimal for data centers because water will ruin large electrical infrastructures and most integrated circuit–based devices—such as computers. Gas-based systems are a good alternative, though they also carry special concerns. Halon was used for many years, and any existing installations may still have it for fire suppression in data centers. Halon displaces oxygen, and any people caught in the gas when the system goes off will need a breathing apparatus to survive. Halon is being replaced with other gas-based suppression systems, such as argon and nitrogen mixing systems or carbon dioxide, but the same danger to people exists, so these systems should be carefully implemented. A more extensive coverage of fire detection and suppression will be covered in Chapter 8.

■ Wireless

When someone talks about wireless communication, they generally are referring to cellular telephones ("cell phones"). These devices have become ubiquitous in today's modern office environment. A cell phone network consists of the phones themselves, the cells with their accompanying base stations that they are used in, and the hardware and software that allow them to communicate. The base stations are made up of antennas, receivers, transmitters, and amplifiers. The base stations communicate with those cell phones that are currently in the geographical area that is serviced by that station. As a person travels across town, they may exit and enter multiple cells. The stations must conduct a handoff to ensure continuous operation for the cell phone. As the individual moves toward the edge of a cell, a mobile switching center notices the power of the signal beginning to drop, checks whether another cell has a stronger signal for the phone (cells frequently overlap), and, if so, switches operation to this new cell and base station. All of this is done without the user ever knowing that they have moved from one cell to another.

Cell phones are a tremendous technology, providing a great service to modern businesses and individuals. Cell phone technology is advancing, and more and more phones are being used for more than just voice communication. Cell phones also provide messaging capability, some provide Internet connectivity, and some can be used as digital cameras.

Wireless technology can also be used for networking. There are two main standards for wireless network technology. **Bluetooth** is designed as a short-range (approximately ten meters) personal area network (PAN) cable-replacement technology that can be built into a variety of devices, such as mobile phones, PDAs, and laptop computers. The idea is to create low-cost wireless technology so that many different devices can communicate with each other. Bluetooth is also interesting because, unlike other wireless

Tech Tip

Wireless Network Security Issues
Due to a number of advantages, such as the ability to take your laptop with you as you move around your building and still stay connected, wireless networks have grown in popularity. They also eliminate the need to string network cables all over the office. At the same time, however, they can be a security nightmare if not adequately protected. The signal for your network doesn't stop at your office door or wall just because it is there. It will continue propagating to areas that may be open to anybody. This provides the opportunity for others to access your network. To avoid this, you must take steps such as encrypting transmissions so that your wireless network doesn't become the weak link in your security chain.

Principles of Computer Security: CompTIA Security+ and Beyond

technology, it is designed so that devices can talk directly with each other without having to go through a central device (such as the base station described previously). This is known as *peer-to-peer communication*.

The other major wireless standard is the **IEEE 802.11** set of standards, which is well suited for the local area network (LAN) environment. 802.11 networks can operate either in an ad hoc peer-to-peer fashion or in infrastructure mode, which is more common. In infrastructure mode, computers with 802.11 network cards communicate with a wireless access point. This access point connects to the network so that the computers communicating with it are essentially also connected to the network.

In an office environment, wireless networks are tremendously useful, as they free the user to take their computer anywhere in the building (as long as an access point is nearby). If a new employee joins the company, wire cable does not need to be strung to connect them; instead, they simply need to be within transmission distance of an access point.

While wireless networks are very useful in today's modern office (and home), they are not without their security problems. Access points are generally placed throughout a building so that all employees can access the corporate network. The transmission and reception areas covered by access points are not easily controlled. Consequently, many publicly accessible areas might fall into the range of one of the organization's access points, or its Bluetooth-enabled systems, and thus the corporate network may become vulnerable to attack. Wireless networks are designed to incorporate some security measures, but all too often the networks are set up without security enabled, and serious security flaws exist in the 802.11 design.

Cross Check

Wireless Networks

Wireless network security is discussed in this chapter in relationship to physical issues such as the placement of wireless access points. There are, however, numerous other issues with wireless security, which are discussed in Chapter 12. Make sure to understand how the physical location of wireless access points affects the other wireless security issues.

■ Electromagnetic Eavesdropping

In 1985, a paper by Wim van Eck of the Netherlands described what became known as the van Eck phenomenon. In the paper van Eck described how eavesdropping on what was being displayed on monitors could be accomplished by picking up and then decoding the electromagnetic interference produced by the monitors. With the appropriate equipment, the exact image of what is being displayed can be re-created some distance away. While the original paper discussed emanations as they applied to video display units (monitors), the same phenomenon applies to other devices such as printers and computers as well.

This phenomenon had actually been known about for quite some time before van Eck published his paper. The U.S. Department of Defense used the term **TEMPEST** (referred to by some as the *Transient ElectroMagnetic Pulse Emanation STandard*) to describe both a program in the military to control these electronic emanations from electrical equipment and the actual process for controlling the emanations. There are three basic ways to prevent these emanations from being picked up by an attacker:

- Put the equipment beyond the point that the emanations can be picked up.
- Provide shielding for the equipment itself.
- Provide a shielded enclosure (such as a room) to put the equipment in.

One of the simplest ways to protect against equipment being monitored in this fashion is to put enough distance between the target and the attacker. The emanations can be picked up from only a limited distance. If the physical security for the facility is sufficient to put enough space between the equipment and publicly accessible areas that the signals cannot be picked up, then the organization doesn't have to take any additional measures to ensure security.

Distance is not the only way to protect against eavesdropping on electronic emanations. Devices can be shielded so their emanations are blocked. Acquiring enough property to provide the necessary distance needed to protect against an eavesdropper may be possible if the facility is in the country with lots of available land surrounding it. If, however, the organization is in the middle of a city, then purchasing additional property may be prohibitive. Indeed, for smaller organizations that occupy only a few offices or floors in a large office building, it would be impossible to acquire enough space.

In this case, the organization may resort to purchasing shielded equipment. A "TEMPEST approved" computer will cost significantly more than what a normal computer would cost. Shielding a room (in what is known as a *Faraday cage*) is also an extremely expensive endeavor. The cost of shielding is so substantial that in most cases it probably cannot be justified. It may be better to carefully select the location in which you put your most sensitive equipment—perhaps it is possible to protect these computers by putting them in the center of your facility and leaving the less-sensitive equipment in the areas closest to public areas.

A natural question to ask is, how prevalent is this form of attack? The equipment needed to perform electromagnetic eavesdropping is not readily available, but it would not cost an inordinate amount of money to produce it. The cost could certainly be afforded by any large corporation, and industrial espionage using such a device is a possibility. While there are no public records of this sort of activity being conducted, it is reasonable to assume that it does take place in large corporations and the government, especially in foreign countries.

One of the challenges in security is determining how much to spend on security without spending too much. Security spending should be based on likely threats to your systems and network. While electronic emanations can be monitored, the likelihood of this taking place in most situations is remote, which makes spending on items to protect against it at best a low priority.

■ Location

Carefully choosing the location in which to place equipment has been mentioned as a possible means to provide security. It has been said that the three most important factors in the success of most businesses are location, location, and location. While the same is not exactly true of security (location is not the most important element in this case), it certainly can play a contributing role. In the case of a wireless network, the location in which you place the wireless access points can make it easier or harder for an attacker to access the network from a publicly accessible area. For electromagnetic emanations, location is also a contributing factor. By placing the most sensitive equipment deep inside the organization, enough space may be obtained to protect the equipment from eavesdropping. Location also plays a significant role in physical security, since some facilities will be easier to protect than others, depending on their proximity to other buildings and roads.

The location of monitors and printers that display information may also be a concern. In some environments, sensitive material may be on monitors or printed pages and also accessible to unauthorized personnel either through shoulder surfing or by grabbing printed pages. Privacy screens can limit shoulder surfing, and there are products that require a user be present at the printer to get their printouts. The bottom line is simple—don't neglect any exposure method when analyzing security requirements.

Chapter 3 Review

■ Chapter Summary

After reading this chapter and completing the exercises, you should understand the following regarding operational and organizational security.

Identify various operational aspects to security in your organization

■ Prevention technologies are designed to keep individuals from being able to gain access to systems or data they are not authorized to use.

■ Previously in operational environments, prevention was extremely difficult and relying on prevention technologies alone was not sufficient. This led to the rise of technologies to detect and respond to events that occur when prevention fails.

■ An important part of any organization's approach to implementing security is to establish policies, procedures, standards, and guidelines to detail what users and administrators should be doing to maintain the security of the systems and network.

■ Environmental issues are important to security because they can affect the availability of a computer system or network.

■ Problems with electrical power and fire are two of the more common environmental conditions that should be considered.

Describe the physical security components that can protect your computers and network

■ Physical security consists of all mechanisms used to ensure that physical access to the computer systems and networks is restricted to only authorized users.

■ The purpose of physical access controls is the same as that of computer and network access controls—to restrict access to only those who are authorized to have it.

■ The careful placement of equipment can provide security for known security problems exhibited by wireless devices and that arise due to electronic emanations.

Identify environmental factors that can affect security

■ Loss of HVAC systems can lead to overheating problems that can affect electronic equipment including security-related devices.

■ The frequency of natural disasters is a contributing factor that must be considered when making contingency processing plans for an installation.

■ Fires are a common problem for organizations. Two general approaches to addressing this problem are fire detection and fire suppression.

Identify factors that affect the security of the growing number of wireless technologies used for data transmission

■ There are two main standards for wireless network technology: Bluetooth and 802.11.

■ Wireless networks have many security issues, including the transmission and reception areas covered by access points, which are not easily controlled and can thus provide easy network access for intruders.

Prevent disclosure through electronic emanations

■ With the appropriate equipment, the exact image of what is being displayed on a computer monitor can be re-created some distance away, allowing eavesdroppers to view what you are doing.

■ Providing a lot of distance between the system you wish to protect and the closest place an eavesdropper could be is one way to protect against eavesdropping on electronic emanations. Devices can also be shielded so that their emanations are blocked.

Key Terms

biometrics *(55)*
Bluetooth *(58)*
guidelines *(51)*
heating, ventilation, and air conditioning
   (HVAC) *(56)*
IEEE 802.11 *(59)*

physical security *(53)*
policies *(51)*
procedures *(51)*
standards *(51)*
TEMPEST *(59)*
uninterruptible power supply (UPS) *(57)*

Key Terms Quiz

Use terms from the Key Terms list to complete the sentences that follow. Don't use the same term more than once. Not all terms will be used.

1. _____ are high-level statements made by management that lay out the organization's position on some issue.

2. The collective term used to refer to the systems that are used to maintain the comfort of an office environment and that are often controlled by computer systems is _____.

3. A(n) _____ is a device designed to provide power to essential equipment for a period of time when normal power is lost.

4. Access control mechanisms in which a physical characteristic, such as a fingerprint or the geometry of an individual's hand, is used to uniquely identify users are called _____.

5. _____ are accepted specifications providing specific details on how a policy is to be enforced.

6. _____ is a wireless technology designed as a short-range (approximately ten meters) personal area network (PAN) cable-replacement technology that may be built into a variety of devices such as mobile phones, PDAs, and laptop computers.

7. The military program to control electronic emanations from electrical equipment is called _____.

8. _____ are step-by-step instructions that describe exactly how employees are expected to act in a given situation or to accomplish a specific task.

9. The set of standards for wireless networks that is well suited for the LAN environment and whose normal mode is to have computers with network cards communicating with a wireless access point is _____.

10. _____ are recommendations relating to a policy that are not mandatory steps.

Multiple-Choice Quiz

1. Which of the following is a physical security threat?
   A. Cleaning crews are allowed unsupervised access because they have a contract.
   B. Employees undergo background criminal checks before being hired.
   C. All data is encrypted before being backed up.
   D. All the above.

2. The benefit of fire detection equipment over fire suppression devices is
   A. Fire detection equipment is regulated whereas fire suppression equipment is not.

   B. Fire detection equipment will often catch fires at a much earlier stage, meaning that the fire can be addressed before significant damage can occur.
   C. Fire detection equipment is much more reliable than fire suppression equipment.
   D. There is no advantage of fire detection over fire suppression other than the cost of fire detection equipment is much less than fire suppression equipment.

3. What security feature is even more common than a lock?

   A. Physical barrier

   B. Card reader

   C. Hand geometry reader

   D. Security guard

4. During which step of the policy lifecycle does training of users take place?

   A. Plan for security

   B. Implement the plans

   C. Monitor the implementation

   D. Evaluate for effectiveness

5. Biometric access controls are typically used in conjunction with another form of access control because:

   A. Biometrics are still expensive.

   B. Biometrics cannot be copied.

   C. Biometrics are not always convenient to use.

   D. Biometrics are not 100 percent accurate, having some level of misidentifications.

6. Procedures can be described as:

   A. High-level, broad statements of what the organization wants to accomplish

   B. Step-by-step instructions on how to implement the policies

   C. Mandatory elements regarding the implementation of a policy

   D. Recommendations relating to a policy

7. What technique can be used to protect against electromagnetic eavesdropping (known as the van Eck phenomenon)?

   A. Provide sufficient distance between the potential target and the nearest location an attacker could be.

   B. Put the equipment that you are trying to protect inside a shielded room.

   C. Purchase "TEMPEST approved" equipment.

   D. All of the above.

8. HVAC systems are important in which of the following locations?

   A. Large cubical farms where many people work in rooms without windows

   B. Network equipment closets

   C. Server rooms

   D. All the above

9. When should a human security guard be used for physical access control?

   A. When other electronic access control mechanisms will not be accepted by employees

   B. When necessary to avoid issues such as piggybacking, which can occur with electronic access controls

   C. When other access controls are too expensive to implement

   D. When the organization wants to enhance its image

10. What device should be used only by organizations to protect sensitive equipment from fluctuations in voltage?

    A. A surge protector

    B. An uninterruptible power supply

    C. A backup power generator

    D. A redundant array of inline batteries (RAIB)

■ Essay Quiz

1. Describe the difference between fire suppression and fire detection systems.

2. Discuss why an "insider" is potentially more dangerous than an external attacker.

3. Why should we be concerned about HVAC systems when discussing security?

4. Outline the various components that make up (or should make up) an organization's security perimeter. Which of these can be found in your organization (or school)?

Lab Projects

• Lab Project 3.1

Take a tour of your building on campus or at work. Record the location and type of physical access points that you find. How are these access points secured at night when workers are absent? What are the policies for visitors and contractors? How does this all impact physical security?

• Lab Project 3.2

Describe the four steps of the policy lifecycle. Obtain a policy from your organization (such as an acceptable-use or Internet usage policy). How are users informed of this policy? How often is it reviewed? How would changes to it be suggested and who would make decisions on whether the changes were accepted?

chapter 4

The Role of People in Security

Even in the common affairs of life, in love, friendship, and marriage, how little security have we when we trust our happiness in the hands of others!
—William Hazlitt

In this chapter, you will learn how to

- **Define basic terminology associated with social engineering**
- **Describe steps organizations can take to improve their security**
- **Describe common user actions that may put an organization's information at risk**
- **Recognize methods attackers may use to gain information about an organization**
- **Determine ways in which users can aid instead of detract from security**

The operational model of computer security discussed in the previous chapter acknowledges that absolute protection of computer systems and networks is not possible and that we need to be prepared to detect and respond to attacks that were able to circumvent our security mechanisms. Another very basic fact that should be recognized is that technology alone will not solve the security problem. No matter how advanced the technology is, it will ultimately be deployed in an environment where humans exist. It is the human element that poses the biggest security challenge. It is hard to compensate for all of the possible ways that humans can deliberately or accidentally cause security problems or circumvent our security mechanisms. Despite all of the technology, despite all of the security procedures we have in place, and despite all of the security training we may provide, somebody will invariably fail to do what they are supposed to do, or do something they are not supposed to do, and create a vulnerability in the organization's security posture. This chapter discusses the human element and the role that people play in security—both the user practices that can aid in securing an organization and the vulnerabilities or holes in security that users can introduce.

People—A Security Problem

The operational model of computer security acknowledges that prevention technologies are not sufficient to protect our computer systems and networks. There are a number of explanations for why this is true, some of them technical, but one of the biggest reasons that prevention technologies are not sufficient is that every network and computer system has at least one human user, and humans are prone to make mistakes and are often easily misled or fooled.

Social Engineering

Social engineering, if you recall from Chapter 2, is the process of convincing an authorized individual to provide confidential information or access to an unauthorized individual. It is a technique in which the attacker uses various deceptive practices to convince the targeted person to divulge information they normally would not divulge or to convince the target of the attack to do something they normally wouldn't do. Social engineering is very successful for two general reasons. The first is the basic desire of most people to be helpful. When somebody asks a question for which we know the answer, our normal response is not to be suspicious but rather to answer the question. The problem with this is that seemingly innocuous information can be used either directly in an attack or indirectly to build a bigger picture that an attacker can use to create an aura of authenticity during an attack—the more information an individual has about an organization, the easier it will be to convince others that he is part of the organization and has a right to even sensitive information. An attacker who is attempting to exploit the natural tendency of people to be helpful may take one of several approaches:

- The attacker may simply ask a question, hoping to immediately obtain the desired information. For basic information that is not considered sensitive, this approach generally works. As an example, an attacker might call and ask who the IT manager is.

- The attacker may first attempt to engage the target in conversation and try to evoke sympathy so that the target feels sorry for the individual and is more prone to provide the information. For information that is even slightly sensitive in nature, the request of which could possibly arouse suspicion, this technique may be tried. As an example, an attacker might call and claim to be under some deadline from a supervisor who is upset for some reason. The target, feeling sorry for an alleged fellow worker, may give up the information, thinking they are helping them avoid trouble with the supervisor.

- The attacker may appeal to an individual's ego. As an example, an attacker might call the IT department, claiming to have some sort of problem, and praising them for work they supposedly did to help another worker. After being told how great they are and how much they helped somebody else, they will often be tempted to demonstrate that they can supply the same level of help to another individual. This technique may be used to obtain sensitive information, such as having the target's password reset.

The second reason that social engineering is successful is that individuals normally seek to avoid confrontation and trouble. If the attacker attempts to intimidate the target, threatening to call the target's supervisor because of a lack of help, the target may give in and provide the information to avoid confrontation. This variation on the attack is often successful in organizations that have a strict hierarchical structure. In the military, for example, a lower-ranking individual may be coerced into providing information to an individual claiming to be of higher rank or to be working for another individual higher up in the chain of command.

Social engineering may also be accomplished using other means besides direct contact between the target and the attacker. For example, an attacker might send a forged e-mail with a link to a bogus web site that has been set up to obtain information from or convince an individual to perform some action. Again, the goal in social engineering is to convince the target to provide information that they normally wouldn't divulge or perform some act that they normally would not do. An example of a slightly different attack that is generally still considered a social engineering attack is one in which an attacker replaces the blank deposit slips in a bank's lobby with ones containing his or her own account number but no name. When an unsuspecting customer uses one of the slips, a teller who is not observant may end up crediting the attacker's account with the deposit.

Cross Check

Social Engineering

Chapters 1 and 2 both discussed social engineering. Electronic versions of social engineering have become very common. What are the different types of social engineering (especially electronic versions) that we have discussed?

Up to this point, social engineering has been discussed in the context of an outsider attempting to gain information about the organization. This does not have to be the case. Insiders may also attempt to gain information they are not authorized to have. In many cases, the insider may be much more successful since they will already have a certain level of information regarding the organization and can therefore better spin a story that may be believable to other employees.

Obtaining Insider Information

An excellent example of social engineering occurred in 1978 when Stanley Mark Rifkin, from Carlsbad, California, stole $10.2 million from the Security Pacific Bank in Los Angeles. Details of the story vary, as Rifkin has never publicly detailed his actions, but a number of facts are known. At the time of the attack, Rifkin was working as a computer consultant for the bank. While working there, he learned details on how money could easily be transferred to accounts anywhere in the United States. The problem would be to actually obtain the money in the first place. In order to do this, he needed to have access to the electronic funds transfer (EFT) code used by the bank to transfer money to other banks. Using the excuse of checking on the computer equipment inside of the room from which the bank made its transfers, Rifkin was able to observe the code for that day. After leaving the room, he used this information to impersonate a bank officer and ordered the transfer of the $10.2 million. Since he had knowledge of the supposedly secret code, the transfer was made with little fanfare (this amount was well below any level that would trigger any suspicion). Earlier Rifkin had set up a bogus account in a New York bank, using a false name, and he deposited the money into that account. He later transferred the money again to another account in Switzerland under a different name. He then used the money to purchase millions of dollars in diamonds, which he then smuggled back into the United States. The crime might have gone undetected if he had not boasted of his exploits to an individual who was more than happy to turn him in. In 1979, Rifkin was sentenced to eight years in prison. At his trial he attempted to convince the judge that he should be released so he could teach others how to protect their systems against the type of activity he perpetrated. The judge denied this request. The diamonds were ultimately turned over to the bank, which tried to recover its loss by selling them.

Phishing

Phishing (pronounced "fishing") is a type of social engineering in which an attacker attempts to obtain sensitive information from a user by masquerading as a trusted entity in an e-mail or instant message sent to a large group of often random users. The attacker attempts to obtain information such as usernames, passwords, credit card numbers, and details about the user's bank accounts. The message sent often encourages the user to go to a web site that appears to be for a reputable entity such as PayPal or eBay, both of which have frequently been used in phishing attempts. The web site the user actually visits is not owned by the reputable organization, however, and asks the user to supply information that can be used in a later attack. Often the message sent to the user will state that the user's account has been compromised and will request, for security purposes, the user to enter their account information to verify the details.

In another very common example of phishing, the attacker sends a bulk e-mail, supposedly from a bank, telling the recipients that a security breach has occurred and instructing them to click a link to verify that their account has not been tampered with. If the individual actually clicks the link, they are taken to a site that appears to be owned by the bank but is actually controlled by the attacker. When they supply their account and password for "verification" purposes, they are actually giving it to the attacker.

The e-mails and web sites generated by the attackers often appear to be legitimate. A few clues, however, can tip off the user that the e-mail might not be what it claims to be. The e-mail may contain grammatical and typographical errors, for example. Organizations that are used in these phishing attempts (such as eBay and PayPal) are careful about their images and will not send a security-related e-mail to users containing obvious errors. In addition, almost unanimously, organizations tell their users that they will never ask for sensitive information (such as a password or account number) via an e-mail. The URL of the web site that the users are taken to may also provide a clue that the site is not what it appears to be. Despite the increasing media coverage concerning phishing attempts, some Internet users still fall for them, which results in attackers continuing to use this relatively cheap method to gain the information they are seeking.

A recent development has been the introduction of a modification to the original phishing attack. *Spear phishing* is the term that has been created to refer to the special targeting of groups with something in common when launching a phishing attack. By targeting specific groups, the ratio of successful attacks (that is, the number of responses received) to the total number of e-mails or messages sent usually increases because a targeted attack will seem more plausible than a message sent to users randomly.

Another recent and related type of attack is *pharming*. In pharming, an attacker attempts to redirect a user to a bogus web site that appears similar to the web site the user had intended to access. The attacker attempts to

> **Exam Tip:** Phishing is now the most common form of social engineering attack related to computer security. The target may be a computer system and access to the information found on it (such as is the case when the phishing attempt asks for a user ID and password) or the target may be personal information, generally financial, about an individual (in the case of phishing attempts that ask for an individual's banking information).

obtain sensitive information (such as credit card numbers) while the user is at the bogus site. The redirection can occur as a result of modifications to a system's hosts file or through attacks on DNS servers, which causes an individual to be taken to the wrong web site because the DNS server returns the incorrect IP address.

Vishing

Vishing is a variation of phishing that uses voice communication technology to obtain the information the attacker is seeking. Vishing takes advantage of the trust that some people place in the telephone network. Users are unaware that attackers can spoof (simulate) calls from legitimate entities using voice over IP (VoIP) technology. Voice messaging can also be compromised and used in these attempts. Generally, the attackers are hoping to obtain credit card numbers or other information that can be used in identity theft. The user may receive an e-mail asking him or her to call a number that is answered by a potentially compromised voice message system. Users may also receive a recorded message that appears to come from a legitimate entity. In both cases, the user will be encouraged to respond quickly and provide the sensitive information so that access to their account is not blocked. If a user ever receives a message that claims to be from a reputable entity and asks for sensitive information, the user should not provide it but instead should use the Internet or examine a legitimate account statement to find a phone number that can be used to contact the entity. The user can then verify that the message received was legitimate or report the vishing attempt.

Shoulder Surfing

Shoulder surfing does not necessarily involve direct contact with the target, but instead involves the attacker directly observing the individual entering sensitive information on a form, keypad, or keyboard. The attacker may simply look over the shoulder of the user at work, for example, or may set up a camera or use binoculars to view the user entering sensitive data. The attacker can attempt to obtain information such as a personal identification number (PIN) at an automated teller machine (ATM), an access control entry code at a secure gate or door, or a calling card or credit card number. Many locations now use a small shield to surround a keypad so that it is difficult to observe somebody entering information. More sophisticated systems can actually scramble the location of the numbers so that the top row at one time includes the numbers 1, 2, and 3 and the next time 4, 8, and 0. While this makes it a bit slower for the user to enter information, it thwarts an attacker's attempt to observe what numbers are pressed and enter the same buttons/pattern, since the location of the numbers constantly changes.

Although methods such as adding shields to block the view or having the pad "scramble" the numbers can help make shoulder surfing more difficult, the best defense is for users to be aware of their surroundings and to not allow individuals to get into a position from which they can observe what the user is entering.

The attacker may attempt to increase the chance of successfully observing the target entering the data by starting a conversation with the target. This provides an excuse for the attacker to be physically closer to the target. Otherwise, the target may be suspicious if the attacker is

---

Tech Tip

Beware of Vishing

Vishing (phishing conducted using voice systems) is generally successful because of the trust that individuals place in the telephone system. With caller ID, people believe they can identify who it is that is calling them. They do not understand that, just like many protocols in the TCP/IP protocol suite, caller ID can be spoofed.

A related, somewhat obvious security precaution is that a person should not use the same PIN for all of their different accounts, gate codes, and so on, since an attacker who learns the PIN for one type of access could then use it for all of the other types of access.

Principles of Computer Security: CompTIA Security+ and Beyond

standing too close. In this sense, shoulder surfing can be considered a social engineering attack.

Reverse Social Engineering

A slightly different approach to social engineering is called **reverse social engineering**. In this technique, the attacker hopes to convince the target to initiate the contact. This obviously differs from the traditional approach, where the target is the one that is contacted. The reason this attack may be successful is that, since the target is the one initiating the contact, attackers may not have to convince the target of their authenticity. The tricky part of this attack is, of course, convincing the target to make that initial contact. Possible methods to accomplish this might include sending out a spoofed e-mail (fake e-mail designed to appear authentic) that claims to be from a reputable source and provides another e-mail address or phone number to call for "tech support," or posting a notice or creating a bogus web site for a legitimate company that also claims to provide "tech support." This may be especially successful if timed to coincide with a company's deployment of a new software or hardware platform. Another potential time to target an organization with this sort of attack is when there is a significant change in the organization itself, such as when two companies merge or a smaller company is acquired by a larger one. During these times, employees are not familiar with the new organization or its procedures, and amidst the confusion, it is easy to conduct either a social engineering or reverse social engineering attack.

Tech Tip

Be Aware of Reverse Social Engineering
Reverse social engineering is not nearly as widely understood as social engineering and is a bit trickier to execute. If the attacker is successful in convincing an individual to make the initial contact, however, the process of convincing them of the authenticity of the attacker is generally much easier than in a social engineering attack.

Hoaxes

At first glance, it might seem that a hoax related to security would be considered a nuisance and not a real security issue. This might be the case for some hoaxes, especially those of the urban legend type, but the reality of the situation is that a hoax can be very damaging if it causes users to take some sort of action that weakens security. One real hoax, for example, described a new, highly destructive piece of malicious software. It instructed users to check for the existence of a certain file and to delete it if the file was found. In reality, the file mentioned was an important file used by the operating system, and deleting it caused problems the next time the system was booted. The damage caused by users modifying security settings can be serious. As with other forms of social engineering, *training and awareness* are the best and first line of defense for both users and administrators. Users should be trained to be suspicious of unusual e-mails and stories and should know who to contact in the organization to verify their validity if they are received. Hoaxes often also advise the user to send it to their friends so they know about the issue as well—and by doing so, they help spread the hoax. Users need to be suspicious of any e-mail telling them to "spread the word."

Poor Security Practices

A significant portion of human-created security problems results from poor security practices. These poor practices may be those of an individual user who is not following established security policies or processes, or they may be caused by a lack of security policies, procedures, or training within the user's organization.

Poor password selection is one of the most common of poor security practices, and one of the most dangerous. Numerous studies that have been conducted on password selection have found that, while overall more users are learning to select good passwords, a significant percentage of users still make poor choices. The problem with this, of course, is that a poor password choice can enable an attacker to compromise a computer system or network more easily. Even when users have good passwords, they often resort to another poor security practice—writing the password down in an easily located place, which can also lead to system compromise if an attacker gains physical access to the area.

Password Selection

For many years, computer intruders have relied on users selecting poor passwords to help them gain unauthorized access to a system or network. If attackers could obtain a list of the users' names, chances were good they could eventually access the system. Users tend to pick passwords that are easy for them to remember, and what easier password could there be than the same sequence of characters that they use for their user ID? If a system has an account with the username *jdoe*, an attacker's reasonable first guess of the account's password would be *jdoe*. If this doesn't work, the attacker would try variations on the same, such as *doej*, *johndoe*, *johnd*, and *eodj*, all of which would be reasonable possibilities.

If the attacker's attempt to use variations on the username does not yield the correct password, they might simply need more information. Users also frequently pick names of family members, pets, or favorite sports team. If the user lives in San Antonio, Texas, for example, a possible password might be *gospursgo* in honor of their professional basketball team. If these don't work for the attacker, then the attacker might next try hobbies of the user, the name of their favorite make or model of car, or similar pieces of information. The key is that the user often picks something easy for them to remember, which means that the more you know about the user, the better your chance of discovering their password.

In an attempt to complicate the attacker's job, organizations have encouraged their users to mix upper- and lowercase characters and to include numbers and special characters in their password. While this does make the password harder to guess, the basic problem still remains: users will pick something that is easy for them to remember. Thus, our user in San Antonio may select the password *G0*Spurs*G0*, capitalizing three of the letters, inserting a special character twice, and substituting the number zero for the letter *O*. This makes the password harder to crack, but there are a finite number of variations on the basic *gospursgo* password, so, while the attacker's job has been made more difficult, it is still possible to guess the password.

Organizations have also instituted additional policies and rules relating to password selection to further complicate an attacker's efforts. Organizations, for example, may require users to frequently change their password. This means that if an attacker is able to guess a password, it is only valid for a limited period of time before a new password is selected, after which the attacker is locked out. All is not lost for the attacker, however, since, again, users will select passwords they can remember. For example, password changes often result in a new password that simply incorporates a number at the end of the old one. Thus, our San Antonio user might select *G0*Spurs*G1* as the new password, in which case the benefit of forcing password changes on a periodic, or even frequent, basis has been totally lost. It is a good bet that the next password chosen will be *G0*Spurs*G2*, followed by *G0Spurs*G3*, and so forth.

Another policy or rule governing password selection often adopted by organizations is that passwords must not be written down. This, of course, is difficult to enforce, and thus users will frequently write them down, often as a result of what we refer to as the "password dilemma." The more difficult we make it for attackers to guess our passwords, and the more frequently we force password changes, the more difficult the passwords are for authorized users to remember and the more likely they are to write them down. Writing them down and putting them in a secure place is one thing, but all too often users will write them on a slip of paper and keep them in their calendar, wallet, or purse. Most security consultants generally agree that if they are given physical access to an office, they will be able to find a password somewhere—the top drawer of a desk, inside of a desk calendar, attached to the underside of the keyboard, or even simply on a yellow "sticky note" attached to the monitor.

With the proliferation of computers, networks, and users, the password dilemma has gotten worse. Today, the average Internet user probably has at least a half dozen different accounts and passwords to remember. Selecting a different password for each account, following the guidelines mentioned previously regarding character selection and frequency of changes, only aggravates the problem of remembering the passwords. This results in users all too frequently using the same password for all accounts. If a user does this, and then one of the accounts is broken, all other accounts are subsequently also vulnerable to attack.

As a final comment, good password selection and the protection of passwords also applies to another common feature of today's electronic world, PINs. Most people have at least one PIN associated with things such as their ATM card or a security code to gain physical access to a room. Again, users will invariably select numbers that are easy to remember. Specific numbers, such as the individual's birth date, their spouse's birth date, or the date of some other significant event, are all common numbers to select. Other people will pick patterns that are easy to remember—2580, for example, uses all of the center numbers on a standard numeric pad on a telephone. Attackers know this, and guessing PINs follows the same sort of process that guessing a password does.

Exam Tip: Know the rules for good password selection. Generally, these are to use eight or more characters in your password, include a combination of upper- and lowercase letters, include at least one number and one special character, do not use a common word, phrase, or name, and choose a password that you can remember so that you do not need to write it down.

Piggybacking

People are often in a hurry and will frequently not follow good physical security practices and procedures. Attackers know this and may attempt to exploit this characteristic in human behavior. **Piggybacking** is the simple tactic of following closely behind a person who has just used their own access card or PIN to gain physical access to a room or building. An attacker can thus gain access to the facility without having to know the access code or having to acquire an access card. It is similar to shoulder surfing in that it relies on the attacker taking advantage of an authorized user not following security procedures. Frequently the attacker may even start a conversation with the target before reaching the door so that the user may be more comfortable with allowing the individual in without challenging them. In this sense piggybacking is related to social engineering attacks. Both the piggybacking and shoulder surfing attack techniques can be easily countered by using simple procedures to ensure nobody follows you too closely or is in a position to observe your actions. Both of these rely on the poor security practices of an authorized user in order to be successful. A more sophisticated countermeasure to piggybacking is a "man trap," which utilizes two doors to gain access to the facility. The second door does not open until the first one is closed and is spaced close enough to the first that an enclosure is formed that only allows one individual through at a time.

Dumpster Diving

As mentioned earlier, attackers need a certain amount of information before launching their attack. One common place to find this information, if the attacker is in the vicinity of the target, is the target's trash. The attacker might find little bits of information that could be useful for an attack. This process of going through a target's trash in hopes of finding valuable information that might be used in a penetration attempt is known in the computer community as **dumpster diving**. The tactic is not, however, unique to the computer community; it has been used for many years by others, such as identity thieves, private investigators, and law enforcement personnel, to obtain information about an individual or organization. If the attackers are very lucky, and the target's security procedures are very poor, they may actually find user IDs and passwords. As mentioned in the discussion on passwords, users sometimes write their password down. If, when the password is changed, they discard the paper the old password was written on without shredding it, the lucky dumpster diver can gain a valuable clue. Even if the attacker isn't lucky enough to obtain a password directly, he undoubtedly will find employee names, from which it's not hard to determine user IDs, as discussed earlier. Manuals from hardware or software that have been purchased may also provide clues as to what vulnerabilities exist on the target's computer systems and networks. Finally, the attacker may gather a variety of information that can be useful in a social engineering attack. In most locations, trash is no longer considered private property after it has been discarded (and even where dumpster diving is illegal, little enforcement occurs). An organization should have policies about discarding materials. Sensitive information should be shredded and the organization should consider securing the trash receptacle so that individuals can't forage through it. People should also consider shredding personal or sensitive information that they wish to discard in their own trash. A reasonable quality shredder is inexpensive and well worth the price when compared with the potential loss that could occur as a result of identity theft.

Try This

Dumpster Diving

The amount of useful information that users throw away in unsecured trash receptacles often amazes security professionals. Hackers know that they can often find manuals, network diagrams, and even user IDs and passwords by rummaging through dumpsters. After coordinating this with your security office, try seeing what you can find that individuals in your organization have discarded (assuming that there is no shredding policy) by either going through your organization's dumpsters or just through the office trash receptacles. What useful information did you find? Is there an obvious suggestion that you might make to enhance the security of your organization?

Installing Unauthorized Hardware and Software

Organizations should have a policy that restricts the ability of normal users to install software and new hardware on their systems. A common example is a user installing unauthorized communication software and a modem to allow them to connect to their machine at work via a modem from their home. Another common example is a user installing a wireless access point so that they can access the organization's network from many different areas. In these examples, the user has set up a backdoor into the network, circumventing all the other security mechanisms in place. The term "rogue modem" or "rogue access point" may be used to describe these two cases. A **backdoor** is an avenue that can be used to access a system while circumventing normal security mechanisms and can often be used to install additional executable files that can lead to more ways to access the compromised system. Security professionals can use widely available tools to scan their own systems periodically for either of these rouge devices to ensure that users haven't created a backdoor.

Another common example of unauthorized software that users install on their systems is games. Unfortunately, not all games come in shrink-wrapped packages. Numerous small games can be downloaded from the Internet. The problem with this is that users don't always know where the software originally came from and what may be hidden inside it. Many individuals have unwittingly installed what seemed to be an innocuous game, only to have downloaded a piece of malicious code capable of many things, including opening a backdoor that allows attackers to connect to, and control, the system from across the Internet.

Because of these potential hazards, many organizations do not allow their users to load software or install new hardware without the knowledge and assistance of administrators. Many organizations also screen, and occasionally intercept, e-mail messages with links or attachments that are sent to users. This helps prevent users from, say, unwittingly executing a hostile program that was sent as part of a worm or virus. Consequently, many organizations have their mail servers strip off executable attachments to e-mail so that users can't accidentally cause a security problem.

Physical Access by Non-Employees

As has been mentioned, if an attacker can gain physical access to a facility, chances are very good that the attacker can obtain enough information to penetrate computer systems and networks. Many organizations require employees to wear identification badges when at work. This is an easy method to quickly spot who has permission to have physical access to the organization and who does not. While this method is easy to implement and can be a significant deterrent to unauthorized individuals, it also requires that employees actively challenge individuals who are not wearing the required identification badge. This is one area where organizations fail. Combine an attacker who slips in by piggybacking off of an authorized individual and an environment where employees have not been encouraged to challenge individuals without appropriate credentials and you have a situation where you might as well not have any badges in the first place. Organizations also frequently become complacent when faced with what appears to be a legitimate reason to access the facility, such as when an individual shows up with a warm pizza claiming it was ordered by an employee. It has often been stated by security consultants that it is amazing what you can obtain access to with a pizza box or a vase of flowers. If the organization doesn't enforce good password policies, a casual stroll through an office may yield passwords or other important information.

Another aspect that must be considered is personnel who have legitimate access to a facility but also have intent to steal intellectual property or otherwise exploit the organization. Physical access provides an easy opportunity for individuals to look for the occasional piece of critical information carelessly left out. With the proliferation of devices such as cell phones with built-in cameras, an

 It has already been mentioned that gaining physical access to a computer system or network often guarantees an attacker success in penetrating the system or the network it is connected to. At the same time, there may be a number of individuals who have access to a facility but are not authorized to access the information the systems store and process. We become complacent to the access these individuals have because they often quietly go about their job so as to not draw attention to themselves and to minimize the impact on the operation of the organization. They may also be overlooked because their job does not impact the core function of the organization. A prime example of this is the custodial staff. Becoming complacent about these individuals and not paying attention to what they may have access to, however, could be a big mistake, and users should not believe that everybody who has physical access to the organization has the same level of concern for or interest in the welfare of the organization.

individual could easily photograph information without it being obvious to employees. Contractors, consultants, and partners frequently not only have physical access to the facility but may also have network access. Other individuals who typically have unrestricted access to the facility when no one is around are nighttime custodial crewmembers and security guards. Such positions are often contracted out. As a result, hackers have been known to take temporary custodial jobs simply to gain access to facilities.

■ People as a Security Tool

An interesting paradox when speaking of social engineering attacks is that people are not only the biggest problem and security risk but also the best tool in defending against a social engineering attack. The first step a company should take to fight potential social engineering attacks is to create the policies and procedures that establish the roles and responsibilities for not only security administrators but for all users. What is it that management expects, security-wise, from all employees? What is it that the organization is trying to protect, and what mechanisms are important for that protection?

Security Awareness

Probably the single most effective method to counter potential social engineering attacks, after establishment of the organization's security goals and policies, is an active security awareness program. The extent of the training will vary depending on the organization's environment and the level of threat, but initial employee training on social engineering at the time a person is hired is important, as well as periodic refresher training. Many government organizations have created security awareness posters to constantly remind individuals of this possible avenue of attack. Security newsletters, often in the form of e-mail, have also been used to remind employees of their security responsibilities.

An important element that should be stressed in training about social engineering is the type of information that the organization considers sensitive and which may be the target of a social engineering attack. There are undoubtedly signs that the organization could point to as indicative of an attacker attempting to gain access to sensitive corporate information. All employees should be aware of these indicators. The scope of information that an attacker may ask for is very large, and many questions attackers pose might also be legitimate in another context (asking for the phone number for somebody, for example). Employees should be taught to be cautious about revealing personal information and should especially be alert for questions regarding account information, personally identifiable information, or passwords.

Try This

Security Awareness Programs

A strong security education and awareness training program can go a long way toward reducing the chance that a social engineering attack will be successful. Awareness programs and campaigns, which might include seminars, videos, posters, newsletters, and similar materials, are also fairly easy to implement and not very costly. There is no reason for an organization to not have an awareness program in place. A lot of information and ideas are available on the Internet. See what you can find that might be usable for your organization that you can obtain at no charge from various organizations on the Internet. (Tip: Check organizations such as NIST and NSA, which have developed numerous security documents and guidelines.)

Individual User Responsibilities

Individual user responsibilities vary between organizations and the type of business the organization is involved in, but there are certain very basic responsibilities that all users should be instructed to adopt:

- Lock the door to your office or workspace.

- Do not leave sensitive information inside your car unprotected.

- Secure storage media containing sensitive information in a secure storage device.

- Shred paper containing organizational information before discarding it.

- Do not divulge sensitive information to individuals (including other employees) who do not have an authorized need to know it.

- Do not discuss sensitive information with family members. (The most common violation of this rule occurs in regard to HR information, as employees, especially supervisors, may complain to their spouse about other employees or problems that are occurring at work.)

- Protect laptops that contain sensitive or important organization information wherever the laptop may be stored or left. (It's a good idea to ensure that sensitive information is encrypted on the laptop so that, should the equipment be lost or stolen, the information remains safe.)

- Be aware of who is around you when discussing sensitive corporate information. Does everybody within earshot have the need to hear this information?

- Enforce corporate access control procedures. Be alert to, and do not allow, piggybacking, shoulder surfing, or access without the proper credentials.

- Be aware of the correct procedures to report suspected or actual violations of security policies.

- Follow procedures established to enforce good password security practices. Passwords are such a critical element that they are frequently the ultimate target of a social engineering attack. Though such password procedures may seem too oppressive or strict, they are often the best line of defense.

As a final note on user responsibilities, corporate security officers must cultivate an environment of trust in their office, as well as an understanding of the importance of security. If users feel that security personnel are only there to make their life difficult or dredge up information that will result in an employee's termination, the atmosphere will quickly turn adversarial and be transformed into an "us versus them" situation. Security personnel need the help of all users and should strive to cultivate a team environment in which users, when faced with a questionable situation, will not hesitate to call the security office. In situations like this, security offices should remember the old adage of "don't shoot the messenger."

Chapter 4 Review

■ Chapter Summary

After reading this chapter and completing the exercises, you should understand the following regarding the role people can play in security.

Define basic terminology associated with social engineering

■ Social engineering is a technique in which the attacker uses various deceptive practices to convince the targeted person to divulge information they normally would not divulge, or to convince the target to do something they normally wouldn't do.

■ In reverse social engineering, the attacker hopes to convince the target to initiate contact.

Describe steps organizations can take to improve their security

■ Organizations should have a policy that restricts the ability of normal users to install new software and hardware on their systems.

■ Contractors, consultants, and partners may frequently have not only physical access to the facility but also network access. Other groups that are given unrestricted, and unobserved, access to a facility are nighttime custodial crewmembers and security guards. Both are potential security problems and organizations should take steps to limit these individuals' access.

■ The single most effective method to counter potential social engineering attacks, after establishing the organization's security goals and policies, is an active security awareness program.

Describe common user actions that may put an organization's information at risk

■ No matter how advanced security technology is, it will ultimately be deployed in an environment where the human element may be its greatest weakness.

■ Attackers know that employees are frequently very busy and don't stop to think about security. They may attempt to exploit this work characteristic through piggybacking or shoulder surfing.

Recognize methods attackers may use to gain information about an organization

■ For many years computer intruders have relied on users selecting poor passwords to help them in their attempts to gain unauthorized access to a system or network.

■ One common way to find useful information (if the attacker is in the vicinity of the target, such as a company office) is to go through the target's trash looking for bits of information that could be useful to a penetration attempt.

Determine ways in which users can aid instead of detract from security

■ An interesting paradox of social engineering attacks is that people are not only the biggest problem and security risk, but also the best line of defense against a social engineering attack.

■ A significant portion of employee-created security problems arise from poor security practices.

■ Users should always be on the watch for attempts by individuals to gain information about the organization and should report suspicious activity to their employer.

■ Key Terms

backdoor *(75)*
dumpster diving *(74)*
phishing *(69)*
piggybacking *(73)*

reverse social engineering *(71)*
shoulder surfing *(70)*
social engineering *(67)*
vishing *(70)*

Key Terms Quiz

Use terms from the Key Terms list to complete the sentences that follow. Don't use the same term more than once. Not all terms will be used.

1. A _____ is an avenue that can be used to access a system while circumventing normal security mechanisms.

2. _____ is a procedure in which attackers position themselves in such a way as to be able to observe an authorized user entering the correct access code.

3. The process of going through a target's trash searching for information that can be used in an attack, or to gain knowledge about a system or network, is known as _____.

4. _____ is the simple tactic of following closely behind a person who has just used their access card or PIN to gain physical access to a room or building.

5. In _____, the attacker hopes to convince the target to initiate contact.

Multiple-Choice Quiz

1. Which of the following are considered good practices for password security?

   A. Using a combination of upper- and lowercase characters, a number, and a special character in the password itself

   B. Not writing the password down

   C. Changing the password on a regular basis

   D. All of the above

2. The password dilemma refers to the fact that:

   A. Passwords that are easy for users to remember are also easy for attackers to guess.

   B. The more difficult we make it for attackers to guess our passwords, and the more frequently we force password changes, the more difficult the passwords are for authorized users to remember and the more likely they are to write them down.

   C. Users will invariably attempt to select passwords that are words they can remember. This means they may select things closely associated with them, such as their spouse's or child's name, a beloved sports team, or a favorite model of car.

   D. Passwords assigned by administrators are usually better and more secure, but are often harder for users to remember.

3. The simple tactic of following closely behind a person who has just used their own access card or PIN to gain physical access to a room or building is called:

   A. Shoulder surfing

   B. Tagging-along

   C. Piggybacking

   D. Access drafting

4. The process of going through a target's trash in hopes of finding valuable information that might be used in a penetration attempt is known as:

   A. Dumpster diving

   B. Trash trolling

   C. Garbage gathering

   D. Refuse rolling

5. An avenue that can be used to access a system while circumventing normal security mechanisms is known as a:

   A. Master-key code

   B. Secret door

   C. Backdoor

   D. Covert channel

6. Reverse social engineering involves:

   A. Contacting the target, eliciting some sensitive information, and convincing them that nothing out of the ordinary has occurred

   B. Contacting the target in an attempt to obtain information that can be used in a second attempt with a different individual

   C. An individual lower in the chain of command convincing somebody at a higher level to divulge information that the attacker is not authorized to have

   D. An attacker attempting to somehow convince the target to initiate contact in order to avoid questions about authenticity

7. The reason for not allowing users to install new hardware or software without the knowledge of security administrators is:

   A. They may not complete the installation correctly and the administrator will have to do more work, taking them away from more important security tasks.

   B. They may inadvertently install more than just the hardware or software; they may accidentally install a backdoor into the network.

   C. They may not have paid for it and thus may be opening the organization up to civil penalties.

   D. Unauthorized hardware and software are usually for leisure purposes and will distract employees from the job they were hired to perform.

8. Once an organization's security policies have been established, the single most effective method of countering potential social engineering attacks is:

   A. An active security awareness program

   B. A separate physical access control mechanism for each department in the organization

   C. Frequent testing of both the organization's physical security procedures and employee telephone practices

   D. Implementing access control cards and the wearing of security identification badges

9. Security administrators should be concerned about security guards and custodial crews because:

   A. These individuals may not have had a thorough background investigation.

   B. These individuals have access to facilities at times when nobody else is around to view their activities.

   C. These individuals are frequently paid minimal salaries.

   D. These individuals are frequently contracted and are not actually employees of the company.

10. In what ways are PINs similar to passwords?

    A. Users will normally pick a PIN that is easy to remember, such as a date or specific pattern.

    B. Attackers know common PINs and will try to use them or will attempt to learn more about the user in order to make an educated guess as to what their PIN might be.

    C. Users may write them down to remember them.

    D. All of the above are true.

■ Essay Quiz

1. Explain the difference between social engineering and reverse social engineering.

2. Describe the process of piggybacking. Is this common attack technique possible in your work or school environment?

3. How might shoulder surfing be a threat in your school or work environment? What can be done to make this sort of activity more difficult?

4. For an environment familiar to you (such as work or school), describe the different non-employees who may have access to facilities that could contain sensitive information.

5. Describe some of the user security responsibilities that you feel are most important for users to remember.

Lab Projects

• Lab Project 4.1

If possible at either your place of employment or school, attempt to determine how easy it would be to perform dumpster diving in order to gain access to information at the site. Are trash receptacles easy to gain access to? Are documents shredded before being discarded? Are areas where trash is stored easily accessible?

• Lab Project 4.2

Perform a search on the Web for articles and stories about social engineering attacks or reverse social engineering attacks. How many were successful? How many failed and why? How could those that may have initially succeeded been prevented?

Cryptography

Using encryption on the Internet is the equivalent of arranging an armored car to deliver credit card information from someone living in a cardboard box to someone living on a park bench.

—GENE SPAFFORD

In this chapter, you will learn how to

- **Identify and describe the three types of cryptography**
- **List and describe current cryptographic algorithms**
- **Explain how cryptography is applied for security**

Cryptography is the science of *encrypting,* or hiding, information— something people have sought to do since they began using language. Although language allowed people to communicate with one another, those in power attempted to hide information by controlling who was taught to read and write. Eventually, more complicated methods of concealing information by shifting letters around to make the text unreadable were developed. These complicated methods are cryptographic algorithms, also known as *ciphers.* The word cipher comes from the Arabic word *sifr,* meaning empty or zero.

The Spartans of ancient Greece would write on a ribbon wrapped around a cylinder with a specific diameter. When the ribbon was unwrapped, it revealed a strange string of letters. The message could be read only when the ribbon was wrapped around the same diameter cylinder. This is an example of a **transposition cipher**, where the same letters are used but the order is changed. In all these cipher systems, the unencrypted input text is known as the *plaintext* and the encrypted output is known as *ciphertext.*

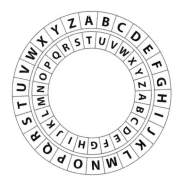

• **Figure 5.1**   Any shift cipher can easily be encoded and decoded on a wheel of two pieces of paper with the alphabet set as a ring; by moving one circle the specified number in the shift, you can translate the characters.

The Romans typically used a different method known as a **shift cipher**. In this case, one letter of the alphabet is shifted a set number of places in the alphabet for another letter. A common modern-day example of this is the ROT13 cipher, in which every letter is rotated 13 positions in the alphabet: *n* is written instead of *a*, *o* instead of *b*, and so on. These types of ciphers are commonly encoded on an alphabet wheel, as shown in Figure 5.1

These ciphers were simple to use and also simple to break. Because hiding information was still important, more advanced transposition and substitution ciphers were required. As systems and technology became more complex, ciphers were frequently automated by some mechanical or electromechanical device. A famous example of a modern encryption machine is the German Enigma machine from World War II (see Figure 5.2). This machine used a complex series of substitutions to perform encryption, and interestingly enough it gave rise to extensive research in computers.

Cryptanalysis, the process of analyzing available information in an attempt to return the encrypted message to its original form, required advances in computer technology for complex encryption methods. The birth of the computer made it possible to easily execute the calculations required by more complex encryption algorithms. Today, the computer almost exclusively powers how encryption is performed. Computer technology has also aided cryptanalysis, allowing new methods to be developed, such as linear and differential cryptanalysis. **Differential cryptanalysis** is done by comparing the input plaintext to the output ciphertext to try and determine the key used to encrypt the information. **Linear cryptanalysis** is similar in that it uses both plaintext and ciphertext, but it puts the plaintext through a simplified cipher to try and deduce what the key is likely to be in the full version of the cipher.

This chapter examines the most common symmetric and asymmetric algorithms in use today, as well as some uses of encryption on computer networks.

• **Figure 5.2**   One of the surviving German Enigma machines

■ Algorithms

Every current encryption scheme is based upon an **algorithm**, a step-by-step, recursive computational procedure for solving a problem in a finite number of steps. The cryptographic algorithm—what is commonly called the *encryption algorithm* or *cipher*—is made up of mathematical steps for encrypting and decrypting information. The following illustration shows a diagram of the encryption and decryption process and its parts.

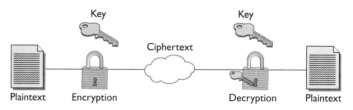

Key   Ciphertext   Key

Plaintext   Encryption   Decryption   Plaintext

The best algorithms are always public algorithms that have been published for peer review by other cryptographic and mathematical experts. Publication is important, as any flaws in the system can be revealed by others before actual use of the system. Several proprietary algorithms have been reverse-engineered, exposing the confidential data the algorithms try to protect. Examples of this include the decryption of Nikon's proprietary RAW format, white-balance encryption, and the cracking of the ExxonMobil Speedpass RFID encryption. The use of a proprietary system can actually be less secure than using a published system. Whereas proprietary systems are not made available to be tested by potential crackers, public systems are made public for precisely this purpose.

A system that maintains its security after public testing can be reasonably trusted to be secure. A public algorithm can be more secure because good systems rely on the *encryption key* to provide security, not the algorithm itself. The actual steps for encrypting data can be published, because without the key, the protected information cannot be accessed (Figure 5.3).

A **key** is a special piece of data used in both the encryption and decryption processes. The algorithms stay the same in every implementation, but a different key is used for each, which ensures that even if someone knows the algorithm you use to protect your data, he cannot break your security. A classic example of this is the early shift cipher, known as *Caesar's cipher*.

Caesar's cipher uses an algorithm and a key: the algorithm specifies that you offset the alphabet either to the right (forward) or to the left (backward), and the key specifies how many letters the offset should be. For example, if the algorithm specifies offsetting the alphabet to the right, and the key is 3, the cipher substitutes an alphabetic letter three to the right for the real letter, so *d* is used to represent *a*, *f* represents *c*, and so on. In this example, both the algorithm and key are simple, allowing for easy cryptanalysis of the cipher and easy recovery of the plaintext message.

The ease with which shift ciphers were broken led to the development of *substitution ciphers*, which were popular in Elizabethan England (roughly the second half of the sixteenth century) and more complex than shift ciphers. Substitution ciphers work on the principle of substituting a different

● **Figure 5.3**   While everyone knows how to use a knob to open a door, without the key to unlock the knob, that knowledge is useless.

letter for every letter: *a* becomes *g*, *b* becomes *d*, and so on. This system permits 26 possible values for every letter in the message, making the cipher many times more complex than a standard shift cipher. Simple analysis of the cipher could be performed to retrieve the key, however. By looking for common letters such as *e* and patterns found in words such as *ing*, you can determine which cipher letter corresponds to which plaintext letter. The examination of ciphertex for frequent letters is known as *frequency analysis*. Making educated guesses about words will eventually allow you to determine the system's key value (see Figure 5.4).

To correct this problem, more complexity had to be added to the system. The **Vigenère cipher** works as a *polyalphabetic substitution cipher* that depends on a password. This is done by setting up a substitution table like this one:

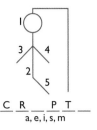

• **Figure 5.4**   Making educated guesses is much like playing hangman— correct guesses can lead to more or all of the key being revealed.

```
A B C D E F G H I J K L M N O P Q R S T U V W X Y Z
B C D E F G H I J K L M N O P Q R S T U V W X Y Z A
C D E F G H I J K L M N O P Q R S T U V W X Y Z A B
D E F G H I J K L M N O P Q R S T U V W X Y Z A B C
E F G H I J K L M N O P Q R S T U V W X Y Z A B C D
F G H I J K L M N O P Q R S T U V W X Y Z A B C D E
G H I J K L M N O P Q R S T U V W X Y Z A B C D E F
H I J K L M N O P Q R S T U V W X Y Z A B C D E F G
I J K L M N O P Q R S T U V W X Y Z A B C D E F G H
J K L M N O P Q R S T U V W X Y Z A B C D E F G H I
K L M N O P Q R S T U V W X Y Z A B C D E F G H I J
L M N O P Q R S T U V W X Y Z A B C D E F G H I J K
M N O P Q R S T U V W X Y Z A B C D E F G H I J K L
N O P Q R S T U V W X Y Z A B C D E F G H I J K L M
O P Q R S T U V W X Y Z A B C D E F G H I J K L M N
P Q R S T U V W X Y Z A B C D E F G H I J K L M N O
Q R S T U V W X Y Z A B C D E F G H I J K L M N O P
R S T U V W X Y Z A B C D E F G H I J K L M N O P Q
S T U V W X Y Z A B C D E F G H I J K L M N O P Q R
T U V W X Y Z A B C D E F G H I J K L M N O P Q R S
U V W X Y Z A B C D E F G H I J K L M N O P Q R S T
V W X Y Z A B C D E F G H I J K L M N O P Q R S T U
W X Y Z A B C D E F G H I J K L M N O P Q R S T U V
X Y Z A B C D E F G H I J K L M N O P Q R S T U V W
Y Z A B C D E F G H I J K L M N O P Q R S T U V W X
Z A B C D E F G H I J K L M N O P Q R S T U V W X Y
```

Then the password is matched up to the text it is meant to encipher. If the password is not long enough, the password is repeated until one character of the password is matched up with each character of the plaintext. For example, if the plaintext is *Sample Message* and the password is *password*, the resulting match is

SAMPLEMESSAGE
PASSWORDPASSW

The cipher letter is determined by use of the grid, matching the plaintext character's row with the password character's column, resulting in a single ciphertext character where the two meet. Consider the first letters *S* and *P*: when plugged into the grid they output a ciphertext character of *H*. This process is repeated for every letter of the message. Once the rest of the letters are processed, the output is HAEHHSDHHSSYA.

In this example, the key in the encryption system is the password. The example also illustrates that an algorithm can be simple and still provide strong security. If someone knows about the table, they can determine how the encryption was performed, but they still will not know the key to decrypting the message.

The more complex the key, the greater the security of the system. The Vigenère cipher system and systems like it make the algorithms rather simple but the key rather complex, with the best keys comprising very long and very random data. Key complexity is achieved by giving the key a large number of possible values. The **keyspace** is every possible key value. When dealing with computer-based cryptographic algorithms, this value is usually defined as a numeric size of bits, such as 1024 bits, meaning 2^{1024} different keys. When an algorithm lists a certain number of bits as a key, it is defining the keyspace.

A larger keyspace allows the use of keys of greater complexity, and therefore more security, assuming the algorithm is well designed. It is easy to see how key complexity affects an algorithm when you look at some of the encryption algorithms that have been broken. The Data Encryption Standard (DES) uses a 56-bit key, allowing 72,000,000,000,000,000 possible values, but it has been broken by modern computers. The modern implementation of DES, Triple DES (3DES), uses a 128-bit key, or 340,000,000,000,000,000,000,000,000,000,000,000,000 possible values. You can see the difference in the possible values, and why 128 bits is generally accepted as the minimum required to protect sensitive information.

Because the security of the algorithms relies on the key, **key management** is of critical concern. Key management includes anything having to do with the exchange, storage, safeguarding, and revocation of keys. It is most commonly associated with asymmetric encryption, since asymmetric encryption uses both public and private keys. To be used properly for authentication, a key must be current and verified. If you have an old or compromised key, you need a way to check to see that the key has been revoked.

Key management is also important for symmetric encryption, because symmetric encryption relies on both parties having the same key for the algorithm to work. Since these parties are usually physically separate, key management is critical to ensure keys are shared and exchanged easily. They must also be securely stored to provide appropriate confidentiality of the encrypted information. While keys can be stored in many different ways, new PC hardware often includes the Trusted Platform Module (TPM), which provides a hardware-based key storage location that is used by many applications, including the BitLocker Drive Encryption featured in Microsoft Windows Vista. (More specific information about the management of keys is provided in Chapter 6.)

The same algorithms cannot be used indefinitely to secure information; eventually an algorithm is either broken as a result of the algorithm being faulty or having been based on poor math or, more likely, rendered obsolete by advancing technology. All encryption ciphers other than a "one-time pad" cipher are susceptible to brute-force attacks, in which a cracker attempts every possible key until he gains access. With a very small key, such as a 2-bit key, trying every possible value is a simple matter, with only four possibilities: 00, 01, 10, or 11. 56-bit DES, on the other hand, has 72 quadrillion values, and while that seems like a lot, today's computers can attempt billions of keys every second. This makes brute-forcing a key only a matter of time; large keys are required to make brute-force attacks against the cipher take longer than the effective value of the information that is enciphered by them. One-time pad ciphers are interesting, because their keys are equal to the length of the messages they protect, and *completely* random characters *must be used* for the keys. This allows the keyspace to be unlimited, therefore making a brute-force attack practically impossible.

Computers in cryptography and cryptanalysis must handle all this data in bit format. They would have difficulty in using the substitution table shown earlier, so many encryption functions use a logical function to perform the encipherment. This function is typically **XOR**, which is the bitwise *exclusive OR*. XOR is used because

if $(P \text{ XOR } K) = C$ then $(C \text{ XOR } K) = P$

This works because in an XOR function, the bits 0 and 1 represent false and true, respectively, and when run through XOR, any *single* true value for P or K will result in C being true. However, when both P and K are either true or false, then C will be false.

If P is the plaintext and K is the key, then C is the ciphertext, making a simple symmetric key cipher in the case where the sender and the receiver both have a shared secret (key) to encrypt and decrypt data.

While symmetric encryption is the most common type of encryption, there are two other types of encryption. These two types are public key or asymmetric encryption, and hashing or one-way functions. Each type is best suited for particular situations.

Tech Tip

One-Time Pad Cipher

A one-time pad with a good random key is considered unbreakable. In addition, since keys are never reused, even if a key is broken, no information can be accessed using the key other than the message used by that key.

Hashing Functions

Hashing functions are commonly used encryption methods. A *hashing function* or *hash function* is a special mathematical function that performs *one-way encryption*, which means that once the algorithm is processed, there is no feasible way to use the ciphertext to retrieve the plaintext that was used to generate it. Also, ideally, there is no feasible way to generate two different plaintexts that compute to the same **hash** value. The hash value is the output of the hashing algorithm for a specific input. The illustration shows the one-way nature of these functions.

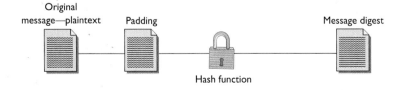

Original
message—plaintext   Padding   Message digest

Hash function

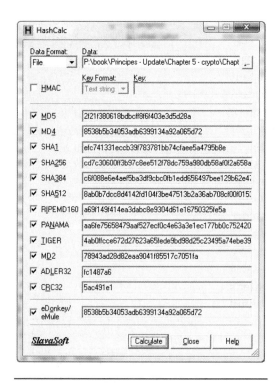

Common uses of hashing functions are to store computer passwords and to ensure message integrity. The idea is that hashing can produce a unique value that corresponds to the data entered, but the hash value is also reproducible by anyone else running the same algorithm against the same data. So you could hash a message to get a message authentication code (MAC), and the computational number of the message would show that no intermediary has modified the message. This process works because hashing algorithms are typically public, and anyone can hash data using the specified algorithm. It is computationally simple to generate the hash, so it is simple to check the validity or integrity of something by matching the given hash to one that is locally generated. Several programs can compute hash values for an input file, as shown in Figure 5.5.

A hash algorithm can be compromised with what is called a **collision attack**, in which an attacker finds two different messages that hash to the same value. This type of attack is very difficult and requires generating a separate algorithm that attempts to find a text that will hash to the same value of a known hash. This must occur faster than simply editing characters until you hash to the same value, which is a brute-force type attack. The consequence of a hash function that suffers from collisions is a loss of integrity. If an attacker can make two different inputs purposefully hash to the same value, she might trick people into running malicious code and cause other problems. Two popular hash algorithms are the Secure Hash Algorithm (SHA) series and Message Digest (MD) hash of varying versions (MD2, MD4, MD5).

Hashing functions are very common and play an important role in the way information, such as passwords, is stored securely, and the way in which messages can be signed. By computing a digest of the message, less data needs to be signed by the more complex asymmetric encryption, and this still maintains assurances about message integrity. This is the primary purpose for which the protocols were designed, and their success will allow greater trust in electronic protocols and digital signatures.

• **Figure 5.5**   There are several programs available that will accept an input and produce a hash value, letting you independently verify the integrity of downloaded content.

Tech Tip

Hashing Algorithms

The hashing algorithms in common use are MD2, MD4, and MD5, and SHA-1, SHA-256, SHA-384, and SHA-512.

SHA

Secure Hash Algorithm (SHA) refers to a set of four hash algorithms designed and published by the National Institute of Standards and Technology (NIST) and the National Security Agency (NSA). These algorithms are included in the SHA standard Federal Information Processing Standards (FIPS) 180-2. The individual standards are named SHA-1, SHA-256, SHA-384, and SHA-512. The latter three variants are occasionally referred to collectively as SHA-2.

SHA-1

SHA-1, developed in 1993, was designed as the algorithm to be used for secure hashing in the U.S. Digital Signature Standard (DSS). It is modeled on the MD4 algorithm and implements fixes in that algorithm discovered by the NSA. It creates message digests 160 bits long that can be used by the Digital

Signature Algorithm (DSA), which can then compute the signature of the message. This is computationally simpler, as the message digest is typically much smaller than the actual message—smaller message, less work.

SHA-1 works, as do all hashing functions, by applying a compression function to the data input. It accepts an input of up to 2^{64} bits or less and then compresses down to a hash of 160 bits. SHA-1 works in block mode, separating the data into words first, and then grouping the words into blocks.

The words are 32-bit strings converted to hex; grouped together as 16 words, they make up a 512-bit block. If the data that is input to SHA-1 is not a multiple of 512, the message is padded with zeros and an integer describing the original length of the message.

Once the message has been formatted for processing, the actual hash can be generated. The 512-bit blocks are taken in order until the entire message has been processed. The computation uses eighty 32-bit words labeled W_0, W_1, W_2, …, W_{79} being sent to two, five-word buffers. The first five-word buffer's words are labeled A, B, C, D, E, and the second five-word buffer's words are labeled H_0, H_1, H_2, H_3, and H_4. These buffers are combined until all words have been processed through all blocks of the message, and the entire message is then represented by the 160-bit string $H_0 H_1 H_2 H_3 H_4$.

At one time, SHA-1 was one of the more secure hash functions, but it has been found to be vulnerable to a collision attack. Thus, many security professionals are suggesting that implementations of SHA-1 be moved to one of the other SHA versions. These longer versions, SHA-256, SHA-384, and SHA-512, all have longer hash results, making them more difficult to attack successfully. The added security and resistance to attack in SHA-2 does require more processing power to compute the hash.

SHA-256

SHA-256 is similar to SHA-1 in that it also accepts input of less than 2^{64} bits and reduces that input to a hash. This algorithm reduces to 256 bits instead of SHA-1's 160. Defined in FIPS 180-2 in 2002, SHA-256 is listed as an update to the original FIPS 180 that defined SHA. Similar to SHA-1, SHA-256 accepts 2^{64} bits of input and uses 32-bit words and 512-bit blocks. Padding is added until the entire message is a multiple of 512. SHA-256 uses sixty-four 32-bit words, eight working variables, and results in a hash value of eight 32-bit words, hence 256 bits.

SHA-256 is more secure than SHA-1, but the attack basis for SHA-1 can produce collisions in SHA-256 as well since they are similar algorithms. The SHA standard does have two longer versions, however.

SHA-384

SHA-384 is also similar to SHA-1, but it handles larger sets of data. SHA-384 accepts 2128 bits of input, which it pads until it has several blocks of data in 1024-bit blocks. SHA-384 also uses 64-bit words instead of SHA-1's 32-bit words. It uses six 64-bit words to produce the 284-bit hash value.

SHA-512

SHA-512 is structurally similar to SHA-384. It accepts the same 2128 bits of input and uses the same 64-bit word size and 1024-bit block size. SHA-512

Tech Tip

Block Mode in Hashing
Most algorithms use block mode to process, i.e., they process all input in set blocks of data such as 512-bit blocks. In the case of hashing algorithms, the final hash is typically generated by adding the output blocks together to form the final output string of 160 or 512 bits.

Try to keep attacks on cryptosystems in perspective. While the theory of attacking hashing through collisions is solid, finding a collision still takes enormous amounts of effort. In the case of attacking SHA-1, the collision is able to be found faster than a pure brute-force method, but by most estimates will still take several years.

differs from SHA-384 in that it uses eight 64-bit words for the final hash, resulting in 512 bits.

Message Digest

Message Digest (MD) is the generic version of one of several algorithms that are designed to create a message digest or hash from data input into the algorithm. MD algorithms work in the same manner as SHA in that they use a secure method to compress the file and generate a computed output of a specified number of bits. The MD algorithms were all developed by Ronald L. Rivest of MIT.

MD2

MD2 was developed in 1989 and is in some ways an early version of the later MD5 algorithm. It takes a data input of any length and produces a hash output of 128 bits. It is different from MD4 and MD5 in that MD2 is optimized for 8-bit machines, whereas the other two are optimized for 32-bit machines. As with SHA, the input data is padded to become a multiple—in this case a multiple of 16 bytes. After padding, a 16-byte checksum is appended to the message. The message is then processed in 16-byte blocks. After initialization, the algorithm invokes a compression function. After the function has been run for every 16 bytes of the message, the output result is a 128-bit digest. The only known attack that is successful against MD2 requires that the checksum not be appended to the message before the hash function is run. Without a checksum, the algorithm can be vulnerable to a collision attack. Some collision attacks are based upon the algorithm's initialization vector (IV).

MD4

MD4 was developed in 1990 and is optimized for 32-bit computers. It is a fast algorithm, but it is subject to more attacks than more secure algorithms such as MD5. Like MD2, it takes a data input of some length and outputs a digest of 128 bits. The message is padded to become a multiple of 512, which is then concatenated with the representation of the message's original length.

As with SHA, the message is then divided into blocks and also into 16 words of 32 bits. All blocks of the message are processed in three distinct rounds. The digest is then computed using a four-word buffer. The final four words remaining after compression are the 128-bit hash.

An extended version of MD4 computes the message in parallel and produces two 128-bit outputs—effectively a 256-bit hash. Even though a longer hash is produced, security has not been improved because of basic flaws in the algorithm. Cryptographer Hans Dobbertin has shown how collisions in MD4 can be found in under a minute using just a PC. This vulnerability to collisions applies to 128-bit MD4 as well as 256-bit MD4. Most people are moving away from MD4 to MD5 or a robust version of SHA.

MD5

MD5 was developed in 1991 and is structured after MD4 but with additional security to overcome the problems in MD4. Therefore, it is very similar to the MD4 algorithm, only slightly slower and more secure.

MD5 creates a 128-bit hash of a message of any length. Like MD4, it segments the message into 512-bit blocks and then into sixteen 32-bit words. First, the original message is padded to be 64 bits short of a multiple of 512 bits. Then a 64-bit representation of the original length of the message is added to the padded value to bring the entire message up to a 512-bit multiple.

After padding is complete, four 32-bit variables, A, B, C, and D, are initialized. A, B, C, and D are copied into a, b, c, and d, and then the main function begins. This has four rounds, each using a different nonlinear function 16 times. These functions operate on three of a, b, c, and d, adding the result to the fourth variable, the fourth variable being a sub-block of the text and a constant, and then rotating the result of that addition to the right a variable number of bits, specified by the round of the algorithm. After adding the result of this operation to one of a, b, c, and d, that sum replaces one of a, b, c, and d. After the four rounds are completed, a, b, c, and d are added to A, B, C, and D, and the algorithm moves on to the next block. After all blocks are completed, A, B, C, and D are concatenated to form the final output of 128 bits.

MD5 has been a fairly common integrity standard and was most commonly used as part of the NTLM (NT LAN Manager) challenge/response authentication protocol. Recently, successful attacks on the algorithm have occurred. Cryptanalysis has displayed weaknesses in the compression function. However, this weakness does not lend itself to an attack on MD5 itself. Czech cryptographer Vlastimil Klíma published work showing that MD5 collisions can be computed in about eight hours on a standard home PC. In November 2007, researchers published results showing the ability to have two entirely different Win32 executables with different functionality but the same MD5 hash. This discovery has obvious implications for the development of malware. The combination of these problems with MD5 has pushed people to adopt a strong SHA version for security reasons.

Hashing Summary

Hashing functions are very common, and they play an important role in the way information, such as passwords, is stored securely and the way in which messages can be signed. By computing a digest of the message, less data needs to be signed by the more complex asymmetric encryption, and this still maintains assurances about message integrity. This is the primary purpose for which the protocols were designed, and their success will allow greater trust in electronic protocols and digital signatures.

■ Symmetric Encryption

Symmetric encryption is the older and more simple method of encrypting information. The basis of symmetric encryption is that both the sender and the receiver of the message have previously obtained the same key. This is, in fact, the basis for even the oldest ciphers—the Spartans needed the exact same size cylinder, making the cylinder the "key" to the message, and in shift ciphers both parties need to know the direction and amount of shift being performed. All symmetric algorithms are based upon this **shared secret** principle, including the unbreakable one-time pad method.

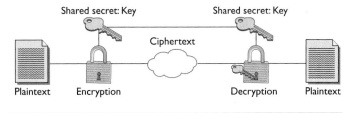

Figure 5.6 Layout of a symmetric algorithm

Figure 5.6 is a simple diagram showing the process that a symmetric algorithm goes through to provide encryption from plaintext to ciphertext. This ciphertext message is, presumably, transmitted to the message recipient, who goes through the process to decrypt the message using the same key that was used to encrypt the message. Figure 5.6 shows the keys to the algorithm, which are the same value in the case of symmetric encryption.

Unlike with hash functions, a cryptographic key is involved in symmetric encryption, so there must be a mechanism for *key management* (discussed earlier in the chapter). Managing the cryptographic keys is critically important in symmetric algorithms because the key unlocks the data that is being protected. However, the key also needs to be known by, or transmitted to in a confidential way, the party to which you wish to communicate. A key must be managed at all stages, which requires securing it on the local computer, securing it on the remote one, protecting it from data corruption, protecting it from loss, and, probably the most important step, protecting it while it is transmitted between the two parties. Later in the chapter we will look at public key cryptography, which greatly eases the key management issue, but for symmetric algorithms the most important lesson is to store and send the key only by known secure means.

Some of the more popular symmetric encryption algorithms in use today are DES, 3DES, AES, and IDEA.

DES

DES, the Data Encryption Standard, was developed in response to the National Bureau of Standards (NBS), now known as the National Institute of Standards and Technology (NIST), issuing a request for proposals for a standard cryptographic algorithm in 1973. NBS received a promising response in an algorithm called Lucifer, originally developed by IBM. The NBS and the NSA worked together to analyze the algorithm's security, and eventually DES was adopted as a federal standard in 1976.

NBS specified that the DES standard had to be recertified every five years. While DES passed without a hitch in 1983, the NSA said it would not recertify it in 1987. However, since no alternative was available for many businesses, many complaints ensued, and the NSA and NBS were forced to recertify it. The algorithm was then recertified in 1993. NIST has now certified the Advanced Encryption Standard (AES) to replace DES.

DES is what is known as a **block cipher**; it segments the input data into blocks of a specified size, typically padding the last block to make it a multiple of the block size required. In the case of DES, the block size is 64 bits, which means DES takes a 64-bit input and outputs 64 bits of ciphertext. This process is repeated for all 64-bit blocks in the message. DES uses a key length of 56 bits, and all security rests within the key. The same algorithm and key are used for both encryption and decryption.

At the most basic level, DES performs a substitution and then a permutation (a form of transposition) on the input, based upon the key. This action is called a *round*, and DES performs this 16 times on every 64-bit block. The algorithm goes step by step, producing 64-bit blocks of ciphertext for each plaintext block. This is carried on until the entire message has been encrypted with DES. As mentioned, the same algorithm and key are used to decrypt and encrypt with DES. The only difference is that the sequence of key permutations is used in reverse order.

Over the years that DES has been a cryptographic standard, a lot of cryptanalysis has occurred, and while the algorithm has held up very well, some problems have been encountered. *Weak keys* are keys that are less secure than the majority of keys allowed in the keyspace of the algorithm. In the case of DES, because of the way the initial key is modified to get the subkey, certain keys are weak keys. The weak keys equate in binary to having all 1's or all 0's, like those shown in Figure 5.7, or to having half the key all 1's and the other half all 0's.

Semiweak keys, with which two keys will encrypt plaintext to identical ciphertext, also exist, meaning that either key will decrypt the ciphertext. The total number of possibly weak keys is 64, which is very small relative to the 2^{56} possible keys in DES.

In addition, multiple successful attacks against DES algorithms have used fewer rounds than 16. Any DES algorithm with fewer than 16 rounds could be analyzed more efficiently with chosen plaintext than via a brute-force attack using differential cryptanalysis. With 16 rounds and not using a weak key, DES is reasonably secure and, amazingly, has been for more than two decades. In 1999, a distributed effort consisting of a supercomputer and 100,000 PCs over the Internet was made to break a 56-bit DES key. By attempting more than 240 billion keys per second, the effort was able to retrieve the key in less than a day. This demonstrates an incredible resistance to cracking a 20-year-old algorithm, but it also demonstrates that more stringent algorithms are needed to protect data today.

```
            Binary Key

       0000000 0000000
       0000000 FFFFFFF
       FFFFFFF 0000000
       FFFFFFF FFFFFFF
```

• **Figure 5.7**   Weak DES keys

3DES

Triple DES (3DES) is a variant of DES. Depending on the specific variant, it uses either two or three keys instead of the single key that DES uses. It also spins through the DES algorithm three times via what's called **multiple encryption**.

Multiple encryption can be performed in several different ways. The simplest method of multiple encryption is just to stack algorithms on top of each other—taking plaintext, encrypting it with DES, then encrypting the first ciphertext with a different key, and then encrypting the second ciphertext with a third key. In reality, this technique is less effective than the technique that 3DES uses, which is to encrypt with one key, then decrypt with a second, and then encrypt with a third, as shown in Figure 5.8.

This greatly increases the number of attempts needed to retrieve the key and is a significant enhancement of security. The additional security comes with a price, however. It can take up to three times longer to compute 3DES than to compute DES. However, the advances in memory and processing power in today's electronics should make this problem irrelevant in all devices except for very small low-power handhelds.

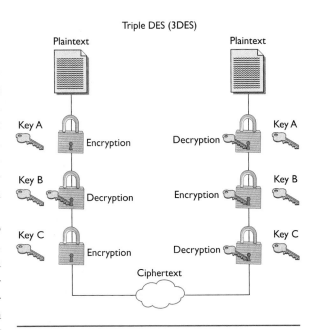

• **Figure 5.8**   Diagram of 3DES

The only weaknesses of 3DES are those that already exist in DES. However, due to the use of different keys in the same algorithm, effecting a longer key length by adding the first keyspace to the second keyspace, and the greater resistance to brute-forcing, 3DES has less actual weakness. 3DES is a good interim step before the new encryption standard, AES, is fully implemented to replace DES.

AES

Because of the advancement of technology and the progress being made in quickly retrieving DES keys, NIST put out a request for proposals for a new Advanced Encryption Standard (AES). It called for a block cipher using symmetric key cryptography and supporting key sizes of 128, 192, and 256 bits. After evaluation, the NIST had five finalists:

- **MARS** IBM
- **RC6** RSA
- **Rijndael** John Daemen and Vincent Rijmen
- **Serpent** Ross Anderson, Eli Biham, and Lars Knudsen
- **Twofish** Bruce Schneier, John Kelsey, Doug Whiting, David Wagner, Chris Hall, and Niels Ferguson

In the fall of 2000, NIST picked Rijndael to be the new AES. It was chosen for its overall security as well as its good performance on limited-capacity devices. Rijndael's design was influenced by Square, also written by John Daemen and Vincent Rijmen. Like Square, Rijndael is a block cipher that separates data input into 128-bit blocks. Rijndael can also be configured to use blocks of 192 or 256 bits, but AES has standardized on 128-bit blocks. AES can have key sizes of 128, 192, and 256 bits, with the size of the key affecting the number of rounds used in the algorithm. Longer key versions are known as AES-192 and AES-256, respectively.

Like DES, AES works in three steps on every block of input data:

1. Add round key, performing an XOR of the block with a subkey.
2. Perform the number of normal rounds required by the key length.
3. Perform a regular round without the mix-column step found in the normal round.

After these steps have been performed, a 128-bit block of plaintext produces a 128-bit block of ciphertext. As indicated in step 2, AES performs multiple rounds. The number is determined by the key size. A key size of 128 bits requires 9 rounds, 192-bit keys require 11 rounds, and 256-bit keys use 13 rounds. Four steps are performed in every round:

1. *Byte sub.* Each byte is replaced by its S-box substitute.
2. *Shift row.* Bytes are arranged in a rectangle and shifted.
3. *Mix column.* Matrix multiplication is performed based upon the arranged rectangle.
4. *Add round key.* This round's subkey is cored in.

These steps are performed until the final round has been completed, and when the final step has been performed, the ciphertext is output.

The Rijndael algorithm is well thought out and has a suitable key length to provide security for many years to come. While no efficient attacks currently exist against AES, more time and analysis will tell if this standard can last as long as DES has.

Tech Tip

AES in Depth

For a more in-depth description of AES, see the NIST document http://csrc.nist.gov/publications/fips/fips197/fips-197.pdf.

CAST

CAST is an encryption algorithm that is similar to DES in its structure. It was designed by Carlisle Adams and Stafford Tavares. CAST uses a 64-bit block size for 64- and 128-bit key versions, and a 128-bit block size for the 256-bit key version. Like DES, it divides the plaintext block into a left half and a right half. The right half is then put through function f and then is XORed with the left half. This value becomes the new right half, and the original right half becomes the new left half. This is repeated for eight rounds for a 64-bit key, and the left and right output is concatenated to form the ciphertext block.

CAST supports longer key lengths than the original 64 bits. Changes to the key length affect the number of rounds: CAST-128 specifies 16 rounds and CAST-256 has 48 rounds. This algorithm in CAST-256 form was submitted for the AES standard but was not chosen. CAST has undergone thorough analysis, with only minor weaknesses discovered that are dependent on low numbers of rounds. Currently, no better way is known to break high-round CAST than by brute-forcing the key, meaning that with sufficient key length, CAST should be placed with other trusted algorithms.

RC

RC is a general term for several ciphers all designed by Ron Rivest—RC officially stands for *Rivest Cipher*. RC1, RC2, RC3, RC4, RC5, and RC6 are all ciphers in the series. RC1 and RC3 never made it to release, but RC2, RC4, RC5, and RC6 are all working algorithms.

RC2

RC2 was designed as a DES replacement, and it is a variable-key-size block-mode cipher. The key size can be from 8 bits to 1024 bits, with the block size being fixed at 64 bits. RC2 breaks up the input blocks into four 16-bit words and then puts them through 18 rounds of either mix or mash operations, outputting 64 bits of ciphertext for 64 bits of plaintext.

According to RSA, RC2 is up to three times faster than DES. RSA maintained RC2 as a trade secret for a long time, with the source code eventually being illegally posted on the Internet. The ability of RC2 to accept different key lengths is one of the larger vulnerabilities in the algorithm. Any key length below 64 bits can be easily retrieved by modern computational power.

RC5

RC5 is a block cipher, written in 1994. It has multiple variable elements, numbers of rounds, key sizes, and block sizes. The algorithm starts by separating the input block into two words, A and B:

$$A = A + S_0$$
$$B = B + S_1$$
$$\text{For} \quad i = 1 \quad \text{to} \quad r$$
$$A = ((A \text{ XOR } B) <<< B) + S_{2i}$$
$$B = ((B \text{ XOR } A) <<< A) + S_{2i+1}$$

A and B represent the ciphertext output. This algorithm is relatively new, but if configured to run enough rounds, RC5 seems to provide adequate security for current brute-forcing technology. Rivest recommends using at least 12 rounds. With 12 rounds in the algorithm, cryptanalysis in a linear fashion proves less effective than brute-force against RC5, and differential analysis fails for 15 or more rounds. A newer algorithm is RC6.

RC6

RC6 is based on the design of RC5. It uses a 128-bit block size, separated into four words of 32 bits each. It uses a round count of 20 to provide security, and it has three possible key sizes: 128, 192, and 256 bits. The four words are named A, B, C, and D, and the algorithm works like this:

$$B = B + S_0$$
$$D = D + S_1$$
$$\text{For} \quad i = 1 - 20$$
$$[t = (B * (2B + 1)) <<< 5$$
$$u = (D * (2D + 1)) <<< 5$$
$$A = ((A \text{ XOR } t) <<< u) + S_{2i}$$
$$C = ((C \text{ XOR } u) <<< t) + S_{2i+1}$$
$$(A, B, C, D) = (B, C, D, A)]$$
$$A = A + S_{42}$$
$$C = C + S_{43}$$

The output of A, B, C, and D after 20 rounds is the ciphertext.

RC6 is a modern algorithm that runs well on 32-bit computers. With a sufficient number of rounds, the algorithm makes both linear and differential cryptanalysis infeasible. The available key lengths make brute-force attacks extremely time-consuming. RC6 should provide adequate security for some time to come.

RC4

RC4 was created before RC5 and RC6, but it differs in operation. RC4 is a **stream cipher**, whereas all the symmetric ciphers we have looked at so far have been *block ciphers*. A stream cipher works by enciphering the plaintext in a stream, usually bit by bit. This makes stream ciphers faster than block-mode ciphers. Stream ciphers accomplish this by performing a bitwise XOR with the plaintext stream and a generated keystream.

RC4 operates in this manner. It was developed in 1987 and remained a trade secret of RSA until it was posted to the Internet in 1994. RC4 can use a key length of 8 to 2048 bits, though the most common versions use 128-bit keys or, if subject to the old export restrictions, 40-bit keys. The key is used to initialize a 256-byte state table. This table is used to generate the pseudo-random stream that is XORed with the plaintext to generate the ciphertext. Alternatively, the stream is XORed with the ciphertext to produce the plaintext.

The algorithm is fast, sometimes ten times faster than DES. The most vulnerable point of the encryption is the possibility of weak keys. One key in 256 can generate bytes closely correlated with key bytes.

Blowfish

Blowfish was designed in 1994 by Bruce Schneier. It is a block-mode cipher using 64-bit blocks and a variable key length from 32 to 448 bits. It was designed to run quickly on 32-bit microprocessors and is optimized for situations with few key changes. Encryption is done by separating the 64-bit input block into two 32-bit words, and then a function is executed every round. Blowfish has 16 rounds; once the rounds are completed, the two words are then recombined to form the 64-bit output ciphertext.

The only successful cryptanalysis to date against Blowfish has been against variants that used a reduced number of rounds. There does not seem to be a weakness in the full 16-round version.

IDEA

IDEA (International Data Encryption Algorithm) started out as PES, or Proposed Encryption Cipher, in 1990, and it was modified to improve its resistance to differential cryptanalysis and its name was changed to IDEA in 1992. It is a block-mode cipher using a 64-bit block size and a 128-bit key. The input plaintext is split into four 16-bit segments, A, B, C, and D. The process uses eight rounds, with a final four-step process. The output of the last four steps is then concatenated to form the ciphertext.

This algorithm is fairly new, but all current cryptanalysis on full, eight-round IDEA shows that the most efficient attack would be to brute-force the key. The 128-bit key would prevent this attack being accomplished, given current computer technology. The only known issue is that IDEA is susceptible to a weak key—a key that is made of all 0's. This weak key is easy to check for, and the weakness is simple to mitigate.

Symmetric Encryption Summary

Symmetric algorithms are important because they are comparatively fast and have few computational requirements. Their main weakness is that two geographically distant parties both need to have a key that matches the other key exactly (see Figure 5.9).

In the past, keys could be much simpler and still be secure, but with today's computational power, simple keys can be brute-forced very quickly. This means that larger and more complex keys must be used and exchanged. This key exchange is difficult because the key cannot be simple, such as a word, but must be shared in a secure manner. It might be easy to exchange a 4-bit key such as b in hex, but exchanging

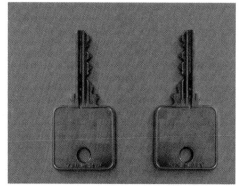

• **Figure 5.9** Symmetric keys must match exactly to encrypt and decrypt the message.

the 128-bit key *4b36402c5727472d5571373d22675b4b* is far more difficult to do securely. This exchange of keys is greatly facilitated by our next subject, asymmetric, or public key cryptography.

■ Asymmetric Encryption

Asymmetric cryptography is in many ways completely different from symmetric cryptography. While both are used to keep data from being seen by unauthorized users, asymmetric cryptography uses two keys instead of one. It was invented by Whitfield Diffie and Martin Hellman in 1975. Asymmetric cryptography is more commonly known as *public key cryptography*. The system uses a pair of keys: a private key that is kept secret, and a public key that can be sent to anyone. The system's security relies upon resistance to deducing one key, given the other, and thus retrieving the plaintext from the ciphertext.

Public key systems typically work by using hard math problems. One of the more common methods relies on the difficulty of factoring large numbers. These functions are often called **trapdoor functions**, as they are difficult to process without the key but easy to process when you have the key—the trapdoor through the function. For example, given a prime number, say 293, and another prime, such as 307, it is an easy function to multiply them together to get 89,951. Given 89,951, it is not simple to find the factors 293 and 307 unless you know one of them already. Computers can easily multiply very large primes with hundreds or thousands of digits but cannot easily factor the product.

The strength of these functions is very important: Because an attacker is likely to have access to the public key, he can run tests of known plaintext and produce ciphertext. This allows instant checking of guesses that are made about the keys of the algorithm. Public key systems, because of their design, also form the basis for *digital signatures*, a cryptographic method for securely identifying people. RSA, Diffie-Hellman, elliptic curve cryptography (ECC), and ElGamal are all popular asymmetric protocols. We will look at all of them and their suitability for different functions.

☑ Cross Check

Digital Certificates

In Chapter 6 you will learn more about digital certificates and how encryption is important to a public key infrastructure. Why is an asymmetric algorithm so important to digital signatures?

RSA

RSA is one of the first public key cryptosystems ever invented. It can be used for both encryption and digital signatures. RSA is named after its inventors, Ron Rivest, Adi Shamir, and Leonard Adleman, and was first published in 1977.

This algorithm uses the product of two very large prime numbers and works on the principle of difficulty in factoring such large numbers. It's best to choose large prime numbers that are from 100 to 200 digits in length and are equal in length. These two primes will be *P* and *Q*. Randomly choose an encryption key, E, so that E is greater than 1, E is less than $P * Q$, and E must be odd. E must also be relatively prime to $(P - 1)$ and $(Q - 1)$. Then compute the decryption key D:

$$D = E^{-1} \bmod ((P - 1)(Q - 1))$$

Now that the encryption key and decryption key have been generated, the two prime numbers can be discarded, but they should not be revealed. To encrypt a message, it should be divided into blocks less than the product of P and Q. Then,

$$C_i = M_i^E \bmod (P * Q)$$

C is the output block of ciphertext matching the block length of the input message, M. To decrypt a message, take ciphertext, C, and use this function:

$$M_i = C_i^D \bmod (P * Q)$$

The use of the second key retrieves the plaintext of the message.

This is a simple function, but its security has withstood the test of more than 20 years of analysis. Considering the effectiveness of RSA's security and the ability to have two keys, why are symmetric encryption algorithms needed at all? The answer is speed. RSA in software can be 100 times slower than DES, and in hardware it can be even slower.

RSA can be used to perform both regular encryption and digital signatures. Digital signatures try to duplicate the functionality of a physical signature on a document using encryption. Typically, RSA and the other public key systems are used in conjunction with symmetric key cryptography. Public key, the slower protocol, is used to exchange the symmetric key (or shared secret), and then the communication uses the faster symmetric key protocol. This process is known as *electronic key exchange*.

Since the security of RSA is based upon the supposed difficulty of factoring large numbers, the main weaknesses are in the implementations of the protocol. Until recently, RSA was a patented algorithm, but it was a de facto standard for many years.

Diffie-Hellman

Diffie-Hellman was created in 1976 by Whitfield Diffie and Martin Hellman. This protocol is one of the most common encryption protocols in use today. It plays a role in the electronic key exchange method of the Secure Sockets Layer (SSL) protocol. It is also used by the TLS, SSH, and IPsec protocols. Diffie-Hellman is important because it enables the sharing of a secret key between two people who have not contacted each other before.

The protocol, like RSA, uses large prime numbers to work. Two users agree to two numbers, P and G, with P being a sufficiently large prime number and G being the generator. Both users pick a secret number, a and b. Then both users compute their public number:

User 1 $X = Ga \bmod P$, with X being the public number
User 2 $Y = Gb \bmod P$, with Y being the public number

The users then exchange public numbers. User 1 knows P, G, a, X, and Y.

User 1 Computes $Ka = Y^a \bmod P$
User 2 Computes $Kb = X^b \bmod P$

With $Ka = Kb = K$, now both users know the new shared secret K.

This is the basic algorithm, and although methods have been created to strengthen it, Diffie-Hellman is still in wide use. It remains very effective because of the nature of what it is protecting—a temporary, automatically generated secret key that is good only for a single communication session.

ElGamal

ElGamal can be used for both encryption and digital signatures. Taher Elgamal designed the system in the early 1980s. This system was never patented and is free for use. It is used as the U.S. government standard for digital signatures.

The system is based upon the difficulty of calculating discrete logarithms in a finite field. Three numbers are needed to generate a key pair. User 1 chooses a prime, P, and two random numbers, F and D. F and D should both be less than P. Then user 1 can calculate the public key A:

$A = D^F \bmod P$

Then A, D, and P are shared with the second user, with F being the private key. To encrypt a message, M, a random key, k, is chosen that is relatively prime to $P - 1$. Then,

$C_1 = D^k \bmod P$
$C_2 = A^k M \bmod P$

C_1 and C_2 make up the ciphertext. Decryption is done by

$M = C_2 / C_1^F \bmod P$

ElGamal uses a different function for digital signatures. To sign a message, M, once again choose a random value k that is relatively prime to $P - 1$. Then,

$C_1 = D^k \bmod P$
$C_2 = (M - C_1 * F)/k \; (\bmod \; P - 1)$

C_1 concatenated to C_2 is the digital signature.

ElGamal is an effective algorithm and has been in use for some time. It is used primarily for digital signatures. Like all asymmetric cryptography, it is slower than symmetric cryptography.

ECC

Elliptic curve cryptography (ECC) works on the basis of elliptic curves. An elliptic curve is a simple function that is drawn as a gently looping curve on the X,Y plane. Elliptic curves are defined by this equation:

$y^2 = x^3 + ax^2 + b$

Elliptic curves work because they have a special property—you can add two points on the curve together and get a third point on the curve, as shown in the illustration.

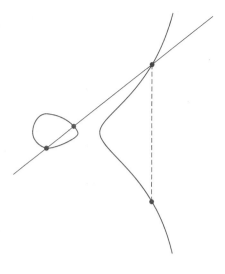

For cryptography, the elliptic curve works as a public key algorithm. Users agree on an elliptic curve and a fixed curve point. This information is not a shared secret, and these points can be made public without compromising the security of the system. User 1 then chooses a secret random number, K_1, and computes a public key based upon a point on the curve:

$$P_1 = K_1 * F$$

User 2 performs the same function and generates P_2. Now user 1 can send user 2 a message by generating a shared secret:

$$S = K_1 * P_2$$

User 2 can generate the same shared secret independently:

$$S = K_2 * P_1$$

This is true because

$$K_1 * P_2 = K_1 * (K_2 * F) = (K_1 * K_2) * F = K_2 * (K_1 * F) = K_2 * P_1$$

The security of elliptic curve systems has been questioned, mostly because of lack of analysis. However, all public key systems rely on the difficulty of certain math problems. It would take a breakthrough in math for any of the mentioned systems to be weakened dramatically, but research has been done about the problems and has shown that the elliptic curve problem has been more resistant to incremental advances. Again, as with all cryptography algorithms, only time will tell how secure they really are.

Asymmetric Encryption Summary

Asymmetric encryption creates the possibility of digital signatures and also corrects the main weakness of symmetric cryptography. The ability to send messages securely without senders and receivers having had prior contact has become one of the basic concerns with secure communication. Digital signatures will enable faster and more efficient exchange of all kinds of documents, including legal documents. With strong algorithms and good key lengths, security can be assured.

■ Steganography

Steganography, an offshoot of cryptography technology, gets its meaning from the Greek word *steganos*, meaning covered. Invisible ink placed on a document hidden by innocuous text is an example of a steganographic message. Another example is a tattoo placed on the top of a person's head, visible only when the person's hair is shaved off.

Hidden writing in the computer age relies on a program to hide data inside other data. The most common application is the concealing of a text message in a picture file. The Internet contains multiple billions of image files, allowing a hidden message to be located almost anywhere without being discovered. Because not all detection programs can detect every kind of steganography, trying to find the message in an Internet image is akin to attempting to find a needle in a haystack the size of the Pacific Ocean; even a Google search for steganography returns thousands of images.

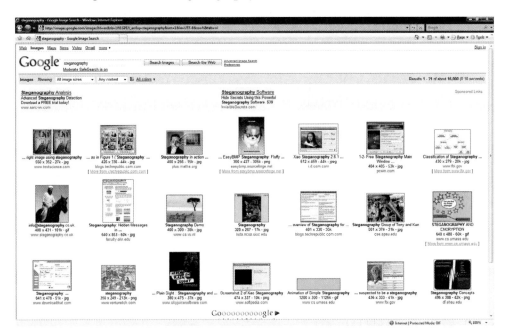

The nature of the image files also makes a hidden message difficult to detect. While it is most common to hide messages inside images, they can also be hidden in video and audio files.

The advantage to steganography over cryptography is that the messages do not attract attention, and this difficulty in detecting the hidden message provides an additional barrier to analysis. The data that is hidden in a steganographic message is frequently also encrypted, so that if it is discovered, the message will remain secure. Steganography has many uses but the most publicized uses are to hide illegal material, often pornography, or allegedly for covert communication by terrorist networks. While there is no direct evidence to support that terrorists use steganography, the techniques have been documented in some of their training materials.

Steganographic encoding can be used in many ways and through many different media. Covering them all is beyond the scope for this book, but we will discuss one of the most common ways to encode into an image file, LSB encoding. LSB, Least Significant Bit, is a method of encoding information into an image while altering the actual visual image as little as possible. A computer image is made up of thousands or millions of pixels, all defined by 1's and 0's. If an image is composed of Red Green Blue (RGB) values, each pixel has an RGB value represented numerically from 0 to 255. For example, 0,0,0 is black, and 255,255,255 is white, which can also be represented as 00000000, 00000000, 00000000 for black and 11111111, 11111111, 11111111 for white. Given a white pixel, editing the least significant bit of the pixel to 11111110, 11111110, 11111110 changes the color. The change in color is undetectable to the human eye, but in an image with a million pixels, this creates a 125KB area in which to store a message.

Some popular steganography detection tools include Stegdetect, StegSecret, StegSpy, and the family of SARC tools. All of these tools use detection techniques based upon the same principle, pattern detection. By looking for known steganographic encoding schemes or artifacts, they can potentially detect embedded data. Additionally, steganography insertion tools can be used to attempt to decode images with suspected hidden messages. Invisible Ink is a small program for steganographic insertion of messages and then the extraction of those messages, as illustrated here.

■ Cryptography Algorithm Use

The use of cryptographic algorithms grows every day. More and more information becomes digitally encoded and placed online, and all of this data needs to be secured. The best way to do that with current technology is to use encryption. This section considers some of the tasks cryptographic algorithms accomplish and those for which they are best suited. Security is typically defined as a product of five components: confidentiality, integrity, availability, authentication, and nonrepudiation. Encryption addresses all of these components except availability. Key escrow will be one of the most important topics as information becomes universally encrypted; otherwise, everyone may be left with useless data. Digital rights management and intellectual property protection are also places where encryption algorithms are heavily used. Digital signatures combine several algorithms to provide reliable identification in a digital form.

Confidentiality

Confidentiality typically comes to mind when the term *security* is brought up. Confidentiality is the ability to keep some piece of data a secret. In the digital world, encryption excels at providing confidentiality.

Maintaining confidentiality often is important for both stored data and transmitted data. In both cases, symmetric encryption is favored because of its speed and because some asymmetric algorithms can significantly increase the size of the object being encrypted. In the case of a stored item, a public key is typically unnecessary, as the item is being encrypted to protect it from access by others. In the case of transmitted data, public key cryptography is typically used to exchange the secret key, and then symmetric cryptography is used to ensure the confidentiality of the data being sent.

Asymmetric cryptography does protect confidentiality, but its size and speed make it more efficient at protecting the confidentiality of small units for tasks such as electronic key exchange. In all cases, the strength of the algorithms and the length of the keys ensure the secrecy of the data in question.

Integrity

Message integrity will become increasingly important as more commerce is conducted digitally. The ability to independently make sure that a document has not been tampered with is very important to commerce. More importantly, once the document is "signed" with a digital signature, it cannot be refuted that the person in question signed it.

Integrity, better known as *message integrity*, is a crucial component of message security. When a message is sent, both the sender and recipient need to know that the message was not altered in transmission. This is especially important for legal contracts—recipients need to know that the contracts have not been altered. Signers also need a way to validate that a contract they sign will not be altered in the future.

Integrity is provided with one-way hash functions and digital signatures. The hash functions compute the message digests, and this guarantees the integrity of the message by allowing easy testing to determine whether any part of the message has been changed. The message now has a computed function (the hash value) to tell the users to resend the message if it was intercepted and interfered with.

This hash value is combined with asymmetric cryptography by taking the message's hash value and encrypting it with the user's private key. This lets anyone with the user's public key decrypt the hash and compare it to the locally computed hash, ensuring not only the integrity of the message but positively identifying the sender.

Try This

Document Integrity

Download a hash calculator that works on your operating system, such as HashCalc, available at www.slavasoft.com/hashcalc/index.htm. Then create a simple document file with any text that you prefer. Save it, and then use the hashing program to generate the hash and save the hash value. Now edit the file, even by simply inserting a single blank space, and resave it. Recalculate the hash and compare.

Nonrepudiation

An item of some confusion, the concept of nonrepudiation is actually fairly simple. Nonrepudiation means that the message sender cannot later deny that they sent the message. This is important in electronic exchanges of data, because of the lack of face-to-face meetings. Nonrepudiation is based upon public key cryptography and the principle of only you knowing your private key. The presence of a message signed by you, using your private key, which nobody else should know, is an example of nonrepudiation. When a third party can check your signature using your public key, that disproves any claim that you were not the one who actually sent the message. Nonrepudiation is tied to asymmetric cryptography and cannot be implemented with symmetric algorithms.

Authentication

Authentication lets you prove you are who you say you are. Authentication is similar to nonrepudiation, except that authentication often occurs as communication begins, not after. Authentication is also typically used in both directions as part of a protocol.

Authentication can be accomplished in a multitude of ways, the most basic being the use of a simple password. Every time you sign in to check your e-mail, you authenticate yourself to the server. This process can grow to need two or three identifying factors, such as a *password*, a *token* (such as a digital certificate), and a *biometric* (such as a fingerprint).

Digital certificates are a form of token. Digital certificates are public encryption keys that have been verified by a trusted third party. When you log into a secure web site, *one-way* authentication occurs. You want to know that you are logging into the server that you intend to log into, so your browser checks the server's digital certificate. This token is digitally signed by a trusted third party, assuring you that the server is genuine. This authentication is one way because the server does not need to know that you are who you say you are—it will authenticate your credit card later on. The other option, *two-way* authentication, can work the same way: you send your digital certificate signed by a third party, and the other entity with which you are communicating sends its certificate.

While symmetric encryption can be used as a simple manner of authentication (only the authorized user should know the secret, after all), asymmetric encryption is better suited to show, via digital signatures and certificates, that you are who you say you are.

Key Escrow

The impressive growth of the use of encryption technology has led to new methods for handling keys. Encryption is adept at hiding all kinds of information, and with privacy and identity protection becoming more of a concern, more information is encrypted. The loss of a key can happen for a multitude of reasons: it might simply be lost, the key holder might be incapacitated or dead, software or hardware might fail, and so on. In many cases, that information is locked up until the cryptography can be broken, and as you have read, that could be millennia. This has raised the topic of **key escrow**, or keeping a copy of the encryption key with a trusted third party. Theoretically, this third party would only release your key to you or your official designate on the event of your being unable to get the key yourself. However, just as the old saying from Benjamin Franklin goes, "Three may keep a secret if two of them are dead." Anytime more than one copy of the key exists, the security of the system is broken. The extent of the insecurity of key escrow is a subject open to debate, and will be hotly contest in the years to come.

Additionally, with computer technology being miniaturized into smartphones and other relatively inexpensive devices, criminals and other ill-willed people have begun using cryptography to conceal communications and business dealings from law enforcement agencies. Because law enforcement agencies have not been able to break the encryption in many cases, government agencies have begun asking for mandatory key escrow legislation. In this sense, *key escrow* is a system by which your private key is kept both by you and by the government. This allows people with a court order to retrieve your private key to gain access to anything encrypted with your public key. The data is essentially encrypted by your key and the government key, giving the government access to your plaintext data. This process is similar to a search warrant of your home, but is used against your computer data. Whether or not this is how things should be is also open to debate, but it does raise the interesting possibility of encryption software that is incompatible with government key escrow being banned. The last major discussion for key escrow legislation was several years ago, but the prospect remains out there waiting for a high profile case to bring encryption into the spotlight.

Key escrow can negatively impact the security provided by encryption, because the government requires a huge, complex infrastructure of systems to hold every escrowed key, and the security of those systems is less efficient than the security of your memorizing the key. However, there are two sides to the key escrow coin. Without a practical way to recover a key if or when it is lost or the key holder dies, for example, some important information will be lost forever. Such issues will affect the design and security of encryption technologies for the foreseeable future.

Digital Signatures

Digital signatures have been touted as the key to truly paperless document flow, and they do have promise for improving the system. Digital signatures are based on both hashing functions and asymmetric cryptography. Both encryption methods play an important role in signing digital documents.

Unprotected digital documents are very easy for anyone to change. If a document is edited after an individual signs it, it is important that any modification can be detected. To protect against document editing, hashing functions are used to create a digest of the message that is unique and easily reproducible by both parties. This ensures that the message integrity is complete.

Protection must also be provided to ensure that the intended party actually did sign the message, and that someone did not edit the message and the hash of the message. This is done by asymmetric encryption. The properties of asymmetric encryption allow anyone to use a person's public key to generate a message that can be read only by that person, as this person is theoretically the only one with access to the private key. In the case of digital signatures, this process works exactly in reverse. When a user can decrypt the hash with the public key of the originator, that user knows that the hash was encrypted by the corresponding private key. This use of asymmetric encryption is a good example of nonrepudiation, because only the signer

Tech Tip

Key Escrow Has Benefits and Hazards

Key escrow can solve many of the problems that result when a key is lost or becomes inaccessible, allowing access to data that otherwise would be impossible to access without key escrow, but it can open up private information to unauthorized access.

would have access to the private key. This is how digital signatures work, by using integrity and nonrepudiation to prove not only that the right person signed the digital document, but also that the digital document was not altered after being signed.

Digital Rights Management

Digital rights management (DRM) is the process for protecting intellectual property from unauthorized use. This is a broad area, but the most concentrated focus is on preventing piracy of software or digital content. Before easy access to computers, or the "digital revolution," the content we came in contact with was analog or print based. While it was possible to copy this content, it was difficult and time-consuming to do so, and usually resulted in a loss of quality. It was also much more difficult to send 1000 pages of a handwritten copy of a book to Europe, for example. Computers and the Internet have made such tasks trivial, and now it is very easy to copy a document, music, or video and quickly send it thousands of miles away.

Cryptography has entered the fray as a solution to protecting digital rights, though it is currently better known for its failures than its successes. The DVD Content Scramble System (CSS) was an attempt to make DVD discs impossible to copy by computer. CSS used an encryption algorithm that was licensed to every DVD player; however, creative programmers were able to retrieve the key to this algorithm by disassembling a software-based DVD player. CSS has been replaced by the Advanced Access Content System (AACS), which is used on the next-generation Blu-ray discs. This system encrypts video content via the symmetric AES algorithm with one or more keys. Several decryption keys have been cracked and released to the Internet, allowing some to freely copy the protected content. Music and computer games have also attempted several different DRM applications, but nearly all of these have eventually been cracked, allowing piracy.

A common example of DRM that is mostly successful is the broadcast stream of digital satellite TV. Since the signal is beamed from space to every home in North America, the satellite TV provider must be able to protect the signal so that it can charge people to receive it. Smartcards are employed to securely hold the decryption keys that allow access to some or all of the content in the stream. This system has been cracked several times, allowing a subset of users free access to the content; however, the satellite TV providers learned from their early mistakes and upgraded new smartcards to correct the old problems.

DRM will also become very important in the industry of Software as a Service (SaaS). Similar to companies that provide satellite TV service, companies that provide SaaS rely on a subscription basis for profitability. If someone could pay for a single license and then distribute that to hundreds of employees, the provider would soon go out of business. Many systems in the past have been cracked because the key was housed inside the software. This has prompted some systems to use specific hardware to store and protect the key. Smartcards are one example of this technology. Another example is hardware token USB keys that must be inserted into the machine for the software to decrypt and run. Placing the keys in hardware makes an attack to retrieve them much harder, a concept that is employed in the Trusted Platform Module; in fact, one of the primary complaints against the TPM is its ability to enforce DRM restrictions.

The profitability of many corporations depends on protecting trade secrets. With the continuing rise of corporate espionage, computer security takes a center-stage role in protection of those assets. This protection of intellectual property (IP) is another offshoot of DRM and can rely on cryptography. Regular symmetric encryption can be used in a variety of places to assist in keeping trade secrets protected against a security breach. However, asymmetric encryption must be used when sending sensitive materials through e-mail and other transmission mediums. There are also applications to encrypt executable code so that attempts to reverse-engineer an application are much more difficult.

Cryptographic Applications

A few applications can be used to encrypt data conveniently on your personal computer. (This is by no means a complete list of every application.)

Pretty Good Privacy (PGP) is mentioned in this book because it is a useful protocol suite. Created by Philip Zimmermann in 1991, it passed through several versions that were available for free under a noncommercial license. PGP applications can be plugged into popular e-mail programs to handle the majority of day-to-day encryption tasks using a combination of symmetric and asymmetric encryption protocols. One of the unique features of PGP is its ability to use both symmetric and asymmetric encryption methods, accessing the strengths of each method and avoiding the weaknesses of each as well. Symmetric keys are used for bulk encryption, taking advantage of the speed and efficiency of symmetric encryption. The symmetric keys are passed using asymmetric methods, capitalizing on the flexibility of this method. PGP is now sold as a commercial application, with home and corporate versions. Depending on the version, PGP can perform file encryption, whole disk encryption, and public key encryption to protect e-mail.

TrueCrypt is an open source solution for encryption. It is designed for symmetric disk-based encryption of your files. It features AES ciphers and the ability to create a *deniable volume*, encryption stored within encryption so that volume cannot be reliably detected. TrueCrypt can perform file encryption and whole disk encryption. Whole disk encryption encrypts the entire hard drive of a computer, including the operating system.

FreeOTFE is similar to TrueCrypt. It offers "on-the-fly" disk encryption as an open source, freely downloadable application. It can encrypt files up to entire disks with several popular ciphers, including AES.

GnuPG, or *Gnu Privacy Guard*, is an open source implementation of the OpenPGP standard. This command line–based tool is a public key encryption program designed to protect electronic communications such as e-mail. It operates similarly to PGP and includes a method for managing public/private keys.

Cross Check

PGP

In Chapter 7 you will learn some additional details about PGP. Why is the ability to use asymmetric and symmetric encryption in the same program important?

File system encryption is becoming a standard means of protecting data while in storage. Even hard drives are available with built-in AES encryption. Microsoft expanded its Encrypting File System (EFS), available since the Windows 2000 operating system, with BitLocker, a boot-sector encryption method that protects data on the Windows Vista operating system. BitLocker is also used in Windows Server 2008 as well as the forthcoming Windows 7 operating system. BitLocker utilizes AES encryption to encrypt every file on the hard drive automatically. All encryption occurs in the background, and decryption occurs seamlessly when data is requested. The decryption key can be stored in the TPM or on a USB key.

Chapter 5 Review

■ Chapter Summary

After reading this chapter and completing the exercises, you should understand the following about cryptography.

Identify and describe the three types of cryptography

- Symmetric cryptography is based upon the concept of a shared secret or key.

- Asymmetric cryptography is based upon a key that can be made openly available to the public, yet still provide security.

- One-way, or hashing, cryptography takes data and enciphers it. However, there is no way to decipher it and no key.

List and describe current cryptographic algorithms

- Hashing is the use of a one-way function to generate a message summary for data integrity.

- Hashing algorithms include SHA and MD (Message Digest).

- Symmetric is a shared secret form of encrypting data for confidentiality; it is fast and reliable, but needs secure key management.

- Symmetric algorithms include DES (Data Encryption Standard), 3DES, AES (Advanced Encryption Standard), CAST, Blowfish, IDEA, and RC (Rivest Cipher) variants.

- Asymmetric is a public/private keypair encryption used for authentication, nonrepudiation, and confidentiality.

- Asymmetric algorithms include RSA, Diffie-Hellman, ElGamal, and ECC.

Explain how cryptography is applied for security

- Confidentiality is gained because encryption is very good at scrambling information to make it look like random noise, when in fact a key can decipher the message and return it to its original state.

- Integrity is gained because hashing algorithms are specifically designed to check integrity. They can reduce a message to a mathematical value that can be independently calculated, guaranteeing that any message alteration would change the mathematical value.

- Nonrepudiation is the property of not being able to claim that you did not send the data. This property is gained because of the properties of private keys.

- Authentication, or being able to prove you are you, is achieved through the private keys involved in digital signatures.

- Digital signatures, combining multiple types of encryption, provide an authentication method verified by a third party, allowing you to use them as if you were actually signing the document with your regular signature.

- Digital rights management (DRM) uses some form of asymmetric encryption that allows an application to determine if you are an authorized user of the digital content you are trying to access. For example, things like DVDs and certain digital music formats such as AAC use DRM.

■ Key Terms

algorithm *(84)*

block cipher *(92)*

collision attack *(88)*

cryptanalysis *(83)*

cryptography *(82)*

differential cryptanalysis *(83)*

digital rights management *(107)*

hash *(87)*

key *(84)*

key escrow *(105)*

key management *(86)*

keyspace *(86)*

linear cryptanalysis *(83)*

multiple encryption *(93)*

shared secret *(91)*
shift cipher *(83)*
steganography *(101)*
stream cipher *(96)*

transposition cipher *(82)*
trapdoor functions *(98)*
Vigenère cipher *(85)*
XOR *(87)*

■ Key Terms Quiz

Use terms from the Key Terms list to complete the sentences that follow. Don't use the same term more than once. Not all terms will be used.

1. Making two inputs result in the exact same cryptographic hash is called a(n) _____.

2. A simple way to hide information, the _____ moves a letter a set number of places down the alphabet.

3. A type of math problem that is difficult unless you know a specific value is called a(n) _____.

4. _____ is required for symmetric encryption.

5. _____ is the evaluation of a cryptosystem to test its security.

6. _____ refers to every possible value for a cryptographic key.

7. _____ is the function most commonly seen in cryptography, a "bitwise exclusive" or.

8. When the government keeps a copy of your private key, it is called _____.

9. Processing through an algorithm more than once with different keys is called _____.

10. The basis for symmetric cryptography is the principle of a(n) _____.

■ Multiple-Choice Quiz

1. When a message is sent, no matter what its format, why do we care about its integrity?

    A. To ensure proper formatting

    B. To show that the encryption keys are undamaged

    C. To show that the message has not been edited in transit

    D. To show that no one has viewed the message

2. How is 3DES different from many other types of encryption listed here?

    A. It only encrypts the hash.

    B. It hashes the message before encryption.

    C. It uses three keys and multiple encryption and/or decryption sets.

    D. It can display the key publicly.

3. If a message has a hash, how does the hash protect the message in transit?

    A. If the message is edited, the hash will no longer match.

    B. Hashing destroys the message so that it cannot be read by anyone.

    C. Hashing encrypts the message so that only the private key holder can read it.

    D. The hash makes the message uneditable.

4. What cipher was chosen to be the new AES standard?

    A. IDEA

    B. RC6

    C. ECC

    D. Rijndael

5. What makes asymmetric encryption better than symmetric encryption?

    A. It's more secure.

    B. Key management is part of the algorithm.

    C. Anyone with the public key can decrypt the data.

    D. It uses a hash.

6. What is the biggest drawback to symmetric encryption?

    A. It is too easily broken.

    B. It is too slow to be easily used on mobile devices.

C. It requires a key to be securely shared.

D. It is available only on UNIX.

7. What is Diffie-Hellman most commonly used for?

A. Symmetric encryption key exchange

B. Signing digital contracts

C. Secure e-mail

D. Storing encrypted passwords

8. What is AES meant to replace?

A. IDEA

B. DES

C. Diffie-Hellman

D. MD5

9. What kind of encryption cannot be reversed?

A. Asymmetric

B. Hash functions

C. Linear cryptanalysis

D. Authentication

10. What is public key cryptography a more common name for?

A. Asymmetric encryption

B. SHA

C. An algorithm that is no longer secure against cryptanalysis

D. Authentication

11. How many bits are in a block of the SHA algorithm?

A. 128

B. 64

C. 512

D. 1024

12. How does elliptical curve cryptography work?

A. It multiplies two large primes.

B. It uses the geometry of a curve to calculate three points.

C. It shifts the letters of the message in an increasing curve.

D. It uses graphs instead of keys.

13. A good hash function is resistant to what?

A. Brute-forcing

B. Rainbow tables

C. Interception

D. Collisions

14. How is 3DES an improvement over normal DES?

A. It uses public and private keys.

B. It hashes the message before encryption.

C. It uses three keys and multiple encryption and/or decryption sets.

D. It is faster than DES.

15. What is the best kind of key to have?

A. Easy to remember

B. Long and random

C. Long and predictable

D. Short

■ Essay Quiz

1. Describe how polyalphabetic substitution works.

2. Explain what a trapdoor function is, with examples.

3. Detail why key management is important.

4. Explain why asymmetric encryption is called public key encryption.

5. Describe cryptanalysis.

Lab Projects

• Lab Project 5.1

Using a utility program, demonstrate how single character changes can make substantial changes to hash values.

• Lab Project 5.2

Create a keyset and use it to transfer a file securely.

Public Key Infrastructure

Without trust, there is nothing.

—ANONYMOUS

In this chapter, you will learn how to

- **Implement the basics of public key infrastructures**
- **Describe the roles of certificate authorities and certificate repositories**
- **Describe the role of registration authorities**
- **Explain the relationship between trust and certificate verification**
- **Use digital certificates**
- **Identify centralized and decentralized infrastructures**
- **Describe public and in-house certificate authorities**

Public key infrastructures (PKIs) are becoming a central security foundation for managing identity credentials in many companies. The technology manages the issue of binding public keys and identities across multiple applications. The other approach, without PKIs, is to implement many different security solutions and hope for interoperability and equal levels of protection.

PKIs comprise several components, including certificates, registration and certificate authorities, and a standard process for verification. PKIs are about managing the sharing of trust and using a third party to vouch for the trustworthiness of a claim of ownership over a credential document, called a **certificate**.

The Basics of Public Key Infrastructures

A **public key infrastructure (PKI)** provides all the components necessary for different types of users and entities to be able to communicate securely and in a predictable manner. A PKI is made up of hardware, applications, policies, services, programming interfaces, cryptographic algorithms, protocols, users, and utilities. These components work together to allow communication to take place using public key cryptography and symmetric keys for digital signatures, data encryption, and integrity.

Although many different applications and protocols can provide the same type of functionality, constructing and implementing a PKI boils down to establishing a level of trust. If, for example, John and Diane want to communicate securely, John can generate his own public/private key pair and send his public key to Diane, or he can place his public key

> ### Cross Check
>
>
> **PKIs and Encryption**
>
> The technologies used in PKI include many cryptographic algorithms and mechanisms. Encryption technologies and public key principles were covered in Chapter 5. A basic understanding of public and private keys and their relationship to public key encryption is a prerequisite for this chapter. If needed, review that material performed before you attempt the details of PKI in this chapter.

in a directory that is available to everyone. If Diane receives John's public key, either from him or from a public directory, how does she know the key really came from John? Maybe another individual, Katie, is masquerading as John and has replaced John's public key with her own, as shown in Figure 6.1 (referred to as a man-in-the-middle attack). If this took place, Diane would believe that her messages could be read only by John and that the replies were actually from him. However, she would actually be communicating with Katie. What is needed is a way to verify an individual's identity, to ensure that a person's public key is bound to their identity and thus ensure that the previous scenario (and others) cannot take place.

In PKI environments, entities called registration authorities (RAs) and certificate authorities (CAs) provide services similar to those of the Department of Motor Vehicles (DMV). When John goes to register for a driver's license, he has to prove his identity to the DMV by providing his passport, birth certificate, or other identification documentation. If the DMV is satisfied with the proof John provides (and John passes a driving test), the DMV will create a driver's license that can then be used by John to prove his identity. Whenever John needs to identify himself, he can show his driver's license.

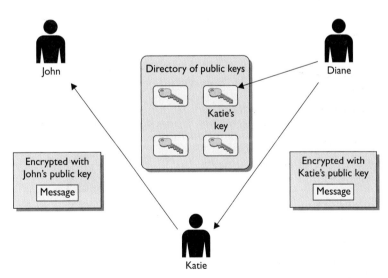

Man-in-the-Middle Attack

1. Katie replaces John's public key with her key in the publicly accessible directory.
2. Diane extracts what she thinks is John's key, but it is in fact Katie's key.
3. Katie can now read messages Diane encrypts and sends to John.
4. After Katie decrypts and reads Diane's message, she encrypts it with John's public key and sends it on to him so he will not be the wiser.

• **Figure 6.1**   Without PKIs, individuals could spoof others' identities.

Try This

Obtaining a Digital Certificate

Obtaining a certificate is as easy as a few mouse clicks on a web page. Go to the Personal E-mail Certificates web page of the CA thawte (www.instantssl.com/ssl-certificate-products/free-email-certificate .html) and create your own free certificate. Notice that the true nature of the technology is hidden from the end user, making the process of obtaining a certificate seem incredibly simple. Then use the certificate with the e-mail client of your choice.

Tech Tip

Public and Private Keys

Recall from Chapter 5 that the public key is the one that you give to others and the private key never leaves your possession. Anything one key does, the other undoes, so if you encrypt something with the public key, only the holder of the private key can decrypt it. If you encrypt something with the private key, then everyone that uses the public key knows that the holder of the private key did the encryption. Certificates do not alter any of this, they only offer a standard means of transferring keys.

Although many people may not trust John to identify himself truthfully, they do trust the third party, the DMV.

In the PKI context, while some variations exist in specific products, the RA will require proof of identity from the individual requesting a certificate and will validate this information. The RA will then advise the CA to generate a certificate, which is analogous to a driver's license. The CA will digitally sign the certificate using its private key. The use of the private key ensures to the recipient that the certificate came from the CA. When Diane receives John's certificate and verifies that it was actually digitally signed by a CA that she trusts, she will believe that the certificate is actually John's—not because she trusts John, but because she trusts the entity that is vouching for his identity (the CA).

This is commonly referred to as a *third-party trust model*. Public keys are components of digital certificates, so when Diane verifies the CA's digital signature, this verifies that the certificate is truly John's and that the public key the certificate contains is also John's. This is how John's identity is bound to his public key.

This process allows John to authenticate himself to Diane and others. Using the third-party certificate, John can communicate with Diane, using public key encryption, without prior communication or a preexisting relationship.

Once Diane is convinced of the legitimacy of John's public key, she can use it to encrypt messages between herself and John, as illustrated in Figure 6.2.

Numerous applications and protocols can generate public/private key pairs and provide functionality similar to what a PKI provides, but no

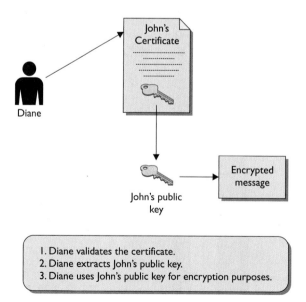

• **Figure 6.2**   Public keys are components of digital certificates.

trusted third party is available for both of the communicating parties. For each party to choose to communicate this way without a third party vouching for the other's identity, the two must choose to trust each other and the communication channel they are using. In many situations, it is impractical and dangerous to arbitrarily trust an individual you do not know, and this is when the components of a PKI must fall into place—to provide the necessary level of trust you cannot, or choose not to, provide on your own.

What does the "infrastructure" in "public key infrastructure" really mean? An infrastructure provides a sustaining groundwork upon which other things can be built. So an infrastructure works at a low level to provide a predictable and uniform environment that allows other, higher-level technologies to work together through uniform access points. The environment that the infrastructure provides allows these higher-level applications to communicate with each other and gives them the underlying tools to carry out their tasks.

Exam Tip: PKIs are composed of several elements:

- Certificates (containing keys)
- Certificate authorities (CAs)
- Registration authorities (RAs)
- Certificate revocation lists (CRLs)
- Trust models

Certificate Authorities

A **certificate authority (CA)** is a trusted authority that certifies individuals' identities and creates electronic documents indicating that individuals are who they say they are. The electronic document is referred to as a **digital certificate**, and it establishes an association between the subject's identity and a public key. The private key that is paired with the public key in the certificate is stored separately.

As noted in Chapter 5, it is important to safeguard the private key. Typically, it should never leave the machine or device where it was created.

A CA is more than just a piece of software, however; it is actually made up of the software, hardware, procedures, policies, and people who are involved in validating individuals' identities and generating the certificates. This means that if one of these components is compromised, it can negatively affect the CA overall and can threaten the integrity of the certificates it produces.

Cross Check

Certificates Stored on a Client PC

Certificates are stored on user PCs. Chapter 17 covers the use of the Internet and associated materials, including the use of certificates by web browsers. Take a moment to explore the certificates stored on your PC through either Internet Explorer or Firefox. To understand the details behind how certificates are stored and managed, the student is directed to the details in Chapter 17.

Every CA should have a **certification practices statement (CPS)** that outlines how identities are verified; the steps the CA follows to generate, maintain, and transmit certificates; and why the CA can be trusted to fulfill its responsibilities.

The CPS describes how keys are secured, what data is placed within a digital certificate, and how revocations will be handled. If a company is going to use and depend on a public CA, the company's security officers, administrators, and legal department should review the CA's entire CPS to ensure that it will properly meet the company's needs, and to make sure that the level of security claimed by the CA is high enough for their use and environment. A critical aspect of a PKI is the trust between the users and the CA, so the CPS should be reviewed and understood to ensure that this level of trust is warranted.

If you tried the previous Try This! exercise, you should have seen the Comodo CPS. Did you read it or just click past the screen? Clicking past the lengthy licenses and other warning screens does not allow you to claim "I didn't know" or "they didn't tell me," so be careful about accepting without reading.

The **certificate server** is the actual service that issues certificates based on the data provided during the initial registration process. The server constructs and populates the digital certificate with the necessary information and combines the user's public key with the resulting certificate. The certificate is then digitally signed with the CA's private key.

■ Registration Authorities

A **registration authority (RA)** is the PKI component that accepts a request for a digital certificate and performs the necessary steps of registering and authenticating the person requesting the certificate. The authentication requirements differ depending on the type of certificate being requested. Most CAs offer a series of classes of certificates with increasing trust by class. The specific classes are described in the Tech Tip sidebar, "Certificate Classes."

Each higher class of certificate can carry out more powerful and critical tasks than the one below it. This is why the different classes have different requirements for proof of identity. If you want to receive a Class 1 certificate, you may only be asked to provide your name, e-mail address, and physical address. For a Class 2 certification, you may need to provide the RA with more data, such as your driver's license, passport, and company information, that can be verified. To obtain a Class 3 certificate, you will be asked to provide even more information and most likely will need to go to the RA's office for a face-to-face meeting. Each CA will outline the certification classes it provides and the identification requirements that must be met to acquire each type of certificate.

In most situations, when a user requests a Class 1 certificate, the registration process will require the user to enter specific information into a web-based form. The web page will have a section that accepts the user's public key, or it will step the user through creating a public/private key pair, which will allow the user to choose the size of the keys to be created. Once these steps have been completed, the public key is attached to the certificate

Tech Tip

Certificate Classes

The types of certificates available can vary between different CAs, but usually at least three different types are available, and they are referred to as classes:

■ *Class 1 A Class 1 certificate is usually used to verify an individual's identity through e-mail. A person who receives a Class 1 certificate can use his public/ private key pair to digitally sign e-mail and encrypt message contents.*

■ *Class 2 A Class 2 certificate can be used for software signing. A software vendor would register for this type of certificate so that it could digitally sign its software. This provides integrity for the software after it is developed and released, and it allows the receiver of the software to verify from where the software actually came.*

■ *Class 3 A Class 3 certificate can be used by a company to set up its own CA, which will allow it to carry out its own identification verification and generate certificates internally.*

registration form and both are forwarded to the RA for processing. The RA is responsible only for the registration process and cannot actually generate a certificate. Once the RA is finished processing the request and verifying the individual's identity, the RA sends the request to the CA. The CA uses the RA-provided information to generate a digital certificate, integrates the necessary data into the certificate fields (user identification information, public key, validity dates, proper use for the key and certificate, and so on), and sends a copy of the certificate to the user. These steps are shown in Figure 6.3. The certificate may also be posted to a publicly accessible directory so that others can access it.

Note that a 1:1 correspondence does not necessarily exist between identities and certificates. An entity can have multiple key pairs, using separate public keys for separate purposes. Thus, an entity can have multiple certificates, each attesting to separate public key ownership. It is also possible to have different classes of certificates, again with different keys. This flexibility allows entities total discretion in how they manage their keys, and the PKI manages the complexity by using a unified process that allows key verification through a common interface.

If an application creates a key store that can be accessed by other applications, it will provide a standardized interface, called the *application programming interface (API)*. In Netscape and UNIX systems, this interface is usually PKCS #11, and in Microsoft applications the interface is Crypto API (CAPI). As an example, Figure 6.4 shows that application A went through the process of registering a certificate and generating a key pair. It created a

Exam Tip: The RA verifies the identity of the certificate requestor on behalf of the CA. The CA generates the certificate using information forwarded by the RA.

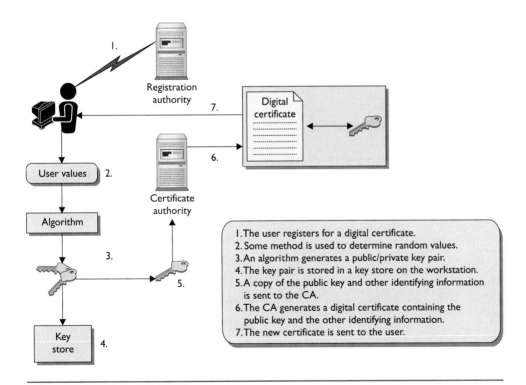

1. The user registers for a digital certificate.
2. Some method is used to determine random values.
3. An algorithm generates a public/private key pair.
4. The key pair is stored in a key store on the workstation.
5. A copy of the public key and other identifying information is sent to the CA.
6. The CA generates a digital certificate containing the public key and the other identifying information.
7. The new certificate is sent to the user.

• **Figure 6.3**   Steps for obtaining a digital certificate

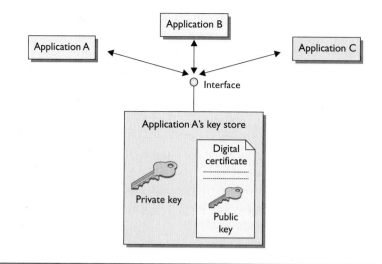

• **Figure 6.4**   Some key stores can be shared by different applications.

key store that provides an interface to allow other applications to communicate with it and use the items held within the store.

The local key store is just one location where these items can be held. Often the digital certificate and public key are also stored in a certificate repository (as discussed in the "Certificate Repositories" section of this chapter) so that it is available to a subset of individuals.

Local Registration Authorities

A **local registration authority (LRA)** performs the same functions as an RA, but the LRA is closer to the end users. This component is usually implemented in companies that have their own internal PKIs and have distributed sites. Each site has users that need RA services, so instead of requiring them to communicate with one central RA, each site can have its own LRA. This reduces the amount of traffic that would be created by several users making requests across wide area network (WAN) lines. The LRA performs identification, verification, and registration functions. It then sends the request, along with the user's public key, to a centralized CA so that the certificate can be generated. It acts as an interface between the users and the CA. LRAs simplify the RA/CA process for entities that desire certificates only for in-house use.

▦ Certificate Repositories

Once the requestor's identity has been proven, a certificate is registered with the public side of the key pair provided by the requestor. Public keys must be available to anybody who requires them to communicate within a PKI environment. These keys, and their corresponding certificates, are usually held in a publicly available repository. **Certificate repository** is a general term that describes a centralized directory that can be accessed by a subset of individuals. The directories are usually Lightweight Directory Access Protocol (LDAP)–compliant, meaning that they can be accessed and searched via an LDAP query from an LDAP client.

When an individual initializes communication with another, the sender can send her certificate and public key to the receiver, which will allow the receiver to communicate with the sender using encryption or digital signatures (or both) without needing to track down the necessary public key in a certificate repository. This is equivalent to the sender saying, "If you would like to encrypt any future messages you send to me, or if you would like the ability to verify my digital signature, here are the necessary components." But if a person wants to encrypt the first message sent to the receiver, the sender needs to find the receiver's public key in a certificate repository.

Cross Check

Certificates and Keys

Certificates are a standardized method of exchanging asymmetric key information. To understand the need for certificates, you should first be able to answer the questions:

- What do I need a public key for?

- How can I get someone's public key, and how do I know it is theirs?

For a refresher on how public and private keys come into play with encryption and digital signatures, refer to Chapter 5.

A certificate repository is a holding place for individuals' certificates and public keys that are participating in a particular PKI environment. The security requirements for repositories themselves are not as high as those needed for actual CAs and for the equipment and software used to carry out CA functions. Since each certificate is digitally signed by the CA, if a certificate stored in the certificate repository is modified, the recipient will be able to detect this change and know not to accept the certificate as valid.

■ Trust and Certificate Verification

We need to use a PKI if we do not automatically trust individuals we do not know. Security is about being suspicious and being safe, so we need a third party that we *do* trust to vouch for the other individual before confidence can be instilled and sensitive communication can take place. But what does it mean that we trust a CA, and how can we use this to our advantage?

When a user chooses to trust a CA, she will download that CA's digital certificate and public key, which will be stored on her local computer. Most browsers have a list of CAs configured to be trusted by default, so when a user installs a new web browser, several of the most well-known and most trusted CAs will be trusted without any change of settings. An example of this listing is shown in Figure 6.5.

• **Figure 6.5**   Browsers have a long list of CAs configured to be trusted by default.

Tech Tip

Distinguished Names

A distinguished name is a label that follows the X.500 standard. This standard defines a naming convention that can be employed so that each subject within an organization has a unique name. An example is {Country = US, Organization = Real Secure, Organizational Unit = R&D, Location = Washington}. CAs use distinguished names to identify the owners of specific certificates.

Because certificates produce chains of trust, having an unnecessary certificate in your certificate store could lead to trust problems. Best practices indicate that you should understand the certificates in your store, and the need for each. When in doubt, remove it. If it is needed, you can add it back later.

In the Microsoft CAPI environment, the user can add and remove CAs from this list as needed. In production environments that require a higher degree of protection, this list will be pruned, and possibly the only CAs listed will be the company's *internal* CAs. This ensures that digitally signed software will be automatically installed only if it was signed by the company's CA. Other products, such as Entrust, use centrally controlled policies to determine which CAs are to be trusted, instead of expecting the user to make these critical decisions.

A number of steps are involved in checking the validity of a message. Suppose, for example, that Maynard receives a digitally signed message from Joyce, who he does not know or trust. Joyce has also included her digital certificate with her message, which has her public key embedded within it. Before Maynard can be sure of the authenticity of this message, he has some work to do. The steps are illustrated in Figure 6.6.

First, Maynard sees which CA signed Joyce's certificate and compares it to the list of CAs he has configured within his computer. He trusts the CAs in his list and no others. (If the certificate was signed by a CA that he does not have in the list, he would not accept the certificate as being valid, and thus he could not be sure that this message was actually sent from Joyce or that the attached key was actually her public key.)

Maynard sees that the CA that signed Joyce's certificate is indeed in his list of trusted CAs, so he now needs to verify that the certificate has not been altered. Using the CA's public key and the digest of the certificate, Maynard can verify the integrity of the certificate. Then Maynard can be assured that

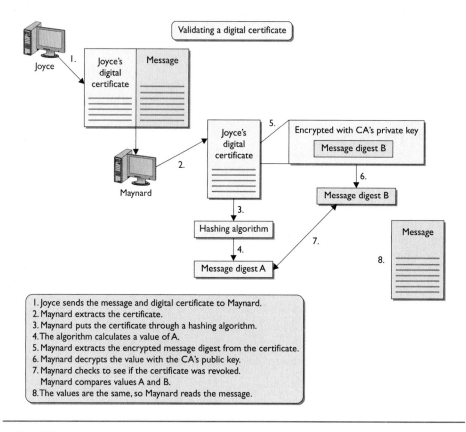

1. Joyce sends the message and digital certificate to Maynard.
2. Maynard extracts the certificate.
3. Maynard puts the certificate through a hashing algorithm.
4. The algorithm calculates a value of A.
5. Maynard extracts the encrypted message digest from the certificate.
6. Maynard decrypts the value with the CA's public key.
7. Maynard checks to see if the certificate was revoked.
   Maynard compares values A and B.
8. The values are the same, so Maynard reads the message.

• **Figure 6.6**   Steps for verifying the authenticity and integrity of a certificate this CA did actually create the certificate, so he can now trust the origin of Joyce's certificate. The use of digital signatures allows certificates to be saved in public directories without the concern of them being accidentally or intentionally altered. If a user extracts a certificate from a repository and creates a message digest value that does not match the digital signature embedded within the certificate itself, that user will know that the certificate has been modified by someone other than the CA, and he will know not to accept the validity of the corresponding public key. Similarly, an attacker could not create a new message digest, encrypt it, and embed it within the certificate because he would not have access to the CA's private key.

But Maynard is not done yet. He needs to be sure that the issuing CA has not revoked this certificate. The certificate also has start and stop dates, indicating a time during which the certificate is valid. If the start date hasn't happened yet or the stop date has been passed, the certificate is not valid. Maynard reviews these dates to make sure the certificate is still deemed valid.

Another step Maynard may go through is to check whether this certificate has been revoked for any reason. To do so, he will refer to a list of revoked certificates, a *certificate revocation list (CRL)*, to see if Joyce's certificate is listed. He could check the CRL directly with the CA that issued the certificate or via a specialized online service that supports the Online Certificate Status Protocol (OCSP). (Certificate revocation and list distribution are explained in the "Certificate Lifecycles" section, later in this chapter.)

Maynard now trusts that this certificate is legitimate and that it belongs to Joyce. Now what does he need to do? The certificate holds Joyce's public key, which he needs to validate the digital signature she appended to her message, so Maynard extracts Joyce's public key from her certificate, runs her message through a hashing algorithm, and calculates a message digest value of X. He then uses Joyce's public key to decrypt her digital signature (remember that a digital signature is just a message digest encrypted with a private key). This decryption process provides him with another message digest of value Y. Maynard compares values X and Y, and if they are the same, he is assured that the

Tech Tip

Validating a Certificate

The following steps are required for validating a certificate:

1. *Compare the CA that digitally signed the certificate to a list of CAs that have already been loaded into the receiver's computer.*

2. *Calculate a message digest for the certificate.*

3. *Use the CA's public key to decrypt the digital signature and recover what is claimed to be the original message digest embedded within the certificate (validating the digital signature).*

4. *Compare the two resulting message digest values to ensure the integrity of the certificate.*

5. *Review the identification information within the certificate, such as the e-mail address.*

6. *Review the validity dates.*

7. *Check a revocation list to see if the certificate has been revoked.*

message has not been modified during transmission. Thus he has confidence in the integrity of the message. But how does Maynard know that the message actually came from Joyce? Because he can decrypt the digital signature using her public key, this indicates that only the associated private key could have been used. There is a miniscule risk that someone could create an identical key pair, but given the enormous keyspace for public keys, this is impractical. The public key can only decrypt something that was encrypted with the related private key, and only the owner of the private key is supposed to have access to it. Maynard can be sure that this message came from Joyce.

After all of this he reads her message, which says, "Hi. How are you?" All of that work just for this message? Maynard's blood pressure would surely go through the roof if he had to do all of this work only to end up with a short and not very useful message. Fortunately, all of this PKI work is performed without user intervention and happens behind the scenes. Maynard didn't have to exert any energy. He simply replies, "Fine. How are you?"

Digital Certificates

A digital certificate binds an individual's identity to a public key, and it contains all the information a receiver needs to be assured of the identity of the public key owner. After an RA verifies an individual's identity, the CA generates the digital certificate, but how does the CA know what type of data to insert into the certificate?

The certificates are created and formatted based on the X.509 standard, which outlines the necessary fields of a certificate and the possible values that can be inserted into the fields. As of this writing, X.509 version 3 is the most current version of the standard. X.509 is a standard of the International Telecommunication Union (www.itu.int). The IETF's Public-Key Infrastructure (X.509), or PKIX, working group has adapted the X.509 standard to the more flexible organization of the Internet, as specified in RFC 3280, and is commonly referred to as PKIX for Public Key Infrastructure X.509.

Figure 6.7 shows the actual values of the different certificate fields for a particular certificate in Internet Explorer. The version of this certificate is V3 (X.509 v3) and the serial number is also listed—this number is unique for

• **Figure 6.7**   Fields within a digital certificate

each certificate that is created by a specific CA. The CA used the MD5 hashing algorithm to create the message digest value, and it then signed using the CA's private key using the RSA algorithm. The actual CA that issued the certificate is Root SGC Authority, and the valid dates indicate how long this certificate is valid. The subject is MS SGC Authority, which is the entity that registered this certificate and that is bound to the embedded public key. The actual public key is shown in the lower window and is represented in hexadecimal.

The subject of a certificate is commonly a person, but it does not have to be. The subject can be a network device (router, web server, firewall, and so on), an application, a department, a company, or a person. Each has its own identity that needs to be verified and proven to another entity before secure, trusted communication can be initiated. If a network device is using a certificate for authentication, the certificate may contain the network address of that device. This means that if the certificate has a network address of 10.0.0.1, the receiver will compare this to the address from which it received the certificate to make sure a man-in-the-middle attack is not being attempted.

Certificate Attributes

Four main types of certificates are used:

- End-entity certificates
- CA certificates
- Cross-certification certificates
- Policy certificates

End-entity certificates are issued by a CA to a specific subject, such as Joyce, the Accounting department, or a firewall, as illustrated in Figure 6.8. An end-entity certificate is the identity document provided by PKI implementations.

A **CA certificate** can be self-signed, in the case of a standalone or root CA, or it can be issued by a superior CA within a hierarchical model. In the model in Figure 6.8, the superior CA gives the authority and allows the subordinate CA to accept certificate requests and generate the individual certificates itself. This may be necessary when a company needs to have multiple internal CAs, and different departments within an organization need to have their own CAs servicing their specific end-entities in their sections. In these

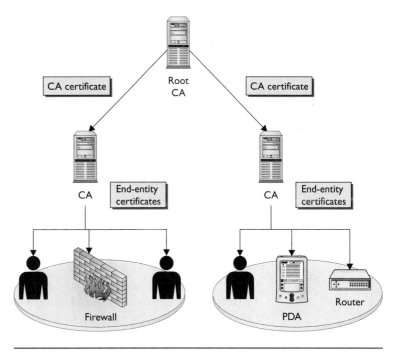

● **Figure 6.8**　End-entity and CA certificates

situations, a representative from each department requiring a CA registers with the higher trusted CA and requests a Certificate Authority certificate. (Public and private CAs are discussed in the "Public Certificate Authorities" and "In-house Certificate Authorities" sections later in this chapter, as are the different trust models that are available for companies.)

A **cross-certification certificate**, or *cross-certificate*, is used when independent CAs establish peer-to-peer trust relationships. Simply put, cross-certificates are a mechanism through which one CA can issue a certificate allowing its users to trust another CA.

Within sophisticated CAs used for high-security applications, a mechanism is required to provide centrally controlled policy information to PKI clients. This is often done by placing the policy information in a **policy certificate**.

Certificate Extensions

Certificate extensions allow for further information to be inserted within the certificate, which can be used to provide more functionality in a PKI implementation. Certificate extensions can be standard or private. *Standard certificate extensions* are implemented for every PKI implementation. *Private certificate extensions* are defined for specific organizations (or domains within one organization), and they allow companies to further define different, specific uses for digital certificates to best fit their business needs.

Several different extensions can be implemented, one being *key usage extensions*, which dictate how the public key that is held within the certificate can be used. Remember that public keys can be used for different functions: symmetric key encryption, data encryption, verifying digital signatures, and more.

A nonrepudiation service can be provided by a third-party notary. In this situation, the sender's digital signature is verified and then signed by the notary so that the sender cannot later deny signing and sending the message. This is basically the same function performed by a traditional notary using paper—validate the sender's identity and validate the time and date of an item being signed and sent. This is required when the receiver needs to be *really* sure of the sender's identity and wants to be legally protected against possible fraud or forgery.

If a company needs to be sure that accountable nonrepudiation services will be provided, a trusted time source needs to be used, which can be a trusted third party called a *time stamp authority (TSA)*. Using a trusted time source gives users a higher level of confidence as to *when* specific messages were digitally signed. For example, suppose Barry sends Ron a message and digitally signs it, and Ron later civilly sues Barry over a dispute. This digitally signed message may be submitted by Ron as evidence pertaining to an earlier agreement that Barry now is not fulfilling. If a trusted time source was not used in their PKI environment, Barry could claim that his private key had been compromised before that message was sent. If a trusted time source was implemented, then it could be shown that the message was signed *before* the date on which Barry claims his key was compromised. If a trusted time source is not used, no activity that was carried out within a PKI environment can be truly proven because it is so easy to change system and software time settings.

Critical and Noncritical Extensions

Certificate extensions are considered either *critical* or *noncritical*, which is indicated by a specific flag within the certificate itself. When this flag is set to

---

Tech Tip

X.509 Digital Certificate Extensions

Following are some key examples of certificate extensions:

- **DigitalSignature** *The key used to verify a digital signature*

- **KeyEncipherment** *The key used to encrypt other keys used for secure key distribution*

- **DataEncipherment** *The key used to encrypt data, which cannot be used to encrypt other keys*

- **CRLSign** *The key used to verify a CA signature on a CRL*

- **KeyCertSign** *The key used to verify CA signatures on certificates*

- **NonRepudiation** *The key used when a nonrepudiation service is being provided*

---

critical, it means that the extension *must* be understood and processed by the receiver. If the receiver is not configured to understand a particular extension marked as critical, and thus cannot process it properly, the certificate cannot be used for its proposed purpose. If the flag does not indicate that the extension is critical, the certificate can be used for the intended purpose, even if the receiver does not process the appended extension.

Certificate Lifecycles

Keys and certificates should have lifetime settings that force the user to register for a new certificate after a certain amount of time. Determining the proper length of these lifetimes is a trade-off: shorter lifetimes limit the ability of attackers to crack them, but longer lifetimes lower system overhead. More-sophisticated PKI implementations perform automated and often transparent key updates to avoid the time and expense of having users register for new certificates when old ones expire.

This means that the certificate and key pair has a lifecycle that must be managed. Certificate management involves administrating and managing each of these phases, including registration, certificate and key generation, renewal, and revocation. Additional management functions include CRL distribution, certificate suspension, and key destruction.

Registration and Generation

A key pair (public and private keys) can be generated locally by an application and stored in a local key store on the user's workstation. The key pair can also be created by a central key-generation server, which will require secure transmission of the keys to the user. The key pair that is created on the centralized server can be stored on the user's workstation or on the user's smart card, which will allow for more flexibility and mobility.

The act of verifying that an individual indeed has the corresponding private key for a given public key is referred to as *proof of possession*. Not all public/private key pairs can be used for digital signatures, so asking the individual to sign a message and return it to prove that she has the necessary private key will not always work. If a key pair is used for encryption, the RA can send a challenge value to the individual, who, in turn, can use her private key to encrypt that value and return it to the RA. If the RA can successfully decrypt this value with the public key that was provided earlier, the RA can be confident that the individual has the necessary private key and can continue through the rest of the registration phase.

Key regeneration and replacement is usually done to protect against these types of threats, although as computers increase in processing power and our knowledge of cryptography and new possible cryptanalysis-based attacks expands, key lifetimes may drastically decrease. As with everything within the security field, it is better to be safe now than to be surprised later and sorry.

The PKI administrator usually configures the minimum required key size that users must use to have a key generated for the first time, and then for each renewal. In most applications, there is a drop-down list of possible algorithms to choose from, and possible key sizes. The key size should provide the necessary level of security for the current environment. The lifetime

Tech Tip

Critical Flag and Certificate Usage

When an extension is marked as critical, it means that the CA is certifying the key for only that specific purpose. If Joe receives a certificate with a DigitalSignature key usage extension and the critical flag is set, Joe can use the public key only within that certificate to validate digital signatures, and no more. If the extension was marked as noncritical, the key can be used for purposes outside of those listed in the extensions, so in this case it is up to Joe (and his applications) to decide how the key will be used.

Setting certificate lifetimes way into the future and using them for long periods of time provides attackers with extended windows to attack the cryptography. As stated in Chapter 5, cryptography merely buys time against an attacker; it is never an absolute guarantee.

Good key management and proper key replacement intervals protect keys from being compromised through human error. Choosing a large key size makes a brute-force attack more difficult.

Once revoked, a certificate cannot be reinstated. This is to prevent an unauthorized reinstatement by someone who has unauthorized access to the key(s). A key pair can be reinstated for use by issuing a new certificate if at a later time the keys are found to be secure. The old certificate would still be void, but the new one would be valid.

of the key should be long enough that continual renewal will not negatively affect productivity, but short enough to ensure that the key cannot be successfully compromised.

Renewal

The certificate itself has its own lifetime, which can be different from the key pair's lifetime. The certificate's lifetime is specified by the validity dates inserted into the digital certificate. These are beginning and ending dates indicating the time period during which the certificate is valid. The certificate cannot be used before the start date, and once the end date is met, the certificate is expired and a new certificate will need to be issued.

A renewal process is different from the registration phase in that the RA assumes that the individual has already successfully completed one registration round. If the certificate has not actually been revoked, the original keys and certificate can be used to provide the necessary authentication information and proof of identity for the renewal phase.

The certificate may or may not need to change during the renewal process; this usually depends on why the renewal is taking place. If the certificate just expired and the keys will still be used for the same purpose, a new certificate can be generated with new validity dates. If, however, the key pair functionality needs to be expanded or restricted, new attributes and extensions may need to be integrated into the new certificate. These new functionalities may require more information to be gathered from the individual renewing the certificate, especially if the class changes or the new key uses allow for more powerful abilities.

This renewal process is required when the certificate has fulfilled its lifetime and its end validity date has been met. This situation differs from that of a certificate revocation.

Revocation

A certificate can be revoked when its validity needs to be ended before its actual expiration date is met, and this can occur for many reasons: for example, a user may have lost a laptop or a smart card that stored a private key; an improper software implementation may have been uncovered that directly affected the security of a private key; a user may have fallen victim to a social engineering attack and inadvertently given up a private key; data held within the certificate may no longer apply to the specified individual; or perhaps an employee left a company and should not be identified as a member of an in-house PKI any longer. In the last instance, the certificate, which was bound to the user's key pair, identified the user as an employee of the company, and the administrator would want to ensure that the key pair could not be used in the future to validate this person's affiliation with the company. Revoking the certificate does this.

If any of these things happens, a user's private key has been compromised or should no longer be mapped to the owner's identity. A different individual may have access to that user's private key and could use it to impersonate and authenticate as the original user. If the impersonator used the key to digitally sign a message, the receiver would verify the authenticity of the sender by verifying the signature by using the original user's public key, and the verification would go through perfectly—the receiver would believe it came from the proper sender and not the impersonator. If receivers could look at a list of certificates that had been revoked before verifying the digital signature, however, they would know not to trust the digital signatures on the list. Because of issues associated with the private key being compromised, revocation is permanent and final—once revoked, a certificate cannot be reinstated. If reinstatement was allowed and a user revoked his certificate, then the unauthorized holder of the private key could use it to restore the certificate validity.

For example, if Joe stole Mike's laptop, which held, among other things, Mike's private key, Joe might be able to use that key to impersonate Mike. Suppose Joe writes a message, digitally signs it with Mike's private key, and sends it to Stacy. Stacy communicates with Mike periodically and has his public key, so she uses it to verify the digital signature. It computes properly, so Stacy is assured that this message came from Mike, but in truth it did not. If, before validating any certificate or digital signature, Stacy could check a list of revoked certificates, she might not fall victim to Joe's false message.

The CA provides this type of protection by maintaining a **certificate revocation list (CRL)**, a list of serial numbers of certificates that have been revoked. The CRL also contains a statement indicating why the individual certificates were revoked and a date when the revocation took place. The list usually contains all certificates that have been revoked within the lifetime of the CA. Certificates that have expired are not the same as those that have been revoked. If a certificate has expired, it means that its end validity date was reached. The format of the CRL message is also defined by X.509. The list is signed, to prevent tampering, and contains information on certificates that have been revoked and the reasons for their revocation. These lists can grow quite long, and as such, there are provisions for date timestamping the

 Exam Tip: A certificate cannot be assumed to be valid without checking for revocation before each use.

Tech Tip

CRL Reason Codes

Per the X.509 v2 CRL standard, the following reasons for revocation are used:

Reason Code	Reason
0	*Unspecified*
1	*All keys compromised; indicates compromise or suspected compromise*
2	*CA compromise; used only to revoke CA keys*
3	*Affiliation changed; indicates a change of affiliation on the certificate*
4	*Superseded; the certificate has been replaced by a more current one*
5	*Cessation; the certificate is no longer needed, but no reason exists to suspect it has been compromised*
6	*Certificate hold; indicates the certificate will not be issued at this point in time*
7	*Remove from CRL; used with delta CRL to indicate a CRL entry should be removed*

list and for issuing delta lists, which show changes since the last list was issued.

The CA is the entity that is responsible for the status of the certificates it generates; it needs to be told of a revocation, and it must provide this information to others. The CA is responsible for maintaining the CRL and posting it in a publicly available directory.

What if Stacy wants to get back at Joe for trying to trick her earlier, and she attempts to revoke Joe's certificate herself? If she is successful, Joe's participation in the PKI can be negatively affected because others will not trust his public key. Although we might think Joe may deserve this, we need to have some system in place to make sure people cannot arbitrarily have others' certificates revoked, whether for revenge or for malicious purposes.

When a revocation request is submitted, the individual submitting the request must be authenticated. Otherwise, this could permit a type of denial-of-service attack, in which someone has another person's certificate revoked. The authentication can involve an agreed-upon password that was created during the registration process, but authentication should not be based on the individual proving that he has the corresponding private key, because it may have been stolen, and the CA would be authenticating an imposter.

The CRL's integrity needs to be protected to ensure that attackers cannot modify data pertaining to a revoked certification on the list. If this were allowed to take place, anyone who stole a private key could just delete that key from the CRL and continue to use the private key fraudulently. The integrity of the list also needs to be protected to ensure that bogus data is not added to it. Otherwise, anyone could add another person's certificate to the list and effectively revoke that person's certificate. The only entity that should be able to modify any information on the CRL is the CA.

The mechanism used to protect the integrity of a CRL is a *digital signature*. The CA's revocation service creates a digital signature for the CRL, as shown in Figure 6.9. To validate a certificate, the user accesses the directory where the CRL is posted, downloads the list, and verifies the CA's digital signature to ensure that the proper authority signed the list and to ensure that the list was not modified in an unauthorized manner. The user then looks through the list to determine whether the serial number of the certificate that he is trying to validate is listed. If the serial number is on the list, the private key should no longer be trusted, and the public key should no longer be used. This can be a cumbersome process, so it has been automated in several ways, which are described in the next section.

One concern is how up-to-date the CRL is— how often is it updated and does it actually reflect *all* the certificates currently revoked? The actual frequency with which the list is updated depends upon the CA and its certification practices statement (CPS). It is important that the list is updated in a timely manner so that anyone using the list has the most current information.

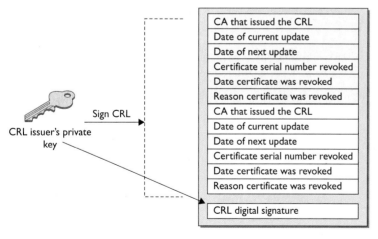

• **Figure 6.9**   The CA digitally signs the CRL to protect its integrity.

Principles of Computer Security: CompTIA Security+ and Beyond

CRL Distribution

CRL files can be requested by individuals who need to verify and validate a newly received certificate, or the files can be periodically pushed down (sent) to all users participating within a specific PKI. This means the CRL can be pulled (downloaded) by individual users when needed or pushed down to all users within the PKI on a timed interval.

The actual CRL file can grow substantially, and transmitting this file and requiring PKI client software on each workstation to save and maintain it can use a lot of resources, so the smaller the CRL is, the better. It is also possible to first push down the full CRL and subsequently push down only *delta* CRLs, which contain only the changes to the original or base CRL. This can greatly reduce the amount of bandwidth consumed when updating CRLs.

In implementations where the CRLs are not pushed down to individual systems, the users' PKI software needs to know where to look for the posted CRL that relates to the certificate it is trying to validate. The certificate might have an extension that points the validating user to the necessary *CRL distribution point*. The network administrator sets up the distribution points, and one or more points can exist for a particular PKI. The distribution point holds one or more lists containing the serial numbers of revoked certificates, and the user's PKI software scans the list(s) for the serial number of the certificate the user is attempting to validate. If the serial number is not present, the user is assured that it has not been revoked. This approach helps point users to the right resource and also reduces the amount of information that needs to be scanned when checking that a certificate has not been revoked.

One last option for checking distributed CRLs is an *online service*. When a client user needs to validate a certificate and ensure that it has not been revoked, he can communicate with an online service that will query the necessary CRLs available within the environment. This service can query the lists for the client instead of pushing down the full CRL to each and every system. So if Joe receives a certificate from Stacy, he can contact an online service and send to it the serial number listed in the certificate Stacy sent. The online service would query the necessary CRLs and respond to Joe, indicating whether that serial number was listed as being revoked or not.

One of the protocols used for online revocation services is the **Online Certificate Status Protocol (OCSP)**, a request and response protocol that obtains the serial number of the certificate that is being validated and reviews revocation lists for the client. The protocol has a responder service that reports the status of the certificate back to the client, indicating whether it has been revoked, is valid, or has an unknown status. This protocol and service saves the client from having to find, download, and process the right lists.

Suspension

Instead of being revoked, a certificate can be *suspended*, meaning it is temporarily put on hold. If, for example, Bob is taking an extended vacation and wants to ensure that his certificate will not be compromised or used during that time, he can make a suspension request to the CA. The CRL would list this certificate and its serial number, and in the field that describes why the certificate is revoked, it would instead indicate a hold state. Once Bob returns to work, he can make a request to the CA to remove his certificate from the list.

Tech Tip

Authority Revocation Lists

*In some PKI implementations, a separate revocation list is maintained for CA keys that have been compromised or should no longer be trusted. This list is known as an **authority revocation list (ARL)**. In the event that a CA's private key is compromised or a cross-certification is cancelled, the relevant certificate's serial number is included in the ARL. A client can review an ARL to make sure the CA's public key can still be trusted.*

A certificate suspension can be a useful process tool to use while investigating whether or not a certificate should be considered to be valid.

Relying on an expiration date on a certificate to "destroy" the utility of a key will not work. A new certificate can be issued with an "extended date." To end the use of a key set, an entry in a CRL is the only sure way to prevent reissuance and re-dating of a certificate.

Another reason to suspend a certificate is if an administrator is suspicious that a private key might have been compromised. While the issue is under investigation, the certificate can be suspended to ensure that it cannot be used.

Key Destruction

Key pairs and certificates have set lifetimes, meaning that they will expire at some specified time. It is important that the certificates and keys are properly destroyed when that time comes, wherever the keys are stored (on users' workstations, centralized key servers, USB token devices, smart cards, and so on).

The goal is to make sure that no one can gain access to a key after its lifetime has ended and use that key for malicious purposes. An attacker might use the key to digitally sign or encrypt a message with the hopes of tricking someone else about his identity (this would be an example of a man-in-the-middle attack). Also, if the attacker is performing some type of brute-force attack on your cryptosystem, trying to figure out specific keys that were used for encryption processes, obtaining an old key could give him more insight into how your cryptosystem generates keys. The less information you supply to potential hackers, the better.

■ Centralized and Decentralized Infrastructures

Keys used for authentication and encryption within a PKI environment can be generated in a centralized or decentralized manner. In a *decentralized* approach, software on individual computers generates and stores cryptographic keys local to the systems themselves. In a *centralized* infrastructure, the keys are generated and stored on a central server, and the keys are transmitted to the individual systems as needed. You might choose one type over the other for several reasons.

If a company uses an asymmetric algorithm that is resource-intensive to generate the public/private key pair, and if large (and resource-intensive) key sizes are needed, then the individual computers may not have the necessary processing power to produce the keys in an acceptable fashion. In this situation, the company can choose a centralized approach in which a very high-end server with powerful processing abilities is used, probably along with a hardware-based random number generator.

Central key generation and storage offers other benefits as well. For example, it is much easier to back up the keys and implement key recovery procedures with central storage than with a decentralized approach. Implementing a key recovery procedure on each and every computer holding one or more key pairs is difficult, and many applications that generate their own key pairs do not usually interface well with a centralized archive system. This means that if a company chooses to allow its individual users to create and maintain their own key pairs on their separate workstations, no real key recovery procedure can be put in place. This puts the company at risk. If an employee leaves the organization or is unavailable for one reason or another, the company may not be able to access its own business information that was encrypted by that employee.

So a centralized approach seems like the best approach, right? Well, the centralized method has some drawbacks to consider, too. Secure key distribution is a tricky event. This can be more difficult than it sounds. A technology needs to be employed that will send the keys in an encrypted manner, ensure the keys' integrity, and make sure that only the intended user is receiving the key.

Also, the server that centrally stores the keys needs to be highly available and is a potential single point of failure, so some type of fault tolerance or redundancy mechanism may need to be put into place. If that one server goes down, users could not access their keys, which might prevent them from properly authenticating to the network, resources, and applications. Also, since all the keys are in one place, the server is a prime target for an attacker—if the central key server is compromised, the whole environment is compromised.

One other issue pertains to how the keys will actually be used. If a public/private key pair is being generated for digital signatures, and if the company wants to ensure that it can be used to provide *true* authenticity and nonrepudiation, the keys should not be generated at a centralized server. This would introduce doubt that only the one person had access to a specific private key. It is better to generate end-user keys on a local machine to eliminate doubt about who did the work and "owns" the keys.

If a company uses smart cards to hold users' private keys, each private key often has to be generated on the card itself and cannot be copied for archiving purposes. This is a disadvantage of the centralized approach. In addition, some types of applications have been developed to create their own public/private key pairs and do not allow other keys to be imported and used. This means the keys would have to be created locally by these applications, and keys from a central server could not be used. These are just some of the considerations that need to be evaluated before any decision is made and implementation begins.

Hardware Storage Devices

PKIs can be constructed in software without special cryptographic hardware, and this is perfectly suitable for many environments. But software can be vulnerable to viruses, hackers, and hacking. If a company requires a higher level of protection than a purely software-based solution can provide, several hardware-based solutions are available.

In most situations, hardware key-storage solutions are used only for the most critical and sensitive keys, which are the root and possibly the intermediate CA private keys. If those keys are compromised, the whole security of the PKI is gravely threatened. If a person obtained a root CA private key, she could digitally sign any certificate, and that certificate would be quickly accepted by all entities within the environment. Such an attacker might be able to create a certificate that has extremely high privileges, perhaps allowing her to modify bank account information in a financial institution, and no alerts or warnings would be initiated because the ultimate CA, the root CA, signed it.

Private Key Protection

Although a PKI implementation can be complex, with many different components and options, a critical concept common to all PKIs must be understood and enforced: the private key needs to stay private. A digital signature is created solely for the purpose of proving who sent a particular message by using a private key. This rests on the assumption that only one person has access to this private key. If an imposter obtains a user's private key, authenticity and nonrepudiation can no longer be claimed or proven.

When a private key is generated for the first time, it must be stored somewhere for future use. This storage area is referred to as a *key store*, and it is usually created by the application registering for a certificate, such as a web browser, smart card software, or other application. In most implementations, the application will prompt the user for a password, which will be used to create an encryption key that protects the key store. So, for example, if Cheryl used her web browser to register for a certificate, her private key would be generated and stored in the key store. Cheryl would then be prompted for a password, which the software would use to create a key that will encrypt the key store. When Cheryl needs to access this private key later that day, she will be prompted for the same password, which will decrypt the key store and allow her access to her private key.

Unfortunately, many applications do not require that a strong password be created to protect the key store, and in some implementations the user can choose not to provide a password at all. The user still has a private key available, and it is bound to the user's identity, so why is a password even necessary? If, for example, Cheryl decided not to use a password, and another person sat down at her computer, he could use her web browser and her private key and digitally sign a message that contained a nasty virus. If Cheryl's co-worker Cliff received this message, he would think it came from Cheryl, open the message, and download the virus. The moral to this story is that users should be required to provide some type of authentication information (password, smart card, PIN, or the like) before being able to use private keys. Otherwise, the keys could be used by other individuals or imposters, and authentication and nonrepudiation would be of no use.

Because a private key is a crucial component of any PKI implementation, the key itself should contain the necessary characteristics and be protected at each stage of its life. The following list sums up the characteristics and requirements of proper private key use:

- The key size should provide the necessary level of protection for the environment.
- The lifetime of the key should correspond with how often it is used and the sensitivity of the data it is protecting.
- The key should be changed at the end of its lifetime and not used past its allowed lifetime.
- Where appropriate, the key should be properly destroyed at the end of its lifetime.
- The key should never be exposed in clear text.
- No copies of the private key should be made if it is being used for digital signatures.

- The key should not be shared.

- The key should be stored securely.

- Authentication should be required before the key can be used.

- The key should be transported securely.

- Software implementations that store and use the key should be evaluated to ensure they provide the necessary level of protection.

If digital signatures will be used for legal purposes, these points and others may need to be audited to ensure that true authenticity and nonrepudiation are provided.

Key Recovery

One individual could have one, two, or many key pairs that are tied to his or her identity. That is because users may have different needs and requirements for public/private key pairs. As mentioned earlier, certificates can have specific attributes and usage requirements dictating how their corresponding keys can and cannot be used. For example, David can have one key pair he uses to encrypt and transmit symmetric keys, another key pair that allows him to encrypt data, and yet another key pair to perform digital signatures. David can also have a digital signature key pair for his work-related activities and another key pair for personal activities, such as e-mailing his friends. These key pairs need to be used only for their intended purposes, and this is enforced through certificate attributes and usage values.

If a company is going to perform key recovery and maintain a key recovery system, it will generally back up only the key pair used to encrypt data, not the key pairs that are used to generate digital signatures. The reason that a company archives keys is to ensure that if a person leaves the company, falls off a cliff, or for some reason is unavailable to decrypt important company information, the company can still get to its company-owned data. This is just a matter of the organization protecting itself. A company would not need to be able to recover a key pair that is used for digital signatures, since those keys are to be used only to prove the authenticity of the individual who sent a message. A company would not benefit from having access to those keys and really should not have access to them, since they are tied to one individual for a specific purpose.

Two systems are important for backing up and restoring cryptographic keys: key archiving and key recovery. **Key archiving** is a way of backing up keys and securely storing them in a repository; **key recovery** is the process of restoring lost keys to the users or the company.

If keys are backed up and stored in a centralized computer, this system must be tightly controlled, because if it were compromised, an attacker would have access to all keys for the entire infrastructure. Also, it is usually unwise to authorize a single person to be able to recover all the keys within the environment, because that person could use this power for evil purposes instead of just recovering keys when they are needed for legitimate purposes. In security systems, it is best not to fully trust anyone.

Dual control can be used as part of a system to back up and archive data encryption keys. PKI systems can be configured to require multiple individuals to be involved in any key recovery process. When a key recovery is

Tech Tip

CA Private Keys
The most sensitive and critical public/private key pairs are those used by CAs to digitally sign certificates. These need to be highly protected because if they were ever compromised, the trust relationship between the CA and all of the end-entities would be threatened. In high-security environments, these keys are often kept in a tamper-proof hardware encryption store, only accessible to individuals with a need to know.

Exam Tip: Key archiving is the process of storing a set of keys to be used as a backup should something happen to the original set. Key recovery is the process of using the backup keys.

required, at least two people can be required to authenticate by the key recovery software before the recovery procedure is performed. This enforces *separation of duties*, which means that one person cannot complete a critical task by himself. Requiring two individuals to recover a lost key together is called **dual control**, which simply means that two people have to be present to carry out a specific task.

This approach to key recovery is referred to as the *m of n authentication*, where *n* number of people can be involved in the key recovery process, but at least *m* (which is a smaller number than *n*) *must* be involved before the task can be completed. The goal is to minimize fraudulent or improper use of access and permissions. A company would not require all possible individuals to be involved in the recovery process, because getting all the people together at the same time could be impossible considering meetings, vacations, sick time, and travel. At least some of all possible individuals must be available to participate, and this is the subset *m* of the number *n*. This form of secret splitting can increase security by requiring multiple people to perform a specific function. Requiring too many people for the *m* subset increases issues associated with availability, whereas requiring too few increases the risk of a small number of people colluding to compromise a secret.

All key recovery procedures should be highly audited. The audit logs should capture at least what keys were recovered, who was involved in the process, and the time and date. Keys are an integral piece of any encryption cryptosystem and are critical to a PKI environment, so you need to track who does what with them.

Key Escrow

Key recovery and key escrow are terms that are often used interchangeably, but they actually describe two different things. You should not use them interchangeably after you have read this section.

Key escrow is the process of giving keys to a third party so that they can decrypt and read sensitive information if the need arises. Key escrow almost always pertains to handing over encryption keys to the government, or to another higher authority, so that the keys can be used to collect evidence during investigations. A key pair used in a person's place of work may be required to be escrowed by the employer for two reasons. First, the keys are property of the enterprise, issued to the worker for use. Second, the firm may have need for them after an employee leaves the firm.

Several movements, supported by parts of the U.S. government, would require all or many people residing in the United States to hand over copies of the keys they use to encrypt communication channels. The movement in the late '90s behind the Clipper chip is the most well-known effort to implement this requirement and procedure. It was suggested that all American-made communication devices should have a hardware encryption chip within them. The chip could be used to encrypt data going back and forth between two individuals, but if a government agency decided that it should be able to eavesdrop on this dialog, it would just need to obtain a court order. If the court order was approved, a law enforcement agent would take the order to two escrow agencies, each of which would have a piece of the key that was necessary to decrypt this communication information. The agent would obtain both pieces of the key and combine them, which would allow the agent to listen in on the encrypted communication outlined in the court order.

The Clipper chip standard never saw the light of day because it seemed too "Big Brother" to many American citizens. But the idea was that the encryption keys would be escrowed to two agencies, meaning that each agency would hold one piece of the key. One agency could not hold the whole key, because it could then use this key to wiretap people's conversations illegally. Splitting up the key is an example of separation of duties, put into place to try and prevent fraudulent activities. The current issue of governments demanding access to keys to decrypt information is covered in Chapter 24.

Public Certificate Authorities

An individual or company may decide to rely on a CA that is already established and being used by many other individuals and companies—a *public CA*. A company, on the other hand, may decide that it needs its own CA for internal use, which gives the company more control over the certificate registration and generation process and allows it to configure items specifically for its own needs. This second type of CA is referred to as a *private CA* (or *in-house CA*).

A public CA specializes in verifying individual identities and creating and maintaining their certificates. These companies issue certificates that are not bound to specific companies or intracompany departments. Instead, their services are to be used by a larger and more diversified group of people and organizations. If a company uses a public CA, the company will pay the CA organization for individual certificates and for the service of maintaining these certificates. Some examples of public CAs are VeriSign (including GeoTrust and thawte), Entrust, and Go Daddy.

One advantage of using a public CA is that it is usually well known and easily accessible to many people. Most web browsers have a list of public CAs installed and configured by default, along with their corresponding root certificates. This means that if you install a web browser on your computer, it is already configured to trust certain CAs, even though you might have never heard of them before. So, if you receive a certificate from Bob, and his certificate was digitally signed by a CA listed in your browser, you automatically trust the CA and can easily walk through the process of verifying Bob's certificate. This has raised some eyebrows among security professionals, however, since trust is installed by default, but the industry has deemed this is a necessary approach that provides users with transparency and increased functionality.

 Users can remove CAs from their browser list if they want to have more control over who their system trusts and who it doesn't.

Earlier in the chapter, the different certificate classes and their uses were explained. No global standard defines these classes, the exact requirements for obtaining these different certificates, or their uses. Standards are in place, usually for a particular country or industry, but this means that public CAs can define their own certificate classifications. This is not necessarily a good thing for companies that depend on public CAs, because it does not provide to the company enough control over how it should interpret certificate classifications and how they should be used.

This means another component needs to be carefully developed for companies that use and depend on public CAs, and this component is referred to as the *certificate policy (CP)*. This policy allows the company to decide what certification classes are acceptable and how they will be used within the organization. This is different from the CPS, which explains how the CA verifies entities, generates certificates, and maintains these certificates. The CP is generated and owned by an individual company that uses an external CA, and it allows the company to enforce *its* security decisions and control how certificates are used with its applications.

■ In-House Certificate Authorities

An *in-house CA* is implemented, maintained, and controlled by the company that implemented it. This type of CA can be used to create certificates for internal employees, devices, applications, partners, and customers. This approach gives the company complete control over how individuals are identified, what certification classifications are created, who can and cannot have access to the CA, and how the certifications can be used.

Choosing Between a Public CA and an In-House CA

When deciding between an in-house and public CA, various factors need to be identified and accounted for. Many companies have embarked upon implementing an in-house PKI environment with a rough estimate that would be implemented within x number of months and would cost approximately y amount in dollars. Without doing the proper homework, companies might not understand the current environment, might not completely hammer out the intended purpose of the PKI, and might not have enough skilled staff supporting the project; time estimates can double or triple and the required funds and resources can become unacceptable. Several companies have started on a PKI implementation, only to quit halfway through, resulting in wasted time and money, with nothing to show for it except heaps of frustration and many ulcers.

In some situations, it is better for a company to use a public CA, since public CAs already have the necessary equipment, skills, and technologies. In other situations, companies may decide it is a better business decision to take on these efforts themselves. This is not always a strictly monetary decision—a specific level of security might be required. Some companies do not believe that they can trust an outside authority to generate and maintain their users' and company's certificates. In this situation, the scale may tip toward an in-house CA.

Each company is unique, with various goals, security requirements, functionality needs, budgetary restraints, and ideologies. The decision to use a private or in-house CA depends on the expansiveness of the PKI within the organization, how integrated it will be with different business needs and goals, its interoperability with a company's current technologies, the number of individuals who will be participating, and how it will work with outside entities. This could be quite a large undertaking that ties up

Certificate authorities come in many types: public, in-house, and outsourced. All of them perform the same functions, with the only difference being an organizational one. This can have a bearing on trust relationships, as one is more likely to trust in-house CAs over others for which there is arguably less control.

staff, resources, and funds, so a lot of strategic planning is required, and what will and won't be gained from a PKI should be fully understood before the first dollar is spent on the implementation.

Outsourced Certificate Authorities

The last available option for using PKI components within a company is to outsource different parts of it to a specific service provider. Usually, the more complex parts are outsourced, such as the CA, RA, CRL, and key recovery mechanisms. This occurs if a company does not have the necessary skills to implement and carry out a full PKI environment.

Although outsourced services might be easier for your company to implement, you need to review several factors before making this type of commitment. You need to determine what level of trust the company is willing to give to the service provider and what level of risk it is willing to accept. Often a PKI and its components serve as large security components within a company's enterprise, and allowing a third party to maintain the PKI can introduce too many risks and liabilities that your company is not willing to undertake. The liabilities the service provider is willing to accept, security precautions and procedures the outsourced CAs provide, and the surrounding legal issues need to be examined before this type of agreement is made.

Some large vertical markets have their own outsourced PKI environments set up because they share similar needs and usually have the same requirements for certification types and uses. This allows several companies within the same market to split the costs of the necessary equipment, and it allows for industry-specific standards to be drawn up and followed. For example, although many medical facilities work differently and have different environments, they have a lot of the same functionality and security needs. If several of them came together, purchased the necessary equipment to provide CA, RA, and CRL functionality, employed one person to maintain it, and then each connected its different sites to the centralized components, the medical facilities could save a lot of money and resources. In this case, not every facility would need to strategically plan its own full PKI, and each would not need to purchase redundant equipment or employ redundant staff members. Figure 6.10 illustrates how one outsourced service provider can offer different PKI components and

Tech Tip

Outsourced CA vs. Public CA

An outsourced CA is different from a public CA in that it provides dedicated services, and possibly equipment, to an individual company. A public CA, in contrast, can be used by hundreds or thousands of companies—the CA doesn't maintain specific servers and infrastructures for individual companies.

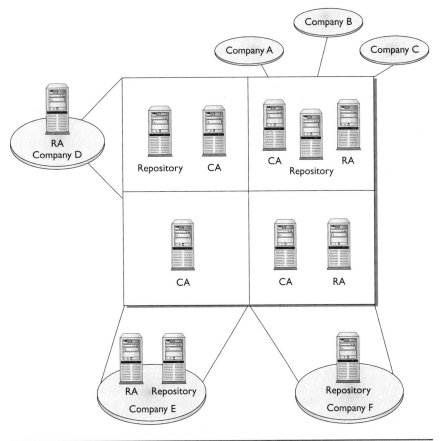

• **Figure 6.10** A PKI service provider (represented by the four boxes) can offer different PKI components to companies.

services to different companies, and how companies within one vertical market can share the same resources.

A set of standards can be drawn up about how each different facility should integrate its own infrastructure and how it should integrate with the centralized PKI components. This also allows for less-complicated inter-communication to take place between the different medical facilities, which will ease information-sharing attempts.

Tying Different PKIs Together

In some cases, more than one CA may be needed for a specific PKI to work properly, and several requirements must be met for different PKIs to inter-communicate. Here are some examples:

- A company wants to be able to communicate seamlessly with its suppliers, customers, or business partners via a PKI.

- One department within a company has higher security requirements than all other departments and thus needs to configure and control its own CA.

- One department needs to have specially constructed certificates with unique fields and usages.

- Different parts of an organization want to control their own pieces of the network and the CA that is encompassed within it.

- The number of certificates that need to be generated and maintained would overwhelm one CA, so multiple CAs must be deployed.

- The political culture of a company inhibits one department from being able to control elements of another department.

- Enterprises are partitioned geographically, and different sites need their own local CA.

These situations can add much more complexity to the overall infra-structure, intercommunication capabilities, and procedures for certificate generation and validation. To control this complexity properly from the be-ginning, these requirements need to be understood, addressed, and planned for. Then the necessary trust model needs to be chosen and molded for the company to build upon. Selecting the right trust model will give the company a solid foundation from the beginning, instead of trying to add structure to an inaccurate and inadequate plan later on.

Trust Models

Potential scenarios exist other than just having more than one CA—each of the companies or each department of an enterprise can actually represent a trust domain itself. A *trust domain* is a construct of systems, personnel, applications, protocols, technologies, and policies that work together to provide a certain level of protection. All of these components can work to-gether seamlessly within the same trust domain because they are known to the other components within the domain and are trusted to some degree. Different trust domains are usually managed by different groups of

Tech Tip

Trust Models
There are several forms of trust models associated with certifi-cates. Hierarchical, peer-to-peer, and hybrid are the primary forms, with the web of trust being a form of hybrid. Each of these models has a useful place in the PKI ar-chitecture under different circum-stances.

administrators, have different security policies, and restrict outsiders from privileged access.

Most trust domains (whether individual companies or departments) usually are not islands cut off from the world—they need to communicate with other, less-trusted domains. The trick is to figure out how much two different domains should trust each other, and how to implement and configure an infrastructure that would allow these two domains to communicate in a way that will not allow security compromises or breaches. This can be more difficult than it sounds.

In the nondigital world, it is difficult to figure out who to trust, how to carry out legitimate business functions, and how to ensure that one is not being taken advantage of or lied to. Jump into the digital world and add protocols, services, encryption, CAs, RAs, CRLs, and differing technologies and applications, and the business risks can become overwhelming and confusing. So start with a basic question: What criteria will we use to determine who we trust and to what degree?

One example of trust considered earlier in the chapter is the driver's license issued by the DMV. Suppose, for example, that Bob is buying a lamp from Carol and he wants to pay by check. Since Carol does not know Bob, she does not know if she can trust him or have much faith in his check. But if Bob shows Carol his driver's license, she can compare the name to what appears on the check, and she can choose to accept it. The *trust anchor* (the agreed-upon trusted third party) in this scenario is the DMV, since both Carol and Bob trust it more than they trust each other. Bob had to provide documentation to the DMV to prove his identity, that organization trusted him enough to generate a license, and Carol trusts the DMV, so she decides to trust Bob's check.

Consider another example of a trust anchor. If Joe and Stacy need to communicate through e-mail and would like to use encryption and digital signatures, they will not trust each other's certificate alone. But when each receives the other's certificate and sees that it has been digitally signed by an entity they both do trust—the CA—they have a deeper level of trust in each other. The trust anchor here is the CA. This is easy enough, but when we need to establish trust anchors between different CAs and PKI environments, it gets a little more complicated.

If two companies need to communicate using their individual PKIs, or if two departments within the same company use different CAs, two separate trust domains are involved. The users and devices from these different trust domains need to communicate with each other, and they need to exchange certificates and public keys, which means that trust anchors need to be identified and a communication channel must be constructed and maintained.

A trust relationship must be established between two issuing authorities (CAs). This happens when one or both of the CAs issue a certificate for the other CA's public key, as shown in Figure 6.11. This means that each CA registers for a certificate and public key from the other CA. Each CA validates the other CA's identification information and generates a certificate containing a public key for that CA to use. This establishes a trust path between the two entities that can then be used when users need to verify other users' certificates that fall within the different trust domains. The trust path can be unidirectional or bidirectional, so either the two CAs trust each other (bidirectional) or only one trusts the other (unidirectional).

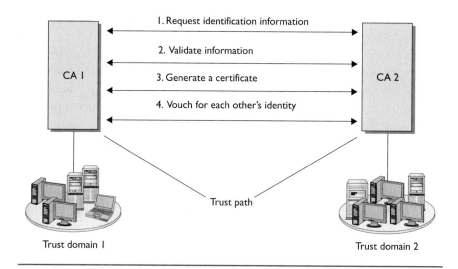

1. Request identification information

2. Validate information

3. Generate a certificate

4. Vouch for each other's identity

CA 1

CA 2

Trust path

Trust domain 1

Trust domain 2

• **Figure 6.11** A trust relationship can be built between two trust domains to set up a communication channel.

As illustrated in Figure 6.11, all the users and devices in trust domain 1 trust their own CA, CA 1, which is their trust anchor. All users and devices in trust domain 2 have their own trust anchor, CA 2. The two CAs have exchanged certificates and trust each other, but they do not have a common trust anchor between them.

The trust models describe and outline the trust relationships between the different CAs and different environments, which will indicate where the trust paths reside. The trust models and paths need to be thought out before implementation to restrict and control access properly and to ensure that as few trust paths as possible are used. Several different trust models can be used: the hierarchical, peer-to-peer, and hybrid models are discussed in the following sections.

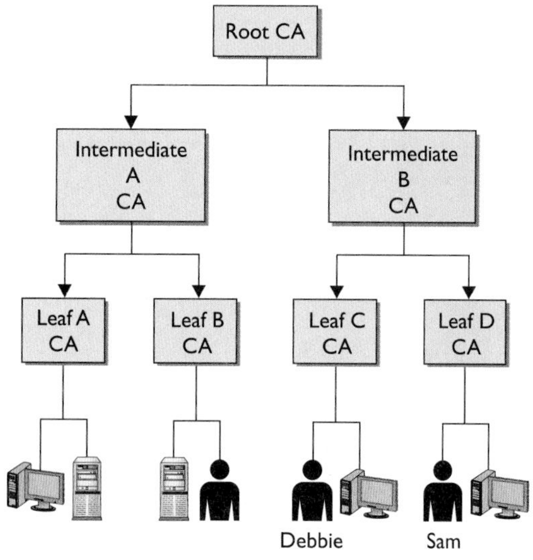

Hierarchical Trust Model

The **hierarchical trust model** is a basic hierarchical structure that contains a root CA, intermediate CAs, leaf CAs, and end-entities. The configuration is that of an inverted tree, as shown in Figure 6.12. The root CA is the ultimate trust anchor for all other entities in this infrastructure, and it generates certificates for the intermediate CAs, which in turn generate certificates for the leaf CAs, and the leaf CAs generate certificates for the end-entities (users, network devices, and applications).

Intermediate CAs function to transfer trust between different CAs. These CAs are referred to as *subordinate CAs* because they are subordinate to the CA that they reference. The path of trust is walked up from the subordinate CA to the higher-level CA; in essence the subordinate CA is using the higher-level CA as a reference.

As shown in Figure 6.12, no bidirectional trusts exist—they are all unidirectional trusts, as indicated by the one-way arrows. Since no other entity can certify and generate certificates for the root CA, it creates a *self-signed certificate*. This means that the certificate's issuer

Root CA

Intermediate A CA

Intermediate B CA

Leaf A CA

Leaf B CA

Leaf C CA

Leaf D CA

Debbie

Sam

• **Figure 6.12** The hierarchical trust model outlines trust paths.

and subject fields hold the same information, both representing the root CA, and the root CA's public key will be used to verify this certificate when that time comes. This root CA certificate and public key are distributed to all entities within this trust model.

Walking the Certificate Path

When a user in one trust domain needs to communicate with a user in another trust domain, one user will need to validate the other's certificate. This sounds simple enough, but what it really means is that each certificate for each CA, all the way up to a shared trusted anchor, also must be validated. If Debbie needs to validate Sam's certificate, as shown in Figure 6.12, she actually also needs to validate the Leaf D CA and Intermediate B CA certificates, as well as Sam's.

So in Figure 6.12, we have a user, Sam, who digitally signs a message and sends it and his certificate to Debbie. Debbie needs to validate this certificate before she can trust Sam's digital signature. Included in Sam's certificate is an issuer field, which indicates that the certificate was issued by Leaf D CA. Debbie has to obtain Leaf D CA's digital certificate and public key to validate Sam's certificate. Remember that Debbie validates the certificate by verifying its digital signature. The digital signature was created by the certificate issuer using its private key, so Debbie needs to verify the signature using the issuer's public key.

Debbie tracks down Leaf D CA's certificate and public key, but she now needs to verify this CA's certificate, so she looks at the issuer field, which indicates that Leaf D CA's certificate was issued by Intermediate B CA. Debbie now needs to get Intermediate B CA's certificate and public key.

Debbie's client software tracks this down and sees that the issuer for Intermediate B CA is the root CA, for which she already has a certificate and public key. So Debbie's client software had to follow the **certificate path**, meaning it had to continue to track down and collect certificates until it came upon a self-signed certificate. A self-signed certificate indicates that it was signed by a root CA, and Debbie's software has been configured to trust this entity as her trust anchor, so she can stop there. Figure 6.13 illustrates the steps Debbie's software had to carry out just to be able to verify Sam's certificate.

Tech Tip

Root CA
If the root CA's private key were ever compromised, all entities within the hierarchical trust model would be drastically affected, because this is their sole trust anchor. The root CA usually has a small amount of interaction with the intermediate CAs and end-entities, and can therefore be taken offline much of the time. This provides a greater degree of protection for the root CA, because when it is offline it is basically inaccessible.

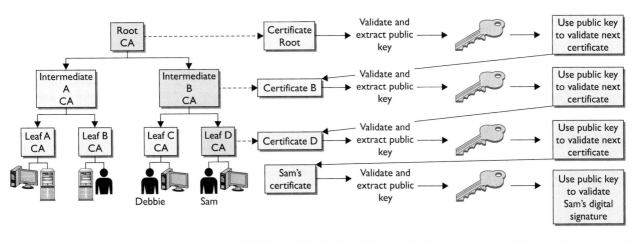

• **Figure 6.13**   Verifying each certificate in a certificate path

This type of simplistic trust model works well within an enterprise that easily follows a hierarchical organizational chart, but many companies cannot use this type of trust model because different departments or offices require their own trust anchors. These demands can be derived from direct business needs or from interorganizational politics. This hierarchical model might not be possible when two or more companies need to communicate with each other. Neither company will let the other's CA be the root CA, because each does not necessarily trust the other entity to that degree. In these situations, the CAs will need to work in a peer-to-peer relationship instead of in a hierarchical relationship.

Peer-to-Peer Model

In a **peer-to-peer trust model**, one CA is not subordinate to another CA, and no established trusted anchor between the CAs is involved. The end-entities will look to their issuing CA as their trusted anchor, but the different CAs will not have a common anchor.

Figure 6.14 illustrates this type of trust model. The two different CAs will certify the public key for each other, which creates a bidirectional trust. This is referred to as *cross-certification*, since the CAs are not receiving their certificates and public keys from a superior CA, but instead are creating them for each other.

One of the main drawbacks to this model is scalability. Each CA must certify every other CA that is participating, and a bidirectional trust path must be implemented, as shown in Figure 6.15. If one root CA were certifying all the intermediate CAs, scalability would not be as much of an issue.

Figure 6.15 represents a fully connected *mesh architecture*, meaning that each CA is directly connected to and has a bidirectional trust relationship with every other CA. As you can see in this illustration, the complexity of this setup can become overwhelming.

Hybrid Trust Model

A company can be internally complex, and when the need arises to communicate properly with outside partners, suppliers, and customers in an authorized and secured manner, this complexity can make sticking to either the

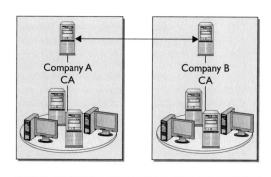

● **Figure 6.14** Cross-certification creates a peer-to-peer PKI model.

In any network model, fully connected mesh architectures are wasteful and expensive. In trust transfer models, the extra level of redundancy is just that: redundant and unnecessary.

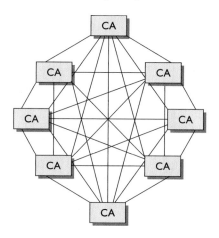

● **Figure 6.15** Scalability is a drawback in cross-certification models.

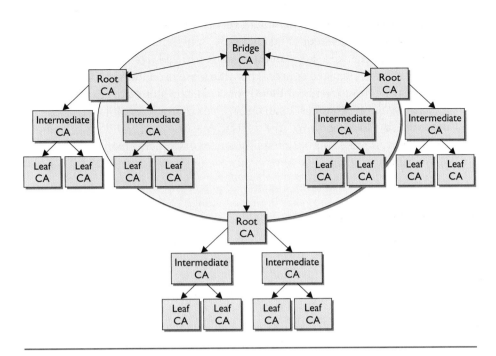

• **Figure 6.16**   A bridge CA can control the cross-certification procedures.

hierarchical or peer-to-peer trust model difficult, if not impossible. In many implementations, the different model types have to be combined to provide the necessary communication lines and levels of trust. In a **hybrid trust model**, the two companies have their own internal hierarchical models and are connected through a peer-to-peer model using cross-certification.

Another option in this hybrid configuration is to implement a *bridge CA*. Figure 6.16 illustrates the role that a bridge CA could play—it is responsible for issuing cross-certificates for all connected CAs and trust domains. The bridge is not considered a root or trust anchor, but merely the entity that generates and maintains the cross-certification for the connected environments.

 Exam Tip: Three trust models exist: hierarchical, peer-to-peer, and hybrid. Hierarchical trust is like an upside down tree, peer-to-peer is a lateral series of references, and hybrid is a combination of hierarchical and peer-to-peer trust.

Certificate-Based Threats

Although certificates bring much capability to security through practical management of trust, they also can present threats. Because much of the actual work is done behind the scenes, without direct user involvement, a false sense of security might ensue. End users might assume that if an HTTPS connection was made with a server, they are securely connected to the proper server. Spoofing, phishing, pharming, and a wide range of sophisticated attacks prey on this assumption. Today, industry has responded with a high-assurance certificate that is signed and recognized by browsers. Using this example, we can examine how an attacker might prey on a user's trust in software getting things correct.

If a hacker wishes to have something recognized as legitimate, he may have to obtain a certificate that proves this point to the end-user machine. One avenue would be to forge a false certificate, but this is challenging because of the public key signing of certificates by CAs. To overcome this problem, the hacker needs to install a false, self-signed root certificate on the end-user PC. This false key can then be used to validate malicious software as coming from a trusted source. This attack preys on the fact that end users do not know the contents of their root certificate store, nor do they have a means to validate changes. In an enterprise environment, this attack can be thwarted by locking down the certificate store and validating changes against a white list. This option really is not very practical for end users outside of an enterprise.

■ Chapter Summary

After reading this chapter and completing the exercises, you should understand the following about public key infrastructures.

Implement the basics of public key infrastructures

- PKI solutions include certificate authorities (CAs) and registration authorities (RAs).
- PKIs form the central management functionality used to enable encryption technologies.
- Understand the steps a user performs to obtain a certificate for use.

Describe the roles of certificate authorities and certificate repositories

- CAs create certificates for identified entities and maintain records of their issuance and revocation.
- CRLs provide a means of letting users know when certificates have been revoked before their end-of-life date.

Describe the role of registration authorities

- RAs verify identities to be used on certificates.
- RAs pass identity information to CAs for use in binding to a certificate.

Explain the relationship between trust and certificate verification

- Trust is based on an understanding of the needs of the user and what the item being trusted offers.

- Certificate verification provides assurance that the data in the certificate is valid, not whether it meets the needs of the user.

Use digital certificates

- Certificates are handled via a certificate server and client software.
- There are three classes of certificates and they have the following typical uses:
  - **Class 1** Personal e-mail use
  - **Class 2** Software signing
  - **Class 3** Used to set up a CA

Identify centralized and decentralized infrastructures

- There are three different architectures of CAs:
  - Hierarchical
  - Peer-to-peer
  - Hybrid
- Multiple CAs can be used together to create a web of trust.

Describe public and in-house certificate authorities

- Public CAs exist as a service that allows entities to obtain certificates from a trusted third party.
- In-house certificates provide certificates that allow a firm a means to use certificates within company borders.

■ Key Terms

authority revocation list (ARL) *(131)*
CA certificate *(125)*
certificate *(114)*
certificate authority (CA) *(117)*
certificate path *(143)*
certificate repository *(120)*
certificate revocation list (CRL) *(129)*
certificate server *(118)*

certification practices statement (CPS) *(117)*
cross-certification certificate *(126)*
digital certificate *(117)*
dual control *(136)*
end-entity certificates *(125)*
hierarchical trust model *(142)*
hybrid trust model *(145)*
key archiving *(135)*

key escrow *(136)*
key recovery *(135)*
local registration authority (LRA) *(120)*
Online Certificate Status Protocol (OCSP) *(131)*

peer-to-peer trust model *(144)*
policy certificate *(126)*
public key infrastructure (PKI) *(115)*
registration authority (RA) *(118)*

■ Key Terms Quiz

Use terms from the Key Terms list to complete the sentences that follow. Don't use the same term more than once. Not all terms will be used.

1. The _____ is the trusted authority for certifying individuals' identities and creating an electronic document indicating that individuals are who they say they are.

2. Requiring two individuals to recover a lost key together is called _____, which simply means that two people have to be present to carry out a specific task.

3. The _____ is a method of determining whether a certificate has been revoked that does not require local machine storage of CRLs.

4. The _____ is the actual service that issues certificates based on the data provided during the initial registration process.

5. Allowing another party to possess a copy of a private key is referred to as _____.

6. A(n) _____ is a holding place for individuals' certificates and public keys that are participating in a particular PKI environment.

7. A(n) _____ is used when independent CAs establish peer-to-peer trust relationships.

8. A(n) _____ is a structure that provides all of the necessary components for different types of users and entities to be able to communicate securely and in a predictable manner.

9. _____ is the mechanism that allows keys to be retrieved in the event of a user losing access.

10. In a(n) _____, one CA is not subordinate to another CA, and there is no established trust anchor between the CAs involved.

■ Multiple-Choice Quiz

1. When a user wants to participate in a PKI, what component does he or she need to obtain, and how does that happen?

    A. The user submits a certificate request to the CA.

    B. The user submits a key pair request to the CRL.

    C. The user submits a certificate request to the RA.

    D. The user submits proof of identification to the CA.

2. How does a user validate a digital certificate that is received from another user?

    A. The user first sees whether her system has been configured to trust the CA that digitally signed the other user's certificate and then validates that CA's digital signature.

    B. The user calculates a message digest and compares it to the one attached to the message.

    C. The user first sees whether her system has been configured to trust the CA that digitally signed the certificate and then validates the public key that is embedded within the certificate.

    D. The user validates the sender's digital signature on the message.

3. What is the purpose of a digital certificate?

    A. It binds a CA to a user's identity.

    B. It binds a CA's identity to the correct RA.

    C. It binds an individual to an RA.

    D. It binds an individual to a public key.

4. What steps does a user's software take to validate a CA's digital signature on a digital certificate?

   A. The user's software creates a message digest for the digital certificate and decrypts the encrypted message digest included within the digital certificate. If the decryption performs properly and the message digest values are the same, the certificate is validated.

   B. The user's software creates a message digest for the digital signature and encrypts the message digest included within the digital certificate. If the encryption performs properly and the message digest values are the same, the certificate is validated.

   C. The user's software creates a message digest for the digital certificate and decrypts the encrypted message digest included within the digital certificate. If the user can encrypt the message digest properly with the CA's private key and the message digest values are the same, the certificate is validated.

   D. The user's software creates a message digest for the digital signature and encrypts the message digest with its private key. If the decryption performs properly and the message digest values are the same, the certificate is validated.

5. What is a bridge CA, and what is its function?

   A. It is a hierarchical trust model that establishes a root CA, which is the trust anchor for all other CAs.

   B. It is an entity that creates and maintains the CRL for several CAs at one time.

   C. It is a CA that handles the cross-certification certificates for two or more CAs in a peer-to-peer relationship.

   D. It is an entity that validates the user's identity information for the RA before the request goes to the CA.

6. Why would a company implement a key archiving and recovery system within the organization?

   A. To make sure all data encryption keys are available for the company if and when it needs them

   B. To make sure all digital signature keys are available for the company if and when it needs them

   C. To create session keys for users to be able to access when they need to encrypt bulk data

   D. To back up the RA's private key for retrieval purposes

7. Within a PKI environment, where does the majority of the trust actually lie?

   A. All users and devices within an environment trust the RA, which allows them to indirectly trust each other.

   B. All users and devices within an environment trust the CA, which allows them to indirectly trust each other.

   C. All users and devices within an environment trust the CRL, which allows them to indirectly trust each other.

   D. All users and devices within an environment trust the CPS, which allows them to indirectly trust each other.

8. Which of the following properly explains the *m of n control*?

   A. This is the process a user must go through to properly register for a certificate through the RA.

   B. This ensures that a certificate has to be fully validated by a user before he can extract the public key and use it.

   C. This is a control in key recovery to enforce separation of duties.

   D. This is a control in key recovery to ensure that the company cannot recover a user's key without the user's consent.

9. Which of the following certificate characteristics was expanded upon with version 3 of the X.509 standard?

   A. Subject

   B. Extensions

   C. Digital signature

   D. Serial number

10. What is a certification practices statement (CPS), and what is its purpose?

   A. A CPS outlines the steps a CA goes through to validate identities and generate certificates. Companies should review this document to ensure that the CA follows the necessary steps the company requires and provides the necessary level of protection.

   B. A CPS outlines the steps a CA goes through to communicate with other CAs in other states. Companies should review this document to ensure that the CA follows the necessary steps the company requires and provides the necessary level of protection.

   C. A CPS outlines the steps a CA goes through to set up an RA at a company's site. Companies should review this document to ensure that the CA follows the necessary steps the company requires and provides the necessary level of protection.

   D. A CPS outlines the steps a CA goes through to become a business within a vertical market. Companies should review this document to ensure that the CA follows the necessary steps the company requires and provides the necessary level of protection.

11. Which of the following properly describes what a public key infrastructure (PKI) actually is?

   A. A protocol written to work with a large subset of algorithms, applications, and protocols

   B. An algorithm that creates public/private key pairs

   C. A framework that outlines specific technologies and algorithms that must be used

   D. A framework that does not specify any technologies, but provides a foundation for confidentiality, integrity, and availability services

12. Once an individual validates another individual's certificate, what is the use of the public key that is extracted from this digital certificate?

   A. The public key is now available to use to create digital signatures.

   B. The user can now encrypt session keys and messages with this public key and can validate the sender's digital signatures.

   C. The public key is now available to encrypt future digital certificates that need to be validated.

   D. The user can now encrypt private keys that need to be transmitted securely.

13. Why would a digital certificate be added to a certificate revocation list (CRL)?

   A. If the public key had become compromised in a public repository

   B. If the private key had become compromised

   C. If a new employee joined the company and received a new certificate

   D. If the certificate expired

14. If an extension is marked as critical, what does this indicate?

   A. If the CA is not programmed to understand and process this extension, the certificate and corresponding keys can be used for their intended purpose.

   B. If the end-entity is programmed to understand and process this extension, the certificate and corresponding keys cannot be used.

   C. If the RA is not programmed to understand and process this extension, communication with the CA is not allowed.

   D. If the end-entity is not programmed to understand and process this extension, the certificate and corresponding keys cannot be used.

15. How can users have faith that the CRL was not modified to present incorrect information?

   A. The CRL is digitally signed by the CA.

   B. The CRL is encrypted by the CA.

   C. The CRL is open for anyone to post certificate information to.

   D. The CRL is accessible only to the CA.

■ Essay Quiz

1. Describe the pros and cons of establishing a key archiving system program for a small- to medium-sized business.

2. Why would a small- to medium-sized firm implement a PKI solution? What business benefits would ensue from such a course of action?

3. Describe the steps involved in verifying a certificate's validity.

4. Describe the steps in obtaining a certificate.

5. Compare and contrast the hierarchical trust model, peer-to-peer trust model, and hybrid trust model.

Lab Projects

• Lab Project 6.1

Investigate the process of obtaining a personal certificate or digital ID for e-mail usage. What information is needed, what are the costs, and what protection is afforded based on the vendor?

• Lab Project 6.2

Determine what certificates are registered with the browser instance on your computer.

Standards and Protocols

*Innovation distinguishes
between a leader and a follower.*
—STEVE JOBS

**In this chapter, you will learn
how to**

- **Identify the standards involved in
  establishing an interoperable
  Internet PKI**

- **Explain interoperability issues
  with PKI standards**

- **Describe how the common
  Internet protocols implement the
  PKI standards**

One of the biggest growth industries since the 1990s has been the commercial use of the Internet. None of the still steadily growing Internet commerce would be possible without the use of standards and protocols that provide a common, interoperable environment for exchanging information securely. Due to the wide distribution of Internet users and businesses, the most practical solution to date has been the commercial implementation of public key infrastructures (PKIs).

This chapter examines the standards and protocols involved in secure Internet transactions and e-business using a PKI. Although you may use only a portion of the related standards and protocols on a daily basis, you should understand how they interact to provide the services that are critical for security: confidentiality, integrity, availability, authentication, and nonrepudiation.

Chapter 6 introduced the algorithms and techniques used to implement a public PKI, but, as you probably noticed, there is a lot of room for interpretation. Various organizations have developed and implemented standards and protocols that have been accepted as the basis for secure interaction in a PKI environment. These standards fall into three general categories:

- **Standards that define the PKI**   These standards define the data and data structures exchanged and the means for managing that data to provide the functions of the PKI (certificate issuance, storage, revocation, registration, and management).

- **Standards that define the interface between applications and the underlying PKI**   These standards use the PKI to establish the services required by applications (S/MIME, SSL, and TLS).

- **Other standards**   These standards don't fit neatly in either of the other two categories. They provide bits and pieces that glue everything together; they not only can address the PKI structure and the methods and protocols for using it, but can also provide an overarching business process environment for PKI implementation (for example, ISO/IEC 27002, Common Criteria, and the Federal Information Processing Standards Publications [FIPS PUBS]).

Figure 7.1 shows the relationships between these standards and protocols and conveys the interdependence of the standards and protocols discussed in this chapter. The Internet **public key infrastructure (PKI)** relies on three main standards for establishing interoperable PKI services: PKI X.509 (PKIX), Public Key Cryptography Standards (PKCS), and X.509. Other protocols and standards help define the management and operation of the PKI and related services—Internet Security Association and Key Management Protocol (ISAKMP) and XML Key Management Specification (XKMS) are both key management protocols, while Certificate Management Protocol (CMP) is used for managing certificates. Wired Equivalent Privacy (WEP) is used to encrypt wireless communications in 802.11 environments to support some of the more application-oriented standards and protocols: Secure/Multipurpose Internet Mail Extensions (S/MIME) for e-mail; Secure Sockets Layer (SSL), Transport Layer Security (TLS), and Wireless Transport Layer Security (WTLS) for secure packet transmission; and IP Security (IPsec) and Point-to-Point Tunneling Protocol (PPTP) to support virtual private networks. Hypertext Transfer Protocol Secure (HTTPS) is commonly used by web browsers. ISO/IEC 27002 and FIPS PUBS each address security at the business process, application, protocol, and PKI implementation levels. Certificate Enrollment Protocol (CEP) is an alternative certificate issuance, distribution,

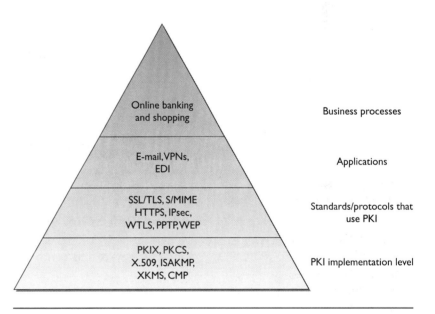

• **Figure 7.1**   Relationships between PKI standards and protocols

and revocation mechanism. Finally, Pretty Good Privacy (PGP) provides an alternative method spanning the protocol and application levels.

This chapter examines each standard from the bottom up, starting with building an infrastructure through protocols and applications, and finishing with some of the inherent weaknesses of and potential attacks on a PKI.

■ PKIX and PKCS

Two main standards have evolved over time to implement PKIs on a practical level on the Internet. Both are based on the X.509 certificate standard (discussed shortly in the "X.509" section) and establish complementary standards for implementing PKIs. PKIX and PKCS intertwine to define the most commonly used set of standards.

PKIX was produced by the Internet Engineering Task Force (IETF) and defines standards for interactions and operations for four component types: the user (end-entity), certificate authority (CA), registration authority (RA), and the repository for certificates and certificate revocation lists (CRLs). PKCS defines many of the lower-level standards for message syntax, cryptographic algorithms, and the like. The PKCS set of standards is a product of RSA Security.

The PKIX working group was formed in 1995 to develop the standards necessary to support PKIs. At the time, the X.509 Public Key Certificate (PKC) format was proposed as the basis for a PKI. X.509 includes information regarding data formats and procedures used for CA-signed PKCs, but it doesn't specify values or formats for many of the fields within the PKC. X.509 v1 (version 1) was originally defined in 1988 as part of the X.500 Directory standard. After being co-opted by the Internet community for implementing certificates for secure Internet communications, X.509's shortcomings became apparent. The current version, X.509 v3, was adopted in 1996. X.509 is very complex, allowing a great deal of flexibility in implementing certificate features. PKIX provides standards for extending and using X.509 v3 certificates and for managing them, enabling interoperability between PKIs following the standards.

PKIX uses the model shown in Figure 7.2 for representing the components and users of a PKI. The user, called an *end-entity*, is not part of the PKI,

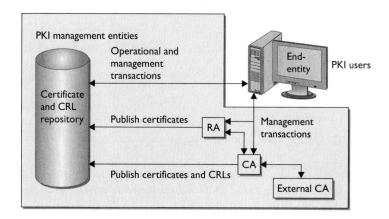

• **Figure 7.2**   The PKIX model

but end-entities are either users of the PKI certificates, the subject of a certificate (an entity identified by it), or both. The **Certificate Authority (CA)** is responsible for issuing, storing, and revoking certificates—both PKCs and Attribute Certificates (ACs). The RA is responsible for management activities designated by the CA. The RA can, in fact, be a component of the CA rather than a separate component. The final component of the PKIX model is the repository, a system or group of distributed systems that provides certificates and CRLs to the end-entities. The **Certificate Revocation List (CRL)** is a digitally signed object that lists all of the current but revoked certificates issued by a CA.

PKIX Standards

Now that we have looked at how PKIX is organized, let's take a look at what PKIX does. Using X.509 v3, the PKIX working group addresses five major areas:

- *PKIX outlines certificate extensions and content not covered by X.509 v3 and the format of version 2 CRLs, thus providing compatibility standards for sharing certificates and CRLs between CAs and end-entities in different PKIs.* The PKIX profile of the X.509 v3 PKC describes the contents, required extensions, optional extensions, and extensions that need not be implemented. The PKIX profile suggests a range of values for many extensions. In addition, PKIX provides a profile for version 2 CRLs, allowing different PKIs to share revocation information. (For more information on PKIX, see "Internet X.509 Public Key Infrastructure Certificate and CRL Profile" [RFC 5280].)

- *PKIX provides certificate management message formats and protocols, defining the data structures, management messages, and management functions for PKIs.* The working group also addresses the assumptions and restrictions of their protocols. This standard identifies the protocols necessary to support online interactions between entities in the PKIX model. The management protocols support functions for entity registration, initialization of the certificate (possibly key-pair generation), issuance of the certificate, key-pair update, certificate revocation, cross-certification (between CAs), and key-pair recovery if available.

- *PKIX outlines certificate policies and certification practices statements (CPSs), establishing the relationship between policies and CPSs.* A policy is a set of rules that helps determine the applicability of a certificate to an end-entity. For example, a certificate for handling routine information would probably have a policy on creation, storage, and management of key pairs quite different from a policy for certificates used in financial transactions, due to the sensitivity of the financial information. A CPS explains the practices used by a CA to issue certificates. In other words, the CPS is the method used to get the certificate, while the policy defines some characteristics of the certificate and how it will be handled and used.

- *PKIX specifies operational protocols, defining the protocols for certificate handling.* In particular, protocol definitions are specified for using File Transfer Protocol (FTP) and Hypertext Transfer Protocol (HTTP) to retrieve certificates from repositories. These are the most common protocols for applications to use when retrieving certificates.

- *PKIX includes time-stamping and data certification and validation services, which are areas of interest to the PKIX working group, and which will probably grow in use over time.* A time stamp authority (TSA) certifies that a particular entity existed at a particular time. A Data Validation and Certification Server (DVCS) certifies the validity of signed documents, PKCs, and the possession or existence of data. These capabilities support nonrepudiation requirements and are considered building blocks for a nonrepudiation service.

PKCs are the most commonly used certificates, but the PKIX working group has been working on two other types of certificates: Attribute Certificates and Qualified Certificates.

An Attribute Certificate (AC) is used to grant permissions using rule-based, role-based, and rank-based access controls. ACs are used to implement a privilege management infrastructure (PMI). In a PMI, an entity (user, program, system, and so on) is typically identified as a client to a server using a PKC. There are then two possibilities: either the identified client pushes an AC to the server, or the server can query a trusted repository to retrieve the attributes of the client. This situation is modeled in Figure 7.3.

The client push of the AC has the effect of improving performance, but no independent verification of the client's permissions is initiated by the server. The alternative is to have the server pull the information from an AC issuer or a repository. This method is preferable from a security standpoint, because the server or server's domain determines the client's access rights. The pull method has the added benefit of requiring no changes to the client software.

The Qualified Certificate (QC) is based on the term used within the European Commission to identify certificates with specific legislative uses. This concept is generalized in the PKIX QC profile to indicate a certificate used to identify a specific individual (a single human rather than the *entity* of the PKC) with a high level of assurance in a nonrepudiation service.

Table 7.1 summarizes the Internet Requests for Comment (RFCs) that have been produced by the PKIX working group for each of these five areas.

Other documents have been produced by the IETF PKIX working group, but those listed in Table 7.1 cover the major implementation details for PKIX. For a complete list of current and pending documents, see the Internet draft for the PKIX working group roadmap (https://datatracker.ietf.org/drafts/draft-ietf-pkix-roadmap/).

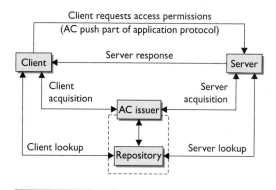

● **Figure 7.3**　The PKIX PMI model

PKCS

RSA Laboratories created the Public Key Cryptography Standards (PKCS) to fill some of the gaps in the standards that existed in PKI implementation. As they have with the PKIX standards, PKI developers have adopted many

Table 7.1		PKIX Subjects and Related RFCs	
Subject	**RFC Number**	**Title**	**Notes**
Certificates and CRL profiles	RFC 3281	An Internet Attribute Certificate Profile for Authorization	
	RFC 3739	Internet X.509 Public Key Infrastructure: Qualified Certificates Profile	Obsoletes RFC 3039
	RFC 4055	Additional Algorithms and Identifiers for RSA Cryptography for Use in the Internet X.509 Public Key Infrastructure Certificate and Certificate Revocation List (CRL) Profile	
	RFC 4476	Attribute Certificate (AC) Policies Extension	
	RFC 5055	Server-based Certificate Validation Protocol (SCVP)	
	RFC 5280	Internet X.509 Public Key Infrastructure Certificate and Certificate Revocation List (CRL) Profile	Obsoletes RFC 4630, RFC 4325, RFC 3280
Certificate management protocols	RFC 2560	X.509 Internet Public Key Infrastructure Online Certificate Status Protocol – OCSP	
	RFC 3709	Internet X.509 Public Key Infrastructure: Logotypes in X.509 Certificates	
	RFC 3820	Internet X.509 Public Key Infrastructure Proxy Certificate Profile	
	RFC 4043	Internet X.509 Public Key Infrastructure Permanent Identifier	
	RFC 4059	Internet X.509 Public Key Infrastructure Warranty Certificate Extension	
	RFC 4158	Internet X.509 Public Key Infrastructure: Certification Path Building	
	RFC 4210	Internet X.509 Public Key Infrastructure Certificate Management Protocols	Obsoletes RFC 2510
	RFC 4211	Internet X.509 Public Key Infrastructure Certificate Request Message Format (CRMF)	Obsoletes RFC 2511
	RFC 4386	Internet X.509 Public Key Infrastructure Repository Locator Service	
	RFC 4387	Internet X.509 Public Key Infrastructure Operational Protocols: Certificate Store Access via HTTP	
	RFC 4683	Internet X.509 Public Key Infrastructure Subject Identification Method (SIM)	
	RFC 4985	Internet X.509 Public Key Infrastructure Subject Alternative Name for Expression of Service Name	
	RFC 5272	Certificate Management Messages over CMS	Obsoletes RFC 2797
	RFC 5273	Certificate Management over CMS (CMC): Transport Protocols	
	RFC 5274	Certificate Management Messages over CMS (CMC): Compliance Requirements	
Certificate policies and CPSs	RFC 3647	Internet X.509 Public Key Infrastructure Certificate Policy and Certification Practices Framework	Obsoletes RFC 2527

(continued)

Table 7.1   **PKIX Subjects and Related RFCs (continued)**

Subject	RFC Number	Title	Notes
Operational protocols	RFC 2528	Internet X.509 Public Key Infrastructure Representation of Key Exchange Algorithm (KEA) Keys in Internet X.509 Public Key Infrastructure Certificates	
	RFC 2585	Internet X.509 Public Key Infrastructure Operational Protocols: FTP and HTTP	
	RFC 3779	X.509 Extensions for IP Addresses and AS Identifiers	
	RFC 4334	Certificate Extensions and Attributes Supporting Authentication in Point-to-Point Protocol (PPP) and Wireless Local Area Networks (WLAN)	Obsoletes RFC 3770
	RFC 5019	The Lightweight Online Certificate Status Protocol (OCSP) Profile for High-Volume Environments	
Time-stamp and data validation	RFC 2875	Diffie-Hellman Proof-of-Possession Algorithms	
	RFC 3029	Internet X.509 Public Key Infrastructure Data Validation and Certification Server Protocols	
	RFC 3161	Internet X.509 Public Key Infrastructure Time Stamp Protocols (TSP)	
	RFC 3628	Policy Requirements for Time-Stamping Authorities	
Other PKIX topics	RFC 3279	Algorithms and Identifiers for the Internet X.509 Public Key Infrastructure Certificate and CRI Profile	Updated by RFC 4491
	RFC 3379	Delegated Path Validation and Delegated Path Discovery Protocol Requirements	
	RFC 3874	A 224-bit One-way Hash Function: SHA-224	
	RFC 4491	Using the GOST R 34.10-94, GOST R 34.10-2001 and GOST R 34.11-94 Algorithms with the Internet X.509 Public Key Infrastructure Certificate and CRL Profile	Updates RFC 3279

of these standards as a basis for achieving interoperability between different CAs. PKCS is composed of a set of (currently) 13 active standards, with 2 other standards that are no longer active. The standards are referred to as PKCS #1 through PKCS #15, as listed in Table 7.2. The standards combine to establish a common base for services required in a PKI.

Though adopted early in the development of PKIs, some of these standards are being phased out. For example, PKCS #6 is being replaced by X.509 v3 (covered shortly in the "X.509" section) and PKCS #7 and PKCS #10 are being used less, as their PKIX counterparts are being adopted.

Why You Need to Know the PKIX and PKCS Standards

If your company is planning to use one of the existing certificate servers to support e-commerce, you may not need to know the specifics of these standards (except perhaps for your exam). However, if you plan to implement a private PKI to support secure services within your organization, you need

Table 7.2	PKCS Standards
Standard	**Title and Description**
PKCS #1	RSA Cryptography Standard: Definition of the RSA encryption standard.
PKCS #2	No longer active; it covered RSA encryption of message digests and was incorporated into PKCS #1.
PKCS #3	Diffie-Hellman Key Agreement Standard: Definition of the Diffie-Hellman key-agreement protocol.
PKCS #4	No longer active; it covered RSA key syntax and was incorporated into PKCS #1.
PKCS #5	Password-Based Cryptography Standard: Definition of a password-based encryption (PBE) method for generating a secret key.
PKCS #6	Extended-Certificate Syntax Standard: Definition of an extended certificate syntax that is made obsolete by X.509 v3.
PKCS #7	Cryptographic Message Syntax Standard: Definition of the cryptographic message standard for encoded messages, regardless of encryption algorithm. Commonly replaced with PKIX Cryptographic Message Syntax.
PKCS #8	Private-Key Information Syntax Standard: Definition of a private key information format, used to store private key information.
PKCS #9	Selected Attribute Types: Definition of attribute types used in other PKCS standards.
PKCS #10	Certification Request Syntax Standard: Definition of a syntax for certification requests.
PKCS #11	Cryptographic Token Interface Standard: Definition of a technology-independent programming interface for cryptographic devices (such as smart cards).
PKCS #12	Personal Information Exchange Syntax Standard: Definition of a format for storage and transport of user privates keys, certificates, and other personal information.
PKCS #13	Elliptic Curve Cryptography Standard: Description of methods for encrypting and signing messages using elliptic curve cryptography.
PKCS #14	Pseudo-random Number Generation: A standard for pseudo-random number generation.
PKCS #15	Cryptographic Token Information Format Standard: Definition of a format for storing cryptographic information in cryptographic tokens.

to understand what standards are out there and how the decision to use a particular PKI implementation (either home grown or commercial) may lead to incompatibilities with other certificate-issuing entities. You must consider your business-to-business requirements when you're deciding how to implement a PKI within your organization.

 Exam Tip: All of the standards and protocols discussed in this chapter are the "vocabulary" of the computer security industry. You should be well versed in all these titles and their purposes and operations.

■ X.509

What is a **certificate**? A certificate is merely a data structure that binds a public key to subjects (unique names, DNS entries, or e-mails) and is used to authenticate that a public key indeed belongs to the subject. In the late 1980s, the X.500 OSI Directory Standard was defined by the International Organization for Standardization (ISO) and the International Telecommunication Union (ITU). It was developed for implementing a network directory system, and part of this directory standard was the concept of authentication of entities within the directory. **X.509** is the portion of the X.500 standard that addresses the structure of certificates used for authentication.

Several versions of the X.509 certificates have been created, with version 3 being the current version (as this is being written). Each version has extended the contents of the certificates to include additional information necessary to use certificates in a PKI. The original ITU X.509 definition was published in 1988, was formerly referred to as CCITT X.509, and is sometimes referred to as ISO/IEC/ITU 9594-8. The 1988 certificate format, version 1, was revised in 1993 as the ITU-T X.509 definition when two more fields were added to support directory access control. ITU-T is the Standards Section of the ITU created in 1992.

The 1993, version 2 specification was revised following lessons learned from implementing Internet Privacy Enhanced Mail (PEM). Version 3 added additional optional extensions for more subject identification information, key attribute information, policy information, and certification path constraints. In addition, version 3 allowed additional extensions to be defined in standards or to be defined and registered by organizations or communities. Table 7.3 gives a description of the fields in an X.509 certificate.

Table 7.3	X.509 Certificate Fields
Field Name	**Field Description**
Certificate Signature	X.509 version used for this certificate: Version 1 = 0 Version 2 = 1 Version 3 = 2
Serial Number	A nonnegative integer assigned by the certificate issuer that must be unique to the certificate.
Signature Algorithm Algorithm Parameters (optional)	The algorithm identifier for the algorithm used by the CA to sign the certificate. The optional Parameters field is used to provide the cryptographic algorithm parameters used in generating the signature.
Issuer	Identification for the entity that signed and issued the certificate. This must be a distinguished name within the hierarchy of CAs.
Validity Not valid before time Not valid after time	Validity specifies a period of time during which the certificate is valid, using a "not valid before" time and a "not valid after" time (expressed in UTC or in a generalized time).
Subject	The name for the certificate owner.
Subject Public Key Info	This field consists of an encryption algorithm identifier followed by a bit string for the public key.
Issuer Unique ID	Optional for versions 2 and 3—a unique bit-string identifier for the CA that issued the certificate.
Subject Unique ID	Optional for versions 2 and 3—a unique bit-string identifier for the subject of the certificate.
Extensions Extension ID Critical Extension Value	Optional for version 3—the extension area consists of a sequence of extension fields containing an extension identifier, a Boolean field indicating whether the extension is critical, and an octet string representing the value of the extension. Extensions can be defined in standards or defined and registered by organizations or communities.
Thumbprint Algorithm Algorithm Parameters (optional)	This field identifies the algorithm used by the CA to sign this certificate. This field must match the algorithm identified in the Signature Algorithm field.
Thumbprint	The signature is the bit-string hash value obtained when the CA signed the certificate. The signature certifies the contents of the certificate, binding the public key to the subject.

Certificates are used to encapsulate the information needed to authenticate an entity. The X.509 specification defines a hierarchical certification structure that relies on a root CA that is *self-certifying* (meaning it issues its own certificate). All other certificates can be traced back to such a root through a *path*. A CA issues a certificate to a uniquely identifiable entity (person, corporation, computer, and so on)—issuing a certificate to "John Smith" would cause some real problems if that were all the information the CA had when issuing the certificate. We are saved somewhat by the requirement that the CA determines what identifier is unique (the distinguished name), but when certificates and trust are extended between CAs, the unique identification becomes critical.

Some other extensions to the X.509 certificate have been proposed for use in implementing a PKI. For example, PKIX identified several extensions for use in the certificate policy framework (see RFC 2427). It is essential that you ensure that your PKI ignores extensions that it is not prepared to handle.

SSL/TLS

Secure Sockets Layer (SSL) and **Transport Layer Security (TLS)** provide the most common means of interacting with a PKI and certificates. The older, SSL protocol was introduced by Netscape as a means of providing secure connections for web transfers using encryption. These two protocols provide secure connections between the client and server for exchanging information. They also provide server authentication (and optionally, client authentication) and confidentiality of information transfers. See Chapter 17 for a detailed explanation.

The IETF established the TLS working group in 1996 to develop a standard transport layer security protocol. The working group began with SSL version 3.0 as its basis and released RFC 2246, TLS Protocol Version 1.0, in 1999 as a proposed standard. The working group also published RFC 2712, "Addition of Kerberos Cipher Suites to Transport Layer Security (TLS)," as a proposed standard, and two RFCs on the use of TLS with HTTP. Like its predecessor, TLS is a protocol that ensures privacy between communicating applications and their users on the Internet. When a server and client communicate, TLS ensures that no third party can eavesdrop or tamper with any message.

TLS is composed of two parts: the TLS Record Protocol and the TLS Handshake Protocol. The TLS Record Protocol provides connection security by using supported encryption methods. The TLS Record Protocol can also be used without encryption. The TLS Handshake Protocol allows the server and client to authenticate each other and to negotiate a session encryption algorithm and cryptographic keys before data is exchanged.

Though TLS is based on SSL and is sometimes referred to as SSL, they are not interoperable. However, the TLS protocol does contain a mechanism that allows a TLS implementation to back down to SSL 3.0. The difference between the two is the way they perform key expansion and message authentication computations. TLS uses the MD5 and SHA1 hashing algorithms XORed together to determine the session key. The most recent

Tech Tip

SSL/TLS Simplified
SSL and TLS are cryptographic protocols to provide data integrity and security over networks by encrypting network connections at the transport layer.

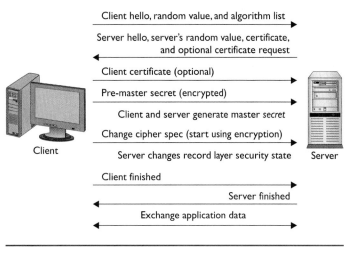

Client hello, random value, and algorithm list

Server hello, server's random value, certificate, and optional certificate request

Client certificate (optional)

Pre-master secret (encrypted)

Client and server generate master *secret*

Change cipher spec (start using encryption)

Server changes record layer security state

Client finished

Server finished

Exchange application data

Client

Server

● **Figure 7.4**   TLS Handshake Protocol

browser versions support TLS. Though SSL also uses both hashing algorithms, SSL is considered less secure because the way it uses them forces a reliance on MD5 rather than SHA1.

The TLS Record Protocol is a layered protocol. At each layer, messages may include fields for length, description, and content. The Record Protocol takes messages to be transmitted, fragments the data into manageable blocks, optionally compresses the data, applies a message authentication code (MAC) to the data, encrypts it, and transmits the result. Received data is decrypted, verified, decompressed, and reassembled, and then delivered to higher-level clients.

The TLS Handshake Protocol involves the following steps, which are summarized in Figure 7.4:

1. Exchange hello messages to agree on algorithms, exchange random values, and check for session resumption.

2. Exchange the necessary cryptographic parameters to allow the client and server to agree on a pre-master secret.

3. Exchange certificates and cryptographic information to allow the client and server to authenticate themselves.

4. Generate a master secret from the pre-master secret and exchanged random values.

5. Provide security parameters to the record layer.

6. Allow the client and server to verify that their peer has calculated the same security parameters and that the handshake occurred without tampering by an attacker.

Though it has been designed to minimize this risk, TLS still has potential vulnerabilities to a man-in-the-middle attack. A highly skilled and well-placed attacker can force TLS to operate at lower security levels. Regardless, through the use of validated and trusted certificates, a secure cipher suite can be selected for the exchange of data.

Once established, a TLS session remains active as long as data is being exchanged. If sufficient inactive time has elapsed for the secure connection to time out, it can be reinitiated.

■ ISAKMP

The **Internet Security Association and Key Management Protocol (ISAKMP)** provides a method for implementing a key exchange protocol and for negotiating a security policy. It defines procedures and packet formats to negotiate, establish, modify, and delete security associates. Because it is a framework, it doesn't define implementation-specific protocols, such as the key exchange protocol or hash functions. Examples of ISAKMP are the

Internet Key Exchange (IKE) protocol and IPsec, which are used widely throughout the industry.

An important definition for understanding ISAKMP is that of the term *security association*. A security association (SA) is a relationship in which two or more entities define how they will communicate securely. ISAKMP is intended to support SAs at all layers of the network stack. For this reason, ISAKMP can be implemented on the transport layer using TCP or User Datagram Protocol (UDP), or it can be implemented on IP directly.

Negotiation of an SA between servers occurs in two stages. First, the entities agree on how to secure negotiation messages (the ISAKMP SA). Once the entities have secured their negotiation traffic, they then determine the SAs for the protocols used for the remainder of their communications. Figure 7.5 shows the structure of the ISAKMP header. This header is used during both parts of the ISAKMP negotiation.

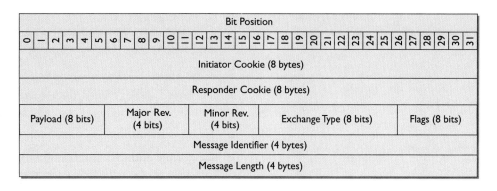

• **Figure 7.5**   ISAKMP header format

The Initiator Cookie is set by the entity requesting the SA, and the responder sets the Responder Cookie. The Payload byte indicates the type of the first payload to be encapsulated. Payload types include security associations, proposals, key transforms, key exchanges, vendor identities, and other things. The Major and Minor Revision fields refer to the major version number and minor version number for the ISAKMP. The Exchange Type helps determine the order of messages and payloads. The Flags bits indicate options for the ISAKMP exchange, including whether the payload is encrypted, whether the initiator and responder have "committed" to the SA, and whether the packet is to be authenticated only (and is not encrypted). The final fields of the ISAKMP header indicate the Message Identifier and a Message Length. Payloads encapsulated within ISAKMP use a generic header, and each payload has its own header format.

Once the ISAKMP SA is established, multiple protocol SAs can be established using the single ISAKMP SA. This feature is valuable due to the overhead associated with the two-stage negotiation. SAs are valid for specific periods of time, and once the time expires, the SA must be renegotiated. Many resources are also available for specific implementations of ISAKMP within the IPsec protocol.

CMP

The PKIX Certificate Management Protocol (CMP) is specified in RFC 4210. This protocol defines the messages and operations required to provide certificate management services within the PKIX model. Though part of the

IETF PKIX effort, CMP provides a framework that works well with other standards, such as PKCS #7 and PKCS #10.

CMP provides for the following certificate operations:

- CA establishment, including creation of the initial CRL and export of the public key for the CA
- Certification of an end-entity, including the following:
  - Initial registration and certification of the end-entity (registration, certificate issuance, and placement of the certificate in a repository)
  - Updates to the key pair for end-entities, required periodically and when a key pair is compromised or keys cannot be recovered
  - End-entity certificate updates, required when a certificate expires
  - Periodic CA key-pair updates, similar to end-entity key-pair updates
  - Cross-certification requests, placed by other CAs
  - Certificate and CRL publication, performed under the appropriate conditions of certificate issuance and certificate revocation
  - Key-pair recovery, a service to restore key-pair information for an end-entity; for example, if a certificate password is lost or the certificate file is lost
  - Revocation requests, supporting requests by authorized entities to revoke a certificate

CMP also defines mechanisms for performing these operations, either online or offline using files, e-mail, tokens, or web operations.

XKMS

The XML Key Management Specification defines services to manage PKI operations within the Extensible Markup Language (XML) environment. These services are provided for handling PKI keys and certificates automatically. Developed by the World Wide Web Consortium (W3C), XKMS is intended to simplify integration of PKIs and management of certificates in applications. As well as responding to problems of authentication and verification of electronic signatures, XKMS also allows certificates to be managed, registered, or revoked.

XKMS services reside on a separate server that interacts with an established PKI. The services are accessible via a simple XML protocol. Developers can rely on the XKMS services, making it less complex to interface with the PKI. The services provide for retrieving key information (owner, key value, key issuer, and the like) and key management (such as key registration and revocation).

Retrieval operations rely on the XML signature for the necessary information. Three tiers of service are based on the client requests and application requirements. Tier 0 provides a means of retrieving key information by embedding references to the key within the XML signature. The signature contains an element called a *retrieval method* that indicates ways to resolve the key. In this case, the client sends a request, using the retrieval method, to obtain the desired key information. For example, if the verification key contains a long chain of X.509 v3 certificates, a retrieval method could be included to avoid sending the certificates with the document. The client would use the retrieval method to obtain the chain of certificates. For tier 0, the server indicated in the retrieval method responds directly to the request for the key, possibly bypassing the XKMS server. The tier 0 process is shown in Figure 7.6.

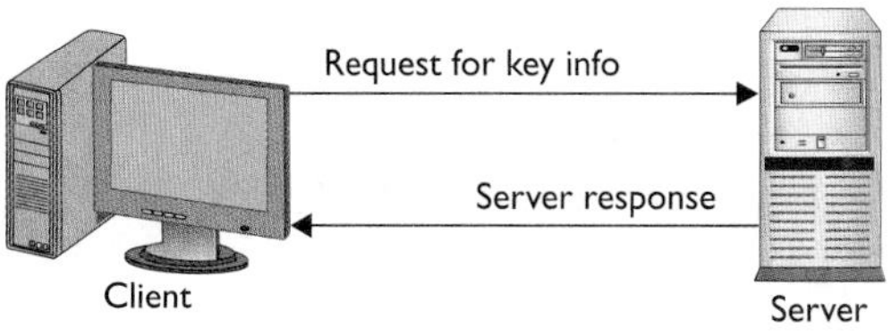

With tier 1 operations, the client forwards the key-information portions of the XML signature to the XKMS server, relying on the server to perform the retrieval of the desired key information. The desired information can be local to the XKMS server, or it can reside on an external PKI system. The XKMS server provides no additional validation of the key information, such as checking whether the certificate has been revoked or is still valid. Just as in tier 0, the client performs final validation of the document. Tier 1 is called the *locate service* because it locates the appropriate key information for the client, as shown in Figure 7.7.

Tier 2 is called the *validate service* and is illustrated in Figure 7.8. In this case, just as in tier 1, the client relies on the XKMS service to retrieve the relevant key information from the external PKI. The XKMS server also performs data validation on a portion of the key information provided by the client for this purpose. This validation verifies the binding of the key information with the data indicated by the key information contained in the XML signature.

The primary difference between tier 1 and tier 2 is the level of involvement of the XKMS server. In tier 1, it can serve only as a relay or gateway between the client and the PKI. In tier 2, the XKMS server is actively involved in verifying the relation between the PKI information and the document containing the XML signature.

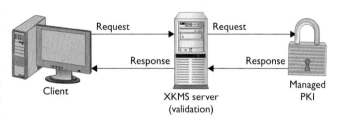

● **Figure 7.6** XKMS tier 0 retrieval

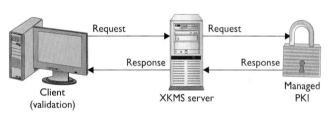

● **Figure 7.7** XKMS tier 1 locate service

● **Figure 7.8** XKMS tier 2 validate service

XKMS relies on the client or underlying communications mechanism to provide for the security of the communications with the XKMS server. The specification suggests using one of three methods for ensuring server authentication, response integrity, and relevance of the response to the request: digitally signed correspondence, a transport layer security protocol (such as SSL, TLS, or WTLS), or a packet layer security protocol (such as IPsec). Obviously, digitally signed correspondence introduces its own issues regarding validation of the signature, which is the purpose of XKMS.

It is possible to define other tiers of service. Tiers 3 and 4, an *assertion service* and an *assertion status service*, respectively, are mentioned in the defining XKMS specification, but they are not defined. The specification states they "could" be defined in other documents.

XKMS also provides services for key registration, key revocation, and key recovery. Authentication for these actions is based on a password or passphrase, which is provided when the keys are registered and when they must be recovered.

S/MIME

The **Secure/Multipurpose Internet Mail Extensions (S/MIME)** message specification is an extension to the MIME standard that provides a way to send and receive signed and encrypted MIME data. RSA Security created the first version of the S/MIME standard, using the RSA encryption algorithm and the PKCS series of standards. The second version dates from 1998 but had a number of serious restrictions, including the restriction to 40-bit Data Encryption Standard (DES). The current version of the IETF standard is dated July 2004 and requires the use of Advanced Encryption Standard (AES).

Cross Check

E-mail Encryption

Want to understand e-mail encryption? Flip ahead to Chapter 16 on e-mail and instant messaging for more details on e-mail encryption. Then answer these questions:

- Why is it important to encrypt e-mail?

- What impacts can malicious code have on a business?

- Why is instant messaging higher risk than e-mail?

The changes in the S/MIME standard have been so frequent that the standard has become difficult to implement. Far from having a stable standard for several years that product manufacturers could have time to gain experience with, there have been changes to the encryption algorithms being used. Just as importantly, and not immediately clear from the IETF documents, the standard places reliance upon more than one other standard for it to function. Key among these is the format of a public key certificate as expressed in the X.509 standard.

IETF S/MIME History

The S/MIME v2 specifications outline a basic strategy for providing security services for e-mail but lack many security features required by the Department of Defense (DoD) for use by the military. In early 1996, the Internet Mail Consortium (IMC) was formed as a technical trade association pursuing cooperative use and enhancement of Internet e-mail and messaging. An early goal of the IMC was to bring together the DoD (along with its vendor community) and commercial industry in order to devise a standard security protocol acceptable to both. Several existing security protocols were considered, including: MIME Object Security Services (MOSS), Pretty Good Privacy (PGP), and S/MIME v2. After examining these protocols, the group determined that none met the requirements of both the military and commercial communities. Instead of launching into a development of an entirely new set of specifications, however, the group decided that with certain enhancements the S/MIME set of specifications could be used. It also decided that, since the discussion was about a common set of specifications to be used throughout the Internet community, this resulting specification should be brought under the control of the IETF.

Shortly after the decision was made to revise the S/MIME v2 specifications, the DoD, its vendor community, and commercial industry met to begin development of the enhanced specifications. These new specifications would be known as S/MIME v3. Participants agreed that backward compatibility between S/MIME v3 and v2 should be preserved; otherwise, S/MIME v3–compatible applications would not be able to work with older S/MIME v2–compatible applications.

A minimum set of cryptographic algorithms was mandated so that different implementations of the new S/MIME v3 set of specifications could be interoperable. This minimum set must be implemented in an application for it to be considered S/MIME-compliant. Applications can implement additional cryptographic algorithms to meet their customers' needs, but the minimum set must also be present in the applications for interoperability with other S/MIME applications. Thus, users are not forced to use S/MIME-specified algorithms; they can choose their own, but if the application is to be considered S/MIME-compliant, the standard algorithms must also be present.

IETF S/MIME v3 Specifications

Building upon the original work by the IMC-organized group, the IETF has worked hard to enhance the S/MIME v3 specifications. The ultimate goal is to have the S/MIME v3 specifications receive recognition as an Internet standard. The current IETF S/MIME v3 set of specifications includes the following:

- Cryptographic Message Syntax (CMS)
- S/MIME v3 message specification
- S/MIME v3 certificate-handling specification
- Enhanced security services (ESS) for S/MIME

The CMS defines a standard syntax for transmitting cryptographic information about contents of a protected message. Originally based on the PKCS #7 version 1.5 specification, the CMS specification was enhanced by the IETF S/MIME working group to include optional security components. Just as the S/MIME v3 provides backward compatibility with v2, CMS provides backward compatibility with PKCS #7, so applications will be interoperable even if the new components are not implemented in a specific application.

Integrity, authentication, and nonrepudiation security features are provided by using digital signatures using the SignedData syntax described by the CMS. CMS also describes what is known as the EnvelopedData syntax to provide confidentiality of the message's content through the use of encryption. The PKCS #7 specification supports key encryption algorithms, such as RSA. Algorithm independence is promoted through the addition of several fields to the EnvelopedData syntax in CMS, which is the major difference between the PKCS #7 and CMS specifications. The goal was to be able to support specific algorithms such as Diffie-Hellman and the Key Exchange Algorithm (KEA), which is implemented on the Fortezza Crypto Card developed for the DoD. One final significant change to the original specifications is the ability to include X.509 Attribute Certificates in the SignedData and EnvelopedData syntaxes for CMS.

CMS Triple-Encapsulated Message

An interesting feature of CMS is the ability to nest security envelopes to provide a combination of security features. As an example, a CMS triple-encapsulated message can be created in which the original content and associated attributes are signed and encapsulated within the inner SignedData object. The inner SignedData object is in turn encrypted and encapsulated within an EnvelopedData object. The resulting EnvelopedData object is then also signed and finally encapsulated within a second SignedData object, the outer SignedData object. Usually the inner SignedData object is signed by the original user and the outer SignedData object is signed by another entity, such as a firewall or a mail list agent, providing an additional level of security.

This triple encapsulation is not required of every CMS object. All that is required is a single SignedData object created by the user to sign a message or an EnvelopedData object if the user desired to encrypt a message.

■ PGP

Pretty Good Privacy (PGP) is a popular program that is used to encrypt and decrypt e-mail and files. It also provides the ability to digitally sign a message so the receiver can be certain of the sender's identity. Taken together, encrypting and signing a message allows the receiver to be assured of who sent the message and to know that it was not modified during transmission. Public-domain versions of PGP have been available for years, as have inexpensive commercial versions. PGP is one of the most widely used programs and is frequently used by both individuals and businesses to ensure data and e-mail privacy. It was developed by Philip R. Zimmermann in 1991 and quickly became a de facto standard for e-mail security.

How PGP Works

PGP uses a variation of the standard public key encryption process. In public key encryption, an individual (here called the *creator*) uses the encryption program to create a pair of keys. One key is known as the *public key* and is designed to be given freely to others. The other key is called the *private key* and is designed to be known only by the creator. Individuals who want to send a private message to the creator encrypt the message using the creator's public key. The algorithm is designed such that only the private key can decrypt the message, so only the creator will be able to decrypt it.

This method, known as *public key* or *asymmetric encryption*, is time consuming. *Symmetric encryption* uses only a single key and is generally faster. It is because of this that PGP is designed the way it is. PGP uses a symmetric encryption algorithm to encrypt the message to be sent. It then encrypts the symmetric key used to encrypt this message with the public key of the

Tech Tip

A PGP Personal Note

After distributing PGP in 1991, including (indirectly) internationally, Zimmermann became a formal target of a criminal investigation by the U.S. government in 1993 for exporting munitions without a license, because cryptosystems using keys larger than 40 bits were considered "munitions" under U.S. export law. Zimmermann proceeded to publish the entire source code of PGP in a hardback book, which, unlike software, is protected from export laws by the First Amendment of the U.S. Constitution. The investigation of Zimmermann was dropped after several years.

intended recipient. Both the encrypted key and message are then sent. The receiver's version of PGP first decrypts the symmetric key with the private key supplied by the recipient and then uses the resulting decrypted key to decrypt the rest of the message.

PGP can use two different public key algorithms—Rivest-Shamir-Adleman (RSA) and Diffie-Hellman. The RSA version uses the International Data Encryption Algorithm (IDEA) to generate a short symmetric key to be used to encrypt the message and uses RSA to encrypt the short IDEA key. The Diffie-Hellman version uses the Carlisle Adams and Stafford Tavares (CAST) algorithm to encrypt the message and the Diffie-Hellman algorithm to encrypt the CAST key.

To generate a digital signature, PGP takes advantage of another property of public key encryption schemes. Normally, the sender encrypts using the receiver's public key and the message is decrypted at the other end using the receiver's private key. The process can be reversed so that the sender encrypts (signs) with his own private key. The receiver then decrypts the message with the sender's public key. Since the sender is the only individual who has a key that will correctly be decrypted with the sender's public key, the receiver knows that the message was created by the sender who claims to have sent it. The way PGP accomplishes this task is to generate a hash value from the user's name and other signature information. This hash value is then encrypted with the sender's private key known only by the sender. The receiver uses the sender's public key, which is available to everyone, to decrypt the hash value. If the decrypted hash value matches the hash value sent as the digital signature for the message, then the receiver is assured that the message was sent by the sender who claims to have sent it.

Typically, versions of PGP contain a user interface that works with common e-mail programs such as Microsoft Outlook. If you want others to be able to send you an encrypted message, you need to register your public key, generated by your PGP program, with a PGP public key server. Alternatively, you have to either send your public key to all those who want to send you an encrypted message or post your key to some location from which they can download it, such as your web page. Note that using a public key server is the better method, for all the reasons of trust described in the discussion of PKIs in Chapter 6.

Tech Tip

Where Can You Use PGP?

For many years the U.S. government waged a fight over the exportation of PGP technology, and for many years its exportation was illegal. Today, however, PGP encrypted e-mail can be exchanged with most users outside the United States, and many versions of PGP are available from numerous international sites. Of course, being able to exchange PGP-encrypted e-mail requires that the individuals on both sides of the communication have valid versions of PGP. Interestingly, international versions of PGP are just as secure as domestic versions—a feature that is not true of other encryption products. It should be noted that the freeware versions of PGP are not licensed for commercial purposes.

HTTPS

Most web activity occurs using the Hypertext Transfer Protocol (HTTP), but this protocol is prone to interception. HTTPS uses the Secure Sockets Layer (SSL) to transfer information. Originally developed by Netscape Communications and implemented in its browser, HTTPS has since been incorporated into most common browsers. It uses the open standard SSL to encrypt data at the application layer. In addition, HTTPS uses the standard TCP port 443 for TCP/IP communications rather than the standard port 80 used for HTTP. Early HTTPS implementations made use of the 40-bit RC4 encryption algorithm, but with the relaxation of export restrictions, most implementations now use 128-bit encryption.

IPsec

IPsec is a collection of IP security features designed to introduce security at the network or packet-processing layer in network communication. Other approaches have attempted to incorporate security at higher levels of the TCP/IP suite such as at the level where applications reside. IPsec is designed to provide secure IP communications over the Internet. In essence, IPsec provides a secure version of the IP by introducing authentication and encryption to protect layer 4 protocols. IPsec is optional for IPv4 but is required for IPv6. Obviously, both ends of the communication need to use IPsec for the encryption/decryption process to occur.

IPsec provides two types of security service to ensure authentication and confidentiality for either the data alone (referred to as IPsec *transport mode*) or for both the data and header (referred to as *tunnel mode*). See Chapter 11 for more detail on tunneling and IPsec operation. IPsec introduces several new protocols, including the Authentication Header (AH), which basically provides authentication of the sender, and the Encapsulating Security Payload (ESP), which adds encryption of the data to ensure confidentiality. IPsec also provides for payload compression before encryption using the IP Payload Compression Protocol (IPcomp). Frequently, encryption negatively impacts the ability of compression algorithms to fully compress data for transmission. By providing the ability to compress the data before encryption, IPsec addresses this issue.

CEP

Certificate Enrollment Protocol (CEP) was originally developed by VeriSign for Cisco Systems. It was designed to support certificate issuance, distribution, and revocation using existing technologies. Its use has grown in client and CA applications. The operations supported include CA and RA public key distribution, certificate enrollment, certificate revocation, certificate query, and CRL query.

One of the key goals of CEP was to use existing technology whenever possible. It uses both PKCS #7 (Cryptographic Message Syntax Standard) and PKCS #10 (Certification Request Syntax Standard) to define a common message syntax. It supports access to certificates and CRLs using either the Lightweight Directory Access Protocol (LDAP) or the CEP-defined certificate query.

FIPS

The Federal Information Processing Standards Publications (FIPS PUBS or simply FIPS) describe various standards for data communication issues. These documents are issued by the U.S. government through the National Institute of Standards and Technology (NIST), which is tasked with their development. NIST creates these publications when a compelling government need requires a standard for use in areas such as security or system interoperability and no recognized industry standard exists. Three categories of FIPS PUBS are currently maintained by NIST:

- Hardware and software standards/guidelines
- Data standards/guidelines
- Computer security standards/guidelines

These documents require that products sold to the U.S. government comply with one (or more) of the FIPS standards. The standards can be obtained from www.itl.nist.gov/fipspubs.

Common Criteria for Information Technology Security (Common Criteria or CC)

The Common Criteria (CC) is the result of an effort to develop a joint set of security processes and standards that can be used by the international community. The major contributors to the CC are the governments of the United States, Canada, France, Germany, the Netherlands, and the United Kingdom. The CC also provides a listing of laboratories that apply the criteria in testing security products. Products that are evaluated by one of the approved laboratories receive an Evaluation Assurance Level of EAL1 through EAL7 (EAL7 is the highest level), with EAL4, for example, designed for environments requiring a moderate to high level of independently assured security, and EAL1 being designed for environments in which some confidence in the correct operation of the system is required but where the threats to the system are not considered serious. The CC also provides a listing of products by function that have performed at a specific EAL.

WTLS

The **Wireless Transport Layer Security (WTLS)** protocol is based on the Transport Layer Security (TLS) protocol. WTLS provides reliability and security for wireless communications using the **Wireless Application Protocol (WAP)**. WTLS is necessary due to the limited memory and processing abilities of WAP-enabled phones.

WTLS can be implemented in one of three classes: Class 1 is called *anonymous* authentication but is not designed for practical use. Class 2 is called *server* authentication and is the most common model. The clients and server may authenticate using different means. Class 3 is *server and client* authentication. In Class 3 authentication, the client's and server's WTLS certificates are authenticated. Class 3 is the strongest form of authentication and encryption.

PPTP

Point to Point Tunneling Protocol (PPTP) allows the encapsulation of one packet inside another to hide the original packet. Its use is widespread, and it is easy to configure.

WEP

The **Wired Equivalent Privacy (WEP)** algorithm is part of the 802.11 standard and is used to protect wireless communications from interception. A secondary function is to prevent unauthorized access to a wireless network. WEP relies on a secret key that is shared between a mobile station and an access point. In most installations, a single key is used by all of the mobile stations and access points.

WEP Security Issues

In modern corporate environments, it's common for wireless networks to be created in which systems with 802.11 network interface cards communicate with wireless access points that connect the computer to the corporation's network. WEP is an optional security protocol specified in the 802.11 standard and is designed to address the security needs in this wireless environment. It uses a 24-bit initialization vector as a seed value to begin the security association. This, in itself, is a potential security problem because more than 16 million vectors are possible with 24 bits. At the speeds at which modern networks operate, it does not take long for initialization vectors to repeat. The secret key is only 40 bits in length (for 64-bit encryption; 104 bits for 128-bit encryption), which is another problem because it does not take too long to brute-force encryption schemes using key lengths this short.

Some vendors provide 128-bit WEP 2 keys in their products to overcome the short encryption key length, but that only increases the complexity in a linear manner and is almost equally vulnerable. In addition, the WEP keys are static. It is up to the system administrator to change WEP keys manually.

One final problem with WEP is that many wireless network implementations do not even come with WEP enabled. Due to the rapid growth of the wireless industry, standards have not been strongly implemented. WPA and WPA2 of the 802.11i standard provide significantly increased wireless security.

 Cross Check

Wireless Security

Want to understand WEP, WPA, WPA2, and 802.11x in more detail? Flip ahead to Chapter 12 on wireless security for more in-depth discussion. Then answer these questions:

- What is the primary reason for WEP's security weakness?
- What are the differences among each of the 802.11x standards?
- What is the purpose of WPA?

ISO/IEC 27002 (Formerly ISO 17799)

ISO/IEC 27002 is a very popular and detailed standard for creating and implementing security policies. ISO/IEC 27002 was formerly ISO 17799, which was based on version 2 of the British Standard 7799 (BS7799) published in May 1999. With the increased emphasis placed on security in both the government and industry over the last few years, many organizations are now training their audit personnel to evaluate their organizations against the ISO/IEC 27002 standard. The standard is divided into 12 sections, each containing more detailed statements describing what is involved for that topic:

- **Risk assessment**   Determine the impact of risks
- **Security policy**   Guidance and policy provided by management
- **Organization of information security**   Governance structure to implement security policy
- **Asset management**   Inventory and classification of assets
- **Human resources security**   Policies and procedures addressing security for employees including hires, changes, and departures
- **Physical and environmental security**   Protection of the computer facilities
- **Communications and operations management**   Management of technical security controls in systems and networks
- **Access control**   Restriction of access rights to networks, systems, applications, functions, and data
- **Information systems acquisition, development, and maintenance**   Building security into applications
- **Information security incident management**   Anticipating and responding appropriately to information security breaches
- **Business continuity management**   Protecting, maintaining, and recovering business-critical processes and systems
- **Compliance**   Ensuring conformance with information security policies, standards, laws, and regulations

Chapter 7 Review

■ Chapter Summary

After reading this chapter and completing the exercises, you should understand the following about standards and protocols.

Identify the standards involved in establishing an interoperable Internet PKI

- PKIX and PKCS define the most commonly used PKI standards.

- PKIX, PKCS, X.509, ISAKMP, XKMS, and CMP combine to implement PKI.

- SSL/TLS, S/MIME, HTTPS, IPsec, WTLS, PPTP, and WEP are protocols that use PKI.

Explain interoperability issues with PKI standards

- Standards and protocols are important because they define the basis for how communication will take place.

- The use of standards and protocols provides a common, interoperable environment for securely exchanging information.

- Without these standards and protocols, two entities may independently develop their own method to implement the various components for a PKI, and the two will not be compatible.

- On the Internet, not being compatible and not being able to communicate is not an option.

Describe how the common Internet protocols implement the PKI standards

- Three main standards have evolved over time to implement PKIs on the Internet.

- Two of the main standards are based on a third standard, the X.509 standard, and establish complementary standards for implementing PKIs. These two standards are Public Key Infrastructure X.509 (PKIX) and Public Key Cryptography Standards (PKCS).

- PKIX defines standards for interactions and operations for four component types: the user (end-entity), certificate authority (CA), registration authority (RA), and the repository for certificates and certificate revocation lists (CRLs).

- PKCS defines many of the lower-level standards for message syntax, cryptographic algorithms, and the like.

- There are other protocols and standards that help define the management and operation of the PKI and related services, such as ISAKMP, XKMS, and CMP.

- WEP is used to encrypt wireless communications in an 802.11 environment and S/MIME is used to encrypt e-mail.

- SSL, TLS, and WTLS are used for secure packet transmission.

- IPsec and PPTP are used to support virtual private networks.

- The Common Criteria establishes a series of criteria from which security products can be evaluated.

- The ISO/IEC 27002 standard provides a point from which security policies and practices can be developed in ten areas.

- Various types of publications are available from NIST such as those found in the FIPS series.

■ Key Terms

certificate (160)
Certificate Authority (CA) (155)
Certificate Revocation List (CRL) (155)
Internet Security Association and Key Management Protocol (ISAKMP) (162)
IPsec (170)

Point to Point Tunneling Protocol (PPTP) (172)
Pretty Good Privacy (PGP) (168)
public key infrastructure (PKI) (153)
Secure/Multipurpose Internet Mail Extensions (S/MIME) (166)
Secure Sockets Layer (SSL) (161)

■ Key Terms Quiz

Use terms from the Key Terms list to complete the sentences that follow. Don't use the same term more than once. Not all terms will be used.

1. _____ is a protocol used to secure IP packets during transmission across a network. It offers authentication, integrity, and confidentiality services. It uses Authentication Headers (AHs) and Encapsulating Security Payload (ESP) to accomplish this functionality.

2. An encryption capability designed to encrypt above the transport layer, enabling secure sessions between hosts, is called _____.

3. A(n) _____ is an entity that is responsible for issuing and revoking certificates. This term is also applied to server software that provides these services.

4. A digitally signed object that lists all of the current but revoked certificates issued by a given certificate authority is called the _____. It allows users to verify whether a certificate is currently valid even if the expiration date hasn't passed.

5. _____ is a format that has been adopted to standardize digital certificates.

6. Infrastructure for binding a public key to a known user through a trusted intermediary, typically a certificate authority, is called the _____.

7. The _____ is a protocol framework that defines the mechanics of implementing a key exchange protocol and negotiation of a security policy.

8. The encryption protocol that is used on Wireless Application Protocol (WAP) networks is called _____.

9. A protocol for transmitting data to small handheld devices like cellular phones is the _____.

10. _____ is a popular encryption program that has the ability to encrypt and digitally sign e-mail and files.

■ Multiple-Choice Quiz

1. Which organization created PKCS?
   A. OSI
   B. ISO
   C. RSA
   D. IEEE

2. Which of the following is not part of a public key infrastructure?
   A. A substitution cipher
   B. The Certificate Revocation List (CRL)
   C. The Certificate Authority (CA)
   D. Certificates

3. Which of the following is used to grant permissions using rule-based, role-based, and rank-based access controls?
   A. A Qualified Certificate
   B. A Control Certificate
   C. An Attribute Certificate
   D. An Optional Certificate

4. Which of the following is subject to reuse of its initialization vector?
   A. Certificate Enrollment Protocol (CEP)
   B. Wireless Transport Layer Security (WTLS)
   C. Wireless Access Protocol (WAP)
   D. Wired Equivalent Privacy (WEP)

5. Transport Layer Security consists of which two protocols?

    A. The TLS Record Protocol and TLS Handshake Protocol

    B. The TLS Record Protocol and TLS Certificate Protocol

    C. The TLS Certificate Protocol and TLS Handshake Protocol

    D. The TLS Key Protocol and TLS Handshake Protocol

6. Which of the following provides connection security by using common encryption methods?

    A. The TLS Certificate Protocol

    B. The TLS Handshake Protocol

    C. The TLS Key Protocol

    D. The TLS Record Protocol

7. Which of the following provides a method for implementing a key exchange protocol?

    A. EISA

    B. ISAKMP

    C. ISA

    D. ISAKEY

8. Which of the following is a detailed standard for creating and implementing security policies?

    A. PKIX

    B. ISO/IEC 27002

    C. FIPS

    D. X.509

9. A relationship where two or more entities define how they will communicate securely is known as what?

    A. A three-way handshake

    B. A security association

    C. A three-way agreement

    D. A security agreement

10. The entity requesting an SA sets what?

    A. The session number

    B. The session ID

    C. The initiator cookie

    D. The process ID

11. What protocol is used to establish a CA?

    A. The Internet Key Exchange Protocol

    B. The Secure Sockets Layer Protocol

    C. The Public Key Infrastructure Protocol

    D. The Certificate Management Protocol

12. What is the purpose of XKMS?

    A. Extends session associations over many transport protocols

    B. Encapsulates session associations over TCP/IP

    C. Defines services to manage heterogeneous PKI operations via XML

    D. Designed to replace SSL

13. Which of the following is a secure e-mail standard?

    A. POP3

    B. IMAP

    C. SMTP

    D. S/MIME

14. Which of the following is a joint set of security processes and standards used by approved laboratories to award an Evaluation Assurance Level (EAL) from EAL1 to EAL7?

    A. Common Criteria

    B. FIPS

    C. ISO 17700

    D. IEEE X.509

15. Secure Sockets Layer uses what port to communicate?

    A. 53

    B. 80

    C. 143

    D. 443

■ Essay Quiz

1. You are the Information Security Officer at a medium-sized company (1500 employees). The CIO has asked you to explain why you recommend using commercial PKIs rather than implementing such a capability in-house with the software developers you already have. Write three succinct sentences that would get your point across and address three key issues.

2. You're still the Information Security Officer and you're still in the office with the CIO. Even though the Wired Equivalent Privacy (WEP) has some known shortcomings/vulnerabilities, explain to your CIO what you can do with WEP to make your wireless network more secure.

3. Imagine you are a web developer for a small locally owned business. Explain when using HTTP would be satisfactory and why, and when you should use HTTPS and why.

4. Explain in your own words how, by applying both asymmetric and symmetric encryption, your browser uses SSL to protect the privacy of the information passing between your browser and a web server.

5. It is well understood that asymmetric encryption consumes more computing resources than symmetric encryption. Explain how PGP uses both asymmetric and symmetric encryption to be both secure and efficient.

Lab Projects

Note that for these lab projects, it would be best to have a partner so that you can each have your own pair of public/private keys to confirm the operation of PGP.

• Lab Project 7.1

Visit www.pgp.com/downloads/desktoptrial/desktoptrial2.html and download PGP Desktop Trial software (after 30 days the trial software reverts to the equivalent of PGP Freeware). Install it and create a public/private key pair for yourself. Create a document using a word processor and encrypt it using the receiver's public key. Send it to a partner (or yourself) and then decrypt it using the corresponding private key.

• Lab Project 7.2

Create another document different from the one used in Lab Project 7.1. This time use your private key to digitally sign the document and send it to a partner (or yourself) who can then use the public key to confirm that it really is from the indicated sender.

Physical Security

chapter

8

> *If you think technology can solve your security problems, then you don't understand the problems and you don't understand the technology.*
>
> —BRUCE SCHNEIER

In this chapter, you will learn how to

- Describe how physical security directly affects computer and network security
- Discuss steps that can be taken to help mitigate risks
- Identify the different types of fires and the various fire suppression systems designed to limit the damage caused by fires
- Explain electronic access controls and the principles of convergence

For most American homes, locks are the primary means of achieving physical security, and almost every American locks the doors to his or her home upon leaving the residence. Some go even further and set up intrusion alarm systems in addition to locks. All these precautions are considered necessary because people believe they have something significant inside the house that needs to be protected, such as important possessions and important people.

Physical security is an important topic for businesses dealing with the security of networks and information systems. Businesses are responsible for securing their profitability, which requires securing a combination of assets: employees, product inventory, trade secrets, and strategy information. These and other important assets affect the profitability of a company and its future survival. Companies therefore perform many activities to attempt to provide physical security—locking doors, installing alarm systems, using safes, posting security guards, setting access controls, and more.

Most companies today have invested a large amount of time, money, and effort in both network security and information systems security. In this chapter, you will learn about how the strategies for securing the network and for securing information systems are linked, and you'll learn several methods by which companies can minimize their exposure to physical security events that can diminish their network security.

The Security Problem

The problem that faces professionals charged with securing a company's network can be stated rather simply: physical access negates all other security measures. No matter how impenetrable the firewall and intrusion detection system (IDS), if an attacker can find a way to walk up to and touch a server, he can break into it. The more remarkable thing is that gaining physical access to machines in many organizations is not that difficult.

Consider that most network security measures are, from necessity, directed at protecting a company from Internet-based threats. Consequently, a lot of companies allow any kind of traffic on the local area network (LAN). So if an attacker attempts to gain access to a server over the Internet and fails, he may be able to gain physical access to the receptionist's machine and, by quickly compromising it, use it as a remotely controlled zombie to attack what he is really after. Figure 8.1 illustrates the use of a lower-privilege machine to obtain sensitive information. Physically securing information assets doesn't mean just the servers; it means protecting physical access to all the organization's computers and its entire network infrastructure.

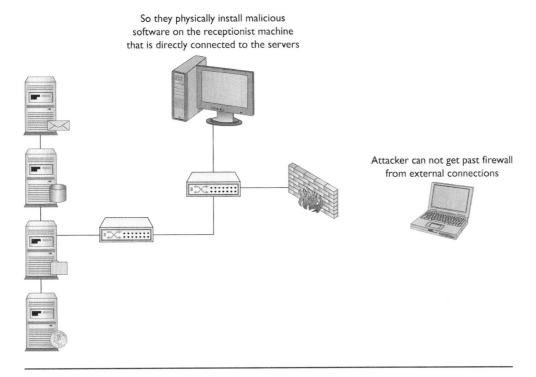

So they physically install malicious software on the receptionist machine that is directly connected to the servers

Attacker can not get past firewall from external connections

• **Figure 8.1**   Using a lower-privilege machine to get at sensitive information

Physical access to a corporation's systems can allow an attacker to perform a number of interesting activities, starting with simply plugging into an open Ethernet jack. The advent of handheld devices with the ability to run operating systems with full networking support has made this attack scenario even more feasible. Prior to handheld devices, the attacker would have to work in a secluded area with dedicated access to the Ethernet for a time. The attacker would sit down with a laptop and run a variety of tools against the network, and working internally typically put the attacker inside the firewall and IDS. Today's capable personal digital assistants (PDAs) can assist these efforts by allowing attackers to place the small device onto the network to act as a *wireless bridge*, as shown in Figure 8.2.

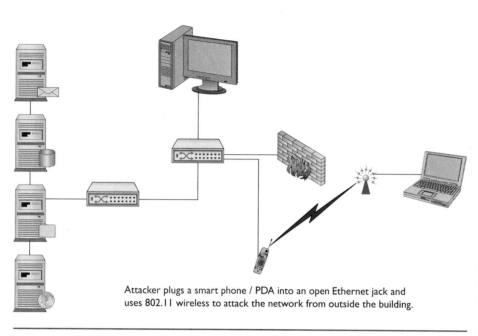

Attacker plugs a smart phone / PDA into an open Ethernet jack and uses 802.11 wireless to attack the network from outside the building.

• **Figure 8.2**   A wireless bridge can allow remote access.

The attacker can then use a laptop to attack a network remotely via the bridge from outside the building. If power is available near the Ethernet jack, this type of attack can also be accomplished with an off-the-shelf access point. The attacker's only challenge is finding an Ethernet jack that isn't covered by furniture or some other obstruction.

Another simple attack that can be used when an attacker has physical access is called a **bootdisk**. Any media used to boot a computer into an operating system that is not the native OS on its hard drive could be classified as a bootdisk. These can be in the form of a floppy disk, CD, DVD, or a USB flash drive. As the new Blu-ray standard becomes more popular, we may see bootable media for that as well. Before bootable CDs or DVDs were available, a boot floppy was used to start the system and prepare the hard drives to load the operating system. Since some machines still have floppy drives, boot floppies might still be used. These floppies can contain a number of programs, but the most typical ones would be NTFSDOS or a floppy-based Linux distribution that can be used to perform a number of tasks, including mounting the hard drives and performing at least read operations. Once an attacker is able to read a hard drive, the password file can be copied off the machine for offline password-cracking attacks. If write access to the drive is obtained, the attacker could alter the password file or place a remote-control program to be executed automatically upon the next boot, guaranteeing continued access to the machine. Most new machines do not include floppy drives, so this attack is rapidly being replaced by the same concept with a CD or DVD.

The bootable CD-ROMs and DVD-ROMs are actually more of a threat, because they can carry a variety of software and can utilize the much greater storage capacity of the CD or DVD media. This capacity can store an entire operating system and a complete tool set for a variety of tasks. An operating system designed to run the entire machine from an optical disc without using the hard drive is commonly referred to as a LiveCD. A **LiveCD** contains a bootable version of an entire operating system, typically a variant of Linux, complete with drivers for most devices. LiveCDs give an attacker a greater array of tools than could be loaded onto a floppy disk, such as scanners, sniffers, vulnerability exploits, forensic tools, drive imagers, password crackers, and so on. These sets of tools are too numerous to list them all here and are changing every day. The best resource is to search the Internet for popular LiveCD distributions like BackTrack, knoppix, and PHLAK. A sample collection of LiveCDs is shown in Figure 8.3.

For example, with a LiveCD an attacker would likely have access to the hard disk and also to an operational network interface that would allow him to send the drive data over the Internet if properly connected. These bootable operating systems could also be custom built to contain any tool that runs under Linux, allowing an attacker to build a standard bootable attack image or a standard bootable forensics image, or something customized for the tools he likes to use.

The use of bootdisks, whether floppy based or disc based, leads to the next area of concern: an attacker creating an image of the hard drive for later investigation. Some form of bootable media is often used to load the imaging software.

Drive imaging is the process of copying the entire contents of a hard drive to a single file on a different media. This process is often used by people who perform forensic investigations of computers. Typically, a bootable media is used to start the computer and load the drive imaging software. This software is designed to make a bit-by-bit copy of the hard drive in a file on another media, usually another hard drive or CD-R/DVD-R media. Drive imaging is used in investigations to make an exact copy that can be observed and taken apart, while keeping the original exactly as it was for evidence purposes.

From an attacker's perspective, drive imaging software is useful because it pulls *all* information from a computer's hard drive while still leaving the machine in its original state. The information contains every bit of data that is on the computer: any locally stored documents, locally stored e-mails, and every other piece of information that the hard drive contains. This data could be very valuable if the machine holds sensitive information about the company.

Try This

Create a Bootdisk

Bootdisks allow you to boot a computer to the disk rather than the OS that is on the hard drive. Create a bootdisk for your own personal computer. The steps differ between different OSs and depending upon the media that you wish to make bootable. Making a floppy disk into a bootdisk is the easiest, followed by CDs and DVDs, and then USB flash drives. Perform a little research to determine the correct procedure for your OS and give it a try.

• **Figure 8.3**   A collection of sample LiveCDs

Exam Tip: Drive imaging is a threat because all existing access controls to data can be bypassed and all the data stored on the drive can be read from the image.

Tech Tip

Encryption to TPM-Based Keys

Some newer PCs come with a security chip that follows the Trusted Platform Module standard. This TPM chip allows for the creation and storage of encryption keys. One of the strengths associated with this level of security is that if a copy of a drive, or even the drive itself, is stolen, the contents are unusable without the key. Having this key locked in hardware prevents hackers from stealing a copy of the key from a memory location.

Physical access is the most common way of imaging a drive, and the biggest benefit for the attacker is that drive imaging leaves absolutely no trace of the crime. Besides physically securing access to your computers, you can do very little to prevent drive imaging, but you can minimize its impact. The use of encryption even for a few important files provides protection. Full encryption of the drive protects all files stored on it. Alternatively, placing files on a centralized file server keeps them from being imaged from an individual machine, but if an attacker is able to image the file server, the data will be copied.

An even simpler version of the drive imaging attack is to steal the computer outright. Computer theft typically occurs for monetary gain—the thief's goal being to sell the computer itself. We're concerned here with the theft of a computer to obtain the data it holds, however. While physical thievery is not a technical attack, it is often carried out in conjunction with a bit of social engineering—for example, the thief might appear to be a legitimate computer repair person and may be allowed to walk out of the building with a laptop or other system in his possession. For anyone who discounts this type of attack, consider this incident: In Australia, two individuals entered a government computer room and managed to walk off with two large servers. They not only escaped with two valuable computers, but they got the data they contained as well. In more unusual cases, thieves will open the case and steal the hard drive. While some cases include switches and CMOS settings to indicate that the case has been opened, this type of attack can only be mitigated through drive encryption.

Many of the methods mentioned so far can be used to perform a denial-of-service (DoS) attack. Physical access to the computers can be much more effective than a network-based DoS attack. Stealing a computer, using a bootdisk to erase all data on the drives, or simply unplugging computers are all effective DoS attacks. Depending on the company's quality and frequency of backing up critical systems, a DoS attack can have lasting effects.

Physical access can negate almost all the security that the network attempts to provide. Considering this, you must determine the level of physical access that attackers might obtain. Of special consideration are persons with authorized access to the building but who are not authorized users of the systems. Janitorial personnel and others have authorized access to many areas, but they do not have authorized system access. An attacker could pose as one of these individuals or attempt to gain access to the facilities through them.

Physical Security Safeguards

While it is difficult, if not impossible, to make an organization's computer systems totally secure, many steps can be taken to mitigate the risk to information systems from a physical threat. The following sections discuss policies and procedures that should be implemented as well as access control methods. Then the chapter explores various authentication methods and how they can help protect against physical threats.

Walls and Guards

The primary defense against a majority of physical attacks are the barriers between the assets and a potential attacker—walls, fences, gates, and doors. Some organizations also employ full- or part-time private security staff to attempt to protect their assets. These barriers provide the foundation upon which all other security initiatives are based, but the security must be designed carefully, as an attacker has to find only a single gap to gain access.

• A gated access featuring cameras and a guardhouse

Exam Tip: All entry points to server rooms and wiring closets should be closely controlled, and, if possible, access should be logged through an access control system.

Another method of preventing surreptitious access is through the use of windows. Many high-security areas have a significant number of windows so that people's activities within the area can't be hidden. A closed server room with no windows makes for a quiet place for someone to achieve physical access to a device without worry of being seen. Windows remove this privacy element that many criminals depend upon to achieve their entry and illicit activities.

The bigger challenge associated with capturing surveillance or other attempted break-in efforts is their clandestine nature. These efforts are designed to be as low profile and nonobvious as possible to increase the chances of success. Training and awareness is necessary not just for security personnel but for all personnel. If an employee hears multiple extensions all start ringing in the middle of the night, do they know who to notify? If a security guard notes such activity, how does this information get reported to the correct team?

Walls may have been one of the first inventions of man. Once he learned to use natural obstacles such as mountains to separate him from his enemy, he next learned to build his *own* mountain for the same purpose. Hadrian's Wall in England, the Great Wall of China, and the Berlin Wall are all famous examples of such basic physical defenses. The walls of any building serve the same purpose, but on a smaller scale: they provide barriers to physical access to company assets. In the case of information assets, as a general rule the most valuable assets are contained on company servers. To protect the physical servers, you must look in all directions: Doors and windows should be safeguarded and a minimum number of each should be used in a server room. Less obvious entry points should also be considered: Is a drop ceiling used in the server room? Do the interior walls extend to the actual roof, raised floors, or crawlspaces? Access to the server room should be limited to the people who need access, not to all employees of the organization. If you are going to use a wall to protect an asset, make sure no obvious holes appear in that wall.

Guards provide an excellent security measure, because guards are a visible presence with direct responsibility for security. Other employees expect security guards to behave a certain way with regard to securing the facility. Guards typically monitor entrances and exits and can maintain access logs of who has entered and departed the building. Everyone who passes through security as a visitor should sign the log, which can be useful in tracing who was at what location and why.

Security personnel are helpful in physically securing the machines on which information assets reside, but to get the most benefit from their presence, they must be trained to take a holistic approach to security. The value of data typically can be many times that of the machines on which the data is stored. Security guards typically are not computer security experts, so they need to be educated about the value of the data and be trained in network security as well as physical security involving users. They are the company's eyes and ears for suspicious activity, so the network security department needs to train them to notice suspicious network activity as well. Multiple extensions ringing in sequence during the night, computers rebooting all at once, or strange people parked in the parking lot with laptop computers are all indicators of a network attack that might be missed without proper training.

Many traditional physical security tools such as access controls and CCTV camera systems are transitioning from closed hardwired systems to Ethernet- and IP-based systems. This transition opens up the devices to network attacks traditionally performed on computers. With physical security systems being implemented using the IP network, everyone in physical security must become smarter about network security.

Policies and Procedures

A policy's effectiveness depends on the culture of an organization, so all of the policies mentioned here should be followed up by functional procedures that are designed to implement them. Physical security **policies and procedures** relate to two distinct areas: those that affect the computers themselves and those that affect users.

To mitigate the risk to computers, physical security needs to be extended to the computers themselves. To combat the threat of bootdisks, begin by removing or disabling the floppy drive from any desktop system that has but does not require it. The continuing advance of hard drive capacity has pushed file sizes beyond what floppies can typically hold. LANs with constant Internet connectivity have made network services the focus of how files are moved and distributed. These two factors have reduced floppy usage to the point where computer manufacturers are making floppy drives accessory options instead of standard features (see Figure 8.4).

The second boot device to consider is the CD/DVD drive. This device can probably also be removed from or disabled on a number of machines. A DVD not only can be used as a boot device, but also can be exploited via the **autorun** feature that some operating systems support. Autorun was designed as a convenience for users, so that when a CD containing an application is inserted, the computer instantly prompts for input versus requiring the user to explore the CD filesystem and find the executable file. Unfortunately, since the autorun file runs an executable, it can be programmed to do anything an attacker wants. If autorun is programmed maliciously, it could run an executable that installs malicious code that could allow an attacker to later gain remote control of the machine. Figure 8.5 illustrates an autorun message prompt in Windows Vista, giving a user at least minimal control over whether to run an item or not.

Since the optical drive can be used as a boot device, a CD loaded with its own operating system (called a *LiveCD*) could be used to boot the computer with malicious system code (see Figure 8.6). This separate

• **Figure 8.4**   The nearly obsolete floppy disk

• **Figure 8.5**   Autorun on a Vista system

• **Figure 8.6**   A LiveCD boots its own OS and bypasses any built-in security of the native operating system.

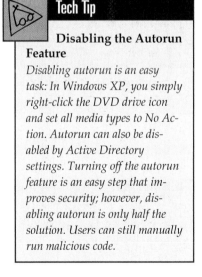

Tech Tip

Disabling the Autorun Feature
Disabling autorun is an easy task: In Windows XP, you simply right-click the DVD drive icon and set all media types to No Action. Autorun can also be disabled by Active Directory settings. Turning off the autorun feature is an easy step that improves security; however, disabling autorun is only half the solution. Users can still manually run malicious code.

operating system will bypass any passwords on the host machine and can access locally stored files.

Some users will undoubtedly insist on having DVD drives in their machines, but, if possible, the drives should be removed from every machine. If removal is not feasible, particularly on machines that require CD-ROM/DVD use, you can remove the optical drive from the boot sequence in the computer's BIOS. While this operation depends on the BIOS software of the individual machine, one step that must also be taken is to set a BIOS password. Nearly all BIOS software will support password protection that allows you to boot the machine but requires a password to edit any BIOS settings. While disabling the optical drive and setting a BIOS password are both good measures, do not depend on this strategy exclusively because, in some cases, BIOS manufacturers will have a default BIOS password that still works.

Try This

Exploring Your BIOS Settings

Next time you boot your PC, explore the BIOS settings. Usually, pressing the F2 key immediately on power-up will allow you to enter the BIOS setup screens. Most PCs will also have a brief time when they prompt for "Setup" and give a key to press, most commonly F2. Explore elements such as the boot order for devices, options for adding passwords, and other options. For safety, do not save changes unless you are absolutely certain that you want to make those changes and are aware of the consequences.

Depending upon BIOS passwords is also not a guaranteed security measure. For many machines, it is trivial to remove and then replace the BIOS battery, which will reset the BIOS to the "no password" or default password state.

To prevent an attacker from editing the boot order, you should set **BIOS passwords**. These passwords should be unique to the machine and, if possible, complex, using multiple upper- and lowercase characters as well as numerics. Considering how rarely these passwords will be used, it is a good idea to list them all in an encrypted file so that a master passphrase will provide access to them.

As mentioned, floppy drives are being eliminated from manufacturers' machines because of their limited usefulness, but new devices are being adopted in their place, such as **USB devices**, as illustrated in Figure 8.7.

• **Figure 8.7**   Assorted USB drives

Principles of Computer Security: CompTIA Security+ and Beyond

USB ports have greatly expanded users' ability to connect devices to their computers. USB ports automatically recognize a device being plugged into the system and usually work without the user needing to add drivers or configure software. This has spawned a legion of USB devices, from MP3 players to CD burners.

The most interesting of these, for security purposes, are the USB flash memory–based storage devices. USB drive keys, which are basically flash memory with a USB interface in a device about the size of your thumb, provide a way to move files easily from computer to computer. When plugged into a USB port, these devices automount and behave like any other drive attached to the computer. Their small size and relatively large capacity, coupled with instant read-write ability, present security problems. They can easily be used by an individual with malicious intent to conceal the removal of files or data from the building or to bring malicious files into the building and onto the company network.

In addition, well-intentioned users could accidentally introduce malicious code from USB devices by using them on an infected home machine and then bringing the infected device to the office, allowing the malware to bypass perimeter protections and possibly infect the organization. If USB devices are allowed, aggressive virus scanning should be implemented throughout the organization. The devices can be disallowed via Active Directory policy settings or with a Windows Registry key entry. USB can also be completely disabled, either through BIOS settings or by unloading and disabling the USB drivers from users' machines, either of which will stop all USB devices from working—however, doing this can create more trouble if users have USB keyboards and mice. Editing the Registry key is probably the most effective solution for users who are not authorized to use these devices. Users who do have authorization for USB drives must be educated about the potential dangers of their use.

The outright theft of a computer is a simple physical attack. This attack can be mitigated in a number of ways, but the most effective method is to lock up equipment that contains important data. Insurance can cover the loss of the physical equipment, but this can do little to get a business up and running again quickly after a theft. Therefore, implementing special access controls for server rooms and simply locking the racks when maintenance is not being performed are good ways to secure an area. From a data standpoint, mission-critical or high-value information should be stored on a server only. This can mitigate the risk of a desktop or laptop being stolen for the data it contains. Loss of laptops has been the cause of multiple recent information breaches, including the loss of personal information by the U.S. Department of Veterans Affairs and the loss of employee information by Hewlett-Packard.

Users are often mentioned as the "weakest link in the security chain," and that can also apply to physical security. Fortunately, in physical security, users are often one of the primary beneficiaries of the security itself. A security program protects a company's information assets, but it also protects the people of the organization. A good security program will provide tangible benefits to employees, helping them to support and reinforce the security program. Users need to be aware of security issues, and they need to be involved in security enforcement. A healthy company culture of security will go a long way toward assisting in this effort. If, for example,

Exam Tip: USB devices can be used to inject malicious code onto any machine to which they are attached. They can be used to transport malicious code from machine to machine without using the network.

Laptops are popular targets for thieves and should be locked inside a desk when not in use, or secured with special computer lockdown cables. Laptop thefts from cars can occur in seconds, and thieves have been caught taking them from security screening areas at airports while the owner was distracted in screening. If desktop towers are used, use computer desks that provide a space in which to lock the computer. All of these measures can improve the physical security of the computers themselves, but most of them can be defeated by attackers if users are not knowledgeable about the security program and do not follow it.

workers in the office notice an unfamiliar person visiting their work areas, they should challenge the individual's presence—this is especially important if visitor badges are required for entry to the facility. A policy of requiring employees to wear a visible badge with the employee's photo on it also assists everyone in recognizing people who do not belong. Users should be briefed on the proper departments or personnel to contact when they suspect a security violation. Users can perform one of the most simple, yet important, information security tasks: lock a workstation immediately before they step away from it.

Please swipe your finger.
Computer is locked
Press ESC for the Welcome screen

Other Credentials

Windows Vista Ultimate

• A biometric-based lockout screen in Vista

Although use of a self-locking screensaver is a good policy, setting it to lock at any point less than 10 to 15 minutes after becoming idle is often counterproductive to active use of the computer on the job as the computer will often lock while the employee is still actively using the computer. Thus, computers typically sit idle for at least 15 minutes before automatically locking under this type of policy. An attacker only needs to be lucky enough to catch a machine that has been left alone for 5 minutes.

It is also important to screen new employees as well as workers who typically are overlooked in the organization, such as third-party contractors. New hires should undergo a background check before being given access to network resources. This policy should also apply to all personnel who will have unescorted physical access to the facility, including janitorial and maintenance workers.

Access Controls and Monitoring

Access control means control of doors and entry points. The design and construction of all types of access control systems, as well as the physical barriers to which they are most complementary, are fully discussed in other texts. Here, we explore a few important points to help you safeguard the information infrastructure, especially where it meets with the physical access control system. This section talks about layered access systems and electronic door control systems. It also discusses closed circuit television (CCTV) systems and the implications of different CCTV system types.

Locks have been discussed as a primary element of security. Although locks have been used for hundreds of years, their design has not changed much: a metal "token" is used to align pins in a mechanical device. As all mechanical devices have tolerances, it is possible to *sneak through* these tolerances by "picking" the lock. Most locks can be easily picked with simple tools, some of which are shown in Figure 8.8.

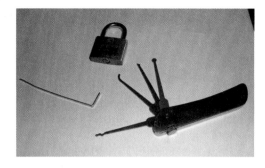

● **Figure 8.8** Lockpicking tools

As we humans are always trying to build a better mousetrap, high-security locks have been designed to defeat attacks, such as the one shown in Figure 8.9; these locks are more sophisticated than a standard home deadbolt system. Typically found in commercial applications that require high security, these locks are produced by two primary manufacturers: Medeco and ASSA. (Medeco's locks, for example, require that the pins in the lock not only be set to a specific depth, but also individually rotated to set direction: left, right, or center.)

High-end lock security is more important now that attacks such as "bump keys" are well known and widely available. A bump key is a key cut with all notches to the maximum depth, also known as "all nines." This key uses a technique that has be around a long time, but has recently gained a lot of popularity. The key is inserted into the lock and then sharply struck, bouncing the lock pins up above the shear line and allowing the lock to open.

● **Figure 8.9** A high-security lock and its key

Layered access is an important concept in security. It is often mentioned in conversations about network security perimeters, but in this chapter it relates to the concept of physical security perimeters. To help prevent an attacker from gaining access to important assets, these assets should be placed inside multiple perimeters. Servers should be placed in a separate secure area, ideally with a separate authentication mechanism. For example, if an organization has an electronic door control system using **contactless access cards** (such as the example shown in Figure 8.10) as well as a keypad, a combination of the card and a separate PIN code would be required to open the door to the server room.

Access to the server room should be limited to staff with a legitimate need to work on the servers. To layer the protection, the area surrounding the server room should also be limited to people who need to work in that area.

Many organizations use electronic access control systems to control the opening of doors. Doorways are electronically controlled via electronic door strikes and magnetic locks. These devices rely on an electronic signal from the control panel to release the mechanism that keeps the door closed. These devices are integrated into an access control system that controls and logs entry into all the doors connected to

● **Figure 8.10** Contactless access cards act as modern keys to a building.

it, typically through the use of access tokens. Security is improved by having a centralized system that can instantly grant or refuse access based upon a token that is given to the user. This kind of system also logs user access, providing nonrepudiation of a specific user's presence in a controlled environment. The system will allow logging of personnel entry, auditing of personnel movements, and real-time monitoring of the access controls.

One caution about these kinds of systems is that they usually work with a software package that runs on a computer, and as such this computer should not be attached to the company network. While attaching it to the network can allow easy administration, the last thing you want is for an attacker to have control of the system that allows physical access to your facility. With this control, an attacker could input the ID of a badge that she owns, allowing full, legitimate access to an area the system controls. Another problem with such a system is that it logs only the person who initially used the card to open the door—so no logs exist for doors that are propped open to allow others access, or of people "tailgating" through a door opened with a card. The implementation of a **mantrap** is one way to combat tailgating. A mantrap comprises two doors closely spaced that require the user to card through one and then the other *sequentially*. Mantraps make it nearly impossible to trail through a doorway undetected—if you happen to catch the first door, you will be trapped in by the second door.

Closed circuit television (CCTV) cameras are similar to the door control systems—they can be very effective, but how they are implemented is an important consideration. The use of CCTV cameras for surveillance purposes dates back to at least 1961, when cameras were installed in the London Transport train station. The development of smaller camera components and lower costs has caused a boon in the CCTV industry since then.

Traditional cameras are analog based and require a video multiplexer to combine all the signals and make multiple views appear on a monitor. IP-based cameras are changing that, as most of them are standalone units viewable through a web browser, such as the camera shown in Figure 8.11.

These IP-based systems add useful functionality, such as the ability to check on the building from the Internet. This network functionality, however, makes the cameras subject to normal IP-based network attacks. A DoS attack launched at the CCTV system just as a break-in is occurring is the last thing that anyone would want (other than the criminals). For this reason, IP-based CCTV cameras should be placed on their own physically separate network that can be accessed only by security personnel. The same physical separation applies to any IP-based camera infrastructure. Older time-lapse tape recorders are slowly being replaced with digital video recorders. While the advance in technology is significant, be careful if and when these devices become IP-enabled, since they will become a security issue, just like everything else that touches the network.

If you depend on the CCTV system to protect your organization's assets, carefully consider camera placement and the type of cameras used. Different iris types, focal lengths, and color or infrared capabilities are all options that make one camera superior over another in a specific location.

The issues discussed so far are especially prevalent when physical access control devices are connected to network resources. But no access controls, network or physical, work without some form of authentication.

● **Figure 8.11** IP-based cameras leverage existing IP networks instead of needing a proprietary CCTV cable.

Environmental Controls

While the confidentiality of information is important, so is its availability. Sophisticated environmental controls are needed for current data centers. Fire suppression is also an important consideration when dealing with information systems.

Heating ventilating and air conditioning (HVAC) systems are critical for keeping data centers cool, because typical servers put out between 1000 and 2000 BTUs of heat.

Enough servers in a confined area will create conditions too hot for the machines to continue to operate. The failure of HVAC systems for any reason is cause for concern. Properly securing these systems is important in helping prevent an attacker from performing a physical DoS attack on your servers.

Fire Suppression

According to the Fire Suppression Systems Association (www.fssa.net), 43 percent of businesses that close as a result of a significant fire never reopen. An additional 29 percent fail within three years of the event. The ability to respond to a fire quickly and effectively is thus critical to the long-term success of any organization. Addressing potential fire hazards and vulnerabilities has long been a concern of organizations in their risk analysis process. The goal obviously should be never to have a fire, but in the event that one does occur, it is important that mechanisms are in place to limit the damage the fire can cause.

Water-Based Fire Suppression Systems

Water-based fire suppression systems have long been, and still are today, the primary tool to address and control structural fires. Considering the amount of electrical equipment found in today's office environment and the fact that, for obvious reasons, this equipment does not react well to large applications of water, it is important to know what to do with equipment if it does become subjected to a water-based sprinkler system. The 2009 *NFPA 75: Standard for the Protection of Information Technology Equipment* outlines measures that can be taken to minimize the damage to electronic equipment exposed to water. This guidance includes these suggestions:

- Open cabinet doors, remove side panels and covers, and pull out chassis drawers to allow water to run out of equipment.

- Set up fans to move room-temperature air through the equipment for general drying. Move portable equipment to dry air-conditioned areas.

- Use compressed air at no higher than 50 psi to blow out trapped water.

- Use handheld dryers on lowest setting to dry connectors, backplane wirewraps, and printed circuit cards.

BTU stands for British Thermal Unit; a single BTU is defined as the amount of energy required to raise the temperature of one pound of liquid water one degree Fahrenheit.

Tech Tip

Environment and Fires

While it may at first seem to the security professional that environmental controls and natural disasters such as fires don't have anything to do with computer security, think of it in terms of availability. If the goal of the attacker is not information but rather to deny an organization the use of its resources, environmental factors, and disasters such as fires, can be used to deny the target the use of its own computing resources. This, then, becomes a security issue as well as an operational issue.

Keep the dryer well away from components and wires. Overheating of electrical components can cause permanent damage.

The NFPA 75 list outlined here provides useful guidance. Users will probably not see wirewrap terminals, and other compounds are now available to replace the Freon-alcohol mixture described. Overall, however, the guidance is still sound and provides a useful starting point to begin cleanup operations from.

■ Use cotton-tipped swabs for hard-to-reach places. Lightly dab the surfaces to remove residual moisture. Do not use cotton-tipped swabs on wirewrap terminals.

■ Water-displacement aerosol sprays containing Freon-alcohol mixtures are effective as a first step in drying critical components. Follow up with professional restoration as soon as possible.

Even if these guidelines are followed, damage to the systems may have already occurred. Since water is so destructive to electronic equipment, not only because of the immediate problems of electronic shorts to the system but also because of longer-term corrosive damage water can cause, alternative fire suppression methods have been sought. One of the more common alternative methods used was halon-based systems.

Halon-Based Fire Suppression Systems

A fire needs fuel, oxygen, and high temperatures for the chemical combustion to occur. If you remove any of these, the fire will not continue. Halon interferes with the chemical combustion present in a fire. Even though halon production was banned in 1994, a number of these systems still exist today. They were originally popular because halon will mix quickly with the air in a room and will not cause harm to computer systems. Halon is also dangerous to humans, especially when subjected to extremely hot temperatures (such as might be found during a fire), when it can degrade into other toxic chemicals. As a result of these dangers, and also because halon has been linked with the issue of ozone depletion, halon is banned in new fire suppression systems. It is important to note that under the Environmental Protection Agency (EPA) rules that mandated no further production of halon, existing systems were not required to be destroyed. Replacing the halon in a discharged system, however, will be a problem, since only existing stockpiles of halon may be used and the cost is becoming prohibitive. For this reason, many organizations are switching to alternative solutions. These alternatives are known as *clean-agent fire suppression systems*, since they not only provide fire suppression capabilities but also protect the contents of the room, including people, documents, and electronic equipment. Examples of clean agents include carbon dioxide, argon, Inergen, and FM-200 (heptafluoropropane).

Clean-Agent Fire Suppression Systems

Carbon dioxide (CO_2) has been used as a fire suppression agent for a long time. The Bell Telephone Company used portable CO_2 extinguishers in the early part of the 20th century. Carbon dioxide extinguishers attack all three necessary elements for a fire to occur. CO_2 displaces oxygen so that the amount of oxygen remaining is insufficient to sustain the fire. It also provides some cooling in the fire zone and reduces the concentration of "gasified" fuel. Argon extinguishes fire by lowering the oxygen concentration below the 15 percent level required for combustible items to burn. Argon systems are designed to reduce the oxygen content to about 12.5 percent, which is below the 15 percent needed for the fire but is still above the 10 percent required by the EPA for human safety. Inergen, a product of

Ansul Corporation, is composed of three gases: 52 percent nitrogen, 40 percent argon, and 8 percent carbon dioxide. In a manner similar to pure argon systems, Inergen systems reduce the level of oxygen to about 12.5 percent, which is sufficient for human safety but not sufficient to sustain a fire. Another chemical used to phase out halon is FE-13, or trifluoromethane. This chemical was originally developed as a chemical refrigerant and works to suppress fires by inhibiting the combustion chain reaction. FE-13 is gaseous, leaves behind no residue that would harm equipment, and is considered safe to use in occupied areas. Other Halocarbons are also approved for use in replacing halon systems, including FM-200 (heptafluoropropane), a chemical used as a propellant for asthma medication dispensers.

Try This

Handheld Fire Extinguishers

Computer security professionals typically do not have much influence over the type of fire suppression system that their office includes. It is, however, important that they are aware of what type has been installed, what they should do in case of an emergency, and what needs to be done to recover after the release of the system. One area that they can influence, however, is the type of handheld fire extinguisher that is located in their area. Check your facility to see what type of fire suppression system is installed. Also check to see where the fire extinguishers are in your office and what type of fires they are designed to handle.

Handheld Fire Extinguishers

Automatic fire suppression systems designed to discharge when a fire is detected are not the only systems you should be aware of. If a fire can be caught and contained before the automatic systems discharge, it can mean significant savings to the organization in terms of both time and equipment costs (including the recharging of the automatic system). Handheld extinguishers are common in offices, but the correct use of them must be understood or disaster can occur. There are four different types of fire, as shown in Table 8.1. Each type of fire has its own fuel source and method for extinguishing it. Type A systems, for example, are designed to extinguish fires with normal combustible material as the fire's source. Water can be used in an extinguisher of this sort, since it is effective against fires of this type. Water, as we've discussed, is not appropriate for fires involving wiring or electrical equipment. Using a type A extinguisher against an electrical fire will not only be ineffective but can result in additional damage. Some

 Exam Tip: The type of fire distinguishes the type of extinguisher that should be used to suppress it. Remember that the most common type is the ABC fire extinguisher, which is designed to handle all types of fires except flammable-metal fires, which are rare.

Table 8.1		Types of Fire and Suppression Methods	
Class of Fire	**Type of Fire**	**Examples of Combustible Materials**	**Example Suppression Method**
A	Common combustibles	Wood, paper, cloth, plastics	Water or dry chemical
B	Combustible liquids	Petroleum products, organic solvents	CO_2 or dry chemical
C	Electrical	Electrical wiring and equipment, power tools	CO_2 or dry chemical
D	Flammable metals	Magnesium, titanium	Copper metal or sodium chloride

extinguishers are designed to be effective against more than one type of fire, such as the common ABC fire extinguishers. This is probably the best type of system to have in a data processing facility. All fire extinguishers should be easily accessible and should be clearly marked. Before anybody uses an extinguisher, they should know what type of extinguisher it is and what the source of the fire is. When in doubt, evacuate and let the fire department handle the situation.

Fire Detection Devices

An essential complement to fire suppression systems and devices are fire detection devices (fire detectors). Detectors may be able to detect a fire in its very early stages, before a fire suppression system is activated, and sound a warning that potentially enables employees to address the fire before it becomes serious enough for the fire suppression equipment to kick in.

There are several different types of fire detectors. One type, of which there are two varieties, is activated by smoke. The two varieties of smoke detector are ionization and photoelectric. A photoelectric detector is good for potentially providing advance warning of a smoldering fire. This type of device monitors an internal beam of light. If something degrades the light, for example by obstructing it, the detector assumes it is something like smoke and the alarm sounds. An ionization style of detector uses an ionization chamber and a small radioactive source to detect fast-burning fires. Shown in Figure 8.12, the chamber consists of two plates, one with a positive charge and one with a negative charge. Oxygen and nitrogen particles in the air become "ionized" (an ion is freed from the molecule). The freed ion, which has a negative charge, is attracted to the positive plate, and the remaining part of the molecule, now with a positive charge, is attracted to the negative plate. This movement of particles creates a very small electric current that the device measures. Smoke inhibits this process, and the detector will detect the resulting drop in current and sound an alarm. Both of these devices are often referred to generically as smoke detectors, and combinations of both varieties are possible. For more information on smoke detectors, see http://home.howstuffworks.com/home-improvement/household-safety/fire/smoke2.htm.

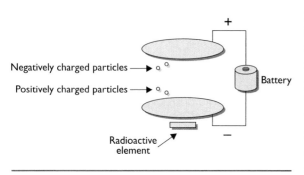

Negatively charged particles

Positively charged particles

Battery

Radioactive element

• **Figure 8.12** An ionization chamber for an ionization type of smoke detector

Another type of fire detector is activated by heat. These devices also come in two varieties. Fixed-temperature or fixed-point devices activate if the temperature in the area ever exceeds some predefined level. Rate-of-rise or rate-of-increase temperature devices activate when there is a sudden increase in local temperature that may indicate the beginning stages of a fire. Rate-of-rise sensors can provide an earlier warning but are also responsible for more false warnings.

A third type of detector is flame activated. This type of device relies on the flames from the fire to provide a change in the infrared energy that can be detected. Flame-activated devices are generally more expensive than the other two types but can frequently detect a fire sooner.

Authentication

Authentication is the process by which a user proves that she is who she says she is. Authentication is performed to allow or deny a person access to a physical space. The heart of any access control system is to allow access to authorized users and to make sure access is denied to unauthorized people. Authentication is required because many companies have grown so large that not every employee knows every other employee, making it difficult to tell by sight who is supposed to be where.

Electronic access control systems were spawned from the need to have more logging and control than provided by the older method of metallic keys. Most electronic systems currently use a token-based card that if passed near a reader, and if you have permission from the system, will unlock the door strike and let you pass into the area. Newer technology attempts to make the authentication process easier and more secure.

Authentication can traditionally be separated into four broad categories: something you have, something you are, something you know, and, less utilized, somewhere you are. Tokens are examples of something you have, biometrics measure something you are, and password-style systems demonstrate something you know. The somewhere you are is more complicated; at a basic level, it prohibits two logins from different areas, or the login from a country or location you could not possibly be in. The combination of two or more of these systems is known as multiple-factor authentication. Authentication is described in detail in Chapter 11.

The following sections discuss how tokens and biometrics are being used for authentication. It also looks into how multiple-factor authentication can be used for physical access.

Access Tokens

Access tokens are defined as "something you have." An access token is a physical object that identifies specific access rights. Your house key, for example, is a basic physical access token that allows you access into your home. Although keys have been used to unlock devices for centuries, they do have several limitations. Keys are paired exclusively with a lock or a set of locks, and they are not easily changed. It is easy to add an authorized user by giving the user a copy of the key, but it is far more difficult to give that user selective access unless that specified area is already set up as a separate key. It is also difficult to take access away from a single key or key holder, which usually requires a rekey of the whole system.

In many businesses, physical access authentication has moved to contactless radio frequency cards and readers. When passed near a card reader, the card sends out a code using radio waves. The reader picks up this code and transmits it to the control panel. The control panel checks the code against the reader from which it is being read and the type of access the card has in its database. One of the advantages of this kind of token-based system is that any card can be deleted from the system without affecting any other card or the rest of the system. The RFID-based contactless entry card shown in Figure 8.13 is a common form of this token device employed

● **Figure 8.13**   Smart cards have an internal chip as well as multiple external contacts for interfacing with a smart card reader.

for door controls and is frequently put behind an employee badge. In addition, all doors connected to the system can be segmented in any form or fashion to create multiple access areas, with different permissions for each one. The tokens themselves can also be grouped in multiple ways to provide different access levels to different groups of people. All of the access levels or segmentation of doors can be modified quickly and easily if building space is retasked. Newer technologies are adding capabilities to the standard token-based systems. The advent of **smart cards** (cards that contain integrated circuits capable of generating and storing cryptographic keys) has enabled cryptographic types of authentication.

The primary drawback of token-based authentication is that only the token is being authenticated. Therefore, the theft of the token could grant anyone who possessed the token access to what the system protects. The risk of theft of the token can be offset by the use of multiple-factor authentication. One of the ways that people have tried to achieve multiple-factor authentication is to add a biometric factor to the system.

Biometrics

Biometrics use the measurements of certain biological factors to identify one specific person from others. These factors are based on parts of the human body that are unique. The most well known of these unique biological factors is the fingerprint. Fingerprint readers have been available for several years in laptops, such as shown in Figure 8.14, and as standalone USB devices.

However, many other biological factors can be used, such as the retina or iris of the eye, the geometry of the hand, and the geometry of the face. When these are used for authentication, there is a two-part process: enrollment and then authentication. During enrollment, a computer takes the image of the biological factor and reduces it to a numeric value. When the user attempts to authenticate, their feature is scanned by the reader, and the computer compares the numeric value being read to the one stored in the database. If they match, access is allowed. Since these physical factors are unique, theoretically only the actual authorized person would be allowed access.

In the real world, however, the theory behind biometrics breaks down. Tokens that have a digital code work very well because everything remains in the digital realm. A computer checks your code, such as 123, against the database; if the computer finds 123 and that number has access, the computer opens the door. Biometrics, however, take an analog signal, such as a fingerprint or a face, and attempt to digitize it, and it is then matched against the digits in the database. The problem with an analog signal is that it might not encode the exact same way twice. For example, if you came to work with a bandage on your chin, would the face-based biometrics grant you access or deny it?

Engineers who designed these systems understood that if a system was set to exact checking, an encoded biometric might never grant access since it might never scan the biometric exactly the same way twice. Therefore, most systems have tried to allow a certain amount of error in the scan, while not allowing too much. This leads to the concepts of false positives and false negatives. A **false positive** occurs when a biometric is scanned and allows

● **Figure 8.14** Newer laptop computers often include a fingerprint reader.

access to someone who is not authorized—for example, two people who have very similar fingerprints might be recognized as the same person by the computer, which grants access to the wrong person. A **false negative** occurs when the system denies access to someone who is actually authorized— for example, a user at the hand geometry scanner forgot to wear a ring he usually wears and the computer doesn't recognize his hand and denies him access. For biometric authentication to work properly, and also be trusted, it must minimize the existence of both false positives and false negatives. To do that, a balance between exacting and error must be created so that the machines allow a little physical variance—but not too much.

False Positives and False Negatives   When a decision is made on information and an associated range of probabilities, the conditions exist for a false decision. Figure 8.15 illustrates two overlapping probabilities; an item belongs to either the red curve or the blue curve, but not both. The problem in deciding which curve an item belongs to occurs when the curves overlap.

When there is an overlapping area, it is typically referred to as the false positive and false negative rate. Note that in the accompanying figures, the size of overlap is greatly exaggerated to make it easy to see. Figure 8.16 illustrates a false positive detection. If the value observed is the dotted line, then it could be considered either a match or a nonmatch. If in fact it should not match, and the system tags it as a match, it is a false positive. In biometrics, a false positive would allow access to an unauthorized party.

Figure 8.17 illustrates a false negative detection. If the value observed is the dotted line, then it could be considered either a match or a nonmatch. If in fact it should match, and the system tags it as a nonmatch, it is a false negative. A false negative would prevent an authorized user from obtaining access.

To solve the false positive and false negative issue, the probabilistic engine must produce two sets of curves that do not overlap. This is equivalent to very low, <0.001%, false positive and false negative rates.

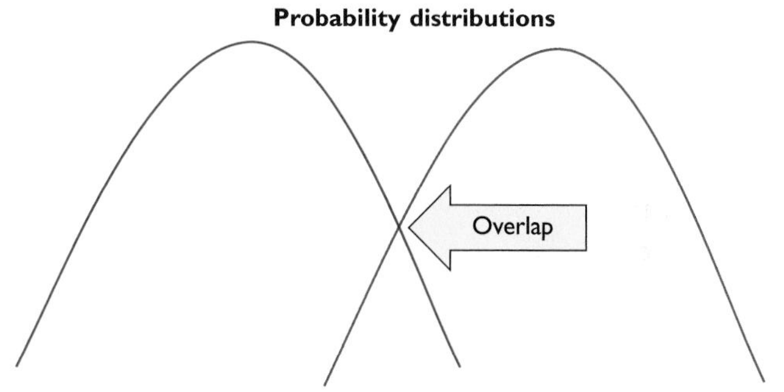

Probability distributions

Overlap

• **Figure 8.15**   Overlapping probabilities

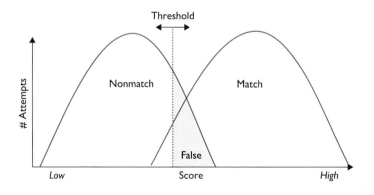

• **Figure 8.16**   False positive

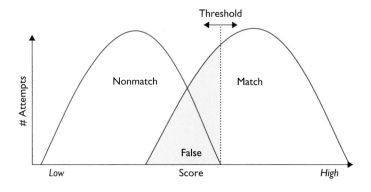

● **Figure 8.17** False negative

Because the curves technically have tails that go forever, there will always be some false rates, but the numbers have to be exceedingly small to assure security. Figure 8.18 illustrates the desired, but typically impractical, separation of the curves.

Another concern with biometrics is that if someone is able to steal the uniqueness factor that the machine scans—your fingerprint from a glass, for example—and is able to reproduce that factor in a substance that fools the scanner, that person now has your access privileges. This idea is compounded by the fact that it is impossible for you to change your fingerprint if it gets stolen. It is easy to replace a lost or stolen token and delete the missing one from the system, but it is far more difficult to replace a human hand. Another problem with biometrics is that parts of the human body can change. A human face can change, through scarring, weight loss or gain, or surgery. A fingerprint can be changed through damage to the fingers. Eye retinas can be affected by some types of diabetes or by pregnancy. All of these changes force the biometric system to allow a higher tolerance for variance in the biometric being read. This has led the way for high-security installations to move toward multiple-factor authentication.

Multiple-Factor Authentication

Multiple-factor authentication is simply the combination of two or more types of authentication. Three broad categories of authentication can be used: what you are (for example, biometrics), what you have (for instance,

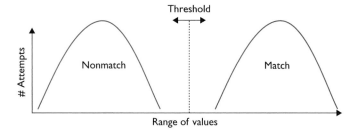

● **Figure 8.18** Desired situation

tokens), and what you know (passwords and other information). Two-factor authentication combines any two of these before granting access. An example would be a card reader that then turns on a fingerprint scanner—if your fingerprint matches the one on file for the card, you are granted access. Three-factor authentication would combine all three types, such as a smart card reader that asks for a PIN before enabling a retina scanner. If all three correspond to a valid user in the computer database, access is granted.

Multiple-factor authentication methods greatly enhance security by making it very difficult for an attacker to obtain all the correct materials for authentication. They also protect against the risk of stolen tokens, as the attacker must have the correct biometric, password, or both. More important, multiple-factor authentication enhances the security of biometric systems, by protecting against a stolen biometric. Changing the token makes the biometric useless unless the attacker can steal the new token. It also reduces false positives by trying to match the supplied biometric with the one that is associated with the supplied token. This prevents the computer from seeking a match using the entire database of biometrics. Using multiple factors is one of the best ways to ensure proper authentication and access control.

Exam Tip: Two-factor authentication combines any two methods of authentication, matching items such as a token with a biometric. Three-factor authentication combines any three, such as a passcode, biometric, and a token.

Chapter 8 Review

■ Chapter Summary

After reading this chapter and completing the exercises, you should understand the following facts about how physical security impacts network security.

Describe how physical security directly affects computer and network security

■ Physical access defeats all network security protections.

■ Bootdisks allow file system access.

■ Drive imaging is simple to accomplish with physical access.

■ Access to the internal network is simple with physical access.

■ Theft of hardware can be an attack in and of itself.

Discuss steps that can be taken to help mitigate risks

■ Removal of floppy drives when they are unnecessary can help mitigate bootdisk attacks.

■ Removal of CD-ROM devices also makes physical access attacks more difficult.

■ BIOS passwords should be used to protect the boot sequence.

■ USB devices are a threat and thus, if possible, USB drivers should be removed.

■ All users need security training.

■ Background checks of new hires help ensure security.

■ Authentication systems should use multiple factors when feasible.

Identify the different types of fires and the various fire suppression systems designed to limit the damage caused by fires

■ Fires can be caused by and can consume a number of different materials. It is important to recognize what type of fire is occurring, because the extinguisher to use depends on the type of fire.

■ The ABC fire extinguisher is the most common type and is designed to handle most types of fires. The only type of fire it is not designed to address is one with combustible metals.

Explain electronic access controls and the principles of convergence

■ Access controls should have layered areas and electronic access control systems.

■ Electronic physical security systems need to be protected from network-based attacks.

■ Key Terms

access control *(188)*
access tokens *(195)*
autorun *(185)*
biometrics *(196)*
BIOS passwords *(186)*
bootdisk *(180)*
closed circuit television (CCTV) *(190)*
contactless access cards *(189)*
drive imaging *(181)*

false negative *(197)*
false positive *(196)*
layered access *(189)*
LiveCD *(181)*
mantrap *(190)*
multiple-factor authentication *(198)*
policies and procedures *(184)*
smart cards *(196)*
USB devices *(186)*

Key Terms Quiz

Use terms from the Key Terms list to complete the sentences that follow. Don't use the same term more than once. Not all terms will be used.

1. A door system designed to only allow a single person through is called a(n) _____.

2. _____ include MP3 players and flash drives.

3. A(n) _____ happens when an unauthorized user is allowed access.

4. Removable media from which a computer can be booted is called a(n) _____.

5. _____ forces a user to authenticate again when entering a more secure area.

6. Items carried by the user to allow them to be authenticated are called _____.

7. _____ is the measurement of unique biological properties, like the fingerprint.

8. _____ prevent an attacker from making the machine boot off the DVD drive.

9. _____ is a system where the camera and monitor are directly linked.

10. Using a token, fingerprint reader, and PIN keypad would be an example of _____.

Multiple-Choice Quiz

1. What is the most common example of an access token?

   A. Smart card

   B. Handwriting sample

   C. PDA

   D. Key

2. Which one is not commonly used as a biometric?

   A. Eye retina

   B. Hand geometry

   C. Shoulder-to-waist geometry

   D. Fingerprint

3. Probably the simplest physical attack on the computer system is:

   A. Accessing an Ethernet jack to attack the network

   B. Using an imitation to fool a biometric authenticator

   C. Installing a virus on the CCTV system

   D. Outright theft of the computers

4. What is a common threat to token-based access controls?

   A. The key

   B. Demagnetization of the strip

   C. A system crash

   D. Loss or theft of the token

5. What about physical security makes it more acceptable to other employees?

   A. It is more secure.

   B. Computers are not important.

   C. It protects the employees themselves.

   D. It uses encryption.

6. Why can USB flash drives be a threat?

   A. They use too much power.

   B. They can bring malicious code past other security mechanisms.

   C. They can be stolen.

   D. They can be encrypted.

7. Why is water not used for fire suppression in data centers?

   A. It would cause a flood.

   B. Water cannot put out an electrical fire.

   C. Water would ruin all the electronic equipment.

   D. Building code prevents it.

8. Why is HVAC important to computer security?

   A. Sabotage of the AC unit could take out the electrical power.

   B. Sabotage of the AC unit would make the computers overheat and shut down.

   C. The AC units could be connected to the network.

   D. HVAC is not important to security.

9. Which fire detection device relies on the temperature in an area rising above some predefined level to activate it?

   A. Smoke detector

   B. Rate-of-rise fire detector

   C. Fixed-temperature fire detector

   D. Flame-activated fire detector

10. Why should security guards get cross-training in network security?

    A. They are the eyes and ears of the corporation when it comes to security.

    B. They are the only people in the building at night.

    C. They are more qualified to know what a security threat is.

    D. They have the authority to detain violators.

11. Why is enrollment important to biometrics?

    A. Fingerprints are unique.

    B. It adds another layer to the layered access model.

    C. If enrollment is not done carefully, false positives will increase.

    D. It completely prevents false positives.

12. On whom should a company perform background checks?

    A. System administrators only.

    B. Contract personnel only.

    C. Background checks are not needed outside of the military.

    D. All individuals who have unescorted physical access to the facility.

13. Why is physical security so important to good network security?

    A. Because encryption is not involved

    B. Because physical access defeats nearly all network security measures

    C. Because an attacker can steal biometric identities

    D. Authentication

14. A perfect bit-by-bit copy of a drive is called what?

    A. Drive picture

    B. Drive image

    C. Drive copy

    D. Drive partition

15. How does multiple-factor authentication improve security?

    A. By using biometrics, no other person can authenticate.

    B. It restricts users to smaller spaces.

    C. By using a combination of authentications, it is more difficult for someone to gain illegitimate access.

    D. It denies access to an intruder multiple times.

■ Essay Quiz

1. You have been asked to report on the feasibility of installing an IP CCTV camera system at your organization. Detail the pros and cons of an IP CCTV system and how you would implement the system.

2. Write a memo justifying layered access for certain areas of the organization.

3. Write a memo justifying more user education about security.

4. Your supervisor has asked you for a report detailing some of the problems associated with biometrics and how these problems could be minimized.

5. Write a sample policy regarding the use of USB devices in an organization.

Lab Projects

• Lab Project 8.1

Load a LiveCD on your machine and examine the tools it provides. You will need the following materials:

- A computer with a version of Windows installed and a CD/DVD burner

- An empty CD or DVD

Then do the following:

1. Download a copy of BackTrack. A good site from which to obtain this is www.remote-exploit.org/backtrack.html.

2. Burn the ISO file to the CD/DVD.

3. Reboot the machine, allowing the LiveCD to start the machine in Linux.

4. Once BackTrack is running, open a terminal window and type **wireshark**.

5. With Wireshark open as a sniffing program, record the traffic to and from this computer.

   a. Open Capture | Options.

   b. Select Start on your Ethernet interface, usually eth0.

   c. Stop Capture by selecting Capture | Stop.

   d. Click any packet listed to view the analysis.

6. View the other tools on the CD under KDE | BackTrack.

• Lab Project 8.2

Disable autorun on your system for several types of media. You will need the following materials:

- A computer with Windows XP

- A USB flash drive

- A CD/DVD with an autorun file

Then do the following:

1. Insert the CD/DVD and verify that autorun is on and working.

2. Follow this chapter's instructions on disabling autorun.

3. Reinsert the CD and verify that autorun is disabled—nothing should appear when the CD is inserted now.

4. Insert the USB flash drive and see if autorun works for it; if it does, disable it using the same method.

Network Fundamentals

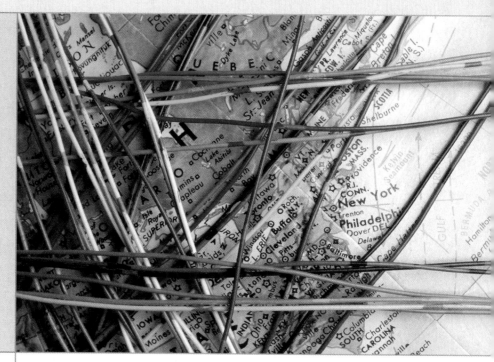

In all large corporations, there is a pervasive fear that someone, somewhere is having fun with a computer on company time. Networks help alleviate that fear.

—John C. Dvorak

In this chapter, you will learn how to

- Identify the basic network architectures
- Define the basic network protocols
- Explain routing and address translation
- Classify security zones

The term "network" has different meanings depending on the context and usage. A network can be a group of friends and associates, a series of interconnected tunnels, or, from a computer-oriented perspective, a collection of interconnected devices. For the purposes of this discussion, we'll focus on the more widely accepted definition of a network to mean any series of interconnected information systems and devices. Networks are all around us, and they enable the computers we use to interact—exchanging information on everything from credit card transactions to the latest news and weather. Essentially the Internet itself is one giant network consisting of interconnected PCs, servers, routers, and switches.

By the simplest definition in the data world, a **network** is a means to connect two or more computers together for the purposes of sharing information. Network sizes and shapes vary drastically—from two personal computers connected with a crossover cable or wireless router to the Internet, encircling the globe and linking together untold numbers of individual, distributed systems. Though data networks vary widely in size and scope, they are generally defined in terms of their architecture, topology, and protocol.

Network Architectures

Every network has an architecture—whether by design or accident. Defining or describing a specific network's architecture involves identifying the network's physical configuration, logical operation, structure, procedures, data formats, protocols, and other components. For the sake of simplicity and categorization, people tend to divide network architectures into two main categories: LANs and WANs. A **local area network (LAN)** typically is smaller in terms of size and geographic coverage and consists of two or more connected devices. Home networks and most small office networks can be classified as LANs. A **wide area network (WAN)** tends to be larger, covering more geographic area, and consists of two or more systems in geographically separated areas connected by any of a variety of methods such as leased lines, radio waves, satellite relays, microwaves, or even dial-up connections. With the advent of wireless networking, optical, and cellular technology, the lines between LAN and WAN sometimes blur, merging seamlessly into a single network entity. For example, most corporations have multiple LANs within each office location that all connect to a WAN that provides intercompany connectivity. Figure 9.1 shows an example of a corporate network. Each office location will typically have one or more LANs, which are connected to the other offices and the company headquarters through a corporate WAN.

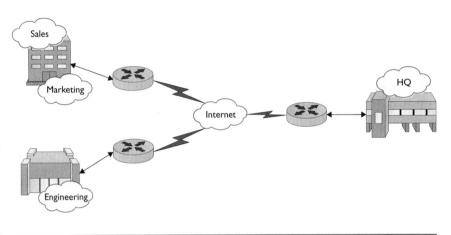

• **Figure 9.1**   Corporate WAN connecting multiple offices

Over time, as networks have grown, diversified, and multiplied, the line between LAN and WAN has become blurred. To better describe emerging, specialized network structures, new terms have been coined to classify networks based on size and use:

- **Campus area network (CAN)**   A network connecting any number of buildings in an office or university complex (also referred to as a campus wide area network).

- **Intranet**   A "private" network that is accessible only to authorized users. Many large corporations host an intranet to facilitate information sharing within their organization.

- **Internet**   The "global network" connecting hundreds of millions of systems and users.

- **Metropolitan area network (MAN)**   A network designed for a specific geographic locality such as a town or a city.

- **Storage area network (SAN)**   A high-speed network connecting a variety of storage devices such as tape systems, RAID arrays, optical drives, file servers, and others.

> **Exam Tip:** A LAN is a local area network—an office building, home network, and so on. A WAN is a wide area network—a corporate network connecting offices in Dallas, New York, and San Jose, for example.

- **Virtual local area network (VLAN)** A logical network allowing systems on different physical networks to interact as if they were connected to the same physical network.

- **Client/server** A network in which powerful, dedicated systems called *servers* provide resources to individual workstations or *clients*.

- **Peer-to-peer** A network in which every system is treated as an equal, such as a home network.

■ Network Topology

One major component of every network's architecture is the network's **topology**—how the network is physically or logically arranged. Terms to classify a network's topology have been developed, often reflecting the physical layout of the network. The main classes of network topologies are star, ring, bus, and mixed.

- **Star topology** Network components are connected to a central point. (See Figure 9.2.)

- **Bus topology** Network components are connected to the same cable, often called "the bus" or "the backbone." (See Figure 9.3.)

- **Ring topology** Network components are connected to each other in a closed loop with each device directly connected to two other devices. (See Figure 9.4.)

Larger networks, such as those inside an office complex, may use more than one topology at the same time. For example, an office complex may have a large ring topology that interconnects all the buildings in the

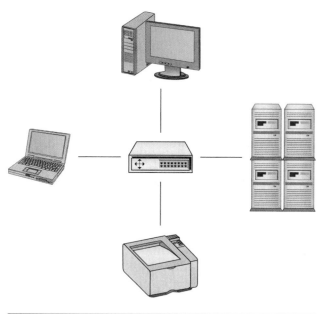

• **Figure 9.2** Star topology

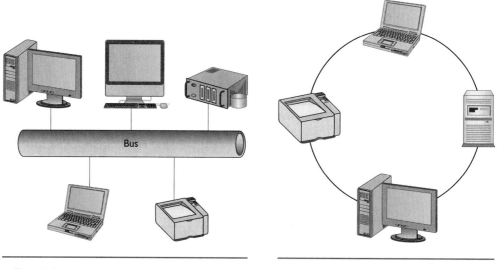

• **Figure 9.3** Bus topology

• **Figure 9.4** Ring topology

complex. Each building may have a large bus topology to interconnect star topologies located on each floor of the building. This is called a mixed topology or hybrid topology. (See Figure 9.5.)

With recent advances in technology, these topology definitions often break down. While a network consisting of five computers connected to the same coaxial cable is easily classified as a bus topology, what about those same computers connected to a switch using Cat-5 cables? With a switch, each com-

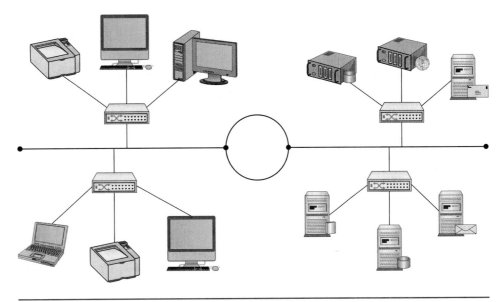

● **Figure 9.5**   Mixed topology

puter is connected to a central node, much like a star topology, but the backplane of the switch is essentially a shared medium. With a switch, each computer has its own exclusive connection to the switch like a star topology, but has to share the switch's communications backbone with all the other computers, much like a bus topology. To avoid this type of confusion, many people use topology definitions only to identify the physical layout of the network, focusing on how the devices are connected to the network. If we apply this line of thinking to our example, the five-computer network becomes a star topology whether we use a hub or a switch.

■ Network Protocols

How do all these interconnected devices communicate? What makes a PC in China able to view web pages on a server in Brazil? When engineers first started to connect computers together via networks, they quickly realized they needed a commonly accepted method for communicating—a protocol. A **protocol** is an agreed-upon format for exchanging or transmitting data between systems. A protocol defines a number of agreed-upon parameters, such as the data compression method, the type of error checking to use, and mechanisms for systems to signal when they have finished either receiving or transmitting data. There is a wide variety of protocols, each designed with certain benefits and uses in mind. Some of the more common protocols are

■ **AppleTalk**   The communications protocol developed by Apple to connect Macintosh computers and printers.

■ **Asynchronous Transfer Mode (ATM)**   A protocol based on transferring data in fixed-size packets. The fixed packet sizes help ensure that no single data type monopolizes the available bandwidth.

Wireless networks use radio waves as their medium to transmit packets, and those radio waves don't stop at the walls of your house or your organization. Anyone within range can "see" those radio waves and attempt to either sniff your traffic or connect to your network. Encryption, MAC address filtering, and suppression of beacon frames are all security mechanisms to consider when using wireless networks.

- **DECnet** Protocol developed by Digital Equipment Corporation that's used to connect PDP and VAX systems.

- **Ethernet** The LAN protocol developed jointly by Xerox, DEC, and Intel—the most widely implemented LAN standard.

- **Fiber Distributed Data Interface (FDDI)** The protocol for sending digital data over fiber-optic cabling.

- **Internet protocols (IP)** The protocols for managing and transmitting data between packet-switched computer networks originally developed for the Department of Defense. Most users are familiar with Internet protocols such as e-mail, File Transfer Protocol (FTP), Telnet, and Hypertext Transfer Protocol (HTTP).

- **Internetwork Packet Exchange (IPX)** The networking protocol created by Novell for use with Novell NetWare operating systems.

- **Signaling System 7 (SS7)** The telecommunications protocol used between private branch exchanges (PBXs) to handle tasks such as call setup, routing, and teardown.

- **Systems Network Architecture (SNA)** A set of network protocols developed by IBM, originally used to connect IBM's mainframe systems.

- **Token Ring** A LAN protocol developed by IBM that requires systems to possess the network "token" before transmitting data.

- **Transmission Control Protocol/Internet Protocol (TCP/IP)** The collection of communications protocols used to connect hosts on the Internet. TCP/IP is by far the most commonly used network protocol and is a combination of the TCP and IP protocols.

- **X.25** A protocol developed by the Comité Consultatif International Téléphonique et Télégraphique (CCITT) for use in packet-switched networks. The CCITT was a subgroup within the International Telecommunication Union (ITU) before the CCITT was disbanded in 1992.

In most cases, communications protocols were developed around the Open System Interconnection (OSI) model. The OSI model, or OSI Reference Model, is an International Organization for Standardization (ISO) standard for worldwide communications that defines a framework for implementing protocols and networking components in seven distinct layers. Within the OSI model, control is passed from one layer to another (top-down) before it exits one system and enters another system, where control is passed bottom-up to complete the communications cycle. It is important to note that most protocols only loosely follow the OSI model; several protocols combine one or more layers into a single function. The OSI model also provides a certain level of abstraction and isolation for each layer, which only needs to know how to interact with the layer above and below it. The application layer, for example, only needs to know how to communicate with the presentation layer—it does not need to talk directly to the physical layer. Figure 9.6 shows the different layers of the OSI model.

A little history on the IP protocol from Wikipedia: "In May, 1974, the Institute of Electrical and Electronic Engineers (IEEE) published a paper entitled 'A Protocol for Packet Network Interconnection.' The paper's authors, Vint Cerf and Bob Kahn, described an internetworking protocol for sharing resources using packet-switching among the nodes."

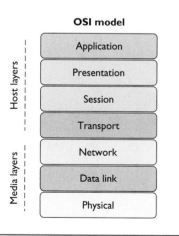

• **Figure 9.6** The OSI Reference Model

Packets

Networks are built to share information and resources, but like other forms of communication, networks and the protocols they use have limits and rules that must be followed for effective communication. For example, large chunks of data must typically be broken up into smaller, more manageable chunks before they are transmitted from one computer to another. Breaking the data up has advantages—you can more effectively share bandwidth with other systems and you don't have to retransmit the entire dataset if there is a problem in transmission. When data is broken up into smaller pieces for transmission, each of the smaller pieces is typically called a **packet**. Each protocol has its own definition of a packet—dictating how much data can be carried, what information is stored where, how the packet should be interpreted by another system, and so on. A standard packet structure is a crucial element in a protocol definition. Without a standard packet structure, systems would not be able to interpret the information coming to them from other systems. To better understand packet structure, let's examine the packet structure defined by the IP protocol. An IP packet, often called a **datagram**, has two main sections: the header and the data section (sometimes called the payload). The header section contains all of the information needed to describe the packet (see Figure 9.7).

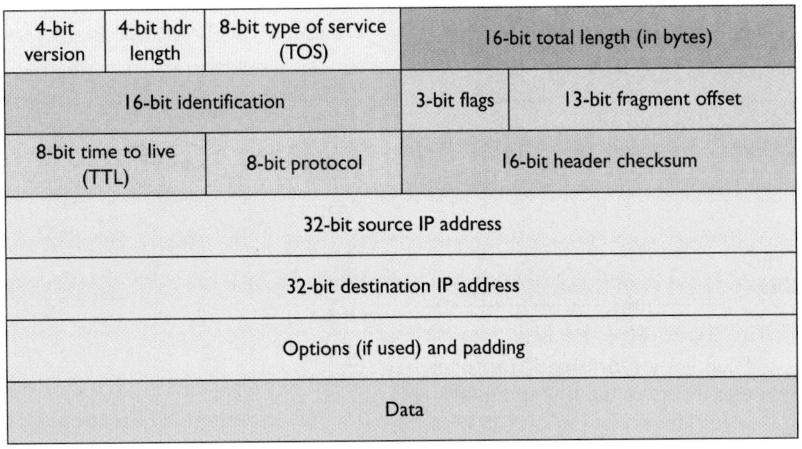

4-bit version	4-bit hdr length	8-bit type of service (TOS)	16-bit total length (in bytes)	
16-bit identification			3-bit flags	13-bit fragment offset
8-bit time to live (TTL)		8-bit protocol	16-bit header checksum	
32-bit source IP address				
32-bit destination IP address				
Options (if used) and padding				
Data				

• **Figure 9.7**   Logical layout of an IP packet

- What kind of packet it is (protocol version number)
- How large the header of the packet is (packet header length)
- How to process this packet (type of service telling the network whether or not to use options such as minimize delay, maximize throughput, maximize reliability, and minimize cost)
- How large the entire packet is (overall length of packet—since this is a 16-bit field, the maximum size of an IP packet is 65,535 bytes, but in practice most packets are around 1500 bytes)
- A unique identifier so that this packet can be distinguished from other packets
- Whether or not this packet is part of a longer data stream and should be handled relative to other packets
- Flags that indicate whether or not special handling of this packet is necessary
- A description of where this packet fits into the data stream as compared to other packets (the fragment offset)
- A "time to live" field that indicates the packet should be discarded if the value is zero

Exam Tip: TCP is a "connection-oriented" protocol and offers reliability and guaranteed delivery of packets. UDP is a "connectionless" protocol with no guarantees of delivery.

- A protocol field that describes the encapsulated protocol

- A checksum of the packet header (to minimize the potential for data corruption during transmission)

- Where the packet is from (source IP address, such as 10.10.10.5)

- Where the packet is going (destination IP address, such as 10.10.10.10)

- Option flags that govern security and handling restrictions, whether or not to record the route this packet has taken, whether or not to record time stamps, and so on

- The data this packet carries

As you can see, this standard packet definition allows systems to communicate. Without this type of "common language," the global connectivity we enjoy today would be impossible—the IP protocol is the primary means for transmitting information across the Internet.

TCP vs. UDP

Protocols are typically developed to enable a certain type of communication or solve a specific problem. Over the years, this approach has lead to the development of many different protocols, each critical to the function or process it supports. However, there are two protocols that have grown so much in popularity and use that without them, the Internet as we know it would cease to exist. These two protocols, the **Transmission Control Protocol (TCP)** and **User Datagram Protocol (UDP)**, are protocols that run on top of the IP network protocol. As separate protocols, they each have their own packet definitions, capabilities, and advantages, but the most important difference between TCP and UDP is the concept of "guaranteed" reliability and delivery.

UDP is known as a "connectionless" protocol as it has very few error-recovery services and no guarantee of packet delivery. With UDP, packets are created and sent on their way. The sender has no idea whether the packets were successfully received or whether they were received in order. In that respect, UDP packets are much like postcards—you address them and drop them in the mailbox, not really knowing if, when, or how the postcards reach your intended audience. Even though packet loss and corruption are relatively rare on modern networks, UDP is considered to be an unreliable protocol and is often only used for network services that are not greatly affected by the occasional lost or dropped packet. Time synchronization requests, name lookups, and streaming audio are good examples of network services based on the UDP protocol. UDP also happens to be a fairly "efficient" protocol in terms of content delivery versus overhead. With UDP, more time and space is dedicated to content (data) delivery than with other protocols such as TCP. This makes UDP a good candidate for streaming protocols, as more of the available bandwidth and resources are used for data delivery than with other protocols.

TCP is a "connection-oriented" protocol and was specifically designed to provide a reliable connection between two hosts exchanging data. TCP was also designed to ensure that packets are processed in the same order in which they were sent. As part of the TCP protocol, each packet has a sequence number to show where that packet fits into the overall conversation. With the sequence numbers, packets can arrive in any order and at different times and the receiving system will still know the correct order for processing them. The sequence numbers also let the receiving system know if packets are missing—receiving packets 1, 2, 4, and 7 tells us that packets 3, 5, and 6 are missing and needed as part of this conversation. The receiving system can then request retransmission of packets from the sender to fill in any gaps.

The "guaranteed and reliable" aspect of the TCP protocol makes it very popular for many network applications and services such as HTTP, FTP, and Telnet. As part of the connection, TCP requires that systems follow a specific pattern when establishing communications. This pattern, often called the **three-way handshake** (shown in Figure 9.8), is a sequence of very specific steps:

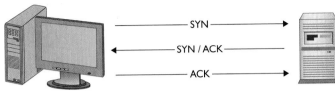

• **Figure 9.8**   TCP's three-way handshake

1. The originating host (usually called the client) sends a SYN (synchronize) packet to the destination host (usually called the server). The SYN packet tells the server what port the client wants to connect to and the initial packet sequence number of the client.

2. The server sends a SYN/ACK packet back to the client. This SYN/ACK (synchronize/acknowledge) tells the client "I received your request" and also contains the server's initial packet sequence number.

3. The client responds to the server with an ACK packet to complete the connection establishment process.

 Think of the three-way handshake as being similar to a phone call. You place a call to your friend—that's the SYN. Your friend answers the phone and says "hello"—that's the SYN/ACK. Then you say "Hi, it's me"—that's the ACK. Your connection is established and you can start your conversation.

ICMP

While TCP and UDP are arguably the most common protocols, the **Internet Control Message Protocol (ICMP)** is probably the third most commonly used protocol. During the early development of large networks, it was quickly discovered that there needed to be some mechanism for managing the overall infrastructure—handling connection status, traffic flow, availability, and errors. This mechanism is the ICMP protocol. ICMP is a control and information protocol and is used by network devices to determine such things as a remote network's availability, the length of time to reach a remote network, and the best route for packets to take when traveling to that remote network (using ICMP redirect messages, for example). ICMP can also be used to handle the flow of

Tech Tip

TCP Packet Flags

TCP packets contain flags—dedicated fields that are used to help the TCP protocol control and manage the TCP session. There are eight different flags in a TCP packet, and when a flag is "set," it is set to a value of 1. The eight different flags are

- **CWR (Congestion Window Reduced)** *Set by a host to indicate that it received a packet with the ECE flag set and is taking action to help reduce congestion.*

- **ECE (ECN-Echo)** *Indicates that the TCP peer is ECN capable when used during the three-way handshake. During normal traffic, this flag means that a packet with a Congestion Experienced flag in its IP header was received by the host sending this packet.*

- **URG (Urgent)** *When set, the urgent pointer in the packets should be read as valid and followed for additional data.*

- **ACK (Acknowledgment)** *Indicates that the data in the ACK field should be processed.*

- **PSH (Push)** *Indicates that data delivery should start immediately rather than waiting for buffers to fill up first.*

- **RST (Reset)** *Resets the current connection—a start-over feature often used by IPS/IDS devices to interrupt sessions.*

- **SYN (Synchronize)** *Used to help synchronize sequence numbers.*

- **FIN (Finish)** *Indicates the sender is finished and has no more data to send.*

Tech Tip

ICMP Type Codes

With ICMP packets, the real message of the packet is contained in the "type and code" fields, not the data field. Here are some of the more commonly seen ICMP type codes:

Type	Name
0	Echo reply
3	Destination unreachable
4	Source quench
5	Redirect
8	Echo
11	Time exceeded
13	Timestamp
30	Traceroute

Some of the types have associated code values that make the message more specific. For example, ICMP messages with a type of 3 can have any of the following codes:

Code	Name
1	Net unreachable
2	Host unreachable
3	Protocol unreachable
4	Port unreachable
5	Fragmentation needed and DF bit set
6	Source route failed
7	Destination network unknown
8	Destination host unknown
9	Source host isolated
10	Communication with destination network is administratively prohibited
11	Communication with destination host is administratively prohibited
12	Destination network unreachable for TOS
13	Destination host unreachable for TOS

As a security professional, knowing how protocols, such as ICMP, work and how to interpret them is extremely important. Imagine you're configuring a firewall. You could configure it to drop all ICMP packets, but that would prevent your users from being able to receive echo replies, traceroute results, and so on. If you know how ICMP works, you could block most ICMP packets and only allow the ones you're really interested in, such as echo replies, past your firewall. This gives you the ability to keep using parts of the protocol and reject others.

traffic, telling other network devices to "slow down" transmission speeds if packets are coming in too fast.

ICMP, like UDP, is a connectionless protocol. ICMP was designed to carry small messages quickly with minimal overhead or impact to bandwidth. ICMP packets are sent using the same header structure as IP packets, with the protocol field set to 1 to indicate that it is an ICMP packet. ICMP packets also have their own header, which follows the IP header and contains type, code, checksum, sequence number, identifier, and data fields. The "type" field indicates what type of ICMP message it is, and the "code" field tells us what the message really means. For example, an ICMP packet with a type of 3 and a code of 2 would tell us this is a "destination unreachable" message and, more specifically, a "host unreachable" message—usually indicating that we are unable to communicate with the intended destination.

Unfortunately, the ICMP protocol has been greatly abused by attackers over the last few years to execute **denial-of-service (DoS)** attacks. Because ICMP packets are very small and connectionless, thousands and thousands of ICMP packets can be generated by a single system in a very short period of time. Attackers have developed methods to trick many systems into generating thousands of ICMP packets with a common destination—the attacker's target. This creates a literal flood of traffic that the target, and in most cases the network the target sits on, is incapable of dealing with. The ICMP flood drowns out any other legitimate traffic and prevents the target from accomplishing its

Cross Check

Ping Sweep

In Chapter 1 you learned about a "ping sweep." What is a ping sweep and what is it used for? What types of ICMP packets could you use to conduct a ping sweep?

 In February 2000 a 17-year-old Canadian script kiddie brought down 11 sites using 75 computers in 52 countries to send 10,700 ICMP messages in 10 seconds. The targeted sites included Yahoo, Buy.com, eBay, CNN, Amazon.com, ZDNet, ETrade, Dell, and Excite.

normal duties—denying access to the service the target normally provides. This has lead to many organizations blocking all external ICMP traffic at the perimeter of their organization.

■ Packet Delivery

Protocols are designed to help information get from one place to another, but in order to deliver a packet we have to know where it is going. Packet delivery can be divided into two sections: local and remote packet delivery. Local delivery applies to packets being sent out on a local network while remote delivery applies to packets being delivered to a remote system, such as across the Internet. Ultimately, packets may follow a local delivery, remote delivery, local delivery pattern before reaching their intended destination. The biggest difference in local versus remote delivery is how packets are addressed. Network systems have addresses, not unlike office numbers or street addresses, and before a packet can be successfully delivered, the sender needs to know the address of the destination system.

Local Packet Delivery

Packets delivered on a network, such as an office LAN, are usually sent using the destination system's hardware address, or **Media Access Control (MAC) address**. Each network card or network device is supposed to have a unique hardware address so that it can be specifically addressed for network traffic. MAC addresses are assigned to a device or network card by the manufacturer, and each manufacturer is assigned a specific block of MAC addresses to prevent two devices from sharing the same MAC address. MAC addresses are usually expressed as six pairs of hexadecimal digits, such as 00:07:e9:7c:c8:aa. In order for a system to send data to another system on the network, it must first find out the destination system's MAC address.

Maintaining a list of every local system's MAC address is both costly and time consuming, and although a system may store MAC addresses temporarily for convenience, in many cases the sender must find the destination MAC address before sending any packets. To find another system's MAC address, the **Address Resolution Protocol (ARP)** is used. Essentially, this is the computer's way of finding out "who owns the blue convertible with license number 123JAK."

 Tech Tip

MAC Addresses
Every network device should have a unique MAC address. Manufacturers of network cards and network chipsets have blocks of MAC addresses assigned to them, so you can often tell what type of equipment is sending packets by looking at the first three pairs of hexadecimal digits in a MAC address. For example "00-00-0C" would indicate the network device was built by Cisco Systems.

 Try This

Finding MAC Addresses on Windows Systems
Open a command prompt on a Windows system. Type the command **ipconfig /all** and find your system's MAC address. *Hint:* It should be listed under "Physical Address" on your network adapters. Now type the command **arp –a** and press ENTER. What information does this display? Can you find the MAC address of your default gateway?

MAC addresses can be "spoofed" or faked. Some operating systems allow users with administrator-level privileges to explicitly set the MAC address for their network card(s). For example, in Linux operating systems you can use the **ifconfig** command to change a network adapter's MAC address. The command **ifconfig eth0 hw ether 00:07:e9:7c:c8:aa** will set the MAC address of adapter eth0 to 00:07:e9:7c:c8:aa. There are also a number of software utilities that allow you to do this through a GUI, such as the GNU MAC Changer. GUI utilities to change MAC addresses on Windows systems are also available.

The Domain Name System is critical to the operation of the Internet—if your computer can't translate www.espn.com into 199.181.132.250, then your web browser won't be able to access the latest scores.

✓ Cross Check

Mandatory Access Control

In Chapter 2 you learned about a different MAC—mandatory access control. What is the difference between mandatory access control and Media Access Control? What is each used for?

In most cases, systems know the IP address they wish to send to, but not the MAC address. Using an ARP request, the sending system will send out a query: Who is 10.1.1.140? This broadcast query is examined by every system on the local network, but only the system whose IP address is 10.1.1.140 will respond. That system will send back a response that says "I'm 10.1.1.140 and my MAC address is 00:07:e9:7c:c8:aa." The sending system will then format the packet for delivery and drop it on the network media, stamped with the MAC address of the destination workstation.

Remote Packet Delivery

While packet delivery on a LAN is usually accomplished with MAC addresses, packet delivery to a distant system is usually accomplished using **Internet Protocol (IP)** addresses. IP addresses are 32-bit numbers that usually are expressed as a group of four numbers (such as 10.1.1.132). In order to send a packet to a specific system on the other side of the world, you have to know the remote system's IP address. Storing large numbers of IP addresses on every PC is far too costly, and most humans are not good at remembering collections of numbers. However, humans are good at remembering names, so the **Domain Name System (DNS)** protocol was created.

DNS translates names into IP addresses. When you enter the name of your favorite web site into the location bar of your web browser and press ENTER, the computer has to figure out what IP address belongs to that name. Your computer takes the entered name and sends a query to a local DNS server. Essentially, your computer asks the DNS server "What IP address goes with www.myfavoritesite.com?" The DNS server, whose main purpose in life is to handle DNS queries, looks in its local records to see if it knows the answer. If it doesn't, the DNS server queries another, higher-level domain server. That server checks its records and queries the server above it, and so on until a match is found. That name-to-IP address matching is passed back down to your computer so it can create the web request, stamp it with the right destination IP address, and send it.

Before sending the packet, your system will first determine if the destination IP address is on a local or remote network. In most cases, it will be on a remote network and your system will not know how to reach that remote network. Again, it would not be practical for your system to know how to directly reach every other system on the Internet, so your system will forward the packet to a network gateway. Network gateways, usually called routers, are devices that are used to interconnect networks and move packets from one network to another. That process of moving packets from one network to another is called **routing** and is critical to the flow of information across the Internet. To accomplish this task, routers use forwarding tables to determine where a packet should go. When a packet reaches a router, the router looks at the destination address to determine where to send the packet. If the router's forwarding tables indicate where the packet should go, the router sends the packet out along the appropriate route. If the router does not know where the destination network is, it forwards the packet to its defined gateway, which repeats the same process. Eventually, after traversing various networks and being passed through various routers, our packet arrives at the router serving the network with the web site we are trying to reach. This router determines the appropriate MAC address of the destination system and forwards the packet accordingly.

IP Addresses and Subnetting

The last section mentioned that IP addresses are 32-bit numbers. Those 32 bits are represented as four groups of 8 bits each (called octets). You will usually see IP addresses expressed as four sets of decimal numbers in dotted-decimal notation, 10.120.102.15 for example. Of those 32 bits in an IP address, some are used for the network portion of the address (the network ID), and some are used for the host portion of the address (the host ID). **Subnetting** is the process that is used to divide those 32 bits in an IP address and tell you how many of the 32 bits are being used for the network ID and how many are being used for the host ID. As you can guess, where and how you divide the 32 bits determines how many networks and how many host addresses you may have. To interpret the 32-bit space correctly, we must use a **subnet mask**, which tells us exactly how much of the space is the network portion and how much is the host portion. Let's look at an example using the IP address 10.10.10.101 with a subnet mask of 255.255.255.0.

First you must convert the address and subnet mask to their binary representations:

Subnet Mask:	11111111.11111111.11111111.00000000
IP Address:	00001010.00001010.00001010.01100101

Then, you perform a bitwise AND operation to get the network address. The bitwise AND operation examines each set of matching bits from the binary representation of the subnet mask and the binary representation of the IP address. For each set where both the mask and address bits are 1, the result of the AND operation is a 1. Otherwise, if either bit is a 0, the result is a 0. So, for our example we get

Network Address: 00001010.00001010.00001010.00000000

which in decimal is 10.10.10.0, the network ID of our IP network address (translate the binary representation to decimal).

The network ID and subnet mask together tell us that the first three octets of our address are network-related (10.10.10.), which means that the last octet of our address is the host portion (101 in this case). In our example, the network portion of the address is 10.10.10 and the host portion is 101. Another shortcut in identifying which of the 32 bits is being used in the network ID is to look at the subnet mask after it's been converted to its binary representation. If there's a 1 in the subnet mask, then the corresponding bit in the binary representation of the IP address is being used

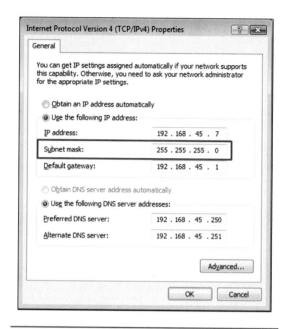

as part of the network ID. In the preceding example, the subnet mask of 255.255.255.0 in binary representation is 11111111.11111111.11111111.00000000. We can see that there's a 1 in the first 24 spots, which means that the first 24 bits of the IP address are being used as the network ID (which is the first three octets of 255.255.255).

Network address spaces are usually divided into one of three classes:

- **Class A** Supports 16,777,214 hosts on each network with a default subnet mask of 255.0.0.0
  Subnets: 0.0.0.0 to 126.255.255.255 (127.0.0.0 to 127.255.255.255 is reserved for loopback)

- **Class B** Supports 65,534 hosts on each network with a default subnet mask of 255.255.0.0
  Subnets: 128.0.0.0 to 191.255.255.255

- **Class C** Supports 253 hosts on each network with a default subnet mask of 255.255.255.0 (see Figure 9.9)
  Subnets: 192.0.0.0 to 223.255.255.255
  Everything above 224.0.0.0 is reserved for either multicasting or future use.

• **Figure 9.9** A subnet mask of 255.255.255.0 indicates this is a Class C address space.

Tech Tip

RFC 1918—Private Address Spaces
RFC 1918 is the technical specification for private address space. RFC stands for "Request For Comment" and there are RFCs for just about everything to do with the Internet—protocols, routing, how to handle e-mail, and so on. You can find RFCs at www.ietf.org/rfc.html.

In addition, certain subnets are reserved for private use and are not routed across public networks such as the Internet:

- 10.0.0.0 to 10.255.255.255
- 172.16.0.0 to 172.31.255.255
- 192.168.0.0 to 192.168.255.255

Finally, when determining the valid hosts that can be placed on a particular subnet, you have to keep in mind that the "all 0s" address of the host portion is reserved for the network address and the "all 1s" address of the host portion is reserved for the broadcast address of that particular subnet. Again from our earlier example:

Subnet Network Address:
10.10.10.**0**
00001010.00001010.00001010.**00000000**

Broadcast Address:
10.10.10.**255**
00001010.00001010.00001010.**11111111**

In their forwarding tables, routers maintain lists of networks and the accompanying subnet mask. With these two pieces, the router can examine the destination address of each packet and then forward the packet on to the appropriate destination.

As mentioned earlier, subnetting allows us to divide networks into smaller logical units, and we use subnet masks to do this. But how does this work? Remember that the subnet mask tells us how many bits are being used to describe the network ID—adjusting the subnet mask (and the number of bits used to describe the network ID) allows us to divide an address space into multiple, smaller logical networks. Let's say you have a single address space of 192.168.45.0 that you need to divide into multiple networks. The default subnet mask is 255.255.255.0, which means you're using 24 bits as the network ID and 8 bits as the host ID. This gives you 254 different hosts addresses. But what if you need more networks and don't need as many host addresses? You can simply adjust your subnet mask to borrow some of the host bits and use them as network bits. If you use a subnet mask of 255.255.255.224, you are essentially "borrowing" the first 3 bits from the space you were using to describe host IDs and using them to describe the network ID. This gives you more space to create different networks but means that each network will now have fewer available host IDs. With a 255.255.255.224 subnet mask, you can create six different subnets, but each subnet can only have 30 unique host IDs. If you borrow 6 bits from the host ID portion and use a subnet mask of 255.255.255.252, you can create 62 different networks but each of them can only have two unique host IDs.

Network Address Translation

If you're thinking that a 32-bit address space that's chopped up and subnetted isn't enough to handle all the systems in the world, you're right. While IP address blocks are assigned to organizations such as companies and universities, there usually aren't enough Internet-visible IP addresses to assign to every system on the planet a unique, Internet-routable IP address. To compensate for this lack of available IP address space, we use **Network Address Translation (NAT)**. NAT translates private (nonroutable) IP addresses into public (routable) IP addresses.

From our discussions earlier in this chapter, you may remember that certain IP address blocks are reserved for "private use," and you'd probably agree that not every system in an organization needs a direct, Internet-routable IP address. Actually, for security reasons, it's much better if most of an organization's systems are hidden from direct Internet access. Most organizations build their internal networks using the private IP address ranges (such as 10.1.1.XXX) to prevent outsiders from directly accessing those internal networks. However, in many cases those systems still need to be able to reach the Internet. This is accomplished by using a NAT device (typically a firewall or router) that translates the many internal IP addresses into one of a small number of public IP addresses.

For example, consider a fictitious company, ACME.com. ACME has several thousand internal systems using private IP addresses in the 10.X.X.X range. To allow those IPs to communicate with the outside world, ACME leases an Internet connection and a few public IP addresses, and deploys a NAT-capable device. ACME administrators configure all their internal hosts to use the NAT device as their default gateway. When internal hosts need to send packets outside the company, they send them to the NAT device. The NAT device removes the internal source IP address out of the outbound packets and replaces it with the NAT device's public, routable address and sends them on their way. When response packets are received from outside sources, the device performs NAT in reverse, stripping off the external, public IP address in the destination address field and replacing it with the correct internal, private IP address before sending it on into the private ACME.com network. Figure 9.10 illustrates this NAT process.

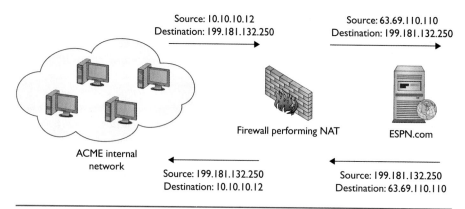

Source: 10.10.10.12
Destination: 199.181.132.250

Source: 63.69.110.110
Destination: 199.181.132.250

Firewall performing NAT

ESPN.com

ACME internal
network

Source: 199.181.132.250
Destination: 10.10.10.12

Source: 199.181.132.250
Destination: 63.69.110.110

 Figure 9.10   Logical depiction of NAT

In Figure 9.10, we see an example of NAT being performed. An internal workstation (10.10.10.12) wants to visit the ESPN web site at www.espn.com. When the packet reaches the NAT device, the device translates the 10.10.10.12 source address to the globally routable 63.69.110.110 address, the IP address of the device's externally visible interface. When the ESPN web site responds, it responds to the device's address just as if the NAT device had originally requested the information. The NAT device must then remember which internal workstation requested the information and route the packet to the appropriate destination.

Security Zones

The first aspect of security is a layered defense. Just as a castle has a moat, an outside wall, an inside wall, and even a keep, so, too, does a modern secure network have different layers of protection. Different zones are designed to provide layers of defense, with the outermost layers providing basic protection and the innermost layers providing the highest level of protection. A constant issue is that accessibility tends to be inversely related to level of protection, so it is more difficult to provide complete

---

Tech Tip

Different Approaches for Implementing NAT

While the concept of NAT remains the same, there are actually several different approaches to implementing NAT. For example:

- **Static NAT**   *Maps an internal, private address to an external, public address. The same public address is always used for that private address. This technique is often used when hosting something you wish the public to be able to get to, such as a web server, behind a firewall.*

- **Dynamic NAT**   *Maps an internal, private IP address to a public IP address selected from a pool of registered (public) IP addresses. This technique is often used when translating addresses for end-user workstations and the NAT device must keep track of internal/external address mappings.*

- **Port Address Translation (PAT)**   *Allows many different internal, private addresses to share a single external IP address. Devices performing PAT replace the source IP address with the NAT IP address and replace the source port field with a port from an available connection pool. PAT devices keep a translation table to track which internal hosts are using which ports so that subsequent packets can be stamped with the same port number. When response packets are received, the PAT device reverses the process and forwards the packet to the correct internal host. PAT is a very popular NAT technique and in use at many organizations.*

---

protection and unfettered access at the same time. Trade-offs between access and security are handled through zones, with successive zones guarded by firewalls enforcing ever-increasingly strict security policies. The outermost zone is the Internet, a free area, beyond any specific controls. Between the inner, secure corporate network and the Internet is an area where machines are considered at risk. This zone has come to be called the **DMZ**, after its military counterpart, the demilitarized zone, where neither side has any specific controls. Once inside the inner, secure network, separate branches are frequently carved out to provide specific functionality; under this heading, we will also discuss intranets, extranets, and virtual LANs (VLANs).

DMZ

The DMZ is a military term for ground separating two opposing forces, by agreement and for the purpose of acting as a buffer between the two sides. A DMZ in a computer network is used in the same way; it acts as a buffer zone between the Internet, where no controls exist, and the inner, secure network, where an organization has security policies in place (see Figure 9.11). To demarcate the zones and enforce separation, a firewall is used on each side of the DMZ. The area between these firewalls is accessible from either the inner, secure network or the Internet. Figure 9.11 illustrates these zones as caused by

firewall placement. The firewalls are specifically designed to prevent access across the DMZ directly, from the Internet to the inner, secure network. It is important to note that typically only filtered Internet traffic is allowed into the DMZ. For example, an organization hosting a web server and an FTP server in its DMZ may want the public to be able to "see" those services but nothing else. In that case the firewall may allow FTP, HTTP, and HTTPS traffic into the DMZ from the Internet and then filter out everything else.

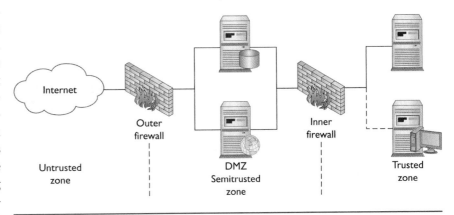

• **Figure 9.11** The DMZ and zones of trust

Special attention should be paid to the security settings of network devices placed in the DMZ, and they should be considered at all times to be at risk for compromise by unauthorized use. A common industry term, *hardened operating system*, applies to machines whose functionality is locked down to preserve security—unnecessary services and software are removed or disabled, functions are limited, and so on. This approach needs to be applied to the machines in the DMZ, and although it means that their functionality is limited, such precautions ensure that the machines will work properly in a less-secure environment.

Many types of servers belong in this area, including web servers that are serving content to Internet users, as well as remote access servers and external e-mail servers. In general, any server directly accessed from the outside, untrusted Internet zone needs to be in the DMZ. Other servers should not be placed in the DMZ. Domain name servers for your inner, trusted network and database servers that house corporate databases should not be accessible from the outside. Application servers, file servers, print servers—all of the standard servers used in the trusted network—should be behind both firewalls and the routers and switches used to connect these machines.

The idea behind the use of the DMZ topology is to provide publicly visible services without allowing untrusted users access to your internal network. If the outside user makes a request for a resource from the trusted network, such as a data element from an internal database that is accessed via a publicly visible web page in the DMZ, then this request needs to follow this scenario:

1. A user from the untrusted network (the Internet) requests data via a web page from a web server in the DMZ.

2. The web server in the DMZ requests the data from the application server, which can be in the DMZ or in the inner, trusted network.

3. The application server requests the data from the database server in the trusted network.

4. The database server returns the data to the requesting application server.

5. The application server returns the data to the requesting web server.

6. The web server returns the data to the requesting user from the untrusted network.

This separation accomplishes two specific, independent tasks. First, the user is separated from the request for data on a secure network. By having intermediaries do the requesting, this layered approach allows significant security levels to be enforced. Users do not have direct access or control over their requests, and this filtering process can put controls in place. Second, scalability is more easily realized. The multiple-server solution can be made to be very scalable, literally to millions of users, without slowing down any particular layer.

Internet

The Internet is a worldwide connection of networks and is used to transport e-mail, files, financial records, remote access—you name it—from one network to another. The Internet is not a single network, but a series of interconnected networks that allows protocols to operate and enable data to flow across it. This means that even if your network doesn't have direct contact with a resource, as long as a neighbor, or a neighbor's neighbor, and so on, can get there, so can you. This large web allows users almost infinite ability to communicate between systems.

Because everything and everyone can access this interconnected web and it is outside of your control and ability to enforce security policies, the Internet should be considered an untrusted network. A firewall should exist at any connection between your trusted network and the Internet. This is not to imply that the Internet is a bad thing—it is a great resource for all networks and adds significant functionality to our computing environments.

The term World Wide Web (WWW) is frequently used synonymously to represent the Internet, but the WWW is actually just one set of services available via the Internet. WWW or "the Web" is more specifically the Hypertext Transfer Protocol (HTTP)–based services that are made available over the

Exam Tip: DMZs act as a buffer zone between unprotected areas of a network (the Internet) and protected areas (sensitive company data stores), allowing for the monitoring and regulation of traffic between these two zones.

 There are over 1.5 billion users on the Internet, English is the most used language, and the average age of an Internet user is 29.7 years.

Internet. This can include a variety of actual services and content, including text files, pictures, streaming audio and video, and even viruses and worms.

Intranet

An **intranet** describes a network that has the same functionality as the Internet for users but lies completely inside the trusted area of a network and is under the security control of the system and network administrators. Typically referred to as *campus* or *corporate* networks, intranets are used every day in companies around the world. An intranet allows a developer and a user the full set of protocols—HTTP, FTP, instant messaging, and so on—that is offered on the Internet, but with the added advantage of trust from the network security. Content on intranet web servers is not available over the Internet to untrusted users. This layer of security offers a significant amount of control and regulation, allowing users to fulfill business functionality while ensuring security.

Two methods can be used to make information available to outside users: Duplication of information onto machines in the DMZ can make it available to other users. Proper security checks and controls should be made prior to duplicating the material to ensure security policies concerning specific data availability are being followed. Alternatively, *extranets* can be used to publish material to trusted partners.

Should users inside the intranet require access to information from the Internet, a proxy server can be used to mask the requestor's location. This helps secure the intranet from outside mapping of its actual topology. All Internet requests go to the proxy server. If a request passes filtering requirements, the proxy server, assuming it is also a cache server, looks in its local cache of previously downloaded web pages. If it finds the page in its cache, it returns the page to the requestor without needing to send the request to the Internet. If the page is not in the cache, the proxy server, acting as a client on behalf of the user, uses one of its own IP addresses to request the page from the Internet. When the page is returned, the proxy server relates it to the original request and forwards it on to the user. This masks the user's IP address from the Internet. Proxy servers can perform several functions for a firm; for example, they can monitor traffic requests, eliminating improper requests such as inappropriate content for work. They can also act as a cache server, cutting down on outside network requests for the same object. Finally, proxy servers protect the identity of internal IP addresses using NAT, although this function can also be accomplished through a router or firewall using NAT as well.

> **Exam Tip:** An intranet is a private, internal network that uses common network technologies (such as HTTP, FTP, and so on) to share information and provide resources to organizational users.

Extranet

An **extranet** is an extension of a selected portion of a company's intranet to external partners. This allows a business to share information with customers, suppliers, partners, and other trusted groups while using a common set of Internet protocols to facilitate operations. Extranets can use public networks to extend their reach beyond a company's own internal network, and some form of security, typically VPN, is used to secure this channel. The use of the term *extranet* implies both privacy and security. Privacy is required for many communications, and security is needed to prevent unauthorized use and events from occurring. Both of these functions can be achieved

> **Exam Tip:** An extranet is a semiprivate network that uses common network technologies (such as HTTP, FTP, and so on) to share information and provide resources to business partners. Extranets can be accessed by more than one company, because they share information between organizations.

through the use of technologies described in this chapter and other chapters in this book. Proper firewall management, remote access, encryption, authentication, and secure tunnels across public networks are all methods used to ensure privacy and security for extranets.

VLANs

A LAN is a set of devices with similar functionality and similar communication needs, typically co-located and operated off a single switch. This is the lowest level of a network hierarchy and defines the domain for certain protocols at the data link layer for communication. A virtual LAN (VLAN) is a logical implementation of a LAN and allows computers connected to different physical networks to act and communicate as if they were on the same physical network. A VLAN has many of the same characteristic attributes of a LAN and behaves much like a physical LAN but is implemented using switches and software. This very powerful technique allows significant network flexibility, scalability, and performance and allows administrators to perform network reconfigurations without having to physically relocate or recable systems.

Trunking

Trunking is the process of spanning a single VLAN across multiple switches. A trunk-based connection between switches allows packets from a single VLAN to travel between switches, as shown in Figure 9.12. Two trunks are shown in the figure: VLAN 10 is implemented with one trunk and VLAN 20 is implemented with the other. Hosts on different VLANs cannot communicate using trunks and thus are switched across the switch network. Trunks enable network administrators to set up VLANs across multiple switches with minimal effort. With a combination of trunks and VLANs, network administrators can subnet a network by user functionality without regard to host location on the network or the need to recable machines.

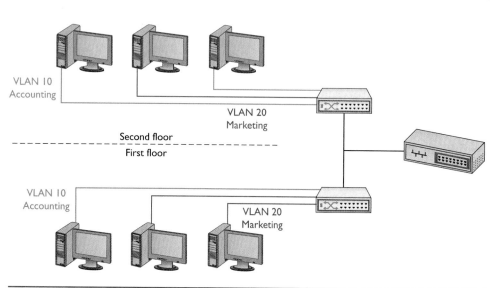

• **Figure 9.12** VLANs and trunks

Security Implications

VLANs are used to divide a single network into multiple subnets based on functionality. This permits accounting and marketing, for example, to share a switch because of proximity yet still have separate traffic domains. The physical placement of equipment and cables is logically and programmatically separated so that adjacent ports on a switch can reference separate subnets. This prevents unauthorized use of physically close devices through separate subnets that are on the same equipment. VLANs also allow a network administrator to define a VLAN that has no users and map all of the unused ports to this VLAN (some managed switches allow administrators to simply disable unused ports as well). Then, if an unauthorized user should gain access to the equipment, that user will be unable to use unused ports, as those ports will be securely defined to nothing. Both a purpose and a security strength of VLANs is that systems on separate VLANs cannot directly communicate with each other.

> ⚠️ Trunks and VLANs have security implications that you need to heed so that firewalls and other segmentation devices are not breached through their use. You also need to understand how to use trunks and VLANs, to prevent an unauthorized user from reconfiguring them to gain undetected access to secure portions of a network.

■ Tunneling

Tunneling is a method of packaging packets so that they can traverse a network in a secure, confidential manner. Tunneling involves encapsulating packets within packets, enabling dissimilar protocols to coexist in a single communication stream, as in IP traffic routed over an Asynchronous Transfer Mode (ATM) network. Tunneling also can provide significant measures of security and confidentiality through encryption and encapsulation methods. The best example of this is a VPN that is established over a public network through the use of a tunnel, as shown in Figure 9.13, connecting a firm's Boston office to its New York City (NYC) office.

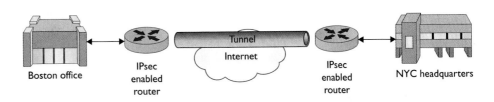

• **Figure 9.13**   Tunneling across a public network

Assume, for example, that a company has multiple locations and decides to use the public Internet to connect the networks at these locations. To make these connections secure from outside unauthorized use, the company can employ a VPN connection between the different networks. On each network, an edge device, usually a router, connects to another edge device on the other network. Then, using IPsec protocols, these routers establish a secure, encrypted path between them. This securely encrypted set of packets cannot be read by outside routers; only the addresses of the edge routers are visible. This arrangement acts as a tunnel across the public Internet and establishes a private connection, secure from outside snooping or use.

Because of ease of use, low-cost hardware, and strong security, tunnels and the Internet are a combination that will see more use in the future. IPsec, VPN, and tunnels will become a major set of tools for users requiring secure network connections across public segments of networks. For more information on VPNs and remote access, refer to Chapter 11.

Chapter 9 Review

For More Information

- **The Internet Engineering Task Force**
  www.ietf.org

- **Wikipedia articles:**
  Routing http://en.wikipedia.org/wiki/Routing
  NAT http://en.wikipedia.org/wiki/Network_address_translation

ICMP http://en.wikipedia.org/wiki/Internet_Control_Message_Protocol
Subnetting http://en.wikipedia.org/wiki/Subnetting

Chapter Summary

After reading this chapter and completing the exercises, you should understand the following about networks.

Identify the basic network architectures

- There are two broad categories of networks: LANs and WANs.

- The physical arrangement of a network is typically called the network's topology.

- There are four main types of network topologies: ring, bus, star, and mixed.

Define the basic network protocols

- Protocols, agreed-upon formats for exchanging or transmitting data between systems, enable computers to communicate.

- When data is transmitted over a network, it is usually broken up into smaller pieces called packets.

- Most protocols define the types and format for packets used in that protocol.

- The TCP protocol is connection oriented, requires the three-way handshake to initiate a connection, and provides guaranteed and reliable data delivery.

- The UDP protocol is connectionless, lightweight, and provides limited error checking and no delivery guarantee.

- Each network device has a unique hardware address known as a MAC address. The MAC address is used for packet delivery.

- Network devices are also typically assigned a 32-bit number known as an IP address.

- The Domain Name Service (DNS) translates names, like www.cnn.com, into IP addresses.

Explain routing and address translation

- The process of moving packets from one end device to another through different networks is called routing.

- Subnetting is the process of dividing a network address space into smaller networks.

- The DHCP protocol allows network devices to be automatically configured on a network and temporarily assigned an IP address.

- Network Address Translation (NAT) converts private, internal IP addresses to public, routable IP addresses and vice versa.

Classify security zones

- A DMZ is a buffer zone between networks with different trust levels. Companies often place public resources in a DMZ so that Internet users and internal users may access those resources without exposing the internal company network to the Internet.

- An intranet is a private, internal network that uses common network technologies (such as HTTP, FTP, and so on) to share information and provide resources to organizational users.

- An extranet is a semiprivate network that uses common network technologies (such as HTTP, FTP, and so on) to share information and provide resources to business partners.

- A VLAN (or virtual LAN) is a group of ports on a switch that is configured to create a logical network of computers that appears to be connected to the same network even if they are located on different physical network segments. Systems on a VLAN can communicate with each other but cannot communicate directly with systems on other VLANs.

- Trunking is the process of spanning a single VLAN across multiple switches.

- Tunneling is a method of packaging packets so that they can traverse a network in a secure, confidential manner.

■ Key Terms

Address Resolution Protocol (ARP) *(213)*
bus topology *(206)*
datagram *(209)*
denial-of-service (DoS) *(212)*
Domain Name System (DNS) *(214)*
DMZ *(219)*
Dynamic Host Configuration Protocol (DHCP) *(217)*
extranet *(221)*
Internet Control Message Protocol (ICMP) *(211)*
Internet Protocol (IP) *(214)*
intranet *(221)*
local area network (LAN) *(205)*
Media Access Control (MAC) address *(213)*
Network Address Translation (NAT) *(217)*
network *(204)*
packet *(209)*

protocol *(207)*
ring topology *(206)*
routing *(214)*
star topology *(206)*
storage area network (SAN) *(205)*
subnetting *(215)*
subnet mask *(215)*
three-way handshake *(211)*
topology *(206)*
Transmission Control Protocol (TCP) *(210)*
trunking *(222)*
tunneling *(223)*
User Datagram Protocol (UDP) *(210)*
virtual local area network (VLAN) *(206)*
wide area network (WAN) *(205)*

■ Key Terms Quiz

Use terms from the Key Terms list to complete the sentences that follow. Don't use the same term more than once. Not all terms will be used.

1. A(n) _____ is a group of two or more devices linked together to share data.

2. A packet in an IP network is sometimes called a _____.

3. Moving packet from source to destination across multiple networks is called _____.

4. The _____ is the hardware address used to uniquely identify each device on a network.

5. A(n) _____ tells you what portion of a 32-bit IP address is being used as the network ID and what portion is being used as the host ID.

6. The shape or arrangement of a network, such as bus, star, ring, or mixed, is known as the _____ of the network.

7. A small, typically local network covering a relatively small area such as a single floor of an office building is called a(n) _____.

8. A(n) _____ is an agreed-upon format for exchanging information between systems.

9. The packet exchange sequence (SYN, SYN/ACK, ACK) that initiates a TCP connection is called the _____.

10. _____ is the protocol that allows the use of private, internal IP addresses for internal traffic and public IP addresses for external traffic.

■ Multiple-Choice Quiz

1. Which of the following topologies connects all the network devices to a central point?

   A. Mixed

   B. Ring

   C. Bus

   D. Star

2. As it relates to networking, what does WAN stand for?

   A. Wide area node

   B. Wide alternate network

   C. Wide area network

   D. Wide automated network

3. What is Layer 1 of the OSI model called?

   A. The physical layer

   B. The network layer

   C. The initial layer

   D. The presentation layer

4. The UDP protocol:

   A. Provides excellent error-checking algorithms

   B. Is a connectionless protocol

   C. Guarantees delivery of packets

   D. Requires a permanent connection between source and destination

5. The process that dynamically assigns an IP address to a network device is called:

   A. NAT

   B. DNS

   C. DHCP

   D. Routing

6. What is the three-way handshake sequence used to initiate TCP connections?

   A. ACK, SYN/ACK, ACK

   B. SYN, SYN/ACK, ACK

   C. SYN, SYN, ACK/ACK

   D. ACK, SYN/ACK, SYN

7. For transmission, large amounts of data are normally broken up into smaller pieces known as:

   A. UDPs

   B. ICMPs

   C. Packets

   D. Subnets

8. Which of the following is a control and information protocol used by network devices to determine such things as a remote network's availability and the length of time required to reach a remote network?

   A. UDP

   B. NAT

   C. TCP

   D. ICMP

9. What is the name of the protocol that translates names into IP addresses?

   A. TCP

   B. DNS

   C. ICMP

   D. DHCP

10. Dividing a network address space into smaller, separate networks is called what?

    A. Translating

    B. Network configuration

    C. Subnetting

    D. Address translation

11. Which protocol translates private (nonroutable) IP addresses into public (routable) IP addresses?

    A. NAT

    B. DHCP

    C. DNS

    D. ICMP

12. The TCP protocol:

    A. Is connectionless

    B. Provides no error checking

    C. Allows for packets to be processed in the order they were sent

    D. Has no overhead

13. What is the most widely used network protocol?

   A. SS7

   B. Token Ring

   C. Ethernet

   D. SNA

14. Which of the following would be a valid MAC address?

   A. 00:07:e9

   B. 00:07:e9:7c:c8

   C. 00:07:e9:7c:c8:aa

   D. 00:07:e9:7c:c8:aa:ba

15. To divide a single switch into multiple broadcast domains and/or multiple network segments, you might use:

   A. DHCP

   B. Tunneling

   C. NAT

   D. VLANs

■ Essay Quiz

1. A developer in your company is building a new application and has asked you if it should use TCP- or UDP-based communications. Provide her with a brief discussion of the advantages and disadvantages of each protocol.

2. Your boss wants to know if DHCP is appropriate for both server and PC environments. Provide her with your opinion and be sure to include a discussion of how DCHP works.

3. Describe the three basic types of network topologies and provide a sample diagram of each type.

4. Describe the three-way handshake process used to initiate TCP connections.

5. Your boss wants to know how subnetting works. Provide her with a brief description and be sure to include an example to illustrate how subnetting works.

Lab Projects

• Lab Project 9.1

A client of yours only has five external, routable IP addresses but has over 50 systems that it wants to be able to reach the Internet for web surfing, e-mail, and so on. Design a network solution for the client that addresses their immediate needs but will still let them grow in the future.

• Lab Project 9.2

Your boss wants you to learn how to use the **arp** and **nslookup** commands. Find a Windows 2000 or XP machine and open a command/DOS prompt. Type in **arp** and press ENTER to see the options for the **arp** command. Use the **arp** command to find the MAC address of your system and at least five other systems on your network. When you are finished with **arp**, type in **nslookup** and press ENTER. At the prompt, type in the name of your favorite web site, such as www.cnn.com. The **nslookup** command will return the IP addresses that match that domain name. Find the IP addresses of at least five different web sites.

chapter
10

Infrastructure Security

The higher your structure is to be, the deeper must be its foundation.

—SAINT AUGUSTINE

In this chapter, you will learn how to

- **Construct networks using different types of network devices**
- **Enhance security using NAC/NAP methodologies**
- **Identify the different types of media used to carry network signals**
- **Describe the different types of storage media used to store information**
- **Use basic terminology associated with network functions related to information security**

Infrastructure security begins with the design of the infrastructure itself. The proper use of components improves not only performance but security as well. Network components are not isolated from the computing environment and are an essential aspect of a total computing environment. From the routers, switches, and cables that connect the devices, to the firewalls and gateways that manage communication, from the network design, to the protocols that are employed—all these items play essential roles in both performance and security.

Devices

A complete network computer solution in today's business environment consists of more than just client computers and servers. *Devices* are needed to connect the clients and servers and to regulate the traffic between them. Devices are also needed to expand this network beyond simple client computers and servers to include yet other devices, such as wireless and handheld systems. Devices come in many forms and with many functions, from hubs and switches, to routers, wireless access points, and special-purpose devices such as virtual private network (VPN) devices. Each device has a specific network function and plays a role in maintaining network infrastructure security.

Workstations

Most users are familiar with the client computers used in the client/server model called *workstation* devices. The **workstation** is the machine that sits on the desktop and is used every day for sending and reading e-mail, creating spreadsheets, writing reports in a word processing program, and playing games. If a workstation is connected to a network, it is an important part of the security solution for the network. Many threats to information security can start at a workstation, but much can be done in a few simple steps to provide protection from many of these threats.

Antivirus Software for Workstations

Antivirus packages are available from a wide range of vendors. Running a network of computers

Cross Check

The Importance of Availability

In Chapter 2, we examined the *CIA* of security: confidentiality, integrity, and availability. Unfortunately, the availability component is often overlooked, even though availability is what has moved computing into the modern networked framework and plays a significant role in security. A failure in availability is a security failure when availability is an essential aspect of the system. A failure in security can easily lead to a failure in availability and hence a failure of the system to meet user needs.

Security failures can occur in two ways. First, a failure can allow unauthorized users access to resources and data they are not authorized to use, compromising information security. Second, a failure can prevent a user from accessing resources and data the user is authorized to use. This second failure is often overlooked, but it can be as serious as the first. The primary goal of network infrastructure security is to allow all authorized use and deny all unauthorized use of resources.

Try This

Securing a Workstation

Workstations are attractive targets for crackers because they are numerous and can serve as entry points into the network and the data that is commonly the target of an attack. Although *safety* is a relative term, following these basic steps will increase workstation security immensely:

- Remove unnecessary protocols such as Telnet, NetBIOS, IPX.
- Remove unnecessary software.
- Remove modems unless needed and authorized.
- Remove all shares that are not necessary.
- Rename the administrator account, securing it with a strong password.
- Disable unnecessary user accounts.
- Disable unnecessary services.
- Install an antivirus program and keep abreast of updates.
- If the floppy drive is not needed, remove or disconnect it.
- Consider disabling USB ports via CMOS to restrict data movement to USB devices.
- If no corporate firewall exists between the machine and the Internet, install a firewall.
- Keep the operating system (OS) patched and up to date.

without this basic level of protection will be an exercise in futility. Even though the number of widespread, indiscriminate broadcast virus attacks has decreased because of the effectiveness of antivirus software, it is still necessary to use antivirus software; the time and money you would spend cleaning up after a virus attack more than equals the cost of antivirus protection. The majority of viruses today exist to create zombie machines for botnets that enable others to control resources on your PC. Even more important, once connected by networks, computers can spread a virus from machine to machine with an ease that's even greater than simple USB flash drive transfer. One unprotected machine can lead to problems throughout a network as other machines have to use their antivirus software to attempt to clean up a spreading infection.

Even secure networks can fall prey to virus and worm contamination, and infection has been known to come from commercial packages. As important as antivirus software is, it is even more important to keep the virus definitions for the software up to date. Out-of-date definitions can lead to a false sense of security, and many of the most potent virus and worm attacks are the newest ones being developed. The risk associated with a new virus is actually higher than for many of the old ones, which have been eradicated to a great extent by antivirus software. In all but the smallest networks, managed antivirus solutions that allow administrators to ensure that all clients have up-to-date definitions are essential to manage multiple workstations efficiently.

A virus is a piece of software that attaches itself to a file and then executes on a machine. Worms can spread without attaching themselves to a file, and thus can be self-replicating. Workstations are the primary mode of entry for viruses into a network. Although a lot of methods can be used to introduce a virus into a network, the two most common are transfer of an infected file from another networked machine and transfer of an infected file via e-mail. Worms do not require a file to transfer and hence can move from machine to machine without file transfer operations. A lot of work has gone into software to clean e-mail while in transit and at the mail server. But transferred files are a different matter altogether. People bring files from home, from friends, from places unknown and then execute them on a PC for a variety of purposes. It doesn't matter whether it is a funny executable, a game, or even an authorized work application—the virus doesn't care what type of file the original file is; it just uses the file to gain access. Even sharing of legitimate work applications can introduce viruses.

Apple Macintosh computers were once considered by many users to be immune because very few examples of malicious software targeting Macs existed. This was not due to anything other than a low market share, and hence the devices were ignored by the malware community as a whole. As Mac has increased in market share, so has its exposure, and today a variety of Mac OS X malware steals files and passwords and is even used to take users' pictures with the computer's built-in webcam. All user machines need to install antivirus software in today's environment, because any computer can become a target.

Additional Precautions for Workstations

A personal firewall is a necessity if a machine has an unprotected interface to the Internet. These firewalls are seen less often in commercial networks because it is more cost effective to connect through a dedicated network firewall. With the advent of broadband connections for homes and small offices, this essential device is frequently overlooked. This can result in penetration of a PC from an outside hacker or a worm infection. Worst of all, the workstation can become part of a larger attack against another network, unknowingly joining forces with other compromised machines in a distributed denial-of-service (DDoS) attack.

Cross Check

Malware

Malware comes in many forms and is covered specifically in Chapter 15. Antivirus solutions and proper workstation configurations are part of a defensive posture against various forms of malware. Additional steps include policy and procedure actions, prohibiting file sharing via USB or external media, and prohibiting access to certain web sites.

The primary method of controlling the security impact of a workstation on a network is to reduce the available attack surface area. Turning off all services that are not needed or permitted by policy will reduce the number of vulnerabilities. Removing methods of connecting additional devices to a workstation to move data—such as CD/DVD drives and USB ports—assists in controlling the movement of data into and out of the device. User-level controls, such as limiting e-mail attachment options, screening all attachments at the e-mail server level, and reducing network shares to needed shares only, can be used to limit the excessive connectivity that can impact security. Having a standard image of a workstation and duplicating it across a bunch of identical workstations will reduce the workload for maintaining these requirements and reduce total cost of operations. Proper security at the workstation level can increase availability of network resources to users, enabling the business to operate as effectively as possible.

Try This

BIOS Settings

There are settings in the BIOS that can also assist in upgrading the security level of a workstation. For example, you can disable the ability to boot from the CD/DVD drive. During a cold boot of your workstation, enter into the BIOS options (usually by pressing the F12 key when the splash screen appears) and explore the options for boot sequence and device disablement.

Finally, restricting physical access to the workstation to only approved personnel is an important issue. If a malicious person were able to access to the workstation, they would be able to modify the computer's BIOS and add programs, including keyloggers and other malware. Physical access can mean compromise for all but the most locked-down machines. For these reasons, it is important to password-protect the BIOS.

Servers

Servers are the computers in a network that host applications and data for everyone to share. Servers come in many sizes, from small single-CPU boxes that may be less powerful than a workstation, to multiple-CPU monsters, up to and including mainframes. The operating systems used by servers range from Windows Server, to UNIX, to Multiple Virtual Storage (MVS) and other mainframe operating systems. The OS on a server tends to be more robust than the OS on a workstation system and is designed to service multiple users over a network at the same time. Servers can host a variety of applications, including web servers, databases, e-mail servers, file servers, print servers, and application servers for middleware applications.

The key management issue behind running a secure server setup is to identify the specific needs of a server for its proper operation and enable only items necessary for those functions. Keeping all other services and users off the system improves system throughput and increases security. Reducing the attack surface area associated with a server reduces the vulnerabilities now and in the future as updates are required.

Once a server has been built and is ready to be placed into operation, the recording of MD5 hash values on all of its crucial files will provide valuable information later in case of a question concerning possible system integrity after a detected intrusion. The use of hash values to detect changes was first developed by Gene Kim and Eugene Spafford at Purdue University in 1992. The concept became the product Tripwire, which is now available in commercial and open source forms. The same basic concept is used by many security packages to detect file-level changes.

Antivirus Software for Servers

The need for antivirus protection on servers depends a great deal on the use of the server. Some types of servers, such as e-mail servers, require extensive antivirus protection because of the services they provide. Other servers (domain controllers and remote access servers, for example) may not require any antivirus software, as they do not allow users to place files on them. File servers need protection, as do certain types of application servers. There is no general rule, so each server and its role in the network will need to be examined to determine whether it needs antivirus software.

Virtualization

A recent trend for both servers and workstations is the addition of a virtualization layer between the hardware and the operating system. This virtualization layer provides many benefits, allowing multiple operating systems to operate concurrently on the same hardware. Virtualization offers many advantages in the form of operational flexibility. It also offers some security advantages. If a browser surfing the Web downloads harmful content, the virtual machine can be deleted at the end of the session, preventing the spread of any malware to the other operating systems.

Network Interface Cards

To connect a server or workstation to a network, a device known as a **network interface card (NIC)** is used. A NIC is a card with a connector port for a particular type of network connection, either Ethernet or Token Ring. The most common network type in use for local area networks (LANs) is the Ethernet protocol, and the most common connector is the RJ-45 connector. Figure 10.1 shows an RJ-45 connector (lower) compared to a standard telephone connector (upper). Additional types of connectors include coaxial cable connectors, frequently used with cable modems and extending from the wall to the cable modem.

• **Figure 10.1** Comparison of RJ-45 (lower) and phone connectors (upper)

A NIC is the physical connection between a computer and the network. The purpose of a NIC is to provide lower-level protocol functionality from the OSI (Open System Interconnection) model. Because the NIC defines the type of physical layer connection, different NICs are used for different physical protocols. NICs come as single-port and multiport, and most workstations use only a single-port NIC, as only a single network connection is needed. Figure 10.2 shows a common form of a NIC. For servers, multiport NICs are used to increase the number of network connections, increasing the data throughput to and from the network.

Each NIC port is serialized with a unique code, 48 bits long, referred to as a Media Access Control address (MAC address). These are created by the manufacturer, with 24 bits representing the manufacturer and 24 bits being a serial number, guaranteeing uniqueness. MAC addresses are used in the addressing and delivery of network packets to the correct machine and in a variety of security situations. Unfortunately, these addresses can be changed, or "spoofed," rather easily. In fact, it is common for personal routers to clone a MAC address to allow users to use multiple devices over a network connection that expects a single MAC.

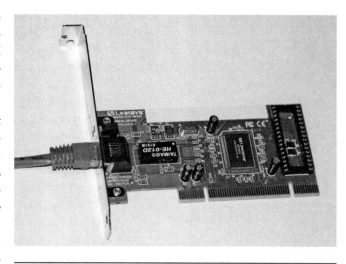

• **Figure 10.2**   Linksys network interface card (NIC)

Hubs

A **hub** is networking equipment that connects devices that are using the same protocol at the physical layer of the OSI model. A hub allows multiple machines in an area to be connected together in a star configuration, with the hub as the center. This configuration can save significant amounts of cable and is an efficient method of configuring an Ethernet backbone. All connections on a hub share a single **collision domain**, a small cluster in a network where collisions occur. As network traffic increases, it can become limited by collisions. The collision issue has made hubs obsolete in newer, higher performance networks, with low-cost switches and switched Ethernet keeping costs low and usable bandwidth high. Hubs also create a security weakness in that all connected devices see all traffic, enabling sniffing and eavesdropping to occur. In today's networks, hubs have all but disappeared, being replaced by low-cost switches.

Bridges

Bridges are networking equipment that connect devices using the same protocol at the data link layer of the OSI model. A **bridge** operates at the data link layer, filtering traffic based on MAC addresses. Bridges can reduce collisions by separating pieces of a network into two separate collision domains, but this only cuts the collision problem in half. Although bridges are useful, a better solution is to use switches for network connections.

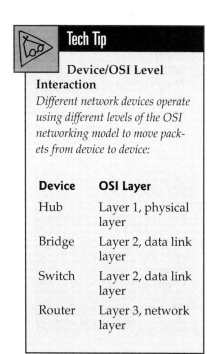

Tech Tip

Device/OSI Level Interaction

Different network devices operate using different levels of the OSI networking model to move packets from device to device:

Device	OSI Layer
Hub	Layer 1, physical layer
Bridge	Layer 2, data link layer
Switch	Layer 2, data link layer
Router	Layer 3, network layer

Switches

A **switch** forms the basis for connections in most Ethernet-based LANs. Although hubs and bridges still exist, in today's high-performance network environment, switches have replaced both. A switch has separate collision domains for each port. This means that for each port, two collision domains exist: one from the port to the client on the downstream side, and one from the switch to the network upstream. When *full duplex* is employed, collisions are virtually eliminated from the two nodes, host and client. This also acts as a security factor in that a sniffer can see only limited traffic, as opposed to a hub-based system, where a single sniffer can see all of the traffic to and from connected devices.

Switches operate at the data link layer, while routers act at the network layer. For intranets, switches have become what routers are on the Internet—the device of choice for connecting machines. As switches have become the primary network connectivity device, additional functionality has been added to them. A switch is usually a Layer 2 device, but Layer 3 switches incorporate routing functionality.

Switches can also perform a variety of security functions. Switches work by moving packets from inbound connections to outbound connections. While moving the packets, it is possible to inspect the packet headers and enforce security policies. Port address security based on MAC addresses can determine whether a packet is allowed or blocked from a connection. This is the very function that a firewall uses for its determination, and this same functionality is what allows an 802.1X device to act as an "edge device."

One of the security concerns with switches is that, like routers, they are intelligent network devices and are therefore subject to hijacking by hackers. Should a hacker break into a switch and change its parameters, he might be able to eavesdrop on specific or all communications, virtually undetected. Switches are commonly administered using the Simple Network Management Protocol (SNMP) and Telnet protocol, both of which have a serious weakness in that they send passwords across the network in clear text. A hacker armed with a sniffer that observes maintenance on a switch can capture the administrative password. This allows the hacker to come back to the switch later and configure it as an administrator. An additional problem is that switches are shipped with default passwords, and if these are not changed when the switch is set up, they offer an unlocked door to a hacker. Commercial-quality switches have a local serial console port for guaranteed access to the switch for purposes of control. Some products in the marketplace enable an out-of-band network, connecting these serial console ports to enable remote, secure access to programmable network devices.

Switches are also subject to electronic attacks, such as ARP poisoning and MAC flooding. ARP poisoning is where a device spoofs the MAC address of another device, attempting to change the ARP tables through spoofed traffic and the ARP table-update mechanism. MAC flooding is where a switch is bombarded with packets from different MAC addresses, flooding the switch table and forcing the device to respond by opening all ports and acting as a hub. This enables devices on other segments to sniff traffic.

Hubs have been replaced by switches because switches perform a number of features that hubs cannot perform. For example, the switch improves

To secure a switch, you should disable all access protocols other than a secure serial line or a secure protocol such as Secure Shell (SSH). Using only secure methods to access a switch will limit the exposure to hackers and malicious users. Maintaining secure network switches is even more important than securing individual boxes, for the span of control to intercept data is much wider on a switch, especially if it's reprogrammed by a hacker.

network performance by filtering traffic. It filters traffic by only sending the data to the port on the switch that the destination system resides on. With a hub, the data is always sent to all ports on the hub, which wastes bandwidth when the destination system resides on only one of the ports. The switch knows what port each system is connected to and sends the data only to that port. The switch also provides security features, such as the option to disable a port so that it cannot be used without authorization. The switch also supports a feature called port security, which allows the administrator to control which systems can send data to each of the ports. The switch uses the MAC address of the systems to incorporate traffic filtering and port security features, which is why it is considered a Layer 2 device.

Routers

A **router** is a network traffic management device used to connect different network segments together. Routers operate at the network layer (Layer 3) of the OSI model, using the network address (typically an IP address) to route traffic and using routing protocols to determine optimal routing paths across a network. Routers form the backbone of the Internet, moving traffic from network to network, inspecting packets from every communication as they move traffic in optimal paths.

Routers operate by examining each packet, looking at the destination address, and using algorithms and tables to determine where to send the packet next. This process of examining the header to determine the next hop can be done in quick fashion.

Routers use access control lists (ACLs) as a method of deciding whether a packet is allowed to enter the network. With ACLs, it is also possible to examine the source address and determine whether or not to allow a packet to pass. This allows routers equipped with ACLs to drop packets according to rules built into the ACLs. This can be a cumbersome process to set up and maintain, and as the ACL grows in size, routing efficiency can be decreased. It is also possible to configure some routers to act as quasi–application gateways, performing stateful packet inspection and using contents as well as IP addresses to determine whether or not to permit a packet to pass. This can tremendously increase the time for a router to pass traffic and can significantly decrease router throughput. Configuring ACLs and other aspects of setting up routers for this type of use are beyond the scope of this book.

One serious security concern regarding router operation is limiting who has access to the router and control of its internal functions. Like a switch, a router can be accessed using SNMP and Telnet and programmed remotely. Because of the geographic separation of routers, this can become a necessity, for many routers in the world of the Internet can be hundreds of miles apart, in separate locked structures. Physical control over a router is absolutely necessary, for if any device, be it server, switch, or router, is physically accessed by a hacker, it should be considered compromised. Thus, such access must be prevented. As with switches, it is important to ensure that the administrator password is never passed in the clear, that only secure mechanisms are used to access the router, and that all of the default passwords are reset to strong passwords.

As with switches, the most assured point of access for router management control is via the serial control interface port. This allows access to the

ACLs can require significant effort to establish and maintain. Creating them is a straightforward task, but their judicious use will yield security benefits with a limited amount of maintenance. Cisco routers have standard and extended ACLs; standard ACLs can filter traffic based only on the source IP address, whereas extended ACLs can filter traffic by source/destination IP address, protocol, and port. This can be very important in security zones such as a DMZ and at edge devices, blocking undesired outside contact while allowing known inside traffic.

control aspects of the router without having to deal with traffic-related issues. For internal company networks, where the geographic dispersion of routers may be limited, third-party solutions to allow out-of-band remote management exist. This allows complete control over the router in a secure fashion, even from a remote location, although additional hardware is required.

Routers are available from numerous vendors and come in sizes big and small. A typical small home office router for use with cable modem/ DSL service is shown in Figure 10.3. Larger routers can handle traffic of up to tens of gigabytes per second per channel, using fiber-optic inputs and moving tens of thousands of concurrent Internet connections across the network. These routers, which can cost hundreds of thousands of dollars, form an essential part of e-commerce infrastructure, enabling large enterprises such as Amazon and eBay to serve many customers concurrently.

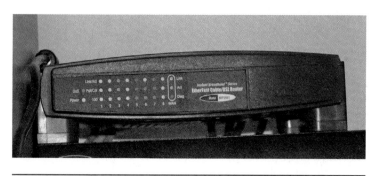

• **Figure 10.3**   A small home office router for cable modem/DSL use

Firewalls

A **firewall** can be hardware, software, or a combination whose purpose is to enforce a set of network security policies across network connections. It is much like a wall with a window: the wall serves to keep things out, except those permitted through the window (see Figure 10.4). Network security policies act like the glass in the window; they permit some things to pass, such as light, while blocking others, such as air. The heart of a firewall is the set of security policies that it enforces. Management determines what is allowed in the form of network traffic between devices, and these policies are used to build rule sets for the firewall devices used to filter network traffic across the network.

Security policies are rules that define what traffic is permissible and what traffic is to be blocked or denied. These are not universal rules, and many different sets of rules are created for a single company with multiple connections. A web server connected to the Internet may be configured to allow traffic only on port 80 for HTTP and have all other ports blocked, for example. An e-mail server may have only necessary ports for e-mail open, with others blocked. The network firewall can be programmed to block all traffic to the web server except for port 80 traffic, and to block all traffic bound to the mail server except for port 25. In this fashion, the firewall acts as a security filter, enabling control over network traffic, by IP address, by protocol, by port, and in

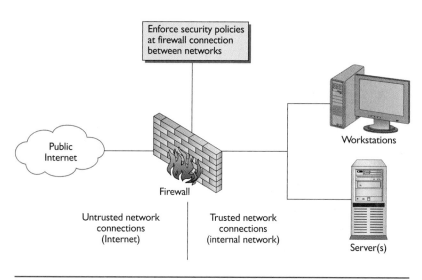

• **Figure 10.4**   How a firewall works

some cases based on application-level detail. A key to setting security policies for firewalls is the same as has been seen for other security policies—the principle of least access. Allow only the necessary access for a function; block or deny all unneeded functionality. How a firm deploys its firewalls determines what is needed for security policies for each firewall.

As will be discussed later, the security topology will determine what network devices are employed at what points in a network. At a minimum, the corporate connection to the Internet should pass through a firewall. This firewall should block all network traffic except that specifically authorized by the firm. This is actually easy to do: Blocking communications on a port is simple—just tell the firewall to close the port. The issue comes in deciding what services are needed and by whom, and thus which ports should be open and which should be closed. This is what makes a security policy useful. The perfect set of network security policies, for a firewall, is one that the end user never sees and that never allows even a single unauthorized packet to enter the network. As with any other perfect item, it will be rare to find the perfect set of security policies for firewalls in an enterprise.

To develop a complete and comprehensive security policy, it is first necessary to have a complete and comprehensive understanding of your network resources and their uses. Once you know how the network will be used, you will have an idea of what to permit. In addition, once you understand what you need to protect, you will have an idea of what to block. Firewalls are designed to block attacks before they reach a target machine. Common targets are web servers, e-mail servers, DNS servers, FTP services, and databases. Each of these has separate functionality, and each has unique vulnerabilities. Once you have decided who should receive what type of traffic and what types should be blocked, you can administer this through the firewall.

One of the most basic security functions provided by a firewall is NAT, which allows you to mask significant amounts of information from outside of the network. This allows an outside entity to communicate with an entity inside the firewall without truly knowing its address. NAT is a technique used in IPv4 to link private IP addresses to public ones. NAT is described in detail in Chapter 9.

Basic packet filtering, the next most common firewall technique, involves looking at packets, their ports, protocols, and source and destination addresses, and checking that information against the rules configured on the firewall. Telnet and FTP connections may be prohibited from being established to a mail or database server, but they may be allowed for the respective service servers. This is a fairly simple method of filtering based on information in each packet header, such as IP addresses and TCP/UDP ports. Packet filtering will not detect and catch all undesired packets, but it is fast and efficient.

To look at all packets and determine the need for each and its data requires stateful packet filtering. *Stateful* means that the firewall maintains, or knows, the context of a conversation. In many cases, rules depend on the context of a specific communication connection. For instance, traffic from an outside server to an inside server may be allowed if it is requested but blocked if it is not. A common example is a request for a web page. This request is actually a series of requests to multiple servers, each of which can be allowed or blocked. Advanced firewalls employ stateful packet filtering to prevent several types of undesired communications. Should a packet come

Tech Tip

How Do Firewalls Work?

Firewalls enforce the established security policies through a variety of mechanisms, including the following:

- *Network Address Translation (NAT)*
- *Basic packet filtering*
- *Stateful packet filtering*
- *ACLs*
- *Application layer proxies*

Tech Tip

Firewall Operations

Application layer firewalls such as proxy servers can analyze information in the header and data portion of the packet, whereas packet-filtering firewalls can analyze only the header of a packet.

from outside the network, in an attempt to pretend that it is a response to a message from inside the network, the firewall will have no record of it being requested and can discard it, blocking the undesired external access attempt. As many communications will be transferred to high ports (above 1023), stateful monitoring will enable the system to determine which sets of high communications are permissible and which should be blocked. A disadvantage of stateful monitoring is that it takes significant resources and processing to perform this type of monitoring, and this reduces efficiency and requires more robust and expensive hardware.

Some high-security firewalls also employ application layer proxies. Packets are not allowed to traverse the firewall, but data instead flows up to an application that in turn decides what to do with it. For example, a Simple Mail Transfer Protocol (SMTP) proxy may accept inbound mail from the Internet and forward it to the internal corporate mail server. While proxies provide a high level of security by making it very difficult for an attacker to manipulate the actual packets arriving at the destination, and while they provide the opportunity for an application to interpret the data prior to forwarding it to the destination, they generally are not capable of the same throughput as stateful packet-inspection firewalls. The trade-off between performance and speed is a common one and must be evaluated with respect to security needs and performance requirements.

Wireless

Wireless devices bring additional security concerns. There is, by definition, no physical connection to a wireless device; radio waves or infrared carry data, which allows anyone within range access to the data. This means that unless you take specific precautions, you have no control over who can see your data. Placing a wireless device behind a firewall does not do any good, because the firewall stops only physically connected traffic from reaching the device. Outside traffic can come literally from the parking lot directly to the wireless device and into the network.

The point of entry from a wireless device to a wired network is performed at a device called a **wireless access point**. Wireless access points can support multiple concurrent devices accessing network resources through the network node they create. A typical wireless access point is shown here:

• A typical wireless access point

Several mechanisms can be used to add wireless functionality to a machine. For PCs, this can be done via an expansion card. For notebooks, a PCMCIA adapter for wireless networks is available from several vendors. For both PCs and notebooks, vendors have introduced USB-based wireless connectors. The following illustration shows one vendor's card—note the extended length used as an antenna. Not all cards have the same configuration, although they all perform the same function: to enable a wireless network connection. The numerous wireless protocols (802.11a, b, g, i, and n) are covered in Chapter 12. Wireless access points and cards must be matched by protocol for proper operation.

 To prevent unauthorized wireless access to the network, configuration of remote access protocols to a wireless access point is common. Forcing authentication and verifying authorization is a seamless method of performing basic network security for connections in this fashion. These protocols are covered in Chapter 11.

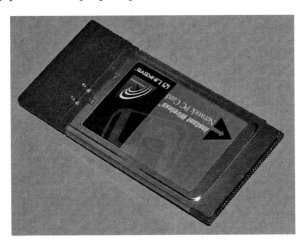

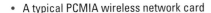

- A typical PCMIA wireless network card

Modems

Modems were once a slow method of remote connection that was used to connect client workstations to remote services over standard telephone lines. **Modem** is a shortened form of *modulator/demodulator*, converting analog signals to digital and vice versa. Connecting a digital computer signal to the analog telephone line required one of these devices. Today, the use of the term has expanded to cover devices connected to special digital telephone lines—DSL modems—and to cable television lines—cable modems. Although these devices are not actually modems in the true sense of the word, the term has stuck through marketing efforts directed to consumers. DSL and cable modems offer broadband high-speed connections and the opportunity for continuous connections to the Internet. Along with these new desirable characteristics come some undesirable ones, however. Although they both provide the same type of service, cable and DSL modems have some differences. A DSL modem provides a direct connection between a subscriber's computer and an Internet connection at the local telephone company's switching station. This private connection offers a degree of security, as it does not involve others sharing the circuit. Cable modems are set up in shared arrangements that theoretically could allow a neighbor to sniff a user's cable modem traffic.

Cable modems were designed to share a party line in the terminal signal area, and the cable modem standard, Data Over Cable Service Interface

Specification (DOCSIS), was designed to accommodate this concept. DOCSIS includes built-in support for security protocols, including authentication and packet filtering. Although this does not guarantee privacy, it prevents ordinary subscribers from seeing others' traffic without using specialized hardware.

Both cable and DSL services are designed for a continuous connection, which brings up the question of IP address life for a client. Although some services originally used a static IP arrangement, virtually all have now adopted the Dynamic Host Configuration Protocol (DHCP) to manage their address space. A static IP address has an advantage of remaining the same and enabling convenient DNS connections for outside users. As cable and DSL services are primarily designed for client services as opposed to host services, this is not a relevant issue. A security issue of a static IP address is that it is a stationary target for hackers. The move to DHCP has not significantly lessened this threat, however, because the typical IP lease on a cable modem DHCP is for days. This is still relatively stationary, and some form of firewall protection needs to be employed by the user.

Cable/DSL Security

The modem equipment provided by the subscription service converts the cable or DSL signal into a standard Ethernet signal that can then be connected to a NIC on the client device. This is still just a direct network connection, with no security device separating the two. The most common security device used in cable/DSL connections is a router that acts as a hardware firewall. The firewall/router needs to be installed between the cable/DSL modem and client computers.

Two common methods to implement firewalls exist in the marketplace. The first is software on each client device. Numerous software companies offer Internet firewall packages, which can cost under $50. Another solution is the use of a cable/DSL router with a built-in firewall. These are also relatively inexpensive, in the $100 range, and can be combined with software for an additional level of protection. Another advantage to the router solution is that most such routers allow multiple clients to share a common Internet connection, and most can also be enabled with other networking protocols such as VPN. A typical small home office cable modem/DSL router was shown earlier, in Figure 10.3. The bottom line is simple: Even if you connect only occasionally and you disconnect between uses, you need a firewall between the client and the Internet connection. Most commercial firewalls for cable/DSL systems come preconfigured for Internet use and require virtually no maintenance other than keeping the system up to date.

Telecom/PBX

A **private branch exchange (PBX)** is an extension of the public telephone network into a business. Although typically considered separate entities from data systems, PBXs are frequently interconnected and have security requirements as part of this interconnection, as well as security requirements of their own. PBXs are computer-based switching equipment designed to connect telephones into the local phone system. Basically digital switching systems, they can be compromised from the outside and used by phone hackers (*phreakers*) to make phone calls at the business's expense. Although this type of hacking has decreased as the cost of long distance calling has decreased, it has not gone away, and as several firms learn every year, voice mail boxes and PBXs can be compromised and the long-distance bills can get very high, very fast.

Another problem with PBXs arises when they are interconnected to the data systems, either by corporate connection or by rogue modems in the hands of users. In either case, a path exists for connection to outside data networks and the Internet. Just as a firewall is needed for security on data connections, one is needed for these connections as well. Telecommunications firewalls are a distinct type of firewall designed to protect both the PBX and the data connections. The functionality of a telecommunications firewall is the same as that of a data firewall: it is there to enforce security policies. Telecommunication security policies can be enforced even to cover hours of phone use, to prevent unauthorized long-distance usage through the implementation of access codes and/or restricted service hours.

VPN

A virtual private network (VPN) is a construct used to provide a secure communication channel between users across public networks such as the Internet. As described in Chapter 11, a variety of techniques can be employed to instantiate a VPN connection. The use of encryption technologies allows either the data in a packet to be encrypted or the entire packet to be encrypted. If the data is encrypted, the packet header can still be sniffed and observed between source and destination, but the encryption protects the contents of the packet from inspection. If the entire packet is encrypted, it is then placed into another packet and sent via tunnel across the public network. Tunneling can protect even the identity of the communicating parties.

The most common implementation of VPN is via IPsec, a protocol for IP security. IPsec is mandated in IPv6 and is optionally back-fitted into IPv4. IPsec can be implemented in hardware, software, or a combination of both and is used to encrypt all IP traffic.

Intrusion Detection Systems

Intrusion detection systems (IDSs) are an important element of infrastructure security. IDSs are designed to detect, log, and respond to unauthorized network or host use, both in real time and after the fact. IDSs are available from a wide selection of vendors and are an essential part of a comprehensive network security program. These systems are implemented using software, but in large networks or systems with significant traffic levels, dedicated hardware is typically required as well. IDSs can be divided into two categories: network-based systems and host-based systems.

Cross Check

Intrusion Detection

From a network infrastructure point of view, network-based IDSs can be considered part of infrastructure, whereas host-based IDSs are typically considered part of a comprehensive security program and not necessarily infrastructure. Two primary methods of detection are used: signature-based and anomaly-based. IDSs are covered in detail in Chapter 13.

Network Access Control

Networks comprise connected workstations and servers. Managing security on a network involves managing a wide range of issues, from various connected hardware and the software operating these devices. Assuming that the network is secure, each additional connection involves risk. Managing the endpoints on a case-by-case basis as they connect is a security methodology known as **network access control**. Two main competing methodologies exist that deal with network access control: **Network Access Protection (NAP)** is a Microsoft technology for controlling network access of a computer host, and **Network Admission Control (NAC)** is Cisco's technology for controlling network admission.

Microsoft's NAP system is based on measuring the system health of the connecting machine, including patch levels of the OS, antivirus protection, and system policies. The objective behind NAP is to enforce policy and governance standards on network devices before they are allowed data-level access to a network. NAP is first utilized in Windows XP Service Pack 3, Windows Vista, and Windows Server 2008, and it requires additional infrastructure servers to implement the health checks. The system includes enforcement agents that interrogate clients and verify admission criteria. Admission criteria can include client machine ID, status of updates, and so forth. Using NAP, network administrators can define granular levels of network access based on multiple criteria; who a client is, what groups a client belongs to, and the degree to which that client is compliant with corporate client health requirements. These health requirements include OS updates, antivirus updates, and critical patches. Response options include rejection of the connection request or restriction of admission to a subnet. NAP also provides a mechanism for automatic remediation of client health requirements and restoration of normal access when healthy.

Cisco's NAC system is built around an appliance that enforces policies chosen by the network administrator. A series of third-party solutions can interface with the appliance, allowing the verification of a whole host of options, including client policy settings, software updates, and client security posture. The use of third-party devices and software makes this an extensible system across a wide range of equipment.

Both Cisco NAC and Microsoft NAP are in their early stages of implementation. The concept of automated admission checking based on client device characteristics is here to stay, as it provides timely control in the ever-changing network world of today's enterprises.

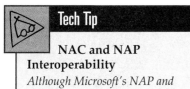

Tech Tip

NAC and NAP Interoperability
Although Microsoft's NAP and Cisco's NAC appear to be competing methodologies, they are in fact complementary. NAP allows much finer-grain control for Windows-based devices, while NAC is a more general-purpose methodology for controlling admission through edge devices. Recognizing how they can work together, Microsoft and Cisco have deployed guides on how to combine these two systems, preserving the advantages and investments in each.

SNMP, Simple Network Management Protocol, is a part of the Internet Protocol suite of protocols. It is an open standard, designed for transmission of management functions between devices. Do not confuse this with SMTP, Simple Mail Transfer Protocol, which is used to transfer mail between machines.

Network Monitoring/Diagnostic

A computer network itself can be considered a large computer system, with performance and operating issues. Just as a computer needs management, monitoring, and fault resolution, so do networks. SNMP was developed to perform this function across networks. The idea is to enable a central monitoring and control center to maintain, configure, and repair network devices, such as switches and routers, as well as other network services, such as firewalls, IDSs, and remote access servers. SNMP has some security limitations, and many vendors have developed software solutions that sit on top of SNMP to provide better security and better management tool suites.

The concept of a network operations center (NOC) comes from the old phone company network days, when central monitoring centers monitored the health of the telephone network and provided interfaces for maintenance and management. This same concept works well with computer networks, and companies with midsize and larger networks employ the same philosophy. The NOC allows operators to observe and interact with the network, using the self-reporting and, in some cases, self-healing nature of network devices to ensure efficient network operation. Although generally a boring operation under normal conditions, when things start to go wrong, as in the case of a virus or worm attack, the NOC can become a busy and stressful place as operators attempt to return the system to full efficiency while not interrupting existing traffic.

As networks can be spread out literally around the world, it is not feasible to have a person visit each device for control functions. Software enables controllers at NOCs to measure the actual performance of network devices and make changes to the configuration and operation of devices remotely. The ability to make remote connections with this level of functionality is both a blessing and a security issue. Although this allows efficient network operations management, it also provides an opportunity for unauthorized entry into a network. For this reason, a variety of security controls are used, from secondary networks to VPNs and advanced authentication methods with respect to network control connections.

Network monitoring is an ongoing concern for any significant network. In addition to monitoring traffic flow and efficiency, monitoring of security-related events is necessary. IDSs act merely as alarms, indicating the possibility of a breach associated with a specific set of activities. These indications still need to be investigated and an appropriate response needs to be initiated by security personnel. Simple items such as port scans may be ignored by policy, but an actual unauthorized entry into a network router, for instance, would require NOC personnel to take specific actions to limit the potential damage to the system. In any significant network, coordinating system changes, dynamic network traffic levels, potential security incidents, and maintenance activities is a daunting task requiring numerous personnel working together. Software has been developed to help manage the information flow required to support these tasks. Such software can enable remote administration of devices in a standard fashion, so that the control systems can be devised in a hardware vendor–neutral configuration.

SNMP is the main standard embraced by vendors to permit interoperability. Although SNMP has received a lot of security-related attention of late due to various security holes in its implementation, it is still an important part of a security solution associated with network infrastructure. Many useful tools have security issues; the key is to understand the limitations and to use the tools within correct boundaries to limit the risk associated with the vulnerabilities. Blind use of any technology will result in increased risk, and SNMP is no exception. Proper planning, setup, and deployment can limit exposure to vulnerabilities. Continuous auditing and maintenance of systems with the latest patches is a necessary part of operations and is essential to maintaining a secure posture.

Mobile Devices

Mobile devices such as personal digital assistants (PDAs) and mobile phones are the latest devices to join the corporate network. These devices can perform significant business functions, and in the future, more of them will enter the corporate network and more work will be performed with them. These devices add several challenges for network administrators. When they synchronize their data with that on a workstation or server, the opportunity exists for viruses and malicious code to be introduced into the network. This can be a major security gap, as a user may access separate e-mail accounts, one personal, without antivirus protection, and the other corporate. Whenever data is moved from one network to another via the PDA, the opportunity to load a virus onto the workstation exists. Although the virus may not affect the PDA or phone, these devices can act as transmission vectors. Currently, at least one vendor offers antivirus protection for PDAs, and similar protection for phones is not far away.

Many mobile devices have significant storage capacity, allowing them to transfer files and data. This makes them no different from any other mobile media source, capable of carrying and delivering viruses, worms, and other forms of malware. They are also capable of removing data from within a network, in the case of an insider attack. Mobile devices are also commonly Bluetooth enabled, making various wireless attacks against the device a risk. One reason to attack the mobile device is to use it to relay the attack onto the internal network when the device is synced up. Bluetooth attacks are covered in Chapter 12.

There is a whole new class of mobile device that can be a threat to the network—consumer digital products. From cell phones to music players, picture frames, cameras, electronic books, and other data-storing devices, these devices all have one element in common: they are capable of storing digital data. When plugged into computers to transfer data, recharge, or move data, they all represent storage technologies that can be used to move data in and out of networks via nontraditional ports. For high-security areas, the only sane way to combat these devices is through securing the USB ports via BIOS disablement, although we have seen the USB ports filled with epoxy as well, acting as a physical barrier.

Device Security, Common Concerns

As more and more interactive devices (that is, devices you can interact with programmatically) are being designed, a new threat source has appeared. In an attempt to build security into devices, typically, a default account and password must be entered to enable the user to access and configure the device remotely. These default accounts and passwords are well known in the hacker community, so one of the first steps you must take to secure such devices is to change the default credentials. Anyone who has purchased a home office router knows the default configuration settings and can check to see if another user has changed theirs. If they have not, this is a huge security hole, allowing outsiders to "reconfigure" their network devices.

Tech Tip

Default Accounts
Always reconfigure all default accounts on all devices before exposing them to external traffic. This is to prevent others from reconfiguring your devices based on known access settings.

Media

The base of communications between devices is the physical layer of the OSI model. This is the domain of the actual connection between devices, whether by wire, fiber, or radio frequency waves. The physical layer separates the definitions and protocols required to transmit the signal physically between boxes from higher level protocols that deal with the details of the data itself. Four common methods are used to connect equipment at the physical layer:

- Coaxial cable
- Twisted-pair cable
- Fiber-optics
- Wireless

Coaxial Cable

Coaxial cable is familiar to many households as a method of connecting televisions to VCRs or to satellite or cable services. It is used because of its high bandwidth and shielding capabilities. Compared to standard twisted-pair lines such as telephone lines, **coaxial cable** ("coax") is much less prone to outside interference. It is also much more expensive to run, both from a cost-per-foot measure and from a cable-dimension measure. Coax costs much more per foot than standard twisted-pair wires and carries only a single circuit for a large wire diameter.

• A coax connector

An original design specification for Ethernet connections, coax was used from machine to machine in early Ethernet implementations. The connectors were easy to use and ensured good connections, and the limited distance of most office LANs did not carry a large cost penalty. The original ThickNet specification for Ethernet called for up to 100 connections over 500 meters at 10 Mbps.

Today, almost all of this older Ethernet specification has been replaced by faster, cheaper twisted-pair alternatives, and the only place you're likely to see coax in a data network is from the cable box to the cable modem.

Because of its physical nature, it is possible to drill a hole through the outer part of a coax cable and connect to the center connector. This is called a "vampire tap" and is an easy method to get access to the signal and data being transmitted.

UTP/STP

Twisted-pair wires have all but completely replaced coaxial cables in Ethernet networks. Twisted-pair wires use the same technology used by the phone company for the movement of electrical signals. Single pairs of twisted wires reduce electrical crosstalk and electromagnetic interference. Multiple groups of twisted pairs can then be bundled together in common groups and easily wired between devices.

Twisted pairs come in two types, shielded and unshielded. **Shielded twisted-pair (STP)** has a foil shield around the pairs to provide extra shielding from electromagnetic interference. **Unshielded twisted-pair (UTP)** relies

• A typical 8-wire UTP line

on the twist to eliminate interference. UTP has a cost advantage over STP and is usually sufficient for connections, except in very noisy electrical areas.

• A typical 8-wire STP line

• A bundle of UTP wires

Twisted-pair lines are categorized by the level of data transmission they can support. Three current categories are in use:

■ **Category 3 (Cat 3)**   Minimum for voice and 10-Mbps Ethernet.

■ **Category 5 (Cat 5/Cat 5e)**   For 100-Mbps Fast Ethernet; Cat 5e is an enhanced version of the Cat 5 specification to address far-end crosstalk and is suitable for 1000 Mbps.

■ **Category 6 (Cat 6/Cat 6a)**   For 10-Gigabit Ethernet over short distances; Cat 6a is used for longer, up to 100m, 10-Gbps cables.

The standard method for connecting twisted-pair cables is via an 8-pin connector, called an RJ-45 connector, that looks like a standard phone jack connector but is slightly larger. One nice aspect of twisted-pair cabling is that it's easy to splice and change connectors. Many a network administrator has made Ethernet cables from stock Cat-5 wire, two connectors, and a crimping tool. This ease of connection is also a security issue; because twisted-pair cables are easy to splice into, rogue connections for sniffing could be made without detection in cable runs. Both coax and fiber are much more difficult to splice because each requires a tap to connect, and taps are easier to detect.

Fiber

Fiber-optic cable uses beams of laser light to connect devices over a thin glass wire. The biggest advantage to fiber is its bandwidth, with transmission capabilities into the terabits per second range. Fiber-optic cable is used to make high-speed connections between servers and is the backbone medium of the Internet and large networks. For all of its speed and bandwidth advantages, fiber has one major drawback—cost.

The cost of using fiber is a two-edged sword. When measured by bandwidth, using fiber is cheaper than using competing wired technologies. The length of runs of fiber can be much longer, and the data capacity of fiber is much higher. But connections to a fiber are difficult and expensive, and fiber is impossible to splice. Making the precise connection on the end of a fiber-optic line is a highly skilled job and is done by specially trained professionals who maintain a level of proficiency. Once the connector is fitted on the end, several forms of connectors and blocks are used, as shown in the images that follow.

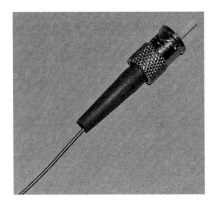

- A typical fiber-optic fiber and terminator

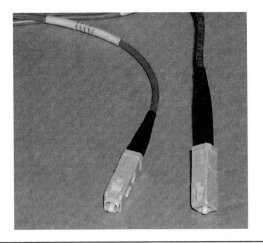

- Another type of fiber terminator

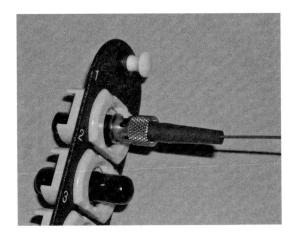

- A connector block for fiber-optic lines

Splicing fiber-optic is practically impossible; the solution is to add connectors and connect through a repeater. This adds to the security of fiber in that unauthorized connections are all but impossible to make. The high cost of connections to fiber and the higher cost of fiber per foot also make it less attractive for the final mile in public networks where users are connected to the public switching systems. For this reason, cable companies use coax and DSL providers use twisted-pair to handle the "last-mile" scenario.

Unguided Media

Electromagnetic waves have been transmitted to convey signals literally since the inception of radio. *Unguided media* is a phrase used to cover all transmission media not guided by wire, fiber, or other constraints; it includes radio frequency, infrared, and microwave methods. Unguided media have one attribute in common: they are unguided and as such can travel to many machines simultaneously. Transmission patterns can be modulated by antennas, but the target machine can be one of many in a reception zone. As such, security principles are even more critical, as they must assume that unauthorized users have access to the signal.

Infrared

Infrared (IR) is a band of electromagnetic energy just beyond the red end of the visible color spectrum. IR has been used in remote-control devices for years. IR made its debut in computer networking as a wireless method to connect to printers. Now that wireless keyboards, wireless mice, and PDAs exchange data via IR, it seems to be everywhere. IR can also be used to connect devices in a network configuration, but it is slow compared to other wireless technologies. IR cannot penetrate walls but instead bounces off them. Nor can it penetrate other solid objects, so if you stack a few items in front of the transceiver, the signal is lost.

RF/Microwave

The use of radio frequency (RF) waves to carry communication signals goes back to the beginning of the 20th century. RF waves are a common method of communicating in a wireless world. They use a variety of frequency bands, each with special characteristics. The term *microwave* is used to describe a specific portion of the RF spectrum that is used for communication and other tasks, such as cooking.

Point-to-point microwave links have been installed by many network providers to carry communications over long distances and rough terrain. Microwave communications of telephone conversations were the basis for forming the telecommunications company MCI. Many different frequencies are used in the microwave bands for many different purposes. Today, home users can use wireless networking throughout their house and enable laptops to surf the Web while they're moved around the house. Corporate users are experiencing the same phenomenon, with wireless networking enabling corporate users to check e-mail on laptops while riding a shuttle bus on a business campus. These wireless solutions are covered in detail in Chapter 12.

One key feature of microwave communications is that microwave RF energy can penetrate reasonable amounts of building structure. This allows you to connect network devices in separate rooms, and it can remove the constraints on equipment location imposed by fixed wiring. Another key feature is broadcast capability. By its nature, RF energy is unguided and can be received by multiple users simultaneously. Microwaves allow multiple users access in a limited area, and microwave systems are seeing application as the last mile of the Internet in dense metropolitan areas. Point-to-multipoint microwave devices can deliver data communication to all the business users in a downtown metropolitan area through rooftop antennas, reducing the need for expensive building-to-building cables. Just as microwaves carry cell phone and other data communications, the same technologies offer a method to bridge the last-mile solution.

The "last mile" problem is the connection of individual consumers to a backbone, an expensive proposition because of the sheer number of connections and unshared line at this point in a network. Again, cost is an issue, as transceiver equipment is expensive, but in densely populated areas, such as apartments and office buildings in metropolitan areas, the user density can help defray individual costs. Speed on commercial microwave links can exceed 10 Gbps, so speed is not a problem for connecting multiple users or for high-bandwidth applications.

■ Security Concerns for Transmission Media

The primary security concern for a system administrator has to be preventing physical access to a server by an unauthorized individual. Such access will almost always spell disaster, for with direct access and the correct tools, any system can be infiltrated. One of the administrator's next major concerns should be preventing unfettered access to a network connection. Access to switches and routers is almost as bad as direct access to a server, and access to network connections would rank third in terms of worst-case scenarios. Preventing such access is costly, yet the cost of replacing a server because of theft is also costly.

■ Physical Security Concerns

A balanced approach is the most sensible approach when addressing physical security, and this applies to transmission media as well. Keeping network switch rooms secure and cable runs secure seems obvious, but cases of using janitorial closets for this vital business purpose abound. One of the keys to mounting a successful attack on a network is information. Usernames, passwords, server locations—all of these can be obtained if someone has the ability to observe network traffic in a process called *sniffing*. A sniffer can record all the network traffic, and this data can be mined for accounts, passwords, and traffic content, all of which can be useful to an unauthorized user. Many common scenarios exist when unauthorized entry to a network occurs, including these:

- Inserting a node and functionality that is not authorized on the network, such as a sniffer device or unauthorized wireless access point
- Modifying firewall security policies
- Modifying ACLs for firewalls, switches, or routers
- Modifying network devices to echo traffic to an external node

One starting point for many intrusions is the insertion of an unauthorized sniffer into the network, with the fruits of its labors driving the remaining unauthorized activities.

Network devices and transmission media become targets because they are dispersed throughout an organization, and physical security of many dispersed items can be difficult to manage. Although limiting physical access is difficult, it is essential. The least level of skill is still more than sufficient to accomplish unauthorized entry into a network if physical access to the network signals is allowed. This is one factor driving many organizations to use fiber-optics, for these cables are much more difficult to tap. Although many tricks can be employed with switches and VLANs to increase security, it is still essential that you prevent unauthorized contact with the network equipment.

Cross Check

Physical Infrastructure Security

The best first effort is to secure the actual network equipment to prevent this type of intrusion. As you should remember from Chapter 8, physical access to network infrastructure provides a myriad of issues, and most of them can be catastrophic with respect to security. Physically securing access to network components is one of the "must dos" of a comprehensive security effort.

Wireless networks make the intruder's task even easier, as they take the network to the users, authorized or not. A technique called *war-driving* involves using a laptop and software to find wireless networks from outside the premises. A typical use of war-driving is to locate a wireless network with poor (or no) security and obtain free Internet access, but other uses can be more devastating. Methods for securing even the relatively weak Wired Equivalent Privacy (WEP) protocol are not difficult; they are just typically not followed by end users. A simple solution is to place a firewall between the wireless access point and the rest of the network and authenticate users before allowing entry. Business users use VPN technology to secure their connection to the Internet and other resources, and home users can do the same thing to prevent neighbors from "sharing" their Internet connections. To ensure that unauthorized traffic does not enter your network through a wireless access point, you must either use a firewall with an authentication system or establish a VPN.

■ Removable Media

One concept common to all computer users is data storage. Sometimes storage occurs on a file server and sometimes it occurs on movable media, allowing it to be transported between machines. Moving storage media represents a security risk from a couple of angles, the first being the potential loss of control over the data on the moving media. Second is the risk of introducing unwanted items, such as a virus or a worm, when the media are attached back to a network. Both of these issues can be remedied through policies and software. The key is to ensure that the policies are enforced and the software is effective. To describe media-specific issues, media can be divided into three categories: magnetic, optical, and electronic.

 Removable and transportable media make the physical security of the data a more difficult task. The only solution to this problem is encryption, which is covered in Chapter 5.

Magnetic Media

Magnetic media store data through the rearrangement of magnetic particles on a nonmagnetic substrate. Common forms include hard drives, floppy disks, zip disks, and magnetic tape. Although the specific format can differ, the basic concept is the same. All these devices share some common characteristics: Each has sensitivity to external magnetic fields. Attach a floppy disk to the refrigerator door with a magnet if you want to test the sensitivity. They are also affected by high temperatures, as in fires, and by exposure to water.

Hard Drives

Hard drives used to require large machines in mainframes. Now they are small enough to attach to PDAs and handheld devices. The concepts remain the same among all of them: a spinning platter rotates the magnetic media beneath heads that read the patterns in the oxide coating. As drives have gotten smaller and rotation speeds have increased, the capacities have also grown. Today gigabytes of data can be stored in a device slightly larger than a bottle cap. Portable hard drives in the 120- to 320GB range are now available and affordable.

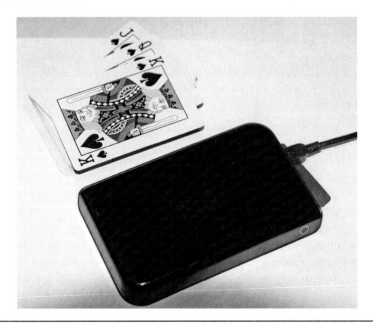

• 320GB USB hard drive

One of the security controls available to help protect the confidentiality of the data is full drive encryption built into the drive hardware. Using a key that is controlled, through a Trusted Platform Module (TPM) interface for instance, this technology protects the data if the drive itself is lost or stolen. This may not be important if a thief takes the whole PC, but in larger storage environments, drives are placed in separate boxes and remotely accessed. In the specific case of notebook machines, this layer can be tied to smart card interfaces to provide more security. As this is built into the controller, encryption protocols such as Advanced Encryption Standard (AES) and Triple Data Encryption Standard (3DES) can be performed at full drive speed.

Diskettes

Floppy disks were the computer industry's first attempt at portable magnetic media. The movable medium was placed in a protective sleeve, and the drive remained in the machine. Capacities up to 1.4MB were achieved, but the fragility of the device as the size increased, as well as competing media, has rendered floppies almost obsolete. A better alternative, the Zip disk from Iomega Corporation, improved on the floppy with a stronger case and higher capacity (250MB); it has been a common backup and file transfer medium. But even the increased size of 250MB is not large enough for some multimedia files, and recordable optical (CD-R) drives have arrived to fill the gap; they will be discussed shortly.

- 3.5" floppy disk and a Zip disk

Tape

Magnetic tape has held a place in computer centers since the beginning of computing. Its primary use has been bulk offline storage and backup. Tape functions well in this role because of its low cost. The disadvantage of tape is its nature as a serial access medium, making it slow to work with for large quantities of data. Several types of magnetic tape are in use today, ranging from quarter inch to digital linear tape (DLT) and digital audio tape (DAT). These cartridges can hold upward of 60GB of compressed data.

Tapes are still a major concern from a security perspective, as they are used to back up many types of computer systems. The physical protection afforded the tapes is of concern, because if a tape is stolen, an unauthorized user could establish a network and recover your data on his system, because it's all stored on the tape. Offsite storage is needed for proper disaster recovery protection, but secure offsite storage and transport is what is really needed. This important issue is frequently overlooked in many facilities.

The simple solution to maintain control over the data even when you can't control the tape is through encryption. Backup utilities can secure the backups with encryption, but this option is frequently not used, for a variety of reasons. Regardless of the rationale for not encrypting data, once a tape is lost, not using the encryption option becomes a lamented decision.

- A magnetic tape cartridge for backups

Optical Media

Optical media involve the use of a laser to read data stored on a physical device. Instead of having a magnetic head that picks up magnetic marks on a disk, a laser picks up deformities embedded in the media that contain the information. As with magnetic media, optical media can be read-write, although the read-only version is still more common.

CD-R/DVD

The compact disc (CD) took the music industry by storm, and then it took the computer industry by storm as well. A standard CD holds more than 640MB of data, in some cases up to 800MB. The digital video disc (DVD) can hold almost 4GB of data. These devices operate as optical storage, with little marks burned in them to represent 1's and 0's on a microscopic scale. The most common type of CD is the read-only version, in which the data is written to the disc once and only read afterward. This has become a popular method for distributing computer software, although higher-capacity DVDs have begun to replace CDs for program distribution.

- A DVD (left) and CD (right)

A second-generation device, the recordable compact disc (CD-R), allows users to create their own CDs using a burner device in their PC and special software. Users can now back up data, make their own audio CDs, and use CDs as high-capacity storage. Their relatively low cost has made them economical to use. CDs have a thin layer of aluminum inside the plastic, upon which bumps are burned by the laser when recorded. CD-Rs use a reflective layer, such as gold, upon which a dye is placed that changes upon impact by the recording laser. A newer type, CD-RW, has a different dye that allows discs to be erased and reused. The cost of the media increases from CD, to CD-R, to CD-RW.

DVDs will eventually occupy the same role that CDs have in the recent past, except that they hold more than seven times the data of a CD. This makes full-length movie recording possible on a single disc. The increased capacity comes from finer tolerances and the fact that DVDs can hold data on both sides. A wide range of formats for DVDs include DVD+R, DVD-R, dual layer, and now HD formats, HD-DVD and Blu-ray. This variety is due to competing "standards" and can result in confusion. DVD+R and -R are distinguishable only when recording, and most devices since 2004 should read both. Dual layers add additional space but require appropriate dual-layer–enabled drives. HD-DVD and Blue-ray are competing formats in the high-definition arena, with devices that currently hold 50GB and with research prototypes promising up to 1TB on a disk. In 2008, Toshiba, the leader of the HD-DVD format, announced it was ceasing production, casting doubts onto its future, although this format is also used in gaming systems such as the Xbox 360.

Electronic Media

The latest form of removable media is electronic memory. Electronic circuits of static memory, which can retain data even without power, fill a niche where high density and small size are needed. Originally used in audio devices and digital cameras, these electronic media come in a variety of vendor-specific types, such as smart cards, SmartMedia, SD cards, flash cards, memory sticks, and CompactFlash devices. These memory devices range from small card-like devices, of which microSD cards are smaller than dimes and hold 2GB, to USB sticks that hold up to 64GB. These devices are becoming ubiquitous, with new PCs and netbooks containing built-in slots to read them like any other storage device. Several recent photo-quality color printers have been released with ports to accept the cards directly, meaning that a computer is not required for printing. Computer readers are also available to permit storing data from the card onto hard drives and other media in a computer. The size of storage on these devices ranges from 256MB to 64GB, making them capable of carrying significant quantities of information.

Although they are used primarily for photos and music, these devices could be used to move any digital information from one machine to another. To a machine equipped with a connector port, these devices look like any other file storage location. They can be connected to a system through a special reader or directly via a USB port. In newer PC systems, a USB boot

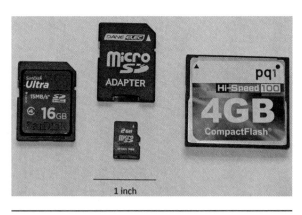

• SD, microSD, and CompactFlash cards

device has replaced the older floppy drive. These devices are small, can hold a significant amount of data—up to 64GB at time of writing—and are easy to move from machine to machine. Another novel interface is a mouse that has a slot for a memory stick. This dual-purpose device conserves space, conserves USB ports, and is easy to use. The memory stick is placed in the mouse, which can then be used normally. The stick is easily removable and transportable. The mouse works with or without the memory stick; it is just a convenient device to use for a portal.

The advent of large-capacity USB sticks has enabled users to build entire systems, OSs, and tools onto them to ensure security and veracity of the OS and tools. With the expanding use of virtualization, a user could carry an entire system on a USB stick and boot it using virtually any hardware. The only downside to this form of mobile computing is the slower speed of the USB 2.0 interface, currently limited to 480 Mbps.

Network Attached Storage

Because of the speed of today's Ethernet networks, it is possible to manage data storage across the network. This has led to a type of storage known as **Network Attached Storage (NAS)**. The combination of inexpensive hard drives, fast networks, and simple application-based servers has made NAS devices in the terabyte range affordable for even home users. Because of the large size of video files, this has become popular for some users as a method of storing TV and video libraries. Because NAS is a network device, it is susceptible to various attacks, including sniffing of credentials and a variety of brute-force attacks to obtain access to the data.

Chapter 10 Review

■ Chapter Summary

After reading this chapter and completing the exercises, you should understand the following aspects of networking and secure infrastructures.

Construct networks using different types of network devices

- Understand the differences between basic network devices, such as hubs, bridges, switches, and routers.

- Understand the security implications of network devices and how to construct a secure network infrastructure.

- Understand the use of security appliances, such as firewalls and intrusion detection systems.

Enhance security using NAC/NAP methodologies

- Cisco NAC protocol and the Microsoft NAP protocol provide security functionality when attaching devices to a network.

- NAC and NAP play a crucial role in the securing of infrastructure as devices enter and leave from the network.

- NAC and NAP can be used together to take advantage of the strengths and investments in each technology to form a strong network admission methodology.

Identify the different types of media used to carry network signals

- Guided and unguided media can both carry network traffic.

- Wired technology from coax cable, through twisted-pair Ethernet, provides a cost-effective means of carrying network traffic.

- Fiber technology is used to carry higher bandwidth.

- Unguided media, including infrared and RF (including wireless and Bluetooth) provide short-range network connectivity.

Describe the different types of storage media used to store information

- Data storage on removable media, because of increased physical access, creates significant security implications.

Use basic terminology associated with network functions related to information security

- Students will understand and use the correct vocabulary for device names and relationships to networking.

- Security appliances add to the terminology, including specific items for IDS and firewalls.

■ Key Terms

basic packet filtering *(237)*
bridge *(233)*
coaxial cable *(245)*
collision domain *(233)*
firewall *(236)*
hub *(233)*
modem *(239)*
network access control *(242)*
Network Access Protection (NAP) *(242)*
Network Admission Control (NAC) *(242)*

Network Attached Storage *(255)*
network interface card (NIC) *(232)*
private branch exchange (PBX) *(240)*
router *(235)*
servers *(231)*
shielded twisted-pair (STP) *(245)*
switch *(234)*
unshielded twisted-pair (UTP) *(245)*
wireless access point *(238)*
workstation *(229)*

■ Key Terms Quiz

Use terms from the Key Terms list to complete the sentences that follow. Don't use the same term more than once. Not all terms will be used.

1. A(n) _____ routes packets based on IP addresses.

2. To add wireless access to your network, you need at least one _____.

3. To connect a computer to a network, you use a(n) _____.

4. A(n) _____ or _____ distributes traffic based on MAC addresses.

5. To verify that a computer is properly configured to connect to a network, the network can use _____.

6. _____ is a name for the typical computer a user uses on a network.

7. A(n) _____ repeats all data traffic across all connected ports.

8. Cat 5 is an example of _____ cable.

9. Basic packet filtering occurs at the _____.

10. A(n) _____ is an extension of the telephone service into a firm's telecommunications network.

■ Multiple-Choice Quiz

1. Switches operate at which layer of the OSI model?

   A. Physical layer

   B. Network layer

   C. Data link layer

   D. Application layer

2. UTP cables are terminated for Ethernet using what type of connector?

   A. A BNC plug

   B. An Ethernet connector

   C. A standard phone jack connector

   D. An RJ-45 connector

3. Coaxial cable carries how many physical channels?

   A. Two

   B. Four

   C. One

   D. None of the above

4. The challenge associated with securing data on removable media is associated with:

   A. Removable media devices are, due to their removable nature, more secure.

   B. Removable media devices are so small in terms of storage capacity that security is not necessary.

   C. The fact that the media can be stolen or moved to another device by an unauthorized party.

   D. Different media have different standards that preclude security.

5. Network access control is associated with which of the following?

   A. NAP

   B. IPsec

   C. IPv6

   D. NAT

6. The purpose of twisting the wires in twisted-pair circuits is to:

   A. Increase speed

   B. Increase bandwidth

   C. Reduce crosstalk

   D. Allow easier tracing

7. The shielding in STP acts as:

   A. A physical barrier strengthening the cable

   B. A way to reduce interference

   C. An amplifier allowing longer connections

   D. None of the above

8. Microsoft NAP permits:

   A. Restriction of connections to a restricted subnet only

   B. Checking of a client OS patch level before a network connection is permitted

   C. Denial of a connection based on client policy settings

   D. All of the above

9. One of the greatest concerns addressed by physical security is preventing unauthorized connections having what intent?

   A. Sniffing

   B. Spoofing

   C. Data diddling

   D. Free network access

10. SNMP is a protocol used for which of the following functions?

    A. Secure e-mail

    B. Secure encryption of network packets

    C. Remote access to user workstations

    D. Remote access to network infrastructure

11. Firewalls can use which of the following in their operation?

    A. Stateful packet inspection

    B. Port blocking to deny specific services

    C. NAT to hide internal IP addresses

    D. All of the above

12. SMTP is a protocol used for which of the following functions?

    A. E-mail

    B. Secure encryption of network packets

    C. Remote access to user workstations

    D. None of the above

13. Microwave communications are limited by:

    A. Speed—the maximum for microwave circuits is 1 Gbps.

    B. Cost—microwaves take a lot of energy to generate.

    C. Line of sight—microwaves don't propagate over the horizon.

    D. Lack of standard operation protocols for widespread use.

14. USB-based flash memory is characterized by:

    A. High cost

    B. Low capacity

    C. Slow access

    D. None of the above

15. Mobile devices connected to networks include what?

    A. Smart phones

    B. Laptops

    C. MP3 music devices

    D. All of the above

■ Essay Quiz

1. Compare and contrast routers and switches by describing what the advantages and disadvantages are of each.

2. Describe the common threats to the transmission media in a network, by type of transmission media.

3. Describe the common data storage technologies and the capabilities of each.

Lab Projects

• Lab Project 10.1

Using two PCs and a small home office–type router, configure them to communicate across the network with each other.

• Lab Project 10.2

Demonstrate network connectivity using Windows command-line tools.

Authentication and Remote Access

We should set a national goal of making computers and Internet access available for every American.

—WILLIAM JEFFERSON CLINTON

In this chapter, you will learn how to

- Discuss the methods and protocols for remote access to networks

- Identify authentication, authorization, and accounting (AAA) protocols

- Explain authentication methods and the security implications in their use

- Implement virtual private networks (VPNs) and their security aspects

- Describe Internet Protocol Security (IPsec) and its use in securing communications

Access is a key issue in today's world of connected computers. Isolated computers, not connected to networks or the Internet, are rare items these days. Except for some special-purpose machines, most computers need interconnectivity to fulfill their purpose. Remote access enables users outside a network to have network access and privileges as if they were inside the network. Being *outside* a network means that the user is working on a machine that is not physically connected to the network and must therefore establish a connection through a remote means, such as by dialing in, connecting via the Internet, or connecting through a wireless connection. A user accessing resources from the Internet through an Internet service provider (ISP) is also connecting remotely to the resources via the Internet.

Authentication is the process of establishing a user's identity to enable the granting of permissions. To establish network connections, a variety of methods are used, the choice of which depends on network type, the hardware and software employed, and any security requirements. Microsoft Windows has a specific server component called the Routing and Remote Access Service (RRAS) that is designed to facilitate the management of remote access connections through dial-up modems. Cisco has implemented a variety of remote access methods through its networking hardware and software. UNIX systems also have built-in methods to enable remote access.

The Remote Access Process

The process of connecting by remote access involves two elements: a temporary network connection and a series of protocols to negotiate privileges and commands. The temporary network connection can occur via a dial-up service, the Internet, wireless access, or any other method of connecting to a network. Once the connection is made, the primary issue is authenticating the identity of the user and establishing proper privileges for that user. This is accomplished using a combination of protocols and the operating system on the host machine.

The three steps in the establishment of proper privileges are authentication, authorization, and accounting, commonly referred to simply as **AAA**. **Authentication** is the matching of user-supplied credentials to previously stored credentials on a host machine, and it usually involves an account username and password. Once the user is authenticated, the authorization step takes place. **Authorization** is the granting of specific permissions based on the privileges held by the account. Does the user have permission to use the network at this time, or is her use restricted? Does the user have access to specific applications, such as mail and FTP, or are some of these restricted? These checks are carried out as part of authorization, and in many cases this is a function of the operating system in conjunction with its established security policies. **Accounting** is the collection of billing and other detail records. Network access is often a billable function, and a log of how much time, bandwidth, file transfer space, or other resources were used needs to be maintained. Other accounting functions include keeping detailed security logs to maintain an audit trail of tasks being performed. All of these standard functions are part of normal and necessary overhead in maintaining a computer system, and the protocols used in remote access provide the necessary input for these functions.

When a user connects to the Internet through an ISP, this is similarly a case of remote access—the user is establishing a connection to her ISP's network, and the same security issues apply. The issue of authentication, the matching of user-supplied credentials to previously stored credentials on a host machine, is usually done via a user account name and password. Once the user is authenticated, the authorization step takes place. Remote authentication usually takes the common form of an end user submitting his credentials via an established protocol to a **remote access server (RAS)**, which acts upon those credentials, either granting or denying access. Much of this

Tech Tip

Securing Remote Connections
By using encryption, remote access protocols can securely authenticate and authorize a user according to previously established privilege levels. The authorization phase can keep unauthorized users out, but after that, encryption of the communications channel becomes very important in preventing nonauthorized users from breaking in on an authorized session and hijacking an authorized user's credentials. As more and more networks rely on the Internet for connecting remote users, the need for and importance of secure remote access protocols and secure communication channels will continue to grow.

chapter is devoted to an examination of the various protocols that can be used for the authentication process.

Access controls define what actions a user can perform or what objects a user is allowed to access. Access controls are built upon the foundation of elements designed to facilitate the matching of a user to a process. These elements are identification, authentication, and authorization. There are a myriad of details and choices associated with setting up remote access to a network, and to provide for the management of these options, it is important for an organization to have a series of remote access policies and procedures spelling out the details of what is permitted and what is not for a given network.

Identification

Identification is the process of ascribing a computer ID to a specific user, computer, network device, or computer process. The identification process is typically performed only once, when a user ID is issued to a particular user. User identification enables authentication and authorization to form the basis for accountability. For accountability purposes, user IDs should not be shared, and for security purposes, they should not be descriptive of job function. This practice enables you to trace activities to individual users or computer processes so that they can be held responsible for their actions. Identification links the logon ID or user ID to credentials that have been submitted previously to either HR or the IT staff. A required characteristic of user IDs is that they must be unique so that they map 1:1 to the credentials presented when the account was established.

 Try This

Identification and Credentials

Using either your school computing resources or work computing environment, explore the basis for an authenticated user. Find the entity that establishes user identities for the institution (for example, the HR department for work or the Registrar of Admissions for school). Find out who authorizes new accounts and ask what the basis for the establishment of credentials is in the environment.

Authentication

Authentication is the process of binding a specific ID to a specific computer connection. Two items need to be presented to cause this binding to occur—the user ID, and some "secret" to prove that the user is the valid possessor of the credentials. Historically, three categories of secrets are used to authenticate the identity of a user: what users know, what users have, and what users are. Today an additional category is used: what users do.

These methods can be used individually or in combination. These controls assume that the identification process has been completed and the identity of the user has been verified. It is the job of authentication mechanisms to ensure that only valid users are admitted. Described another way, authentication is using some mechanism to prove that you are who you claimed to be when the identification process was completed.

The most common method of authentication is the use of a password. For greater security, you can add an element from a separate group, such as a smart card token—something a user has in her possession. Passwords are common because they are one of the simplest forms and use user memory as a prime component. Because of their simplicity, passwords have become ubiquitous across a wide range of authentication systems.

Another method to provide authentication involves the use of something that only valid users should have in their possession. A physical-world example of this would be a simple lock and key. Only those individuals with the correct key will be able to open the lock and thus gain admittance to a house, car, office, or whatever the lock was protecting. A similar method can be used to authenticate users for a computer system or network (though the key may be electronic and could reside on a smart card or similar device). The problem with this technology, however, is that people do lose their keys (or cards), which means not only that the user can't log into the system but that somebody else who finds the key may then be able to access the system, even though they are not authorized. To address this problem, a combination of the something-you-know and something-you-have methods is often used so that the individual with the key is also required to provide a password or passcode. The key is useless unless the user knows this code.

The third general method to provide authentication involves something that is unique about you. We are accustomed to this concept in our physical world, where our fingerprints or a sample of our DNA can be used to identify us. This same concept can be used to provide authentication in the computer world. The field of authentication that uses something about you or something that you are is known as *biometrics*. A number of different mechanisms can be used to accomplish this type of authentication, such as a fingerprint, iris, retinal, or hand geometry scan. All of these methods obviously require some additional hardware in order to operate. The inclusion of fingerprint readers on laptop computers is becoming common as the additional hardware is becoming cost effective.

While these three approaches to authentication appear to be easy to understand and in most cases easy to implement, authentication is not to be taken lightly, since it is such an important component of security. Potential attackers are constantly searching for ways to get past the system's authentication mechanism, and they have employed some fairly ingenious methods to do so. Consequently, security professionals are constantly devising new methods, building on these three basic approaches, to provide authentication mechanisms for computer systems and networks.

Kerberos

Developed as part of MIT's project Athena, **Kerberos** is a network authentication protocol designed for a client/server environment. The current version is Kerberos Version 5 release 1.7 and is supported by all major operating systems. Kerberos securely passes a symmetric key over an insecure network using the Needham-Schroeder symmetric key protocol. Kerberos is built around the idea of a trusted third party, termed a **key distribution center (KDC)**, which consists of two logically separate parts: an **authentication server (AS)** and a **ticket-granting server (TGS)**. Kerberos communicates via "tickets" that serve to prove the identity of users.

Taking its name from the three-headed dog of Greek mythology, Kerberos is designed to work across the Internet, an inherently insecure environment. Kerberos uses strong encryption so that a client can prove its identity to a server and the server can in turn authenticate itself to the client.

> **Tech Tip**
>
> **Categories of Shared Secrets for Authentication**
> *Originally published by the U.S. government in one of the "rainbow series" of manuals on computer security, the categories of shared "secrets" are*
>
> - *What users know (such as a password)*
> - *What users have (such as tokens)*
> - *What users are (static biometrics such as fingerprints or iris pattern)*
>
> *Today, because of technological advances, a new category has emerged, patterned after subconscious behavior:*
>
> - *What users do (dynamic biometrics such as typing patterns or gait)*

> **Exam Tip:** Two tickets are used in Kerberos. The first is a ticket-granting ticket (TGT) obtained from the authentication server (AS). The TGT is presented to a ticket-granting server (TGS) when access to a server is requested and a client-to-server ticket is issued, granting access to the server. Typically both the AS and the TGS are logically separate parts of the Key Distribution Center (KDC).

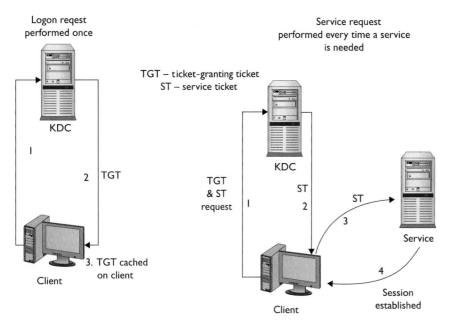

Logon reqest
performed once

Service request
performed every time a service
is needed

TGT – ticket-granting ticket
ST – service ticket

KDC

2 | TGT

3. TGT cached
on client

Client

KDC

TGT
& ST
request

ST

ST

3

Service

4

Session
established

Client

Client Authentication
1. The client sends a cleartext message to the AS requesting services on behalf of the user.
2. The AS checks to see if the client is in its database. If it is, the AS sends back ticket-granting ticket.
3. Once the client receives messages, it decrypts them to obtain the client/TGS session key.

Service Request
1. Using its TGT, client requests a service ticket (ST).
2. Client gets ST.
3. Client submits ST to service provider with request.
4. The server provides the requested services to the client.

• **Figure 11.1**   Kerberos operations

Tech Tip

Kerberos Authentication
Kerberos is a third-party authentication service that uses a series of tickets as tokens for authenticating users. The six steps involved are protected using strong cryptography:

1. *The user presents his credentials and requests a ticket from the Key Distribution Center (KDC).*
2. *The KDC verifies credentials and issues a ticket-granting ticket (TGT).*
3. *The user presents a TGT and request for service to the KDC.*
4. *The KDC verifies authorization and issues a client-to-server ticket (or service ticket).*
5. *The user presents a request and a client-to-server ticket to the desired service.*
6. *If the client-to-server ticket is valid, service is granted to the client.*

A complete Kerberos environment is referred to as a Kerberos *realm*. The Kerberos server contains user IDs and hashed passwords for all users that will have authorizations to realm services. The Kerberos server also has shared secret keys with every server to which it will grant access tickets.

The basis for authentication in a Kerberos environment is the ticket. Tickets are used in a two-step process with the client. The first ticket is a *ticket-granting ticket (TGT)* issued by the AS to a requesting client. The client can then present this ticket to the Kerberos server with a request for a ticket to access a specific server. This *client-to-server ticket* (also called a *service ticket*) is used to gain access to a server's service in the realm. Since the entire session can be encrypted, this eliminates the inherently insecure transmission of items such as a password that can be intercepted on the network. Tickets are time-stamped and have a lifetime, so attempting to reuse a ticket will not be successful. Figure 11.1 details Kerberos operations.

To illustrate how the Kerberos authentication service works, think about the common driver's license. You have received a license that you can present to other entities to prove you are who you claim to be. Because other entities trust the state in which the license was issued, they will accept your license as proof of your identity. The state in which the license was issued is analogous to the Kerberos authentication service realm, and the license acts as a client-to-server ticket. It is the trusted entity both sides rely on to provide valid identifications. This analogy is not perfect, because we all probably have heard of individuals who obtained a phony driver's license, but it serves to illustrate the basic idea behind Kerberos.

Certificates

Certificates are a method of establishing authenticity of specific objects such as an individual's public key or downloaded software. A *digital certificate* is a digital file that is sent as an attachment to a message and is used to verify that the message did indeed come from the entity it claims to have come from. To verify the authenticity of an item, the public key of the signer is needed, and the digital certificate contains this information. A special form of authentication is the *digital signature,* which is an encrypted hash of an item that enables the recipient, using the public key, to verify that the original contents are not changed. The digital certificate can also contain a key that can be used to encrypt future communication.

> **Cross Check**
>
> ### Digital Certificates and Digital Signatures
>
> Kerberos uses tickets to convey messages. Part of the ticket is a certificate that contains requisite keys. Understanding how certificates convey this vital information is an important part of understanding how Kerberos-based authentication works. Certificates and how they are used was covered in Chapter 6, with the protocols associated with PKI covered in Chapter 7. Refer back to these chapters as needed.

Tokens

A *token* is a hardware device that can be used in a challenge/response authentication process. In this way, it functions as both a something-you-have and something-you-know authentication mechanism. Several variations on this type of device exist, but they all work on the same basic principles. The device has an LCD screen and may or may not have a numeric keypad. Devices without a keypad will display a password (often just a sequence of numbers) that changes at a constant interval, usually about every 60 seconds. When an individual attempts to log into a system, he enters his own user ID number and then the number that is showing on the LCD screen. These two numbers are entered either separately or concatenated. The user's own ID number is secret, which prevents someone from using a lost device. The system knows which device the user has and is synchronized with it so that it will know the number that should have been displayed. Since this number is constantly changing, a potential attacker who is able to see the sequence will not be able to use it later, since the code will have changed. Devices with a keypad work in a similar fashion (and may also be designed to function as a simple calculator).

• A one-time password generator token

The individual who wants to log into the system first types his personal identification number into the calculator. He then attempts to log in. The system provides a challenge; the user must enter that challenge into the calculator and press a special function key. The calculator then determines the correct response and displays it. The user provides the response to the system he is attempting to log into, and the system verifies that this is the correct response. Since each user has a different PIN, two individuals receiving the same challenge will have different responses. The device can also use the date or time as a variable for the response calculation so that the same challenge at different times will yield different responses, even for the same individual.

Multifactor

Multifactor authentication is a term that describes the use of more than one authentication mechanism at the same time. An example of this is the hardware token, which requires both a personal ID number (PIN) or password and the device itself to determine the correct response in order to authenticate to the system. This means that both the something-you-have and something-you-know mechanisms are used as factors in verifying authenticity of the user. Biometrics are also often used in conjunction with a PIN so that they, too, can be used as part of a multifactor authentication scheme, in this case something you are as well as something you know. The purpose of multifactor authentication is to increase the level of security, since more than one mechanism would have to be spoofed in order for an unauthorized individual to gain access to a computer system or network. The most common example of multifactor security is the common ATM card most of us carry in our wallets. The card is associated with a PIN that only the authorized cardholder should know. Knowing the PIN without having the card is useless, just as having the card without knowing the PIN will also not provide you access to your account.

Multifactor authentication is sometimes referred to as two-factor authentication or three-factor authentication, referring to the number of different factors used. It is important to note that this implies separate factors for the authentication element; a user ID and password are not two factors, as the user ID is not a shared secret element.

Single Sign-on

Single sign-on is a form of authentication that involves the transferring of credentials between systems. As more and more systems are combined in daily use, users are forced to have multiple sets of credentials. A user may have to log into three, four, five, or even more systems every day just to do her job. Single sign-on allows a user to transfer her credentials, so that logging into one system acts to log her into all of them. Once the user has entered a user ID and password, the single sign-on system passes these credentials transparently to other systems so that repeated logons are not required. This has an advantage of reducing login hassles for the user. It also has a disadvantage of combining the authentication systems in a way such that if one login is compromised, they all are for that user.

Try This

Personal Single Sign-on System

Single sign-on systems require specialized software and the establishment of trust boundaries between separate systems. These are items that are out of the reach of ordinary computer end users. But for many users, a nearly equivalent system has evolved—common user IDs and passwords. The typical end user accesses or has accessed between 30 and 50 password-based systems. Some of these accesses are from work or school, but others represent the user's personal life, such as accessing social networking sites, e-commerce vendors, numerous web sites, banks, stock brokers, and so forth. Everywhere one turns on the Web, they are being asked to log in. Maintaining the myriad of passwords and IDs is a cognitive nightmare, so many users have developed their own standards, such as common user IDs and a limited number of passwords—for example, one password for social networking sites, a different one for most e-commerce sites, and yet another for higher-security sites such as bank sites.

Examine your personal password "policies" and usage patterns—have you adopted a form of single sign-on? If not, would you?

Mutual Authentication

Mutual authentication describes a process in which each side of an electronic communication verifies the authenticity of the other. We are accustomed to the idea of having to authenticate ourselves to our ISP before we access the Internet, generally through the use of a user ID/password pair, but how do we actually know that we are really communicating with our ISP and not some other system that has somehow inserted itself into our communication (a man-in-the-middle attack)? Mutual authentication provides a mechanism for each side of a client/server relationship to verify the authenticity of the other to address this issue. A common method of performing mutual authentication involves using a secure connection, such as Secure Sockets Layer (SSL), to the server and a one-time password generator that then authenticates the client.

 Mutual SSL–based authentication provides the same functions as normal SSL, with the addition of authentication and nonrepudiation of the *client*. This second authentication, the authentication of the client, is done in the same manner as the normal server authentication using digital signatures. The client authentication represents the many sides of a many-to-one relationship. Mutual SSL authentication is not commonly used because of the complexity, cost, and logistics associated with managing the multitude of client certificates. This reduces the effectiveness, and most web applications are not designed to require client-side certificates.

Authorization

Authorization is the process of permitting or denying access to a specific resource. Once identity is confirmed via authentication, specific actions can be authorized or denied. Many types of authorization schemes are used, but the purpose is the same: determine whether a given user who has been identified has permissions for a particular object or resource being requested. This functionality is frequently part of the operating system and is transparent to users.

The separation of tasks, from identification to authentication to authorization, has several advantages. Many methods can be used to perform each task, and on many systems several methods are concurrently present for each task. Separation of these tasks into individual elements allows combinations of implementations to work together. Any system or resource, be it hardware (router or workstation) or a software component (database system), that requires authorization can use its own authorization method once authentication has occurred. This makes for efficient and consistent application of these principles.

Access Control

The term **access control** has been used to describe a variety of protection schemes. It is sometimes used to refer to all security features used to prevent unauthorized access to a computer system or network—or even a network resource such as a printer. In this sense, it may be confused with authentication. More properly, *access* is the ability of a subject (such as an individual or a process running on a computer system) to interact with an object (such as a file or hardware device). Once the individual has verified their identity, access controls regulate what the individual can actually do on the system. Just because a person is granted entry to the system, that does not mean that they should have access to all data the system contains.

To further illustrate, consider another example. When you go to your bank to make a withdrawal, the teller at the window will verify that you are indeed who you claim to be. This is usually done by asking you to provide some form of identification with your picture on it, such as your driver's license. You may also have to provide information such as your bank account number. Once the teller verifies your identity, you will have proved that you are a valid (authorized) customer of this bank. This does not, however, mean that you have the ability to view all information that the bank protects—such as your neighbor's account. The teller controls what information, and funds, you may have access to and grants you access only to that which you are authorized. In this example, your identification and bank account number serve as your method of authentication and the teller serves as the access control mechanism.

In computer systems and networks, there are several ways that access controls can be implemented. An *access control matrix* provides the simplest framework for illustrating the process. An example of an access control matrix is provided in Table 11.1. In this matrix, the system is keeping track of two processes, two files, and one hardware device. Process 1 can read both File 1 and File 2 but can write only to File 1. Process 1 cannot access Process 2, but Process 2 can execute Process 1. Both processes have the ability to write to the printer.

While simple to understand, the access control matrix is seldom used in computer systems because it is extremely costly in terms of storage space and processing. Imagine the size of an access control matrix for a large network with hundreds of users and thousands of files. The actual mechanics

Tech Tip

Access Control vs. Authentication
It may seem that access control and authentication are two ways to describe the same protection mechanism. This, however, is not the case. Authentication provides a way to verify to the computer who the user is. Once the user has been authenticated, the access controls decide what operations the user can perform. The two go hand-in-hand but are not the same thing.

Table 11.1	An Access Control Matrix				
	Process 1	**Process 2**	**File 1**	**File 2**	**Printer**
Process 1	Read, write, execute		Read, write	Read	Write
Process 2	Execute	Read, write, execute	Read, write	Read, write	Write

Principles of Computer Security: CompTIA Security+ and Beyond

of how access controls are implemented in a system varies, though using *access control lists* (*ACLs*) is common. An ACL is nothing more than a list that contains the subjects that have access rights to a particular object. The list identifies not only the subject but the specific access that that subject has for the object. Typical types of access include read, write, and execute, as indicated in the example access control matrix in Table 11.1. No matter what specific mechanism is used to implement access controls in a computer system or network, the controls should be based on a specific model of access. Several different models are discussed in security literature, including discretionary access control (DAC), mandatory access control (MAC), role-based access control (RBAC), and rule-based access control (also RBAC).

Discretionary Access Control

Both discretionary access control and mandatory access control are terms originally used by the military to describe two different approaches to controlling what access an individual has on a system.

While the terminology in the Note may appear to many to be typical "government-speak" and confusing, the principle is really rather simple. In systems that employ discretionary access controls, the owner of an object can decide which other subjects may have access to the object and what specific access they may have. One common method to accomplish this is via the permission bits used in UNIX-based systems. The owner of a file can specify what permissions (read/write/execute) members in the same group may have and also what permissions all others may have. Access control lists are another common mechanism used to implement discretionary access control.

Mandatory Access Control

A less frequently employed system for restricting access is mandatory access control. This system, generally used only in environments where different levels of security classifications exist, is much more restrictive of what a user is allowed to do. Referring to the Orange Book, we can find a definition for **mandatory access control (MAC)**: "A means of restricting access to objects based on the sensitivity (as represented by a label) of the information contained in the objects and the formal authorization (i.e., clearance) of subjects to access information of such sensitivity."

In the case of MAC, the owner or subject can't determine whether access is to be granted to another subject; it is the job of the operating system to decide. In MAC, the security mechanism controls access to all objects, and individual subjects cannot change that access. The key here is the label attached to every subject and object. The label identifies the level of classification for that object and the level that the subject is entitled to. Think of military security classifications such as Secret and Top Secret. A file that has been identified as Top Secret (has a label indicating that it is Top Secret) may be viewed only by individuals with a Top Secret clearance. It is up to the access control mechanism to ensure that an individual with only a Secret clearance never gains access to a file labeled as Top Secret. Similarly, a user cleared for Top Secret access will not be allowed by the access control mechanism to change the classification of a file labeled as Top Secret to Secret or to send that Top Secret file to a user cleared only for Secret information.

As defined by the "Orange Book," a Department of Defense document (in the previously mentioned "rainbow series") that at one time was the standard for describing what constituted a trusted computing system, a **discretionary access control (DAC)** is, "a means of restricting access to objects based on the identity of subjects and/or groups to which they belong. The controls are discretionary in the sense that a subject with a certain access permission is capable of passing that permission (perhaps indirectly) on to any other subject (unless restrained by mandatory access control)."

The complexity of such a mechanism can be further understood when you consider today's windowing environment. The access control mechanism will not allow a user to copy a portion of a Top Secret document and paste it into a window containing a document with only a Secret label. It is this separation of differing levels of classified information that results in this sort of mechanism being referred to as multilevel security. A final comment should be made: just because a subject has the appropriate level of clearance to view a document, that does not mean that they will be allowed to do so. The concept of "need to know," which is a DAC concept, also exists in MAC mechanisms.

Role-Based Access Control

Access control lists can be cumbersome and can take time to administer properly. Another access control mechanism that has been attracting increased attention is **role-based access control (RBAC)**. In this scheme, instead of each user being assigned specific access permissions for the objects associated with the computer system or network, that user is assigned a set of roles that the user may perform. The roles are in turn assigned the access permissions necessary to perform the tasks associated with the role. Users will thus be granted permissions to objects in terms of the specific duties they must perform—not of a security classification associated with individual objects.

Rule-Based Access Control

The first thing that you might notice is the ambiguity that is introduced with this access control method also using the acronym RBAC. **Rule-based access control (RBAC)** again uses objects such as ACLs to help determine whether or not access should be granted, but in this case, a series of rules is contained in the ACL and the determination of whether to grant access is made based on these rules. An example of such a rule is one that states that no employee may have access to the payroll file after hours or on weekends. As with MAC, users are not allowed to change the access rules, and administrators are relied on to enforce this. Rule-based access control can actually be used in addition to or as a method of implementing other access control methods. For example, MAC methods can utilize a rule-based approach for implementation.

IEEE 802.1X

IEEE 802.1X 1X is an authentication standard that supports port-based authentication services between a user and an authorization device, such as an edge router. IEEE 802.1X is used by all types of networks, including Ethernet, Token Ring, and wireless. This standard describes methods used to authenticate a user prior to granting access to network and the authentication server, such as a RADIUS server. 802.1X acts through an intermediate device, such as an edge switch, enabling ports to carry normal traffic if the connection is properly authenticated. This prevents unauthorized clients from accessing the publicly available ports on a switch, keeping unauthorized users out of a LAN. Until a client has successfully authenticated itself to the device, only Extensible Authentication Protocol over LAN (EAPOL) traffic is passed by the switch.

EAPOL is an encapsulated method of passing EAP messages over 802.1 frames. EAP is a general protocol that can support multiple methods of authentication, including one-time passwords, Kerberos, public keys, and security device methods such as smart cards. Once a client successfully authenticates itself to the 802.1X device, the switch opens ports for normal traffic. At this point, the client can communicate with the system's AAA method, such as a RADIUS server, and authenticate itself to the network.

> One security issue associated with 802.1X is that the authentication occurs only upon initial connection, and that another user can insert themselves into the connection by changing packets or using a hub. The secure solution is to pair 802.1X, which authenticates the initial connection, with a VPN or IPsec, which provides persistent security.

Wireless Protocols

802.1X is commonly used on wireless access points as a port-based authentication service prior to admission to the wireless network. 802.1X over wireless uses either 802.11i or EAP-based protocols, such as EAP-TLS or PEAP-TLS.

 Cross Check

Wireless Remote Access

Wireless is a common method of allowing remote access to a network, as it does not require physical cabling and allows mobile connections. Wireless security, including protocols such as 802.11i and EAP-based solutions, is covered in Chapter 12.

■ RADIUS

Remote Authentication Dial-In User Service (RADIUS) is a protocol that was developed originally by Livingston Enterprises (acquired by Lucent) as an AAA protocol. It was submitted to the Internet Engineering Task Force (IETF) as a series of RFCs: RFC 2058 (RADIUS specification), RFC 2059 (RADIUS accounting standard), and updated RFCs 2865–2869, which are now standard protocols. The IETF AAA Working Group has proposed extensions to RADIUS (RFC 2882) and a replacement protocol Diameter (Internet Draft Diameter Base Protocol).

RADIUS is designed as a connectionless protocol that uses the User Datagram Protocol (UDP) as its transport layer protocol. Connection type issues, such as timeouts, are handled by the RADIUS application instead of the transport layer. RADIUS utilizes UDP port 1812 for authentication and authorization and UDP 1813 for accounting functions (see Table 11.2 in the "Connection Summary" section).

RADIUS is a client/server protocol. The RADIUS client is typically a network access server (NAS). Network access servers act as intermediaries, authenticating clients before allowing them access to a network. RADIUS, RRAS (Microsoft), RAS, and VPN servers can all act as network access servers. The RADIUS server is a process or daemon running on a UNIX or Windows Server machine. Communications between a RADIUS client and RADIUS server are encrypted using a shared secret that is manually configured into each entity and not shared over a connection. Hence, communications between a RADIUS client (typically a NAS) and a RADIUS server are secure, but the communications between a user (typically a PC) and the RADIUS client are subject to compromise. This is important to note, for if the user's machine (the PC) is not the RADIUS client (the NAS), then communications between the PC and the NAS are typically not encrypted and are passed in the clear.

RADIUS Authentication

The RADIUS protocol is designed to allow a RADIUS server to support a wide variety of methods to authenticate a user. When the server is given a username and password, it can support Point-to-Point Protocol (PPP), Password Authentication Protocol (PAP), Challenge-Handshake Authentication Protocol (CHAP), UNIX login, and other mechanisms, depending on what was established when the server was set up. A user login authentication consists of a query (Access-Request) from the RADIUS client and a corresponding response (Access-Accept, Access-Challenge or Access-Reject) from the RADIUS server, as you can see in Figure 11.2. (The steps are also detailed in the Tech Tip sidebar, "Steps to Establish a RADIUS Connection.") The Access-Challenge response is the initiation of a challenge/response handshake. If the client cannot support challenge/response, then it treats the Challenge message as an Access-Reject.

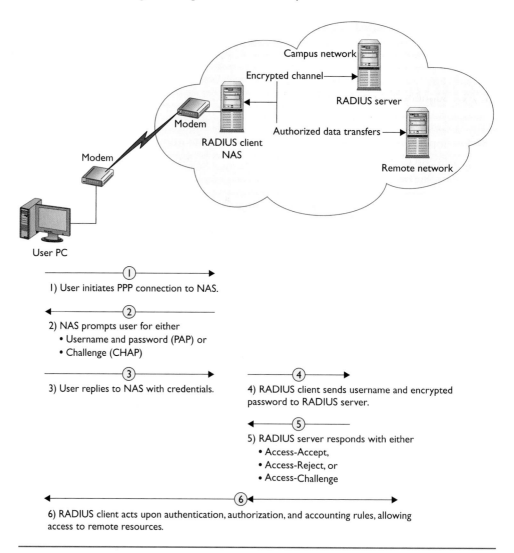

• **Figure 11.2**   RADIUS communication sequence

The Access-Request message contains the username, encrypted password, NAS IP address, and port. The message also contains information concerning the type of session the user wants to initiate. Once the RADIUS server receives this information, it searches its database for a match on the username. If a match is not found, either a default profile is loaded or an Access-Reject reply is sent to the user. If the entry is found or the default profile is used, the next phase involves authorization, for in RADIUS, these steps are performed in sequence. Figure 11.2 shows the interaction between a user and the RADIUS client and RADIUS server and the steps taken to make a connection.

RADIUS Authorization

In the RADIUS protocol, the authentication and authorization steps are performed together in response to a single Access-Request message, although they are sequential steps (see Figure 11.2). Once an identity has been established, either known or default, the authorization process determines what parameters are returned to the client. Typical authorization parameters include the service type allowed (shell or framed), the protocols allowed, the IP address to assign to the user (static or dynamic), and the access list to apply or static route to place in the NAS routing table.

These parameters are all defined in the configuration information on the RADIUS client and server during setup. Using this information, the RADIUS server returns an Access-Accept message with these parameters to the RADIUS client.

RADIUS Accounting

The RADIUS accounting function is performed independently of RADIUS authentication and authorization. The accounting function uses a separate UDP port, 1813 (see Table 11.2 in the "Connection Summary" section at the end of the chapter). The primary functionality of RADIUS accounting was established to support ISPs in their user accounting, and it supports typical accounting functions for time billing and security logging. The RADIUS accounting functions are designed to allow data to be transmitted at the beginning and end of a session, and it can indicate resource utilization, such as time, bandwidth, and so on.

When RADIUS was first designed in the mid 1990s, the role of ISP NASs was relatively simple. Allowing and denying access to a network and timing usage were the major concerns. In the subsequent decade and a half, the Internet and its access methods have changed dramatically, and so have the AAA requirements. As individual firms extended RADIUS to meet these needs, interoperability has become an issue, and a new AAA protocol called Diameter, designed to address these issues in a comprehensive fashion, has been proposed and is entering the final stages of the Internet draft/RFC process.

Diameter

Diameter is a proposed name for the new AAA protocol suite, designated by the IETF to replace the aging RADIUS protocol. Diameter operates in much the same way as RADIUS in a client/server configuration, but it improves upon RADIUS, resolving discovered weaknesses. Diameter is a TCP-based service and has more extensive capabilities in authentication, authorization, and accounting. Diameter is also designed for all types of remote access, not just modem pools. As more and more users adopt broadband and other connection methods, these newer services require more options to determine permissible usage properly and to account for and log the usage. Diameter is designed with these needs in mind.

Diameter also has an improved method of encrypting message exchanges to prohibit replay and man-in-the-middle attacks. Taken all together, Diameter, with its enhanced functionality and security, is an improvement on the proven design of the old RADIUS standard.

■ TACACS+

The *Terminal Access Controller Access Control System+ (TACACS+)* protocol is the current generation of the TACACS family. Originally TACACS was developed by BBN Planet Corporation for MILNET, an early military network, but it has been enhanced by Cisco, which has expanded its functionality twice. The original BBN TACACS system provided a combination process of authentication and authorization. Cisco extended this to Extended Terminal Access Controller Access Control System (XTACACS), which provided for separate authentication, authorization, and accounting processes. The current generation, TACACS+, has extended attribute control and accounting processes.

One of the fundamental design aspects is the separation of authentication, authorization, and accounting in this protocol. Although there is a straightforward lineage of these protocols from the original TACACS, TACACS+ is a major revision and is not backward-compatible with previous versions of the protocol series.

TACACS+ uses TCP as its transport protocol, typically operating over TCP port 49. This port is used for the login process and is reserved in the assigned numbers RFC, RFC 3232, manifested in a database from IANA. In the IANA specification, both UDP port 49 and TCP port 49 are reserved for the TACACS+ login host protocol (see Table 11.2 in the "Connection Summary" section at the end of the chapter).

TACACS+ is a client/server protocol, with the client typically being a NAS and the server being a daemon process on a UNIX, Linux, or Windows server. This is important to note, for if the user's machine (usually a PC) is not the client (usually a NAS), then communications between PC and NAS are typically not encrypted and are passed in the clear. Communications between a TACACS+ client and TACACS+ server are encrypted using a shared secret that is manually configured into each entity and is not shared over a connection. Hence, communications between a TACACS+ client (typically a NAS) and a TACACS+ server are secure, but the communications between a user (typically a PC) and the TACACS+ client are subject to compromise.

TACACS+ Authentication

TACACS+ allows for arbitrary length and content in the authentication exchange sequence, enabling many different authentication mechanisms to be used with TACACS+ clients. Authentication is optional and is determined as a site-configurable option. When authentication is used, common forms include PPP PAP, PPP CHAP, PPP EAP, token cards, and Kerberos. The authentication process is performed using three different packet types: START, CONTINUE, and REPLY. START and CONTINUE packets originate from the client and are directed to the TACACS+ server. The REPLY packet is used to communicate from the TACACS+ server to the client.

The authentication process is illustrated in Figure 11.3, and it begins with a START message from the client to the server. This message may be in response to an initiation from a PC connected to the TACACS+ client. The START message describes the type of authentication being requested (simple plaintext password, PAP, CHAP, and so on). This START message may also contain additional authentication data, such as a username and password. A START message is also sent as a response to a restart request from the server in a REPLY message. A START message always has its sequence number set to 1.

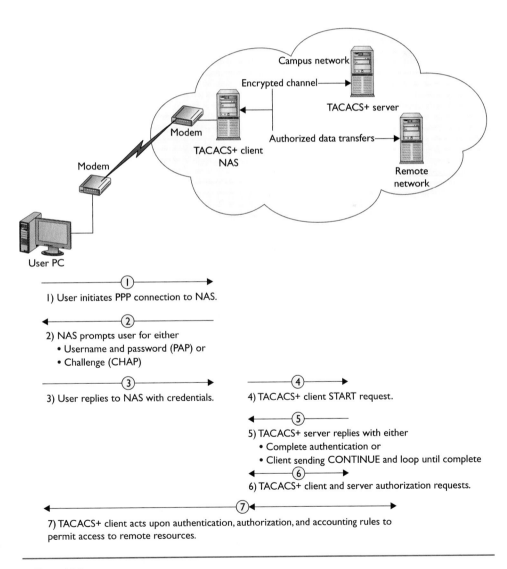

1) User initiates PPP connection to NAS.

2) NAS prompts user for either
  • Username and password (PAP) or
  • Challenge (CHAP)

3) User replies to NAS with credentials.

4) TACACS+ client START request.

5) TACACS+ server replies with either
  • Complete authentication or
  • Client sending CONTINUE and loop until complete

6) TACACS+ client and server authorization requests.

7) TACACS+ client acts upon authentication, authorization, and accounting rules to permit access to remote resources.

• **Figure 11.3**   TACACS+ communication sequence

When a TACACS+ server receives a START message, it sends a REPLY message. This REPLY message indicates whether the authentication is complete or needs to be continued. If the process needs to be continued, the REPLY message also specifies what additional information is needed. The response from a client to a REPLY message requesting additional data is a CONTINUE message. This process continues until the server has all the information needed, and the authentication process concludes with a success or failure.

TACACS+ Authorization

Authorization is defined as the granting of specific permissions based on the privileges held by the account. This generally occurs after authentication, as shown in Figure 11.3, but this is not a firm requirement. A default state of "unknown user" exists before a user is authenticated, and permissions can be determined for an unknown user. As with authentication, authorization is an optional process and may or may not be part of a site-specific operation. When it is used in conjunction with authentication, the authorization process follows the authentication process and uses the confirmed user identity as input in the decision process.

The authorization process is performed using two message types: REQUEST and RESPONSE. The authorization process is performed using an authorization session consisting of a single pair of REQUEST and RESPONSE messages. The client issues an authorization REQUEST message containing a fixed set of fields enumerating the authenticity of the user or process requesting permission and a variable set of fields enumerating the services or options for which authorization is being requested.

The RESPONSE message in TACACS+ is not a simple yes or no; it can also include qualifying information, such as a user time limit or IP restrictions. These limitations have important uses, such as enforcing time limits on shell access or enforcing IP access list restrictions for specific user accounts.

TACACS+ Accounting

As with the two previous services, accounting is also an optional function of TACACS+. When utilized, it typically follows the other services. Accounting in TACACS+ is defined as the process of recording what a user or process has done. Accounting can serve two important purposes:

- It can be used to account for services being utilized, possibly for billing purposes.
- It can be used for generating security audit trails.

TACACS+ accounting records contain several pieces of information to support these tasks. The accounting process has the information revealed in the authorization and authentication processes, so it can record specific requests by user or process. To support this functionality, TACACS+ has three types of accounting records: START, STOP, and UPDATE. Note that these are record types, not message types as earlier discussed.

START records indicate the time and user or process that began an authorized process. STOP records enumerate the same information concerning the stop times for specific actions. UPDATE records act as intermediary notices that a particular task is still being performed. Together these three message types allow the creation of records that delineate the activity of a user or process on a system.

■ Authentication Protocols

Numerous authentication protocols have been developed, used, and discarded in the brief history of computing. Some have come and gone because they did not enjoy market share, others have had security issues, and yet others have been revised and improved in newer versions. Although it's impossible and impractical to cover them all, some of the common ones follow.

L2TP and PPTP

Layer 2 Tunneling Protocol (L2TP) and Point-to-Point Tunneling Protocol (PPTP) are both OSI Layer 2 tunneling protocols. *Tunneling* is the encapsulation of one packet within another, which allows you to hide the original packet from view or change the nature of the network transport. This can be done for both security and practical reasons.

From a practical perspective, assume that you are using TCP/IP to communicate between two machines. Your message may pass over various networks, such as an Asynchronous Transfer Mode (ATM) network, as it moves from source to destination. As the ATM protocol can neither read nor understand TCP/IP packets, something must be done to make them passable across the network. By encapsulating a packet as the payload in a separate protocol, so it can be carried across a section of a network, a mechanism called a *tunnel* is created. At each end of the tunnel, called the tunnel *endpoints*, the payload packet is read and understood. As it goes into the tunnel, you can envision your packet being placed in an envelope with the address of the appropriate tunnel endpoint on the envelope. When the envelope arrives at the tunnel endpoint, the original message (the tunnel packet's payload) is re-created, read, and sent to its appropriate next stop. The information being tunneled is understood only at the tunnel endpoints; it is not relevant to intermediate tunnel points because it is only a payload.

PPP

Point-to-Point Protocol (PPP) is a widely used protocol for establishing dial-in connections over serial lines or Integrated Services Digital Network (ISDN) services. PPP has several authentication mechanisms, including PAP, CHAP, and the Extensible Authentication Protocol (EAP). These protocols are used to authenticate the peer device, not a user of the system. PPP is a standardized Internet encapsulation of IP traffic over point-to-point links, such as serial lines. The authentication process is performed only when the link is established.

PPP is a commonly used data link layer protocol to connect devices. Defined in RFC 1661, PPP originally was created as an encapsulation protocol to carry IP traffic over point-to-point links. PPP has been extended upon with multiple RFCs to carry a variety of network traffic types over a variety of network types. PPP uses Link Control Protocols (LCP) and Network Control Protocols (NCP) to establish the desired connections over a network.

PPP

Microsoft led a consortium of networking companies to extend PPP to enable the creation of virtual private networks (VPNs). The result was the **Point-to-Point Tunneling (PPTP)**, a network protocol that enables the secure transfer of data from a remote PC to a server by creating a VPN across a TCP/IP network. This remote network connection can also span a public switched telephone network (PSTN) and is thus an economical way of connecting remote dial-in users to a corporate data network. The incorporation of PPTP into the Microsoft Windows product line provides a built-in secure method of remote connection using the operating system, and this has given PPTP a large marketplace footprint.

For most PPTP implementations, three computers are involved: the PPTP client, the NAS, and a PPTP server, as shown in Figure 11.4. The connection between the remote client and the network is established in stages, as illustrated in Figure 11.5. First the client makes a PPP connection to a NAS, typically an ISP. (In today's world of widely available broadband, if there is already an Internet connection, then there is no need to perform the PPP connection to the ISP.) Once the PPP connection is established, a second connection is made over the PPP connection to the PPTP server. This second connection creates the VPN connection between the remote client and the PPTP server. A typical VPN connection is one in which the user is in a hotel with a wireless Internet connection, connecting to a corporate network. This connection acts as a tunnel for future data transfers. Although these diagrams illustrate a telephone connection, this first link can be virtually any method. Common in hotels today are wired connections to the Internet. These wired connections typically are provided by a local ISP and offer the same services as a phone connection, albeit at a much higher data transfer rate.

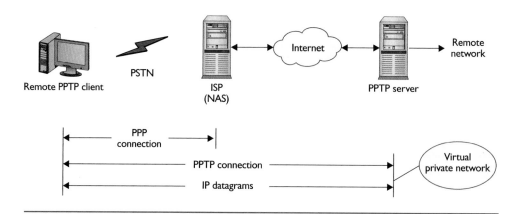

● **Figure 11.4**   PPTP communication diagram

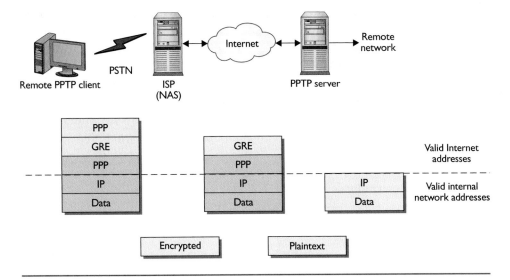

• **Figure 11.5**   PPTP message encapsulation during transmission

As mentioned earlier in this chapter, tunneling is the process of sending packets as data within other packets across a section of a network. This encapsulation enables a network to carry a packet type that it cannot ordinarily route, and it also provides the opportunity to secure the contents of the first packet through encryption. PPTP establishes a tunnel from the remote PPTP client to the PPTP server and enables encryption within this tunnel. This provides a secure method of transport. To do this and still enable routing, an intermediate addressing scheme, Generic Routing Encapsulation (GRE), is used.

To establish the connection, PPTP uses communications across TCP port 1723 (see Table 11.2 in the "Connection Summary" section at the end of the chapter), so this port must remain open across the network firewalls for PPTP to be initiated. Although PPTP allows the use of any PPP authentication scheme, CHAP is used when encryption is specified, to provide an appropriate level of security. For the encryption methodology, Microsoft chose the RSA RC4 cipher, with either a 40- or 128-bit session key length, and this is OS driven. Microsoft Point-to-Point Encryption (MPPE) is an extension to PPP that enables VPNs to use PPTP as the tunneling protocol.

EAP

Extensible Authentication Protocol (EAP) is a universal authentication framework defined by RFC 3748 that is frequently used in wireless networks and point-to-point connections. Although EAP is not limited to wireless and can be used for wired authentication, it is most often used in wireless LANs. EAP is discussed in detail in Chapter 12.

CHAP

Challenge-Handshake Authentication Protocol (CHAP) is used to provide authentication across a point-to-point link using PPP. In this protocol, authentication after the link has been established is not mandatory. CHAP is

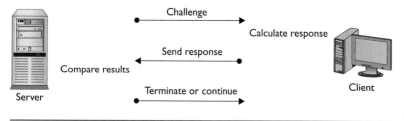

• **Figure 11.6** The CHAP challenge/response sequence

designed to provide authentication periodically through the use of a challenge/response system that is sometimes described as a *three-way handshake*, as illustrated in Figure 11.6. The initial challenge (a randomly generated number) is sent to the client. The client uses a one-way hashing function to calculate what the response should be and then sends this back. The server compares the response to what it calculated the response should be. If they match, communication continues. If the two values don't match, then the connection is terminated. This mechanism relies on a shared secret between the two entities so that the correct values can be calculated.

Microsoft has created two versions of CHAP, modified to increase the usability of CHAP across Microsoft's product line. MSCHAP v1, defined in RFC 2433, has been deprecated and dropped in Windows Vista. The current standard, version 2, defined in RFC 2759, was introduced with Windows 2000.

NTLM

NT LAN Manager (NTLM) is an authentication protocol designed by Microsoft, for use with the Server Message Block (SMB) protocol. SMB is an application-level network protocol primarily used for sharing of files and printers in Windows-based networks. NTLM was designed as a replacement for the LANMAN protocol. The current version is NTLM v2, which was introduced with Windows NT 4.0 SP4. Although Microsoft has adopted the Kerberos protocol for authentication, NTLM v2 is still used when

- Authenticating to a server using an IP address
- Authenticating to a server that belongs to a different Active Directory forest
- Authenticating to a server that doesn't belong to a domain
- No Active Directory domain exists ("workgroup" or "peer-to-peer" connection)

PAP

Password Authentication Protocol (PAP) involves a two-way handshake in which the username and password are sent across the link in clear text. PAP authentication does not provide any protection against playback and line sniffing. PAP is now a deprecated standard.

L2TP

Layer 2 Tunneling Protocol (L2TP) is also an Internet standard and came from the Layer 2 Forwarding (L2F) protocol, a Cisco initiative designed to address issues with PPTP. Whereas PPTP is designed around PPP and IP networks, L2F, and hence L2TP, is designed for use across all kinds of networks, including ATM and Frame Relay. Additionally, whereas PPTP is designed to be implemented in software at the client device, L2TP was conceived as a hardware implementation using a router or a special-purpose appliance. L2TP can be configured in software and is in Microsoft's RRAS servers, which use L2TP to create a VPN.

L2TP works in much the same way as PPTP, but it opens up several items for expansion. For instance, in L2TP, routers can be enabled to concentrate VPN traffic over higher-bandwidth lines, creating hierarchical networks of VPN traffic that can be more efficiently managed across an enterprise. L2TP also has the ability to use IPsec and Data Encryption Standard (DES) as encryption protocols, providing a higher level of data security. L2TP is also designed to work with established AAA services such as RADIUS and TACACS+ to aid in user authentication, authorization, and accounting.

L2TP is established via UDP port 1701, so this is an essential port to leave open across firewalls supporting L2TP traffic. This port is registered with the Internet Assigned Numbers Authority (IANA), as is 1723 for PPTP (see Table 11.2 in the "Connection Summary" section at the end of the chapter). Microsoft supports L2TP in Windows 2000 and above, but because of the computing power required, most implementations will use specialized hardware (such as a Cisco router).

Telnet

One of the methods to grant remote access to a system is through Telnet. Telnet is the standard terminal-emulation protocol within the TCP/IP protocol series, and it is defined in RFC 854. Telnet allows users to log in remotely and access resources as if the user had a local terminal connection. Telnet is an old protocol and offers little security. Information, including account names and passwords, is passed in clear text over the TCP/IP connection.

Telnet makes its connection using TCP port 23. (A list of remote access networking port assignments is provided in Table 11.2 in the "Connection Summary" section at the end of the chapter.) As Telnet is implemented on most products using TCP/IP, it is important to control access to Telnet on machines and routers when setting them up. Failure to control access by using firewalls, access lists, and other security methods, or even by disabling the Telnet daemon, is equivalent to leaving an open door for unauthorized users on a system.

SSH

If you are looking for remote access to a system in a secure manner, you could use Secure Shell (SSH), a protocol series designed to facilitate secure network functions across an insecure network. SSH provides direct support for secure remote login, secure file transfer, and secure forwarding of TCP/IP and X Window System traffic. A SSH connection is an encrypted channel, providing for confidentiality and integrity protection.

SSH has its origins as a replacement for the insecure Telnet application from the UNIX operating system. An original component of UNIX, Telnet allowed users to connect between systems. Although Telnet is still used today, it has some drawbacks, as discussed in the preceding section. Some enterprising University of California, Berkeley, students subsequently developed the **r-** commands, such as **rlogin**, to permit access based on the user and source system, as opposed to passing passwords. This was not perfect either, however, because when a login was required, it was still passed in the clear. This led to the development of the SSH protocol series, designed to eliminate all of the insecurities associated with Telnet, **r-** commands, and other means of remote access.

SSH opens a secure transport channel between machines by using an SSH daemon on each end. These daemons initiate contact over TCP port 22 and then communicate over higher ports in a secure mode. One of the strengths of SSH is its support for many different encryption protocols. SSH 1.0 started with RSA algorithms, but at the time they were still under patent, and this led to SSH 2.0 with extended support for Triple DES (3DES) and other encryption methods. Today, SSH can be used with a wide range of encryption protocols, including RSA, 3DES, Blowfish, International Data Encryption Algorithm (IDEA), CAST128, AES256, and others.

The SSH protocol has facilities to encrypt data automatically, provide authentication, and compress data in transit. It can support strong encryption, cryptographic host authentication, and integrity protection. The authentication services are host-based and not user-based. If user authentication is desired in a system, it must be set up separately at a higher level in the OSI model. The protocol is designed to be flexible and simple, and it is designed specifically to minimize the number of round trips between systems. The key exchange, public key, symmetric key, message authentication, and hash algorithms are all negotiated at connection time. Individual data-packet integrity is assured through the use of a message authentication code that is computed from a shared secret, the contents of the packet, and the packet sequence number.

The SSH protocol consists of three major components:

- **Transport layer protocol** Provides server authentication, confidentiality, integrity, and compression
- **User authentication protocol** Authenticates the client to the server
- **Connection protocol** Provides multiplexing of the encrypted tunnel into several logical channels

SSH is very popular in the UNIX environment, and it is actively used as a method of establishing VPNs across public networks. Because all communications between the two machines are encrypted at the OSI application layer by the two SSH daemons, this leads to the ability to build very secure solutions and even solutions that defy the ability of outside services to monitor. As SSH is a standard protocol series with connection parameters established via TCP port 22, different vendors can build differing solutions that can still interoperate. As such, if SSH is enabled on a UNIX platform, it is a built-in method of establishing secure communications with that system from a wide range of client platforms.

Although Windows Server implementations of SSH exist, this has not been a popular protocol in the Windows environment from a server perspective. The development of a wide array of commercial SSH clients for the

Windows platform indicates the marketplace strength of interconnection from desktop PCs to UNIX-based servers utilizing this protocol.

VPNs

A **virtual private network (VPN)** is a secure *virtual* network built on top of a *physical* network. The security of a VPN lies in the encryption of packet contents between the endpoints that define the VPN. The physical network upon which a VPN is built is typically a public network, such as the Internet. Because the packet contents between VPN endpoints are encrypted, to an outside observer on the public network, the communication is secure, and depending on how the VPN is set up, security can even extend to the two communicating parties' machines.

Virtual private networking is not a protocol per se, but rather a method of using protocols to achieve a specific objective—secure communications—as shown in Figure 11.7. A user who wants to have a secure communication channel with a server across a public network can set up two intermediary devices, VPN endpoints, to accomplish this task. The user can communicate with his endpoint, and the server can communicate with its endpoint. The two endpoints then communicate across the public network. VPN endpoints can be software solutions, routers, or specific servers set up for specific functionality. This implies that VPN services are set up in advance and are not something negotiated on-the-fly.

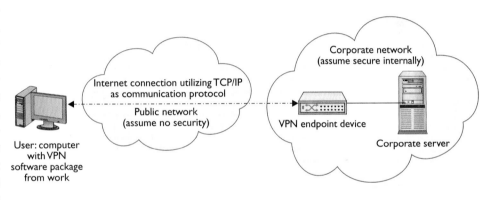

• **Figure 11.7** VPN service over an Internet connection

A typical use of VPN services is a user accessing a corporate data network from a home PC across the Internet. The employee installs VPN software from work on a home PC. This software is already configured to communicate with the corporate network's VPN endpoint; it knows the location, the protocols that will be used, and so on. When the home user wants to connect to the corporate network, she connects to the Internet and then starts the VPN software. The user can then log into the corporate network by using an appropriate authentication and authorization methodology. The sole purpose of the VPN connection is to provide a private connection between the machines, which encrypts any data sent between the home user's PC and the corporate network. Identification, authorization, and all other standard functions are accomplished with the standard mechanisms for the established system.

VPNs can use many different protocols to offer a secure method of communicating between endpoints. Common methods of encryption on VPNs include PPTP, IPsec, SSH, and L2TP, all of which are discussed in this chapter.

The key is that both endpoints know the protocol and share a secret. All of this necessary information is established when the VPN is set up. At the time of use, the VPN only acts as a private tunnel between the two points and does not constitute a complete security solution.

IPsec

Internet Protocol Security (IPsec) is a set of protocols developed by the IETF to securely exchange packets at the network layer (Layer 3) of the OSI model (RFC 2401–2412). Although these protocols work only in conjunction with IP networks, once an IPsec connection is established, it is possible to tunnel across other networks at lower levels of the OSI model. The set of security services provided by IPsec occurs at the network layer of the OSI model, so higher-layer protocols, such as TCP, UDP, Internet Control Message Protocol (ICMP), Border Gateway Protocol (BGP), and the like, are not functionally altered by the implementation of IPsec services.

The IPsec protocol series has a sweeping array of services it is designed to provide, including but not limited to access control, connectionless integrity, traffic-flow confidentiality, rejection of replayed packets, data security (encryption), and data-origin authentication. IPsec has two defined methods—transport and tunneling—that provide different levels of security. IPsec also has three modes of connection: host-to-server, server-to-server, and host-to-host.

The transport method encrypts only the data portion of a packet, thus enabling an outsider to see source and destination IP addresses. The transport method protects the higher-level protocols associated with a packet and protects the data being transmitted but allows knowledge of the transmission itself. Protection of the data portion of a packet is referred to as **content protection**.

Tunneling provides encryption of source and destination IP addresses, as well as of the data itself. This provides the greatest security, but it can be done only between IPsec servers (or routers) because the final destination needs to be known for delivery. Protection of the header information is known as **context protection**.

It is possible to use both methods at the same time, such as using transport within one's own network to reach an IPsec server, which then tunnels to the target server's network, connecting to an IPsec server there, and then using the transport method from the target network's IPsec server to the target host.

Security Associations

A **security association (SA)** is a formal manner of describing the necessary and sufficient portions of the IPsec protocol series to achieve a specific level of protection. Because many options exist, both communicating parties must agree on the use of the protocols that are available, and this agreement is referred to as a security association. SAs exist both for integrity-protecting systems and confidentiality-protecting systems. In each IPsec implementation, a security association database (SAD) defines parameters associated with each SA. The SA is a one-way (simplex) association, and if two-way communication security is desired, two SAs are used—one for each direction.

IPsec Configurations

Four basic configurations can be applied to machine-to-machine connections using IPsec. The simplest is a host-to-host connection between two machines, as shown in Figure 11.8. In this case, the Internet is not a part of the SA between the machines. If bidirectional security is desired, two SAs are used. The SAs are effective from host to host.

The second case places two security devices in the stream, relieving the hosts of the calculation and encapsulation duties. These two gateways have an SA between them. The network is assumed to be secure from each machine to its gateway, and no IPsec is performed across these hops. Figure 11.9 shows the two security gateways with a tunnel across the Internet, although either tunnel or transport mode could be used.

The third case combines the first two. A separate SA exists between the gateway devices, but an SA also exists between hosts. This could be considered a tunnel inside a tunnel, as shown in Figure 11.10.

Remote users commonly connect through the Internet to an organization's network. The network has a security gateway through which it secures traffic to and from its servers and authorized users. In the last

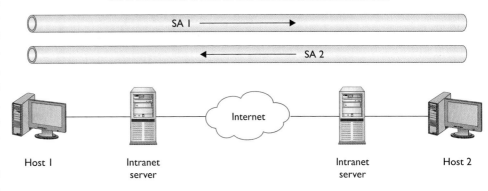

Case 1:
Two SAs from host to host for bidirectional secure communications

• **Figure 11.8**   A host-to-host connection between two machines

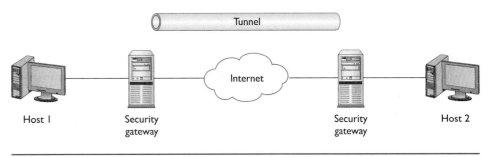

Case 2:
IPsec between machines using gateway security devices

• **Figure 11.9**   Two security gateways with a tunnel across the Internet

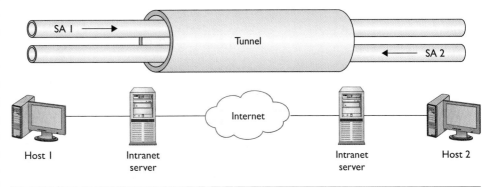

Case 3:
Separate IPsec tunnels, host to host and gateway to gateway

• **Figure 11.10**   A tunnel inside a tunnel

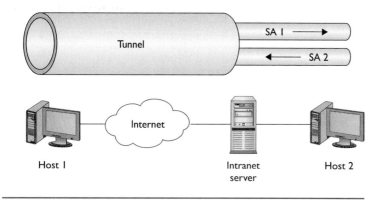

Case 4:
Tunnel from host to gateway
Optional: Two SAs for bidirectional secure communications

Tunnel

SA 1 ⟶

⟵ SA 2

Host 1

Internet

Intranet
server

Host 2

• **Figure 11.11**   Tunnel from host to gateway

case, illustrated in Figure 11.11, the user establishes an SA with the security gateway and then a separate SA with the desired server, if required. This can be done using software on a remote laptop and hardware at the organization's network.

Windows can act as an IPsec server, as can routers and other servers. The primary issue is CPU usage and where the computing power should be implanted. This consideration has led to the rise of IPsec appliances, which are hardware devices that perform the IPsec function specifically for a series of communications. Depending on the number of connections, network bandwidth, and so on, these devices can be inexpensive for small office or home office use or quite expensive for large enterprise-level implementations.

IPsec Security

IPsec uses two protocols to provide traffic security:

- **Authentication Header (AH)**   A header added to a packet for the purposes of integrity checking

- **Encapsulating Security Payload (ESP)**   A method of encrypting the data portion of a datagram to provide confidentiality

For key management and exchange, three protocols exist:

- **Internet Security Association and Key Management Protocol (ISAKMP)**

- **Oakley**

- **Secure Key Exchange Mechanism for Internet (SKEMI)**

These key management protocols can be collectively referred to as *Internet Key Management Protocol (IKMP)* or *Internet Key Exchange (IKE)*.

IPsec does not define specific security algorithms, nor does it require specific methods of implementation. IPsec is an open framework that allows vendors to implement existing industry-standard algorithms suited for specific tasks. This flexibility is key in IPsec's ability to offer a wide range of security functions. IPsec allows several security technologies to be combined into a comprehensive solution for network-based confidentiality, integrity, and authentication. IPsec uses the following:

- Diffie-Hellman key exchange between peers on a public network

- Public key signing of Diffie-Hellman key exchanges to guarantee identity and avoid man-in-the-middle attacks

- Bulk encryption algorithms, such as IDEA and 3DES, for encrypting data

- Keyed hash algorithms, such as HMAC, and traditional hash algorithms, such as MD5 and SHA-1, for packet-level authentication

- Digital certificates to act as digital ID cards between parties

To provide traffic security, two header extensions have been defined for IP datagrams. The AH, when added to an IP datagram, ensures the integrity of the data and also the authenticity of the data's origin. By protecting the nonchanging elements in the IP header, the AH protects the IP address, which enables data-origin authentication. The ESP provides security services for the higher-level protocol portion of the packet only, not the IP header.

AH and ESP can be used separately or in combination, depending on the level and types of security desired. Both also work with the transport and tunnel modes of IPsec protocols. In transport mode, the two communication endpoints provide security primarily for the upper-layer protocols. The cryptographic endpoints, where encryption and decryption occur, are located at the source and destination of the communication channel. When AH is in transport mode, the original IP header is exposed, but its contents are protected via the AH block in the packet, as illustrated in Figure 11.12. When AH is employed in tunnel mode, portions of the outer IP header are given the same header protection that occurs in transport mode, with the entire inner packet receiving protection. This is illustrated in Figure 11.13. The use of tunnel mode allows easier crossing of firewalls, for without it, specific firewall rules would be needed to pass the modified transport packet header.

Tunneling is a means of encapsulating packets inside a protocol that is understood only at the entry and exit points of the tunnel. This provides security during transport in the tunnel, because outside observers cannot decipher packet contents or even the identities of the communicating parties. IPsec has a tunnel mode that can be used from server to server across a public network. Although the tunnel endpoints are referred to as *servers*, these devices can be routers, appliances, or servers. In tunnel mode, the tunnel endpoints merely encapsulate the entire packet with new IP headers to indicate the endpoints, and they encrypt the contents of this new packet. The true source and destination information is contained in the inner IP header, which is encrypted in the tunnel. The outer IP header contains the addresses of the endpoints of the tunnel.

ESP provides a means of encrypting the packet's contents, as shown in Figure 11.14. In this case, in transport mode, the datagram contents are encrypted and authenticated via the ESP header and footer/trailer that are inserted into the datagram. As mentioned, AH and ESP can be employed in tunnel mode. ESP affords the same encryption protection to the contents of the tunneled packet, which is the entire packet from the initial sender, as illustrated in Figure 11.15. Together, in tunnel mode, AH and ESP can provide complete protection across the

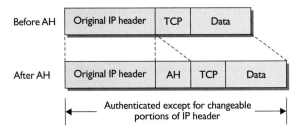

Authentication header in transport mode

• **Figure 11.12**   IPsec use of AH in transport mode

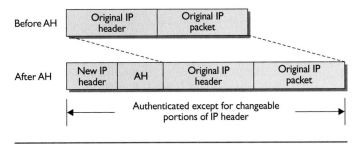

Authentication header in tunnel mode

• **Figure 11.13**   IPsec use of AH in tunnel mode

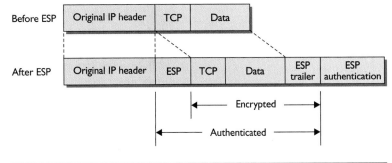

Encapsulating security payload in transport mode

• **Figure 11.14**   IPsec use of ESP in transport mode

Encapsulating security payload in tunnel mode

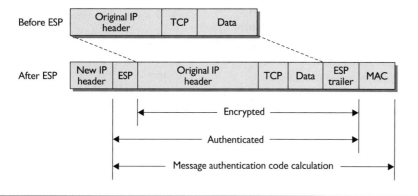

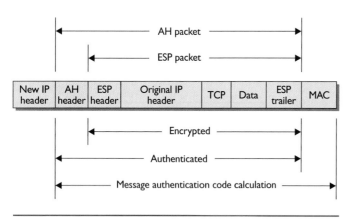

• **Figure 11.15** IPsec use of ESP in tunnel mode

• **Figure 11.16** IPsec ESP and AH packet construction in tunnel mode

packet, as shown in Figure 11.16. The specific combination of AH and ESP is referred to as a *security association* in IPsec.

In IP version 4 (IPv4), IPsec is an add-on, and its acceptance is vendor driven. It is not a part of the original IP—one of the short-sighted design flaws of the original IP. In IPv6, IPsec is integrated into IP and is native on all packets. Its use is still optional, but its inclusion in the protocol suite will guarantee interoperability across vendor solutions when they are compliant with IPv6 standards.

IPsec uses cryptographic keys in its security process and has both manual and automatic distribution of keys as part of the protocol series. Manual key distribution is included, but it is practical only in small, static environments and does not scale to enterprise-level implementations. The default method of key management, **Internet Key Exchange (IKE)**, is automated. IKE authenticates each peer involved in IPsec and negotiates the security policy, including the exchange of session keys. IKE creates a secure tunnel between peers and then negotiates the security association for IPsec across this channel. This is done in two phases: the first develops the channel, and the second develops the security association.

■ Vulnerabilities of Remote Access Methods

The primary vulnerability associated with many of these methods of remote access is the passing of critical data in clear text. Plaintext passing of passwords provides no security if the password is sniffed, and sniffers are easy to use on a network. Even plaintext passing of user IDs gives away information that can be correlated and possibly used by an attacker. Plaintext credential passing is one of the fundamental flaws with Telnet and is why SSH was developed. This is also one of the flaws with RADIUS and TACACS+, as they have a segment unprotected. There are methods for overcoming these limitations, although they require discipline and understanding in setting up a system.

The strength of the encryption algorithm is also a concern. Should a specific algorithm or method prove to be vulnerable, services that rely solely on it are also vulnerable. To get around this dependency, many of the protocols allow numerous encryption methods, so that should one prove vulnerable, a shift to another restores security.

As with any software implementation, there always exists the possibility that a bug could open the system to attack. Bugs have been corrected in most software packages to close holes that made systems vulnerable, and remote access functionality is no exception. This is not a Microsoft-only phenomenon, as one might believe from the popular press. Critical flaws have been found in almost every product, from open system implementations such as OpenSSH to proprietary systems such as Cisco IOS. The important issue is not the presence of software bugs, for as software continues to become more complex, this is an unavoidable issue. The true key is vendor responsiveness to fixing the bugs once they are discovered, and the major players, such as Cisco and Microsoft, have been very responsive in this area.

■ Connection Summary

Table 11.2		Common TCP/UDP Remote Access Networking Port Assignments	
TCP Port Number	**UDP Port Number**	**Keyword**	**Protocol**
20		FTP-Data	File Transfer (Default Data)
21		FTP	File Transfer Control
22		SSH	Secure Shell Login
23		TELNET	Telnet
25		SMTP	Simple Mail Transfer
37	37	TIME	Time
49	49	TACACS+	TACACS+ login
53	53	DNS	Domain Name Server
65	65	TACACS+	TACACS+ database service
88	88	Kerberos	Kerberos
500	500	ISAKMP	ISAKMP
512		rexec	
513		rlogin	UNIX rlogin
	513	rwho	UNIX Broadcast Naming Service
514		rsh	UNIX rsh and rep
	514	SYSLOG	UNIX system logs
614	614	SSHELL	SSL Shell
	1645	RADIUS	RADIUS: Historical
	1646	RADIUS	RADIUS: Historical
	1701	L2TP	L2TP
1723	1723	PPTP	PPTP
1812	1812	RADIUS	RADIUS Authorization
1813	1813	RADIUS-actg	RADIUS Accounting

Chapter 11 Review

▪ Chapter Summary

After reading this chapter and completing the exercises, you should understand the following about authentication and remote access protocols.

Discuss the methods and protocols for remote access to networks

- Remote access protocols provide a mechanism to remotely connect clients to networks.

- A wide range of remote access protocols has evolved to support various security and authentication mechanisms.

- Remote access is granted via remote access servers, such as RRAS or RADIUS.

Identify authentication, authorization, and accounting (AAA) protocols

- Authentication is a cornerstone element of security, connecting access to a previously approved user ID.

- Authorization is the process of determining whether an authenticated user has permission.

- Accounting protocols manage connection time and cost records.

Explain authentication methods and the security implications in their use

- Password-based authentication is still the most widely used because of cost and ubiquity.

- Ticket-based systems, such as Kerberos, form the basis for most modern authentication and credentialing systems.

Implement virtual private networks (VPNs) and their security aspects

- VPNs use protocols to establish a private network over a public network, shielding user communications from outside observation.

- VPNs can be invoked via many different protocol mechanisms and involve either a hardware or software client on each end of the communication channel.

Describe Internet Protocol Security (IPsec) and its use in securing communications

- IPsec is the native method of securing IP packets; it is optional in IPv4 and mandatory in IPv6.

- IPsec uses Authentication Headers (AH) to authenticate packets.

- IPsec uses Encapsulating Security Payload (ESP) to provide confidentiality service at the datagram level.

▪ Key Terms

AAA *(261)*
access control *(268)*
accounting *(261)*
authentication *(261)*
Authentication Header (AH) *(286)*
authentication server (AS) *(263)*
authorization *(261)*
content protection *(284)*
context protection *(284)*
discretionary access control (DAC) *(269)*
Encapsulating Security Payload (ESP) *(286)*
identification *(262)*

Internet Key Exchange (IKE) *(288)*
Internet Protocol Security (IPsec) *(284)*
Internet Security Association and Key Management Protocol (ISAKMP) *(286)*
Kerberos *(263)*
key distribution center (KDC) *(263)*
Layer 2 Tunneling Protocol (L2TP) *(280)*
mandatory access control (MAC) *(269)*
Oakley *(286)*
Point-to-Point Tunneling Protocol (PPTP) *(278)*
remote access server (RAS) *(261)*
role-based access control (RBAC) *(270)*
rule-based access control (RBAC) *(270)*

Secure Key Exchange Mechanism for Internet
   (SKEMI) *(286)*
security association (SA) *(284)*

ticket-granting server (TGS) *(263)*
virtual private network (VPN) *(283)*

■ Key Terms Quiz

Use terms from the Key Terms list to complete the sentences that follow. Don't use the same term more than once. Not all terms will be used.

1. _____ is an authentication model designed around the concept of using tickets for accessing objects.

2. _____ is designed around the type of tasks people perform.

3. A formal manner of describing the necessary and sufficient portions of the IPsec protocol series to achieve a specific level of protection is a(n) _____.

4. _____ describes a system where every resource has access rules set for it all of the time.

5. A(n) _____ is a collection of protocols used to secure network traffic over a nonsecure network.

6. In IPsec, a security association is defined by a specific combination of _____ and _____.

7. The protection of the data portion of a packet is _____.

8. The protection of the header portion of a packet is _____.

9. _____ is a key management and exchange protocol used with IPsec.

10. The process of comparing credentials to those established during the identification process is referred to as _____.

■ Multiple-Choice Quiz

1. Which statement best describes differences between RADIUS and TACACS+?

   A. RADIUS is for Microsoft Windows only.

   B. TACACS+ is faster than RADIUS.

   C. RADIUS is a remote identification service.

   D. TACACS+ separates authentication, authorization, and accounting capabilities.

2. Authentication is typically based upon what?

   A. Something a user possesses

   B. Something a user knows

   C. Something measured on a user, such as a fingerprint

   D. All of the above

3. Passwords are an example of:

   A. Something you have

   B. Something you know

   C. A shared secret

   D. None of the above

4. Which of these protocols is used for carrying authentication, authorization, and accounting information between a network access server and a shared authentication server?

   A. IPsec

   B. VPN

   C. SSH

   D. RADIUS

5. On a VPN, traffic is encrypted and decrypted at:

   A. Endpoints of the tunnel only

   B. Users' machines

   C. Each device at each hop

   D. The data link layer of access devices

6. A ticket-granting server is an important element in which of the following authentication models?

   A. L2TP

   B. RADIUS

   C. PPP

   D. Kerberos

7. What protocol is used for RADIUS?

   A. UDP

   B. NetBIOS

   C. TCP

   D. Proprietary

8. Which protocols are natively supported by Microsoft Windows XP and Vista for use in securing remote connections?

   A. SSH

   B. PPTP

   C. IPsec

   D. RADIUS

9. What are the foundational elements of an access control system?

   A. Passwords, permissions, cryptography

   B. Shared secrets, authorization, authenticators

   C. Authentication, permissions, user IDs

   D. Identification, authorization, authentication

10. IPsec provides which options as security services?

    A. ESP and AH

    B. ESP and AP

    C. EA and AP

    D. EA and AH

11. Secure Shell uses which port to communicate?

    A. TCP port 80

    B. UDP port 22

    C. TCP port 22

    D. TCP port 110

12. Elements of Kerberos include which of the following?

    A. Tickets, ticket-granting server, ticket-authorizing agent

    B. Ticket-granting ticket, authentication server, ticket

    C. Services server, Kerberos realm, ticket authenticators

    D. Client-to-server ticket, authentication server ticket, ticket

13. To establish a PPTP connection across a firewall, you must do which of the following?

    A. Do nothing; PPTP does not need to cross firewalls by design.

    B. Do nothing; PPTP traffic is invisible and tunnels past firewalls.

    C. Open a UDP port of choice and assign it to PPTP.

    D. Open TCP port 1723.

14. To establish an L2TP connection across a firewall, you must do which of the following?

    A. Do nothing; L2TP does not cross firewalls by design.

    B. Do nothing; L2TP tunnels past firewalls.

    C. Open a UDP port of choice and assign it to L2TP.

    D. Open UDP port 1701.

15. IPsec can provide which of the following types of protection?

    A. Context protection

    B. Content protection

    C. Both context and content protection

    D. Neither context nor content protection

■ Essay Quiz

1. Your boss has asked you to compare and contrast several remote access systems. One is based on 802.1X, another is based on TACACS+, and the last is based on RADIUS.

2. How are authentication and authorization alike and how are they different. What is the relationship, if any, between the two?

3. What is a VPN and what technologies are used to create one?

Lab Projects

• Lab Project 11.1

Using two workstations and some routers, set up a simple VPN. Using Wireshark (a shareware network protocol analyzer, available at www.wireshark.com), observe traffic inside and outside the tunnel to demonstrate protection.

• Lab Project 11.2

Using freeSSHd and freeFTPd (both shareware programs, available at www.freesshd.com) and Wireshark, demonstrate the security features of SSH compared to Telnet and FTP.

Wireless Security

chapter 12

We must plan for freedom, and not only for security, if for no other reason than that only freedom can make security secure.

—Karl Popper

In this chapter, you will learn how to

- **Describe the different wireless systems in use today**
- **Detail WAP and its security implications**
- **Identify 802.11's security issues and possible solutions**

Wireless is increasingly the way people access the Internet. Because wireless access is considered a consumer benefit, many businesses have added wireless access points to lure customers into their shops. With the rollout of third-generation (3G) cellular networks, people are also increasingly accessing the Internet from their mobile phones.

As wireless use increases, the security of the wireless protocols has become a more important factor in the security of the entire network. As a security professional, you need to understand wireless network applications because of the risks inherent in broadcasting a network signal where anyone can intercept it. Sending unsecured information across public airwaves is tantamount to posting your company's passwords by the front door of the building.

This chapter looks at several current wireless protocols and their security features.

Introduction to Wireless Networking

Wireless networking is the transmission of packetized data by means of a physical topology that does not use direct physical links. This definition can be narrowed to apply to networks that use radio waves to carry the signals over either public or private bands, instead of using standard network cabling. Although some proprietary applications use point-to-point technology with narrowband radios and highly directional antennas, this technology is not common enough to produce any significant research into its vulnerabilities, and anything that was developed would have limited usefulness. So this chapter focuses on point-to-multipoint systems, the two most common of which are the family of cellular protocols and IEEE 802.11. IEEE 802.11 is a family of protocols instead of a single specification; this is a summary table of the 802.11 family.

Specification	Speed	Frequency Range
802.11a	54 Mbps	5.2 GHz
802.11b	11 Mbps	2.4 GHz
802.11g	11 Mbps/54 Mbps	2.4 GHz
802.11i	11 Mbps/54 Mbps	2.4 GHz
802.11n	124–248 Mbps	2.4 GHz/5.2 GHz

The **IEEE 802.11** protocol has been standardized by the IEEE for wireless local area networks (LANs). Three versions are currently in production—802.11g, 802.11b, and 802.11a. At the time of writing, a fourth standard, 802.11n, has just been ratified. While the fourth standard was an IEEE draft specification, some manufacturers shipped products based on it. With the 802.11n standard due to be ratified in late 2009 and the WiFi alliance certifying 802.11n products, many more manufacturers will release 802.11n-based products. Cellular phone technology has moved rapidly to embrace data transmission and the Internet. The Wireless Application Protocol (WAP) was one of the pioneers of mobile data applications, but it has been overtaken by a variety of protocols pushing us to third-generation (3G) or fourth-generation (4G) mobile networks.

Bluetooth is a short-range wireless protocol typically used on small devices such as mobile phones. Early versions of these phones also had Bluetooth on and discoverable as a default, making the compromise of a nearby phone easy. Security research has focused on finding problems with these devices simply because the devices are so common.

The security world ignored wireless for a long time, and then within the space of a few months, it seemed like everyone was attempting to breach the security of wireless networks and transmissions. One reason wireless suddenly found itself to be such a target is that wireless networks are so abundant and so unsecured. The dramatic proliferation of these inexpensive products has made the security ramifications of the protocol astonishing.

No matter what the system, wireless security is a very important topic as more and more applications are designed to use wireless to send data. Wireless is particularly problematic from a security standpoint, because there is

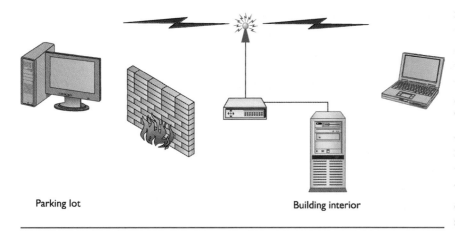

Parking lot   Building interior

• **Figure 12.1**   Wireless transmission extending beyond the facility's walls

no control over the physical layer of the traffic. In most wired LANs, the administrators have physical control over the network and can control to some degree who can actually connect to the physical medium. This prevents large amounts of un-authorized traffic and makes snooping around and listening to the traffic difficult. Wireless does away with the physical limitations. If an attacker can get close enough to the signal's source as it is being broadcast, he can at the very least listen to the access point and clients talking to capture all the packets for examination, as depicted in Figure 12.1.

Attackers can also try to modify the traffic being sent or try to send their own traffic to disrupt the system. In this chapter, you will learn the different types of attacks that wireless networks face.

■ Mobile Phones

When cellular phones first hit the market, security wasn't an issue—if you wanted to keep your phone safe, you'd simply keep it physically secure and not loan it to people you didn't want making calls. Its only function was that of a telephone.

• Early cell phones just allowed you to make calls.

The advance of digital circuitry has added amazing power in smaller and smaller devices, causing security to be an issue as the software becomes more and more complicated. Today's small and inexpensive products have made the wireless market grow by leaps and bounds, as traditional wireless devices such as cellular phones and pagers are being replaced by wireless e-mail devices and PDAs.

- Today's phones allow you to carry computers in your pocket.

Almost all current mobile phones have wireless networking features built in. All these devices have generated a demand for additional services. The **Wireless Application Protocol (WAP)** attempted to satisfy the needs for more data on mobile devices, but it is falling by the wayside as the mobile networks' capabilities increase. The need for more and more bandwidth has pushed carriers to adopt a more IP-centric routing methodology with technologies such as High Speed Packet Access (HSPA) and Evolution Data Optimized (EVDO). Mobile phones have ruthlessly advanced with new technologies and services, causing phones and the carrier networks that support them to be described in generations—1G, 2G, 3G, and 4G. 1G refers to the original analog cellular standard, Advanced Mobile Phone System or AMPS. 2G refers to the digital network that superseded it. 3G is the system of mobile networks that is currently being deployed. They allow carriers to offer a wider array of services to the consumer, including broadband data service up to 14.4 Mbps and video calling. 4G is the planned move to an entirely IP-based network for all services, running voice over IP (VoIP) on your mobile phone.

All of these "gee-whiz" features are nice, but how secure are your bits and bytes going to be when they're traveling across a mobile carrier's network? All the protocols mentioned have their own security implementations—WAP applies its own Wireless Transport Layer Security (WTLS) to attempt to secure data transmissions, but WAP still has issues such as the "WAP gap" (as discussed next). 3G networks have attempted to push a large amount of security down the stack and rely on the encryption designed into the wireless protocol.

WAP

WAP was introduced to compensate for the relatively low amount of computing power on handheld devices as well as the generally poor network throughput of cellular networks. It uses the **Wireless Transport Layer Security (WTLS)** encryption scheme, which encrypts the plaintext data and then sends it over the airwaves as ciphertext. The originator and the recipient both have keys to decrypt the data and reproduce the plaintext. This method of ensuring confidentiality is very common, and if the encryption is well designed and implemented, it is difficult for unauthorized users to take captured ciphertext and reproduce the plaintext that created it. As described in Chapter 5, **confidentiality** is the ability to keep protected data a secret. WTLS uses a modified version of the Transport Layer Security (TLS) protocol, formerly known as Secure Sockets Layer (SSL). The WTLS protocol supports several popular bulk encryption algorithms, including Data Encryption Standard (DES), Triple DES (3DES), RC5, and International Data Encryption Algorithm (IDEA).

WTLS implements integrity through the use of *message authentication codes (MACs)*. A MAC algorithm generates a one-way hash of the compressed WTLS data. WTLS supports the MD5 and SHA MAC algorithms. The MAC algorithm is also decided during the WTLS handshake. The TLS protocol that WTLS is based on is designed around Internet-based computers, machines that have relatively high processing power, large amounts of memory, and sufficient bandwidth available for Internet applications. The PDAs and other devices that WTLS must accommodate are limited in all these respects. Thus, WTLS has to be able to cope with small amounts of memory and limited processor capacity, as well as long round-trip times that TLS could not handle well. These requirements are the primary reasons that WTLS has security issues.

As the protocol is designed around more capable servers than devices, the WTLS specification can allow connections with little to no security. Clients with low memory or CPU capabilities cannot support encryption, and choosing null or weak encryption greatly reduces confidentiality. Authentication is also optional in the protocol, and omitting authentication reduces security by leaving the connection vulnerable to a man-in-the-middle–type attack. In addition to the general flaws in the protocol's implementation, several known security vulnerabilities exist, including those to the chosen-plaintext attack, the PKCS #1 attack, and the alert message truncation attack.

The chosen-plaintext attack works on the principle of a predictable **initialization vector (IV)**. By the nature of the transport medium that it is using, WAP, WTLS needs to support unreliable transport. This forces the IV to be based on data already known to the client, and WTLS uses a linear IV computation. Because the IV is based on the sequence number of the packet, and several packets are sent unencrypted, entropy is severely decreased. This lack of entropy in the encrypted data reduces confidentiality.

Now consider the PKCS #1 attack. Public Key Cryptography Standards (PKCS), used in conjunction with RSA encryption, provide standards for formatting the padding used to generate a correctly formatted block size. When the client receives the block, it will reply to the sender as to the validity of the block. An attacker takes advantage of this by attempting to send multiple guesses at the padding to force a padding error. In vulnerable implementations, WTLS will return error messages providing an Oracle-decrypting RSA with roughly 2^{20} chosen ciphertext queries. Alert messages in WTLS are sometimes sent in plaintext and are not authenticated. This fact could allow an attacker to overwrite an encrypted packet from the actual sender with a plaintext alert message, leading to possible disruption of the connection through, for instance, a truncation attack.

Some concern over the so-called **WAP gap** involves confidentiality of information where the two different networks meet, the WAP gateway, as shown in Figure 12.2.

WTLS acts as the security protocol for the WAP network, and TLS is the standard for the Internet, so the WAP gateway has to perform translation from one encryption standard to the other. This translation forces all messages to be seen by the WAP gateway in plaintext. This is a weak point in the network design, but from an attacker's perspective, it's a much more difficult target than the WTLS protocol itself. Threats to the WAP gateway can be minimized through careful infrastructure design, such as selecting a secure physical location and allowing only outbound traffic from the gateway. A risk of compromise still exists, however, and an attacker would find a WAP gateway an especially appealing target, as plaintext messages are processed through it from all wireless devices, not just a single user. The solution for this is to have end-to-end security layered over anything underlying, in effect creating a VPN from the endpoint to the mobile device, or to standardize on a full implementation of TLS for end-to-end encryption and strong authentication. The limited nature of the devices hampers the ability of the security protocols to operate as intended, compromising any real security to be implemented on WAP networks.

Tech Tip

Weakness in WAP Aggregation
WAP is a point-to-multipoint protocol, but it can face disruptions or attacks because it aggregates at well-known points: the cellular antenna towers.

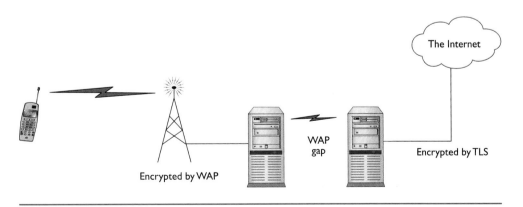

• **Figure 12.2** The WAP gap shows an unencrypted space between two enciphered connections.

3G Mobile Networks

Our cell phones are one of the most visible indicators of advancing technology. Within recent memory, we were forced to switch from old analog phones to digital models. Currently, they are all becoming "smart" as well, integrating personal digital assistant (PDA) and Internet functions. The networks have been or are being upgraded to 3G, greatly enhancing speed and lowering latency. This has reduced the need for lightweight protocols to handle data transmission, and more standard protocols such as IP can be used. The increased power and memory of the handheld devices also reduce the need for lighter-weight encryption protocols. This has caused the protocols used for 3G mobile devices to build in their own encryption protocols. Security will rely on these lower-level protocols or standard application-level security protocols used in normal IP traffic.

Several competing data transmission standards exist for 3G networks, such as HSPA and EVDO. However, all the standards include transport layer encryption protocols to secure the voice traffic traveling across the wireless signal as well as the data sent by the device. The cryptographic standard proposed for 3G is known as *KASUMI*. This modified version of the MISTY1 algorithm uses 64-bit blocks and 128-bit keys. Multiple attacks have been launched against this cipher. While the attacks tend to be impractical, this shows that application layer security is needed for secure transmission of data on mobile devices. WAP and WTLS can be used over the lower-level protocols, but traditional TLS can also be used.

Bluetooth

Bluetooth was originally developed by Ericsson and known as multi-communicator link; in 1998, Nokia, IBM, Intel, and Toshiba joined Ericsson and adopted the Bluetooth name. This consortium became known as the Bluetooth Special Interest Group (SIG). The SIG now has more than 10,000 member companies and drives the development of the technology and controls the specification to ensure interoperability.

Most people are familiar with Bluetooth as it is part of many mobile phones and headsets, such as those shown in Figure 12.3. This short-range, low-power wireless protocol transmits in the **2.4 GHz band**, the same band used for 802.11. The concept for the short-range (approx. 32 feet) wireless protocol is to transmit data in personal area networks (PANs).

Bluetooth transmits and receives data from a variety of devices, the most common being mobile phones, laptops, printers, and audio devices. The mobile phone has driven a lot of Bluetooth growth and has even spread Bluetooth into new cars as a mobile phone hands-free kit.

Bluetooth has gone through a few releases. Version 1.1 was the first commercially successful version, with version 1.2 released in 2007 and correcting some of the problems found in 1.1. Version 1.2 allows speeds up to 721 Kbps and improves resistance to interference. Version 1.2 is backward-compatible with version 1.1. Bluetooth 2.0 introduced enhanced data rate (EDR), which allows the transmission of up to 3.0 Mbps.

● **Figure 12.3** Headsets and cell phones are two of the most popular types of Bluetooth-capable devices.

As Bluetooth became popular, people started trying to find holes in it. Bluetooth features easy configuration of devices to allow communication, with no need for network addresses or ports. Bluetooth uses pairing to establish a trust relationship between devices. To establish that trust, the devices advertise capabilities and require a passkey. To help maintain security, most devices require the passkey to be entered into both devices; this prevents a default passkey–type attack. The Bluetooth's protocol advertisement of services and pairing properties is where some of the security issues start.

Bluejacking is a term used for the sending of unauthorized messages to another Bluetooth device. This involves setting a message as a phonebook contact:

> **Tech Tip**
>
> **Bluetooth Security**
> *Bluetooth should always have discoverable mode turned off unless you're deliberately pairing a device.*

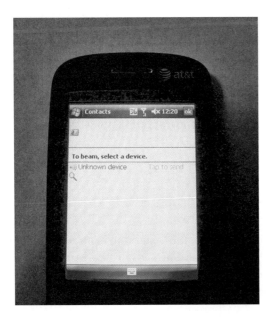

Then the attacker sends the message to the possible recipient via Bluetooth. Originally, this involved sending text messages, but more recent phones can send images or audio as well. A popular variant of this is the transmission of "shock" images, featuring disturbing or crude photos. As Bluetooth is a short-range protocol, the attack and victim must be within roughly 10 yards of each other. The victim's phone must also have Bluetooth enabled and must be in discoverable mode. On some early phones, this was the default configuration, and while it makes connecting external devices easier, it also allows attacks against the phone. If Bluetooth is turned off, or if the device is set to nondiscoverable, bluejacking can be avoided.

Bluesnarfing is similar to bluejacking in that it uses the same contact transmission protocol. The difference is that instead of sending an unsolicited message to the victim's phone, the attacker copies off the victim's information, which can include e-mails, contact lists, calendar, and anything else that exists on that device. More recent phones with media capabilities can be snarfed for private photos and videos. Bluesnarfing used to require a laptop with a Bluetooth adapter, making it relatively easy to identify a possible attacker, but bluesnarfing applications are now available for mobile devices. Bloover, a combination of Bluetooth and Hoover, is one such application that runs as a Java applet. The majority of Bluetooth phones need to be discoverable for the bluesnarf attack to work, but it does not necessarily need to be paired. In theory, an attacker can also brute-force the device's unique 48-bit name. A program called RedFang attempts to perform this brute-force attack by sending all possible names and seeing what gets a response. This approach was addressed in Bluetooth 1.2 with an anonymity mode.

Bluebugging is a far more serious attack than either bluejacking or bluesnarfing. In bluebugging, the attacker uses Bluetooth to establish a serial connection to the device. This allows access to the full AT command set— GSM phones use AT commands similar to Hayes-compatible modems. This connection allows full control over the phone, including the placing of calls to any number without the phone owner's knowledge. Fortunately, this attack requires pairing of the devices to complete, and phones initially vulnerable to the attack have updated firmware to correct the problem. To accomplish the attack now, the phone owner would need to surrender her phone and allow an attacker to physically establish the connection.

Bluetooth technology is likely to grow due to the popularity of mobile phones. Software and protocol updates have helped to improve the security of the protocol. Almost all phones now keep Bluetooth turned off by default, and they allow you to make the phone discoverable for only a limited amount of time. User education about security risks is also a large factor in avoiding security breaches.

■ 802.11

The 802.11b protocol is an IEEE standard ratified in 1999. The standard launched a range of products (such as wireless routers, an example of which is shown in Figure 12.4) that would open the way to a whole new genre of possibilities for attackers and a new series of headaches for security

• **Figure 12.4** A common wireless router

administrators everywhere. 802.11 was a new standard for sending packetized data traffic over radio waves in the unlicensed 2.4 GHz band.

This group of IEEE standards is also called Wi-Fi, which is a certification owned by an industry group. A device marked as Wi-Fi certified adheres to the standards of the alliance. As the products matured and became easy to use and affordable, security experts began to deconstruct the limited security that had been built into the standard.

The 802.11b standard was the first to market, 802.11a followed, and 802.11g products currently are the most common ones being sold. These chipsets have also commonly been combined into devices that support a/b/g standards. 802.11n is on the horizon, with many manufacturers shipping devices based upon the draft specification. This table shows the standards with their frequency ranges.

Specification	Frequency
802.11a	5.180 GHz to 5.320 GHz divided into 8 channels
802.11b	2.401 GHz to 2.473 GHz divided into 11 channels
802.11g	2.401 GHz to 2.473 GHz divided into 11 channels
802.11i	N/A
802.11n	2.401 GHz to 2.473 GHz and the 5 GHz band

802.11a is the wireless networking standard that supports traffic on the **5 GHz band**, allowing faster speeds over shorter ranges. Features of 802.11b and 802.11a were later joined to create 802.11g, an updated standard that allows the faster speeds of the 5 GHz specification on the 2.4 GHz band. Security problems were discovered in the implementations of these early wireless standards, principally involving the Wired Equivalent Privacy (WEP) protocol. These problems included an attacker's ability to break the cryptography and monitor other users' traffic. The security problems in

WEP were a top concern until the adoption of 802.11i-compliant products enhanced the security with Wi-Fi Protected Access (WPA). 802.11n is the latest standard; it focuses on achieving much higher speeds for wireless networks. The following table offers an overview of each protocol, descriptions of which, as well as OFDM and DSSS, follow.

802.11 Protocol	Frequency in GHz	Speed in Mbps	Modulation
-	2.4	2	
a	5	54	OFDM
b	2.4	11	DSSS
g	2.4	54	OFDM
n	2.4, 5	124–248	OFDM
y	3.7	54	OFDM

Exam Tip: The best place for current 802.11 standards and upcoming draft standard information is in the RFCs. You can find them at www.ietf.org/rfc.html.

Direct-sequence spread spectrum (DSSS) is a modulation type that spreads the traffic sent over the entire bandwidth. It does this by injecting a noise-like signal into the information stream and transmitting the normally narrowband information over the wider band available. The primary reason that spread-spectrum technology is used in 802.11 protocols is to avoid interference on the public 2.4 GHz and 5 GHz bands. **Orthogonal frequency division multiplexing (OFDM)** multiplexes, or separates, the data to be transmitted into smaller chunks and then transmits the chunks on several subchannels. This use of subchannels is what the "frequency division" portion of the name refers to. Both of these techniques, multiplexing and frequency division, are used to avoid interference. *Orthogonal* refers to the manner in which the subchannels are assigned, principally to avoid crosstalk, or interference with your own channels.

802.11: Individual Standards

The 802.11b protocol provides for multiple-rate Ethernet over 2.4 GHz spread-spectrum wireless. It provides transfer rates of 1 Mbps, 2 Mbps, 5.5 Mbps, and 11 Mbps and uses DSSS. The most common layout is a point-to-multipoint environment, with the available bandwidth being shared by all users. Typical range is roughly 100 yards indoors and 300 yards outdoors, line of sight. While the wireless transmissions of 802.11 can penetrate some walls and other objects, the best range is offered when both the access point and network client devices have an unobstructed view of each other.

802.11a uses a higher band and has higher bandwidth. It operates in the 5 GHz spectrum using OFDM. Supporting rates of up to 54 Mbps, it is the faster brother of 802.11b; however, the higher frequency used by 802.11a shortens the usable range of the devices and makes it incompatible with 802.11b. The chipsets tend to be more expensive for 802.11a, which has slowed adoption of the standard.

The 802.11g standard uses portions of both of the other standards: it uses the 2.4 GHz band for greater range but uses the OFDM transmission method to achieve the faster 54 Mbps data rates. As it uses the 2.4 GHz band, this standard interoperates with the older 802.11b standard. This allows a 802.11g access point (AP) to give access to both "G" and "B" clients.

The most recent standard, 802.11n, improves on the older standards by greatly increasing speed. It has a data rate of 248 Mbps, gained through the use of wider bands and multiple-input multiple-output (MIMO) processing. MIMO uses multiple antennas and can bond separate channels together to increase data throughput.

All these protocols operate in bands that are "unlicensed" by the FCC. This means that people operating this equipment do not have to be certified by the FCC, but it also means that the devices could possibly share the band with other devices, such as cordless phones, closed-circuit TV (CCTV) wireless transceivers, and other similar equipment. This other equipment can cause interference with the 802.11 equipment, possibly causing speed degradation.

The 2.4 GHz band is commonly used by many household devices that are constantly on, such as cordless phones. It is also the frequency used by microwave ovens to heat food. So if you are having intermittent interference on your Wi-Fi LAN, check to see if the microwave is on.

The 802.11 protocol designers expected some security concerns and attempted to build provisions into the 802.11 protocol that would ensure adequate security. The 802.11 standard includes attempts at rudimentary authentication and confidentiality controls. Authentication is handled in its most basic form by the 802.11 AP, forcing the clients to perform a handshake when attempting to "associate" to the AP. Association is the process required before the AP will allow the client to talk across the AP to the network. Association occurs only if the client has all the correct parameters needed in the handshake, among them the **service set identifier (SSID)**. This SSID setting should limit access only to the authorized users of the wireless network. The SSID is a phrase-based authentication mechanism that helps ensure that you are connecting to the correct AP. This SSID phrase is transmitted in all the access point's **beacon frames**. The beacon frame is an 802.11 management frame for the network and contains several different fields, such as the timestamp and beacon interval, but most importantly the SSID. This allows attackers to scan for the beacon frame and retrieve the SSID.

Try This

Finding Multiple SSIDs

Click (or double-click) the wireless icon in your computer's system tray (you must be using a computer equipped with a wireless network adapter, of course). This should open a network connection window, the look of which differs based upon your computer's wireless adapter drivers. Somewhere on this window will be a Refresh Network List button. Click this button to refresh the list and it will show you all the SSID names that are broadcasting within range of your computer.

The designers of the 802.11 standard also attempted to maintain confidentiality by introducing **Wired Equivalent Privacy (WEP)**, which uses the **RC4 stream cipher** to encrypt the data as it is transmitted through the air. WEP has been shown to have an implementation problem that can be exploited to break security.

To understand all the 802.11 security problems, you must first look at some of the reasons it became such a prominent technology.

Wireless networks came along in 2000 and became very popular. For the first time, it was possible to have almost full-speed network connections without having to be tied down to an Ethernet cable. The technology quickly took off, allowing prices to drop into the consumer range. Once the market shifted to focus on customers who were not necessarily technologists, the products also became very easy to install and operate. Default settings were designed to get the novice users up and running without having to alter anything substantial, and products were described as being able to just plug in and work. These developments further enlarged the market for the low-cost, easy-to-use wireless access points. Then attackers realized that instead of attacking machines over the Internet, they could drive around and seek out these APs. Having physical control of an information asset is critical to its security. Physical access to a machine will enable an attacker to bypass *any* security measure that has been placed on that machine.

Typically, access to actual Ethernet segments is protected by physical security measures. This structure allows security administrators to plan for only internal threats to the network and gives them a clear idea of the types and number of machines connected to it. Wireless networking takes the keys to the kingdom and tosses them out the window and into the parking lot. A typical wireless installation broadcasts the network right through the physical controls that are in place. An attacker can drive up and have the same access as if he plugged into an Ethernet jack inside the building—in fact, better access, because 802.11 is a shared medium, allowing sniffers to view all packets being sent to or from the AP and all clients. These APs are also typically behind any security measures the companies have in place, such as firewalls and intrusion detection systems (IDSs). This kind of access into the internal network has caused a large stir among computer security professionals and eventually the media. War-driving, war-flying, war-walking, war-chalking—all of these terms have been used in security article after security article to describe attacks on wireless networks.

Cross Check

Intrusion Detection Systems

Chapter 13 has a lot more information about intrusion detection systems, whereas this chapter references methods of getting past the IDSs. When you learn more about the different IDSs, how would you design an IDS that can catch wireless attackers?

Attacking 802.11

Wireless is a popular target for several reasons: the access gained from wireless, the lack of default security, and the wide proliferation of devices. However, other reasons also make it attackable. The first of these is *anonymity*: An attacker can probe your building for wireless access from the street. Then he can log packets to and from the AP without giving any indication that an attempted intrusion is taking place. The attacker will announce his presence only if he attempts to associate to the AP. Even then, an attempted association is recorded only by the MAC address of the wireless card associating to it, and most APs do not have alerting functionality to indicate when users associate to it. This fact gives administrators a very limited view of who is gaining access to the network, if they are even paying attention at all. It gives attackers the ability to seek out and compromise wireless networks with relative impunity.

The second reason is the low cost of the equipment needed. A single wireless access card costing less than $100 can give access to any unsecured AP within driving range. Finally, attacking a wireless network is relatively easy compared to attacking other target hosts. Windows-based tools for locating and sniffing wireless-based networks have turned anyone who can download files from the Internet and has a wireless card into a potential attacker.

 Anonymity also works in another way; once an attacker finds an unsecured AP with wireless access, they can use an essentially untraceable IP address to attempt attacks on other Internet hosts.

Locating wireless networks was originally termed *war-driving*, an adaptation of the term *war-dialing*. War-dialing comes from the 1983 movie *WarGames*; it is the process of dialing a list of phone numbers looking for modem-connected computers. *War-drivers* drive around with a wireless locater program recording the number of networks found and their locations. This term has evolved along with *war-flying* and *war-walking*, which mean exactly what you expect. *War-chalking* started with people using chalk on sidewalks to mark some of the wireless networks they find.

The most common tools for an attacker to use are reception-based programs that listen to the beacon frames output by other wireless devices, and programs that promiscuously capture all traffic. The most widely used of these programs is called NetStumbler, created by Marius Milner and shown in Figure 12.5. This program listens for the beacon frames of APs that are within range of the card attached to the NetStumbler computer. When it receives the frames, it logs all available information about the AP for later analysis. Since it listens only to beacon frames, NetStumbler displays only networks that have the SSID broadcast turned on. If the computer has a GPS unit attached to it, the program also logs the AP's coordinates. This information can be used to return to the AP or to plot maps of APs in a city.

> NetStumbler is a Windows-based application, but programs for other operating systems such as Mac, BSD, Linux, and others work on the same principle.

Once an attacker has located a network, and assuming that he cannot directly connect and start active scanning and penetration of the network, he will use the best attack tool there is: a network sniffer. The network sniffer, when combined with a wireless network card it can support, is a powerful attack tool, as the shared medium of a wireless network exposes all packets to interception and logging. Popular wireless sniffers are Wireshark (formerly Ethereal) and Kismet. Regular sniffers used on wireline Ethernet have also been updated to include support for wireless. Sniffers are also important because they allow you to retrieve the MAC addresses of the nodes of the network. APs can be configured to allow access only to prespecified MAC addresses, and an attacker spoofing the MAC can bypass this feature.

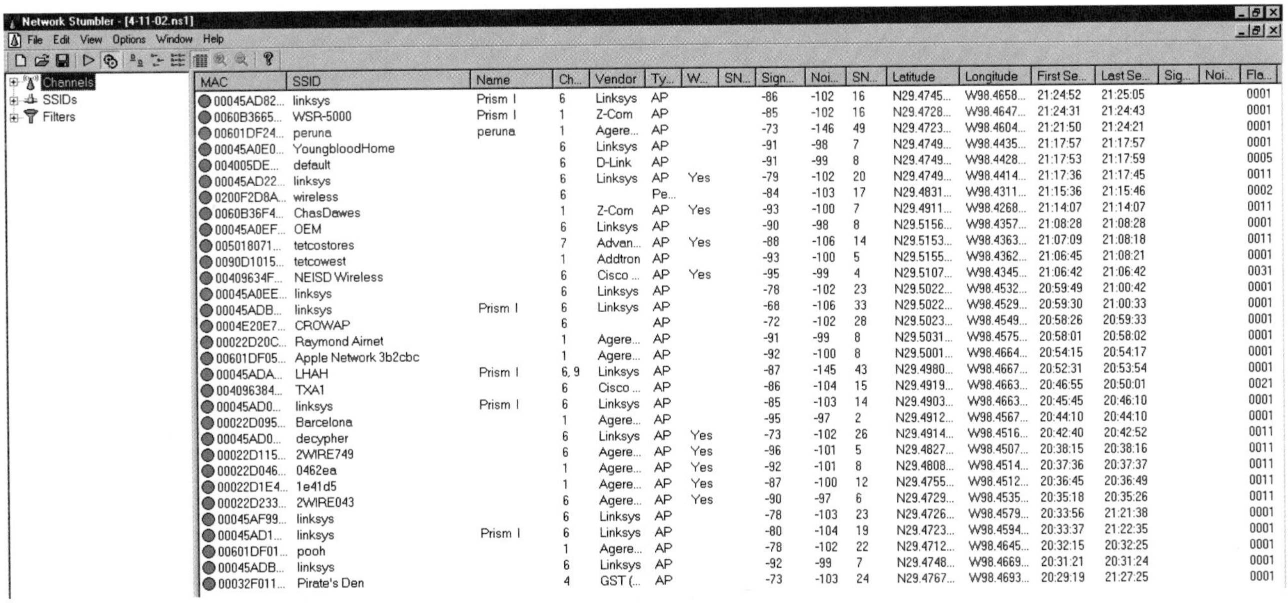

MAC	SSID	Name	Ch.	Vendor	Ty..	W..	SN.	Sign..	Noi..	SN.	Latitude	Longitude	First Se..	Last Se..	Sig..	Noi..	Fla..
00045AD82...	linksys	Prism I	6	Linksys	AP			-86	-102	16	N29.4745...	W98.4658...	21:24:52	21:25:05			0001
0060B3665...	WSR-5000	Prism I	1	Z-Com	AP			-85	-102	16	N29.4728...	W98.4647...	21:24:31	21:24:43			0001
00601DF24...	peruna	peruna	1	Agere..	AP			-73	-146	49	N29.4723...	W98.4604...	21:21:50	21:24:21			0001
00045A0E0...	YoungbloodHome		6	Linksys	AP			-91	-98	7	N29.4749...	W98.4435...	21:17:57	21:17:57			0001
004005DE...	default		6	D-Link	AP			-91	-99	8	N29.4749...	W98.4428...	21:17:53	21:17:59			0005
00045AD22...	linksys		6	Linksys	AP	Yes		-79	-102	20	N29.4749...	W98.4414...	21:17:36	21:17:45			0011
0200F2D8A...	wireless		6	Pe...				-84	-103	17	N29.4831...	W98.4311...	21:15:36	21:15:46			0002
0060B36F4...	ChasDawes		1	Z-Com	AP	Yes		-93	-100	7	N29.4911...	W98.4268...	21:14:07	21:14:07			0011
00045A0EF...	OEM		6	Linksys	AP			-90	-98	8	N29.5156...	W98.4357...	21:08:28	21:08:28			0001
005018071...	tetcostores		7	Advan..	AP	Yes		-88	-106	14	N29.5153...	W98.4363...	21:07:09	21:08:18			0011
0090D1015...	tetcowest		1	Addtron	AP			-93	-100	5	N29.5155...	W98.4362...	21:06:45	21:08:21			0001
00409634F...	NEISD Wireless		6	Cisco ..	AP	Yes		-95	-99	4	N29.5107...	W98.4345...	21:06:42	21:06:42			0031
00045A0EE...	linksys		6	Linksys	AP			-78	-102	23	N29.5022...	W98.4532...	20:59:49	21:00:42			0001
00045ADB...	linksys	Prism I	6	Linksys	AP			-68	-106	33	N29.5022...	W98.4529...	20:59:30	21:00:33			0001
0004E20E7...	CROWAP		6		AP			-72	-102	28	N29.5023...	W98.4549...	20:58:26	20:59:33			0001
00022D20C...	Raymond Airnet		1	Agere..	AP			-91	-99	8	N29.5031...	W98.4575...	20:58:01	20:58:02			0001
00601DF05...	Apple Network 3b2cbc		1	Agere..	AP			-92	-100	8	N29.5001...	W98.4664...	20:54:15	20:54:17			0001
00045ADA...	LHAH	Prism I	6, 9	Linksys	AP			-87	-145	43	N29.4980...	W98.4667...	20:52:31	20:53:54			0001
004096384...	TXA1		6	Cisco ..	AP			-86	-104	15	N29.4919...	W98.4663...	20:46:55	20:50:01			0021
00045AD0...	linksys	Prism I	6	Linksys	AP			-85	-103	14	N29.4903...	W98.4663...	20:45:45	20:46:10			0001
00022D095...	Barcelona		1	Agere..	AP			-95	-97	2	N29.4912...	W98.4567...	20:44:10	20:44:10			0001
00045AD0...	decypher		6	Linksys	AP	Yes		-73	-102	26	N29.4914...	W98.4516...	20:42:40	20:42:52			0011
00022D115...	2WIRE749		6	Agere..	AP	Yes		-96	-101	5	N29.4827...	W98.4507...	20:38:15	20:38:16			0011
00022D046...	0462ea		1	Agere..	AP	Yes		-92	-101	8	N29.4808...	W98.4514...	20:37:36	20:37:37			0011
00022D1E4...	1e41d5		1	Agere..	AP	Yes		-87	-100	12	N29.4755...	W98.4512...	20:36:45	20:36:49			0011
00022D233...	2WIRE043		6	Agere..	AP	Yes		-90	-97	6	N29.4729...	W98.4535...	20:35:18	20:35:26			0011
00045AF99...	linksys		6	Linksys	AP			-78	-103	23	N29.4726...	W98.4579...	20:33:56	21:21:38			0001
00045AD1...	linksys	Prism I	6	Linksys	AP			-80	-104	19	N29.4723...	W98.4594...	20:33:37	21:22:35			0001
00601DF01...	pooh		1	Agere..	AP			-78	-102	22	N29.4712...	W98.4645...	20:32:15	20:32:25			0001
00045ADB...	linksys		6	Linksys	AP			-92	-99	7	N29.4748...	W98.4669...	20:31:20	20:31:24			0001
00032F011...	Pirate's Den		4	GST (..	AP			-73	-103	24	N29.4767...	W98.4693...	20:29:19	21:27:25			0001

• **Figure 12.5**   NetStumbler on a Windows PC

There are specialized sniffer tools designed with a single objective: to crack Wired Equivalent Privacy (WEP) keys. As described earlier, WEP is an encryption protocol that 802.11 uses to attempt to ensure confidentiality of wireless communications. Unfortunately, it has turned out to have several problems. WEP's weaknesses are specifically targeted for attack by the specialized sniffer programs. They work by exploiting weak initialization vectors in the encryption algorithm. To exploit this weakness, an attacker needs a certain number of ciphertext packets; once he has captured enough packets, however, the program can very quickly decipher the encryption key being used. WEPCrack was the first available program to use this flaw to crack WEP keys; however, WEPCrack depends on a dump of actual network packets from another sniffer program. AirSnort is a standalone program that captures its own packets; once it has captured enough ciphertext, it provides the WEP key of the network.

All these tools are used by the wireless attacker to compromise the network. They are also typically used by security professionals when performing wireless site surveys, which identify the existence of a wireless network within the organization. The site survey has a simple purpose: to minimize the available wireless signal being sent beyond the physical controls of the organization. By using the sniffer and finding AP beacons, a security official can determine which APs are transmitting into uncontrolled areas. The APs can then be tuned, either by relocation or through the use of directional antennas, to minimize radiation beyond an organization's walls. This type of wireless data emanation is particularly troubling when the AP is located on the internal network.

Local users of the network are susceptible to having their entire traffic decoded and analyzed. A proper site survey is an important step in securing a wireless network to avoid sending critical data beyond company walls. Recurring site surveys are important because wireless technology is cheap and typically comes unsecured in its default configuration. If anyone attaches a wireless AP to your network, you want to know about it immediately.

If unauthorized wireless is set up, it is known as a *rogue access point*. These can be set up by well-meaning employees or hidden by an attacker with physical access. An attacker might set up a rogue access point if they have a limited amount of physical access to an organization, perhaps by sneaking into the building briefly. The attacker can then set up an AP on the network and, by placing it behind the external firewall or network IDS (NIDS) type of security measures, can attach to the wireless at a later date at their leisure. This approach reduces the risk of getting caught by physical security staff, and if the AP is found, it does not point directly back to any kind of traceable address.

Cross Check

Identifying Rogue Access Points

In Chapter 8 you learned about how physical security can impact information security, and how several different devices can act as a wireless bridge and be a rogue access point. Can you think of some physical security policies that can help reduce the risk of rogue access points? What about some information security policies?

Principles of Computer Security: CompTIA Security+ and Beyond

802.11 networks have two features used primarily for security: one is designed solely for authentication, and the other is designed for authentication and confidentiality. The authentication function, introduced earlier, is known as the service set identifier (SSID). This unique 32-character identifier is attached to the header of the packet. The SSID is broadcast by default as a network name, but broadcasting of this beacon frame can be disabled.

Many APs also use a default SSID; for Cisco APs, this default is *tsunami*, which may indicate an AP that has not been configured for any security. Renaming the SSID and disabling SSID broadcast are both good ideas; however, because the SSID is part of every frame, these measures should not be considered adequate to secure the network. As the SSID is, hopefully, a unique identifier, only people who know the identifier will be able to complete association to the AP. While the SSID is a good idea in theory, it is sent in plaintext in the packets, so in practice SSID offers little security significance—any sniffer can determine the SSID, and some operating systems, such as Windows XP (see Figure 12.6), will display a list of SSIDs active in the area and prompt the user to choose which one to connect to.

This weakness is magnified by most APs' default settings to transmit beacon frames. The beacon frame's purpose is to announce the wireless network's presence and capabilities so that WLAN cards can attempt to associate to it. This can be disabled in software for many APs, especially the more sophisticated ones. From a security perspective, the beacon frame is damaging because it contains the SSID, and this beacon frame is transmitted at a set interval (ten times per second by default). Since a default AP without any other traffic is sending out its SSID in plaintext ten times a second, you can see why the SSID does not provide true authentication. Scanning programs such as NetStumbler work by capturing the beacon frames and thereby the SSIDs of all APs.

• **Figure 12.6**   Windows displaying access points

Most APs also have the ability to lock access in only to known MAC addresses, providing a limited authentication capability. Given sniffers' capacity to grab all active MAC addresses on the network, this capability is not very effective. An attacker simply configures his wireless cards to a known good MAC address.

WEP encrypts the data traveling across the network with an RC4 stream cipher, attempting to ensure confidentiality. This synchronous method of encryption ensures some method of authentication. The system depends on the client and the AP having a shared secret key, ensuring that only authorized people with the proper key have access to the wireless network. WEP supports two key lengths, 40 and 104 bits, though these are more typically referred to as 64 and 128 bits, because 24 bits of the overall key length are used for the initialization vector (IV). In 802.11a and 802.11g, manufacturers have extended this to 152-bit WEP keys, again with 24 bits being used for the IV.

The IV is the primary reason for the weaknesses in WEP. The IV is sent in the plaintext part of the message, and because the total keyspace is approximately 16 million keys, the same key will be reused. Once the key has been repeated, an attacker has two ciphertexts encrypted with the same key stream. This allows the attacker to examine the ciphertext and retrieve the key. This attack can be improved by examining only packets that have weak IVs, reducing the amount of packets needed to crack the key. Using only weak IV packets, the number of required captured packets is reduced to around four or five million, which can take only a few hours to capture on a fairly busy AP. For a point of reference, this means that equipment with an advertised WEP key of 128 bits can be cracked in less than a day, whereas to crack a normal 128-bit key would take roughly 2,000,000,000,000,000,000 years on a computer able to attempt one trillion keys a second. As mentioned, AirSnort is a modified sniffing program that takes advantage of this weakness to retrieve the WEP keys.

The biggest weakness of WEP is that the IV problem exists regardless of key length, because the IV always remains at 24 bits.

After the limited security functions of a wireless network are broken, the network behaves exactly like a regular Ethernet network and is subject to the exact same vulnerabilities. The host machines that are on or attached to the wireless network are as vulnerable as if they and the attacker were physically connected. Being on the network opens up all machines to vulnerability scanners, Trojan horse programs, virus and worm programs, and traffic interception via sniffer programs. Any unpatched vulnerability on any machine accessible from the wireless segment is now open to compromise.

Tech Tip

WEP Isn't Equivalent

WEP should not be trusted alone to provide confidentiality. If WEP is the only protocol supported by your AP, place it outside the corporate firewall and VPN to add more protection.

New Security Protocols

WEP was designed to provide some measure of confidentiality on an 802.11 network similar to what is found on a wired network, but that has not been the case. Accordingly, new standards were developed to improve upon WEP. The 802.11i standard is the IEEE standard for security in wireless networks, also known as Wi-Fi Protected Access (WPA and WPA2). It uses 802.1X to provide authentication and uses Advanced Encryption Standard (AES) as the encryption protocol. The 802.11i standard specifies the use of the Temporal Key Integrity Protocol (TKIP) and the Counter Mode with CBC-MAC Protocol (in full, the Counter Mode with Cipher Block Chaining–Message

Authentication Codes Protocol, or simply CCMP). These two protocols have different functions, but they both serve to enhance security.

TKIP works by using a shared secret combined with the card's MAC address to generate a new key, which is mixed with the IV to make per-packet keys that encrypt a single packet using the same RC4 cipher used by traditional WEP. This overcomes the WEP key weakness, as a key is used on only one packet. The other advantage to this method is that it can be retrofitted to current hardware with only a software change, unlike AES and 802.1X. CCMP is actually the mode in which the AES cipher is used to provide message integrity. Unlike TKIP, CCMP requires new hardware to perform the AES encryption. The advances of 802.11i have corrected the weaknesses of WEP.

The **802.1X** protocol can support a wide variety of authentication methods and also fits well into existing authentication systems such as RADIUS and LDAP. This allows 802.1X to interoperate well with other systems such as VPNs and dial-up RAS. Unlike other authentication methods, such as the Point-to-Point Protocol over Ethernet (PPPoE), 802.1X does not use encapsulation, so the network overhead is much lower. Unfortunately, the protocol is just a framework for providing implementation, so no specifics guarantee strong authentication or key management. Implementations of the protocol vary from vendor to vendor in method of implementation and strength of security, especially when it comes to the difficult test of wireless security.

Implementing 802.1X

Three common methods are used to implement 802.1X: EAP-TLS, EAP-TTLS, and EAP-MD5. EAP-TLS relies on TLS, an attempt to standardize the SSL structure to pass credentials. The standard, developed by Microsoft, uses X.509 certificates and offers dynamic WEP key generation. This means that the organization must have the ability to support the public key infrastructure (PKI) in the form of X.509 digital certificates. Also, per-user, per-session dynamically generated WEP keys help prevent anyone from cracking the WEP keys in use, as each user individually has her own WEP key. Even if a user were logged onto the AP and transmitted enough traffic to allow cracking of the WEP key, access would be gained only to that user's traffic. No other user's data would be compromised, and the attacker could not use the WEP key to connect to the AP. This standard authenticates the client to the AP, but it also authenticates the AP to the client, helping to avoid man-in-the-middle attacks. The main problem with the EAP-TLS protocol is that it is designed to work only with Microsoft's Active Directory and Certificate Services; it will not take certificates from other certificate issuers. Thus a mixed environment would have implementation problems.

EAP-TTLS (the acronym stands for EAP–Tunneled TLS protocol) is a variant of the EAP-TLS protocol. EAP-TTLS works much the same way as EAP-TLS, with the server authenticating to the client with a certificate, but the protocol tunnels the client side of the authentication, allowing the use of legacy authentication protocols such as Password Authentication Protocol (PAP), Challenge-Handshake Authentication Protocol (CHAP), MS-CHAP, or MS-CHAP-V2. This makes the protocol more versatile while still supporting the enhanced security features such as dynamic WEP key assignment.

EAP-MD5, while it does improve the authentication of the client to the AP, does little else to improve the security of your AP. The protocol works by using the MD5 encryption protocol to hash a user's username and password. This protocol, unfortunately, provides no way for the AP to authenticate with the client, and it does not provide for dynamic WEP key assignment. In the wireless environment, without strong two-way authentication, it is very easy for an attacker to perform a man-in-the-middle attack. Normally, these type of attacks are difficult to perform, requiring a traffic redirect of some kind, but wireless changes all those rules. By setting up a rogue AP, an attacker can attempt to get clients to connect to it as if it were authorized and then simply authenticate to the real AP, a simple way to have access to the network and the client's credentials. The problem of not dynamically generating WEP keys is that it simply opens up the network to the same lack of confidentiality to which a normal AP is vulnerable. An attacker has to wait only for enough traffic to crack the WEP key, and he can then observe all traffic passing through the network.

Because the security of wireless LANs has been so problematic, many users have simply switched to a layered security approach—that is, they have moved their APs to untrustworthy portions of the network and have forced all clients to authenticate through the firewall to a third-party VPN system. The additional security comes at a price of putting more load on the firewall and VPN infrastructure and possibly adding cumbersome software to the users' devices. While wireless can be set up in a very secure manner in this fashion, it can also be set up poorly. Some systems lack strong authentication of both endpoints, leading to possibilities of a man-in-the-middle attack. Also, even though the data is tunneled through, IP addresses are still sent in the clear, giving an attacker information about what and where your VPN endpoint is.

Another phenomenon of wireless is borne out of its wide availability and low price. All the security measures of the wired and wireless network can be defeated by the rogue AP. This is the third possible type of rogue access point discussed in this chapter; they all share the same name as they all represent a security breach. However, since they are implemented with different motives and accordingly pose slightly different threats, we discuss them all separately. In this case, a well-intentioned employee who is trying to make the work environment more convenient purchases an AP at a local retailer and installs it. When installed, it works fine, but it typically will have no security installed. Since the IT department doesn't know about it, it is an uncontrolled entry point into the network.

No matter what kind of rogue AP we are dealing with, the rogue AP must be detected and controlled. The most common way to control rogue APs is some form of wireless scanning to ensure only legitimate wireless is

 Try This

Scanning for Rogue Wireless

Once you have completed Lab Project 12.1 and have NetStumbler or Kismet installed on the computer, take it to several locations around your workplace or school and attempt to scan for wireless access points that should not be there.

in place at an organization. While complete wireless IDSs will detect APs, this can also be done with a laptop and free software.

802.11 has enjoyed tremendous growth because of its ease of use and popularity, but that growth is threatened by many organizational rules prohibiting its use due to security measures. As you have seen here, the current state of wireless security is very poor, making attacking wireless a popular activity. With the addition of strong authentication and better encryption protocols, wireless should become both convenient and safe. To help secure wireless access points that you are responsible for, some best practices should be adhered to. The use of encryption should always be employed, typically with WPA or WPA2. Turning off SSID broadcasting can help avoid some scanning. Additionally, regular site surveys will help avoid rogue access points.

Chapter 12 Review

■ Chapter Summary

After reading this chapter and completing the exercises, you should understand the following about wireless and wireless security.

Describe the different wireless systems in use today

- Wireless Application Protocol (WAP) is used on small, handheld devices like cell phones for out-of-the-office connectivity.

- 802.11 is the IEEE standard for wireless local area networks. The standard includes several different specifications of 802.11 networks, such as 802.11b, 802.11a, 802.11g, and 802.11n.

Detail WAP and its security implications

- WAP is the data protocol used by many cellular phones to deliver e-mail and lightweight web services.

- Designers created WTLS as a method to ensure privacy of data being broadcast over WAP.

- WTLS has a number of inherent security problems, such as weak encryption necessitated by the low computing power of the devices and the network transition that must occur at the cellular provider's network, or the WAP gap.

Identify 802.11's security issues and possible solutions

- 802.11 does not allow physical control of the transport mechanism.

- Transmission of all network data wirelessly transmits frames to all wireless machines, not just a single client, similar to Ethernet hub devices.

- Poor authentication is caused by the SSID being broadcast to anyone listening.

- Flawed implementation of the RC4 encryption algorithm makes even encrypted traffic subject to interception and decryption.

■ Key Terms

2.4 GHz band *(300)*
5 GHz band *(303)*
beacon frames *(305)*
bluejacking *(301)*
bluesnarfing *(302)*
bluebugging *(302)*
confidentiality *(298)*
direct-sequence spread spectrum (DSSS) *(304)*
IEEE 802.1X *(311)*
IEEE 802.11 *(295)*

initialization vector (IV) *(298)*
orthogonal frequency division multiplexing (OFDM) *(304)*
RC4 stream cipher *(305)*
service set identifier (SSID) *(305)*
WAP gap *(299)*
Wired Equivalent Privacy (WEP) *(305)*
Wireless Application Protocol (WAP) *(297)*
Wireless Transport Layer Security (WTLS) *(298)*

■ Key Terms Quiz

Use terms from the Key Terms list to complete the sentences that follow. Don't use the same term more than once. Not all terms will be used.

1. An AP uses _____ to advertise its existence to potential wireless clients.

2. The _____ is the part of the RC4 cipher that has a weak implementation in WEP.

3. _____ is a standard for Ethernet authentication.

4. WAP uses the _____ protocol to attempt to ensure confidentiality of data.

5. The 32-character identifier attached to the header of a packet used for authentication to an 802.11 access point is the _____.

6. 802.11g uses frequencies in the _____.

7. 802.11i updates the flawed security deployed in _____.

8. The standard for wireless local area networks is called _____.

9. Cryptography in the WEP protocol is an attempt to guarantee _____.

10. 802.11a uses frequencies in the _____.

■ Multiple-Choice Quiz

1. Why does WTLS support short key lengths?

   A. Security is not necessary in mobile phones.

   B. The algorithm doesn't gain any security with longer keys.

   C. Longer keys cannot be used with the WTLS protocol.

   D. WTLS has to support devices with low processor power and limited RAM.

2. Why should wireless have strong two-way authentication?

   A. So that only the executives can use the wireless system.

   B. Because wireless is especially susceptible to a man-in-the-middle attack.

   C. Because you want to know when you are being attacked.

   D. Strong authentication is needed so that all virus definitions are checked on the client computer.

3. Why is 802.11 wireless more of a security problem than any other type of network?

   A. It has more readily readable frames.

   B. It provides access to the physical layer of Ethernet without needing physical access to the building.

   C. It is the only network that allows sniffing of the traffic.

   D. It draws too much power and the other servers reboot.

4. Bluebugging can give an attacker what?

   A. All of your contacts

   B. The ability to send "shock" photos

   C. Total control over a mobile phone

   D. A virus

5. How does 802.11n improve network speed?

   A. Wider bandwidth

   B. Higher frequency

   C. Multiple-input multiple-output (MIMO)

   D. Both A and C

6. WTLS ensures integrity through what device?

   A. Public key encryption

   B. Message authentication codes

   C. Source IP

   D. Digital signatures

7. WEP has used an implementation of which of the following encryption algorithms?

   A. SHA

   B. ElGamal

   C. RC4

   D. Triple-DES

8. How are the security parameters of WTLS chosen between two endpoints?

   A. Only one option exists for every parameter.

   B. The client dictates all parameters to the server.

   C. The user codes the parameters through DTMF tones.

   D. The WTLS handshake determines what parameters to use.

9. What is bluejacking?

   A. Stealing a person's mobile phone

   B. Sending an unsolicited message via Bluetooth

   C. Breaking a WEP key

   D. Leaving your Bluetooth in discoverable mode

10. Why is it important to scan your own organization for wireless?

   A. It can detect rogue access points.

   B. It checks the installed encryption.

   C. It finds vulnerable mobile phones.

   D. It checks for wireless coverage.

11. While the SSID provides some measure of authentication, why is it not very effective?

   A. It is dictated by the manufacturer of the access point.

   B. It is encrypted.

   C. It is broadcast in every beacon frame.

   D. SSID is not an authentication function.

12. The 802.1X protocol is a new protocol for Ethernet:

   A. Authentication

   B. Speed

   C. Wireless

   D. Cabling

13. What is the best way to avoid problems with Bluetooth?

   A. Keep personal info off your phone

   B. Keep Bluetooth discoverability off

   C. Buy a new phone often

   D. Encryption

14. Why is attacking wireless networks so popular?

   A. There are more wireless networks than wired.

   B. They all run Windows.

   C. It's easy.

   D. It's more difficult and more prestigious than other network attacks.

15. What two key lengths do most implementations of WEP support?

   A. 64 and 56

   B. 104 and 40

   C. 512 and 256

   D. 1024 and 2048

■ Essay Quiz

1. Produce a report on why sensitive information should not be sent over the Wireless Application Protocol.

2. When you want to start scanning for rogue wireless networks, your supervisor asks you to write a memo detailing the threats of rogue wireless access points. What information would you include in the memo?

3. Write a report for the security team on how you would deploy wireless in the organization. Detail the protocols that you propose to use as well as

the frequency bands, how you would chose access point locations, and which network segments you would place the APs on.

4. Write a security policy for company-owned cell phones that use the Bluetooth protocol.

5. Write a memo recommending upgrading your organization's old 802.11b infrastructure to an 802.11i-compliant network, and detail the security enhancements.

Lab Projects

• Lab Project 12.1

Set up NetStumbler or Kismet on a computer, and then use it to find wireless access points. You will need the following:

- A laptop with Windows or Linux installed
- A compatible wireless 802.11 network adapter

Then do the following:

1. Download NetStumbler from www.netstumbler.com or Kismet from www.kismetwireless.net.

2. For NetStumbler, run the Windows Installer. For Kismet, untar the source file and then execute, in order, **./configure**, **make**, and **make install**.

3. Start the program and make sure that it sees your wireless adapter.

4. Take the laptop on your normal commute (or drive around your neighborhood) with NetStumbler/Kismet running.

5. Log any access points you detect.

• Lab Project 12.2

Attempt to scan the area for Bluetooth devices. You will need a cell phone with Bluetooth installed or a computer with a Bluetooth adapter. Then do the following:

1. If you're using a PC, download BlueScanner from Aruba Labs at https://labs.arubanetworks.com.

2. Take your phone or computer to a place with many people, such as a café.

3. Start the program and make sure that it sees your Bluetooth adapter.

4. Attempt to scan for vulnerable Bluetooth devices.

5. If you're using your phone, tell it to scan for Bluetooth devices. Any devices that you find are running in "discoverable" mode and are potentially exploitable.

Intrusion Detection Systems and Network Security

The outcome of any serious research can only be to make two questions grow where only one grew before.

—THORSTEIN VEBLEN

In this chapter, you will learn how to

- Apply the appropriate network tools to facilitate network security
- Determine the appropriate use of tools to facilitate network security
- Apply host-based security applications

Ensuring network security can be fairly easily compared to ensuring physical security—the more you want to protect and restrict access to an asset, the more security you need. In the world of physical security, you can use locks, walls, gates, guards, motion sensors, pressure plates, and so on, to protect physical assets. As you add more protective devices, you add "layers" of security that an intruder would have to overcome or breach to obtain access to whatever you are protecting. Correspondingly, in the network and data security arenas, you use protective layers in the form of passwords, firewalls, access lists, file permissions, and intrusion detection systems. An **intrusion detection system (IDS)** is a security system that detects inappropriate or malicious activity on a computer or network. Most organizations use their own approaches to network security, choosing the layers that make sense for them after they weigh risks, potentials for loss, costs, and manpower requirements.

The foundation for a layered network security approach usually starts with a well-secured system, regardless of the system's function (whether it's a user PC or a corporate e-mail server). A well-secured system uses up-to-date application and operating system patches, requires well-chosen passwords, runs the minimum number of services necessary, and restricts access to available services. On top of that foundation, you can add layers of protective measures such as antivirus products, firewalls, sniffers, and IDSs.

Some of the more complicated and interesting types of network/data security devices are IDSs, which are to the network world what burglar alarms are to the physical world. The main purpose of an IDS is to identify suspicious or malicious activity, note activity that deviates from normal behavior, catalog and classify the activity, and, if possible, respond to the activity. This chapter looks at the history of IDSs and various types of IDSs, considers how they work and the benefits and weaknesses of specific types, and what the future might hold for these systems as we discuss intrusion prevention systems. You'll also look at some topics complementary to network-based IDS such as proxy servers, firewalls, content filters, protocol analyzers, and honeypots. Intrusion detection can also occur at the host level, so we'll analyze host-based intrusion detection systems along with other host-based protections such as malware protection.

History of Intrusion Detection Systems

Like much of the network technology we see today, IDSs grew from a need to solve specific problems. Like the Internet itself, the IDS concept came from U.S. Department of Defense–sponsored research. In the early 1970s, the U.S. government and military became increasingly aware of the need to protect the electronic networks that were becoming critical to daily operations. In 1972, James Anderson published a paper for the U.S. Air Force outlining the growing number of computer security problems and the immediate need to secure Air Force systems (James P. Anderson, "Computer Security Technology Planning Study Volume 2," October 1972, http://seclab.cs.ucdavis.edu/projects/history/papers/ande72.pdf). Anderson continued his research and in 1980 published a follow-up paper outlining methods to improve security auditing and surveillance methods ("Computer Security Threat Monitoring and Surveillance," April 15, 1980, http://csrc.nist.gov/publications/history/ande80.pdf). In this paper, Anderson pioneered the concept of using system audit files to detect unauthorized access and misuse. He also suggested the use of automated detection systems, which paved the way for misuse detection on mainframe systems in use at the time.

While Anderson's work got the efforts started, the concept of a real-time, rule-based IDS didn't really exist until Dorothy Denning and Peter Neumann developed the first real-time IDS model, called "The Intrusion Detection Expert System (IDES)," from their research between 1984 and 1986. In 1987, Denning published "An Intrusion-Detection Model," a paper that laid out the model on which most modern IDSs are based (and which

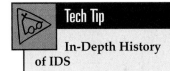

Tech Tip

In-Depth History of IDS
This chapter is far too short to cover the full history of IDS. Google "History of IDS" for a lot more information on the development of IDS over the years.

appears in *IEEE Transactions on Software Engineering*, Vol. SE-13, No. 2 [February 1987]: 222–232).

With a model and definitions in place, the U.S. government continued to fund research that led to projects such as Discovery, Haystack, Multics Intrusion Detection and Alerting System (MIDAS), and Network Audit Director and Intrusion Reporter (NADIR). Finally, in 1989, Haystack Labs released Stalker, the first commercial IDS. Stalker was host-based and worked by comparing audit data to known patterns of suspicious activity. While the military and government embraced the concept, the commercial world was very slow to adopt IDS products, and it was several years before other commercial products began to emerge.

In the early to mid-1990s, as computer systems continued to grow, companies started to realize the importance of IDSs; however, the solutions available were host-based and required a great deal of time and money to manage and operate effectively. Focus began to shift away from host-based systems, and network-based IDSs began to emerge. In 1995, WheelGroup was formed in San Antonio, Texas, to develop the first commercial network-based IDS product, called NetRanger. NetRanger was designed to monitor network links and the traffic moving across the links to identify misuse as well as suspicious and malicious activity. NetRanger's release was quickly followed by Internet Security Systems' RealSecure in 1996. Several other players followed suit and released their own IDS products, but it wasn't until the networking giant Cisco Systems acquired WheelGroup in February 1998 that IDSs were recognized as a vital part of any network security infrastructure. Figure 13.1 offers a timeline for these developments.

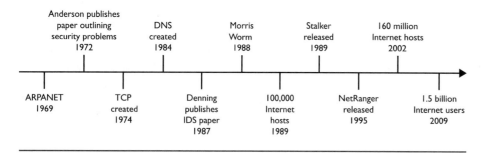

• **Figure 13.1** History of the Internet and IDS

■ IDS Overview

As mentioned, an IDS is somewhat like a burglar alarm. It watches the activity going on around it and tries to identify undesirable activity. IDSs are typically divided into two main categories, depending on how they monitor activity:

- **Host-based IDS (HIDS)** Examines activity on an individual system, such as a mail server, web server, or individual PC. It is concerned only with an individual system and usually has no visibility into the activity on the network or systems around it.

- **Network-based IDS (NIDS)** Examines activity on the network itself. It has visibility only into the traffic crossing the network link it is monitoring and typically has no idea of what is happening on individual systems.

Whether it is network- or host-based, an IDS typically consists of several specialized components working together, as illustrated in Figure 13.2.

These components are often logical and software-based rather than physical and will vary slightly from vendor to vendor and product to product. Typically, an IDS has the following logical components:

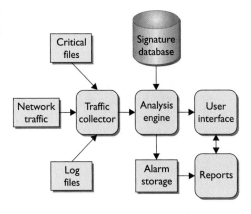

- **Traffic collector (or sensor)**   Collects activity/events for the IDS to examine. On a HIDS, this could be log files, audit logs, or traffic coming to or leaving a specific system. On a NIDS, this is typically a mechanism for copying traffic off the network link—basically functioning as a sniffer. This component is often referred to as a sensor.

- **Analysis engine**   Examines the collected network traffic and compares it to known patterns of suspicious or malicious activity stored in the signature database. The analysis engine is the "brains" of the IDS.

 Figure 13.2   Logical depiction of IDS components

- **Signature database**   A collection of patterns and definitions of known suspicious or malicious activity.

- **User interface and reporting**   Interfaces with the human element, providing alerts when appropriate and giving the user a means to interact with and operate the IDS.

Let's look at an example to see how all these components work together. Imagine a network intruder is scanning your organization for systems running a web server. The intruder launches a series of network probes against every IP address in your organization. The traffic from the intruder comes into your network and passes through the traffic collector (sensor). The traffic collector forwards the traffic to the analysis engine. The analysis engine examines and categorizes the traffic—it identifies a large number of probes coming from the same outside IP address (the intruder). The analysis engine compares the observed behavior against the signature database and gets a match. The intruder's activity matches a TCP port scan. The intruder is sending probes to many different systems in a short period of time. The analysis engine generates an alarm that is passed off to the user interface and reporting mechanisms. The user interface generates a notification to the administrator (icon, log entry, and so on). The administrator sees the alert and can now decide what to do about the potentially malicious traffic. Alarm storage is simply a repository of alarms the IDS has recorded—most IDS products allow administrators to run customized reports that sift through the collected alarms for items the administrator is searching for, such as all the alarms generated by a specific IP address.

In addition to the network versus host distinction, some IDS vendors will further categorize an IDS based on how it performs the detection of suspicious or malicious traffic:

- **Signature-based IDS**   Relies heavily on a predefined set of attack and traffic patterns called signatures. A signature-based IDS can only match against known patterns—if a new attack comes in that the signature-based IDS has never seen before, it won't be able to identify it as suspicious or malicious. This is considered to be one of the primary weaknesses of the signature-based systems, as they can only spot malicious traffic they've "seen before" and have a signature to match against.

Tech Tip

IDS Signatures

An IDS relies heavily on its signature database just like antivirus products rely on their virus definitions. If an attack is something completely new, an IDS may not recognize the traffic as malicious.

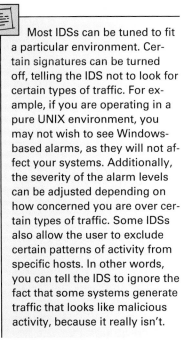

Most IDSs can be tuned to fit a particular environment. Certain signatures can be turned off, telling the IDS not to look for certain types of traffic. For example, if you are operating in a pure UNIX environment, you may not wish to see Windows-based alarms, as they will not affect your systems. Additionally, the severity of the alarm levels can be adjusted depending on how concerned you are over certain types of traffic. Some IDSs also allow the user to exclude certain patterns of activity from specific hosts. In other words, you can tell the IDS to ignore the fact that some systems generate traffic that looks like malicious activity, because it really isn't.

- **Anomaly-based IDS** Monitors activity and attempts to classify it as either "normal" or "anomalous." Anything that falls outside of what the IDS considers to be "normal" system operations is potentially hostile. An anomaly-based IDS must be able to learn what is "normal" and create its own rule sets based on those "normal" traffic and activity patterns. Anomaly-based IDSs are also referred to as behavior or heuristic IDSs because they use heuristic techniques to categorize and classify traffic while developing and refining their internal rule sets. An advantage of anomaly-based IDSs is their ability to potentially detect new attacks or variants of old attacks. Drawbacks of anomaly-based IDSs include the potentially high number of false positives while the system is learning what "normal" is and the fact that networks change a great deal over time. An anomaly-based IDS must either be able to dynamically adapt to changes or be retaught what "normal" behavior is for the network.

■ Network-Based IDSs

Tech Tip

Network Visibility

A network IDS has to be able to see traffic to find the malicious traffic. Encrypted traffic such as SSH or HTTPS sessions must be decrypted before a network IDS can examine them.

Network-based IDSs (NIDSs) actually came along a few years after host-based systems. After running host-based systems for a while, many organizations grew tired of the time, energy, and expense involved with managing the first generation of these systems—the host-based systems were not centrally managed, there was no easy way to correlate alerts between systems, and false-positive rates were high. The desire for a "better way" grew along with the growth in the amount of interconnectivity between systems and, consequently, the amount of malicious activity coming across the networks themselves. This fueled development of a new breed of IDS designed to focus on the source for a great deal of the malicious traffic—the network itself.

The NIDS integrated very well into the concept of **perimeter security**. More and more companies began to operate their computer security like a castle or military base (see Figure 13.3), with attention and effort focused on securing and controlling the ways in and out—the idea being that if you could restrict and control access at the perimeter, you didn't have to worry as much about activity inside the organization. Even though the idea of a security perimeter is somewhat flawed (many security incidents originate inside the perimeter), it caught on very quickly, as it was easy to understand and devices such as firewalls, bastion hosts, and routers were available to define and secure that perimeter. The best way to secure the perimeter from outside attack is to reject all traffic from external entities, but this is impossible and impractical to do, so security personnel needed a way to let traffic in but still be able to determine whether or not the traffic was malicious. This is the problem that NIDS developers were trying to solve.

As its name suggests, a NIDS focuses on network traffic—the bits and bytes traveling along the cables and wires that interconnect the systems. A NIDS must examine the network traffic as it passes by and be able to analyze traffic according to protocol, type, amount, source, destination, content, traffic already seen, and other factors. This analysis must happen quickly, and the NIDS must be able to handle traffic at whatever speed the network operates to be effective.

NIDSs are typically deployed so that they can monitor traffic in and out of an organization's major links: connections to the Internet, remote offices, partners, and so on. Like host-based systems, NIDSs look for certain activities that typify hostile actions or misuse, such as the following:

- Denial-of-service attacks
- Port scans or sweeps
- Malicious content in the data payload of a packet or packets
- Vulnerability scanning
- Trojans, viruses, or worms
- Tunneling
- Brute-force attacks

In general, most NIDSs operate in a fairly similar fashion. Figure 13.4 shows the logical layout of a NIDS. By considering the function and activity of each component, you can gain some insight into how a NIDS operates.

In the simplest form, a NIDS has the same major components: traffic collector, analysis engine, reports, and a user interface.

In a NIDS, the *traffic collector* is specifically designed to pull traffic from the network. This component usually behaves in much the same way as a network traffic sniffer—it simply pulls every packet it can see off the network to which it is connected. In a NIDS, the traffic collector will logically attach itself to a network interface card (NIC) and instruct the NIC to accept every packet it can. A NIC that accepts and processes every packet regardless of the packet's origin and destination is said to be in *promiscuous mode*.

The *analysis engine* in a NIDS serves the same function as its host-based counterpart, with some substantial differences. The network analysis engine must be able to collect packets and examine them individually or, if necessary, reassemble them into an entire traffic session. The patterns and signatures being matched are far more complicated than host-based

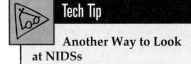

- **Figure 13.3** Network perimeters are a little like castles—firewalls and NIDSs form the gates and the walls to keep malicious traffic out.

> ### Tech Tip
>
> **Another Way to Look at NIDSs**
>
> *In its simplest form, a NIDS is a lot like a motion detector and a video surveillance system rolled into one. The NIDS notes the undesirable activity, generates an alarm, and records what happens.*

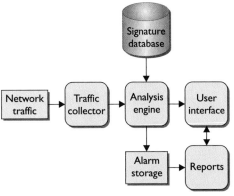

- **Figure 13.4** Network IDS components

Cross Check

NIDS and Encrypted Traffic

You learned about encrypted traffic in Chapter 5, so check your memory with these questions. What is SSH? What is a one-time pad? Can you name at least three different algorithms?

signatures, so the analysis engine must be able to remember what traffic preceded the traffic currently being analyzed so that it can determine whether or not that traffic fits into a larger pattern of malicious activity. Additionally, the network-based analysis engine must be able to keep up with the flow of traffic on the network, rebuilding network sessions and matching patterns in real time.

The NIDS *signature database* is usually much larger than that of a host-based system. When examining network patterns, the NIDS must be able to recognize traffic targeted at many different applications and operating systems as well as traffic from a wide variety of threats (worms, assessment tools, attack tools, and so on). Some of the signatures themselves can be quite large, as the NIDS must look at network traffic occurring in a specific order over a period of time to match a particular malicious pattern.

Using the lessons learned from early host-based systems, NIDS developers modified the logical component design somewhat to distribute the user interface and reporting functions. As many companies had more than one network link, they would need an IDS capable of handling multiple links in many different locations. The early IDS vendors solved this dilemma by dividing the components and assigning them to separate entities. The traffic collector, analysis engine, and signature database were bundled into a single entity, usually called a *sensor* or *appliance*. The sensors would report to and be controlled by a central system or master console. This central system, shown in Figure 13.5, consolidated alarms and provided the user interface and reporting functions that allowed users in one location to manage, maintain, and monitor sensors deployed in a variety of remote locations.

By creating separate components designed to work together, the NIDS developers were able to build a more capable and flexible system. With encrypted communications, network sensors could be placed around both local and remote perimeters and still be monitored and managed securely from a central location. Placement of the sensors very quickly became an issue for most security personnel, as the sensors obviously had to have visibility of the network traffic in order to analyze it. Because most organizations with NIDSs also had firewalls, location of the NIDS relative to the firewall had to be considered as well. Placed before the firewall, as shown in Figure 13.6, the NIDS will see all traffic coming in from the Internet, including attacks against the firewall itself. This includes traffic that the firewall stops and does not permit into the corporate network. With this type of deployment, the NIDS sensor will generate a large number of alarms (including alarms for traffic that the firewall would stop). This tends to overwhelm the human operators managing the system.

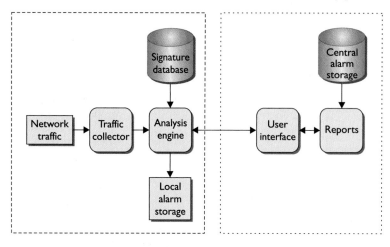

• **Figure 13.5**   Distributed network IDS components

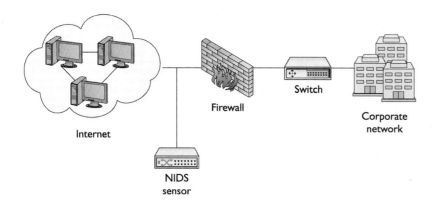

• **Figure 13.6**   NIDS sensor placed in front of firewall

Placed after the firewall, as shown in Figure 13.7, the NIDS sensor sees and analyzes the traffic that is being passed through the firewall and into the corporate network. While this does not allow the NIDS to see attacks against the firewall, it generally results in far fewer alarms and is the most popular placement for NIDS sensors.

As you already know, NIDSs examine the network traffic for suspicious or malicious activity. Here are two examples of suspicious traffic to illustrate the operation of a NIDS:

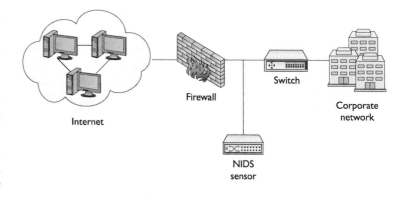

• **Figure 13.7**   NIDS sensor placed behind firewall

- **Port scan**   A port scan is a reconnaissance activity a potential attacker uses to find out information about the systems he wants to attack. Using any of a number of tools, the attacker attempts to connect to various services (web, FTP, SMTP, and so on) to see if they exist on the intended target. In normal network traffic, a single user might connect to the FTP service provided on a single system. During a port scan, an attacker may attempt to connect to the FTP service on every system. As the attacker's traffic passes by the IDS, the IDS will notice this pattern of attempting to connect to different services on different systems in a relatively short period of time. When the IDS compares the activity to its signature database, it will very likely match this traffic against the port scanning signature and generate an alarm.

- **Ping of death**   Toward the end of 1996, it was discovered that certain operating systems, such as Windows, could be crashed by sending a very large Internet Control Message Protocol (ICMP) echo request packet to that system. The vulnerable operating systems did not handle the packet correctly and would subsequently reboot or lock up after receiving the packets. This is a fairly simple traffic pattern for a NIDS to identify, as it simply has to look for ICMP packets over a certain size.

Port scanning activity is rampant on the Internet. Most organizations with NIDS see hundreds or thousands of port scan alarms every day from sources around the world. Some administrators reduce the alarm level of port scan alarms or ignore port scanning traffic because there is simply too much traffic to track down and respond to each alarm.

Advantages of a NIDS

A NIDS has certain advantages that make it a good choice for certain situations:

- *Providing IDS coverage requires fewer systems.* With a few well-placed NIDS sensors, you can monitor all the network traffic going in and out of your organization. Fewer sensors usually equates to less overhead and maintenance, meaning you can protect the same number of systems at a lower cost.

- *Deployment, maintenance, and upgrade costs are usually lower.* The fewer systems that have to be managed and maintained to provide IDS coverage, the lower the cost to operate the IDS. Upgrading and maintaining a few sensors is usually much cheaper than upgrading and maintaining hundreds of host-based processes.

- *A NIDS has visibility into all network traffic and can correlate attacks among multiple systems.* Well-placed NIDS sensors can see the "big picture" when it comes to network-based attacks. The network sensors can tell you whether attacks are widespread and unorganized or focused and concentrated on specific systems.

Disadvantages of a NIDS

A NIDS has certain disadvantages:

- *It is ineffective when traffic is encrypted.* When network traffic is encrypted from application to application or system to system, a NIDS sensor will not be able to examine that traffic. With the increasing popularity of encrypted traffic, this is becoming a bigger problem for effective IDS operations.

- *It can't see traffic that does not cross it.* The IDS sensor can examine only traffic crossing the network link it is monitoring. With most IDS sensors being placed on perimeter links, traffic traversing the internal network is never seen.

- *It must be able to handle high volumes of traffic.* As network speeds continue to increase, the network sensors must be able to keep pace and examine the traffic as quickly as it can pass the network. When NIDSs were introduced, 10-Mbps networks were the norm. Now 100-Mbps and even 1-Gbps networks are commonplace. This increase in traffic speeds means IDS sensors must be faster and more powerful than ever before.

- *It doesn't know about activity on the hosts themselves.* NIDSs focus on network traffic. Activity that occurs on the hosts themselves will not be seen by a NIDS.

Active vs. Passive NIDSs

Most NIDSs can be distinguished by how they examine the traffic and whether or not they interact with that traffic. On a *passive* system, the NIDS simply watches the traffic, analyzes it, and generates alarms. It does not

---

Tech Tip

TCP Reset

The most common defensive ability for an active NIDS is to send a TCP reset message. Within TCP, the reset message (RST) essentially tells both sides of the connection to drop the session and stop communicating immediately. While this mechanism was originally developed to cover situations such as systems accidentally receiving communications intended for other systems, the reset message works fairly well for NIDSs—with one serious drawback: a reset message affects only the current session. Nothing prevents the attacker from coming back and trying again and again. Despite the "temporariness" of this solution, sending a reset message is usually the only defensive measure implemented on NIDS deployments, as the fear of blocking legitimate traffic and disrupting business processes, even for a few moments, often outweighs the perceived benefit of discouraging potential intruders.

---

interact with the traffic itself in any way, and it does not modify the defensive posture of the system to react to the traffic. A passive NIDS is very similar to a simple motion sensor—it generates an alarm when it matches a pattern, much as the motion sensor generates an alarm when it sees movement. An *active* NIDS contains all the same components and capabilities of the passive NIDS with one critical addition—the active NIDS can *react* to the traffic it is analyzing. These reactions can range from something simple, such as sending a TCP reset message to interrupt a potential attack and disconnect a session, to something complex, such as dynamically modifying firewall rules to reject all traffic from specific source IP addresses for the next 24 hours.

■ Signatures

As you have probably deduced from the discussion so far, one of the critical elements of any good IDS is the signature database—the set of patterns the IDS uses to determine whether or not activity is potentially hostile. Signatures can be very simple or remarkably complicated, depending on the activity they are trying to highlight. In general, signatures can be divided into two main groups, depending on what the signature is looking for: content-based and context-based.

Content-based signatures are generally the simplest. They are designed to examine the content of such things as network packets or log entries. Content-based signatures are typically easy to build and look for simple things, such as a certain string of characters or a certain flag set in a TCP packet. Here are some example content-based signatures:

- *Matching the characters /etc/passwd in a Telnet session.* On a UNIX system, the names of valid user accounts (and sometimes the passwords for those user accounts) are stored in a file called *passwd* located in the *etc* directory.

- *Matching the characters "to: decode" in the header of an e-mail message.* On certain older versions of sendmail, sending an e-mail message to "decode" would cause the system to execute the contents of the e-mail.

Context-based signatures are generally more complicated, as they are designed to match large patterns of activity and examine how certain types of activity fit into the other activities going on around them. Context signatures generally address the question, How does this event compare to other events that have already happened or might happen in the near future? Context-based signatures are more difficult to analyze and take more resources to match, as the IDS must be able to "remember" past events to match certain context signatures. Here are some example context-based signatures:

- *Match a potential intruder scanning for open web servers on a specific network.* A potential intruder may use a port scanner to look for any systems accepting connections on port 80. To match this signature, the IDS must analyze all attempted connections to port 80 and then be able to determine which connection attempts are coming from the same source but are going to multiple, different destinations.

- *Identify a Nessus scan*. Nessus is an open-source vulnerability scanner that allows security administrators (and potential attackers) to quickly examine systems for vulnerabilities. Depending on the tests chosen, Nessus typically performs the tests in a certain order, one after the other. To be able to determine the presence of a Nessus scan, the IDS must know which tests Nessus runs as well as the typical order in which the tests are run.

- *Identify a ping flood attack*. A single ICMP packet on its own is generally regarded as harmless, certainly not worthy of an IDS signature. Yet thousands of ICMP packets coming to a single system in a short period of time can have a devastating effect on the receiving system. By flooding a system with thousands of valid ICMP packets, an attacker can keep a target system so busy it doesn't have time to do anything else—a very effective denial-of-service attack. To identify a ping flood, the IDS must recognize each ICMP packet and keep track of how many ICMP packets different systems have received in the recent past.

To function, the IDS must have a decent signature base with examples of known, undesirable activity that it can use when analyzing traffic or events. Any time an IDS matches current events against a signature, the IDS could be considered successful, as it has correctly matched the current event against a known signature and reacted accordingly (usually with an alarm or alert of some type).

■ False Positives and False Negatives

Viewed in its simplest form, an IDS is really just looking at activity (be it host-based or network-based) and matching it against a predefined set of patterns. When it matches activity to a specific pattern, the IDS cannot know the true intent behind that activity—whether or not it is benign or hostile—and therefore it can react only as it has been programmed to do. In most cases, this means generating an alert that must then be analyzed by a human who tries to determine the intent of the traffic from whatever information is available. When an IDS matches a pattern and generates an alarm for benign traffic, meaning the traffic was not hostile and not a threat, this is called a **false positive**. In other words, the IDS matched a pattern and raised an alarm when it didn't really need to do so. Keep in mind that the IDS can only match patterns and has no ability to determine intent behind the activity, so in some ways this is an unfair label. Technically, the IDS is functioning correctly by matching the pattern, but from a human standpoint this is not information the analyst needed to see, as it does not constitute a threat and does not require intervention.

An IDS is also limited by its signature set—it can match only activity for which it has stored patterns. Hostile activity that does not match an IDS signature and therefore goes undetected is called a **false negative**. In this case, the IDS is not generating any alarms, even though it should be, giving a false sense of security.

IDS Models

In addition to being divided along the host and network lines, IDSs are often classified according to the detection model they use: anomaly or misuse. For an IDS, a model is a method for examining behavior so that the IDS can determine whether that behavior is "not normal" or in violation of established policies.

An **anomaly detection model** is the more complicated of the two. In this model, the IDS must know what "normal" behavior on the host or network being protected really is. Once the "normal" behavior baseline is established, the IDS can then go to work identifying deviations from the norm, which are further scrutinized to determine whether or not that activity is malicious. Building the profile of normal activity is usually done by the IDS, with some input from security administrators, and can take days to months. The IDS must be flexible and capable enough to account for things such as new systems, new users, movement of information resources, and other factors, but be sensitive enough to detect a single user illegally switching from one account to another at 3 A.M. on a Saturday.

Anomaly detection was developed to make the system capable of dealing with variations in traffic and better able to determine which activity patterns were malicious. A perfectly functioning anomaly-based system would be able to ignore patterns from legitimate hosts and users but still identify those patterns as suspicious should they come from a potential attacker. Unfortunately, most anomaly-based systems suffer from extremely high false positives, especially during the "break-in" period while the IDS is learning the network. On the other hand, an anomaly-based system is not restricted to a specific signature set and is far more likely to identify a new exploit or attack tool that would go unnoticed by a traditional IDS.

A **misuse detection model** is a little simpler to implement, and therefore it's the more popular of the two models. In a misuse detection model, the IDS looks for suspicious activity or activity that violates specific policies and then reacts as it has been programmed to do. This reaction can be an alarm, e-mail, router reconfiguration, or TCP reset message. Technically, misuse detection is the more efficient model, as it takes fewer resources to operate, does not need to learn what "normal" behavior is, and will generate an alarm whenever a pattern is successfully matched. However, the misuse model's greatest weakness is its reliance on a predefined signature base—any activity, malicious or otherwise, that the misuse-based IDS does not have a signature for will go undetected. Despite that drawback and because it is easier and cheaper to implement, most commercial IDS products are based on the misuse detection model.

> **Exam Tip:** Anomaly detection looks for things that are out of the ordinary, such as a user logging in when he's not supposed to or unusually high network traffic into and out of a workstation.

> **Exam Tip:** Misuse detection looks for things that violate policy. For example, a denial-of-service attack launched at your web server or an attacker attempting to brute-force an SSH session.

Firewalls

A **firewall** is a network device—hardware, software, or a combination thereof—whose purpose is to enforce a security policy across its connections by allowing or denying traffic to pass into or out of the network. A firewall is a lot like a gate guard at a secure facility. The guard examines all the traffic trying to enter the facility—cars with the correct sticker or delivery trucks with the appropriate paperwork are allowed in; everyone else is turned away. The heart of a firewall is the firewall policy that it enforces.

Firewall security policies are a series of rules that defines what traffic is permissible and what traffic is to be blocked or denied. These are not universal rules, and there are many different sets of rules for a single company with multiple connections. A web server connected to the Internet may be configured only to allow traffic on port 80 for HTTP, and have all other ports blocked. An e-mail server may have only necessary ports for e-mail open, with others blocked. A key to security policies for firewalls is the same as has been seen for other security policies—the principle of least access. Only allow the necessary access for a function; block or deny all unneeded functionality. How an organization deploys its firewalls determines what is needed for security policies for each firewall. You may even have a small office–home office firewall at your house, such as the RVS4000 shown in Figure 13.8. This device from Linksys provides both routing and firewall functions.

The security topology determines what network devices are employed at what points in a network. At a minimum, the corporate connection to the Internet should pass through a firewall, as shown in Figure 13.9. This firewall should block all network traffic except that specifically authorized by the security policy. This is actually easy to do: blocking communications on a port is simply a matter of telling the firewall to close the port. The issue comes in deciding what services are needed and by whom, and thus which ports should be open and which should be closed. This is what makes a security policy useful but, in some cases, difficult to maintain.

The perfect firewall policy is one that the end user never sees and one that never allows even a single unauthorized packet to enter the network. As with any other perfect item, it will be rare to find the perfect security policy for a firewall.

• **Figure 13.8**   Linksys RVS4000 SOHO firewall

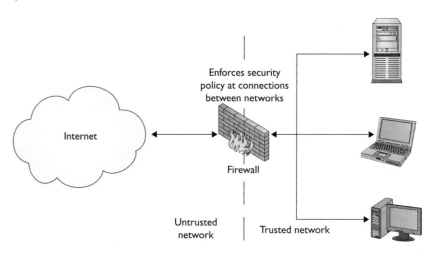

• **Figure 13.9**   Logical depiction of a firewall protecting an organization from the Internet

Principles of Computer Security: CompTIA Security+ and Beyond

To develop a complete and comprehensive security policy, it is first necessary to have a complete and comprehensive understanding of your network resources and their uses. Once you know what your network will be used for, you will have an idea of what to permit. Also, once you understand what you need to protect, you will have an idea of what to block. Firewalls are designed to block attacks before they get to a target machine. Common targets are web servers, e-mail servers, DNS servers, FTP services, and databases. Each of these has separate functionality, and each of these has separate vulnerabilities. Once you have decided who should receive what type of traffic and what types should be blocked, you can administer this through the firewall.

How Do Firewalls Work?

Firewalls enforce the established security policies. They can do this through a variety of mechanisms, including:

- **Network Address Translation (NAT)** As you may remember from Chapter 9, NAT translates private (nonroutable) IP addresses into public (routable) IP addresses.

- **Basic packet filtering** Basic packet filtering looks at each packet entering or leaving the network and then either accepts the packet or rejects the packet based on user-defined rules. Each packet is examined separately.

- **Stateful packet filtering** Stateful packet filtering also looks at each packet, but it can examine the packet in its relation to other packets. Stateful firewalls keep track of network connections and can apply slightly different rule sets based on whether the packet is part of an established session or not.

- **Access control lists (ACLs)** ACLs are simple rule sets that are applied to port numbers and IP addresses. They can be configured for inbound and outbound traffic and are most commonly used on routers and switches.

- **Application layer proxies** An application layer proxy can examine the content of the traffic as well as the ports and IP addresses. For example, an application layer has the ability to look inside a user's web traffic, detect a malicious website attempting to download malware to the user's system, and block the malware.

 NAT is the process of modifying network address information in datagram packet headers while in transit across a traffic routing device, such as a router or firewall, for the purpose of remapping a given address space into another. See Chapter 9 for a more detailed discussion on NAT.

One of the most basic security functions provided by a firewall is NAT. This service allows you to mask significant amounts of information from outside of the network. This allows an outside entity to communicate with an entity inside the firewall without truly knowing its address.

Basic packet filtering, also known as stateless packet inspection, involves looking at packets, their protocols and destinations, and checking that information against the security policy. Telnet and FTP connections may be prohibited from being established to a mail or database server, but they may be allowed for the respective service servers. This is a fairly simple method of filtering based on information in each packet header, like IP addresses and TCP/UDP ports. This will not detect and catch all undesired packets, but it is fast and efficient.

To look at all packets, determining the need for each and its data, requires stateful packet filtering. Advanced firewalls employ stateful packet filtering to prevent several types of undesired communications. Should a packet come from outside the network, in an attempt to pretend that it is a response to a message from inside the network, the firewall will have no record of it being requested and can discard it, blocking access. As many communications will be transferred to high ports (above 1023), stateful monitoring will enable the system to determine which sets of high-port communications are permissible and which should be blocked. The disadvantage to stateful monitoring is that it takes significant resources and processing to do this type of monitoring, and this reduces efficiency and requires more robust and expensive hardware. However, this type of monitoring is essential in today's comprehensive networks, particularly given the variety of remotely accessible services.

As they are in routers, switches, servers, and other network devices, ACLs are a cornerstone of security in firewalls. Just as you must protect the device from physical access, ACLs do the same task for electronic access. Firewalls can extend the concept of ACLs by enforcing them at a packet level when packet-level stateful filtering is performed. This can add an extra layer of protection, making it more difficult for an outside hacker to breach a firewall.

Some high-security firewalls also employ application layer proxies. As the name implies, packets are not allowed to traverse the firewall, but data instead flows up to an application that in turn decides what to do with it. For example, an SMTP proxy may accept inbound mail from the Internet and forward it to the internal corporate mail server, as depicted in Figure 13.10. While proxies provide a high level of security by making it very difficult for an attacker to manipulate the actual packets arriving at the destination, and while they provide the opportunity for an application to interpret the data prior to forwarding it to the destination, they generally are not capable of the same throughput as stateful packet inspection firewalls. The trade-off

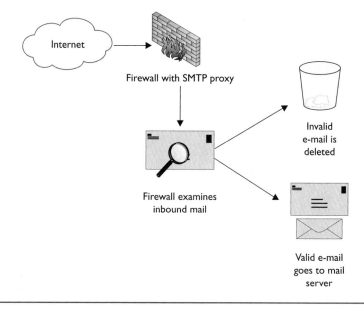

• **Figure 13.10** Firewall with SMTP application layer proxy

Principles of Computer Security: CompTIA Security+ and Beyond

between performance and speed is a common one and must be evaluated with respect to security needs and performance requirements.

Intrusion Prevention Systems

An **intrusion prevention system (IPS)** monitors network traffic for malicious or unwanted behavior and can block, reject, or redirect that traffic in real time. Sound familiar? It should: while many vendors will argue that an IPS is a different animal from an IDS, the truth is that most IPSs are merely expansions of existing IDS capabilities. As a core function, an IPS must be able to monitor for and detect potentially malicious network traffic, which is essentially the same function as an IDS. However, an IPS does not stop at merely monitoring traffic—it must be able to block, reject, or redirect that traffic in real time to be considered a true IPS. It must be able to stop or prevent malicious traffic from having an impact. To qualify as an IDS, a system just needs to see and classify the traffic as malicious. To qualify as an IPS, a system must be able to do something about that traffic. In reality, most products that are called IDSs, including the first commercially available IDS, NetRanger, can interact with and stop malicious traffic, so the distinction between the two is often blurred.

 The term *intrusion prevention system* was originally coined by Andrew Plato in marketing literature developed for NetworkICE, a company that was purchased by ISS and which is now part of IBM. The term IPS has effectively taken the place of the term "active IDS."

Like IDSs, most IPSs have an internal signature database to compare network traffic against known "bad" traffic patterns. IPSs can perform content-based inspections, looking inside network packets for unique packets, data values, or patterns that match known malicious patterns. Some IPSs can perform protocol inspection, in which the IPS decodes traffic and analyzes it as it would appear to the server receiving it. For example, many IPSs can do HTTP protocol inspection, so they can examine incoming and outgoing HTTP traffic and process it as an HTTP server would. The advantage here is that the IPS can detect and defeat popular evasion techniques such as encoding URLs because the IPS "sees" the traffic in the same way the web server would when it receives and decodes it. The IPS can also detect activity that is abnormal or potentially malicious for that protocol, such as passing an extremely large value (over 10,000 characters) to a login field on a web page.

 Exam Tip: An IDS is like a burglar alarm—it watches and alerts you when something bad happens. An IPS is like an armed security guard—it watches, stops the bad activity, and then lets you know what happened.

Unlike a traditional IDS, an IPS must sit inline (in the flow of traffic) to be able to interact effectively with the network traffic. Most IPSs can operate in "stealth mode" and do not require an IP address for the connections they are monitoring. When an IPS detects malicious traffic, it can drop the offending packets, reset incoming or established connections, generate alerts, quarantine traffic to/from specific IP addresses, or even block traffic from offending IP addresses on a temporary or permanent basis. As they are sitting inline, most IPSs can also offer *rate-based monitoring* to detect and mitigate denial-of-service attacks. With rate-based monitoring, the IPS can watch the amount of traffic traversing the network. If the IPS sees too much traffic coming into or going out from a specific system or set of systems, the IPS can intervene and throttle down the traffic to a lower and more acceptable level. Many IPSs perform this function by "learning" what are "normal" network traffic patterns with regard to number of connections per second, amount of packets per connection, packets coming from or going to specific ports, and

The term *wire speed* refers to the theoretical maximum transmission rate of a cable or other medium and is based on a number of factors, including the properties of the cable itself and the connection protocol in use (in other words, how much data can be pushed through under ideal conditions).

so on, and comparing current traffic rates for network traffic (TCP, UDP, ARP, ICMP, and so on) to those established norms. When a traffic pattern reaches a threshold or varies dramatically from those norms, the IPS can react and intervene as needed.

Like a traditional IDS, the IPS has a potential weakness when dealing with encrypted traffic. Traffic that is encrypted will typically pass by the IPS untouched (provided it does not trigger any non-content–related alarms such as rate-based alarms). To counter this problem, some IPS vendors are including the ability to decrypt Secure Sockets Layer (SSL) sessions for further inspection. To do this, some IPS solutions store copies of any protected web servers' private keys on the sensor itself. When the IPS sees a session initiation request, it monitors the initial transactions between the server and the client. By using the server's stored private keys, the IPS will be able to determine the session keys negotiated during the SSL session initiation. With the session keys, the IPS can decrypt all future packets passed between server and client during that web session. This gives the IPS the ability to perform content inspection on SSL-encrypted traffic.

You will often see IPSs (and IDSs) advertised and marketed by the amount of traffic they can process without dropping packets or interrupting the flow of network traffic. In reality, a network will never reach its hypothetical maximum transmission rate, or wire speed, due to errors, collisions, retransmissions, and other factors; therefore, a 1-Gbps network is not actually capable of passing 1 Gbps of network traffic, even if all the components are rated to handle 1 Gbps. When used in a marketing sense, wire speed is the maximum throughput rate the networking or security device equipment can process without impacting that network traffic. For example, a 1-Gbps IPS should be able to process, analyze, and protect 1 Gbps of network traffic without impacting traffic flow. IPS vendors often quote their products' capacity as the combined throughput possible through all available ports on the IPS sensor—a 10-Gbps sensor may have 12 Gigabit Ethernet ports but is capable of handling only 10 Gbps of network traffic.

■ Proxy Servers

Though not strictly a security tool, a **proxy server** (or simply *proxy*) can be used to filter out undesirable traffic and prevent employees from accessing potentially hostile web sites. A proxy server takes requests from a client system and forwards them to the destination server on behalf of the client, as shown in Figure 13.11. Proxy servers can be completely transparent (these are usually called *gateways* or *tunneling proxies*), or a proxy server can modify the client request before sending it on, or even serve the client's request without needing to contact the destination server. Several major categories of proxy servers are in use:

- **Anonymizing proxy** An anonymizing proxy is designed to hide information about the requesting system and make a user's web browsing experience "anonymous." This type of proxy service is often used by individuals who are concerned about the amount of personal information being transferred across the Internet and the use of tracking cookies and other mechanisms to track browsing activity.

- **Caching proxy** This type of proxy keeps local copies of popular client requests and is often used in large organizations to reduce bandwidth usage and increase performance. When a request is made, the proxy server first checks to see whether it has a current copy of the requested content in the cache; if it does, it services the client request immediately without having to contact the destination server. If the content is old or the caching proxy does not have a copy of the requested content, the request is forwarded to the destination server.

- **Content-filtering proxy** Content-filtering proxies examine each client request and compare it to an established acceptable use policy. Requests can usually be filtered in a variety of ways, including by the requested URL, destination system, or domain name or by keywords in the content itself. Content-filtering proxies typically support user-level authentication, so access can be controlled and monitored and activity through the proxy can be logged and analyzed. This type of proxy is very popular in schools, corporate environments, and government networks.

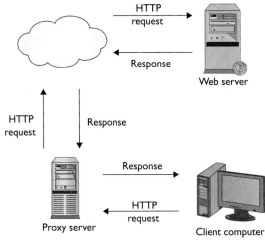

• **Figure 13.11** HTTP proxy handling client requests and web server responses

- **Open proxy** An open proxy is essentially a proxy that is available to any Internet user and often has some anonymizing capabilities as well. This type of proxy has been the subject of some controversy, with advocates for Internet privacy and freedom on one side of the argument, and law enforcement, corporations, and government entities on the other side. As open proxies are often used to circumvent corporate proxies, many corporations attempt to block the use of open proxies by their employees.

- **Reverse proxy** A reverse proxy is typically installed on the server side of a network connection, often in front of a group of web servers. The reverse proxy intercepts all incoming web requests and can perform a number of functions, including traffic filtering and shaping, SSL decryption, serving of common static content such as graphics, and performing load balancing.

- **Web proxy** A web proxy is solely designed to handle web traffic and is sometimes called a *web cache*. Most web proxies are essentially specialized caching proxies.

Deploying a proxy solution within a network environment is usually done either by setting up the proxy and requiring all client systems to configure their browsers to use the proxy or by deploying an intercepting proxy that actively intercepts all requests without requiring client-side configuration.

From a security perspective, proxies are most useful in their ability to control and filter outbound requests. By limiting the types of content and web sites employees can access from corporate systems, many administrators hope to avoid loss of corporate data, hijacked systems, and infections from malicious web sites. Administrators also use proxies to enforce corporate acceptable use policies and track use of corporate resources. Most proxies can be configured to either allow or require individual user authentication—this gives them the ability to log and control activity based on specific users or

> **Exam Tip:** A proxy server is a system or application that acts as a go-between for clients' requests for network services. The client tells the proxy server what it wants and, if the client is authorized to have it, the proxy server connects to the appropriate network service and gets the client what it asked for. Web proxies are the most commonly deployed type of proxy server.

groups. For example, an organization might want to allow the human resources group to browse Facebook during business hours but not allow the rest of the organization to do so.

Internet Content Filters

With the dramatic proliferation of Internet traffic and the push to provide Internet access to every desktop, many corporations have implemented content-filtering systems, called an **Internet content filter**, to protect them from employees' viewing of inappropriate or illegal content at the workplace and the subsequent complications that occur when such viewing takes place. Internet content filtering is also popular in schools, libraries, homes, government offices, and any other environment where there is a need to limit or restrict access to undesirable content. In addition to filtering undesirable content, such as pornography, some content filters can also filter out malicious activity such as browser hijacking attempts or cross-site–scripting attacks. In many cases, content filtering is performed with or as a part of a proxy solution as the content requests can be filtered and serviced by the same device. Content can be filtered in a variety of ways, including via the requested URL, the destination system, the domain name, by keywords in the content itself, and by type of file requested.

Content-filtering systems face many challenges, because the ever-changing Internet makes it difficult to maintain lists of undesirable sites (sometime called black lists); terms used on a medical site can also be used on a pornographic site, making keyword filtering challenging; and determined users are always seeking ways to bypass proxy filters. To help administrators, most commercial content-filtering solutions provide an update service, much like IDS or antivirus products, that updates keywords and undesirable sites automatically.

The term "Internet content filter" or "content filter" is applied to any device, application, or software package that examines network traffic (especially web traffic) for undesirable or restricted content. A content filter could be a software package loaded on a specific PC or a network appliance capable of filtering an entire organization's web traffic.

Protocol Analyzers

A **protocol analyzer** (also known as a *packet sniffer*, *network analyzer*, or *network sniffer*) is a piece of software or an integrated software/hardware system that can capture and decode network traffic. Protocol analyzers have been popular with system administrators and security professionals for decades because they are such versatile and useful tools for a network environment. From a security perspective, protocol analyzers can be used for a number of activities, such as the following:

- Detecting intrusions or undesirable traffic (an IDS/IPS must have some type of capture and decode ability to be able to look for suspicious/malicious traffic)

- Capturing traffic during incident response or incident handling

- Looking for evidence of botnets, Trojans, and infected systems

- Looking for unusual traffic or traffic exceeding certain thresholds
- Testing encryption between systems or applications

From a network administration perspective, protocol analyzers can be used for activities such as these:

- Analyzing network problems
- Detecting misconfigured applications or misbehaving applications
- Gathering and reporting network usage and traffic statistics
- Debugging client/server communications

Regardless of the intended use, a protocol analyzer must be able to see network traffic in order to capture and decode it. A software-based protocol analyzer must be able to place the NIC it is going to use to monitor network traffic in *promiscuous mode* (sometimes called *promisc mode*). Promiscuous mode tells the NIC to process every network packet its sees regardless of the intended destination. Normally, a NIC processes only *broadcast* packets (which go to everyone on that subnet) and packets with the NIC's Media Access Control (MAC) address as the destination address inside the packet. As a sniffer, the analyzer must process every packet crossing the wire, so the ability to place a NIC into promiscuous mode is critical.

<img alt="Exam Tip icon" /> **Exam Tip:** A sniffer must use a NIC placed in promiscuous (promisc) mode or it will not see all the network traffic coming into the NIC.

With older networking technologies, such as hubs, it was easier to operate a protocol analyzer, as the hub broadcast every packet across every interface regardless of the destination. With switches now the standard for networking equipment, placing a protocol analyzer becomes more difficult.

To accommodate protocol analyzers, IDS devices, and IPS devices, most switch manufacturers support **port mirroring** or a **Switched Port Analyzer (SPAN)** port. Depending on the manufacturer and the hardware, a mirrored port will see all the traffic passing through the switch or through a specific VLAN(s), or all the traffic passing through other specific switch ports. The network traffic is essentially copied (or mirrored) to a specific port, which can then support a protocol analyzer.

Another option for traffic capture is to use a **network tap**, a hardware device that can be placed inline on a network connection and that will copy traffic passing through the tap to a second set of interfaces on the tap. Network taps are often used to sniff traffic passing between devices at the network perimeter, such as the traffic passing between a router and a firewall. Many common network taps work by bridging a network connection and passing incoming traffic out one tap port (A) and outgoing traffic out another tap port (B), as shown in Figure 13.12.

A popular, open source protocol analyzer is Wireshark (www.wireshark.org). Available for both UNIX and Windows operating systems, Wireshark is a GUI-based protocol analyzer that allows users to capture and decode network traffic on any available network interface in the system on which the software is running (including wireless interfaces), as demonstrated in Figure 13.13. Wireshark has some interesting features, including the ability to "follow the TCP stream," which allows the user to select a single TCP packet and then see all the other packets involved in that TCP conversation.

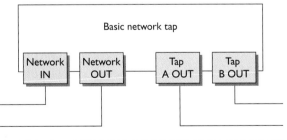

• **Figure 13.12**   A basic network tap

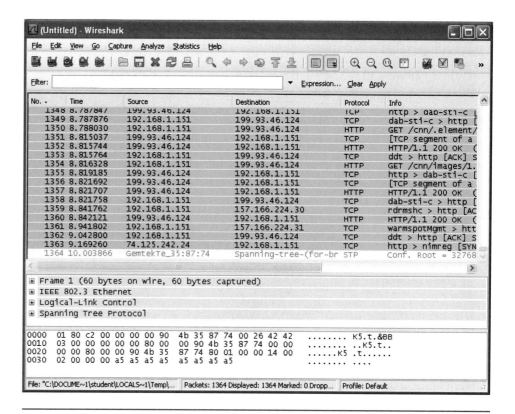

No. ▲	Time	Source	Destination	Protocol	Info
1348	8.787847	199.93.46.124	192.168.1.151	TCP	http > dab-sti-c [
1349	8.787876	192.168.1.151	199.93.46.124	TCP	dab-sti-c > http [
1350	8.788030	192.168.1.151	199.93.46.124	HTTP	GET /cnn/.element/
1351	8.815037	199.93.46.124	192.168.1.151	TCP	[TCP segment of a
1352	8.815744	199.93.46.124	192.168.1.151	HTTP	HTTP/1.1 200 OK (
1353	8.815764	192.168.1.151	199.93.46.124	TCP	ddt > http [ACK] s
1354	8.816328	192.168.1.151	199.93.46.124	HTTP	GET /cnn/images/1.
1355	8.819185	199.93.46.124	192.168.1.151	TCP	http > dab-sti-c [
1356	8.821692	199.93.46.124	192.168.1.151	TCP	[TCP segment of a
1357	8.821707	199.93.46.124	192.168.1.151	HTTP	HTTP/1.1 200 OK (
1358	8.821758	192.168.1.151	199.93.46.124	TCP	dab-sti-c > http [
1359	8.841762	192.168.1.151	157.166.224.30	TCP	rdrmshc > http [AC
1360	8.842121	199.93.46.124	192.168.1.151	HTTP	HTTP/1.1 200 OK (
1361	8.941802	192.168.1.151	157.166.224.31	TCP	warmspotMgmt > htt
1362	9.042800	192.168.1.151	199.93.46.124	TCP	ddt > http [ACK] s
1363	9.169260	74.125.242.24	192.168.1.151	TCP	http > nimreg [SYN
1364	10.003866	GemtekTe_35:87:74	Spanning-tree-(for-br	STP	Conf. Root = 32768

⊞ Frame 1 (60 bytes on wire, 60 bytes captured)
⊞ IEEE 802.3 Ethernet
⊞ Logical-Link Control
⊞ Spanning Tree Protocol

```
0000  01 80 c2 00 00 00 00 90  4b 35 87 74 00 26 42 42   ........ K5.t.&BB
0010  03 00 00 00 00 00 80 00  00 90 4b 35 87 74 00 00   ........ ..K5.t..
0020  00 00 80 00 00 90 4b 35  87 74 80 01 00 00 14 00   ......K5 .t......
0030  02 00 00 00 a5 a5 a5 a5  a5 a5 a5 a5               ........ ....
```

File: "C:\DOCUME~1\student\LOCALS~1\Temp\... | Packets: 1364 Displayed: 1364 Marked: 0 Dropp... | Profile: Default

• **Figure 13.13**   Wireshark—a popular, open source protocol analyzer

■ Honeypots and Honeynets

As is often the case, one of the best tools for information security personnel has always been knowledge. To secure and defend a network and the information systems on that network properly, security personnel need to know what they are up against. What types of attacks are being used? What tools and techniques are popular at the moment? How effective is a certain technique? What sort of impact will this tool have on my network? Often this sort of information is passed through white papers, conferences, mailing lists, or even word of mouth. In some cases, the tool developers themselves provide much of the information in the interest of promoting better security for everyone.

Information is also gathered through examination and forensic analysis, often after a major incident has already occurred and information systems are already damaged. One of the most effective techniques for collecting this type of information is to observe activity first-hand—watching an attacker as he probes, navigates, and exploits his way through a network. To accomplish this without exposing critical information systems, security researchers often use something called a honeypot.

A **honeypot**, sometimes called a **digital sandbox**, is an artificial environment where attackers can be contained and observed without putting real systems at risk. A good honeypot appears to an attacker to be a real network consisting of application servers, user systems, network traffic, and so on, but in most cases it's actually made up of one or a few systems running specialized software to simulate the user and network traffic common to most targeted networks. Figure 13.14 illustrates a simple honeypot layout in which a single system is placed on the network to deliberately attract attention from potential attackers.

Figure 13.14 shows the security researcher's view of the honeypot, while Figure 13.15 shows the attacker's view. The security administrator knows that the honeypot, in this case, actually consists of a single system running software designed to react to probes, reconnaissance attempts, and exploits as if it were an entire network of systems. When the attacker connects to the honeypot, she is presented with an entire "virtual" network of servers and PCs running a variety of applications. In most cases, the honeypot will appear to be running versions of applications that are known to be vulnerable to specific exploits. All this is designed to provide the attacker with an enticing, hopefully irresistible, target.

Any time an attacker has been lured into probing or attacking the virtual network, the honeypot records the activity for later analysis: what the attacker does, which systems and applications she concentrates on, what tools are run, how long the attacker stays, and so on. All this information is collected and analyzed in the hopes that it will allow security personnel to better understand and protect against the threats to their systems.

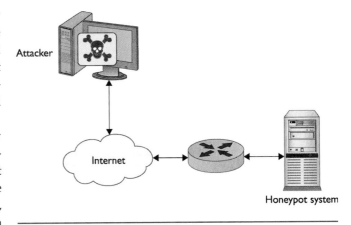

• **Figure 13.14**   Logical depiction of a honeypot

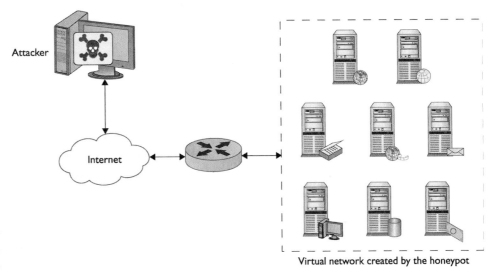

• **Figure 13.15**   Virtual network created by the honeypot

There are many honeypots in use, specializing in everything from wireless to denial-of-service attacks; most are run by research, government, or law enforcement organizations. Why aren't more businesses running honeypots? Quite simply, the time and cost are prohibitive. Honeypots take a lot of time and effort to manage and maintain, and even more effort to sort, analyze, and classify the traffic the honeypot collects. Unless they are developing security tools, most companies focus their limited security efforts on preventing attacks, and in many cases, companies aren't even that concerned with detecting attacks as long as the attacks are blocked, are unsuccessful, and don't affect business operations. Even though honeypots can serve as a valuable resource by luring attackers away from production systems and allowing defenders to identify and thwart potential attackers before they cause any serious damage, the costs and efforts involved deter many companies from using honeypots.

A **honeynet** is a collection of two or more honeypots. Larger, very diverse network environments can deploy multiple honeypots (thus forming a honeynet) when a single honeypot device does not provide enough coverage. Honeynets are often integrated into an organization-wide IDS/IPS because the honeynet can provide relevant information about potential attackers.

Host-Based IDSs

The very first IDSs were host-based and designed to examine activity only on a specific host. A host-based IDS (HIDS) examines log files, audit trails, and network traffic coming into or leaving a specific host. HIDSs can operate in *real time*, looking for activity as it occurs, or in *batch mode*, looking for activity on a periodic basis. Host-based systems are typically self-contained, but many of the newer commercial products have been designed to report to and be managed by a central system. Host-based systems also take local system resources to operate. In other words, a HIDS will use up some of the memory and CPU cycles of the system it is protecting. Early versions of HIDSs ran in batch mode, looking for suspicious activity on an hourly or daily basis, and typically looked only for specific events in the system's log files. As processor speeds increased, later versions of HIDSs looked through the log files in real time and even added the ability to examine the data traffic the host was generating and receiving.

Most HIDSs focus on the log files or audit trails generated by the local operating system. On UNIX systems, the examined logs usually include those created by syslog, such as messages, kernel logs, and error logs. On Windows systems, the examined logs are typically the three event logs: Application, System, and Security. Some HIDSs can cover specific applications, such as FTP or web services, by examining the logs produced by those specific applications or examining the traffic from the services themselves. Within the log files, the HIDS is looking for certain activities that typify hostile actions or misuse, such as the following:

- Logins at odd hours
- Login authentication failures
- Additions of new user accounts
- Modification or access of critical system files
- Modification or removal of binary files (executables)
- Starting or stopping processes
- Privilege escalation
- Use of certain programs

In general, most HIDSs operate in a very similar fashion. (Figure 13.16 shows the logical layout of a HIDS.) By considering the function and activity of each component, you can gain some insight into how HIDSs operate.

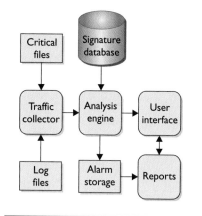

• **Figure 13.16** Host-based IDS components

As on any IDS, the *traffic collector* on a HIDS pulls in the information the other components, such as the analysis engine, need to examine. For most HIDSs, the traffic collector pulls data from information the local system has already generated, such as error messages, log files, and system files. The traffic collector is responsible for reading those files, selecting which items are of interest, and forwarding them to the analysis engine. On some HIDSs, the traffic collector also examines specific attributes of critical files, such as file size, date modified, or checksum.

The *analysis engine* is perhaps the most important component of the HIDS, as it must decide what activity is "okay" and what activity is "bad." The analysis engine is a sophisticated decision and pattern-matching

 Critical files are those that are vital to the system's operation or overall functionality. They may be program (or binary) files, files containing user accounts and passwords, or even scripts to start or stop system processes. Any unexpected modifications to these files could mean the system has been compromised or modified by an attacker. By monitoring these files, the HIDS can warn users of potentially malicious activity.

Tech Tip

Decision Trees

In computer systems, a tree *is a data structure, each element of which is attached to one or more structures directly beneath it (the connections are called* branches*). Structures on the end of a branch without any elements below them are called* leaves*. Trees are most often drawn inverted, with the root at the top and all subsequent elements branching down from the root. Trees in which each element has no more than two elements below it are called* binary trees*.*

In IDSs, a decision tree *is used to help the analysis engine quickly examine traffic patterns. The decision tree helps the analysis engine eliminate signatures that don't apply to the particular traffic or activity being examined, so that the fewest number of comparisons need to be made. For example, as shown in this illustration, the decision tree may contain a section that divides the activity into one of three subsections based upon the origin of the activity (a log entry for an event taken from the system logs, a file change for a modification to a critical file, or a user action for something a user has done):*

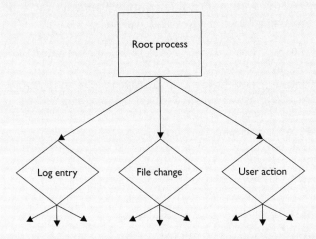

When the analysis engine looks at the activity pattern and starts down the decision tree, it must decide which path to follow. If it is a log entry, the analysis engine can then concentrate on only the signatures that apply to log entries and it does not need to worry about signatures that apply to file changes or user actions. This type of decision tree allows the analysis engine to function much faster, as it does not have to compare activities to every signature in the database, just the signatures that apply to that particular type of activity. It is important to note that HIDSs can look at both activities occurring on the host itself and the network traffic coming into or leaving the host.

---

mechanism—it looks at the information provided by the traffic collector and tries to match it against known patterns of activity stored in the signature database. If the activity matches a known pattern, the analysis engine can react, usually by issuing an alert or alarm. An analysis engine may also be capable of remembering how the activity it is looking at right now compares to traffic it has already seen or may see in the near future, so that it can match more complicated, multistep malicious activity patterns. An analysis engine must also be capable of examining traffic patterns as quickly as possible, as the longer it takes to match a malicious pattern, the less time the HIDS or human operator has to react to malicious traffic. Most HIDS vendors build a decision tree into their analysis engines to expedite pattern matching.

The *signature database* is a collection of predefined activity patterns that have already been identified and categorized—patterns that typically indicate suspicious or malicious activity. When the analysis engine has an activity or traffic pattern to examine, it compares that pattern to the appropriate signatures in the database. The signature database can contain anywhere from a few to a few thousand signatures, depending on the vendor, type of HIDS, space available on the system to store signatures, and other factors.

The user interface is the visible component of the HIDS—the part that humans interact with. The user interface varies widely depending on the product and vendor and could be anything from a detailed GUI to a simple command line. Regardless of the type and complexity, the interface is provided to allow the user to interact with the system: changing parameters, receiving alarms, tuning signatures and response patterns, and so on.

To better understand how a HIDS operates, take a look at the following examples from a UNIX system and a Windows system.

On a UNIX system, the HIDS is likely going to examine any of a number of system logs—basically, large text files containing entries about what is happening on the system. For this example, consider the following lines from the "messages" log on a Red Hat system:

```
Jan 5 18:20:39 jeep su(pam_unix)[32478]: session opened for
    user bob by (uid=0)
Jan 5 18:20:47 jeep su(pam_unix)[32516]: authentication
    failure; logname= uid=502 euid=0 tty= ruser=bob rhost=
    user=root
Jan 5 18:20:53 jeep su(pam_unix)[32517]: authentication
    failure; logname= id=502 euid=0 tty= ruser=bob
    rhost= user=root
Jan 5 18:21:06 jeep su(pam_unix)[32519]: authentication
    failure; logname= uid=502 euid=0 tty= ruser=bob
    rhost= user=root
```

In the first line beginning Jan 5, you see a session being opened by a user named *bob*. This usually indicates that whoever owns the account bob has logged into the system. On the next three lines beginning Jan 5, you see authentication failures as bob tries to become *root*—the superuser account that can do anything on the system. In this case, user bob tries three times to become root and fails on each try. This pattern of activity could mean a number of different things—bob could be an admin who has forgotten the password for the root account, bob could be an admin and someone changed the root password without telling him, bob could be a user attempting to guess the root password, or an attacker could have compromised bob's account and is now trying to compromise the root account on the system. In any case, our HIDS will work through its decision tree to determine whether an authentication failure in the message log is something it needs to examine. In this instance, when the HIDS examines these lines in the log, it will note the fact that three of the lines in the log match one of the patterns it has been told to look for (as determined by information from the decision tree and the signature database), and it will react accordingly, usually by generating an alarm or alert of some type that appears on the user interface or in an e-mail, page, or other form of message.

On a Windows system, the HIDS will likely examine the logs generated by the operating system. The three logs (Application, System, and Security) are similar to the logs on a UNIX system, though the Windows logs are not stored as text files and typically require a utility or application to read them. This example uses the security log from a Windows Vista system:

```
Audit Failure  5/2/2009  6:47:29 PM  Microsoft-Windows-
    Security-Auditing Logon 529
Audit Failure  5/2/2009  6:47:54 PM  Microsoft-Windows-
    Security-Auditing Logon 542
Audit Failure  5/2/2009  6:48:22 PM  Microsoft-Windows-
    Security-Auditing Logon 578
Audit Success  5/2/2009  6:49:14 PM  Microsoft-Windows-
    Security-Auditing Logon 601
```

In the first three main lines of the Security log, you see an **Audit Failure** entry for the **Logon** process. This indicates someone has tried to log into the system three times and has failed each time (much like our UNIX example) and then succeeded on the fourth try. You won't see the name of the account until you expand the log entry within the Windows Event Viewer tool, but for this example, assume it was the administrator account—the Windows equivalent of the root account. Here again, you see three login failures—if the HIDS has been programmed to look for failed login attempts, it will generate alerts when it examines these log entries.

Advantages of HIDSs

HIDSs have certain advantages that make them a good choice for certain situations:

- *They can be very operating system–specific and have more detailed signatures.* A HIDS can be very specifically designed to run on a certain operating system or to protect certain applications. This narrow focus lets developers concentrate on the specific things that affect the specific environment they are trying to protect. With this type of focus, the developers can avoid generic alarms and develop much more specific, detailed signatures to identify malicious traffic more accurately.

- *They can reduce false-positive rates.* When running on a specific system, the HIDS process is much more likely to be able to determine whether or not the activity being examined is malicious. By more accurately identifying which activity is "bad," the HIDS will generate fewer false positives (alarms generated when the traffic matches a pattern but is not actually malicious).

- *They can examine data after it has been decrypted.* With security concerns constantly on the rise, many developers are starting to encrypt their network communications. When designed and implemented in the right manner, a HIDS will be able to examine traffic that is unreadable to a network-based IDS. This particular ability is becoming more important each day as more and more web sites start to encrypt all of their traffic.

- *They can be very application specific.* On a host level, the IDS can be designed, modified, or tuned to work very well on specific applications without having to analyze or even hold signatures for other applications that are not running on that particular system. Signatures can be built for specific versions of web server software, FTP servers, mail servers, or any other application housed on that host.

- *They can determine whether or not an alarm may impact that specific system.* The ability to determine whether or not a particular activity or pattern will really affect the system being protected assists greatly in reducing the number of generated alarms. Because the HIDS resides on the system, it can verify things such as patch levels, presence of certain files, and system state when it analyzes traffic. By knowing what state the system is in, the HIDS can more accurately determine whether an activity is potentially harmful to the system.

Disadvantages of HIDSs

HIDSs also have certain disadvantages that must be weighed in making the decision of whether to deploy this type of technology:

- *The HIDS must have a process on every system you want to watch.* You must have a HIDS process or application installed on every host you want to watch. To watch 100 systems, then, you would need to deploy 100 HIDSs.

- *The HIDS can have a high cost of ownership and maintenance.* Depending on the specific vendor and application, a HIDS can be fairly costly in terms of time and manpower to maintain. Unless some type of central console is used that allows you to maintain remote processes, administrators must maintain each HIDS process individually. Even with a central console, with a HIDS, there will be a high number of processes to maintain, software to update, and parameters to tune.

- *The HIDS uses local system resources.* To function, the HIDS must use CPU cycles and memory from the system it is trying to protect. Whatever resources the HIDS uses are no longer available for the system to perform its other functions. This becomes extremely important on applications such as high-volume web servers, where fewer resources usually means fewer visitors served and the need for more systems to handle expected traffic.

- *The HIDS has a very focused view and cannot relate to activity around it.* The HIDS has a limited view of the world, as it can see activity only on the host it is protecting. It has little to no visibility into traffic around it on the network or events taking place on other hosts. Consequently, a HIDS can tell you only if the system it is running on is under attack.

- *The HIDS, if logged locally, could be compromised or disabled.* When an HIDS generates alarms, it typically stores the alarm information in a file or database of some sort. If the HIDS stores its generated alarm traffic on the local system, an attacker that is successful in breaking into the system may be able to modify or delete those alarms. This makes it difficult for security personnel to discover the intruder and conduct any type of post-incident investigation. A capable intruder may even be able to turn off the HIDS process completely.

A security best practice is to store or make a copy of log information, especially security-related log information, on a separate system. When a system is compromised, the attacker typically hides their tracks by clearing out any log files on the compromised system. If the log files are only stored locally on the compromised system, you'll know an attacker was present (due to the empty log files) but you won't know what they did or when they did it.

Active vs. Passive HIDSs

Most IDSs can be distinguished by how they examine the activity around them and whether or not they interact with that activity. This is certainly true for HIDSs. On a *passive* system, the HIDS is exactly that—it simply watches the activity, analyzes it, and generates alarms. It does not interact with the activity itself in any way, and it does not modify the defensive posture of the system to react to the traffic. A passive HIDS is similar to a simple motion sensor—it generates an alarm when it matches a pattern, much as the motion sensor generates an alarm when it sees movement.

An *active* IDS will contain all the same components and capabilities of the passive IDS with one critical exception—the active IDS can *react* to the activity it is analyzing. These reactions can range from something simple, such as running a script to turn a process on or off, to something as complex as modifying file permissions, terminating the offending processes, logging off specific users, and reconfiguring local capabilities to prevent specific users from logging in for the next 12 hours.

Resurgence and Advancement of HIDSs

The past few years have seen a strong resurgence in the use of HIDSs. With the great advances in processor power, the introduction of multicore processors, and the increased capacity of hard drives and memory systems, some of the traditional barriers to running a HIDS have been overcome. Combine those advances in technology with the widespread adoption of always-on broadband connections, the rise in the use of telecommuting, and a greater overall awareness of the need for computer security, and solutions such as HIDS start to become an attractive and sometimes effective solution for business and home users alike.

The latest generation of HIDSs has introduced new capabilities designed to stop attacks by preventing them from ever executing or accessing protected files in the first place, rather than relying on a specific signature set that only matches known attacks. The more advanced host-based offerings, which most vendors refer to as host-based intrusion prevention systems (HIPS), combine the following elements into a single package:

- **Integrated system firewall** The firewall component checks all network traffic passing into and out of the host. Users can set rules for what types of traffic they want to allow into or out of their system.

- **Behavioral- and signature-based IDS** This hybrid approach uses signatures to match well-known attacks and generic patterns for catching "zero-day" or unknown attacks for which no signatures exist.

- **Application control**   This allows administrators to control how applications are used on the system and whether or not new applications can be installed. Controlling the addition, deletion, or modification of existing software can be a good way to control a system's baseline and prevent malware from being installed.

- **Enterprise management**   Some host-based products are installed with an "agent" that allows them to be managed by and report back to a central server. This type of integrated remote management capability is essential in any large-scale deployment of host-based IDS/IPS.

- **Malware detection and prevention**   Some HIDSs/HIPSs include scanning and prevention capabilities that address spyware, malware, rootkits, and other malicious software.

PC-Based Malware Protection

In the early days of PC use, threats were limited: most home users were not connected to the Internet 24/7 through broadband connections, and the most common threat was a virus passed from computer to computer via an infected floppy disk. But things have changed dramatically over the last decade and current threats pose a much greater risk than ever before. According to SANS Internet Storm Center, the average survival time of an unpatched Windows PC on the Internet is less than two hours (http://isc.sans.org/survivaltime.html). This is the estimated time before an automated probe finds the system, penetrates it, and compromises it. Automated probes from botnets and worms are not the only threats roaming the Internet—viruses and malware spread by e-mail, phishing, infected web sites that execute code on your system when you visit them, adware, spyware, and so on. Fortunately, as the threats increase in complexity and capability, so do the products designed to stop them.

Antivirus Products

Antivirus products attempt to identify, neutralize, or remove malicious programs, macros, and files. These products were initially designed to detect and remove computer viruses, though many of the antivirus products are now bundled with additional security products and features. At the present time, there is no real consensus regarding the first antivirus product. The first edition of Polish antivirus software *mks_vir* was released in 1987, and the first publicly known neutralization of a PC virus was performed by European Bernt Fix (also known as Bernd) early in the same year. By 1990, software giants McAfee and Norton both had established commercial antivirus products.

Although antivirus products have had nearly two decades to refine their capabilities, the purpose of the antivirus products remains the same: to detect and eliminate computer viruses and malware. Most antivirus products combine the following approaches when scanning for viruses:

- **Signature-based scanning** Much like an IDS, the antivirus products scan programs, files, macros, e-mails, and other data for known worms, viruses, and malware. The antivirus product contains a virus dictionary with thousands of known virus signatures that must be frequently updated, as new viruses are discovered daily. This approach will catch known viruses but is limited by the virus dictionary—what it does not know about it cannot catch.

- **Heuristic scanning (or analysis)** Heuristic scanning does not rely on a virus dictionary. Instead, it looks for suspicious behavior—anything that does not fit into a "normal" pattern of behavior for the operating system and applications running on the system being protected.

As signature-based scanning is a familiar concept, let's examine heuristic scanning in more detail. **Heuristic scanning** typically looks for commands or instructions that are not normally found in application programs, such as attempts to access a reserved memory register. Most antivirus products use either a weight-based or rule-based system in their heuristic scanning (more effective products use a combination of both techniques). A weight-based system rates every suspicious behavior based on the degree of threat associated with that behavior. If the set threshold is passed based on a single behavior or combination of behaviors, the antivirus product will treat the process, application, macro, and so on, performing those behaviors as a threat to the system. A rules-based system compares activity to a set of rules meant to detect and identify malicious software. If part of the software matches a rule or a process, application, macro, and so on, and performs a behavior that matches a rule, the antivirus software will treat that as a threat to the local system.

Some heuristic products are very advanced and contain capabilities for examining memory usage and addressing, a parser for examining executable code, a logic flow analyzer, and a disassembler/emulator so they can "guess" what the code is designed to do and whether or not it is malicious.

As with IDS/IPS products, encryption poses a problem for antivirus products: anything that cannot be read cannot be matched against current virus dictionaries or activity patterns. To combat the use of encryption in malware and viruses, many heuristic scanners look for encryption and decryption loops. As malware is usually designed to run alone and unattended, if it uses encryption, it must contain all the instructions to encrypt and decrypt itself as needed. Heuristic scanners look for instructions such as the initialization of a pointer with a valid memory address, manipulation of a counter, or a branch condition based on a counter value. While these actions don't always indicate the presence of an encryption/decryption loop, if the heuristic engine can find a loop, it might be able to decrypt the software in a protected memory space, such as an emulator, and evaluate the software in more detail. Many viruses share common encryption/decryption routines, which helps antivirus developers.

Exam Tip: Heuristic scanning is a method of detecting potentially malicious or "virus-like" behavior by examining what a program or section of code does. Anything that is "suspicious" or potentially "malicious" is closely examined to determine whether or not it is a threat to the system. Using heuristic scanning, an antivirus product attempts to identify new viruses or heavily modified versions of existing viruses before they can damage your system.

Current antivirus products are highly configurable, and most offerings have the following capabilities:

- **Automated updates** Perhaps the most important feature of a good antivirus solution is its ability to keep itself up to date by automatically downloading the latest virus signatures on a frequent basis. This usually requires that the system be connected to the Internet in some fashion and perform updates on a daily (or more frequent) basis.

- **Automated scanning** Most antivirus products allow for the scheduling of automated scans, enabling the antivirus product to routinely examine the local system for infected files. These automated scans can typically be scheduled for specific days and times, and the scanning parameters can be configured to specify what drives, directories, and types of files are scanned.

- **Media scanning** Removable media is still a common method for virus and malware propagation, and most antivirus products can be configured to automatically scan CDs, USB drives, memory sticks, or any other types of removable media as soon as they are connected to or accessed by the local system.

- **Manual scanning** Many antivirus products allow the user to scan drives, files, or directories "on demand."

- **E-mail scanning** E-mail is still a major method of virus and malware propagation. Many antivirus products give users the ability to scan both incoming and outgoing messages as well as any attachments.

- **Resolution** When the antivirus product detects an infected file or application, it can typically perform one of several actions. The antivirus product may quarantine the file, making it inaccessible; it may try and repair the file by removing the infection or offending code; or it may delete the infected file. Most antivirus products allow the user to specify the desired action, and some allow for an escalation in actions, such as cleaning the infected file if possible or quarantining the file if it cannot be cleaned.

Antivirus solutions are typically installed on individual systems (desktops and servers), but network-based antivirus capabilities are also available in many commercial gateway products. These gateway products often combine firewall, IDS/IPS, and antivirus capabilities into a single integrated platform. Most organizations also employ antivirus solutions on e-mail servers, as e-mail continues to be a very popular propagation method for viruses.

While the installation of a good antivirus product is still considered a necessary best practice, there is growing concern about the effectiveness of antivirus products against developing threats. Early viruses often exhibited destructive behaviors; were poorly written, modified files; and were less concerned with hiding their presence than they were with propagation. We are seeing an emergence of viruses and malware created by professionals, sometimes financed by criminal organizations, that go to great lengths to hide their presence. These viruses and malware are often used to steal sensitive information or turn the infected PC into part of a larger botnet for use in spamming or attack operations.

Personal Software Firewalls

Personal firewalls are host-based protective mechanisms that monitor and control traffic passing into and out of a single system. Designed for the end user, software firewalls often have a configurable security policy that allows the user to determine what traffic is "good" and allowed to pass and what traffic is "bad" and is blocked. Software firewalls are extremely commonplace—so much so that most modern operating systems come with some type of personal firewall included.

For example, with the introduction of the Windows XP Professional operating system, Microsoft included a utility called Internet Connection Firewall (ICF). Though disabled by default and hidden in the network configuration screens where most users would never find it, ICF did give users some direct control over the network traffic passing through their systems. When Service Pack 2 was launched, Microsoft renamed ICF to Windows Firewall (see Figure 13.17) and enabled it by default (Vista also enables Windows Firewall by default). Windows Firewall is fairly configurable; it can be set up to block all traffic, make exceptions for traffic you want to allow, and log rejected traffic for later analysis.

With the introduction of the Vista operating system, Microsoft modified Windows Firewall to make it more capable and configurable. More options were added to allow for more granular control of network traffic as well as the ability to detect when certain components are not behaving as expected. For example, if your MS Outlook client suddenly attempts to connect to a remote web server, Windows Firewall can detect this as a deviation from normal behavior and block the unwanted traffic.

• **Figure 13.17** Windows Firewall is enabled by default in XP SP2 and Vista.

UNIX-based operating systems have had built-in software-based firewalls (see Figure 13.18) for a number of years, including TCP Wrappers, ipchains, and iptables.

TCP Wrappers is a simple program that limits inbound network connections based on port number, domain, or IP address and is managed with two text files called hosts.allow and hosts.deny. If the inbound connection is coming from a trusted IP address and destined for a port to which it is allowed to connect, then the connection is allowed.

Ipchains is a more-advanced, rule-based software firewall that allows for traffic filtering, Network Address Translation (NAT), and redirection. Three configurable "chains" are used for handling network traffic: input, output, and forward. The input chain contains rules for traffic that is coming into the local system. The output chain contains rules for traffic that is leaving the local system. The forward chain contains rules for traffic that was received by the local system but is not destined for the local system.

● Figure 13.18   UNIX firewall

Iptables is the latest evolution of ipchains and is designed to work with Linux kernels 2.4 and 2.6. Iptables uses the same three chains for policy rules and traffic handling as ipchains, but with iptables each packet is processed only by the appropriate chain. Under ipchains, each packet passes through all three chains for processing. With iptables, incoming packets are processed only by the input chain, and packets leaving the system are processed only by the output chain. This allows for more granular control of network traffic and enhances performance.

In addition to the "free" firewalls that come bundled with operating systems, many commercial personal firewall packages are available. Programs such as ZoneAlarm from Check Point Software provide additional capabilities not found in some bundled software firewalls. Many commercial software firewalls limit inbound and outbound network traffic, block pop-ups, detect adware, block cookies, block malicious processes, and scan instant messenger traffic. While you can still purchase or even download a free software-based personal firewall, most commercial vendors are bundling the firewall functionality with additional capabilities such as antivirus and antispyware.

Pop-up Blockers

One of the most annoying nuisances associated with web browsing is the pop-up ad. Pop-up ads are online advertisements designed to attract web traffic to specific web sites, capture e-mail addresses, advertise a product, and perform other tasks. If you've spent more than an hour surfing the Web, you've undoubtedly seen them. They're created when the web site you are visiting opens a new web browser window for the sole purpose of displaying an advertisement. Pop-up ads typically appear in front of your current browser window to catch your attention (and disrupt your browsing). Pop-up ads can range from mildly annoying, generating one or two pop-ups, to system crippling if a malicious web site attempts to open thousands of pop-up windows on your system.

Similar to the pop-up ad is the pop-under ad that opens up behind your current browser window. You won't see these ads until your current window is closed, and they are considered by some to be less annoying than pop-ups. Another form of pop-up is the hover ad that uses Dynamic HTML to appear as a floating window superimposed over your browser window. Dynamic HTML can be very CPU-intensive and can have a significant impact on the performance of older systems.

To some users, pop-up ads are as undesirable as spam, and many web browsers now allow users to restrict or prevent pop-ups with functionality called a **pop-up blocker** that is either built into the web browser or available as an add-on. Internet Explorer contains a built-in Pop-up Blocker (shown in Figure 13.19 and available from the Tools menu in Internet Explorer 7).

Firefox also contains a built-in pop-up blocker (available by choosing Tools | Options and then selecting the Content tab). Popular add-ons such as the Google and Yahoo! toolbars also contain pop-up blockers. If these freely available options are not enough for your needs, many commercial security suites from McAfee, Symantec, and Check Point contain pop-up blocking capabilities as well. Users must be careful when selecting a pop-up blocker, as some unscrupulous developers have created adware products disguised as free pop-up blockers or other security tools.

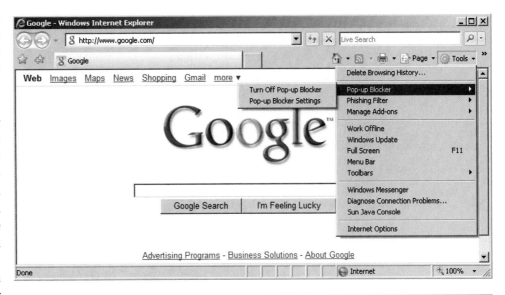

• **Figure 13.19**   Pop-up Blocker in IE 7

Pop-ups ads can be generated in a number of ways, including JavaScript and Adobe Flash, and an effective pop-up blocker must be able to deal with the many methods used to create pop-ups. When a pop-up is created, users typically can click a close or cancel button inside the pop-up or close the new window using a method available through the operating system, such as closing the window from the taskbar in Windows. With the advanced features available to them in a web development environment, some unscrupulous developers program the close or cancel buttons in their pop-ups to launch new pop-ups, redirect the user, run commands on the local system, or even load software.

Windows Defender

As part of its ongoing efforts to help secure its PC operating systems, Microsoft created and released a free utility called Windows Defender in February 2006. The stated purpose of Windows Defender is to protect your computer from spyware and other unwanted software (www.microsoft.com/athome/security/spyware/software/default.mspx). Windows Defender is standard with all versions of the Vista operating system and is available via free download for Windows XP Service Pack 2 or later in both 32- and 64-bit versions. It has the following capabilities:

- **Spyware detection and removal**   Windows Defender is designed to find and remove spyware and other unwanted programs that display pop-ups, modify browser or Internet settings, or steal personal information from your PC.

- **Scheduled scanning** You can schedule when you want your system to be scanned or you can run scans on demand.

- **Automatic updates** Updates to the product can be automatically downloaded and installed without user interaction.

- **Real-time protection** Processes are monitored in real time to stop spyware and malware when they first launch, attempt to install themselves, or attempt to access your PC.

- **Software Explorer** One of the more interesting capabilities within Windows Defender is the ability to examine the various programs running on your computer. Windows Defender allows you to look at programs that run automatically on startup, are currently running on your PC, or are accessing network connections on your PC. Windows Defender provides you with details such as the publisher of the software, when it was installed on your PC, whether or not the software is "good" or considered to be known malware, the file size, publication date, and other information.

- **Configurable responses** Windows Defender lets you choose what actions you want to take in response to detected threats (see Figure 13.20); you can automatically disable the software, quarantine it, attempt to uninstall it, and perform other tasks.

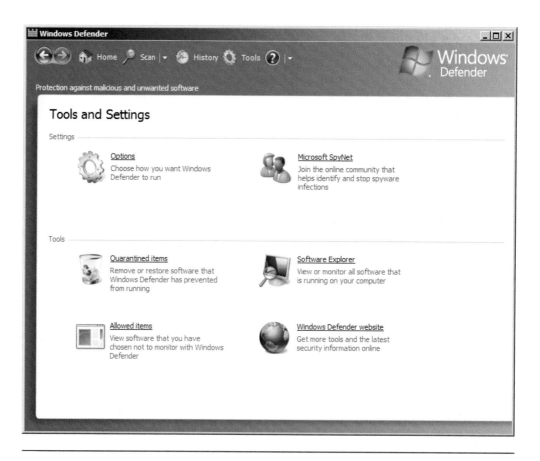

• **Figure 13.20**   Windows Defender configuration options

Antispam

If you have an e-mail account, you've likely received *spam*, that endless stream of unsolicited, electronic junk mail advertising get-rich-quick schemes, asking you to validate your bank account's password, or inviting you to visit one web site or another. Despite federal legislation (such as the CAN-SPAM Act of 2003) and promises from IT industry giants like Bill Gates ("Two years from now, spam will be solved"—2004), spam is alive and well and filling up your inbox as you read this. Industry experts have been fighting the spam battle for years, and while significant progress has been made in the development of antispam products, unfortunately, the spammers have proven to be very creative and very dedicated in their quest to fill your inbox.

Antispam products attempt to filter out that endless stream of junk e-mail so you don't have to. Some antispam products operate at the corporate level, filtering messages as they enter or leave designated mail servers. Other products operate at the host level, filtering messages as they come into your personal inbox. Most antispam products use similar techniques and approaches for filtering out spam:

 Spam is not a new problem. It's reported that the first spam message was sent on May 1, 1978 by a Digital Equipment Corporation sales representative. This sales representative attempted to send a message to all ARPANET users on the West Coast.

- **Blacklisting** Several organizations maintain lists of servers or domains that generate or have generated spam. Most gateway- or server-level products can reference these blacklists and automatically reject any mail coming from servers or domains on the blacklist.

- **Header filtering** The antispam products look at the message headers to see if they are forged. E-mail headers typically contain information such as sender, receiver, servers used to transmit the message, and so on. Spammers often forge information in message headers in an attempt to hide where the message is really coming from.

- **Content filtering** The content of the message is examined for certain key words or phrases that are common to spam but rarely seen in legitimate e-mails ("get rich now" for example). Unfortunately, content filtering does occasionally flag legitimate messages as spam.

- **Language filtering** Some spam products allow you to filter out e-mails written in certain languages.

- **User-defined filtering** Most antispam products allow end users to develop their own filters, such as always allowing e-mail from a specific source even if it would normally be blocked by a content filter.

- **Trapping** Some products will monitor unpublished e-mail addresses for incoming spam—anything sent to an unpublished and otherwise unused account is likely to be spam.

- **Enforcing the specifications of the protocol** Some spam-generation tools don't properly follow the SMTP protocol. By enforcing the technical requirements of SMTP, some spam can be rejected as delivery is attempted.

- **Egress filtering** This technique scans mail as it leaves an organization to catch spam before it is sent to other organizations.

Chapter 13 Review

■ For More Information

- **SANS' Intrusion Detection FAQ** www.sans.org/resources/idfaq/
- **SANS InfoSec Reading Room—Firewalls & Perimeter Protection** www.sans.org/reading_room/whitepapers/firewalls/
- **The Honeynet Project** www.honeynet.org/
- **Fight Spam on the Internet!** http://spam.abuse.net/

■ Chapter Summary

After reading this chapter and completing the exercises, you should understand the following facts about intrusion detection systems and network security.

Apply the appropriate network tools to facilitate network security

- Intrusion detection is a mechanism for detecting unexpected or unauthorized activity on computer systems.
- IDSs can be host-based, examining only the activity applicable to a specific system, or network-based, examining network traffic for a large number of systems.
- Firewalls are security devices that protect an organization's network perimeter by filtering traffic coming into the organization based on an established policy.
- Antivirus technologies scan network traffic, e-mail, files, and removable media for malicious code.
- Proxies service client requests by forwarding requests from users to other servers.
- Proxies can be used to help filter and manage network traffic, particularly web browsing.
- Protocol analyzers, often called sniffers, are tools that capture and decode network traffic.
- Honeypots are specialized forms of intrusion detection that involve setting up simulated hosts and services for attackers to target.
- Honeypots are based on the concept of luring attackers away from legitimate systems by presenting more tempting or interesting systems that, in most cases, appear to be easy targets.

- Antispam products help organizations filter out unsolicited commercial email.

Determine the appropriate use of tools to facilitate network security

- IDSs match patterns known as signatures that can be content- or context-based. Some IDSs are model-based and alert an administrator when activity does not match normal patterns (anomaly based) or when it matches known suspicious or malicious patterns (misuse detection).
- Newer versions of IDSs include prevention capabilities that automatically block suspicious or malicious traffic before it reaches its intended destination. Most vendors call these intrusion prevention systems (IPSs).
- Firewalls can be simple packet-filtering devices or can have more-advanced, application layer–filtering capabilities.
- Antivirus solutions are available in software and appliance form and provide a necessary line of defense against the massive amount of malicious code roaming the Internet.
- Proxies are often combined with a content-filtering capability that administrators can use to block access to malicious or inappropriate content.
- Many organizations and users also employ pop-up blockers, mechanisms that prevent the annoying ads that appear in new browser windows as you visit certain web pages.
- Analyzers must be able to see and capture network traffic to be effective, and many switch vendors support network analysis through the use of mirroring or SPAN ports.

- Network traffic can also be viewed using network taps, a device for replicating network traffic passing across a physical link.
- By monitoring activity within the honeypot, security personnel are better able to identify potential attackers along with their tools and capabilities.
- Antispam tools use a variety of techniques, including blacklisting, content filtering, user-defined rules, header filtering, trapping, and protocol enforcement.

Apply host-based security applications

- IDSs can be host-based, examining only the activity applicable to a specific system, or network-based, examining network traffic for a large number of systems.
- Personal software firewalls are software packages that help protect individual systems by controlling network traffic coming into and out of that individual system.
- Antivirus technologies scan network traffic, e-mail, files, and removable media for malicious code.
- Proxies service client requests by forwarding requests from users to other servers.
- Antispam products help organizations filter out unsolicited commercial email.

■ Key Terms

access control lists (ACLs) *(331)*	**intrusion detection system (IDS)** *(318)*
analysis engine *(321)*	**intrusion prevention system (IPS)** *(333)*
anomaly detection model *(329)*	**misuse detection model** *(329)*
antispam *(353)*	**Network Address Translation (NAT)** *(331)*
antivirus *(346)*	**network tap** *(337)*
content-based signature *(327)*	**network-based IDS (NIDS)** *(320)*
context-based signature *(327)*	**perimeter security** *(322)*
digital sandbox *(338)*	**pop-up blocker** *(351)*
false negative *(328)*	**port mirroring** *(337)*
false positive *(328)*	**protocol analyzer** *(336)*
firewall *(329)*	**proxy server** *(334)*
heuristic scanning *(347)*	**signature database** *(321)*
honeynet *(340)*	**Switched Port Analyzer (SPAN)** *(337)*
honeypot *(338)*	**traffic collector** *(321)*
host-based IDS (HIDS) *(320)*	**user interface** *(321)*
Internet content filter *(336)*	

■ Key Terms Quiz

Use terms from the Key Terms list to complete the sentences that follow. Don't use the same term more than once. Not all terms will be used.

1. A(n) _____ is a piece of software or an integrated software/hardware system that can capture and decode network traffic.

2. When an IDS generates an alarm on "normal" traffic that is actually not malicious or suspicious, that alarm is called a(n) _____.

3. An attacker scanning a network full of inviting, seemingly vulnerable targets might actually be scanning a(n) _____ where the attacker's every move can be watched and monitored by security administrators.

4. A(n) _____ looks at a certain string of characters inside a TCP packet.

5. An IDS that looks for unusual or unexpected behavior is using a(n) _____.

6. _____ allows administrators to send all traffic passing through a network switch to a specific port on the switch.

7. Within an IDS, the _____ examines the collected network traffic and compares it to known patterns of suspicious or malicious activity stored in the signature database.

8. _____ allows an outside system to communicate with a system inside a firewall

without truly knowing the internal system's IP address.

9. _____ are designed to match large patterns of activity and examine how certain types of activity fit into the other activities going on around them.

10. A(n) _____ can be used to filter out undesirable traffic and prevent employees from accessing potentially hostile web sites.

■ Multiple-Choice Quiz

1. What are the three types of event logs generated by Windows 2003 and Vista systems?
   A. Event, Process, and Security
   B. Application, User, and Security
   C. User, Event, and Security
   D. Application, System, and Security

2. What are the two main types of intrusion detection systems?
   A. Network-based and host-based
   B. Signature-based and event-based
   C. Active and reactive
   D. Intelligent and passive

3. What was the first commercial, network-based IDS product?
   A. Stalker
   B. NetRanger
   C. IDES
   D. RealSecure

4. What are the two main types of IDS signatures?
   A. Network-based and file-based
   B. Context-based and content-based
   C. Active and reactive
   D. None of the above

5. Which of the following describes a passive, host-based IDS?
   A. Runs on the local system
   B. Does not interact with the traffic around it
   C. Can look at system event and error logs
   D. All of the above

6. Which of the following is *not* a capability of network-based IDS?
   A. Can detect denial-of-service attacks
   B. Can decrypt and read encrypted traffic
   C. Can decode UDP and TCP packets
   D. Can be tuned to a particular network environment

7. An active IDS can:
   A. Respond to attacks with TCP resets
   B. Monitor for malicious activity
   C. A and B
   D. None of the above

8. Honeypots are used to:
   A. Attract attackers by simulating systems with open network services
   B. Monitor network usage by employees
   C. Process alarms from other IDSs
   D. Attract customers to e-commerce sites

9. Egress filtering is used to detect spam that is:
   A. Coming into an organization
   B. Sent from known spammers outside your organization
   C. Leaving an organization
   D. Sent to mailing lists in your organization

10. Preventative intrusion detection systems:
    A. Are cheaper
    B. Are designed to stop malicious activity from occurring
    C. Can only monitor activity
    D. Were the first types of IDS

11. Which of the following is not a type of proxy?

    A. Reverse

    B. Web

    C. Open

    D. Simultaneous

12. IPS stands for

    A. Intrusion processing system

    B. Intrusion prevention sensor

    C. Intrusion prevention system

    D. Interactive protection system

13. A protocol analyzer can be used to:

    A. Troubleshoot network problems

    B. Collect network traffic statistics

    C. Monitor for suspicious traffic

    D. All of the above

14. Windows Defender is available with every version of the Windows operating system.

    A. True

    B. False

15. Heuristic scanning looks for:

    A. Normal network traffic patterns

    B. Viruses and spam only

    C. Firewall policy violations

    D. Commands or instructions that are not normally found in application programs

■ Essay Quiz

1. Discuss the differences between an anomaly-based and a misuse-based detection model. Which would you use to protect a corporate network of 10,000 users? Why would you choose that model?

2. Define the term heuristic scanning. Discuss how heuristic scanning is used within antivirus products.

3. Pick three technologies discussed in this chapter and describe how you would deploy them to protect a small business network. Describe the protection each technology provides.

Lab Projects

• Lab Project 13.1

Design three content-based and three context-based signatures for use in an IDS. Name each signature and describe what the signature should look for, including traffic patterns or characters that need to be matched. Describe any activity that could generate a false positive for each signature.

• Lab Project 13.2

Use the Internet to research Snort (an open source IDS). With your instructor's permission, download Snort and install it on your classroom network. Examine the traffic and note any alarms that are generated. Research and note the sources of the alarm traffic. See if you can track down the sources of the alarm traffic and discover why they are generating those alarms on your IDS.

• Lab Project 13.3

Research host-based firewalls, including iptables and Windows Firewall. Pick one and install it on your lab system with your instructor's permission. Turn off the firewall and ask your instructor to scan your system using a port scanner. Note what open ports the scanner found. Now turn on the firewall and configure it to block all incoming connections. Ask your instructor to scan your system again. Note what open ports the scanner found. Compare the results from the first and second scan and discuss why the results are different.

Baselines

chapter

14

People can have the Model T in any color—so long as it's black.

—Henry Ford

In this chapter, you will learn how to

- Harden operating systems and network operating systems
- Harden applications
- Establish group policies

Computers are such an integral part of everything we do today that it is difficult to imagine life without them. Operating systems, network devices, and applications all work together on millions of computers to process, transmit, and store the billions of pieces of information exchanged every day. Everything from cars to credit cards require computers to operate.

The many uses for systems and operating systems require flexible components that allow users to design, configure, and implement the systems they need. Yet it is this very flexibility that causes some of the biggest weaknesses in computer systems. Computer and operating system developers often build and deliver systems in "default" modes that do little to secure the system from external attacks. From the view of the developer, this is the most efficient mode of delivery, as there is no way they could anticipate what every user in every situation will need. Even if developers could anticipate every user's needs and their individual security requirements, the amount of effort required to meet every user's needs directly would be time and cost prohibitive. From the user's view, however, this means a good deal of effort must be put into protecting and securing the system before it is ever placed into service. The process of securing and preparing a system for the production environment is called **hardening**. Unfortunately, many users don't understand the steps necessary to secure their systems effectively, resulting in hundreds of compromised systems every day.

 Exam Tip: System hardening is the process of preparing and securing a system and involves the removal of all unnecessary software and network services.

Overview of Baselines

To secure systems effectively and consistently, you must take a structured and logical approach. This starts with an examination of the system's intended functions and capabilities to determine what processes and applications will be housed on the system. As a best practice, anything that is not required for operations should be removed or disabled on the system; then, all the appropriate patches, hotfixes, and settings should be applied to protect and secure it.

This process of establishing a system's security state is called **baselining**, and the resulting product is a security **baseline** that allows the system to run safely and securely. Once the process has been completed for a particular hardware and software combination, any similar systems can be configured with the same baseline to achieve the same level and depth of security and protection. Uniform baselines are critical in large-scale operations, because maintaining separate configurations and security levels for hundreds or thousands of systems is far too costly.

Password Selection

Password selection is one of those critical activities that is often neglected as part of a good security baseline. The heart of the problem is that most systems today are protected only by a simple user ID and password. If an attacker discovers the right user ID and password combination—either by hand or by using any of the numerous, freely available brute-force attack tools—they can access the system, and they have completely bypassed all the normal steps taken to secure the system. Worse still, on a server system supporting multiple users, the attacker only has to guess one correct user ID and password combination to gain access.

This basic security challenge exists for every topic we examine in this chapter, from operating systems to applications. Selecting a good password

Cross Check

Password Policies

Chapter 22 discusses password policies. It lists five major components that should be included in a password policy—what are those five major components?

for all user accounts is critical to protecting information systems. What makes a good password? One that is still relatively easy to remember but still difficult to guess? Unfortunately, no magic answer covers all situations, but if you follow some basic guidelines and principles in choosing passwords, you can ensure that the passwords used on your system will protect your assets.

■ Operating System and Network Operating System Hardening

IBM's OS/2 was the first 32-bit operating system for PCs and was widely available in 1992. Windows NT, Microsoft's first 32-bit operating system, wasn't released until 1993.

Tech Tip

The Term "Operating System"

The term "operating system" is the commonly accepted name for the software that provides the interface between computer hardware and the user and is responsible for the management, coordination, and sharing of limited computer resources such as memory and disk space.

The **operating system (OS)** of a computer is the basic software that handles things such as input, output, display, memory management, and all the other highly detailed tasks required to support the user environment and associated applications. Most users are familiar with the Microsoft family of desktop operating systems: Windows 95, Windows NT, Windows 98, Windows 2000, Windows Me, Windows XP, and Windows Vista. Indeed, the vast majority of home and business PCs run some version of a Microsoft operating system. Other users may be familiar with Mac OS, Solaris, or one of the many varieties of the UNIX operating system.

A **network operating system (NOS)** is an operating system that includes additional functions and capabilities to assist in connecting computers and devices, such as printers, to a local area network (LAN). Some of the more familiar network operating systems include Novell's NetWare and PC Micro's LANtastic. For most modern operating systems, including Windows 2008, Solaris, and Linux, the terms *operating system* and *network operating system* are used interchangeably as they perform all the basic functions and provide enhanced capabilities for connecting to LANs.

Operating system developers and manufacturers all share a common problem. There is no possible way they can anticipate the many different configurations and variations that the user community will require from their products. So, rather than spending countless hours and funds attempting to meet every need, manufacturers provide a "default" installation for their products that usually contains the base operating system and some more commonly desirable options, such as drivers, utilities, and enhancements. As the operating system could be used for any of a variety of purposes, and could be placed in any number of logical locations (local LAN, DMZ, WAN, and so on), the manufacturer typically does little to nothing with security. The manufacturer may provide some recommendations or simplified tools and settings to facilitate securing the system, but in general, the end users are responsible for securing their own systems. Generally this involves removing unnecessary applications and utilities, disabling unneeded services, setting appropriate permissions on files, and updating the operating system and application code to the latest version.

Principles of Computer Security: CompTIA Security+ and Beyond

This process of securing an operating system is called hardening, and it is intended to make the system more resistant to attack, much like armor or steel is hardened to make it less susceptible to breakage or damage. Each operating system has its own approach to security, and while the process of hardening is generally the same, different steps must be taken to secure each operating system.

Hardening Microsoft Operating Systems

For this book, Windows Vista, Server 2003, and Server 2008 are the focus of the discussion. Older Microsoft OSs, such as Windows 3.11, 95, 98, and Me, are no longer supported by Microsoft and won't be covered in this chapter.

Hardening Windows Server 2003

In response to the public outcry demanding better security in its products, Microsoft created the Trustworthy Computing Initiative (TCI) in 2002. To produce more secure products, Microsoft adopted a "secure by design, secure by default" motto to describe its approach to product development, attempted to re-educate its entire development staff, and started creating freely available security resources for administrators. The first OS to benefit from the TCI was Windows 2003 Server: fewer features were installed by default, administrators could pick and choose what functionality they needed on the server more easily, and Microsoft produced a series of hardening guides tailored to various server roles (domain controller, web server, DNS server, and so on). For example, Microsoft's *Windows Server 2003 Security Guide* provides specific recommendations on how to secure a Windows Server 2003 server in various operating environments. This guide, which is freely available for download from the Microsoft Download Center at www.microsoft.com/downloads/en/default.aspx (just search for *Windows Server 2003 Security Guide*), addresses the most common hardening/baselining tasks such as disabling unnecessary services, restricting permissions on files and directories, removing unnecessary software, applying patches, removing unnecessary users, and applying password guidelines.

In its own efforts to secure the Windows Server 2003 OS, Microsoft made some extensive modifications and added some new capabilities:

- *Internet Information Services (IIS) 6 gained the ability to isolate individual web applications into self-contained web service processes*. This prevents one application from disrupting all web services or other web applications running on the server. In addition, third-party application code runs in isolated worker processes within IIS, which by default use a lower-privileged Network Service logon account. This makes it possible to restrict a web site or application to its root directory through access control lists (ACLs).

- *By default, 19 services running under Windows 2000 were disabled in Windows Server 2003*. For example, IIS 6 must be installed by administrators; it is not part of the "default" installation, as it was in Windows 2000 Server.

- *Two new service accounts with lower privilege levels were introduced.* The Network Service account can be used to run IIS processes, and the Local Service account can be used to run a service such as Secure Shell (SSH). These lower-privilege accounts help isolate processes and prevent a compromise in one service from escalating into a system-level compromise.

- *The Security Configuration Wizard (SCW) was introduced with Service Pack 1.* This tool allows administrators to configure their servers with the minimal amount of functionality required. The SCW also allows administrators to run lockdown tests to ensure their security policies are achieving the desired effect.

- *The Software Restriction Policy (SRP) was introduced.* This tool gives administrators a policy-driven mechanism to identify software and control its ability to execute.

- *Enhanced audit capabilities were provided.* These allow auditing of specific users, enhanced logon/logoff auditing with IP address tracking, and operations-based auditing.

- *Network Access Quarantine Control was introduced.* This allows administrators to prevent computers from connecting to the network until their configuration has been reviewed and deemed "safe."

Try This

Examining File and Directory Permissions

Open a command prompt as either administrator or a user with administrator privileges on a PC running Windows Vista. Type the command **cd c:** and press ENTER (this should change your current directory to the C: drive on your system). Type the command **icacls Windows** and press ENTER. The **icacls** command can be used to display or set the discretionary access control lists on folders and files (for more information, search for "icacls" on Microsoft's TechNet site or visit http://technet .microsoft.com/en-us/library/cc753525(WS.10).aspx). What do the results of the **icacls Windows** command mean? Can you tell which accounts have Full Control permissions on the Windows folder?

Hardening Windows Vista

With the release of Windows Vista, Microsoft tried to make similar security improvements to its mainstream desktop OS as it did to its main server OS, Windows 2003. As a desktop OS, Vista is available in several different versions: Home Basic, Home Premium, Business, Enterprise, and Ultimate. While each of the "higher end" versions has exclusive functionality and capability, many of the security features in Vista are available to all versions of the desktop OS.

Here are some of the security capabilities introduced with Vista:

- *User Account Control allows users to operate the system without requiring administrative privileges.* If you've used Vista, you've undoubtedly seen the "Windows needs your permission to continue" pop-ups. While annoying to many users (one of Apple's "I'm a Mac" commercials focuses specifically on this feature), this feature does help prevent users from "accidentally" making changes to their system configuration. Figure 14.1 shows the User Account Control feature in Vista.

• **Figure 14.1**   Vista's User Account Control in action

- *An outbound filtering capability was added to Windows Firewall.* Vista allows filtering of traffic coming into and leaving the system, which is useful for controlling things like peer-to-peer applications.

- *BitLocker allows encryption of all data on a server, including any data volumes.* This capability is only available in Vista Enterprise and Vista Ultimate.

- *Vista clients work with Network Access Protection.* See the discussion of NAP in the following "Hardening Windows Server 2008" section for more details.

- *Windows Defender is a built-in malware detection and removal tool.* Windows Defender detects many types of potentially suspicious software and can prompt the user before allowing applications to make potentially malicious changes.

- *A new, more-secure version of Internet Explorer is included.* Internet Explorer now has limited capabilities to detect and prevent spoofing and phishing attacks as well as a "protected mode" that is designed to prevent settings and configurations from being altered by malicious websites.

Hardening Windows Server 2008

Microsoft claims that its Windows 2008 OS is its "most secure server" to date. Building on the changes it made to the Windows Server 2003 and Vista OSs, Microsoft attempted to add more defense-in-depth protections to the newest server OS. As with the Server 2003 OS, Microsoft has a free hardening guide for the 2008 OS available from its Download Center.

Here are some of the new security capabilities in Windows 2008:

- *BitLocker allows encryption of all data on a server, including any data volumes.* This capability is also available in certain versions of Vista.

- *Role-based installation of functions and capabilities minimizes the server's footprint.* For example, if a server is going to be a web server, it does not need DNS or SMTP software, and thus those features are no longer installed by default.

- *Network Access Protection (NAP) controls access to network resources based on a client computer's identity and compliance with corporate governance policy.* NAP allows network administrators to define granular levels of network access based on client identity, group membership, and the degree to which that client is compliant with corporate policies. NAP can also ensure that clients comply with corporate policies. Suppose, for example, that a sales manager connects her laptop to the corporate network. NAP can be used to examine the laptop and see if it is fully patched and running a company-approved antivirus product with updated signatures. If the laptop does not meet those standards, network access for that laptop can be restricted until the laptop is brought back into compliance with corporate standards.

- *Read-only domain controllers can be created and deployed in high-risk locations, but they can't be modified to add new users, change access levels, and so on.* This new ability to create and deploy "read-only" domain controllers can be very useful in high threat environments.

- *More-granular password policies allow for different password policies on a group or user basis.* This allows administrators to assign different password policies and requirements for the sales group and the engineering group if that capability is needed.

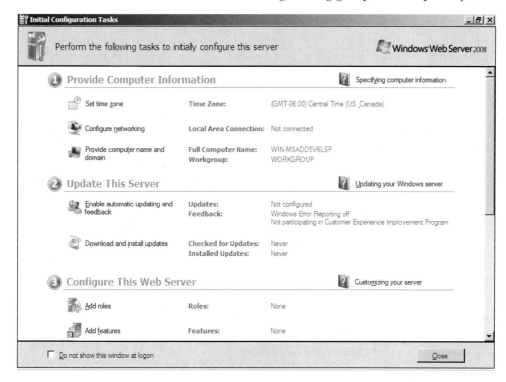

- *Web sites or web applications can be administered within IIS 7. This allows administrators quicker and more convenient administration capabilities, such as the ability to turn on or off specific modules through the IIS management interface. For example, removing CGI support from a web application is a quick and simple operation in IIS 7.*

Figure 14.2 lists the initial configuration tasks.

• **Figure 14.2** Windows 2008 Initial Configuration Tasks

Hardening UNIX- or Linux-Based Operating Systems

While you do not have the advantage of a single manufacturer for all UNIX operating systems (like you do with Windows operating systems), the concepts behind securing different UNIX- or Linux-based operating systems are similar whether the manufacturer is Red Hat or Sun Microsystems. Indeed, the overall tasks involved with hardening all operating systems are remarkably similar.

Establishing General UNIX Baselines

General UNIX baselining is the same as baselining for Windows OSs: disable unnecessary services, restrict permissions on files and directories, remove unnecessary software, apply patches, remove unnecessary users, and apply password guidelines. Some versions of UNIX provide GUI-based tools for these tasks, while others require administrators to edit configuration files manually. In most cases, anything that can be accomplished through a GUI can be accomplished from the command line or by manually editing configuration files.

Like Windows systems, UNIX systems are easiest to secure and baseline if they are providing a single service or performing a single function, such as acting as a Simple Mail Transfer Protocol (SMTP) server or web server. Prior to performing any software installations or baselining, the administrator should define the purpose of the system and identify all required capabilities and functions. One nice advantage of UNIX systems is that you typically have complete control over what does or does not get installed on the system. During the installation process, the administrator can select which services and applications are placed on the system, offering an opportunity to not install services and applications that will not be required. However, this assumes that the administrator knows and understands the purpose of this system, which is not always the case. In other cases, the function of the system itself may have changed.

Regardless of the installation decisions, the administrator may need to remove applications or components that are no longer needed. With UNIX systems, no "add/remove program" wizard is usually available, unlike Windows, but you will often encounter package managers that help you remove unneeded components and applications automatically. On some UNIX versions, though, you must manually delete the files associated with the applications or services you want to remove.

Services on a UNIX system can be controlled through a number of different mechanisms. As the root user, an administrator can start and stop services manually from the command line or through a GUI tool. The OS can also stop and start services automatically through configuration files (usually contained in the /etc directory). (Note that UNIX systems vary a good deal in this regard, as some use a super-server process, such as inetd, while others have individual configuration files for each network service.) Unlike Windows, UNIX systems can also have different **run levels**, in which the system can be configured to bring up different services depending on the run level selected.

On a running UNIX system, you can see which processes, applications, and services are running by using the process status, or **ps**, command, as shown in Figure 14.3. To stop a running service, an administrator can identify the service by its unique **process identifier (PID)** and then use the **kill** command to stop the service. For example, if you wanted to stop the bluetooth-applet service in Figure 14.3, you would use the command **kill 2443**. To prevent this service from starting again when the system is rebooted, you would have to modify the appropriate run levels to remove this service, as shown in Figure 14.4, or modify the configuration files that control this service.

Accounts on a UNIX system can also be controlled via GUIs in some cases and command-line interfaces in others. On most popular UNIX versions, the user information can be found in the passwd file located in

Tech Tip

Run Levels
Run levels are used to describe the state of init (initialization) and what system services are operating in UNIX systems. For example, run level 0 is shutdown. Run level 1 is single-user mode (typically for administrative purposes). Run levels 2 through 5 are user defined (that is, administrators can define what services are running at each level). Run level 6 is for reboot.

```
                        root@localhost:~                          _ + x
 File  Edit  View  Terminal  Tabs  Help
student   2369      1   0 13:47 ?        00:00:00 /usr/libexec/trashapplet --oaf-a
student   2373      1   0 13:47 ?        00:00:00 /usr/libexec/gvfsd-burn --spawne
student   2375      1   0 13:47 ?        00:00:00 /usr/libexec/mixer_applet2 --oaf
student   2377      1   0 13:47 ?        00:00:00 /usr/libexec/clock-applet --oaf-
student   2379      1   0 13:47 ?        00:00:00 /usr/libexec/gdm-user-switch-app
student   2381      1   0 13:47 ?        00:00:00 /usr/libexec/notification-area-a
student   2383      1   3 13:47 ?        00:00:00 mono /usr/lib/tomboy/Tomboy.exe
student   2398      1   1 13:47 ?        00:00:00 gnome-terminal
student   2403   2398   0 13:47 ?        00:00:00 gnome-pty-helper
student   2404   2398   0 13:47 pts/0    00:00:00 bash
student   2433   2043   1 13:47 ?        00:00:00 python /usr/share/system-config-
student   2437   2043   0 13:47 ?        00:00:00 kerneloops-applet
root      2439   2404   0 13:47 pts/0    00:00:00 su -
student   2443   2043   0 13:47 ?        00:00:00 bluetooth-applet
student   2446   2043   0 13:47 ?        00:00:00 gpk-update-icon
student   2448   2043   0 13:47 ?        00:00:00 imsettings-applet --disable-xset
student   2449   2043   0 13:47 ?        00:00:00 nm-applet --sm-disable
student   2454      1   0 13:47 ?        00:00:00 gnome-power-manager
root      2469      1   0 13:47 ?        00:00:00 /usr/sbin/packagekitd
student   2472      1   2 13:47 ?        00:00:00 /usr/bin/python -E /usr/bin/seal
student   2474      1   1 13:47 ?        00:00:00 /usr/libexec/notification-daemon
root      2489   2439   0 13:47 pts/0    00:00:00 -bash
root      2527   2489   0 13:47 pts/0    00:00:00 ps -eaf
[root@localhost ~]#
```

• **Figure 14.3**   **ps** command run on a Fedora 10 system

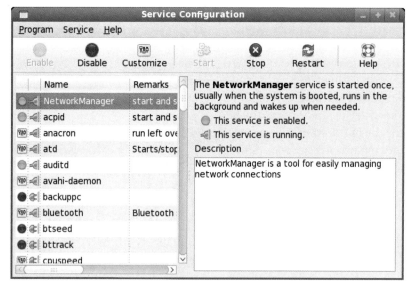

the /etc directory. By manually editing this file, you can add, delete, or modify user accounts on the system. By examining this file, an administrator can see which user accounts exist on the system and then determine which accounts to remove or disable. On most UNIX systems, if you remove the user account from the passwd file, you must manually remove any files that belong to that user, including home directories. Most modern UNIX versions store the actual password associated with a user account in a **shadow file** located in the /etc directory. The shadow file contains the actual password hashes for each user account and is readable only by the root user (or a process with root-level permissions).

How you patch a UNIX system depends a great deal on the UNIX version in use and the patch being applied. In some cases, a patch will consist of a series of manual steps requiring the administrator to replace files, change permissions, and alter directories. In other cases, the patches are executable scripts or utilities that perform the patch actions automatically. Some UNIX versions, such as Red Hat and Solaris, have built-in utilities that handle the patching process. In those cases, the administrator downloads a specifically formatted file that the patching utility then processes to perform any modifications or updates that need to be made.

To better illustrate UNIX baselines, we will examine two popular UNIX-based operating systems: Solaris and Red Hat Linux.

Hardening Solaris   The Solaris OS, developed and distributed by Sun Microsystems, has been an extremely popular choice in high-performance and high-availability environments. As a commercial OS, Solaris is typically bundled with a hardware platform from Sun, but it can be purchased separately and is even available for Intel-based processor platforms (Solaris x86). For more secure environments, a specially hardened version called Trusted Solaris is available, though this is typically used only by the government, military, and banking communities.

Baselining a Solaris system is fairly simple. Once the system's purpose is defined, installation is typically done through a graphical interface that allows the administrator to select which applications and services should be loaded on the system. On a running Solaris system, patches and services can be added or removed using the **pkgadd** command, which adds binary packages, and the **pkgrm** command, which removes binary packages.

The binary packages themselves are unusable in the format in which they are downloaded or delivered on removable media. The pkg utilities take care of interpreting the package's software control files to determine where to install or remove files or directories. Any package handled by the Solaris system is stored in a package information database, so administrators can easily obtain a list of currently installed software. Software can also be installed or removed using the Solaris Product Registry tool, shown in Figure 14.5.

A crucial step in baselining a Solaris system is to ensure that all the latest patches and fixes are in place. Patches for Solaris systems are typically distributed from Sun and are available from Sun's web site but can also be obtained on CD-ROM, floppy disk, or tape in some cases. Once obtained, patches must be processed, and Solaris provides several tools to assist administrators in managing and maintaining patches:

- **patchadd**   Can be used to add patches to the system as well as obtain information about what patches are currently installed on the system

- **patchrm**   Can be used to remove installed patches from the system

- **smpatch**   Can be used to process signed patches

- **pkgparam**   Can be used to show patches installed for a specific software package

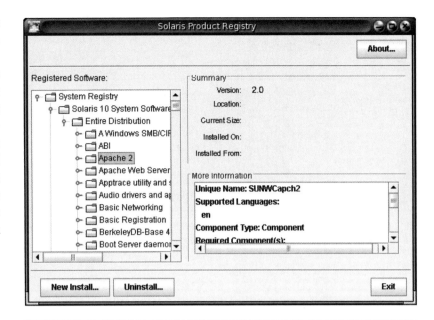

- Figure 14.5   Solaris Product Registry tool can be used to add or remove software.

Newer versions of Solaris have a graphical utility for managing patches and updates called Sun Update Manager, shown in Figure 14.6.

Obtaining a list of running services on a Solaris system is much the same as on all UNIX systems. You can use the **ps** command to view running processes, and you can examine the Internet servers configuration file, called inetd.conf in Solaris. The inetd.conf file, located in the /etc directory, contains a list of services controlled by the Internet services daemon, simply called *inetd*. On Solaris and many other UNIX variants, inetd listens for incoming connections on the TCP and UDP ports associated with each of the services listed in its configuration file, inetd.conf. When a connection request is received, inetd will launch the program or process associated with that service, if necessary,

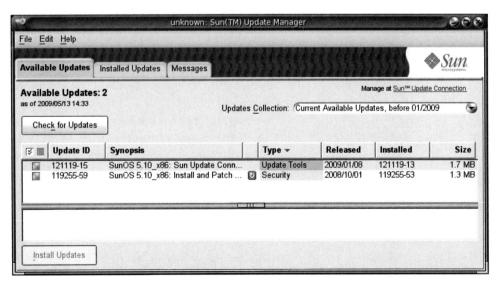

- Figure 14.6   Sun Update Manager

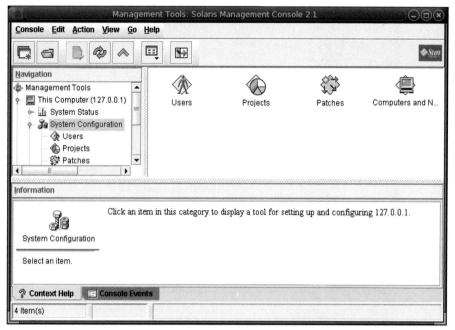

● **Figure 14.7** Solaris Management Console

and pass the connection request to the appropriate service. To prevent unwanted services from running and processing requests, administrators can edit inetd.conf and either comment out or remove the lines for the services they want to disable. On most UNIX systems, you can simply add the # character to the beginning of each line you want to comment out.

In recent versions of Solaris, Sun has migrated a number of administrative functions into a single tool called Solaris Management Console. Users, groups, services, storage, devices, and so on can all be managed from a single GUI, as shown in Figure 14.7.

In addition to disabling or removing unnecessary network services, Solaris (like most UNIX systems) allows administrators to use local security mechanisms called **TCP wrappers** that provide additional layers of security for network services. TCP wrappers are essentially filters that compare incoming connection requests to lists of authorized and unauthorized connections. If a connection is authorized, it is permitted to reach the network service it is attempting to contact. If a connection is unauthorized, it is dropped by the TCP wrappers. These functions are controlled by two files: hosts.allow and hosts.deny. The hosts.allow file contains a list of IP addresses or subnets that are allowed to connect to a specific service, such as **10.0.0.0: FTP**, which would allow any address in the 10.X.X.X network to connect to the FTP service on the local machine. In more secure installations, the hosts.allow file is populated, and the entry **ALL: ALL** is placed in the hosts.deny file. This type of configuration will reject any inbound connections to the local system unless they are specifically authorized by the hosts.allow file.

Securing access to files and directories in Solaris is done in the same manner as in most UNIX variants. Each file and directory has a list of associated permissions for the owner of the file or directory, the group of users to which the owner of the file or directory belongs, and anyone else (often called the "world"). The permissions are listed in owner-group-world order and consist of three values for each grouping: read, write, and execute. The logical representation looks like this: **rwx rwx rwx**. Read (**r**) allows for viewing of the file or listing of the directory. Write (**w**) allows for modification of the file or directory. Execute (**x**) allows the file, usually an executable or script, to be run. If you want a file to have read, write, and execute permissions for the owner, read and write permissions for the group, and no permissions for the world, the permissions could be logically represented as shown to the left.

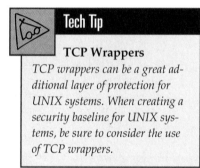

Owner	Group	World
rwx	rw-	---

In Solaris, you can use the **chmod** command to modify the permissions associated with a file or directory. Similarly, the **chown** command allows you to modify the ownership of a file or directory, and **chgrp** allows you to change the group ownership of a file or directory. To adequately secure a Solaris system, you should ensure that all configuration and system files have appropriately restrictive permissions—you don't want any user on the system to be able to modify inted.conf without appropriate access. To assist you in securing files and directories, there are many different resources available on Sun's web site, as well as on security-related web sites.

In spite of the security efforts identified so far, a Solaris system can still be easily compromised if the user base is not effectively managed and maintained. The keys to protecting accounts and system access are to remove or disable unused accounts and to ensure that all accounts are secured with a good, strong password. In Solaris, user accounts are maintained in the passwd file, and groups are maintained in the groups file, both of which are located in the /etc directory. There are three main methods for maintaining users and groups on a Solaris system: manually editing the required configuration files, using command-line interface tools such as **useradd**, and using the management console. Each method can be used interchangeably, offering a level of flexibility not found on Windows systems. Removing unused user accounts can be accomplished through any of these methods—the end result is the same.

The second step to effectively managing your user base is to ensure that users select good passwords. On Solaris systems, passwords are generally stored in a separate file called shadow. This file contains the encrypted password for each account on the system, and it must therefore be guarded and protected appropriately. An administrator can use any of a number of popular password-cracking programs to check the user passwords to ensure that they are not easily guessed or based on a simple dictionary word. Additionally, Solaris already imposes some restrictions on what is considered a "suitable" password for users. In most implementations, a password must be at least six characters long, must contain at least two letters and one number or symbol, must not be the same as the login ID, and must be different than the previous password. If these are not strict enough guidelines, the administrator can alter these parameters by using the **passwd** command and the appropriate option flag or by modifying the parameters in /etc/default/passwd. Solaris also supports **Pluggable Authentication Modules (PAM)**, a mechanism for providing interoperation and secure access to a variety of services on different platforms.

Hardening Linux   Linux is a rather unique operating system. It is UNIX-based, very powerful, open source, can be obtained for free, and is available in many different "distributions" from several vendors. Linux was initially conceived and written by Linus Torvalds in 1991. His concept of creating a lightweight, flexible, and free operating system gave rise to an entirely new operating system that is very popular and is installed on millions of computers around the world. Due to its open nature, the entire source-code base for the operating system is available to anyone who wants to examine it, modify it, or recompile it for their own specific uses. Linux is a favored operating system among security professionals, system administrators, and other highly technical users who enjoy the flexibility and power that Linux provides.

From Wikipedia, "Pluggable authentication modules, or PAM, is a mechanism to integrate multiple low-level authentication schemes into a high-level application programming interface (API). It allows programs that rely on authentication to be written independently of the underlying authentication scheme. PAM was first proposed by Sun Microsystems in an Open Software Foundation Request for Comments (RFC) dated October 1995."

While most versions of Linux can be obtained for free simply by downloading them from the Internet (including major commercial distributions), you can also purchase commercial versions of the Linux operating system from vendors, such as Red Hat, Slackware, SuSE, and Debian, who have built a business out of providing custom versions of Linux along with support and training. We will use Fedora, a popular (and free) Linux distribution, as the example for the rest of this section. Regardless of which Linux version you prefer, baselining a Linux system follows the same guidelines as any other UNIX system: disable unnecessary services, restrict permissions on files and directories, remove unnecessary software, apply patches, remove unnecessary users, and apply password guidelines.

Services under Linux are normally controlled by their own configuration files or by xinetd, the extended Internet services daemon. Instead of starting all Internet services, such as FTP servers, at system startup, some Linux distributions use xinetd to listen for incoming connections. Xinetd listens to all the appropriate ports (those that match the services in its configuration files), and when a connection request comes in, xinetd starts the appropriate server and hands over the connection request. This "master process" approach makes it fairly simple to disable unwanted services—all the configuration information for each server is located in /etc/xinetd.d, with a configuration file for each process.

Permissions under Linux are the same as for other UNIX-based operating systems. There are permissions for owner, group, and others (or world). Permissions are based on the same read-write-execute principle and can be adjusted using the **chmod** command. Individual and group ownership information can be changed using **chown** and **chgrp**, respectively. As with other baselining exercises, permissions should be as restrictive as functionally possible, giving read-only access when possible and write or execute access when necessary.

Adding and removing software under Linux is typically done through a package manager. In Fedora Core Linux, the package manager is called Red Hat Package Manager, or rpm for short. Using rpm, you can add, modify, update, or remove software packages from your system. Using the **rpm –qa** command will give you a list of all the software packages installed on your Red Hat system. You can remove any packages you do not wish to leave installed by using the **rpm -e** command. As with most things under Linux, there is a GUI-based utility to accomplish this same task. The GUI-based Add/Remove Software utility is shown in Figure 14.8.

Patching and keeping a Fedora Linux system up to date is a fairly simple exercise, as well. Fedora has provided an Update Agent that, once configured, will examine your system, obtain the list of available updates, and, if desired, install those updates on your system. Like any other operating system, it is important to maintain the patch level of your Fedora system. For more information on the Fedora Update Agent, see the "Updates (a.k.a. Hotfixes, Service Packs, and Patches)" section later in this chapter.

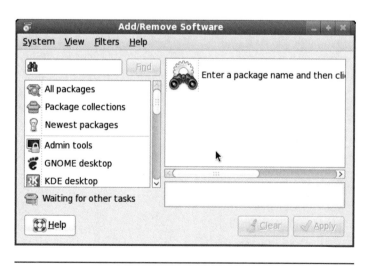

• **Figure 14.8**   Fedora Add/Remove Software utility

Managing and maintaining user accounts under Linux can be accomplished with either the command line or a GUI. Unlike certain other operating systems, there's really only one default account for Linux systems—the root, or superuser, account. The root account has complete and total control over the system and should therefore be protected with an exceptionally strong password. Many administrators will configure their systems to prevent anyone from logging in directly as root; instead they must log in with their own personal accounts and switch to the root account using the **su** command. Adding user accounts can be done with the **useradd** command, and unwanted user accounts can be removed using the **userdel** command. Additionally you can manually edit /etc/passwd to add or remove user accounts. User accounts can also be managed via a GUI, as shown in Figure 14.9.

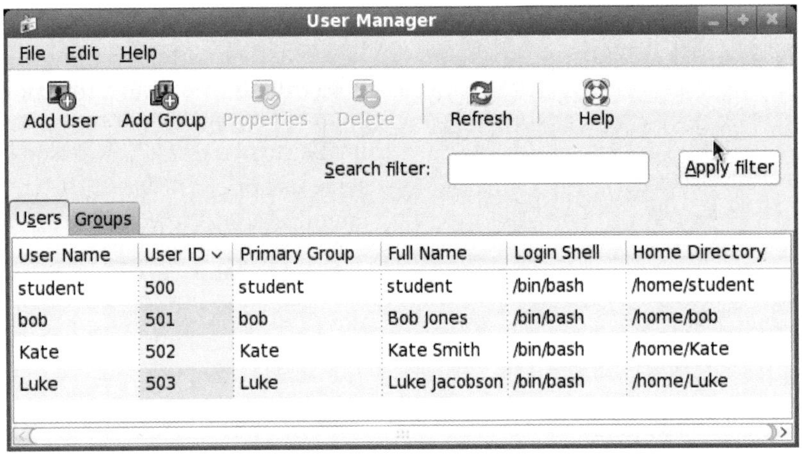

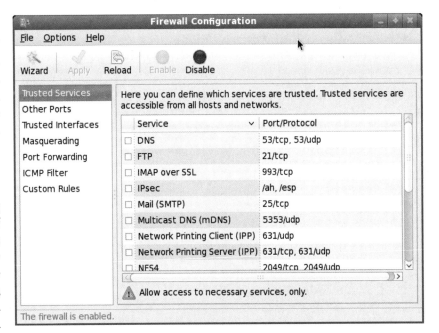

• **Figure 14.9**   Fedora User Manager

For increased local security, Fedora also provides a built-in firewall function that can be managed either via the command line or through a GUI, as shown in Figure 14.10. To protect network access to the local system, administrators can control which ports external users may connect to, such as mail, FTP, or web. Administrators may choose a security level, from high, medium, off, or a customized option that enables them to individually select which ports on which interfaces external users may connect to.

In addition to the built-in firewall functions, administrators may also use TCP wrappers like those discussed earlier in the "Hardening Solaris" section of this chapter. By specifying host and port combinations in /etc/ hosts.allow, administrators can allow certain hosts to connect on certain ports. The firewall function and hosts.allow must work together if both functions are used on the same system. The connection must be allowed by both utilities or it will be dropped.

Hardening Mac OS

Apple's latest iteration of its operating system is essentially a new variant of the UNIX operating system. While this POSIX-compliant OS brings a new level of power, flexibility, and stability to Mac users everywhere, it also brings a new level of security concerns. Traditionally, the Mac OS was largely ignored by the hacker community—the deployment was relatively small and

• **Figure 14.10**   Fedora Firewall Configuration GUI

largely being restricted to individual users or departments. With the migration to a UNIX-based OS and a rise in the number of Macs on the market, Mac users should anticipate a sharp increase in unwanted attention and scrutiny from potential attackers.

Because it is a UNIX-based OS, the same rough guidelines for all UNIX systems apply to Mac OS X. In the Mac OS X 10.5 (Leopard) release, Apple included some new security-specific features to help protect its user base:

- **Mandatory access controls for access to system resources** Only processes that are explicitly granted access are allowed to access system resources such as networking, file systems, process execution, and so on.

- **Tagged downloads** Any file downloaded with Safari, iChat, or Mail is automatically tagged with metadata, including the source URL, date and time of download, and so on. If the download was an archive (such as a zip file), the same metadata is tagged to any file extracted from the archive. Users are prompted with this information the first time they try to run or open the downloaded file.

- **Execute disable** Leopard provides no execute stack protection. Essentially this means that certain portions of the stack have been marked as "data only" and the OS will not execute any instructions in regions marked as data only. This helps protect against buffer-overflow attacks.

- **Library randomization** In another attempt to help defeat buffer-overflow attacks, Leopard loads system libraries into random locations, making it harder for attackers to reference static system library locations in their exploit code.

- **FileVault** FileVault encrypts files with AES encryption. When this feature is enabled, everything in the user's home directory is automatically encrypted.

- **Application-aware firewall** The new Apple Application firewall, shown in Figure 14.11, allows users to restrict network access on both a per-application and a per-port basis.

File permissions in Mac OS X are nearly identical to those in any other UNIX variant and are based on separate read, write, and execute permissions for owner, group, and world. While these permissions can be adjusted manually from a command-line interface, with the standard **chown**, **chmod**, and **chgrp** commands, Apple again provides some nice interface capabilities for viewing and managing

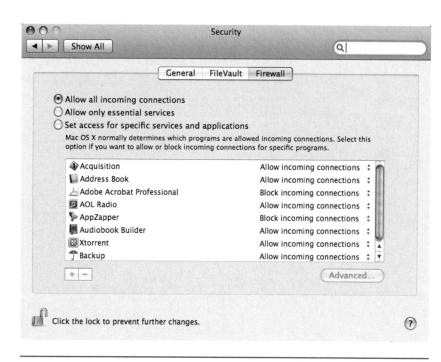

• **Figure 14.11**   Firewall utility in Mac OS X 10.5

file and directory permissions. By selecting the properties of any given file or folder, the user can view and modify the permissions for that file or folder, as shown in Figure 14.12. Note that the GUI follows the same user-group-world pattern of permissions that other UNIX variants follow, though Apple uses the term *others* as opposed to *world*.

This GUI allows users to restrict access to sensitive files and directories quickly and effectively. By default, Mac OS X limits a user's ability to access or modify certain areas of the file system, including those areas containing system binaries. However, these restrictions can be circumvented by a user with the appropriate permissions or by certain third-party applications.

Removing unwanted or unnecessary programs in Mac OS X is usually done through the program's own uninstaller utility or by simply using the Finder to locate and then delete the folder containing the program and associated utilities. Like Windows, Mac OS X maps certain file extensions to specific programs, so deleting a program that handles specific extension types may require that an administrator clear up associated extensions.

Like most UNIX-based OSs, Mac OS X is a multiuser platform. As part of the baselining effort, the active user accounts should be examined to ensure they have the right level of access, permissions, group memberships, and so on. Mac OS X also permits administrators to lock accounts so that they can be modified only by users with administrative-level privileges.

● **Figure 14.12** Setting file permissions in Mac OS X

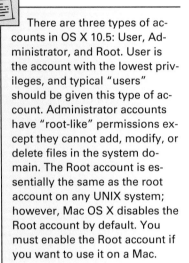

There are three types of accounts in OS X 10.5: User, Administrator, and Root. User is the account with the lowest privileges, and typical "users" should be given this type of account. Administrator accounts have "root-like" permissions except they cannot add, modify, or delete files in the system domain. The Root account is essentially the same as the root account on any UNIX system; however, Mac OS X disables the Root account by default. You must enable the Root account if you want to use it on a Mac.

Updates (a.k.a. Hotfixes, Service Packs, and Patches)

Operating systems are large and complex mixes of interrelated software modules written by dozens or even thousands of separate individuals. With the push toward GUI-based functionality and enhanced capabilities that has occurred over the past several years, operating systems have continued to grow and expand. Windows Vista contains approximately 50 million lines of code, and though it may be one of the largest in that respect, other modern operating systems are not far behind. As operating systems continue to grow and introduce new functions, the potential for problems with the code grows as well. It is almost impossible for an operating system vendor to test its product on every possible platform under every possible circumstance, so functionality and security issues do arise after an operating system has been released. To the average user or system administrator, this means a fairly constant stream of updates designed to correct problems, replace sections of code, or even add new features to an installed operating system.

Vendors typically follow a hierarchy for software updates:

■ **Hotfix** This is a term given to a (usually) small software update designed to address a specific problem, such as a buffer overflow in an application that exposes the system to attacks. Hotfixes are typically developed in reaction to a discovered problem and are produced and then released rather quickly. Hotfixes typically address critical, security-related issues and should be applied to the affected application or operating system as soon as possible.

■ **Patch** This term is usually applied to a more formal, larger software update that may address several or many software problems. Patches often contain enhancements or additional capabilities as well as fixes for known bugs. Patches are usually developed over a longer period of time.

- **Service pack**   This term is usually given to a large collection of patches and hotfixes rolled into a single, rather large package. Service packs are designed to bring a system up to the latest known, good level all at once, rather than requiring the user or system administrator to download dozens or hundreds of updates separately.

Every operating system, from Linux to Solaris to Windows, requires software updates, and each operating system has different methods of assisting users in keeping their systems up to date. Microsoft, for example, typically makes updates available for download from its web site. While most administrators or technically proficient users may prefer to identify and download updates individually, Microsoft recognizes that nontechnical users prefer a simpler approach, which Microsoft has built into its operating systems. In Windows Vista, Server 2003, and Server 2008, Microsoft provides an automated update functionality that will, once configured, locate any required updates, download them to your system, and even install the updates if that is your preference. Figure 14.13 shows the Automatic Updates window, which can be found in the Control Panel. Note that both the web-based updates and Automatic Updates require active Internet connections to retrieve information and updates from Microsoft.

In Vista, the Windows Update utility (see Figure 14.14) can perform an on-demand search for updates or be

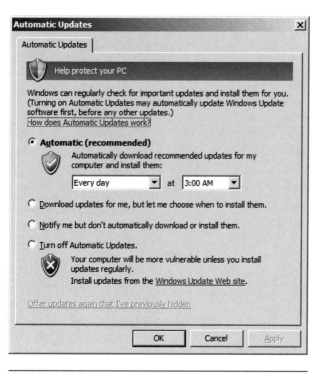

• **Figure 14.13**   Automatic Updates utility from Windows XP

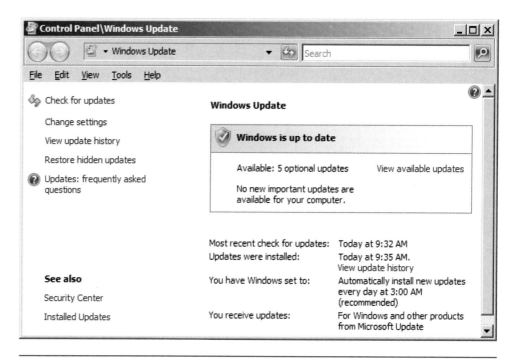

• **Figure 14.14**   Windows Update utility in Vista

Principles of Computer Security: CompTIA Security+ and Beyond

configured to scan for, download, and even install updates automatically—essentially the same functions as Automatic Updates with a new look. An especially nice feature of Windows Update is the ability to scan for and download patches for other Microsoft software, such as Office, as well as updates and patches for the operating system itself.

Microsoft is not alone in providing utilities to assist users in keeping their systems up to date and secure. The latest versions of Fedora Linux contain a utility called the Package Updater, shown in Figure 14.15, which does essentially the same thing. Running the utility will show you which updates are available and allow you to select which updates to download and apply. As with most operating systems, you can configure Fedora to automatically download and apply available updates.

Regardless of the method you use to update the operating system, it is critically important to keep systems up to date. New security advisories come out every day, and while a buffer overflow may be a "potential" problem today, it will almost certainly become a "definite" problem in the near future. Much like the steps taken to baseline and initially secure an operating system, keeping every system patched and up to date is critical to protecting the system and the information it contains.

• **Figure 14.15** Fedora software package update utility

■ Network Hardening

While considering the baseline security of systems, you must consider the role the network connection plays in the overall security profile. The tremendous growth of the Internet and the affordability of multiple PCs and Ethernet networking have resulted in almost every computer being attached to some kind of network, and once computers are attached to a network, they are open to access from any other user on that network. Proper controls over network access must be established on computers by controlling the services that are running and the ports that are opened for network access. In addition to servers and workstations, however, network devices must also be examined: routers, switches, and modems, as well as various other components.

Today's network infrastructure components are similar to other computing devices on the network—they have dedicated hardware that runs an OS, typically with one or more open ports for direct connection to the OS, as well as ports supporting various network services. Any flaws in the coding of the OS can be exploited to gain access as with any "regular" computer. These network devices should be configured with very strict parameters to maintain network security. Like normal computer OSs that need to be patched and updated, the software that runs network infrastructure components needs to be updated regularly. Finally, an outer layer of security should be added by implementing appropriate firewall rules and router access control lists (ACLs).

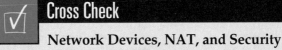

Cross Check

Network Devices, NAT, and Security

Chapter 9 discussed NAT (Network Address Translation). How do network devices that perform NAT services help secure private networks from Internet-based attacks?

Software Updates

Maintaining current vendor patch levels for your software is one of the most important things you can do to maintain security. This is also true for the infrastructure that runs the network. While some equipment is unmanaged and typically has no network presence and few security risks, any managed equipment that is responding on network ports will have some software or firmware controlling it. This software or firmware needs to be updated on a regular basis.

The most common device that connects people to the Internet is the network router. Dozens of brands of routers are available on the market, but Cisco Systems products dominate. The popular Cisco Internetwork Operating System (IOS) runs on more than 70 of Cisco's devices and is installed countless times at countless locations. Its popularity has fueled research into vulnerabilities in the code, and over the past few years quite a few vulnerabilities have been reported. These vulnerabilities can take many forms because routers send and receive several different kinds of traffic, from the standard Telnet remote terminal, to routing information in the form of Routing Information Protocol (RIP) or Open Shortest Path First (OSPF) packets, to Simple Network Management Protocol (SNMP) packets. This highlights the need to update the Cisco IOS software on a regular basis.

Cisco IOS also runs on many of its Ethernet switching products. Like routers, these have capabilities for receiving and processing protocols such as Telnet and SNMP. Smaller network components do not usually run large software suites and typically have smaller software loaded on internal non-volatile RAM (NVRAM). While the update process for this kind of software is typically called a **firmware update**, this does not change the security implications of keeping it up to date. In the case of a corporate network with several devices, someone must take ownership of updating the devices, and updates must be performed regularly according to security and administration policies.

> While we focused on Cisco in our discussion, it's important to note that every network device, regardless of the manufacturer, needs to be maintained and patched to remain secure.

Device Configuration

As important as it is to keep software up to date, properly configuring network devices is equally, if not more, important. Many network devices, such as routers and switches, now have advanced remote management capabilities, with multiple open ports accepting network connections. Proper configuration is necessary to keep these devices secure. Choosing a good password is very important in maintaining external and internal security, and closing or limiting access to any open ports is also a good step for securing the devices. On the more advanced devices, you must carefully consider what services the device is running, just as with a computer. Here are some general steps to take when securing networking devices:

- **Limit access to only those who need it** If your networking device allows management via a web interface, SSH, or any other method, limit who can connect to those services. Many networking devices allow you to specify which IP addresses are allowed to connect to those management services.

- **Choose good passwords** Always change default passwords and follow good password selection guidelines. If the device supports encryption, ensure passwords are stored in encrypted format on the device.

- **Password-protect console and remote access** If the device supports password protection, ensure that all local and remote access capabilities are password protected.

- **Turn off unnecessary services** If your networking equipment supports Telnet but your organization doesn't need it, turn that service off. It's always a good idea to disable or remove unused services. Your device may also support the use of access control lists to limit access to services such as Telnet or SSH on the device itself.

- **Change SNMP community strings** SNMP is widely used to manage networking equipment and typically allows a "public" string, which can typically only read information from a device, and a "private" string, which can often read and write to a device's configuration. Some manufacturers use default or well-known strings (such as "public" for the public string)—always change both the public and private strings if you are using SNMP.

 Exam Tip: The use of the word "public" as a public SNMP community string is an extremely well-known vulnerability. Any system using an SNMP community string of "public" should be changed immediately.

Application Hardening

Perhaps as important as OS and network hardening is **application hardening**—securing an application against local and Internet-based attacks. Hardening applications is fairly similar to hardening operating systems—you remove the functions or components you don't need, restrict access where you can, and make sure the application is kept up to date with patches. In most cases, the last step in that list is the most important for maintaining application security. After all, applications must be accessible to users or they serve no purpose. As most problems with applications tend to be buffer overflows in legitimate user input fields, patching the application is often the only way to secure it from attack.

Application Patches

As obvious as this seems, application patches are most likely going to come from the vendor that sells the application. After all, who else has access to the source code? In some cases, such as with Microsoft's IIS, this is the same company that sold the OS that the application runs on. In other cases, such as Apache, the vendor is OS independent and provides an application with versions for many different OSs.

Application patches are likely to come in three varieties: hotfixes, patches, and upgrades. As described for OSs earlier in the chapter, hotfixes are usually small sections of code designed to fix a specific problem. For example, a hotfix may address a buffer overflow in the login routine for an application. Patches are usually collections of fixes, tend to be much larger, and are usually released on a periodic basis or whenever enough problems have been addressed to warrant a patch release. Upgrades are another popular method of patching applications, and they tend to be presented with a more positive spin than patches. Even the term *upgrade* has a positive connotation—you are moving up to a better, more functional, and more secure application. For this reason, many vendors release "upgrades" that consist mainly of fixes rather than new or enhanced functionality.

Application patches can come in a variety of forms. They can be downloaded from the vendor's web site or FTP site, or they can be received on a CD-ROM. In many cases, a patch is a small binary application that, when run, automatically replaces defective application binaries with updated ones. The patch may also change settings or modify configuration files. In other cases, the patch will be a zipped archive of files, with instructions that require the user or administrator to replace defective applications with the updated ones manually. Some advanced applications will have automatic update routines that update the application automatically in much the same fashion as an OS is automatically updated.

Patch Management

In the early days of network computing, things were easy—fewer applications existed, vendor patches came out annually or quarterly, and access was restricted to authorized individuals. Updates were few and easy to handle. Now application and OS updates are pushed constantly as vendors struggle to provide new capabilities, fix problems, and address vulnerabilities. Microsoft has created "Patch Tuesday" in an effort to condense the update cycle and reduce the effort required to maintain its products. As the number of patches continues to rise, many organizations struggle to keep up with patches—which patches should be applied immediately, which are compatible with the current configuration, which will not affect current business operations, and so on. To help cope with this flood of patches, many organizations have adopted **patch management**, the process of planning, testing, and deploying patches in a controlled manner.

Patch management is a disciplined approach to the acquisition, testing, and implementation of OS and application patches and requires a fair amount of resources to implement properly. To implement patch management effectively, you must first have a good inventory of the software used in your environment, including all OSs and applications. Then you must set up a process to monitor for updates to those software packages. Many vendors provide the ability to update their products automatically or to automatically check for updates and inform the user when updates are available. For example, Windows Update, shown in Figure 14.16, allows the user to choose to receive completely automatic updates on a scheduled basis, to download new updates but choose when to install them, or to be notified when updates are available. Some vendors provide notification of all patches that they release and some vendors provide a service that will alert you when patches that apply to your environment are available.

Keeping track of patch availability is merely the first step; in many environments, patches must be analyzed and tested. Does the patch apply to the software you are running? Does the patch address a vulnerability or critical issue that must be addressed immediately? What is the impact of applying that patch or group of patches? Will it break something else if you apply this patch? To address these issues, it is recommended that you use development or test platforms, where you can carefully analyze and test patches before placing them into a production environment. While patches are generally "good," they are not always exhaustively tested; some have been known to "break" other products or functions within the product being patched; and some have introduced new vulnerabilities while attempting to address an existing vulnerability. The extent of analysis and testing varies widely from organization to organization. Testing and analysis will also vary depending on the application or OS and the extent of the patch.

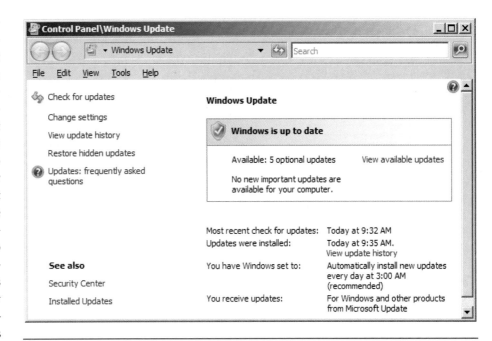

• **Figure 14.16**   Windows Update utility

Once a patch has been analyzed and tested, administrators have to determine when to apply the patch. As many patches require a restart of applications or services or even a reboot of the entire system, most operational environments apply patches only at specific times, to reduce downtime and possible impact and to ensure administrators are available if something goes wrong. Many organizations will also have a rollback plan that allows them to recover the systems back to a known good configuration prior to the patch, in case the patch has unexpected or undesirable effects. Some organizations require extensive coordination and approval of patches prior to implementation, and some institute "lockout" dates where no patching or system changes (with few exceptions) can be made, to ensure business operations are not disrupted. For example, an e-commerce site might have a lockout between the Thanksgiving and Christmas holidays to ensure the site is always available to holiday shoppers.

With any environment, but especially with larger environments, it can be a challenge to track the update status of every desktop and server in the organization. Documenting and maintaining patch status can be a challenge. However, with a disciplined approach, training, policies, and procedures, even the largest environments can be managed. To assist in their patch-management efforts, many organizations use a patch-management product that automates many of the mundane and manpower-intensive tasks associated with patch management. For example, many patch-management products provide the following:

- Ability to inventory applications and operating systems in use
- Notification of patches that apply to your environment

Exam Tip: Patch management is the process of planning, testing, and deploying patches in a controlled manner.

- Periodic or continual scanning of systems to validate patch status and identify missing patches
- Ability to select which patches to apply and to which systems to apply them
- Ability to push patches to systems on an on-demand or scheduled basis
- Ability to report patch success or failure
- Ability to report patch status on any or all systems in the environment

Patch-management solutions can also be useful to satisfy audit or compliance requirements, as they can show a structured approach to patch management, show when and how systems are patched, and provide a detailed accounting of patch status within the organization.

Microsoft provides a free patch-management product called Windows Server Update Services (WSUS), shown in Figure 14.17. Using the WSUS product, administrators can manage updates for any compatible Windows-based system in their organization. The WSUS product can be configured to download patches automatically from Microsoft based on a variety of factors (such as OS, product family, criticality, and so on). When updates are downloaded, the administrator can determine whether or not to push out the patches and when to apply them to the systems in their environment. The WSUS product can also help administrators track patch status on their systems, which is a useful and necessary feature.

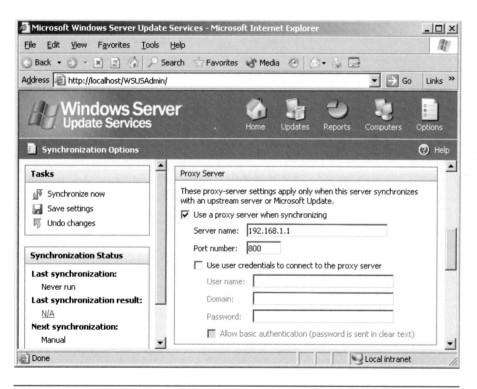

• **Figure 14.17** Windows Server Update Services

■ Group Policies

Microsoft defines a **group policy** as "an infrastructure used to deliver and apply one or more desired configurations or policy settings to a set of targeted users and computers within an Active Directory environment. This infrastructure consists of a Group Policy engine and multiple client-side extensions (CSEs) responsible for writing specific policy settings on target client computers." Introduced with the Windows 2000 operating system, group polices are a great way to manage and configure systems centrally in an Active Directory environment (Windows NT had policies—but technically not "group policies"). Group policies can also be used to manage users, making these policies valuable tools in any large environment.

Within the Windows environment, group policies can be used to refine, set, or modify a system's Registry settings, auditing and security policies, user environments, logon/logoff scripts, and so on. Policy settings are stored in a **group policy object (GPO)** and are referenced internally by the OS using a **globally unique identifier (GUID)**. A single policy can be linked to a single user, a group of users, a group of machines, or an entire organizational unit (OU), which makes updating common settings on large groups of users or systems much easier. Users and systems can have more than one GPO assigned and active, which can create conflicts between policies that must then be resolved at an attribute level. Group policies can also overwrite local policy settings. Group policies should not be confused with local policies. *Local* policies are created and applied to a specific system (locally),

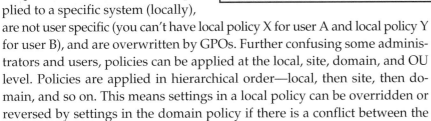

Try This

Windows Local Security Policies

Open a command prompt as either administrator or a user with administrator privileges on a Windows system. Type the command **secpol** and press ENTER (this should bring up the Local Security Policy utility). Expand Account Policies on the left side of the Local Security Policy window (which should have a + next to it). Click Password Policy. Look in the right side of the Local Security Policy window. What is the minimum password length? What is the maximum password age in days? Now explore some of the policy settings—but be careful! Changes made to the local security policy can affect the functionality or usability of your system.

are not user specific (you can't have local policy X for user A and local policy Y for user B), and are overwritten by GPOs. Further confusing some administrators and users, policies can be applied at the local, site, domain, and OU level. Policies are applied in hierarchical order—local, then site, then domain, and so on. This means settings in a local policy can be overridden or reversed by settings in the domain policy if there is a conflict between the two policies. If there is no conflict, the policy settings are aggregated.

Creating GPOs is usually done through either the Group Policy Object Editor, shown in Figure 14.18, or the Group Policy Management Console (GPMC). The GPMC is a more powerful GUI-based tool that can summarize GPO settings; simplify security filtering settings; backup, clone, restore, and edit GPOs; and perform other tasks. After creating a GPO, administrators will associate it with the desired targets. After association, group policies operate on a *pull model*. At a semi-random interval, the Group Policy client will collect and apply any policies associated to the system and the currently logged-on user.

With the most recent implementation of group policies, Microsoft has added some interesting and effective new capabilities:

- **Network location awareness** Systems are now "aware" of which network they are connected to and can apply different GPOs as needed. For example, a system can have a very restrictive GPO when connected to a public network and a less restrictive GPO when connected to an internal, trusted network.

Exam Tip: Group policies are the mechanism that allows for centralized management and configuration of computers and remote users in an Active Directory environment.

In Windows, policies are applied in hierarchical order. Local policies get applied first, then site policies, then domain polices, and finally OU policies. If a setting from a later policy conflicts with a setting from an earlier policy, the setting from the later policy "wins" and is applied. Keep this in mind when building group policies.

• **Figure 14.18**   Group Policy Object Editor

- **Ability to process without ICMP**   Older group policy processes would occasionally time out or fail completely if the targeted system did not respond to ICMP packets. Current implementations in Vista do not rely on ICMP during the GPO update process.

- **VPN compatibility**   As a side benefit of network location awareness, mobile users who connect through VPNs can receive a GPO update in the background after connecting to the corporate network via VPN.

- **Power management**   Under Vista, power management settings can be configured using GPOs.

- **Device access blocking**   Under Vista, policy settings have been added that allow administrators to restrict user access to USB drives, CD-RW drives, DVD-RW drives, and other removable media.

- **Location-based printing**   Users can be assigned to various printers based on their location. As mobile users move, their printer locations can be updated to the closest local printer.

■ Security Templates

A **security template** is simply a collection of security settings that can be applied to a system. Within the Windows OSs, security templates can contain hundreds of settings that control or modify system settings such as password length, auditing of user actions, or restrictions on network access. Security templates can be standalone files that are applied manually to each system, but they can also be part of a group policy, allowing common security settings to be applied to systems on a much wider scale.

As an administrator, when you are creating a security template, all settings are initially "not configured," which means the template will make no changes to whatever settings are already in place. By selecting the settings you want to modify, you can fine-tune the template to create a more (or less) secure system. Security templates typically configure settings in the following areas:

- **Account policies**   Settings for user accounts, such as password length, complexity requirements, account lockouts, and so on.

- **Event log settings**   Settings that apply to the three main audit logs within Windows (Application, System, and Security), such as log file size, retention of older entries, and so on.

- **File permissions**   Settings that apply to files and folders, such as permission inheritance, locking permissions, and so on.

- **Registry permissions**   Settings that control who can access the Registry and how it can be accessed.

- **Restricted groups**   Settings that control who should be allowed to join or be part of certain groups. If the user is not already a member of a group as defined in the policy, you will not be able to add that user to the corresponding group on the local system.

- **System services**   Settings for services that run on the system, such as startup mode, whether or not users can stop/start the service, and so on.

- **User rights**   Settings that control what a user can and cannot do on the system.

You can create and/or modify security templates on your local system through the Microsoft Management Console (if you have the Security Templates snap-in installed). Microsoft includes a series of predefined security templates (usually stored in \WINDOWS\security\templates) that will appear under Security Templates in your MMC window. These templates range from minimal to maximal security and can all be applied as-is or modified as needed. You can also create a completely new security template and then customize each of the settings to your specifications. Figure 14.19 shows the MMC with the Security Templates snap-in enabled.

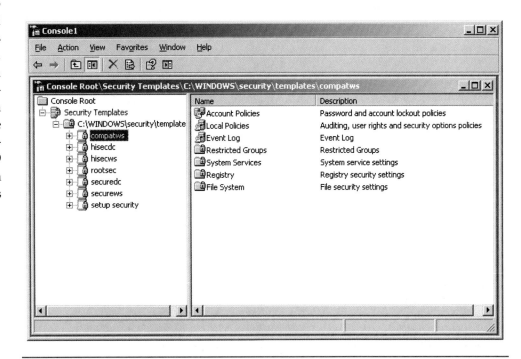

• **Figure 14.19**   MMC with Security Templates snap-in

Chapter 14 Review

■ For More Information

- **Microsoft's Security Central** www.microsoft.com/security/default.mspx

- **SANS Reading Room: Application/Database Security** www.sans.org/reading_room/whitepapers/application/

- **Best Practices** www.sans.org/reading_room/whitepapers/bestprac/

- **Network Devices** www.sans.org/reading_room/whitepapers/networkdevs/

■ Chapter Summary

After reading this chapter and completing the exercises, you should understand the following about baselines.

Harden operating systems and network operating systems

- Security baselines are critical to protecting information systems, particularly those allowing connections from external users.

- The process of establishing a system's security state is called baselining, and the resulting product is a security baseline that allows the system to run safely and securely.

- Hardening is the process by which operating systems, network resources, and applications are secured against possible attacks.

- Securing operating systems consists of removing or disabling unnecessary services, restricting permissions on files and directories, removing unnecessary software (or not installing it in the first place), applying the latest patches, removing unnecessary user accounts, and ensuring strong password guidelines are in place.

- Securing network resources consists of disabling unnecessary functions, restricting access to ports and services, ensuring strong passwords are used, and ensuring the code on the network devices is patched and up to date.

- Securing applications depends heavily on the application involved but typically consists of removing samples and default materials,

preventing reconnaissance attempts, and ensuring the software is patched and up to date.

Harden applications

- Patch management is a disciplined approach to the acquisition, testing, and implementation of OS and application patches.

- A hotfix is a single package designed to address a specific, typically security-related, problem in an operating system or application.

- A patch is a fix or collection of fixes that addresses vulnerabilities or errors in operating systems or applications.

- A service pack is a large collection of fixes, corrections, and enhancements for an operating system, application, or group of applications.

Establish group policies

- Group policies are a method for managing the settings and configurations of many different users and systems in an Active Directory environment.

- Group policies can be used to refine, set, or modify a system's Registry settings, auditing and security policies, user environments, logon/logoff scripts, and so on.

- Security templates are collections of security settings that can be applied to a system. Security templates can contain hundreds of settings that control or modify settings on a system, such as password length, auditing of user actions, or restrictions on network access.

■ Key Terms

■ Key Terms Quiz

Use terms from the Key Terms list to complete the sentences that follow. Don't use the same term more than once. Not all terms will be used.

1. _____ is the process of establishing a system's security state.

2. Securing and preparing a system for the production environment is called _____.

3. A(n) _____ is a small software update designed to address a specific, often urgent, problem.

4. The basic software on a computer that handles input and output is called the _____.

5. The Simple Network Management Protocol (SNMP) uses two kinds of strings: _____ and _____. One allows you "read-only" access and the other may allow you to change configuration information on a compatible remote device.

6. A(n) _____ is a bundled set of software updates, fixes, and additional functions contained in a self-installing package.

7. In most UNIX operating systems, each running program is given a unique number called a _____.

8. When a user or process supplies more data than was expected, a(n) _____ may occur.

9. _____ are used to describe the state of init and what system services are operating in UNIX systems.

10. A(n) _____ is a collection of security settings that can be applied to a system.

■ Multiple-Choice Quiz

1. A small software update designed to address an urgent or specific problem is called a:

   A. Hotfix

   B. Service pack

   C. Patch

   D. None of the above

2. In a UNIX operating system, which run level describes single-user mode?

   A. 0

   B. 6

   C. 4

   D. 1

3. TCP wrappers do what?

   A. Help secure the system by restricting network connections

   B. Help prioritize network traffic for optimal throughput

   C. Encrypt outgoing network traffic

   D. Strip out excess input to defeat buffer-overflow attacks

4. File permissions under UNIX consist of what three types?

   A. Modify, read, and execute

   B. Read, write, and execute

   C. Full control, read-only, and run

   D. Write, read, and open

5. The combination of hardware and software running on most routers, switches, and network devices is called:

   A. inetd

   B. A network operating system

   C. An operating system

   D. Firmware

6. The mechanism that allows for centralized management and configuration of computers and remote users in an Active Directory environment is called:

   A. Baseline

   B. Group policies

   C. Simple Network Management Protocol

   D. Security templates

7. Under Windows Vista, the User Account Control function:

   A. Allows for the use of passwords longer than 14 characters

   B. Implements group policies

   C. Automatically downloads and applies patches and service packs

   D. Allows users to operate the system without requiring administrative privileges

8. What feature in Windows Server 2008 controls access to network resources based on a client computer's identity and compliance with corporate governance policy?

   A. BitLocker

   B. Network Access Protection

   C. inetd

   D. Process identifiers

9. Microsoft's way of bundling updates, fixes, and new functions into a large, self-installing package is called a(n):

   A. Service pack

   B. Hotfix

   C. Upgrade

   D. Firmware update

10. Applying the latest patches is important for maintaining the security of:

    A. Applications only

    B. Operating systems and applications

    C. Firmware only

    D. Buffer overflows

11. To stop a particular service or program running on a UNIX operating system, you might use the _____ command.

    A. netstat

    B. ps

    C. kill

    D. inetd

12. Updating the software loaded on nonvolatile RAM is called:

    A. A buffer overflow

    B. A firmware update

    C. A hotfix

    D. A service pack

13. The shadow file on a UNIX system contains

    A. Password associated with a user account

    B. Group policy information

    C. File permissions for system files

    D. Network services started when the system is booted

14. An attack conducted by supplying more data than is expected is called:

    A. A buffer overflow

    B. Relaying

    C. Smurfing

    D. Access list trashing

15. On a UNIX system, if a file has the permissions **rwx r-x rw-**, what permissions does the owner of the file have?

    A. Read only

    B. Read and write

    C. Read, write, and execute

    D. None

■ Essay Quiz

1. Explain the difference between a "hotfix" and a "service pack" and describe why both are so important.

2. A new administrator needs some help creating a security baseline. Create a checklist/template that covers the basic steps in creating a security baseline to assist them, and explain why each step is important.

3. Your boss doesn't understand why patches need to be "tested" and can't just be applied as they come in. Explain to your boss why testing of patches is important.

4. An administrator wants to build a "security template" she can apply to all the workstations in a computing lab but needs some help. Outline for her the areas she might want to address in her security template.

Lab Projects

• Lab Project 14.1

Find a lab system running Linux with at least one open service such as FTP, Telnet, or SMTP. From another lab system, connect to the Linux system and observe your results. Configure TCP wrappers on the Linux system to reject all connection attempts from the other lab system. Now try to reconnect, and observe your results. Document your steps and explain how TCP wrappers work.

• Lab Project 14.2

Find a system running Windows XP or Vista and experiment with the Password Policy settings under the Local Security Policy (Settings | Control Panel | Administrative Tools | Local Security Policy). Find the setting for Passwords Must Meet Complexity Requirements and make sure it is disabled. Set the password on the account you are using to **bob**. Now enable the Passwords Must Meet Complexity Requirements settings and attempt to change your password to **jane**. Were you able to change it to "jane"? Explain why or why not. Set your password to something the system will allow and explain how you selected that password and how it meets the complexity requirements.

• Lab Project 14.3

Use the Internet to research group policies. Imagine you are creating a group policy for systems that will be used as Internet kiosks in a public library. Describe three settings you would implement in your group policy and why you would implement those three settings.

Types of Attacks and Malicious Software

If you know the enemy and know yourself you need not fear the results of a hundred battles.

—SUN TZU

In this chapter, you will learn how to

■ **Describe various types of computer and network attacks, including denial-of-service, spoofing, hijacking, and password guessing**

■ **Identify the different types of malicious software that exist, including viruses, worms, Trojan horses, logic bombs, time bombs, and rootkits**

■ **Explain how social engineering can be used as a means to gain access to computers and networks**

■ **Describe the importance of auditing and what should be audited**

Attacks can be made against virtually any layer or level of software, from network protocols to applications. When an attacker finds a vulnerability in a system, he exploits the weakness to attack the system. The effect of an attack depends on the attacker's intent and can result in a wide range of effects, from minor to severe. An attack on one system might not be visible on the user's system because the attack is actually occurring on a different system, and the data the attacker will manipulate on the second system is obtained by attacking the first system. For example, an attack on a DNS cache can result in widespread effects for other processes, many times without any specific warning to a user.

■ Avenues of Attack

A computer system is attacked for one of two general reasons: it is specifically targeted by the attacker, or it is a target of opportunity. In the first case, the attacker has chosen the target not because of the hardware or software the organization is running but for another reason, such as a political reason. For example, an individual in one country might attack a government system in another country to gather secret information. Or the attacker might target an organization as part of a "hacktivist" attack—the attacker could deface the web site of a company that sells fur coats because the attacker believes using animals in this way is unethical, for example. Perpetrating some sort of electronic fraud is another reason a specific system might be targeted for attack. Whatever the reason, the attacker usually begins an attack of this nature before he knows which hardware and software the organization uses.

The second type of attack, an attack against a target of opportunity, is launched against a site that has hardware or software that is vulnerable to a specific exploit. The attacker, in this case, is not targeting the organization; he has instead learned of a specific vulnerability and is simply looking for an organization with this vulnerability that he can exploit. This is not to say that an attacker might not be targeting a given sector and looking for a target of opportunity in that sector. For example, an attacker who wants to obtain credit card or other personal information may search for any exploitable company that stores credit card information on its system to accomplish the attack.

Targeted attacks are more difficult and take more time and effort than attacks on a target of opportunity. The latter type of attack simply relies on the fact that, with any piece of widely distributed software, somebody in the organization will not have patched the system as they should have.

The Steps in an Attack

Attackers are like bank robbers in the sense that they execute an organized process when performing an attack. The steps an attacker takes in attempting to penetrate a targeted network are similar to those that a security consultant performs during a penetration test and are detailed in the Tech Tip, "Anatomy of a Hack."

Reconnaissance

The attacker can gather as much information about the organization as possible via several means, including studying the organization's own web site, looking for postings on news groups, or consulting resources such as the U.S. Securities and Exchange Commission's (SEC's) Filings & Forms (EDGAR) web site (www.sec.gov/edgar.shtml). A number of different financial reports are available through the EDGAR site that can provide information about an organization that can prove useful for an attack, especially for social engineering attacks. The attacker wants information about IP addresses, phone numbers, names of important individuals, and what networks the organization maintains. The attacker can also use tools such as Whois.Net (www.whois.net) to link IP addresses to registrants.

Tech Tip

Defense Begins with Eliminating Vulnerabilities
Defense against attacks begins with elimination of vulnerabilities. Vulnerabilities are exploited by attackers to gain access to a system. Minimization of vulnerabilities is one of the foundational elements of defense.

Tech Tip

Anatomy of a Hack
Although the movies make you think a hacker can sit at a keyboard and just do anything he wants, there is more to a hack than typing. Hacking a computer system is a multistep, fairly complicated process, and over time a "standard" method has emerged. The common steps of the hacking process are:

1. *Perform reconnaissance (also known as profiling) on the target organization.*
2. *Scan the target organization's network.*
3. *Research vulnerabilities.*
4. *Perform the attack.*
5. *Create a backdoor.*
6. *Cover their tracks.*

Google is also a good source of information during the reconnaissance phase. Google can assist the attacker in determining the organization's web pages, ftp sites, and many more Internet-facing surfaces.

Scanning

The next step begins the technical part of an attack that determines what target systems are accessible and active. This is often done using a **ping sweep**, which simply sends a ping (an Internet Control Message Protocol echo request) to the target machine. If the machine responds, the attacker knows it is reachable.

The attacker's next step is often to perform a **port scan** to help identify which ports are open, which indicates which services may be running on the target machine. The program nmap is the de facto standard for ping sweeping and port scanning. Running nmap with the –sv option performs a *banner grab* in an attempt to determine the version of the software behind open ports. An alternative GUI program for Windows is SuperScan (www.foundstone.com/us/resources/proddesc/superscan.htm).

After the attacker determines which services are available, the next step is to determine which operating system is running on the target machine, as well as any specific application programs. The attacker can use various techniques to send specifically formatted packets to the ports on a target system to view the response.

This response often provides clues as to which operating system and specific applications are running on the target system. Then the attacker should have a list of possible target machines, the operating system running on them, and some specific applications or services to target.

Researching Vulnerabilities

After the hacker has a list of software running on the systems, he will start researching the Internet for vulnerabilities associated with that software. Numerous web sites provide information on vulnerabilities in specific application programs and operating systems. This information is valuable to administrators who need to know what problems exist and how to patch them.

In addition to information about specific vulnerabilities, some sites also provide tools that can be used to exploit the vulnerabilities. An attacker can search for known vulnerabilities and tools to exploit them, download the information and tools, then use them against a site. If the administrator for the targeted system has not installed the correct patch, the attack may be successful; if the patch has been installed, the attacker will move on to the next possible vulnerability. If the administrator has installed all the appropriate patches so that all known vulnerabilities have been addressed, the attacker may have to resort to a brute-force attack, which involves calculating user ID and password combinations. Unfortunately, this type of attack, which could be easily prevented, sometimes proves successful.

Performing the Attack

Now the attacker is ready to execute an attack, which could have many different results—the system could crash, information could be stolen off the system, or a web site could be defaced. Hackers often install a backdoor and build their own user accounts with administrative privileges so that even when you do patch the system, they can still gain access.

This discussion of attack steps is by no means complete. A system can be attacked in many different ways. The driving force behind the type of attack is the attacker's objective; if activism can be accomplished by a web site defacement, he may consider this a sufficient attack. If the target is more sinister, such as intellectual property theft or identity theft, data theft may be the hacker's objective and hence guide his attack.

Creating a Backdoor

Many times a hacker will create a specific backdoor so that he can later access the machine without having to go through the hack process he used to get this far. This can be as simple as creating an account and password or as complex as installing a sophisticated agent that initiates calls out of the system back to the hacker. (See "Backdoors and Trapdoors" later in the chapter.) The rationale behind this step is simple: the vulnerability that was exploited once may not be there in the future, so, to maintain the ability to access a machine, the attacker creates his own backdoor into the machine.

Covering Their Tracks

After a long day's hard work compromising a machine, the last thing a hacker wishes to be discovered. In years past, a hacker's motivation often was to achieve notoriety; hence they defaced web sites and made other publicly apparent hacks. Today, much of the hacking is performed for monetary gain. When engaging in this type of criminal activity, not being seen or caught is important to the hacker. Erasing log files and changing file time stamps are two common methods used to escape detection.

Exam Tip: A good defense against a hacker modifying or erasing log files is to maintain them on a separate, remote log file server, with restricted access.

Minimizing Possible Avenues of Attack

By understanding the steps an attacker can take, you can limit the exposure of your system and minimize the possible avenues an attacker can exploit. Your first step to minimize possible attacks is to ensure that all patches for the operating system and applications are installed. Many security problems, such as viruses and worms, exploit known vulnerabilities for which patches actually exist. These attacks are successful only because administrators have not taken the appropriate actions to protect their systems.

The next step is to limit the services that are running on the system. As mentioned in earlier chapters, limiting the number of services to those that are absolutely necessary provides two safeguards: it limits the possible avenues of attack (the possible services for which a vulnerability may exist and be exploited), and it reduces the number of services the administrator has to worry about patching in the first place.

Another step is to limit public disclosure of private information about your organization and its

Cross Check

Baseline Analysis and Patching of Systems

Keeping a system patched and up to date for the operating system and applications is the best defense against exposed vulnerabilities. How up to date is the system you are currently using? How do you know? Chapter 14 covers the baselining and patching of systems to understand and remove vulnerabilities. Refer to this chapter for more in-depth information on how to perform these activities.

computing resources. Since the attacker is after this information, don't make it easy to obtain.

■ Attacking Computer Systems and Networks

Although hackers and viruses receive the most attention in the news (due to the volume of these forms of attack), they are not the only avenues of attack against computer systems and networks. This chapter addresses many different ways computers and networks are attacked on a daily basis. Each type of attack threatens at least one of the three security requirements mentioned in Chapter 2: confidentiality, integrity, and availability (the CIA of security). Attacks are thus attempts by unauthorized individuals to access or modify information, to deceive the system so that an unauthorized individual can take over an authorized session, or to disrupt service to authorized users.

From a high-level standpoint, attacks on computer systems and networks can be grouped into two broad categories: attacks on specific software (such as an application or the operating system) and attacks on a specific protocol or service. Attacks on a specific application or operating system are generally possible because of an oversight in the code (and possibly in the testing of that code) or because of a flaw, or bug, in the code (again indicating a lack of thorough testing). Attacks on specific protocols or services are attempts either to take advantage of a specific feature of the protocol or service or to use the protocol or service in a manner for which it was not intended. This section discusses various forms of attacks of which security professionals need to be aware.

Denial-of-Service Attacks

A **denial-of-service (DoS) attack** is an attack designed to prevent a system or service from functioning normally. A DoS attack can exploit a known vulnerability in a specific application or operating system, or it can attack features (or weaknesses) in specific protocols or services. In a DoS attack, the attacker attempts to deny authorized users access either to specific information or to the computer system or network itself. This can be accomplished by crashing the system—taking it offline—or by sending so many requests that the machine is overwhelmed.

The purpose of a DoS attack can be simply to prevent access to the target system, or the attack can be used in conjunction with other actions to gain unauthorized access to a computer or network. For example, a **SYN flood** attack can be used to prevent service to a system temporarily in order to take advantage of a trusted relationship that exists between that system and another.

SYN flooding is an example of a DoS attack that takes advantage of the way TCP/IP networks were designed to function, and it can be used to illustrate the basic principles of any DoS attack. SYN flooding uses the TCP three-way handshake that establishes a connection between two systems.

Under normal circumstances, the first system sends a SYN packet to the system with which it wants to communicate. The second system responds with a SYN/ACK if it is able to accept the request. When the initial system receives the SYN/ACK from the second system, it responds with an ACK packet, and communication can then proceed. This process is shown in Figure 15.1.

In a SYN flooding attack, the attacker sends fake communication requests to the targeted system. Each of these requests will be answered by the target system, which then waits for the third part of the handshake. Since the requests are fake (a nonexistent IP address is used in the requests, so the target system is responding to a system that doesn't exist), the target will wait for responses that never come, as shown in Figure 15.2. The target system will drop these connections after a specific time-out period, but if the attacker sends requests faster than the time-out period eliminates them, the system will quickly be filled with requests. The number of connections a system can support is finite, so when more requests come in than can be processed, the system will soon be reserving all its connections for fake requests. At this point, any further requests are simply dropped (ignored), and legitimate users who want to connect to the target system will not be able to do so, because use of the system has been denied to them.

> A SYN/ACK is actually the SYN packet sent to the first system combined with an ACK packet acknowledging the first system's SYN packet.

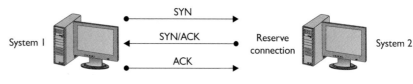

• **Figure 15.1**   The TCP three-way handshake

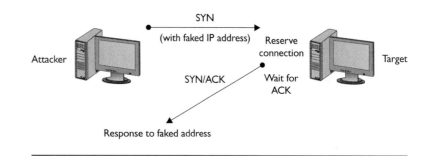

• **Figure 15.2**   A SYN flooding–based DoS attack

Another simple DoS attack is the infamous *ping of death (POD)*, and it illustrates the other type of attack—one targeted at a specific application or operating system, as opposed to SYN flooding, which targets a protocol. In the POD attack, the attacker sends an Internet Control Message Protocol (ICMP) ping packet equal to, or exceeding, 64KB (which is to say, greater than $64 \times 1024 = 65,536$ bytes). This type of packet should not occur naturally (there is no reason for a ping packet to be larger than 64KB). Certain systems are not able to handle this size of packet, and the system will hang or crash.

DoS attacks are conducted using a single attacking system. A DoS attack employing multiple attacking systems is known as a **distributed denial-of-service (DDoS) attack**. The goal of a DDoS attack is also to deny the use of or access to a specific service or system. DDoS attacks were made famous in 2000 with the highly publicized attacks on eBay, CNN, Amazon, and Yahoo!.

In a DDoS attack, service is denied by overwhelming the target with traffic from many different systems. A network of attack agents (sometimes called *zombies*) is created by the attacker, and upon receiving the attack command from the attacker, the attack agents commence sending a specific type of traffic against the target.

If the attack network is large enough, even ordinary web traffic can quickly overwhelm the largest of sites, such as those targeted in 2000.

 A **botnet** is a network of machines controlled by a malicious user. Each of these controlled machines is commonly referred to as a **zombie**.

Creating a DDoS attack network is no simple task. The attack agents are not willing agents—they are systems that have been compromised and on which the DDoS attack software has been installed. To compromise these agents, the attacker has to have gained unauthorized access to the system or tricked authorized users to run a program that installed the attack software. The creation of the attack network may in fact be a multistep process in which the attacker first compromises a few systems and then uses those systems as *handlers* or *masters*, which in turn compromise other systems. Once the network has been created, the agents wait for an attack message, which will include data on the specific target, before launching the attack. One important aspect of a DDoS attack is that with just a few messages to the agents, the attacker can have a flood of messages sent against the targeted system. Figure 15.3 illustrates a DDoS network with agents and handlers.

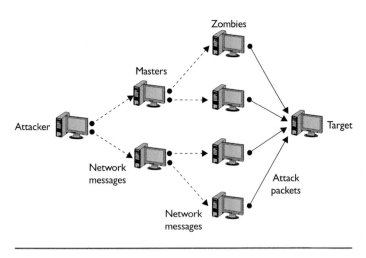

• **Figure 15.3**   DDoS attack

How can you stop or mitigate the effects of a DoS or DDoS attack? One important precaution is to ensure that you have applied the latest patches and upgrades to your systems and the applications running on them. Once a specific vulnerability is discovered, it does not take long before multiple exploits are written to take advantage of it. Generally you will have a small window of opportunity in which to patch your system between the time the vulnerability is discovered and the time exploits become widely available. A vulnerability can also be discovered by hackers, and exploits provide the first clues that a system has been compromised. Attackers can also reverse-engineer patches to learn what vulnerabilities have been patched, allowing them to attack unpatched systems.

Another approach involves changing the time-out option for TCP connections so that attacks such as the SYN flooding attack are more difficult to perform, because unused connections are dropped more quickly.

For DDoS attacks, much has been written about distributing your own workload across several systems so that any attack against your system would have to target several hosts to be completely successful. While this is effective against some DDoS attacks, if large enough DDoS networks are created (with tens of thousands of zombies, for example), any network, no matter how much the load is distributed, can be successfully attacked. Such an approach also involves additional costs to your organization to establish this distributed environment. Addressing the problem in this manner is actually an attempt to mitigate the effect of the attack, rather than preventing or stopping an attack.

To prevent a DDoS attack, you must either be able to intercept or block the attack messages or keep the DDoS network from being established in the first place. Tools have been developed that will scan your systems, searching for sleeping zombies waiting for an attack signal. Many of the current antivirus/spyware security suite tools will detect known zombie-type infections. The problem with this type of prevention approach, however, is that it is not something you can do to prevent an attack on your network—it is something you can do to keep your network from being used to attack other networks or systems. You have to rely on the community of network administrators to test their own systems to prevent attacks on yours.

A final option you should consider that will address several forms of DoS and DDoS attacks is to block ICMP packets at your border, since many attacks rely on ICMP. Blocking ICMP packets at the border devices prevents external ICMP packets from entering your network, and while this may block some functionality, it will leave internal ICMP functionality intact. It is also possible to block specific forms of ICMP; blocking Type 8, for instance, will block ICMP-based ping sweeps. It is worth noting that not all pings occur via ICMP; some tools, such as hping2, use TCP to carry ping messages.

> **Tech Tip**
>
> **Edge Blocking of ICMP**
> *Blocking ICMP at the edge device of the network will prevent ICMP-based attacks from external sites while still allowing full ICMP functionality for traffic inside the network.*

Backdoors and Trapdoors

Backdoors were originally (and sometimes still are) nothing more than methods used by software developers to ensure that they could gain access to an application even if something were to happen in the future to prevent normal access methods. An example would be a hard-coded password that could be used to gain access to the program in the event that administrators forgot their own system password. The obvious problem with this sort of backdoor (also sometimes referred to as a *trapdoor*) is that, since it is hard-coded, it cannot be removed. Should an attacker learn of the backdoor, all systems running that software would be vulnerable to attack.

The term **backdoor** is also, and more commonly, used to refer to programs that attackers install after gaining unauthorized access to a system, to ensure that they can continue to have unrestricted access to the system even if their initial access method is discovered and blocked. Backdoors can also be installed by authorized individuals inadvertently, should they run software that contains a Trojan horse (more on this later in this chapter).

A variation on the backdoor is the *rootkit*, which is established not to gain root access but rather to ensure continued root access.

> Common backdoors include NetBus and Back Orifice. Either of these, if running on your system, can allow an attacker remote access to your system—access that allows them to perform any function on your system.

Null Sessions

Microsoft Windows systems prior to XP and Server 2003 exhibited a vulnerability in their Server Message Block (SMB) system that allowed users to establish null sessions. A **null session** is a connection to a Windows interprocess communications share (IPC$). There is good news and bad news associated with this vulnerability. The good news is that Windows XP, Server 2003, and beyond are not susceptible to this vulnerability by default. The bad news is that the millions of previous version machines are vulnerable and patching will not solve the problem. This vulnerability can be used to glean many useful pieces of information from a machine, including user IDs, share names, Registry settings, and security settings. A wide range of tools and malware use this vulnerability to achieve their aim.

Hardening an affected system from the null session vulnerability requires a bit of work. The seemingly obvious path of upgrading systems to XP and beyond is not a perfect solution, for they too can be tweaked by a malicious user to become susceptible to null sessions. There are Registry settings to restrict anonymous connections, but these will not limit all types. The best method is to limit access to TCP ports 139 and 445 to only trusted users.

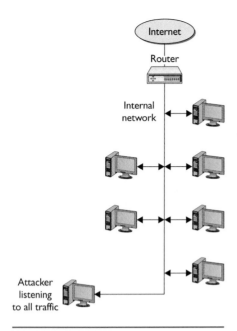

Internet

Router

Internal
network

Attacker
listening
to all traffic

● **Figure 15.4**   Network sniffers listen to all
network traffic.

Exam Tip: A network interface card (NIC) that is listening
to all network traffic and not just
its own is said to be in "promiscuous mode."

Sniffing

The group of protocols that makes up the TCP/IP suite was designed to
work in a friendly environment in which everybody who connected to
the network used the protocols as they were designed. The abuse of this
friendly assumption is illustrated by network-traffic sniffing programs,
sometimes referred to as *sniffers*. **Sniffing** is when someone examines all
the network traffic that passes their NIC, whether addressed for them or
not.

A network sniffer is a software or hardware device that is used to observe traffic as it passes through a network on shared broadcast media.
The device can be used to view all traffic, or it can target a specific protocol, service, or even string of characters (looking for logins, for example).
Normally, the network device that connects a computer to a network is
designed to ignore all traffic that is not destined for that computer. Network sniffers ignore this friendly agreement and observe all traffic on
the network, whether destined for that computer or others, as shown in
Figure 15.4. Some network sniffers are designed not just to observe all
traffic but to modify traffic as well.

Network sniffers can be used by network administrators to monitor
network performance. They can be used to perform traffic analysis, for
example, to determine what type of traffic is most commonly carried on
the network and to determine which segments are most active. They can
also be used for network bandwidth analysis and to troubleshoot certain
problems (such as duplicate MAC addresses).

Network sniffers can also be used by attackers to gather information that
can be used in penetration attempts. Information such as an authorized
username and password can be viewed and recorded for later use. The contents of e-mail messages can also be viewed as the messages travel across the
network. It should be obvious that administrators and security professionals will not want unauthorized network sniffers on their networks because
of the security and privacy concerns they introduce. Fortunately, for network sniffers to be most effective, they need to be on the internal network,
which generally means that the chances for outsiders to use them against
you are extremely limited. This is another reason that physical security is an
important part of information security in today's environment.

Cross Check

Physical Access and Security

One of the challenges in a modern network is getting a connection to a
point in the network where your sniffing will result in the discovery of interesting information. Getting access to an open port, or to an equipment
room where routers and switches are maintained, is a failure of physical
security. Physical security is an important component of a comprehensive information security program. At this point ask yourself—where can
I connect into my company network? Can I get connections near high-
value targets such as database servers? Details on physical security measures are covered in Chapter 8.

Spoofing

Spoofing is nothing more than making data look like it has come from a different source. This is possible in TCP/IP because of the friendly assumptions behind the protocols. When the protocols were developed, it was assumed that individuals who had access to the network layer would be privileged users who could be trusted.

When a packet is sent from one system to another, it includes not only the destination IP address and port but the source IP address as well. You are supposed to fill in the source with your own address, but nothing stops you from filling in another system's address. This is one of the several forms of spoofing.

Spoofing E-Mail

In e-mail spoofing, a message is sent with a From address that differs from that of the sending system. This can be easily accomplished in several different ways using several programs. To demonstrate how simple it is to spoof an e-mail address, you can Telnet to port 25 (the port associated with e-mail) on a mail server. From there, you can fill in any address for the From and To sections of the message, whether or not the addresses are yours or even actually exist.

You can use several methods to determine whether an e-mail message was sent by the source it claims to have been sent from, but most users do not question their e-mail and will accept as authentic where it appears to have originated. A variation on e-mail spoofing, though not technically spoofing, is for the attacker to acquire a URL similar to the URL they want to spoof so that e-mail sent from their system appears to have come from the official site—until you read the address carefully. For example, if attackers want to spoof XYZ Corporation, which owns XYZ.com, the attackers might gain access to the URL XYZ.Corp.com. An individual receiving a message from the spoofed corporation site would not normally suspect it to be a spoof but would take it to be official. This same method can be, and has been, used to spoof web sites. The most famous example of this is probably www.whitehouse.com. The www.whitehouse.gov site is the official site for the White House. The www.whitehouse.com URL takes you to a pornographic site. In this case, nobody is likely to take the pornographic site to be the official government site, and it was not intended to be taken that way. If, however, the attackers made their spoofed site appear similar to the official one, they could easily convince many potential viewers that they were at the official site.

IP Address Spoofing

IP is designed to work so that the originators of any IP packet include their own IP address in the From portion of the packet. While this is the intent, nothing prevents a system from inserting a different address in the From portion of the packet. This is known as *IP address spoofing*. An IP address can be spoofed for several reasons. In a specific DoS attack known as a **smurf attack**, the attacker sends a spoofed packet to the broadcast address for a network, which distributes the packet to all systems on that network. In the smurf attack, the packet sent by the attacker to the broadcast address is an

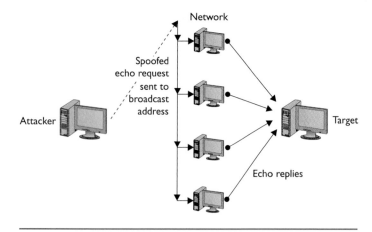

Network

Spoofed
echo request
sent to
broadcast
address

Attacker

Target

Echo replies

• **Figure 15.5** Smurfing used in a smurf DOS attack

echo request with the From address forged so that it appears that another system (the target system) has made the echo request. The normal response of a system to an echo request is an echo reply, and it is used in the ping utility to let a user know whether a remote system is reachable and is responding. In the smurf attack, the request is sent to all systems on the network, so all will respond with an echo reply to the target system, as shown in Figure 15.5. The attacker has sent one packet and has been able to generate as many as 254 responses aimed at the target. Should the attacker send several of these spoofed requests, or send them to several different networks, the target can quickly become overwhelmed with the volume of echo replies it receives.

Spoofing and Trusted Relationships

Spoofing can also take advantage of a *trusted relationship* between two systems. If two systems are configured to accept the authentication accomplished by each other, an individual logged onto one system might not be forced to go through an authentication process again to access the other system. An attacker can take advantage of this arrangement by sending a packet to one system that appears to have come from a trusted system. Since the trusted relationship is in place, the targeted system may perform the requested task without authentication.

Since a reply will often be sent once a packet is received, the system that is being impersonated could interfere with the attack, since it would receive an acknowledgment for a request it never made. The attacker will often initially launch a DoS attack (such as a SYN flooding attack) to temporarily take out the spoofed system for the period of time that the attacker is exploiting the trusted relationship. Once the attack is completed, the DoS attack on the spoofed system would be terminated, and the system administrators, apart from having a temporarily nonresponsive system, might never notice that the attack occurred. Figure 15.6 illustrates a spoofing attack that includes a SYN flooding attack.

Because of this type of attack, administrators are encouraged to strictly limit any trusted relationships between hosts. Firewalls should also be configured to discard any packets from outside of the firewall that have From addresses indicating they originated from inside the network (a situation that should not occur normally and that indicates spoofing is being attempted).

Spoofing and Sequence Numbers

How complicated the spoofing is depends heavily on several factors, including whether the traffic is encrypted and where the attacker is located relative to the target. Spoofing attacks from inside a network, for example, are

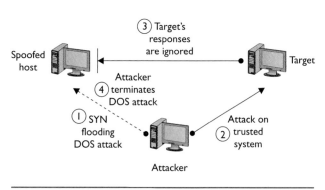

Spoofed
host

③ Target's
responses
are ignored

Target

Attacker
④ terminates
DOS attack

① SYN
flooding
DOS attack

Attack on
② trusted
system

Attacker

• **Figure 15.6** Spoofing to take advantage of a trusted relationship much easier to perform than attacks from outside of the network, because the inside attacker can observe the traffic to and from the target and can do a better job of formulating the necessary packets.

Formulating the packets is more complicated for external attackers because a sequence number is associated with TCP packets. A **sequence number** is a 32-bit number established by the host that is incremented for each packet sent. Packets are not guaranteed to be received in order, and the sequence number can be used to help reorder packets as they are received and to refer to packets that may have been lost in transmission.

In the TCP three-way handshake, two sets of sequence numbers are created, as shown in Figure 15.7. The first system chooses a sequence number to send with the original SYN packet. The system receiving this SYN packet acknowledges with a SYN/ACK. It sends an acknowledgment number back, which is based on the first sequence number plus one (that is, it increments the sequence number sent to it by one). It then also creates its own sequence number and sends that along with it. The original system receives the SYN/ACK with the new sequence number. It increments the sequence number by one and uses it as the acknowledgment number in the ACK packet with which it responds.

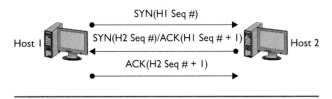

• **Figure 15.7**   Three-way handshake with sequence numbers

The difference in the difficulty of attempting a spoofing attack from inside a network and from outside involves determining the sequence number. If the attacker is inside of the network and can observe the traffic with which the target host responds, the attacker can easily see the sequence number the system creates and can respond with the correct sequence number. If the attacker is external to the network and the sequence number the target system generates is not observed, it is next to impossible for the attacker to provide the final ACK with the correct sequence number. So the attacker has to guess what the sequence number might be.

Sequence numbers are somewhat predictable. Sequence numbers for each session are not started from the same number, so that different packets from different concurrent connections will not have the same sequence numbers. Instead, the sequence number for each new connection is incremented by some large number to keep the numbers from being the same. The sequence number may also be incremented by some large number every second (or some other time period). An external attacker has to determine what values are used for these increments. The attacker can do this by attempting connections at various time intervals to observe how the sequence numbers are incremented. Once the pattern is determined, the attacker can attempt a legitimate connection to determine the current value, and then immediately attempt the spoofed connection. The spoofed connection sequence number should be the legitimate connection incremented by the determined value or values.

Sequence numbers are also important in session hijacking, which is discussed later in the "TCP/IP Hijacking" section of this chapter. When an attacker spoofs addresses and imposes his packets in the middle of an existing connection, this is the man-in-the-middle attack.

Man-in-the-Middle Attacks

A **man-in-the-middle attack**, as the name implies, generally occurs when attackers are able to place themselves in the middle of two other hosts that are communicating. Ideally, this is done by ensuring that all communication going to or from the target host is routed through the attacker's host (which can be accomplished if the attacker can compromise the router for the target host). The attacker can then observe all traffic before relaying it and can actually modify or block traffic. To the target host, it appears that communication is occurring normally, since all expected replies are received. Figure 15.8 illustrates this type of attack.

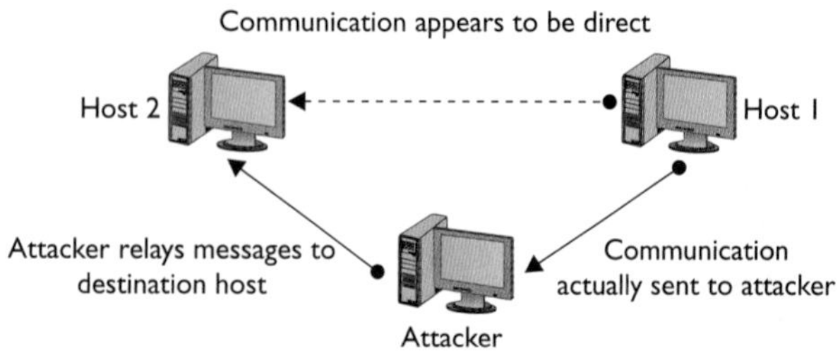

The amount of information that can be obtained in a man-in-the-middle attack will obviously be limited if the communication is encrypted. Even in this case, however, sensitive information can still be obtained, since knowing what communication is being conducted, and between which individuals, may in fact provide information that is valuable in certain circumstances.

• Figure 15.8   A man-in-the-middle attack

Communication appears to be direct

Host 2   Host 1

Attacker relays messages to destination host   *Communication actually sent to attacker*

Attacker

Man-in-the-Middle Attacks on Encrypted Traffic

The term "man-in-the-middle attack" is sometimes used to refer to a more specific type of attack—one in which the encrypted traffic issue is addressed.

If you wanted to communicate securely with your friend Bob, you might ask him for his public key so you could encrypt your messages to him. You, in turn, would supply Bob with your public key. An attacker can conduct a man-in-the-middle attack by intercepting your request for Bob's public key and the sending of your public key to him. The attacker would replace your public key with their public key, and she would send this on to Bob. The attacker's public key would also be sent to you by the attacker instead

> ### ☑ Cross Check
>
> #### Encryption
> Cryptography and encryption are tools that can solve many of our secrecy problems. The challenges solved through encryption and the new problems associated with the use of encryption require an understanding of the technical details. Public key encryption, discussed in detail in Chapters 5 and 6, uses two keys: a public key, which anybody can use to encrypt or "lock" your message, and a private key, which only you know and which is used to "unlock" or decrypt a message locked with your public key. One of the key challenges associated with the use of public keys and corresponding private keys is determining who has what key values. Do you have your own key pair? If so, do you know the public key value that you need to share with others?

of Bob's public key. Now when either you or Bob encrypts a message, it will be encrypted using the attacker's public key, enabling the attacker to intercept it, decrypt it, and then send it on by re-encrypting it with the appropriate key for either you or Bob. Each of you thinks you are transmitting messages securely, but in reality your communication has been compromised. Well-designed cryptographic products use techniques such as mutual authentication to avoid this problem.

Replay Attacks

A **replay attack** occurs when the attacker captures a portion of a communication between two parties and retransmits it at a later time. For example, an attacker might replay a series of commands and codes used in a financial transaction to cause the transaction to be conducted multiple times. Generally replay attacks are associated with attempts to circumvent authentication mechanisms, such as the capturing and reuse of a certificate or ticket.

The best way to prevent replay attacks is with encryption, cryptographic authentication, and time stamps. If a portion of the certificate or ticket includes a date/time stamp or an expiration date/time, and this portion is also encrypted as part of the ticket or certificate, replaying it at a later time will prove useless, since it will be rejected as having expired.

Exam Tip: The best method for defending against replay attacks is through the use of encryption and short time frames for legal transactions. Encryption can protect the contents from being understood, and a short time frame for a transaction prevents subsequent use.

TCP/IP Hijacking

TCP/IP hijacking and *session hijacking* are terms used to refer to the process of taking control of an already existing session between a client and a server. The advantage to an attacker of hijacking over attempting to penetrate a computer system or network is that the attacker doesn't have to circumvent any authentication mechanisms, since the user has already authenticated and established the session. Once the user has completed the authentication sequence, the attacker can then usurp the session and carry on as if the attacker, and not the user, had authenticated with the system. To prevent the user from noticing anything unusual, the attacker can decide to attack the user's system and perform a DoS attack on it, taking it down so that the user, and the system, will not notice the extra traffic that is taking place.

Hijack attacks generally are used against web and Telnet sessions. Sequence numbers as they apply to spoofing also apply to session hijacking, since the hijacker will need to provide the correct sequence number to continue the appropriated sessions.

Drive-by Download Attacks

Browsers are used to navigate the Internet, using HTTP and other protocols to bring files to users' computers. Some of these files are images, some are scripts, and some are text based, and together they form the web pages that we see. Users don't ask for each component—it is the job of the browser to identify the needed files and fetch them. A new type of attack takes advantage of this mechanism by initiating downloads of malware, whether a user clicks it or not. This automated download of materials is referred to as a **drive-by download attack**.

Drive-by downloads can occur from a couple of different mechanisms. It is possible for an ad that is rotated into content on a reputable site to contain a drive-by download. Users don't have control over what ads are presented. A second, more common method is a web site that the user gets to either by mistyping a URL or by following a search link without vetting where they are clicking first. Just like cities can have bad neighborhoods, so too does the Internet, and surfing in a bad neighborhood can result in bad outcomes.

Phishing and Pharming Attacks

Phishing is the use of fraudulent e-mails or instant messages that appear to be genuine but are designed to trick users. The goal of a phishing attack is to obtain from the user information that can be used in an attack, such as login credentials or other critical information. When the attacker includes information that should be known only to the entity that they are impersonating, the attack is called **spear phishing**.

Pharming is the impersonation of a web site in an effort to deceive a user into entering their credentials. Phishing and pharming are two tools used for identity theft and are common attack methods used to steal credentials.

The Anti-Phishing Working Group (APWG) is "an industry association focused on eliminating the identity theft and fraud that result from the growing problem of phishing and email spoofing." APWG is located at www.antiphishing.org.

Attacks on Encryption

Cryptography is the art of "secret writing," and *encryption* is the process of transforming *plaintext* into an unreadable format known as *ciphertext* using a specific technique or algorithm. Most encryption techniques use some form of key in the encryption process. The key is used in a mathematical process to scramble the original message to arrive at the unreadable ciphertext. Another key (sometimes the same one and sometimes a different one) is used to decrypt or unscramble the ciphertext to re-create the original plaintext. The length of the key often directly relates to the strength of the encryption.

Cryptanalysis is the process of attempting to break a cryptographic system—it is an attack on the specific method used to encrypt the plaintext. Cryptographic systems can be compromised in various ways.

Cross Check

Cryptography and Encryption

Understanding the basics of cryptography is important to understanding various defenses from malware. If you are not familiar with encryption, decryption, hashes, and signatures, it would be wise to review them now. The various elements of cryptography and encryption are discussed in detail in Chapter 5.

Weak Keys

Certain encryption algorithms may have specific keys that yield poor, or easily decrypted, ciphertext. Imagine an encryption algorithm that consists solely of a single XOR function (an exclusive OR function where two bits are compared and a 1 is returned if either of the original bits, but not both, is a 1), where the key is repeatedly used to XOR with the plaintext. A key where all bits are 0's, for example, would result in ciphertext that is the same as the original plaintext. This would obviously be a weak key for this encryption algorithm. In fact, any key with long strings of 0's would yield portions of the ciphertext that were the same as the plaintext. In this simple example, many keys could be considered weak.

Encryption algorithms used in computer systems and networks are much more complicated than a simple, single XOR function, but some algorithms have still been found to have weak keys that make cryptanalysis easier.

Exhaustive Search of Key Space

Even if the specific algorithm used to encrypt a message is complicated and has not been shown to have weak keys, the key length will still play a significant role in how easy it is to attack the method of encryption. Generally speaking, the longer a key, the harder it will be to attack. Thus, a 40-bit encryption scheme will be easier to attack using a brute-force technique (which tests all possible keys, one by one) than a 256-bit based scheme. This is easily demonstrated by imagining a scheme that employs a 2-bit key. Even if the resulting ciphertext were completely unreadable, performing a brute-force attack until one key is found that can decrypt the ciphertext would not take long, since only four keys are possible. Every bit that is added to the length of a key doubles the number of keys that have to be tested in a brute-force attack on the encryption. It is easy to understand why a scheme utilizing a 40-bit key would be much easier to attack than a scheme that utilizes a 256-bit key.

The bottom line is simple: an exhaustive search of the keyspace will decrypt the message. The strength of the encryption method is related to the sheer size of the keyspace, which with modern algorithms is large enough to provide significant time constraints when using this method to break an encrypted message. Algorithmic complexity is also an issue with respect to brute force, and you cannot immediately compare different key lengths from different algorithms and assume relative strength.

Indirect Attacks

One of the most common ways of attacking an encryption system is to find weaknesses in mechanisms surrounding the cryptography. Examples include poor random-number generators, unprotected key exchanges, keys stored on hard drives without sufficient protection, and other general programmatic errors, such as buffer overflows. In attacks that target these types of weaknesses, it is not the cryptographic algorithm itself that is being attacked, but rather the implementation of that algorithm in the real world.

Address System Attacks

Many aspects of a computer system are controlled by the use of addresses. IP addresses can be manipulated as shown earlier, and the other address schemes can be manipulated as well. In the summer of 2008, much was made of a serious Domain Name System (DNS) vulnerability that required the simultaneous patching of systems by over 80 vendors. This coordinated effort was to close a technical loophole in the domain name resolution infrastructure that would allow the hijacking and man-in-the-middle attack on the DNS system worldwide.

The DNS system has been the target of other attacks. One attack, **DNS kiting**, is an economic attack against the terms of using a new DNS entry. New DNS purchases are allowed a five-day "test period" during which the name can be relinquished for no fee. Creative users learned to register a name, use it for less than five days, relinquish the name, and then get the name and begin all over, repeating this cycle many times to use a name without paying for it. Typical registration versus permanent entry ratios of 15:1 occur, and in February 2007 GoDaddy reported that out of 55.1 million requests only 3.6 million were not canceled.

Exam Tip: The process of using a new domain name for the five-day "test" period and then relinquishing the name, only to repeat the process again—in essence, obtaining a domain name for free—is called DNS kiting.

Another twist on this scheme is the concept of domain name front running, where a registrar places a name on a five-day hold after someone searches for it, and then offers it for sale at a higher price. In January 2008, Network Solutions was accused of violating the trust as a registrar by forcing people to purchase names from them after they engaged in domain name tasting (www.domainnamenews.com/featured/domain-registrar-network-solutions-front-running-on-whois-searches/1359).

Another attack on a DNS is through the concept of DNS poisoning, the unauthorized changing of DNS tables on a machine. When an IP address needs to be resolved, a check against the local cache is first performed. If the address is present, this alleviates the need to ask an outside DNS resource. If the local cache is tampered with, this can result in the hijacking of information because the computer will connect to the wrong site.

Local MAC addresses can also be poisoned in the same manner, although it is called ARP poisoning. This can cause miscommunications locally. Poisoning attacks can be used to steal information, establish man-in-the-middle attacks, and even create DoS opportunities.

Password Guessing

The most common form of authentication is the user ID and password combination. While it is not inherently a poor mechanism for authentication, the combination can be attacked in several ways. All too often, these attacks yield favorable results for the attacker not as a result of a weakness in the scheme but usually due to the user not following good password procedures.

Poor Password Choices

The least technical of the various password-attack techniques consists of the attacker simply attempting to guess the password of an authorized user of the system or network. It is surprising how often this simple method works, and the reason it does is because people are notorious for picking poor passwords. Users need to select a password that they can remember, so they create simple passwords, such as their birthday, their mother's maiden name, the name of their spouse or one of their children, or even simply their user ID itself. All it takes is for the attacker to obtain a valid user ID (often a simple matter, because organizations tend to use an individual's names in some combination—first letter of their first name combined with their last name, for example) and a little bit of information about the user before guessing can begin. Organizations sometimes make it even easier for attackers to obtain this sort of information by posting the names of their "management team" and other individuals, sometimes with short biographies, on their web sites.

Even if the person doesn't use some personal detail as her password, the attacker may still get lucky, since many people use a common word for their password. Attackers can obtain lists of common passwords—a number of such lists exist on the Internet. Words such as "password" and "secret" have often been used as passwords. Names of favorite sports teams also often find their way onto lists of commonly used passwords.

Dictionary Attack

Another method of determining passwords is to use a password-cracking program that uses a list of dictionary words to try to guess the password. The dictionary words can be used by themselves, or two or more smaller words can be combined to form a single possible password. A number of commercial and public-domain password-cracking programs employ a variety of methods to crack passwords, including using variations on the user ID.

Rules can also be defined so that the cracking program will substitute special characters for other characters or combine words. The ability of the attacker to crack passwords is directly related to the method the user employs to create the password in the first place, as well as the dictionary and rules used.

Brute-Force Attack

If the user has selected a password that is not found in a dictionary, even if simply by substituting various numbers or special characters for letters, the only way the password can be cracked is for an attacker to attempt a brute-force attack, in which the password-cracking program attempts all possible character combinations.

The length of the password and the size of the set of possible characters in the password will greatly affect the time a brute-force attack will take. A few years ago, this method of attack was very time consuming, since it took considerable time to generate all possible combinations. With the increase in computer speed, however, generating password combinations is much faster, making it more feasible to launch brute-force attacks against certain computer systems and networks.

A brute-force attack on a password can take place at two levels: The attacker can use a password-cracking program to attempt to guess the password directly at a login prompt, or the attacker can first steal a password file, use a password-cracking program to compile a list of possible passwords based on the list of password hashes contained in the password file (offline), and then use that narrower list to attempt to guess the password at the login prompt. The first attack can be made more difficult if the account locks after a few failed login attempts. The second attack can be thwarted if the password file is securely maintained so that others cannot obtain a copy of it.

Hybrid Attack

A hybrid password attack is an attack that combines the preceding dictionary and brute-force methods. Most cracking tools have this option built in, first attempting a dictionary attack, and then moving to brute-force methods.

The programs often permit the attacker to create various rules that tell the program how to combine words to form new possible passwords. Users commonly substitute certain numbers for specific letters. If the user wanted to use the word *secret* as a base for a password, for example, she could replace the letter *e* with the number *3*, yielding *s3cr3t*. This password will not be found in the dictionary, so a pure dictionary attack would not crack it, but the password is still easy for the user to remember. If the attacker created a rule that instructed the program to try all words in the dictionary and then try the same words substituting the number *3* for the letter *e*, however, the password would be cracked.

Birthday Attack

The **birthday attack** is a special type of brute-force attack that gets its name from something known as the *birthday paradox*, which states that in a group of at least 23 people, the chance that two individuals will have the same birthday is greater than 50 percent. Mathematically, the equation is $1.25 \times k^{1/2}$, where k equals the size of the set of possible values, which in the birthday paradox is 365 (the number of possible birthdays). This same phenomenon applies to passwords, with k (number of passwords) being quite a bit larger.

Software Exploitation

An attack that takes advantage of bugs or weaknesses in software is referred to as *software exploitation*. These bugs and weaknesses can be the result of poor design, poor testing, or poor coding practices. They can also result from what are sometimes called "features." An example of this might be a

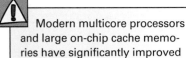

Modern multicore processors and large on-chip cache memories have significantly improved the speed of password-cracking programs, making brute-force methods practical in many cases.

Tech Tip

Offline Password Attacks

Because an attacker who obtains a password file has unlimited time offline to prepare for the online attack, and can prepare without tipping off the target, all passwords should be considered to be vulnerable over extended periods of time. For this reason, even batch passwords (used for system-run batch jobs) should be changed periodically to prevent offline attacks.

debugging feature, which when used during debugging might allow unauthenticated individuals to execute programs on a system. If this feature remains in the program when the final version of the software is shipped, it creates a weakness that is just waiting to be exploited.

Buffer-Overflow Attack

A common weakness that has often been exploited is a **buffer overflow**, which occurs when a program is provided more data for input than it was designed to handle. For example, what would happen if a program that asks for a 7- to 10-character phone number instead receives a string of 150 characters? Many programs will provide some error checking to ensure that this will not cause a problem. Some programs, however, cannot handle this error, and the extra characters continue to fill memory, overwriting other portions of the program. This can result in a number of problems, including causing the program to abort or the system to crash. Under certain circumstances, the program can execute a command supplied by the attacker. Buffer overflows typically inherit the level of privilege enjoyed by the program being exploited. This is why programs that use root-level access are so dangerous when exploited with a buffer overflow, as the code that will execute does so at root-level access.

> Buffer overflows were one of the most common vulnerabilities over the past ten years, although awareness and efforts to eradicate them over the past couple of years has been very successful in new code.

Malicious Code

Malicious code, or **malware**, refers to software that has been designed for some nefarious purpose. Such software can be designed to cause damage to a system, such as by deleting all files, or it can be designed to create a backdoor in the system to grant access to unauthorized individuals. Most malware instances attack vulnerabilities in programs or operating systems. This is why patching of vulnerabilities is so important, for it closes the point of entry for most malware. Generally the installation of malicious code is done in such a way that it is not obvious to the authorized users. Several different types of malicious software can be used, such as viruses, Trojan horses, logic bombs, spyware, and worms, and they differ in the ways they are installed and their purposes.

Viruses

The best-known type of malicious code is the virus. Much has been written about viruses as a result of several high-profile security events that involved them. A virus is a piece of malicious code that replicates by attaching itself to another piece of executable code. When the other executable code is run, the virus also executes and has the opportunity to infect other files and perform any other nefarious actions it was designed to do. The specific way that a virus infects other files, and the type of files it infects, depends on the type of virus. The first viruses created were of two types—boot sector viruses and program viruses.

Boot Sector Virus   A boot sector virus infects the boot sector portion of either a floppy disk or a hard drive (years ago, not all computers had hard drives, and many booted from a floppy). When a computer is first turned on, a small portion of the operating system is initially loaded from hardware. This small operating system then attempts to load the rest of the operating system from a specific location (sector) on either the floppy or the hard drive. A boot sector virus infects this portion of the drive.

An example of this type of virus was the Stoned virus, which moved the true Master Boot Record (MBR) from the first to the seventh sector of the first cylinder and replaced the original MBR with the virus code. When the system was turned on, the virus was first executed, which had a one-in-seven chance of displaying a message stating the computer was "stoned"; otherwise, it would not announce itself and would instead attempt to infect other boot sectors. This virus was rather tame in comparison to other viruses of its time, which were often designed to delete the entire hard drive after a period of time in which they would attempt to spread.

Program Virus   A second type of virus is the program virus, which attaches itself to executable files—typically files ending in .exe or .com on Windows-based systems. The virus is attached in such a way that it is executed before the program executes. Most program viruses also hide a nefarious purpose, such as deleting the hard drive data, which is triggered by a specific event, such as a date or after a certain number of other files are infected. Like other types of viruses, program viruses are often not detected until after they execute their malicious payload. One method that has been used to detect this sort of virus before it has an opportunity to damage a system is to calculate checksums for commonly used programs or utilities. Should the checksum for an executable ever change, it is quite likely that it is due to a virus infection.

Macro Virus   In the late 1990s, another type of virus appeared that now accounts for the majority of viruses. As systems and operating systems became more powerful, the boot sector virus, which once accounted for most reported infections, became less common. Systems no longer commonly booted from floppies, which were the main method for boot sector viruses to spread. Instead, the proliferation of software that included macro-programming languages resulted in a new breed of virus—the macro virus.

The Concept virus was the first known example of this new breed. It appeared to be created to demonstrate the possibility of attaching a virus to a document file, something that had been thought to be impossible before the introduction of software that included powerful macro language capabilities. By this time, however, Microsoft Word documents could include segments of code written in a derivative of Visual Basic. Further development of other applications that allowed macro capability, and enhanced versions of the original macro language, had the side effect of allowing the proliferation of viruses that took advantage of this capability.

This type of virus is so common today that it is considered a security best practice to advise users never to open a document attached to an e-mail if it seems at all suspicious. Many organizations now routinely have their mail servers eliminate any attachments containing Visual Basic macros.

Avoiding Virus Infection   Always being cautious about executing programs or opening documents sent to you is a good security practice. "If you don't know where it came from or where it has been, don't open or run it" should be the basic mantra for all computer users. Another security best practice for protecting against virus infection is to install and run an

Tech Tip

Modern Virus and Worm Threats
Early virus and worm attacks would cause damage to PCs, but they were generally visible to users. Many modern viruses and worms are used to deliver payloads that lead to machines becoming zombies in a botnet, controlled by an attacker. This type of attack is typically invisible to the end user, so as not to alert them to the malware.

antivirus program. Since these programs are designed to protect against known viruses, it is also important to maintain an up-to-date listing of virus signatures for your antivirus software. Antivirus software vendors provide this information, and administrators should stay on top of the latest updates to the list of known viruses.

Two advances in virus writing have made it more difficult for antivirus software to detect viruses. These advances are the introduction of *stealth virus* techniques and *polymorphic viruses*. A stealthy virus employs techniques to help evade being detected by antivirus software that uses checksums or other techniques. Polymorphic viruses also attempt to evade detection, but they do so by changing the virus itself (the virus "evolves"). Because the virus changes, signatures for that virus may no longer be valid, and the virus may escape detection by antivirus software.

Virus Hoaxes Viruses have caused so much damage to systems that many Internet users become extremely cautious anytime they hear a rumor of a new virus. Many users will not connect to the Internet when they hear about a virus outbreak, just to be sure their machines don't get infected. This has given rise to virus hoaxes, in which word is spread about a new virus and the extreme danger it poses. It may warn users to not read certain files or connect to the Internet.

A good example of a virus hoax was the Good Times virus warning, which has been copied repeatedly and can still be seen in various forms today. It caused widespread panic as users read about this extremely dangerous virus, which allegedly could actually cause the processor to overheat (from being put into an "nth complexity infinite binary loop") and be destroyed. Many folks saw through this hoax, but many less experienced users did not, and they passed the warning along to all of their friends.

Hoaxes can actually be even more destructive than just wasting time and bandwidth. Some hoaxes warning of a dangerous virus have included instructions to delete certain files if they're found on the user's system. Unfortunately for those who follow the advice, the files may actually be part of the operating system, and deleting them could keep the system from booting properly. This suggests another good piece of security advice: make sure of the authenticity and accuracy of any virus report before following somebody's advice. Antivirus software vendors are a good source of factual data for this sort of threat as well. (See www.symantec.com/business/security_response/threatexplorer/risks/hoaxes.jsp or http://vil.mcafee.com/hoax.asp for examples of hoaxes.)

Trojan Horses

A Trojan horse, or simply *Trojan*, is a piece of software that appears to do one thing (and may, in fact, actually do that thing) but hides some other functionality. The analogy to the famous story of antiquity is very accurate. In the original case, the object appeared to be a large wooden horse, and in fact it was. At the same time, it hid something much more sinister and dangerous to the occupants of the city of Troy. As long as the horse was left outside the city walls, it could cause no damage to the inhabitants. It had to be taken in by the inhabitants, and it was inside that the hidden purpose was activated. A computer Trojan works in much the same way. Unlike a virus, which reproduces by attaching itself to other files or programs, a Trojan is a standalone program that must be copied and installed by the user—it must be "brought inside" the system by an authorized user. The challenge for the attacker is enticing the user to copy and run the program. This generally means that the program must be disguised as something that the user would want to run—a special utility or game, for example. Once it has been copied and is inside the system, the Trojan will perform its hidden purpose, with the user often still unaware of its true nature.

A good example of a Trojan is Back Orifice (BO), originally created in 1999 and now offered in several versions. BO can be attached to a number of types of programs. Once it is attached, and once an infected file is run, BO will create a way for unauthorized individuals to take over the system remotely, as if they were sitting at the console. BO is designed to work with Windows-based systems. Many Trojans communicate to the outside through a port that the Trojan opens, and this is one of the ways Trojans can be detected.

The single best method to prevent the introduction of a Trojan to your system is never to run software if you are unsure of its origin, security, and integrity. A virus-checking program may also be useful in detecting and preventing the installation of known Trojans.

Spyware

Spyware is software that "spies" on users, recording and reporting on their activities. Typically installed without user knowledge, spyware can do a wide range of activities. It can record keystrokes (commonly called keylogging) when the user logs into specific web sites. It can monitor how a user uses a specific piece of software (for example, monitor attempts to cheat at games).

Many uses of spyware seem innocuous at first, but the unauthorized monitoring of a system can be abused very easily. In other cases, the spyware is specifically designed to steal information. Many states have passed legislation banning the unapproved installation of software, but many cases of spyware circumvent this issue through complex and confusing end-user license agreements.

Keylogging is one of the holy grails for attackers, for if they can get a keylogger on a machine, the capturing of user-typed credentials is a quick win for the attacker.

Logic Bombs

Logic bombs, unlike viruses and Trojans, are a type of malicious software that is deliberately installed, generally by an authorized user. A logic bomb is a piece of code that sits dormant for a period of time until some event invokes its malicious payload. An example of a logic bomb might be a program that is set to load and run automatically, and that periodically checks an organization's payroll or personnel database for a specific employee. If the employee is not found, the malicious payload executes, deleting vital corporate files.

Logic bombs are difficult to detect because they are often installed by authorized users and, in particular, by administrators who are also often responsible for security. This demonstrates the need for a separation of duties and a periodic review of all programs and services that are running on a system. It also illustrates the need to maintain an active backup program so that if your organization loses critical files to this sort of malicious code, it loses only transactions that occurred since the most recent backup and no permanent loss of data results.

If the event invoking the logic bomb is a specific date or time, the program will often be referred to as a *time bomb.* In one famous example of a time bomb, a disgruntled employee left a time bomb in place just prior to being fired from his job. Two weeks later, thousands of client records were deleted. Police were eventually able to track the malicious code to the disgruntled ex-employee, who was prosecuted for his actions. He had hoped that the two weeks that had passed since his dismissal would have caused investigators to assume he could not have been the individual who had caused the deletion of the records.

Rootkits

A *rootkit* is a form of malware that is specifically designed to modify the operation of the operating system in some fashion to facilitate nonstandard functionality. The history of rootkits goes back to the beginning of the UNIX operating system, where they were sets of modified administrative tools. Originally designed to allow a program to take greater control over operating system function when it fails or becomes unresponsive, the technique has evolved and is used in a variety of ways.

A rootkit can do many things—in fact, it can do virtually anything that the operating system does. Rootkits modify the operating system kernel and supporting functions, changing the nature of the system's operation. Rootkits are designed to avoid, either by subversion or evasion, the security functions of the operating system to avoid detection. Rootkits act as a form of malware that can change thread priorities to boost an application's performance, perform keylogging, act as a sniffer, hide other files from other applications, or create backdoors in the authentication system. The use of rootkit functionality to hide other processes and files enables an attacker to use a portion of a computer without the user or other applications knowing what is happening. This hides exploit code from antivirus and antispyware programs, acting as a cloak of invisibility.

Rootkits can load before the operating system loads, acting as a virtualization layer, as in SubVirt and Blue Pill. Rootkits can exist in firmware, and these have been demonstrated in both video cards and PCI expansion cards. Rootkits can exist as loadable library modules, effectively changing portions of the operating system outside the kernel. Further information on specific rootkits in the wild can be found at www.antirootkit.com.

Once a rootkit is detected, it needs to be removed and cleaned up. Because of rootkits' invasive nature, and the fact that many aspects of rootkits are not easily detectable, most system administrators don't even attempt to clean up or remove a rootkit. It is far easier to use a previously captured clean system image and reimage the machine than to attempt to determine the depth and breadth of the damage and fix individual files.

Worms

It was once easy to distinguish between a worm and a virus. Recently, with the introduction of new breeds of sophisticated malicious code, the distinction has blurred. Worms are pieces of code that attempt to penetrate networks and computer systems. Once a penetration occurs, the worm will create a new copy of itself on the penetrated system. Reproduction of a worm thus does not rely on the attachment of the virus to another piece of code or to a file, which is the definition of a virus.

Viruses were generally thought of as a system-based problem, and worms were network-based. If the malicious code is sent throughout a network, it may subsequently be called a worm. The important distinction, however, is whether the code has to attach itself to something else (a virus) or if it can "survive" on its own (a worm).

Some recent examples of worms that have had high profiles include the Sobig worm of 2003, the SQL Slammer worm of 2003, the 2001 attacks of Code Red and Nimba, and the 2005 Zotob worm, which took down CNN Live. Nimba was particularly impressive in that it used five different methods to spread: via e-mail, via open network shares, from browsing infected web sites, using directory-traversal vulnerability of Microsoft IIS 4.0/5.0, and most impressively through the use of backdoors left by Code Red II and sadmind worms.

Morris Worm   The most famous example of a worm was the Morris worm in 1988. Also sometimes referred to as the Internet worm, because of its effect on the early Internet, the worm was able to insert itself into so many systems connected to the Internet that it has been repeatedly credited with "bringing the Internet to its knees" for several days. This worm provided the impetus for the creation of what was once called the Computer Emergency Response Team Coordination Center, now the CERT Coordination Center (CERT/CC), located at Carnegie Mellon University.

The Morris worm was created by Robert Morris, at the time a graduate student at Cornell University. It utilized several known vulnerabilities to gain access to a new system, and it also relied on password guessing to obtain access to accounts. Once a system was penetrated, a small bootstrap program was inserted into the new system and executed. This program then downloaded the rest of the worm to the new system. The worm had some stealth characteristics to make determining what it was doing harder, and it suffered from one major miscalculation. The worm would not be loaded if a copy of it was already found on the new system, but it was designed to ignore this check periodically, reportedly to ensure that the worm could not be easily eliminated. The problem with this plan was that interconnected systems were constantly being reinfected. Eventually the systems were running so many copies of the worm that the system response time ground to a stop. It took a concerted effort by many individuals to eliminate the worm. While the Morris worm carried no malicious payload, it is entirely possible for worms to do so.

Protection Against Worms   How you protect your system against worms depends on the type of worm. Those attached and propagated through e-mail can be avoided by following the same guidelines about not opening files and not running attachments unless you are absolutely sure of their origin and integrity. Protecting against the Morris type of Internet worm involves securing systems and networks against penetration in the same way you would protect your systems against human attackers: install patches, eliminate unused and unnecessary services, enforce good password security, and use firewalls and intrusion detection systems. More sophisticated attacks, such as the Samy worm, are almost impossible to avoid.

Botnets

Malware can have a wide range of consequences on a machine, from relatively benign to extremely serious. One form of malware that is seemingly benign to a user is a botnet zombie. Hackers create armies of machines by installing malware agents on the machines, which then are called zombies. These zombies are controlled in large networks, called botnets, and are used to conduct other attacks and to spread spam and other malware. Botnets have grown into networks of over a million nodes and are responsible for tens of millions of spam messages daily.

Tech Tip

Samy Worm (The MySpace Worm)
MySpace is a popular social networking site with a feature that allows people to list other users as friends. In 2005, a clever MySpace user looking to expand his friends list created the first self-propagating cross-site scripting (XSS) worm. In less than a day, the worm had gone viral and user Samy had amassed more than 1 million friends on the popular online community. The worm's code, now posted at http://namb.la/popular/tech.html, used a fairly sophisticated JavaScript script. Fortunately the script was written for fun and didn't try to take advantage of unpatched security holes in Internet Explorer to create a massive MySpace botnet. MySpace was taken down because the worm replicated too efficiently, eventually surpassing several thousand replications per second.

Malware Defenses

Malware in all forms—virus, worm, spyware, botnet, and so on—can be defended against in a couple of simple steps:

- **Use an antivirus program** Most major-vendor antivirus suites are designed to catch most widespread forms of malware. In some markets, the antivirus software is being referred to as anti-*x* software, indicating that it covers more than viruses. But because the threat environment changes literally daily, the signature files for the software need regular updates, which most antivirus programs offer to perform automatically.

- **Keep your software up to date** Many forms of malware achieve their objectives through exploitation of vulnerabilities in software, both in the operating system and applications. Although operating system vulnerabilities were the main source of problems, today application-level vulnerabilities pose the greatest risk. Unfortunately, while operating system vendors are becoming more and more responsive to patching, most application vendors are not, and some, like Adobe, have very large footprints across most machines.

One of the challenges in keeping a system up to date is keeping track of the software that is on the system, and keeping track of all vendor updates. There are software products, such as Secunia's Personal Software Inspector (PSI) program, that can scan your machine to enumerate all the software installed and verify the vendor status of each product. For standalone machines, such as the one in your home, this type of program is a great time-saving item. In even small enterprises, these tools are essential to manage the complexity of patches needed across the machines.

Application-Level Attacks

Attacks against a system can occur at the network level, at the operating system level, at the application level, or at the user level (social engineering). Early attack patterns were against the network, but most of today's attacks are aimed at the applications. This is primarily because this is where the objective of most attacks resides; in the infamous words of bank robber Willie Sutton, "because that's where the money is." In fact, many of today's attacks on systems are combinations of using vulnerabilities in networks, operating systems, and applications, all means to an end to obtain the desired objective of an attack, which is usually some form of data.

Application-level attacks take advantage of several facts associated with computer applications. First, most applications are large programs written by groups of programmers and, by their nature, have errors in design and coding that create vulnerabilities. For a list of typical vulnerabilities, see the Common Vulnerability and Exposures (CVE) list maintained by Mitre, http://cve.mitre.org. Second, even when vulnerabilities are discovered and

 Cross Check

Application Vulnerabilities

Applications are a common target of attacks, as attackers have shifted to easier targets as the network and OS have become more hardened. What applications are not up to date on the PC you use every day? How would you know? How would you update them? A more complete examination of common application vulnerabilities is presented in Chapter 18.

patched by software vendors, end users are slow to apply patches, as evidenced by the SQL Slammer incident in January 2003. The vulnerability exploited was a buffer overflow, and the vendor supplied a patch six months prior to the outbreak, yet the worm still spread quickly due to the multitude of unpatched systems.

War-Dialing and War-Driving

War-dialing is the term used to describe an attacker's attempt to discover unprotected modem connections to computer systems and networks. The term's origin is the 1983 movie *War Games*, in which the star has his machine systematically call a sequence of phone numbers in an attempt to find a computer connected to a modem. In the case of the movie, the intent was to find a machine with games the attacker could play, though obviously an attacker could have other purposes once access is obtained.

War-dialing is surprisingly successful, mostly because of *rogue modems*—unauthorized modems attached to computers on a network by authorized users. Generally the reason for attaching the modem is not malicious—an individual may simply want to be able to go home and then connect to the organization's network to continue working. The problem, however, is that if a user can connect, so can an attacker. If the authorized user has not implemented any security protection, this means of access could be totally open. This is often the case. Most organizations enact strict policies against connecting unauthorized modems, but it is difficult to enforce this kind of policy. Recently, new technology has been developed to address this common backdoor into corporate networks. Telephone firewalls have been created, which block any unauthorized modem connections into an organization. These devices make it impossible for an unauthorized modem connection to be established and can also enforce strict access policies on any authorized modems.

Another avenue of attack on computer systems and networks has seen a tremendous increase over the last few years because of the increase in the use of wireless networks. War-driving is the unauthorized scanning for and connecting to wireless access points, frequently done while driving near a facility. Wireless networks have some obvious advantages—they free employees from the cable connection to a port on their wall, allowing them to move throughout the building with their laptops and still be connected. An employee could, for example, leave her desk with her laptop and move to a conference room where she could then make a presentation, all without ever having to disconnect her machine from the wall or find a connection in the conference room.

The problem with wireless networks is that it is difficult to limit access to them. Since no physical connection exists, the distance that a user can go and still remain connected is a function of the wireless network itself and where the various components of the network are placed. To ensure access throughout a facility, wireless access points are often placed at numerous locations, some of which may actually provide access to areas outside of the organization to ensure that the farthest offices in the organization can be reached. Frequently, access extends into adjacent offices or into the parking lot or street. Attackers can locate these access areas that fall outside of the organization and attempt to gain unauthorized access.

Cross Check

Wireless Vulnerabilities

Wireless systems have their own vulnerabilities unique to the wireless protocols. Wireless systems are becoming very common. If your machine is wireless capable, how many wireless access points can you see from your current location? Securing wireless systems from unauthorized access is an essential element of a comprehensive security program. This material is covered in depth in Chapter 12.

The term *war-driving* has been used to refer to the activity in which attackers wander throughout an area (often in a car) with a computer with wireless capability, searching for wireless networks they can access. Some security measures can limit an attacker's ability to succeed at this activity, but, just as in war-dialing, the individuals who set up the wireless networks don't always activate these security mechanisms.

Social Engineering

Social engineering relies on lies and misrepresentation, which an attacker uses to trick an authorized user into providing information or access the attacker would not normally be entitled to. The attacker might, for example, contact a system administrator and pretend to be an authorized user, asking to have a password reset. Another common ploy is to pose as a representative from a vendor who needs temporary access to perform some emergency maintenance. Social engineering also applies to physical access. Simple techniques include impersonating pizza or flower delivery personnel to gain physical access to a facility.

Attackers know that, due to poor security practices, if they can gain physical access to an office, the chances are good that, given a little unsupervised time, a user ID and password pair might be found on a notepad or sticky note. Unsupervised access might not even be required, depending on the quality of the security practices of the organization. One of the authors of this book was once considering opening an account at a bank near his home. As he sat down at the desk across from the bank employee taking his information, the author noticed one of the infamous little yellow notes attached to the computer monitor the employee was using. The note read "password for June is junejune." It probably isn't too hard to guess what July's password might be. Unfortunately, this is all too often the state of security practices in most organizations. With that in mind, it is easy to see how social engineering might work and might provide all the information an attacker needs to gain unauthorized access to a system or network.

■ Auditing

Auditing, in the financial community, is done to verify the accuracy and integrity of financial records. Many standards have been established in the financial community about how to record and report a company's financial status correctly. In the computer security world, auditing serves a similar function. It is a process of assessing the security state of an organization compared against an established standard.

The important elements here are the standards. Organizations from different communities may have widely different standards, and any audit will need to consider the appropriate elements for the specific community. Audits differ from security or vulnerability assessments in that assessments measure the security posture of the organization but may do so without any mandated standards against which to compare them. In a security assessment, general security "best practices" can be used, but they may lack the regulatory teeth that standards often provide. Penetration tests can also be encountered—these tests are conducted against an organization to determine whether any holes in the organization's security can be found. The goal of the penetration test is to penetrate the security rather than measure it against some standard. Penetration tests are often viewed as *white-hat hacking* in that the methods used often mirror those that attackers (often called *black hats*) might use.

You should conduct some form of security audit or assessment on a regular basis. Your organization might spend quite a bit on security, and it is important to measure how effective the efforts have been. In certain communities, audits can be regulated on a periodic basis with very specific standards that must be measured against. Even if your organization is not part of such a community, periodic assessments are important.

Many particulars can be evaluated during an assessment, but at a minimum, the security perimeter (with all of its components, including host-based security) should be examined, as well as the organization's policies, procedures, and guidelines governing security. Employee training is another aspect that should be studied, since employees are the targets of social engineering and password-guessing attacks.

Security audits, assessments, and penetration tests are a big business, and a number of organizations can perform them for you. The costs of these varies widely depending on the extent of the tests you want, the background of the company you are contracting with, and the size of the organization to be tested.

■ Chapter Summary

After reading this chapter and completing the exercises, you should understand the following aspects of attacks and malware.

Describe the various types of computer and network attacks, including denial-of-service, spoofing, hijacking, and password guessing

- Understand how denial-of-service (DoS) and distributed denial-of-service (DDoS) attacks are performed and the defenses against them.

- Understand spoofing of both packet headers and e-mail headers.

- Understand how session hijacking and man-in-the-middle attacks are performed and what the defenses are against these attacks.

- Understand the vulnerabilities of password systems.

Identify the different types of malicious software that exist, including viruses, worms, Trojan horses, logic bombs, time bombs, and rootkits

- Viruses are pieces of malware that require a file to infect a system.

- Worms are pieces of malware that can exist without infecting a file.

- Trojan horses are pieces of malware disguised as something else, something the user wants or finds useful.

- Logic bombs trigger when specific events occur in code, allowing an attack to be timed against an event.

- Time bombs are delayed malware designed to occur after a set period of time or on a specific date.

- Rootkits are pieces of malware designed to alter the lower-level functions of a system in a manner to escape detection.

Explain how social engineering can be used as a means to gain access to computers and networks

- Social engineering attacks are attacks against the operators and users of a system.

- Training and awareness is the best defensive measure against social engineering.

Describe the importance of auditing and what should be audited

- Logging is important because logs can provide information associated with attacks.

- Auditing is an essential component of a comprehensive security system.

■ Key Terms

backdoor *(395)*
birthday attack *(405)*
botnet *(393)*
buffer overflow *(406)*
denial-of-service (DoS) attack *(392)*
distributed denial-of-service (DDoS) attack *(393)*
DNS kiting *(403)*
drive-by download attack *(401)*
malware *(406)*
man-in-the-middle attack *(400)*
null session *(395)*
pharming *(401)*
phishing *(401)*

ping sweep *(390)*
port scan *(390)*
replay attack *(400)*
sequence number *(399)*
smurf attack *(397)*
sniffing *(396)*
spear phishing *(401)*
spoofing *(397)*
spyware *(409)*
SYN flood *(392)*
TCP/IP hijacking *(401)*
zombie *(393)*

■ Key Terms Quiz

Use terms from the Key Terms list to complete the sentences that follow. Don't use the same term more than once. Not all terms will be used.

1. Changing a source IP address for malicious purpose is an example of _____.

2. A(n) _____ is a way back into a machine via an unauthorized channel of access.

3. A malicious proxy could create a(n) _____ attack.

4. Abusing the TCP handshake in an effort to overuse server resources can be done using a(n) _____.

5. The main TCP/IP defense against a man-in-the-middle attack is the use of a(n) _____.

6. Holding a DNS name without paying is called _____.

7. When a keylogger is installed as malware, it is referred to as _____.

8. Rendering a resource useless is called a(n) _____.

9. An attack designed to match any user's password as opposed to a specific user's password is an example of a(n) _____.

10. A NIC can be set in promiscuous mode to enable _____.

■ Multiple-Choice Quiz

1. A SYN flood is an example of what type of attack?
   A. Malicious code
   B. Denial-of-service
   C. Man-in-the-middle
   D. Spoofing

2. An attack in which the attacker simply listens for all traffic being transmitted across a network, in the hope of viewing something such as a user ID and password combination, is known as:
   A. A man-in-the-middle attack
   B. A denial-of-service attack
   C. A sniffing attack
   D. A backdoor attack

3. Which attack takes advantage of a trusted relationship that exists between two systems?
   A. Spoofing
   B. Password guessing
   C. Sniffing
   D. Brute-force

4. In what type of attack does an attacker resend the series of commands and codes used in a financial transaction to cause the transaction to be conducted multiple times?
   A. Spoofing
   B. Man-in-the-middle

   C. Replay
   D. Backdoor

5. The trick in both spoofing and TCP/IP hijacking is in trying to:
   A. Provide the correct authentication token.
   B. Find two systems between which a trusted relationship exists.
   C. Guess a password or brute-force a password to gain initial access to the system or network.
   D. Maintain the correct sequence numbers for the response packets.

6. Rootkits are challenging security problems because:
   A. They can be invisible to the operating system and end user.
   B. Their true functionality can be cloaked, preventing analysis.
   C. They can do virtually anything an operating system can do.
   D. All of the above.

7. The ability of an attacker to crack passwords is directly related to the method the user employed to create the password in the first place, as well as:
   A. The length of the password
   B. The size of the character set used in generating the password

C. The speed of the machine cracking the password

D. The dictionary and rules used by the cracking program

8. A piece of malicious code that must attach itself to another file to replicate itself is known as:

A. A worm

B. A virus

C. A logic bomb

D. A Trojan

9. A piece of malicious code that appears to be designed to do one thing (and may in fact do that thing) but that hides some other payload (often malicious) is known as:

A. A worm

B. A virus

C. A logic bomb

D. A Trojan

10. An attack in which an attacker attempts to lie and misrepresent himself in order to gain access to information that can be useful in an attack is known as:

A. Social science

B. White-hat hacking

C. Social engineering

D. Social manipulation

11. The first step in an attack on a computer system consists of:

A. Gathering as much information about the target system as possible

B. Obtaining as much information about the organization in which the target lies as possible

C. Searching for possible exploits that can be used against known vulnerabilities

D. Searching for specific vulnerabilities that may exist in the target's operating system or software applications

12. The best way to minimize possible avenues of attack for your system is to:

A. Install a firewall and check the logs daily.

B. Monitor your intrusion detection system for possible attacks.

C. Limit the information that can be obtained on your organization and the services that are run by your Internet-visible systems.

D. Ensure that all patches have been applied for the services that are offered by your system.

13. A war-driving attack is an attempt to exploit what technology?

A. Fiber-optic networks, whose cables often run along roads and bridges

B. Cellular telephones

C. The public switched telephone network (PSTN)

D. Wireless networks

14. How can you protect against worms of the type that Robert Morris unleashed on the Internet?

A. Follow the same procedures you'd use to secure your system from a human attacker.

B. Install antivirus software.

C. Ensure that no executable attachments to e-mails are executed unless their integrity has been verified.

D. Monitor for changes to utilities and other system software.

15. Malicious code that is set to execute its payload on a specific date or at a specific time is known as:

A. A logic bomb

B. A Trojan horse

C. A virus

D. A time bomb

■ Essay Quiz

1. Compare and contrast port scanning and ping sweeps.

2. Describe the steps in an attack and the rationale for using these general terms.

3. What is the best practice to employ to mitigate malware effects on a machine?

Lab Projects

• Lab Project 15.1

Using the Internet, research password-cracking tools. Then, using a tool of choice, examine how easy it is to crack passwords on Windows- and UNIX-based systems. Create a series of accounts with different complexities of passwords and see how well they fare.

• Lab Project 15.2

Obtain a copy of the nmap scanning tool. Explore the various command-line options to scan networks, fingerprint operating systems, and perform other network-mapping functions.

chapter 16

E-Mail and Instant Messaging

The "free" distribution of unwelcome or misleading messages to thousands of people is an annoying and sometimes destructive use of the Internet's unprecedented efficiency.

—BILL GATES, New York Times, 1998

In this chapter, you will learn how to

■ **Describe security issues associated with e-mail**

■ **Implement security practices for e-mail**

■ **Detail the security issues of instant messaging protocols**

E-mail is the most popular application on the Internet. It is also by far the most popular application on intracompany networks. Roughly 12 million e-mails were sent each day in 2001, meaning that about 4.38 billion e-mails were sent in that year. In 2000, 569 million e-mail inboxes existed in the world. A Pew report from 2007 states that 91 percent of U.S. Internet users use e-mail (Deborah Fallows, "Adjusting to a Diet of Spam," May 23, 2007, http://pewresearch.org/pubs/487/spam). Several sources indicate that in 2007, more than a billion active e-mail accounts sent more than 150 billion e-mail messages every day, or more than 50 trillion e-mails a year. In 2008 the estimates were increased to 210 billion e-mail messages every day.

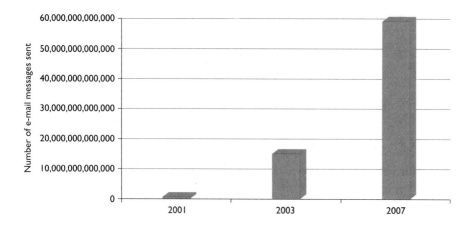

Security of E-Mail

E-mail started with mailbox programs on early time-sharing machines, allowing researchers to leave messages for others using the same machine. The first intermachine e-mail was sent in 1972, and a new era in person-to-person communication was launched. E-mail proliferated, but it remained unsecured, only partly because most e-mail is sent in plaintext, providing no privacy in its default form. Current e-mail in its use is not different from its earlier versions; it's still a simple way to send a relatively short text message to another user. Users' dependence on e-mail has grown with the number of people accessing the Internet.

Internet e-mail depends on three primary protocols, SMTP, POP3, and IMAP. **Simple Mail Transfer Protocol (SMTP)** is the method by which mail is sent to the server as well as from server to server. SMTP by default uses TCP port 25. POP3 stands for Post Office Protocol version 3, which by default uses TCP port 110. POP3 is a method by which a client computer may connect to a server and download new messages. POP3 has been partly replaced by IMAP, or Internet Message Access Protocol, which uses port TCP 143 by default. IMAP is similar to POP3 in that it allows the client to retrieve messages from the server, but IMAP typically works in greater synchronization; for example, e-mails are left on the server until the client deletes them in the client, at which time IMAP instructs the server to delete them. As e-mail services became more standardized, the methods of transmission became easier to attack as they were not strange proprietary protocols. Also, as the world became more connected, there were many more available targets for the malware and commercial e-mails.

Viruses started as simple self-replicating programs that spread via the transfer of floppy disks, but the introduction of e-mail gave virus files a passport to travel. Sending themselves to every user that they possibly can, viruses have achieved record-breaking infection rates. Trojan horse programs are also often sent through e-mail, with computer owners as unwitting accomplices, compromising hundreds of machines every day. These programs seem to be innocuous, but if you install the malicious code, you become the installer of the program that compromises your machine.

The **e-mail hoax** has become another regular occurrence; Internet-based urban legends are spread through e-mail, with users forwarding them in seemingly endless loops around the globe. And, of course, people still haven't found a good way to block ubiquitous spam e-mails (a sampling of which is shown in Figure 16.1), despite the remarkable advance of every other technology.

E-mail security is ultimately the responsibility of users themselves, because they are the ones who will actually be sending and receiving the messages. However, security administrators can give users the tools they need to fight malware, spam, and hoaxes. Secure/Multipurpose Internet Mail Extensions (S/MIME) and Pretty Good Privacy (PGP) are two popular methods used for encrypting e-mail, as discussed later in the chapter. Server-based and desktop-based virus protection can help against malicious code, and spam filters attempt to block all unsolicited commercial e-mail. E-mail users need to be educated about security as well, however, because the popularity and functionality of e-mail is only going to increase with time.

Instant messaging (IM), while not part of the e-mail system, is similar to e-mail in many respects, particularly in the sense that it is commonly plaintext and can transmit files. IM's handling of files opens the application to virus exploitation just like e-mail. IM has experienced a boom in popularity in the last few years, so we will look at some popular IM programs later in this chapter, such as AOL Instant Messenger, shown in Figure 16.2.

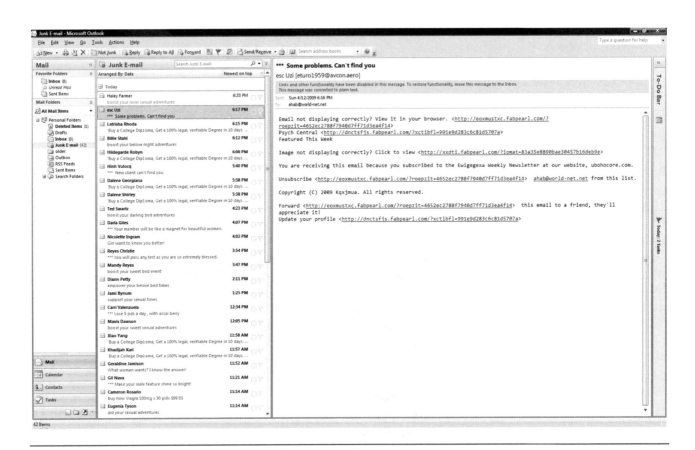

• **Figure 16.1** A typical list of spam e-mails

• **Figure 16.2**   AOL Instant Messenger is a popular instant messaging program.

■ Malicious Code

Viruses and worms are popular programs because they make themselves popular. When viruses were constrained only to one computer, they attempted to spread by attaching themselves to every executable program that they could find. This worked out very well for the viruses, because they could piggyback onto a floppy disk with a program that was being transferred to another computer. (For example, back in its day, Windows 3.11 could be transferred from one computer to another only via a series of floppy disks such as those shown in Figure 16.3.) The virus would infect the next computer, and the next computer after that. While often successful, virus propagation was slow, and floppies could be scanned for viruses.

The advent of computer networks was a computer virus writer's dream, allowing viruses to attempt to infect every network share to which the computer was attached. This extended the virus's reach from a set of machines that might share a floppy disk to every

• **Figure 16.3**   Floppy disks are the old method of transferring files (and viruses) from computer to computer.

machine on the network. Because the e-mail protocol permits users to attach files to e-mail messages (see Figure 16.4), viruses can travel by e-mail from one local network to another, anywhere on the Internet. This changed the nature of virus programs, since they once were localized but now could spread virtually everywhere. E-mail gave the virus a global reach.

Viruses spread by e-mail further and faster than they ever spread before, but viruses also evolved. This evolution started with viruses that were scripted to send themselves to other users, and this type of virus was known as a **worm**. A worm uses its code to automate the infection process. For example, when a worm program is executed, the code may seek out the user's e-mail address book and mail itself to as many people as the worm's programming dictates. This method of transmission depends on the user actually executing the worm file. Some worms use multiple methods of attack. They not only send multiple infected e-mails, but also scan hosts on the Internet, looking for a specific vulnerability. Upon finding the vulnerability, the worm infects the remote host and, with a new launching point, starts the process all over again.

Viruses and worms are a danger not only to the individual user's machine, but also to network security, because they can introduce all kinds of malicious traffic to other machines. This can cause not only loss of data, but it can sometimes send data out to other users. The Sircam worm, for example, attached random files from the infected user's hard drive to the e-mails the worm sent out.

Worms can also carry Trojan horse payloads, as can any e-mail message. A **Trojan horse program** is a program that seems to be safe but actually has a

> **Exam Tip:** Viruses and worms both can carry malicious payloads and cause damage. The difference is in how they are transmitted: viruses require a file to infect, whereas worms can exist independently of a file.

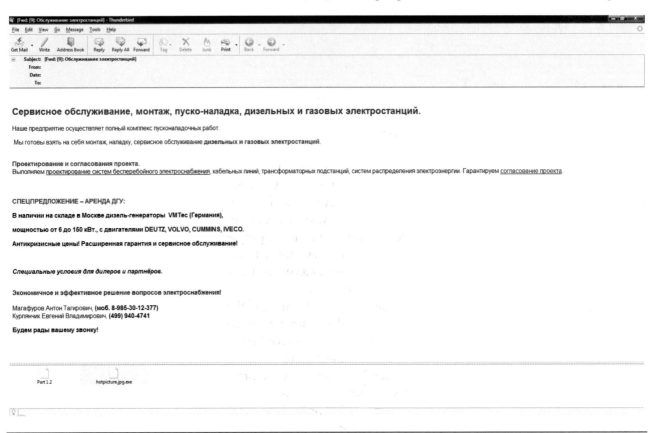

• **Figure 16.4**   Viruses commonly spread through e-mail attachments.

sinister hidden purpose. For example, an executable game program or an executable self-playing movie could be a Trojan. These programs will run and do what they claim, but they typically also install some other program, such as a remote-control package such as SubSeven or Back Orifice. These programs allow an attacker to remotely control an infected machine. Once control is achieved, the attacker can use the machine to perform a number of tasks, such as using it in distributed denial-of-service (DDoS) attacks, using it as a launching point to compromise other machines, or using it as a remote place to store some extra files. The most common thing an attacker does with an infected computer is to make it part of a **botnet** (from ro*bot net*work), making it a robot or "zombie" computer. A botnet typically is remotely controlled to act as a single attacker.

While the distribution of malicious code in e-mail is tied to the files that are attached to the e-mail messages, in the past a user actually had to execute the attached file. The original system of e-mail used regular text to send messages, but the advent of the World Wide Web changed this. Hypertext Markup Language (HTML) was created to allow regular text to represent complex page designs in a standardized way. HTML was soon adopted by e-mail programs so that users could use different fonts and colors and embed pictures in their e-mails. E-mail programs then grew more advanced and, like web browsers, were designed to automatically open files attached to e-mails.

When active content was designed for the Web, in the form of Java and ActiveX scripts, these scripts were interpreted and run by the web browser. E-mail programs also would run these scripts, and that's when the trouble began. Some e-mail programs, most notably Microsoft Outlook, use a preview pane, which allows users to read e-mails without opening them in the full screen (see Figure 16.5).

Unfortunately, this preview still activates all the content in the e-mail message, and because Outlook supports Visual Basic scripting, it is vulnerable to e-mail worms. A user doesn't need to run the program or even open the e-mail to activate the worm—simply previewing the e-mail in the preview pane can launch the malicious content. This form of automatic execution was the primary reason for the spread of the ILOVEYOU worm.

All malware is a security threat, with the several different types having different countermeasures. The antivirus systems that we have used for years have progressed to try and stop all forms of malicious software, but they are not a panacea. Worm prevention also relies on patch management of the operating system and applications. Viruses are user-launched, and since one of the most common transfer methods for viruses is through e-mail, the people using the e-mail system create the front line of defense against viruses. In addition to antivirus scanning of the user's system, and possibly an e-mail virus filter, users need to be educated about the dangers of viruses.

Although the great majority of users are now aware of viruses and the damage they can cause, more education may be needed to instruct them on the specific things that need to be addressed when a virus is received via e-mail. These can vary from organization to organization and from e-mail software to e-mail software; however, some useful examples of good practices involve examining all e-mails for a known source as well as a known destination, especially if the e-mails have attachments. Strange files or unexpected attachments should always be checked with an antivirus program before execution. Users also need to know that some viruses can be executed

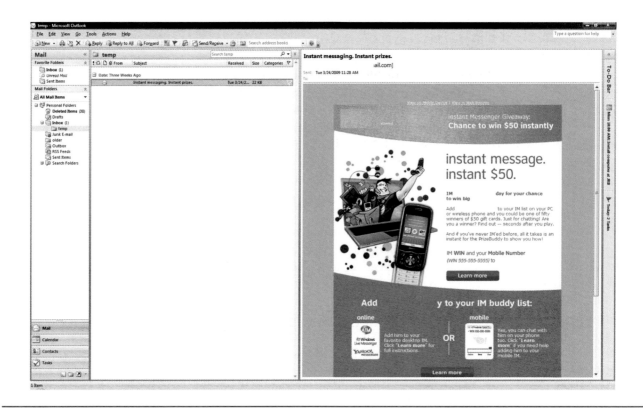

• Figure 16.5   The preview pane on the right can execute code in e-mails without opening them.

simply by opening the e-mail or viewing it in the preview pane. Education and proper administration is also useful in configuring the e-mail software to be as virus resistant as possible—turning off scripting support and the preview pane are good examples. Many organizations outline specific user responsibilities for e-mail, similar to network acceptable use policies. Some examples include using e-mail resources responsibly, avoiding the installation of untrusted programs, and using localized antivirus scanning programs, such as AVG.

Another protection is to carefully create virus scanning procedures. If possible, perform virus scans on every e-mail as it comes into the company's e-mail server. Some users will also attempt to retrieve e-mail offsite from a normal Internet service provider (ISP) account, which can bypass the server-based virus protection, so every machine should also be protected with a host-based virus protection program that scans all files on a regular basis and performs checks of files upon their execution. While these steps will not eliminate the security risks of malicious code in e-mail, they will limit infection and help to keep the problem to manageable levels.

■ Hoax E-Mails

An interesting offshoot of e-mail viruses is the phenomenon of e-mail hoaxes. If you've had an Internet e-mail address for more than a couple of months, you've probably received at least one of these—the Neiman-Marcus cookie recipe sent to you because someone was charged $250 for it, the "famous" commencement speech by Kurt Vonnegut, and the plea from the young dying boy whose last wish is to make it into the record books by receiving the most get well cards ever. These are the most famous of the e-mail hoaxes, though many others exist.

E-mail hoaxes are mostly a nuisance, but they do cost everyone, not only in the time wasted by receiving and reading the e-mails, but also in the Internet bandwidth and server processing time they take up. E-mail hoaxes are global urban legends, perpetually traveling from one e-mail account to the next, and most have a common theme of some story you must tell ten other people about right away for good luck or some virus that will harm your friends unless you tell them immediately. Hoaxes are similar to chain letters, but instead of promising a reward, the story in the e-mail is typically what produces the action. Whether it's a call for sympathy from a dying boy, or an overly expensive recipe sent to the masses in the name of justice, all hoaxes prompt action of some sort, and this call for action is probably what keeps them going.

Hoaxes have been circling the Internet for many years, and many web sites are dedicated to debunking them, such as Snopes.com (see Figure 16.6).

Forwarding hoax e-mails and other jokes, funny movies, and non-work-related e-mails at work can be a violation of your company's acceptable use policy and result in disciplinary actions.

● **Figure 16.6**   Snopes is an online reference for urban legends common in hoax e-mails.

The power of the e-mail hoax is actually quite amazing. The Neiman-Marcus story, in which someone gets charged $250 for a chocolate chip cookie recipe, thinking that she is only being charged $2.50, used to have a fatal flaw: Neiman-Marcus did not sell chocolate chip cookies (but it does now simply because of the hoax, and has posted the recipe on its web site). The Kurt Vonnegut hoax was convincing enough to fool his wife, and the "dying" boy, who is now 20, still receives cards in the mail. The power of these hoaxes probably means that they will never be stopped, though they might be slowed down.

The most important thing to do in this case is educate e-mail users: They should be familiar with a hoax or two before they go online, and they should know how to search the Internet for hoax information. Users need to apply the same common sense on the Internet that they would in real life: If it sounds too outlandish to be true, it probably is a fabrication. The goal of education about hoaxes should be to change user behavior to delete the hoax e-mail and not send it on.

Unsolicited Commercial E-Mail (Spam)

Exam Tip: Unsolicited commercial e-mail is referred to as spam.

Every e-mail user has received spam, and usually does on a daily basis. Spam refers to **unsolicited commercial e-mail** whose purpose is the same as the junk mail you get in your physical mailbox—it tries to persuade you to buy something. The term **spam** comes from a skit on *Monty Python's Flying Circus*, where two people are in a restaurant that serves only the potted meat product. This concept of the repetition of unwanted things is the key to e-mail spam.

The first spam e-mail was sent in 1978 by a DEC employee. However, the first spam that really captured everyone's attention was in 1994, when two lawyers posted a commercial message to every Usenet newsgroup. This was the origin of using the Internet to send one message to as many recipients as possible via an automated program. Commercial e-mail programs have taken over, resulting in the variety of spam that most users receive in their inboxes every day. In 2000, AOL estimated that nearly 30 percent of e-mail sent to its systems was spam, accounting for nearly 24 million messages a day (according to *The Industry Standard*, www.thestandard.com/article/ 0,1902,15586,00.html). Botnet researchers have reported that 1 million–plus infected machines send more than 100 billion spam e-mails every day. According to the Symantec monthly State of Spam report in July 2009, over 90 percent of e-mail sent worldwide is spam.

The appeal to the people generating the spam is the extremely low cost per advertising impression. The senders of spam e-mail can generally send the messages for less than a cent apiece. This is much less expensive than more traditional direct mail or print advertisements, and this low cost will ensure the continued growth of spam e-mail unless something is done about it. The amount of spam being transmitted eventually spurred federal authorities into action. In late 2003 the Controlling the Assault of Non-Solicited Pornography and Marketing Act (CAN-SPAM) was signed into law. This law gave the Federal Trade Commission (FTC) authority to define the standards of spam e-mail and enforce the other provisions of the act. While several spammers have been caught and prosecuted under this act, it has not been restrictive enough to severely limit spam. This has forced most people to seek out technical solutions to the spam problem.

For more information on spam, see the FTC's web site on spam, www.ftc.gov/spam/.

The front line of the war against spam e-mail is filtering. Almost all e-mail providers filter spam at some level; however, bandwidth is still used to send the spam, and the recipient e-mail server still has to process the message. To reduce spam, it must be fought on several fronts. The first thing to do is educate users about spam. A good way for users to fight spam is to be cautious about where on the Internet they post their e-mail address. However, you can't keep e-mail addresses secret just to avoid spam. One of the steps that the majority of system administrators running Internet e-mail servers have taken to reduce spam, and which is also a good e-mail security principle, is to shut down mail relaying. Port scanning occurs across all hosts all the time, typically with a single host scanning large subnets for a single port, and some of these people could be attempting to send spam e-mail. When they scan for TCP port 25, they are looking for SMTP servers, and once they find a host that is an **open relay** (a mail server that will accept mail from anyone), they can use that host to send as many commercial e-mails as possible. The reason that they look for an open relay is that spammers typically do not want the e-mails traced back to them. **Mail relaying** is similar to dropping a letter off at a post office instead of letting the postal carrier pick it up at your mailbox. On the Internet, that consists of sending e-mail from a separate IP address, making it more difficult for the mail to be traced back to you. SMTP server software is typically configured to accept mail only from specific hosts or domains. All SMTP software can and should be configured to accept only mail from known hosts, or to known mailboxes; this closes down mail relaying and helps to reduce spam.

Since it may not be possible to close all mail relays, and because some spammers will mail from their own mail servers, software must be used to combat spam at the recipient's end. Spam can be filtered at two places: at the host itself or at the server. Filtering spam at the host level is done by the e-mail client software and usually employs basic pattern matching, focusing on the sender, subject, or text of the e-mail. This fairly effective system uses an inordinate amount of bandwidth and processing power on the host computer, however. These problems can be solved by filtering spam at the mail server level.

The server-based approach can be beneficial because other methods of filtering spam can be used at the server: pattern matching is still used, but SMTP software can also use a process called Domain Name Service (DNS) blacklisting, or DNSBL. The **Realtime Blackhole List (RBL)** was the first list to utilize the concept of using DNS records to filter, or "blackhole," spam-sending IP addresses and domains. Started in 1997, this list was and is maintained in real time specifically for blocking spam e-mail. While the RBL was the first DNSBL, there are now many blackhole lists. The DNSBL service is so popular that many programs, such as sendmail, Postfix, and Eudora Internet Mail Server, include support for it by default.

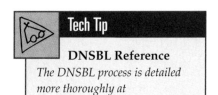
In addition to the RBL, multiple other DNS-based blacklist services can assist filtering based upon DNS sources of mail. Commercial packages can block spam at the server level using both methods mentioned, maintaining their own blacklists and pattern-matching algorithms.

Many additional techniques exist for server-based spam filtering—enough to fill an entire book on the subject. One technique is to use a *challenge/response system*: once an e-mail is received by a "new" contact, a challenge is sent back to the originating address to confirm the contact. Since spammers send e-mails in bulk, the response mechanism is too cumbersome and they will not respond.

Another technique is known as *greylisting*. When an e-mail is received, it is bounced as a temporary rejection. SMTP servers that are RFC5321-compliant will wait a configurable amount of time and attempt retransmission of the message. Obviously, spammers will not retry sending of any messages, so spam is reduced.

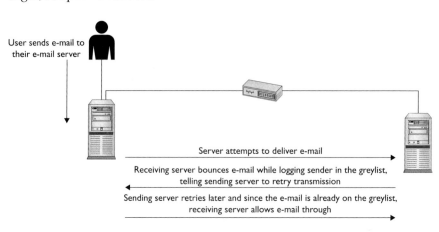

User sends e-mail to their e-mail server

Server attempts to deliver e-mail

Receiving server bounces e-mail while logging sender in the greylist, telling sending server to retry transmission

Sending server retries later and since the e-mail is already on the greylist, receiving server allows e-mail through

All these techniques have advantages and disadvantages, and most people will run some combination of techniques to attempt to filter as much spam as possible while not rejecting legitimate messages.

A side benefit of filtering spam at the receiving server is reduced e-mail. In enterprises, performing backups of information is a significant task. Backups are size-dependent, both in cost and time, and reducing e-mail by eliminating spam can have significant impacts on e-mail backups. Spam reduction will also have a significant impact on the e-discovery process as it reduces the quantity of material that needs to be searched. *E-discovery* is a term for electronic discovery, the electronic component of a legal discovery process. The discovery process is court mandated and, when applied to a corporate environment, can cause the shutdown of corporate operations until the process is complete. For this reason, anything that makes the process easier or faster will benefit the corporation.

Microsoft offers another server-based solution to spam, called the Sender ID Framework (SIDF). SIDF attempts to authenticate messages by checking the sender's domain name against a list of IP addresses authorized to send e-mail by the domain name listed. This list is maintained in a text (TXT) record published by the DNS, called a **Sender Policy Framework (SPF)** record. So when a mail server receives an e-mail, it will check the sender's domain name in the DNS; if the outbound server's IP matches, the message gets a "pass" rating by SIDF. This is similar to the idea that routers should drop any outbound port 25 traffic that does not come from known e-mail servers on the subnet managed by the router. However, the SIDF system handles the authentication of the e-mail server when it is received, not when it is sent. This system still allows wasted bandwidth from the sender of the message to the receiver, and since bandwidth is increasingly a metered service, this means the cost of spam is still paid by the recipient.

These methods will take care of 90 percent of the junk mail clogging our networks, but they cannot stop it entirely. Better control of port 25 traffic is required to slow the tide of spam hitting our inboxes. This would stop spammers using remote open relays and, hopefully, prevent many users from running unauthorized e-mail servers of their own. Because of the low cost of generating spam, until serious action is taken, or spam is somehow made unprofitable, it will remain with us.

■ Mail Encryption

The e-mail concerns discussed so far in this chapter are all global issues involving security, but e-mail suffers from a more important security problem—the lack of confidentiality, or, as it is sometimes referred to, privacy. As with many Internet applications, e-mail has always been a plaintext protocol. When many people first got onto the Internet, they heard a standard lecture about not sending anything through e-mail that they wouldn't want posted on a public bulletin board. Part of the reason for this was that e-mail is sent with the clear text of the message exposed to anyone who is sniffing the network. Any attacker at a choke point in the network could read all e-mail passing through that network segment.

Some tools can be used to solve this problem by using **encryption** on the e-mail's content. The first method is S/MIME and the second is PGP.

S/MIME

Secure/Multipurpose Internet Mail Extensions (S/MIME) is a *secure* implementation of the MIME protocol specification. MIME was created to allow Internet e-mail to support new and more creative features. The original e-mail RFC specified only text e-mail, so any nontext data had to be handled by a new specification—MIME. MIME handles audio files, images, applications, and multipart e-mails. MIME allows e-mail to handle multiple types of content in a message, including file transfers. Every time you send a file as an e-mail attachment, you are using MIME. S/MIME takes this content and specifies a framework for encrypting the message as a MIME attachment.

Cross Check

X.509 Certificates

In Chapter 7 you learned about X.509 certificate standards. Why is it important to have a standardized certificate format?

S/MIME was developed by RSA Data Security and uses the X.509 format for certificates. The specification supports both 40-bit RC2 and 3DES for symmetric encryption. The protocol can affect the message in one of two ways: the host mail program can encode the message with S/MIME, or the server can act as the processing agent, encrypting all messages between servers.

The host-based operation starts when the user clicks Send; the mail agent then encodes the message using the generated symmetric key. Then the symmetric key is encoded with the remote user's public key for confidentiality or signed with the local user's private key for authentication/nonrepudiation. This enables the remote user to decode the symmetric key and then decrypt the actual content of the message. Of course, all of this is handled by the user's mail program, requiring the user simply to tell the program to decode the message. If the message is signed by the sender, it will be signed with the sender's public key, guaranteeing the source of the message. The reason that both symmetric and asymmetric encryption are used in the mail is to increase the speed of encryption and decryption. As encryption is based on difficult mathematical problems, it takes time to encrypt and decrypt. To speed this up, the more difficult process, asymmetric encryption, is used only to encrypt a relatively small amount of data, the symmetric key. The symmetric key is then used to encrypt the rest of the message.

The S/MIME process of encrypting e-mails provides integrity, privacy, and, if the message is signed, authentication. Several popular e-mail programs support S/MIME, including the popular Microsoft products, Outlook and Windows Mail. They both manage S/MIME keys and functions through the E-mail Security screen, shown in Figure 16.7. This figure shows the different settings that can be used to encrypt

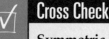

Cross Check

Symmetric Encryption

In Chapter 5 you learned about symmetric encryption, including RC2 and the 3DES algorithms supported by S/MIME. What part of the CIA of security does symmetric encryption attempt to provide in this instance?

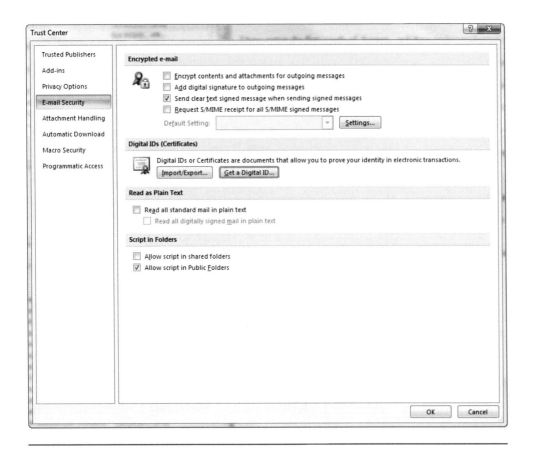

• **Figure 16.7**   S/MIME options in Outlook

messages and use X.509 digital certificates. This allows interoperability with web certificates, and trusted authorities are available to issue the certificates. Trusted authorities are needed to ensure the senders are who they claim to be, an important part of authentication. In Windows Mail, the window is more simplistic (see Figure 16.8), but the same functions of key management and secure e-mail operation are available.

While S/MIME is a good and versatile protocol for securing e-mail, its implementation can be problematic. S/MIME allows the user to select low strength (40-bit) encryption, which means a user can send a message that is thought to be secure but that can be more easily decoded than messages sent with 3DES encryption. Also, as with any protocol, bugs can exist in the software itself. Just because an application is designed for security does not mean that it, itself, is secure. Despite its potential flaws, however, S/MIME is a tremendous leap in security over regular e-mail.

• **Figure 16.8**   S/MIME options in Windows Mail

PGP

Pretty Good Privacy (PGP) implements e-mail security in a similar fashion to S/MIME, but PGP uses completely different protocols. The basic framework is the same: The user sends the e-mail, and the mail agent applies encryption as specified in the mail program's programming. The content is encrypted with the generated symmetric key, and that key is encrypted with the public key of the recipient of the e-mail for confidentiality. The sender can also choose to sign the mail with a private key, allowing the recipient to authenticate the sender. Currently PGP supports public key infrastructure (PKI) provided by multiple vendors, including X.509 certificates, Lightweight Directory Access Protocol (LDAP) key sources such as Microsoft's Active Directory, and Novell's NDS, now called eDirectory.

In Figure 16.9, you can see how PGP manages keys locally in its own software. This is where a user stores not only local keys, but also any keys that were received from other users. A free key server is available for storing PGP public keys. PGP can generate its own keys using either Diffie-Hellman or RSA, and it can then transmit the public keys to the PGP LDAP server so other PGP users can search for and locate your public key to communicate with you. This key server is convenient, as each person using PGP for communications does not have to implement a server to handle key management. For the actual encryption of the e-mail content itself, PGP supports International Data Encryption Algorithm (IDEA), 3DES, and Carlisle Adams and Stafford Tavares (CAST) for symmetric encryption. PGP provides pretty good security against brute-force attacks by using a 3DES key length of 168 bits, an IDEA key length of 128 bits, and a CAST key length of 128 bits. All of these algorithms are difficult to brute-force with existing hardware, requiring well over a million years to break the code. While this is not a promise of future security against brute-force attacks, the security is reasonable today.

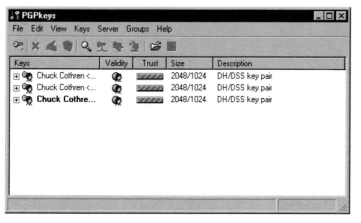

• **Figure 16.9**   PGP key management

PGP has plug-ins for many popular e-mail programs, including Outlook and Qualcomm's Eudora. These plug-ins handle the encryption and decryption behind the scenes, and all that the user must do is enter the encryption key's passphrase to ensure that they are the owner of the key. In Figure 16.10, you can see the string of encrypted text that makes up the MIME attachment. This text includes the encrypted content of the message and the encrypted symmetric key. You can also see that the program does not decrypt the message upon receipt; it waits until instructed to decrypt it. PGP also stores encrypted messages in the encrypted format, as does S/MIME. This is important, since it provides end-to-end security for the message.

Like S/MIME, PGP is not problem-free. You must be diligent about keeping the software up to date and fully patched, because vulnerabilities are occasionally found. For example, a buffer overflow was found in the way PGP was handled in Outlook, causing the overwriting of heap memory and leading to possible malicious code execution. There is also a lot of discussion about the way PGP handles key recovery, or key escrow. PGP uses what's called an *Additional Decryption Key (ADK)*, which is basically an additional public key stacked upon the original public key. An ADK, in theory, would give the proper organization a private key that would be used to

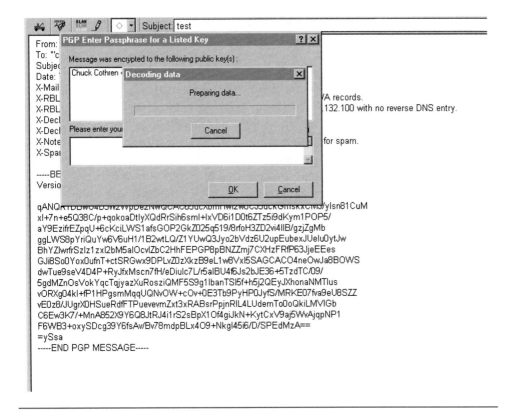

● **Figure 16.10** Decoding a PGP-encoded message in Eudora

retrieve the secret messages. In practice, the ADK is not always controlled by a properly authorized organization, and the danger exists for someone to add an ADK and then distribute it to the world. This creates a situation in which other users will be sending messages that they believe can be read only by the first party, but that can actually be read by the third party who modified the key. These are just examples of the current vulnerabilities in the product, showing that PGP is just a tool, not the ultimate answer to security.

 **Cross Check**

Key Escrow

In Chapter 5 you learned about symmetric encryption, including RC2, and the 3DES algorithms supported by S/MIME. What part of the CIA of security does symmetric encryption attempt to provide in this instance?

■ Instant Messaging

Instant messaging (IM) is another technology that has seen widespread acceptance in recent years. With the growth of the Internet pulling customers away from AOL, one of the largest dial-up providers in the United States, the company had to look at new ways of providing content. It started **AOL Instant Messenger (AIM)**, which was conceived as a way to find people of like interests online, and it was modeled after earlier chat programs.

With GUI features and enhanced ease of use, it quickly became popular enough for AOL to release to regular users of the Internet. With several competing programs, AIM was feeding the tremendous growth of the instant messaging segment.

The programs had to appeal to a wide variety of users, so ease of use was paramount, and security was not a priority. Now that people are accustomed to IM applications, they see the benefit of using them not only for personal chatting on the Internet, but also for legitimate business use. When people install these applications, they unwittingly expose the corporate network to security breaches through many of the same malicious software problems as e-mail. Instant messages traverse the Internet in plaintext and also cross third-party servers—be it Yahoo, MSN/Windows Live, Google, or AOL.

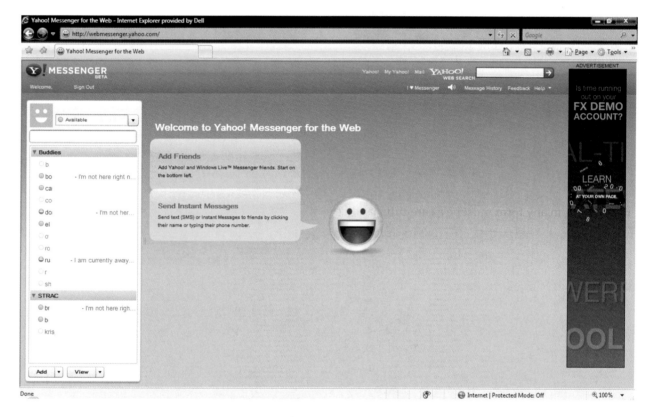

IM programs are designed to attach to a server, or a network of servers, and allow you to talk with other people on the same network of servers in near real time. The nature of this type of communication opens several holes in a system's security. First, the program has to attach to a server, typically announcing the IP address of the originating client. This is not a problem in most applications, but IM identifies a specific user associated with the IP address, making attacks more likely. Also associated with this fact is that for other users to be able to send you messages, the program is forced to announce your presence on the server. So now a user is displaying that his or her computer is on and is possibly broadcasting the source IP address to anyone who is looking. This problem is compounded by the tendency for people to run these programs in the background so that they don't miss any messages.

Popular IM clients were not implemented with security in mind. All support sending files as attachments, few currently support encryption, and currently none have a virus scanner built into the file-sharing utility.

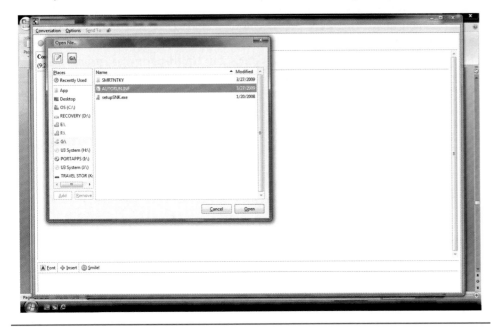

• File sharing in IM programs

File sharing in any form must be a carefully handled application to prevent the spread of viruses and other malicious code. Chat programs produce security risks, because the sharing is done ad hoc between end users, administrators have no control over the quality of the files being sent, and there is no monitoring of the original sources of those files. The only authentication for the files is the human interaction between the two users in question. This kind of vulnerability coupled with a social engineering attack can produce dramatic enough results that the CERT Coordination Center (CERT/CC) was compelled to issue an incident note (CERT Incident Note IN-2002-03: Social Engineering Attacks via IRC and Instant Messaging). This personal type of authentication was abused, tricking people into downloading and executing backdoor or Trojan horse programs.

A user can also be persuaded autonomously to download and run a file via IM. Several worms exist that attempt, via IM, to get users to download and run the payload. W32.pipeline uses AIM to install a rootkit. Goner, running via ICQ, another IM program, asks users to download a screen saver. Choke, spreading via MSN/Windows Live Messenger, attempts to get users to download a game; if the game is downloaded, the worm attempts to spread to any user the infected user chats with. These worms and others all depend on user interaction to run the payload. This file-sharing mechanism bypasses all the server-side virus protection that is part of most organizations' e-mail infrastructure. This pushes more of the responsibility for malware protection onto the local users' antivirus system. This can be problematic for users who do not regularly update their systems or who fail to perform regular antivirus scans.

One of the largest problems with IM programs is the lack of support for encryption. AIM, ICQ, MSN/Windows Live Messenger, and Yahoo Messenger all currently do not natively support encryption of the text messages traveling between users. However, some third-party programs will add encryption as a plug-in. The lack of encryption was not a significant concern while these IM programs were still used primarily for personal communication, but with businesses moving to adopt the systems, people are not aware of the infrastructure difference between IM and e-mail. Intracompany e-mail never leaves the company's network, but an intracompany instant message typically will do so unless the organization purchases a product and operates an internal IM server. This can and does expose large amounts of confidential business information to anyone who is physically in a spot to monitor and has the desire to capture the traffic.

If you think about how often client information is sent in e-mail between two people at a company, you start to see the danger that sending it via IM creates. IM is an application that is typically installed by the end user, without the knowledge of the administrator. These types of rogue applications have always been a danger to a network's security, but administrators have typically been able to control them by eliminating the applications' ports through the firewall.

The protocols used for these chat applications have default TCP ports—AIM uses 5190, Jabber uses 5222 and 5269, Yahoo Messenger uses 5050, and MSN/Windows Live Messenger uses 1863. Some IM applications have been programmed for use as *rogue apps*. In the event that they can't reach a server on the default ports, they begin to scan all ports looking for one that is allowed out of the firewall. As these applications can connect on any port, including common ones such as Telnet port 23 and HTTP port 80, they are very hard to control. These types of security risks go above and beyond the routine security holes generated in IM software that arise as in any other piece of software, through coding errors.

IM applications work only in a networked environment and therefore are forced to accept traffic as well as send it, giving attackers a way to exploit flaws in the code of the program. AIM has encountered two buffer-overflow problems that allow a remote attacker to gain control of the user's computer. These flaws, which have been patched, are just the beginning—with the proliferation of these applications, many more bugs are out there waiting to be exploited.

You can improve the security of IM now, however, and new programs will offer improved security features. Businesses that use IM should use a local IM server, as illustrated next. Keeping messages within the perimeter of the organization goes a long way toward ensuring that confidential information does not get out. Microsoft Exchange 2000 provided a built-in IM server, and this capability was later moved into the company's Live Communications Server.

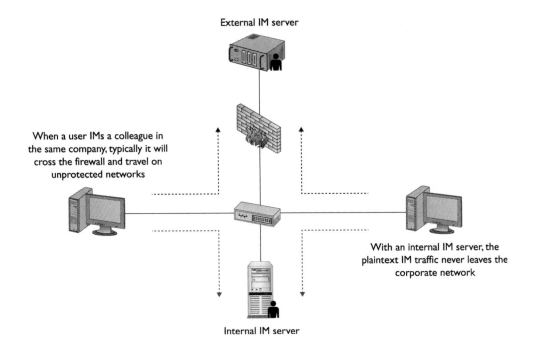

External IM server

When a user IMs a colleague in the same company, typically it will cross the firewall and travel on unprotected networks

With an internal IM server, the plaintext IM traffic never leaves the corporate network

Internal IM server

This server can act as an internal IM server, routing employee-to-employee IMs within the organization, and it also provides presence management, so the system will know what device you are available to communicate with. This capability has now been renamed Office Communications Server 2007, with IM, presence, and voice and video capabilities. It supports Microsoft Office Live Meeting clients and the Office Communicator clients.

Trillian is a third-party chat client program that works with multiple chat networks; its most significant feature is that it can encrypt the chat messages, on AIM and ICQ networks, that the client sends to the server. While this does not help with file-sharing problems, it provides confidentiality in one direction. To protect the method of file exchange, the clients have to be changed to integrate a virus scanner. These solutions and others should be applied widely to ensure that IM occurs securely.

Instant messaging is an application that can increase productivity by saving communication time, but it's not without risks. The protocol sends messages in plaintext and thus fails to preserve their confidentiality. It also allows for sharing of files between clients, allowing a backdoor access method for files. There are some methods to minimize security risks, but more development efforts are required before IM is ready to be implemented in a secure fashion. The best ways in which to protect yourself on an IM network are similar to those for almost all Internet applications: avoid communication with unknown persons, avoid running any program you are unsure of, and do not write anything you wouldn't want posted with your name on it.

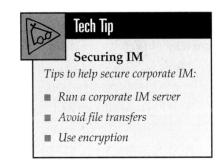

Tech Tip

Securing IM
Tips to help secure corporate IM:

- *Run a corporate IM server*
- *Avoid file transfers*
- *Use encryption*

Chapter 16 Review

■ Chapter Summary

After reading this chapter and completing the exercises, you should understand the following about e-mail and IM security.

Describe security issues associated with e-mail

- Malicious code is code that performs something harmful to the computer it runs on. Malicious code is often sent through e-mail.

- Viruses are pieces of malicious code that require user action to spread.

- Trojan programs deceive the user into thinking that a program is something innocuous, when it is actually a piece of malicious code.

- Worms are pieces of malicious code that use automated methods to spread.

- Spam, or unsolicited commercial e-mail, is e-mail that is sent to you without you requesting it, attempting to sell you something. It is the electronic equivalent of a telemarketing call.

- Hoax e-mails are e-mails that travel from user to user because of the compelling story contained in them.

Implement security practices for e-mail

- Protecting your e-mail system from virus code requires several measures:
  - Don't execute any attachment from an unknown source.
  - Use antivirus programs that run on the server to filter all e-mails.
  - Use client-side antivirus programs to catch any viruses that might come from web-based e-mail accounts.

- Keeping all software up to date helps to prevent worm propagation.

- Server-side filtering software and the application of spam blackhole lists help limit the amount of unsolicited e-mail.

- E-mail encryption is a great way to protect the privacy of communication since e-mail is a cleartext medium.

- PGP, or Pretty Good Privacy, is a good specific application for e-mail encryption.

- S/MIME, or Secure/Multipurpose Internet Mail Extension, is the e-mail protocol that allows encryption applications to work.

- Antivirus software is important to protect against malware.

Detail the security issues of instant messaging protocols

- AOL Instant Messenger, ICQ, and MSN Messenger are all different versions of instant messaging programs.

- The most popular IM programs all send messages in the clear, without a native encryption built into the default clients.

- All the IM clients need to attach to a server to communicate. Therefore, when attached to the server, they announce the source IP of a particular user.

- Instant messaging can also transfer files. This activity typically bypasses any security built into the network, especially mail server virus protections.

■ Key Terms

AOL Instant Messenger (AIM) *(435)*
botnet *(425)*
e-mail *(421)*
e-mail hoax *(422)*
encryption *(432)*
instant messaging (IM) *(422)*

mail relaying *(429)*
open relay *(429)*
Pretty Good Privacy (PGP) *(433)*
Realtime Blackhole List (RBL) *(430)*
Secure/Multipurpose Internet Mail Extensions (S/MIME) *(432)*

■ Key Terms Quiz

Use terms from the Key Terms list to complete the sentences that follow. Don't use the same term more than once. Not all terms will be used.

1. Spam is the popular term for _____.

2. A(n)_____ is a malicious code program that automates the infection process.

3. A large source of spam is zombie computers that are part of a(n) _____.

4. A program that looks like a normal application but contains malicious code is a(n) _____.

5. A(n) _____ is a compilation of servers that are blocked because they have been known to send spam.

6. _____ is one of the most popular chat programs.

7. A(n) _____ is a malicious code program that needs user intervention to spread.

8. A(n) _____ is a false e-mail that tells a compelling story, and typically prompts the user to forward it to other users.

9. _____ _____ can have the same virus risks as e-mail.

10. The most prevalent protocol that e-mail is sent by is _____.

■ Multiple-Choice Quiz

1. What is end-to-end security?

   A. When e-mail messages are stored in encrypted format until the user instructs decryption.

   B. When e-mail messages remain encrypted, no matter how many e-mail servers they pass through.

   C. When e-mail messages are sent through special secure servers.

   D. When e-mail is sent directly from the local host to the remote host, bypassing servers entirely.

2. What is one of the largest reasons spam is prevalent today?

   A. Criminals use zombie botnets.

   B. Regular mail is too slow.

   C. Spam is popular among recipients.

   D. Spam is sent from the government.

3. What is spam?

   A. Unsolicited commercial e-mail

   B. A Usenet archive

   C. A computer virus

   D. An encryption algorithm

4. How many bits are needed in a symmetric encryption algorithm to give decent protection from brute-force attacks?

   A. 24 bits

   B. 40 bits

   C. 56 bits

   D. 128 bits

5. Why is an open e-mail relay bad?

   A. It allows anyone to remotely control the server.

   B. It makes the e-mail server reboot once a day.

   C. No e-mail will go through.

   D. It will allow anyone to send spam through the server.

6. What makes e-mail hoaxes popular enough to keep the same story floating around for years?

   A. They are written by award-winning authors.

   B. The story prompts action on the reader's part.

   C. The story will grant the user good luck only if he or she forwards it on.

   D. The hoax e-mail forwards itself.

7. What is greylisting?

   A. E-mail messages are temporarily rejected so that the sender is forced to resend.

   B. E-mail messages are run through a strong set of filters before delivery.

   C. E-mail messages are sent through special secure servers.

   D. E-mail is sent directly from the local host to the remote host, bypassing servers entirely.

8. Why are instant messaging protocols dangerous for file transfer?

   A. They bypass server-based virus protections.

   B. File sharing is never dangerous.

   C. They allow everyone you chat with to view all your files.

   D. You'll end up receiving many spam files.

9. Why do PGP and S/MIME need public key cryptography?

   A. Public keys are necessary to determine whether the e-mail is encrypted.

   B. The public key is necessary to encrypt the symmetric key.

   C. The public key unlocks the password to the e-mail.

   D. The public key is useless and gives a false sense of privacy.

10. What symmetric encryption protocols does S/MIME support?

    A. AES and RC4

    B. IDEA and 3DES

    C. 3DES and RC2

    D. RC4 and IDEA

11. What instant messaging client currently supports encryption?

    A. Yahoo Messenger

    B. MSN/Windows Live Messenger

    C. Trillian

    D. AIM

12. Why is HTML e-mail dangerous?

    A. It can't be read by some e-mail clients.

    B. It sends the content of your e-mails to web pages.

    C. It can allow launching of malicious code from the preview pane.

    D. It is the only way spam can be sent.

13. What is a Trojan horse program?

    A. A program that encrypts e-mail for security

    B. A program that appears legitimate but is actually malicious code

    C. A program that runs only on a single computer

    D. A program that self-compiles before it runs

14. If they are both text protocols, why is instant messaging traffic riskier than e-mail?

    A. More viruses are coded for IM.

    B. IM has no business purpose.

    C. IM traffic has to travel outside of the organization to a server.

    D. Emoticons.

15. What makes spam so popular as an advertising medium?

    A. Its low cost per impression

    B. Its high rate of return

    C. Its ability to canvass multiple countries

    D. Its quality of workmanship

■ Essay Quiz

1. The marketing department wants to start using IM instead of e-mail, claiming that it will increase productivity, but the CIO has doubts about the security of IM. Describe how you would secure an IM implementation in the organization.

2. How would you implement a successful spam filtering policy?

3. You realize that a new e-mail game has been making the rounds at your company, and you are concerned that it is a Trojan horse program. Describe a few of the steps that can be used to prevent malicious code from infecting systems.

4. Draft a memo describing malware risks to the common user and what the user can do to avoid infection.

Lab Projects

• Lab Project 16.1

Show that instant messaging is an insecure protocol. You will need a lab computer with Windows installed, an IM program, and a sniffer. Then do the following:

1. If you need to install an IM program, download AIM from www.aim.com.

2. Run the Installer program.

3. Generate a username and password and log in.

4. Start the sniffer program and set it to capture all traffic.

5. Start a chat session with a partner in the class.

6. Decode the sniff trace to view the cleartext messages of the chat.

• Lab Project 16.2

Find at least ten pieces of spam mail from any account, whether it be home, work, school, or something else. Using the e-mail headers, and any web site that might provide information, attempt to trace the spam mail back to its original source.

You will need the following materials:

- Ten separate spam mails
- An Internet connection

Then do the following:

1. Collect the e-mails and view the e-mail header information in your e-mail program.

2. Find the "Received:" field in the headers and write down as many DNS names or IP addresses as you can. Also look for common details in the header elements of the different messages, such as the same e-mail servers and spammers.

3. Using the Internet, research the physical locations of the IP addresses.

4. Report the different locations from which your spam e-mail originated. What did you learn about tracing e-mail and spam?

chapter 17

Web Components

It is the framework which changes with each new technology and not just the picture within the frame.

—MARSHALL MCLUHAN

In this chapter, you will learn how to

- Describe the functioning of the SSL/TLS protocol suite
- Explain web applications, plug-ins, and associated security issues
- Describe secure file transfer options
- Explain directory usage for data retrieval
- Explain scripting and other Internet functions that present security concerns
- Use cookies to maintain parameters between web pages
- Examine web-based application security issues

The World Wide Web was invented by Tim Berners-Lee to give physicists a convenient method of exchanging information. What began in 1990 as a physics tool in the European Laboratory for Particle Physics (CERN, the acronym for the original French name) has grown into a complex system that is used by millions of computer users for tasks from e-commerce, to e-mail, chatting, games, and even the original intended use—file and information sharing. Before the Web, plenty of methods were used to perform these tasks, and they were already widespread in use. File Transfer Protocol (FTP) was used to move files, and Telnet allowed users access to other machines. What was missing was the common architecture brought by Berners-Lee: First, a common addressing scheme, built around the concept of a **Uniform Resource Locator (URL)**; second, the concept of linking documents to other documents by URLs through the **Hypertext Markup Language (HTML)**.

Although these elements might seem minor, they formed a base that spread like wildfire. Berners-Lee developed two programs to demonstrate the usefulness of his vision: a web server to serve documents to users, and a web browser to retrieve documents for users. Both of these key elements contributed to the spread of this new technological innovation. The success of these components led to network after network being connected together in a "network of networks" known today as the Internet. Much of this interconnection was developed and funded through grants from the U.S. government to further technological and economic growth.

What enabled the Web's explosive growth into the PC market were the application programs, called browsers, that were developed to use these common elements and allow users ease of access to the new world of connected resources. Browsers became graphically based, and as more users began to use them, a market for more services via the web channel was born. Out of this market, standards emerged to provide the required levels of security necessary as the user base and functionality of the Web expanded.

Current Web Components and Concerns

The usefulness of the Web is due not just to browsers, but also to web components that enable services for end users through their browser interfaces. These components use a wide range of protocols and services to deliver the desired content to end users. From a security perspective, they offer users an easy-to-use, secure method of conducting data transfers over the Internet. Many protocols have been developed to deliver this content, although for most users, the browser handles the details.

From a systems point of view, many security concerns have arisen, but they can be grouped into three main tasks:

- Securing a server that delivers content to users over the Web
- Securing the transport of information between users and servers over the Web
- Securing the user's computer from attack over a web connection

This chapter presents the components used on the Web to request and deliver information securely over the Internet.

Web Protocols

When two people communicate, several things must happen for the communication to be effective: They must use a language that both parties understand, and they must correctly use the language—that is, structure and syntax—to express their thoughts. The mode of communication is a separate entity entirely, for the previous statements are important in both spoken and written forms of communication. The same requirements are present with respect to computer communications, and they are addressed through *protocols*, agreed-upon sets of rules that allow different vendors to produce hardware and software that can interoperate with hardware and software developed by other vendors. Because of the worldwide nature of the Internet, protocols are very important and form the basis by which all the separate parts can work together. The specific instantiation of protocols is done through hardware and software components. The majority of this chapter concentrates on protocols related to the Internet as instantiated by software components.

Encryption (SSL and TLS)

Secure Sockets Layer (SSL) is a general-purpose protocol developed by Netscape for managing the encryption of information being transmitted over the Internet. It began as a competitive feature to drive sales of Netscape's web server product, which could then send information securely to end users. This early vision of securing the transmission channel between the web server and the browser became an Internet standard. Today, SSL is almost ubiquitous with respect to e-commerce—all browsers support it as do web servers, and virtually all e-commerce web sites use this method to protect sensitive financial information in transit between web servers and browsers.

The **Internet Engineering Task Force (IETF)** embraced SSL in 1996 through a series of RFCs and named the group of RFCs **Transport Layer Security (TLS)**. Starting with SSL 3.0, in 1999 the IETF issued RFC 2246, "TLS Protocol Version 1.0," followed by RFC 2712, which added Kerberos authentication, and then RFCs 2817 and 2818, which extended TLS to HTTP version 1.1 (HTTP/1.1). Although SSL has been through several versions, TLS begins with an equivalency to SSL 3.0, so today SSL and TLS are essentially the same although not interchangeable.

SSL/TLS is a series of functions that exists in the OSI (Open System Interconnection) model between the application layer and the transport and network layers. The goal of TCP is to send an unauthenticated, error-free stream of information between two computers. SSL/TLS adds message integrity and authentication functionality to TCP through the use of cryptographic methods. Because cryptographic methods are an ever-evolving field, and because both parties must agree on an implementation method, SSL/TLS has embraced an open, extensible, and adaptable method to allow flexibility and strength. When two programs initiate an SSL/TLS connection, one of their first tasks is to compare available protocols and agree on an appropriate common cryptographic protocol for use in this particular communication. As SSL/TLS can use separate algorithms and methods for encryption, authentication, and data integrity, each of these is negotiated and determined depending upon need at the beginning of a communication. Currently, the browsers from Mozilla (Firefox) and Microsoft (Internet Explorer 8) allow fairly extensive SSL/TLS setup options, as illustrated in Figure 17.1 (Internet Explorer 8), Figure 17.2 (Firefox), and Figure 17.3 (Firefox).

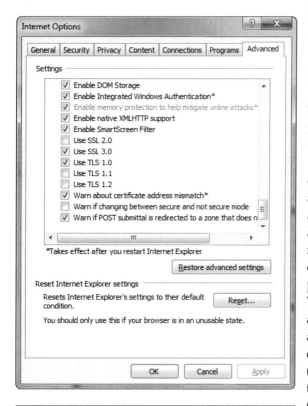

• **Figure 17.1**   IE 8 security options

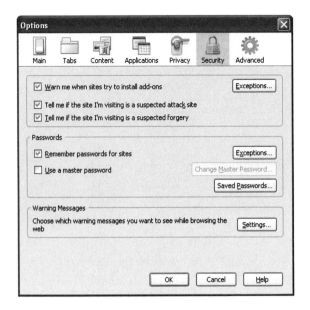

● **Figure 17.2** Firefox SSL security options

● **Figure 17.3** Firefox SSL cipher options

How SSL/TLS Works

SSL/TLS uses a wide range of cryptographic protocols. To use these protocols effectively between a client and a server, an agreement must be reached on which protocol to use, which is done via the SSL handshake process. The process begins with a client request for a secure connection and a server's response.

The questions asked and answered are which protocol and which cryptographic algorithm will be used. For the client and server to communicate, both sides must agree on a commonly held protocol (SSL v1, v2, v3, or TLS v1). Commonly available cryptographic algorithms include Diffie-Hellman and RSA. The next step is to exchange certificates and keys as necessary to enable authentication.

Once authentication is established, the channel is secured with symmetric key cryptographic methods and hashes, typically RC4 or 3DES for symmetric key and MD5 or SHA-1 for the hash functions.

Exam Tip: Authentication was a one-way process for SSL v1 and v2, with only the server providing authentication. In SSL v3/TLS, mutual authentication of both client and server is possible.

Cross Check

X.509 Certificates

As we explored in Chapters 5 and 6, certificates are used as a way to exchange trusted cryptographic data. The certificate exchange is via X.509 certificates, and public key cryptography is used to establish authentication. This is an operational example of the principles from Chapter 6. When making a secure connection to your bank, what information would you expect on the certificate?

SSL/TLS Handshake

The following steps, depicted in the illustration, establish an SSL/TLS secured channel (SSL handshake):

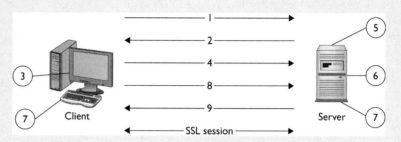

1. *The client sends to the server the client's SSL version number, cipher settings, and session-specific data.*

2. *The server sends to the client the server's SSL version number, cipher settings, session-specific data, and its own certificate. If the resource requested requires client authentication, the server requests the client's certificate.*

3. *The client authenticates the server using the information it has received. If the server cannot be authenticated, the user is warned of the problem and informed that an encrypted and authenticated connection cannot be established.*

4. *The client encrypts a seed value with the server's public key (from certificate—step 2) and sends it to the server. If the server requested client authentication, the client also sends the client certificate.*

5. *If the server requested client authentication, the server attempts to authenticate the client certificate. If the client certificate cannot be authenticated, the session ends.*

6. *The server uses its private key to decrypt the secret, and then performs a series of steps (which the client also performs) to generate a master secret. The required steps depend on the cryptographic method used for key exchange.*

7. *Both the client and the server use the master secret to generate the session key, which is a symmetric key used to encrypt and decrypt information exchanged during the SSL session.*

8. *The client sends a message informing the server that future messages from the client will be encrypted with the session key. It then sends a separate (encrypted) message indicating that the client portion of the handshake is finished.*

9. *The server sends a message informing the client that future messages from the server will be encrypted with the session key. It then sends a separate (encrypted) message indicating that the server portion of the handshake is finished.*

10. *The SSL handshake is now complete and the session can begin.*

At this point, the authenticity of the server and possibly the client has been established, and the channel is protected by encryption against eavesdropping. Each packet is encrypted using the symmetric key before transfer across the network, and then decrypted by the receiver. All of this work requires CPU time; hence, SSL/TLS connections require significantly more overhead than unprotected connections. Establishing connections is particularly time consuming, so even stateless web connections are held in a stateful fashion when secured via SSL/TLS, to avoid repeating the handshake process for each request. This makes some web server functionality more difficult, such as implementing web farms, and requires that either an SSL/TLS appliance be used before the web server to maintain state or the SSL/TLS state information be maintained in a directory-type service accessible by all of the web farm servers. Either method requires additional infrastructure and equipment. However, to enable secure e-commerce and other private data transactions over the Internet, this is a cost-effective method to establish a specific level of necessary security.

The use of certificates could present a lot of data and complication to a user. Fortunately, browsers have incorporated much of this desired functionality into a seamless operation. Once you have decided always to accept code from XYZ Corporation, subsequent certificate checks are handled by the browser. The ability to manipulate certificate settings is under the Options menus in both Internet Explorer (Figures 17.4 and 17.5) and Mozilla Firefox (Figures 17.6 and 17.7).

Tech Tip

Certificates

A certificate is merely a standard set of formatted data that represents the authenticity of the public key associated with the signer. The use of certificates allows a third party to act as a notary in the electronic world. A person using a notary assumes the notary is honest, and states have regulations and notaries have insurance to protect against fraud. The same idea is true with certificates, although the legal system has not caught up to the electronic age, nor has the business of liability insurance. Still, certificates provide a method of proving who someone is, provided you trust the issuer. If the issuer is a third party of stature, such as VeriSign or AT&T, you can rest your faith upon that authenticity. If the issuer is a large firm such as Microsoft, you can probably trust it since you are downloading its code. If the issuer is Bob's Certificate Shack—well, unless you know Bob, you may have cause for concern. Certificates do not vouch for code security, they only say that the person or entity that is signing them is actually the person or entity they claim to be. Details of certificates and PKI elements to support their use are covered in Chapter 6, and you are encouraged to brush up on them if needed.

SSL/TLS Attacks

SSL/TLS is specifically designed to provide protection from man-in-the-middle attacks. By authenticating the server end of the connection, SSL/TLS was designed to prevent the initial hijacking of a session. By encrypting all of the conversations between the client and the server, SSL/TLS prevents eavesdropping. Even with all of this, however, SSL/TLS is not a complete security solution and can be defeated.

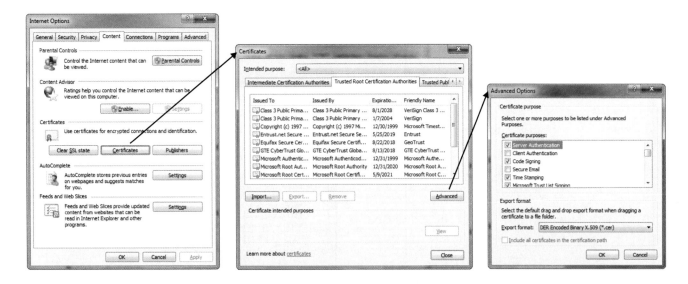

● **Figure 17.4**   IE 8 certificate management options

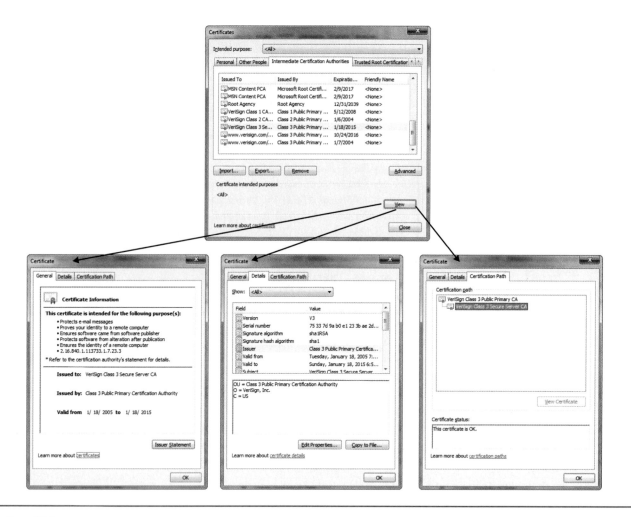

• **Figure 17.5** IE 8 certificate store

Once a communication is in the SSL/TLS channel, it is very difficult to defeat the SSL protocol. Before data enters the secured channel, however, defeat is possible. A Trojan program that copies keystrokes and echoes them to another TCP/IP address in parallel with the intended communication can

• **Figure 17.6** Firefox certificate options

• **Figure 17.7** Firefox certificate store

Tech Tip

SSL Proxy Attack

SSL-based security is not foolproof. It can be defeated, as in the case of a proxy-based attack. Examining the handshake, the following steps could occur, as shown in this illustration:

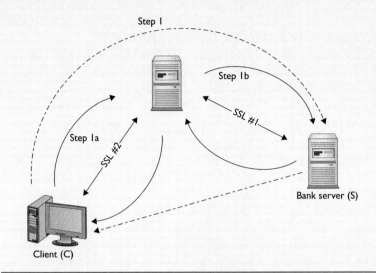

- SSL man-in-the-middle attack

1. *The client (C) initiates an SSL session with their bank server (S) through a proxy (P).*

2. *P acts by echoing the information sent to it by C (step 1a) to S (step 1b), imitating C to S, and establishing a secure channel between P and S (SSL #1).*

3. *P creates a second secure channel to C (SSL #2), using information received from S, pretending to be S.*

4. *The user assumes that the dotted lines occur—a secure channel to the bank directly—when in fact the client only has a secure channel to the proxy. In fact, the proxy has the secure channel to the bank, and as far as the bank is concerned, the proxy is the client, and using the client's credentials. For a proxy that is not completely trusted, this could be a nightmare for the client.*

The advent of high-assurance certificates in Internet Explorer 7 and later prevents the proxy from imitating the bank, as it cannot give the correct set of credentials back to the client to complete the high-assurance handshake. Mutual authentication is also designed to prevent this, as the proxy cannot simultaneously imitate both sides of the handshake. Mutual authentication is rarely used, as there is the issue of maintaining client certificates that are trusted to a server—a challenge for broad-reach sites like financial institutions and e-commerce sites.

defeat SSL/TLS, for example, provided that the Trojan program copies the data prior to SSL/TLS encapsulation. This type of attack has occurred and has been used to steal passwords and other sensitive material from users, performing the theft as the user actually types in the data.

The Web (HTTP and HTTPS)

HTTP is used for the transfer of hyperlinked data over the Internet, from web servers to browsers. When a user types a URL such as http://www.example .com into a browser, the http:// portion indicates that the desired method of data transfer is HTTP. Although it was initially created just for HTML pages, today many protocols deliver content over this connection protocol. HTTP traffic takes place over TCP port 80 by default, and this port is typically left open on firewalls because of the extensive use of HTTP.

One of the primary drivers behind the development of SSL/TLS was the desire to hide the complexities of cryptography from end users. When using an SSL/TLS-enabled browser, this can be done simply by requesting a secure connection from a web server instead of a nonsecure connection. With respect to HTTP connections, this is as simple as using https:// in place of http://.

When a browser is SSL/TLS-aware, the entry of an SSL/TLS-based protocol will cause the browser to perform the necessary negotiations with the web server to establish the required level of security. Once these negotiations have been completed and the session is secured by a session key, a closed padlock icon is displayed in the lower right of the screen to indicate that the session is secure. If the protocol is *https:*, your connection is secure; if it is *http:*, then the connection is carried by plaintext for anyone to see. Figure 17.8 shows a secure connection in Internet Explorer 8, and Figure 17.9 shows the equivalent in Firefox. As of Internet Explorer 7, Microsoft places the padlock icon in an obvious position, next to the URL, instead of in the lower-right corner of the screen, where users could more easily miss it. Another new security feature that begins with Internet Explorer 7 and Firefox 3 is the use of high-assurance SSL, a combination of an extended-validation SSL certificate and a high-security browser. If a high-security browser, Internet Explorer 7 or Firefox 3 and beyond, establishes a connection with a vendor that has registered with a certificate authority for an extended-validation SSL certificate, then the URL box will be colored green and the box next to it will display the registered entity and additional validation information when clicked. These improvements were in response to phishing sites and online fraud, and although they require additional costs and registration on the part of the vendors, this is a modest up-front cost to help reduce fraud and provide confidence to customers.

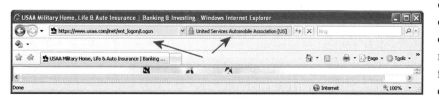

● **Figure 17.8**   High-assurance notification in IE 7

● **Figure 17.9**   High-assurance notification in Firefox

The objective of enabling cryptographic methods in this fashion is to make it easy for end users to use these protocols. SSL/TLS is designed to be *protocol agnostic*. Although designed to run on top of TCP/IP, it can operate on top of other, lower-level protocols, such as X.25. SSL/TLS requires a reliable lower-level protocol, so it is not designed and cannot properly function on top of a nonreliable protocol such as the User Datagram Protocol (UDP). Even with this limitation, SSL/TLS has been used to secure many common TCP/IP-based services, as shown in Table 17.1.

Table 17.1	SSL/TLS-Protected Services	
Protocol	TCP Port	Use
HTTPS	443	SSL/TSL-secured HTTP traffic
SSMTP	465	SSL/TLS-secured SMTP for mail sending
SPOP3 (Secure POP3)	995	SSL/TLS-secured POP3 for mail receiving
sNEWS	563	SSL/TLS-secured Usenet news
SSL = LDAP	636	SSL/TLS-secured LDAP services

Directory Services (DAP and LDAP)

A *directory* is a data storage mechanism similar to a database, but it has several distinct differences designed to provide efficient data retrieval services compared to standard database mechanisms. A directory is designed and optimized for reading data, offering very fast search and retrieval operations. The types of information stored in a directory tend to be descriptive attribute data. A directory offers a static view of data that can be changed without a complex update transaction. The data is hierarchically described in a treelike structure, and a network interface for reading is typical.

> As directories are optimized for read operations, they are frequently employed where data retrieval is desired. Common uses of directories include e-mail address lists, domain server data, and resource maps of network resources.

To enable interoperability, the **X.500** standard was created as a standard for directory services. The primary method for accessing an X.500 directory is through the Directory Access Protocol (DAP), a heavyweight protocol that is difficult to implement completely, especially on PCs and more constrained platforms. This led to the **Lightweight Directory Access Protocol (LDAP)**, which contains the most commonly used functionality. LDAP can interface with X.500 services, and, most importantly, LDAP can be used over TCP with significantly less computing resources than a full X.500 implementation. LDAP offers all of the functionality most directories need and is easier and more economical to implement, hence LDAP has become the Internet standard for directory services. LDAP standards are governed by two separate entities depending upon use: the International Telecommunication Union (ITU) governs the X.500 standard, and LDAP is governed for Internet use by the IETF. Many RFCs apply to LDAP functionality, but some of the most important are RFCs 2251 through 2256 and RFCs 2829 and 2830.

> LDAP over TCP is a plaintext protocol, meaning data is passed in the clear and is susceptible to eavesdropping. Encryption can be used to remedy this problem, and the application of SSL/TLS-based service will protect directory queries and replies from eavesdroppers.

SSL/TLS LDAP

SSL/TLS provides several important functions to LDAP services. It can establish the identity of a data source through the use of certificates, and it can also provide for the integrity and confidentiality of the data being presented from an LDAP source. As LDAP and SSL/TLS are two separate independent protocols, interoperability is more a function of correct setup than anything else. To achieve LDAP over SSL/TLS, the typical setup is to establish an SSL/TLS connection and then open an LDAP connection over the protected channel. To do this requires that both the client and the server be enabled for SSL/TLS. In the case of the client, most browsers are already enabled. In the case of an

LDAP server, this specific function must be enabled by a system administrator. As this setup initially is complicated, it's definitely a task for a competent system administrator.

Once an LDAP server is set up to function over an SSL/TLS connection, it operates as it always has. The LDAP server responds to specific queries with the data returned from a node in the search. The SSL/TLS functionality operates to secure the channel of communication, and it is transparent to the data flow from the user's perspective. From the outside, SSL/TLS prevents observation of the data request and response, ensuring confidentiality.

File Transfer (FTP and SFTP)

One of the original intended uses of the Internet was to transfer files from one machine to another in a simple, secure, and reliable fashion, which was needed by scientific researchers. Today, file transfers represent downloads of music content, reports, and other data sets from other computer systems to a PC-based client. Until 1995, the majority of Internet traffic was file transfers. With all of this need, a protocol was necessary so that two computers could agree on how to send and receive data. As such, FTP is one of the older protocols.

FTP

File Transfer Protocol (FTP) is an application-level protocol that operates over a wide range of lower-level protocols. FTP is embedded in most operating systems and provides a method of transferring files from a sender to a receiver. Most FTP implementations are designed to operate both ways, sending and receiving, and can enable remote file operations over a TCP/IP connection. FTP clients are used to initiate transactions, and FTP servers are used to respond to transaction requests. The actual request can be either to upload (send data from client to server) or to download (send data from server to client).

Clients for FTP on a PC can range from an application program to the command-line FTP program in Windows/DOS to most browsers. To open an FTP data store in a browser, you can enter **ftp://url** in the browser's address field to indicate that you want to see the data associated with the URL via an FTP session—the browser handles the details.

Blind FTP (Anonymous FTP)

To access resources on a computer, an account must be used to allow the operating system–level authorization function to work. In the case of an FTP server, you may not wish to control who gets the information, so a standard account called *anonymous* exists. This allows unlimited public access to the files and is commonly used when you want to have unlimited distribution. On a server, access permissions can be established to allow only downloading or only uploading or both, depending on the system's function.

As FTP servers can present a security risk, they are typically not permitted on workstations and are disabled on servers without need for this functionality.

As FTP can be used to allow anyone access to upload files to a server, it is considered a security risk and is commonly implemented on specialized servers isolated from other critical functions.

SFTP

FTP operates in a plaintext mode, so an eavesdropper can observe the data being passed. If confidential transfer is required, Secure FTP (SFTP) combines both the Secure Shell (SSH) protocol and FTP to accomplish this task. SFTP operates as an application program that encodes both the commands and the data being passed and requires SFTP to be on both the client and the server. SFTP is not interoperable with standard FTP—the encrypted commands cannot be read by the standard FTP server program. To establish SFTP data transfers, the server must be enabled with the SFTP program, and then clients can access the server, provided they have the correct credentials. One of the first SFTP operations is the same as that of FTP: an identification function that uses a username and an authorization function that uses a password. There is no anonymous SFTP account by definition, so access is established and controlled from the server using standard access control lists (ACLs), IDs, and passwords.

Vulnerabilities

Modern encryption technology can provide significant levels of privacy, up to military-grade secrecy. The use of protocols such as SSL/TLS provides a convenient method for end users to use cryptography without having to understand how it works. This can result in complacency—the impression that once SSL/TLS is enabled, the user is safe, but this is not necessarily the case. If a Trojan program is recording keystrokes and sending the information to another unauthorized user, for example, SSL/TLS cannot prevent the security breach. If the user is connecting to an untrustworthy site, the mere fact that the connection is secure does not prevent the other site from running a scam.

Using SSL/TLS and other encryption methods will not guard against your credit card information being "lost" by a company with which you do business, as in the Egghead.com credit card hack of 2000. In December 2000, Egghead.com's credit card database was hacked, and as many as 3.7 million credit card numbers were exposed. Other similar stories include 55,000 credit card records being compromised by Creditcards.com in 2000 and more than 300,000 records being compromised by the CD Universe hack in 1999.

The key to understanding what is protected and where it is protected requires an understanding of what these protocols can and cannot do. The SSL/TLS suite can protect data in transit, but not on either end in storage. It can authenticate users and servers, provided that the certificate mechanisms are established and used by both parties. Properly set up and used, SSL/TLS can provide a very secure method of authentication, followed by confidentiality in data transfers and data integrity checking. But again, all of this occurs during transit, and the protection ends once the data is stored.

> SSL is not a guarantee of security. All SSL can do is secure the transport link between the computer and the server. There are still a number of vulnerabilities that can affect the security of the system. A keylogger on the client can copy the secrets before they go to the SSL-protected link. Malware on either end of the secure communication can copy and/or alter transmissions outside the secure link.

■ Code-Based Vulnerabilities

The ability to connect many machines together to transfer data is what makes the Internet so functional for so many users. Browsers enable much of this functionality, and as the types of data have grown on the Internet, browser functionality has grown as well. But not all functions can be anticipated or included in each browser release, so the idea of extending browser functions through plug-ins became a standard. Browsers can perform many types of data transfer, and in some cases, additional helper programs, or plug-ins, can increase functionality for specific types of data transfers. In other cases, separate application programs may be called by a browser to handle the data being transferred. Common examples of these plug-ins and programs include Shockwave plug-ins, RealOne player (both plug-in and standalone application), Windows Media Player, and Adobe Acrobat (both plug-in and standalone). The richness that enables the desired functionality of the Internet has also spawned some additional types of interfaces in the form of ActiveX components and Java applets.

In essence, all of these are pieces of code that can be written by third parties, distributed via the Internet, and run on your PC. If the code does what the user wants, the user is happy. But the opportunity exists for these applications or plug-ins to include malicious code that performs actions not desired by the end user. Malicious code designed to operate within a web browser environment is a major tool for computer crackers to use to obtain unauthorized access to computer systems. Whether delivered by HTML-based e-mail, by getting a user to visit a web site, or even delivery via an ad server, the result is the same: malware performs malicious tasks in the browser environment.

Buffer Overflows

One of the most common exploits used to hack into software is the **buffer overflow**. The buffer overflow vulnerability is a result of poor coding practices on the part of software programmers—when any program reads input into a buffer (an area of memory) and does not validate the input for correct length, the potential for a buffer overflow exists. The buffer-overflow vulnerability occurs when an application can accept more input than it has assigned storage space and the input data overwrites other program areas. The exploit concept is simple: An attacker develops an executable program that performs some action on the target machine and appends this code to a legitimate response to a program on the target machine. When the target machine reads through the too-long response, a buffer-overflow condition causes the original program to fail. The extra malicious code fragment is now in the machine's memory, awaiting execution. If the attacker executed it correctly, the program will skip into the attacker's code, running it instead of crashing.

Buffer overflows have been shown to be exploitable in a wide range of programs, from UNIX, to Windows, to applications such as Internet Explorer, Netscape Communicator, and many more. Historically, more than 50 percent of

Cross Check

Dangers of Software Vulnerabilities

Errors in software lead to vulnerabilities associated with the code being run. These vulnerabilities are exploited by hackers to perform malicious activity on a machine. These errors are frequently related to web-enabled programs, as the Internet provides a useful conduit for hackers to achieve access to a system. The problem of code vulnerabilities, from buffer overflows, to arithmetic overflows, to cross-site request forgeries, cross-site scripting, and injection attacks, is a serious issue that has many faces. It is noted in this chapter because web components are involved, but full details on the severity of and steps to mitigate this issue are in Chapter 18. The next time you provide input to a web-based application, think of what malicious activity you could perform on the server in question.

the security incidents by type are due to buffer-overflow exploits. It is one of the most common hacks used, and the primary defense users have is to keep their machines up to date with patches from software manufacturers. Unfortunately, patching has not proven to be a very effective method of protection. Many people don't keep up to date with the patches, as demonstrated by the Slammer worm attack, which took place almost six months after Microsoft had released a patch specifically for the vulnerability. Even with the patch widely available, both in a hotfix and in a service pack, many SQL servers had not received the patch and were affected by this worm, which used a buffer overflow to propagate.

Java and JavaScript

Java is a computer language invented by Sun Microsystems as an alternative to Microsoft's development languages. Designed to be platform-independent and based on C, Java offered a low learning curve and a way of implementing programs across an enterprise, independent of platform. Although platform independence never fully materialized, and the pace of Java language development was slowed by Sun, Java has found itself to be a leader in object-oriented programming languages.

Java operates through an interpreter called a Java Virtual Machine (JVM) on each platform that interprets the Java code, and this JVM enables the program's functionality for the specific platform. JavaScript works through the browser environment using JScript (in Internet Explorer), SpiderMonkey (in Firefox), and V8 (in Google Chrome). Java's reliance on an interpretive step has led to performance issues, and Java is still plagued by poor performance when compared to most other languages. Security was one of the touted advantages of Java, but in reality, security is not a built-in function but an afterthought and is implemented independently of the language core. This all being said, properly coded Java can operate at reasonable rates, and when properly designed can act in a secure fashion. These facts have led to the wide dependence on Java for much of the server-side coding for e-commerce and other web-enabled functionality. Servers can add CPUs to address speed concerns, and the low learning curve has proven cost efficient for enterprises.

Java was initially designed to be used in trusted environments, and when it moved to the Internet for general use, safety became one of its much-hyped benefits. Java has many safety features, such as type checking and garbage collection, that actually improve a program's ability to run safely on a machine and not cause operating system–level failures. This isolates the user from many common forms of operating system faults that can end in the "blue screen of death" in a Windows environment, where the operating system crashes and forces a reboot of the system. Safety is not security, however, and although safe, a malicious Java program can still cause significant damage to a system.

The primary mode of a computer program is to interact with the operating system and perform functional tasks for a user, such as getting and displaying data, manipulating data, storing data, and so on. Although these functions can seem benign, when enabled across the Web they can have some unintended consequences. The ability to read data from a hard drive and display it on the screen is essential for many programs, but when the

> Java is designed for safety, reducing the opportunity for system crashes. Java can still perform malicious activities, and the fact that many users falsely believe it is safe increases its usefulness to attackers.

program is downloaded and run from the Internet and the data is, without the knowledge of the user, sent across the Internet to an unauthorized user, this enables a program to spy on a user and steal data. Writing data to the hard drive can also cause deletions if the program doesn't write the data where the user expects. Sun recognized these dangers and envisioned three different security policies for Java that would be implemented via the browser and JVM, providing different levels of security. The first policy is not to run Java programs at all. The second restricts Java program functionality when the program is not run directly from the system's hard drive—programs being directly executed from the Internet have severe restrictions that block disk access and force other security-related functions to be performed. The last policy runs any and all Java programs as presented.

Most browsers adopted the second security policy, restricting Java functionality on a client unless the program was loaded directly from the client's hard drive. Although this solved many problems initially, it also severely limited functionality. Today, browsers allow much more specific granularity on security for Java, based on security zones and user settings.

JavaScript is a scripting language developed by Netscape and designed to be operated within a browser instance. The primary purpose of JavaScript is to enable features such as validation of forms before they are submitted to the server. Enterprising programmers found many other uses for JavaScript, such as manipulating the browser history files, now prohibited by design. JavaScript actually runs within the browser, and the code is executed by the browser itself. This has led to compatibility problems, and not just between vendors, such as Microsoft and Mozilla, but between browser versions. Security settings in Internet Explorer are done by a series of zones, allowing differing levels of control over .NET functionality, ActiveX functionality, and Java functionality (see Figure 17.10). Unfortunately, these settings can be changed by a Trojan program, altering the browser (without alerting the user) and lowering the security settings. In Firefox, using the NoScript plug-in is a solution to this, but the reduced functionality leads to other issues, as shown in Figure 17.11, and requires more diligent user intervention.

Although JavaScript was designed not to be able to access files or network resources directly, except through the browser functions, it has not proven to be as secure as desired. This fault traces back to a similar fault in the Java language, where security was added on,

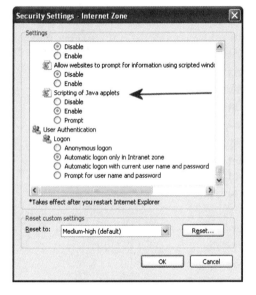

• **Figure 17.10** Java configuration settings in Microsoft Internet Explorer 7

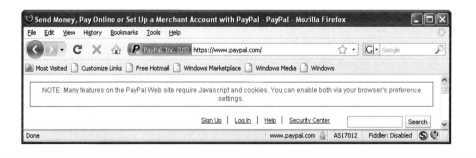

• **Figure 17.11** Security setting functionality issues

without the benefit of a comprehensive security model. So, although designers put thought and common sense into the design of JavaScript, the lack of a comprehensive security model left some security holes. For instance, a form could submit itself via e-mail to an undisclosed recipient, either eavesdropping, spamming, or causing other problems—imagine your machine sending death threat e-mails to high-level government officials from a rogue JavaScript implementation.

Further, most browsers do not have a mechanism to halt a running script, short of aborting the browser instance, and even this may not be possible if the browser has stopped responding to commands. Malicious JavaScripts can do many things, including opening two new windows every time you close one, each with the code to open two more. There is no way out of this one, short of killing the browser process from the operating system.

JavaScripts can also trick users into thinking they are communicating with one entity when in fact they are communicating with another. For example, a window may open asking whether you want to download and execute the new update from "http://www.microsoft.com..../update.exe," and what is covered by the ellipsis (…) is actually "www.microsoft.com.attacker.org/"—the user assumes this is a Microsoft address that is cut short by space restrictions on the display.

As a browser scripting language, JavaScript is here to stay. Its widespread popularity for developing applets such as animated clocks, mortgage calculators, simple games, and the like will overcome its buggy nature and poor level of security. Similarly, Java as a development language is also here to stay, although it may never live up to its initial hype and will continue to have security issues. Both of these technologies boast many skilled developers, low learning curves (because of their heritage in the C language), and popularity in computer science courses. When viewed as a total package, the marketplace has decided that the benefits outweigh the drawbacks, and these two technologies will be a cornerstone for much Internet programming development.

> Many web sites may have behaviors that users deem less than desirable, such as popping open additional windows, either on top (pop-up) or underneath (pop-under). To prevent these behaviors, a class of applet referred to as a pop-up blocker may be employed. Although they may block some desired pop-ups, most pop-up blockers have settings to allow pop-ups on selected sites. The use of a pop-up blocker assists in retaining strict control over browser behavior and enhances security for the user.

ActiveX

ActiveX is the name given to a broad collection of application programming interfaces (APIs), protocols, and programs developed by Microsoft to download and execute code automatically over an Internet-based channel. The code is bundled together into an ActiveX control with an .ocx extension. These controls are referenced in HTML using the **<object>** tag. ActiveX is a tool for the Windows environment and can be extremely powerful. It can do simple things, such as enable a browser to display a custom type of information in a particular way, and it can also perform complex tasks, such as update the operating system and application programs. This range of abilities gives ActiveX a lot of power, but this power can be abused as well as used for good purposes. Internet Explorer has several options to control the execution of ActiveX controls, as illustrated in Figure 17.12.

To enable security and consumer confidence in downloaded programs such as ActiveX controls, Microsoft developed **Authenticode**, a system that uses digital signatures and allows Windows users to determine who produced a specific piece of code and whether or not the code has been altered. As in the case of Java, safety and security are different things, and Authenticode

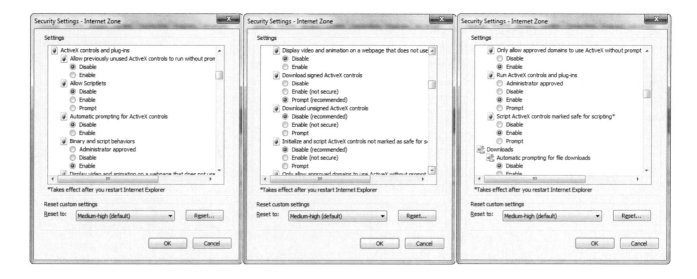

• Figure 17.12   ActiveX security settings in IE 8

Exam Tip: ActiveX technology can be used to create complex application logic that is then embedded into other container objects such as a web browser. ActiveX components have very significant capabilities and thus malicious ActiveX objects can be very dangerous. Authenticode is a means of signing an ActiveX control so that a user can judge trust based on the control's creator.

promotes neither in reality. Authenticode provides limited accountability at the time of download and provides reasonable assurance that the code has not been changed since the time of signing. Authenticode does not identify whether a piece of code will cause damage to a system, nor does it regulate how code is used, so a perfectly safe ActiveX control under one set of circumstances may be malicious if used improperly. As with a notary's signature, recourse is very limited—if code is signed by a terrorist organization and the code ruins your machine, all Authenticode did was make it seem legitimate. It is still incumbent upon the users to know from whom they are getting code and to determine whether or not they trust that organization.

Critics of Authenticode and other code-signing techniques are not against code signing, for this is a universally recognized good thing. What the critics argue is that code signing is not a panacea for security issues and that marketing it as doing more than it really does is irresponsible. Understanding the nuances of security is important in today's highly technical world, and leaving the explanations to marketing departments is not the ideal solution.

Securing the Browser

A great deal of debate concerns the relative security issue of browser extensions versus the rich user interaction that they provide. There is no doubt that the richness of the environment offered by ActiveX adds to the user experience. But as is the case in most coding situations, added features means weaker security, all other things being constant. If nothing else, a development team must spend some portion of its time on secure development practices, time that some developers and marketers would prefer to spend on new features. Although no browser is 100 percent safe, the use of Firefox coupled with the NoScript plug-in comes the closest to fitting the bill. Firefox will not execute ActiveX, so that threat vector is removed. The NoScript plug-in allows the user to determine from which domains to trust scripts. The use of NoScript puts the onus back on the user as to which domain scripts they choose to trust, and although it's not perfect from a security perspective, this at least allows a measure of control over what code you want to run on your machine.

CGI

The **Common Gateway Interface (CGI)** was the original method for having a web server execute a program outside the web server process, yet on the same server. The intent was to pass information via environment variables to an independent program, execute the program, and return the results to the web server for display. Web servers are presentation and display engines, and they provide less than stellar results when used for other purposes. For example, a web server instance can have numerous independent connections, and a program failure that results in a process bounce can affect multiple users if it is run within the web server process. Separating into processes any time-consuming and more risky programming cores, such as database lookups and manipulation, complex calculations, and other tasks, was and still is a prudent idea.

CGI offers many advantages to web-based programs. The programs can be written in a number of languages, although Perl is a favorite. These scripted programs embrace the full functionality of a server, allowing access to databases, UNIX commands, other programs, and so on. This provides a wide range of functionality to the web environment. With this unrestrained capability, however, come security issues. Poorly written scripts can cause unintended consequences at runtime.

The problem with poorly written scripts is that their defects are not always obvious. Sometimes scripts appear to be fine, but unexpected user inputs can have unintended consequences. The addition of extra elements on a command line, for example, can result in dramatically different outputs. The use of the Perl backquote function, for example, allows a user to programmatically encode user input to a UNIX shell, and this works properly given proper user input, but if the user appends **& /bin/ls –l** to a proper input, this could generate a directory listing of the cgi-bin directory, which in turn gives away script names for future exploitation attempts. Permitting users to execute other programs in such an uncontrolled fashion led many ISPs to prohibit the use of CGI scripts unless they were specifically approved by the ISP. This led to considerable overhead and code checking to ensure clean code and validated user inputs.

A variety of books have been written on how to write secure code, and CGI has benefited. Properly coded, CGI offers no more and no less risk than any other properly coded solution. CGI's loss was that it was first and thus was abused first, and many developers learned by making mistakes early on CGI. On UNIX systems, CGI offers the ultimate in programmable diversity and capability, and now that security standard practices have been learned and put to use, the system is experiencing new popularity.

Server-Side Scripts

CGI has been replaced in many web sites through newer **server-side scripting** technologies such as Java, **Active Server Pages (ASP)**, **ASP.NET**, and **PHP**. All these technologies operate in much the same fashion as CGI: they allow programs to be run outside the web server and to return data to the web server to be served to end users via a web page. The term *server-side script* is actually a misnomer, as these are actually executable programs that are either interpreted or run in virtual machines. Each of these newer technologies has advantages and disadvantages, but all of them have stronger security models than CGI. With these security models come reduced functionality and, as each is based on a different language, a steeper learning curve. Still, the need for adherence to programming fundamentals exists in these technologies—code must be well designed and well written to avoid the same vulnerabilities that exist in all forms of code. Buffer overflows are still an issue. Changing languages or technologies does not eliminate the basic security problems associated with incorporating open-ended user input into code. Understanding and qualifying user responses before blindly using them programmatically is essential to the security of a system.

Cookies

Cookies are small chunks of ASCII text passed within an HTTP stream to store data temporarily in a web browser instance. Invented by Netscape, cookies pass back and forth between web server and browser and act as a mechanism to maintain state in a stateless world. *State* is a term that describes the dependence on previous actions. By definition, HTTP traffic served by a web server is *stateless*—each request is completely independent of all previous requests, and the server has no memory of previous requests. This dramatically simplifies the function of a web server, but it also significantly complicates the task of providing anything but the most basic functionality in a site. Cookies were developed to bridge this gap. Cookies are passed along with HTTP data through a Set-Cookie message in the header portion of an HTTP message.

> Cookies come in two types, session and persistent. Session cookies last only during a web browsing session with a web site. Persistent cookies are stored on the user's hard drive and last until an expiration date.

A cookie is actually a series of name-value pairs that is stored in memory during a browser instance. The specification for cookies established several specific name-value pairs for defined purposes. Additional name-value pairs may be defined at will by a developer. The specified set of name-value pairs include the following:

- **Expires** This field specifies when the cookie expires. If no value exists, the cookie is good only during the current browser session and will not be persisted to the user's hard drive. Should a value be given, the cookie will be written to the user's machine and persisted until this datetime value occurs.

- **Domain** This name-value pair specifies the domain where the cookie is used. Cookies were designed as memory-resident objects, but as the user or data can cause a browser to move between domains, say from comedy.net to jokes.org, some mechanism needs to tell the browser which cookies belong to which domains.

- **Path** This name-value pair further resolves the applicability of the cookie into a specific path within a domain. If path = /directory, the cookie will be sent only for requests within /directory on the given domain. This allows a level of granular control over the information being passed between the browser and server, and it limits unnecessary data exchanges.

- **Secure** The presence of the keyword **[secure]** in a cookie indicates that it is to be used only when connected in an SSL/TLS session. This does not indicate any other form of security, as cookies are stored in plaintext on the client machine. In fact, one browser-based security issue was the ability to read another site's cookies from the browser cache and determine the values by using a script.

Cookie management on a browser is normally an invisible process, but both Internet Explorer and Firefox have methods for users to examine and manipulate cookies on the client side. Firefox users can examine, delete, and block individual cookies through the interface shown in Figure 17.13.

Internet Explorer has a much simpler interface, with just a Delete Cookies option in the browser (see Figure 17.14). Additional cookie manipulation is done through the file processing system, because cookies are stored as individual files, as shown in Figure 17.15. This combination allows easier bulk manipulation, which is a useful option because cookies can become quite numerous in short order.

So what good are cookies? Disable cookies in your browser and go to some common sites that you visit, and you'll quickly learn the usefulness of cookies. Cookies store a variety of information, from customer IDs to data about previous visits. Because cookies are stored on a user's machine in a form that will allow simple manipulation, they must always be

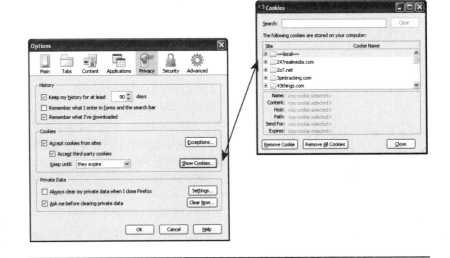

• **Figure 17.13** Firefox cookie management

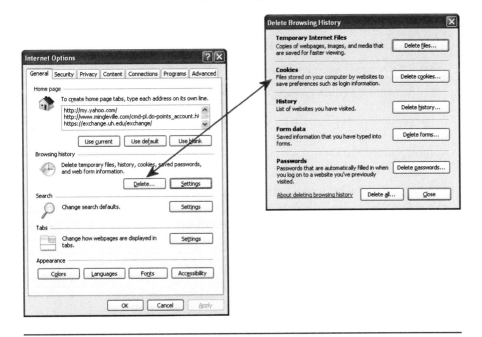

• **Figure 17.14** Microsoft Internet Explorer 7 cookie management

• Figure 17.15 Microsoft Internet Explorer 7 cookie store

considered suspect and are not suitable for use as a security mechanism. They can, however, allow the browser to provide crucial pieces of information to a web server. Advertisers can use them to control which ads you are shown, based on previous ads you have viewed, and regardless of ad location by site. Specific sites can use cookies to pass state information between pages, enabling functionality at the user's desired levels. Cookies can also remember your ZIP code for a weather site, your ID for a stock tracker site, the items in your shopping cart—these are all typical cookie uses. In the end analysis, cookies are a part of the daily web experience, here to stay and useful if not used improperly (such as to store security data and to provide ID and authentication).

Disabling Cookies

If the user disables cookies in a browser, this type of information will not be available for the web server to use. IETF RFC 2109 describes the HTTP state-management system (cookies) and specifies several specific cookie functions to be enabled in browsers, specifically

- The ability to turn on and off cookie usage
- An indicator as to whether cookies are in use
- A means of specifying cookie domain values and lifetimes

Several of these functions have already been discussed, but to surf cookie-free requires more than a simple step. Telling a browser to stop accepting cookies is a setup option available through an Options menu, but this has no effect on cookies already received and stored on the system. To prevent the browser from sending cookies already received, the user must delete the cookies from the system. This bulk operation is easily performed, and then the browser can run cookie-free. Several third-party tools enable even a finer granularity of cookie control.

Signed Applets

Code signing was an attempt to bring the security of shrink-wrapped software to software downloaded from the Internet. Code signing works by adding a digital signature and a digital certificate to a program file to demonstrate file integrity and authenticity. The certificate identifies the author, and the digital signature contains a hash value that covers code, certificate, and signature to prove integrity, and this establishes the integrity of the code and publisher via a standard browser certificate check. The purpose of a company signing the code is to state that it considers the code it created to be safe, and it is stating that the code will not do any harm to the system (to the company's knowledge). The digital signature also tells the user that the stated company is, indeed, the creator of the code.

The ability to use a certificate to sign an applet or a control allows the identity of the author of a control or applet to be established. This has many benefits. For instance, if a user trusts content from a particular vendor, such as Sun Microsystems, the user can trust controls that are signed by Sun Microsystems. This signing of a piece of code does not do anything other than identify the code's manufacturer and guarantee that the code has not been modified since it was signed.

A signed applet can be hijacked as easily as a graphic or any other file. The two ways an attacker could hijack a signed control are by inline access or copying the file in its entirety and republishing it. **Inlining** is using an embedded control from another site with or without the other site's permission. Republishing a signed control is done much like stealing a GIF or JPEG image—a copy of the file is maintained on the unauthorized site and served from there instead of from the original location. If a signed control cannot be modified, why be concerned with these thefts, apart from the issue of intellectual property? The primary security concern comes from how the control is used. A cracker may be able to use a control in an unintended fashion, resulting in file loss or buffer overflow—conditions that weaken a system and can allow exploitation of other vulnerabilities. A common programming activity is cleaning up installation files from a computer's hard drive after successfully installing a software package. If a signed control is used for this task and permission has already been granted, then improperly using the control could result in the wrong set of files being deleted. The control will still function as designed, but the issue becomes who it is used by and how. These are concerns not addressed simply by signing a control or applet.

Browser Plug-ins

The addition of browser scripting and ActiveX components allows a browser to change how it handles data, tremendously increasing its functionality as a user interface. But all data types and all desired functionality cannot be offered through these programming technologies. Plug-ins are used to fill these gaps.

Plug-ins are small application programs that increase a browser's ability to handle new data types and add new functionality. Sometimes these plug-ins are in the form of ActiveX components, which is the form Microsoft chose for its Office plug-in, which enables a browser to manipulate various Office files, such as pivot tables from Excel, over the Web. Adobe has developed Acrobat Reader, a plug-in that enables a browser to read and display Portable Document Format (PDF) files directly in a browser. PDF files offer platform independence for printed documents and are usable across a wide array of platforms—they are a compact way to provide printed information.

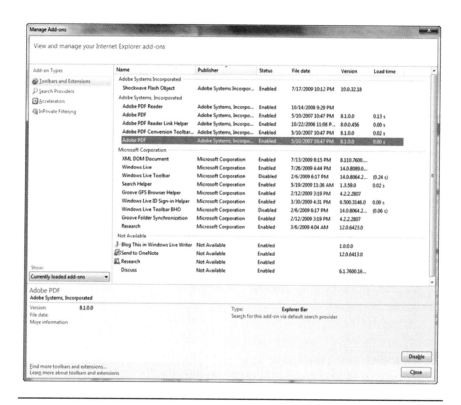

• **Figure 17.16**   Add-ons for IE 8

Figure 17.16 illustrates the various plug-ins and browser helper objects enabled in Internet Explorer 8.

Dynamic data such as movies and music can be manipulated by a wide variety of plug-ins, and one of the most popular comes from Real Networks. RealPlayer can either operate as a standalone program or run video and audio files in a web page. QuickTime from Apple provides the same type of functionality, and not just for Apple computers, but for Windows PCs as well. Microsoft has responded with its own viewer technology, Windows Media Player, which also acts as a standalone application in addition to enhancing browser capabilities.

Two strikingly different plug-ins that few computers are without are the Flash and Shockwave plug-ins. These plug-ins from Adobe enable developers to develop striking graphic and cartoon animations that greatly enhance the look and feel of a web experience. The combination of a development environment for developers and plug-in–enabled browsers that can display the content has caused these technologies to see widespread use. The result is a tremendous increase in visual richness in web communications, and this, in turn, has made the Web more popular and has increased usage in various demographic segments.

Until recently, these plug-ins have had a remarkable safety record. As Flash-based content has grown more popular, crackers have examined the Flash plug-ins and software, determined vulnerabilities, and developed exploit code to use against the Flash protocol. Adobe has patched the issue, but as more and more third-party plug-ins become popular, expect data losses to occur as crackers investigate the more popular plug-ins and protocols for vulnerabilities.

Application-Based Weaknesses

Web browsers are not the only aspect of software being abused by crackers. The application software written to run on servers and serve up the content for users is also a target. Web application security is a fairly hot topic in security, as it has become a prime target for professional crackers. Criminal hackers typically are after some form of financial reward, whether from stolen data, stolen identity, or some form of extortion. Attacking web-based applications has proven to be a lucrative venture for several reasons. First, the target is a rich environment, as company after company has developed a customer-facing web presence, often including custom-coded functionality that permits customer access to back-end systems for legitimate business purposes. Second, building these custom applications to high levels of security is a difficult if not impossible feat, especially given the corporate pressure on delivery time and cost.

The same programmatic errors that plague operating systems, such as buffer overflows, can cause havoc with web-based systems. But web-based systems have a new history of rich customer interactions, including the collection of information from the customer and dynamically using

Cross Check

Common Application Vulnerabilities

There are some common application vulnerabilities that hackers use to attack web sites, including injection attacks, cross-site request forgeries, cross-site scripting attacks, and numeric attacks. These are attacks that use the browser's ability to submit input to a back-end server program, and they take advantage of coding errors on the back-end system, enabling behavior outside the desired program response. These errors are covered in more detail in Chapter 18, as they are fundamentally programming errors on the server side. Have you ever downloaded a Flash applet from a site you really don't trust?

customer-supplied information to modify the user experience. This makes the customer a part of the application, and when proper controls are not in place, errors such as the MySpace-based Samy worm can occur. Different types of errors are commonly observed in the deployment of web applications, and these have been categorized into six logical groupings of vulnerabilities: authentication, authorization, logical attacks, information disclosure, command execution, and client-side attacks. A total of 24 different types of vulnerabilities have been classified by the Web Application Security Consortium (WASC), an international organization that establishes best practices for web application security. This list is sure to grow as different methods of attack are developed by the hacker community.

The changing nature of the web-based vulnerabilities is demonstrated by the changing of the OWASP Top Ten list of web application vulnerabilities maintained by The Open Web Application Security Project. OWASP is a worldwide free and open community focused on improving the security of application software and has published a series of Top Ten vulnerability lists highlighting the current state of the art and threat environment facing web application developers. OWASP maintains a web site (www.owasp .org) with significant resources to help firms build better software and eliminate these common and pervasive problems. The true challenge in this area is not just about coding, but also about developing an understanding of the nature of web applications and the difficulty of using user-supplied inputs for crucial aspects in a rich, user experience–based web application. The errors included in the OWASP Top Ten list have plagued some of the largest sites and those with arguably the best talent, including Amazon, eBay, MySpace, and Google.

Open Vulnerability and Assessment Language (OVAL)

The Mitre Corporation, a government-funded research group (www.mitre .org), has done extensive research into software vulnerabilities. To enable collaboration between the many different parties involved in software development and maintenance, Mitre has developed a taxonomy of vulnerabilities, the **Common Vulnerabilities and Exposures (CVE)**. This is just one of the many related enumerations that Mitre has developed, in an effort to make machine-readable data exchanges to facilitate system management across large enterprises. The CVE led to efforts such as the development of the Open Vulnerability and Assessment Language (OVAL). OVAL comprises two main elements: an XML-based machine-readable language for describing vulnerabilities, and a repository; see oval.mitre.org.

In addition to the CVE and OVAL efforts, Mitre has developed a wide range of enumerations and standards designed to ease the automation of security management at the lowest levels across an enterprise. Additional efforts include

- Common Attack Pattern Enumeration and Classification (CAPEC)
- Extensible Configuration Checklist Description Format (XCCDF)
- Security Content Automation Protocol (SCAP)
- Common Configuration Enumeration (CCE)
- Common Platform Enumeration (CPE)
- **Common Weakness Enumeration (CWE)**
- Common Event Expression (CEE)
- Common Result Format (CRF)

Additional information can be obtained from the Mitre Making Security Measurable web site, http://measurablesecurity.mitre.org.

Web 2.0 and Security

A relatively new phenomenon has swept the Internet, Web 2.0, a collection of technologies that is designed to make web sites more useful for users. From new languages and protocols, such as AJAX, to user-provided content, to social networking sites through mash-ups, the Internet has changed dramatically from its static HTML roots. There is a wide range of security issues associated with this new level of deployed functionality.

The new languages and protocols add significant layers of complexity into a web site's design, and errors can have significant consequences. Early efforts by Google to add Web 2.0 functionality to its applications created

CVE provides security personnel with a common language to use when discussing vulnerabilities. If one is discussing a specific vulnerability in the Flash object that allows an arbitrary execution of code, then using the nomenclature CVE-2005-2628 records the specifics of the vulnerability and ensures everyone is discussing the same problem.

holes that allowed hackers access to a logged-in user's Gmail account and password. Google has fixed these errors, but they illustrate the dangers of rushing into new functionality without adequate testing. Social networking sites, such as Facebook, operate by enabling users to add and change content on their own pages on the site. This functionality has been abused in some high-profile cases like the Samy worm, where a user made a worm that "friended" everyone it came across, resulting in millions of friends for Samy and a bogged-down MySpace until the worm was cleared.

The fine details of Web 2.0 security concerns are far too numerous to detail here—in fact, they could comprise their own book. The important thing to remember is that the foundations of security apply the same way in Web 2.0 as they do elsewhere. In fact, with more capability and greater complexity comes a greater need for strong foundational security efforts, and Web 2.0 is no exception.

Chapter 17 Review

■ Chapter Summary

After reading this chapter and completing the exercises, you should understand the following about web components.

Describe the functioning of the SSL/TLS protocol suite

- SSL and TLS use a combination of symmetric and asymmetric cryptographic methods to secure traffic.
- Before an SSL session can be secured, a handshake occurs to exchange cryptographic information and keys.

Explain web applications, plug-ins, and associated security issues

- Web browsers have mechanisms to enable plug-in programs to manage applications such as Flash objects and videos.
- Firefox has a No-Script helper that blocks scripts from functioning.
- Plug-ins that block pop-up windows and phishing sites can improve end-user security by permitting greater control over browser functionality.

Describe secure file transfer options

- FTP operations occur in plaintext, allowing anyone that sees the traffic to read it.
- SFTP combines the file transfer application with the Secure Shell (SSH) application to provide for a means of confidential FTP operations.

Explain directory usage for data retrieval

- LDAP is a protocol describing interaction with directory services.

- Directory services are data structures optimized for retrieval and are commonly used where data is read many times more than written, such as ACLs.

Explain scripting and other Internet functions that present security concerns

- Scripts are pieces of code that can execute within the browser environment.
- ActiveX is a robust programming language that acts like a script in Microsoft Internet Explorer browsers to provide a rich programming environment.
- Some scripts or code elements can be called from the server side, creating the web environment of ASP.NET and PHP.

Use cookies to maintain parameters between web pages

- Cookies are small text files used to maintain state between web pages.
- Cookies can be set for persistent (last for a defined time period) or session (expire when the session is closed).

Examine web-based application security issues

- As more applications are moving to a browser environment to ease programmatic deployment, it makes it easier for users to work with a familiar user environment.
- Browsers have become powerful programming environments that perform many actions behind the scenes for a user, and malicious programmers can exploit this hidden functionality to perform actions on a user's PC without their obvious consent.

■ Key Terms

Active Server Pages (ASP) *(461)*
ActiveX *(459)*
ASP.NET *(461)*
Authenticode *(459)*
buffer overflow *(456)*

code signing *(464)*
Common Gateway Interface (CGI) *(461)*
Common Vulnerabilities and Exposures (CVE) *(468)*
Common Weakness Enumeration (CWE) *(468)*
cookies *(462)*

File Transfer Protocol (FTP) *(454)*
Hypertext Markup Language (HTML) *(444)*
inlining *(465)*
Internet Engineering Task Force (IETF) *(446)*
Java *(457)*
JavaScript *(458)*
Lightweight Directory Access Protocol (LDAP) *(453)*

PHP *(461)*
plug-ins *(465)*
Secure Sockets Layer (SSL) *(446)*
server-side scripting *(461)*
Transport Layer Security (TLS) *(446)*
Uniform Resource Locator (URL) *(444)*
X.500 *(453)*

■ Key Terms Quiz

1. The use of _____ can validate input responses from clients and prevent certain attack methodologies.

2. _____ are small text files used to enhance web surfing by creating a link between pages visited on a web site.

3. _____ or _____ is a technology used to support confidentiality across the Internet for web sites.

4. _____ are small application programs that increase a browser's ability to handle new data types and add new functionality.

5. An application-level protocol that operates over a wide range of lower-level protocols and is used to transfer files is _____.

6. _____ files have the .ocx extension to identify them.

7. _____ is the standard for directory services.

8. Adding a digital signature and a digital certificate to a program file to demonstrate file integrity and authenticity is _____.

9. A(n) _____ is a descriptor where content is located on the Internet.

10. _____ is a system that uses digital signatures and allows Windows users to determine who produced a specific piece of code and whether or not the code has been altered.

■ Multiple-Choice Quiz

1. What is a cookie?
   A. A piece of data in a database that enhances web browser capability
   B. A small text file used in some HTTP exchanges
   C. A segment of script to enhance a web page
   D. A program that runs when you visit a web site so it remembers you

2. The use of certificates in SSL is similar to:
   A. A receipt proving purchase
   B. Having a notary notarize a signature
   C. A historical record of a program's lineage
   D. None of the above

3. SSL can be used to secure:
   A. POP3 traffic
   B. HTTP traffic

   C. SMTP traffic
   D. All of the above

4. SFTP uses which method to secure its transmissions?
   A. IPsec
   B. VPN
   C. SSH
   D. SSL

5. Security for JavaScript is established by whom?
   A. The developer at the time of code development.
   B. The user at the time of code usage.
   C. The user through browser preferences.
   D. Security for JavaScript is not necessary—the Java language is secure by design.

6. ActiveX can be used for which of the following purposes?

   A. Add functionality to a browser

   B. Update the operating system

   C. Both A and B

   D. Neither A nor B

7. CGI has a weakness in its implementation because:

   A. It offers almost unlimited operating system access and functionality on a UNIX box.

   B. It is limited to Windows operating systems only.

   C. It is difficult to program in.

   D. It has a proprietary interface.

8. The keyword [secure] in a cookie:

   A. Causes the system to encrypt its contents

   B. Prevents it from passing over HTTP connections

   C. Tells the browser that the cookie is a security upgrade

   D. None of the above

9. Code signing is used to:

   A. Allow authors to take artistic credit for their hard work

   B. Provide a method to demonstrate code integrity

   C. Guarantee code functionality

   D. Prevent copyright infringement by code copying

10. SSL provides which of the following functionality?

    A. Data integrity services

    B. Authentication services

    C. Data confidentiality services

    D. All of the above

11. SSL uses which port to carry HTTPS traffic?

    A. TCP port 80

    B. UDP port 443

    C. TCP port 443

    D. TCP port 8080

12. High-security browsers can use what to validate SSL credentials for a user?

    A. AES encrypted links to a root server

    B. An extended-validation SSL certificate

    C. MD-5 hashing to ensure integrity

    D. SSL v3.0

13. To establish an SSL connection for e-mail and HTTP across a firewall, you must:

    A. Open TCP ports 80, 25, 443, and 223.

    B. Open TCP ports 443, 465, and 995.

    C. Open a TCP port of choice and assign it to all SSL traffic.

    D. Do nothing; SSL tunnels past firewalls.

14. Directories are characterized by:

    A. Being optimized for read-only data

    B. Being optimized for attribute type data

    C. More functionality than a simple database

    D. Better security model than a database

15. To prevent the use of cookies in a browser, a user must:

    A. Tell the browser to disable cookies via a setup option.

    B. Delete all existing cookies.

    C. Both A and B.

    D. The user need do nothing; by design, cookies are necessary and cannot be totally disabled.

■ Essay Quiz

1. Much has been made of the new Web 2.0 phenomenon, including social networking sites and user-created mash-ups. How does Web 2.0 change security for the Internet?

2. SSL and TLS use elements of both symmetric and asymmetric encryption. Describe the relationship between these methods and their roles in securing the communication channel.

Lab Project

• Lab Project 17.1

Cookies and scripts can both enhance web browsing experiences. They can also represent a risk, and as such the option exists to turn them off. Using Firefox with the NoScript plug-in to disable scripts, compare the browsing experience at the following sites with and without cookies, and with and without scripts.

- E-commerce site like Amazon
- A bank
- An information site like Wikipedia
- A news site

chapter 18

Secure Software Development

Security Features != Secure Features

—MICHAEL HOWARD, MICROSOFT CORPORATION

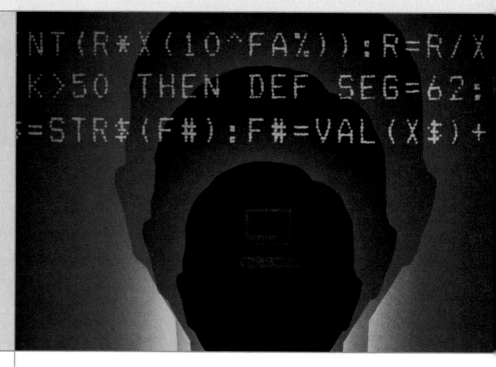

In this chapter, you will learn how to

- Describe how secure coding can be incorporated into the software development process
- List the major types of coding errors and their root causes
- Describe good software development practices and explain how they impact application security
- Describe how using a software development process enforces security inclusion in a project

$\mathbf{S}$oftware engineering is the systematic development of software to fill a variety of functions, such as business, recreational, scientific, and educational functions, which are just a few of the many areas where software comes in handy. Regardless of the type of software, there is a universal requirement that the software work properly, perform the desired functions, and perform them in the correct fashion. The functionality of software ranges from spreadsheets that accurately add figures, to pacemakers that stimulate the heart. Developers know that functional specifications must be met for the software to be satisfactory. Software engineering, then, fits as many requirements as possible into the project management schedule timeline. But with analysts and developers working overtime to get as many functional elements correct as possible, the issue of nonfunctional requirements often gets pushed to the back burner, or neglected entirely.

Security has been described as a nonfunctional requirement. This places it into a category of secondary importance for many developers. Their view is that if timelines, schedules, and budgets are all in the green, then maybe there will be time to devote to security programming. With computing becoming ubiquitous and our daily lives now supported by a wide assortment of computer programs, this viewpoint must change. Getting security right in a program is essential if we are going to rely on computing in our lives. Trust is built upon an expectation that the software will work, and keep working, meeting our needs and not changing its behavior or functionality because of outside influence. People get vaccinated not to improve their health but to prevent a downturn in their current well-being due to outside influence. As we depend more and more on computers driven by software, we will need systems to do the same—to not only function now, but to be protected from malfunction in the future.

■ The Software Engineering Process

Software does not build itself. This is good news for software designers, analysts, programmers, and the like, for the complexity of designing and building software enables them to engage in well-paying careers. To achieve continued success in this difficult work environment, software engineering processes have been developed. Rather than just sitting down and starting to write code at the onset of a project, software engineers use a complete development process. There are several major categories of software engineering processes. The waterfall model, the spiral model, and the evolutionary model are major examples. Within each of these major categories, there are numerous variations, and each group then personalizes the process to their project requirements and team capabilities.

Traditionally, security is an add-on item that is incorporated into a system after the functional requirements have been met. It is not an integral part of the software development lifecycle process. This places it at odds with both functional and lifecycle process requirements. The resolution to all of these issues is relatively simple: incorporate security into the process model and build it into the product along with each functional requirement. The challenge is in how to accomplish this goal. There are two separate and required elements needed to achieve this objective. First, the inclusion of security requirements and measures in the specific process model being used. Second, the use of secure coding methods to prevent opportunities to introduce security failures into the software's design.

> ⚠ This chapter contains many details of how to test for exploitable vulnerabilities in software. Do not perform or attempt these steps outside of systems for which you either are the owner or have explicit permission from the owner. Otherwise, you may find yourself being accused of hacking and possibly even facing legal charges.

Process Models

There are several major software engineering process models, each with slightly different steps and sequences, yet they all have many similar items. The **waterfall model** is characterized by a multistep process in which steps follow each other in a linear, one-way fashion, like water over a waterfall. The **spiral model** has steps in phases that execute in a spiral fashion, repeating at different levels with each revolution of the model. The **agile model** is characterized by iterative development, where requirements and solutions evolve through an ongoing collaboration between self-organizing cross-functional teams. The **evolutionary model** is an iterative model designed to enable the construction of increasingly complex versions of a project. There are numerous other models and derivations of software development models in use today. The details of these process models are outside the scope of this book, and most of the detail is not significantly relevant to the issue of security. From a secure coding perspective, a **secure development lifecycle (SDL) model** is essential to success. From requirements to system architecture to coding to testing, security is an embedded property in all aspects of the process. There are several specific items of significance with respect to security. Four primary items of interest, regardless of the particular model or methodology employed in software creation, are requirements, design, coding, and testing phases.

Secure Development Lifecycle

There may be as many different software engineering methods as there are software engineering groups. But an analysis of these methods indicates that most share common elements from which an understanding of a universal methodology can be obtained. For decades, secure coding—that is, creating code that does what it is supposed to do, and only what it is supposed to do—has not been high on the radar for most organizations. The past decade of explosive connectivity and the rise of malware and hackers have raised awareness of this issue significantly. A recent alliance of several major software firms concerned with secure coding principles revealed several interesting patterns. First, they were all attacking the problem using different methodologies, but yet in surprisingly similar fashions. Second, they found a series of principles that appears to be related to success in this endeavor.

First and foremost, recognition of the need to include secure coding principles into the development process is a common element among all firms. Microsoft has been very open and vocal about its implementation of its Security Development Lifecycle (SDL) and has published significant volumes of information surrounding its genesis and evolution (http://msdn.microsoft.com/en-us/security/cc448177.aspx).

The Software Assurance Forum for Excellence in Code (SAFECode) is an organization formed from some of the leading software development firms with the objective of advancing software assurance through better development methods. SAFECode (www.safecode.org) members include EMC, Microsoft, and Nokia. An examination of SAFECode members' processes reveals an assertion that secure coding must be treated as an issue that exists throughout the development process and cannot be effectively treated at a few checkpoints with checklists. Regardless of the software development process used, the first step down the path to secure coding is to infuse the process with secure coding principles.

Requirements Phase

The **requirements phase** should define the specific security requirements if there is any expectation of them being designed into the project. Regardless of the methodology employed, the process is all about completing the requirements. Secure coding does not refer to adding security functionality into a piece of software. Security functionality is a standalone requirement. The objective of the secure coding process is to properly implement this and all other requirements, so that the resultant software performs as desired and only as desired.

The requirements process is a key component of security in software development. Security-related items enumerated during the requirements process are visible throughout the rest of the software development process. They can be architected into the systems and subsystems, addressed during coding, and tested. For the subsequent steps to be effective, the security requirements need to be both specific and positive. Requirements such as "make secure code" or "no insecure code" are nonspecific and not helpful in the overall process. Specific requirements such as "prevent unhandled buffer overflows, or unhandled input exceptions" can be specifically coded for in each piece of code.

During the requirements activity, it is essential that the project/program manager and any business leaders who set schedules and allocate resources are aware of the need and requirements of the secure development process. The cost of adding security in later rises exponentially, with the most expensive form being the common release and patch process used by many firms. The development of both functional and nonfunctional security requirements occurs in tandem with other requirements through the development of use cases, analysis of customer inputs, implementation of company policies, and compliance with industry best practices. Depending on the nature of a particular module, special attention may be focused on sensitive issues such as personally identifiable information (PII), sensitive data, or intellectual property data.

One of the outputs of the requirements phase is a security document that helps guide the remaining aspects of the development process, ensuring that secure code requirements are being addressed. These requirements can be infused into design, coding, and testing, ensuring they are addressed throughout the development process.

Tech Tip

Common Secure Coding Requirements
Common secure coding requirements include

- *Analysis of security and privacy risk*
- *Authentication and password management*
- *Audit logging and analysis*
- *Authorization and role management*
- *Code integrity and validation testing*
- *Cryptography and key management*
- *Data validation and sanitization*
- *Network and data security*
- *Ongoing education and awareness*
- *Team staffing requirements*
- *Third-party component analysis*

Design Phase

Coding without designing first is like building a house without using plans. This might work fine on small projects, but as the scope grows, so do complexity and the opportunity for failure. Designing a software project is a multifaceted process. Just as there are many ways to build a house, there are many ways to build a program. Design is a process involving trade-offs and choices, and the criteria used during the design decisions can have lasting impacts on program construction. There are two secure coding principles that can be applied at design time that can have a large influence on the code quality. The first of these is the concept of *minimizing attack surface area*. Reducing the avenues of attack available to a hacker can have obvious benefits to the software. Minimizing attack surface area is a concept that tends to run counter to the way software has been designed—most designs come as a result of incremental accumulation, adding features and functions without regard to maintainability.

Threat Modeling and Attack Surface Area Minimization   Two important tools have come from the secure coding revolution: threat modeling and attack surface area minimization. Threat modeling is a communication tool designed to communicate to everyone on the development team the threats and dangers facing the code. Attack surface area minimization is a strategy to reduce the places where code can be attacked.

The second major design effort is one built around *threat modeling*, the process of analyzing threats and their potential effects on software in a very detailed, granular fashion. The output of the threat model process is a compilation of threats and how they interact with the software. This information is communicated across the design and coding team, so that potential weaknesses can be mitigated before the software is released.

Step by Step 18.1

Threat Modeling Steps

In this exercise, you will follow the steps used to conduct threat modeling.

Step 1

Define scope. Communicate what is in scope and out of scope with respect to the threat modeling effort. This includes both attacks and software components.

Step 2

Enumerate assets. List all of the component parts of the software being examined.

Step 3

Decompose assets. Break apart the software into small subsystems composed of inputs and outputs. This is to simplify data flow analysis and to capture internal entry points.

Step 4

Enumerate threats. List all the threats to the software.

Step 5

Classify threats. Classify the threats by their mode of operation.

Step 6

Associate threats to assets. Connect specific threats and modes to specific software subsystems.

Step 7

Score and rank threats. Score each specific threat–asset pair and then rank them from most dangerous to least dangerous.

Step 8

Create threat trees. Create a graphical representation of the required elements for an attack vector.

Step 9

Determine and score mitigation. Score the mitigation efforts associated with each attack vector.

For more details on threat modeling, see http://msdn.microsoft.com/en-us/security/aa570411.aspx.

Coding Phase

The point at which the design is implemented is the coding step in the software development process. The act of instantiating an idea into code is a point where an error can enter the process. These errors are of two types: the failure to include desired functionality, and the inclusion of undesired behavior in the code. Testing for the first type of error is relatively easy if the requirements are enumerated in a previous phase of the process.

Testing for the inclusion of undesired behavior is significantly more difficult. Testing for an *unknown* is a virtually impossible task. What makes this possible at all is the concept of testing for categories of previously determined errors. Several classes of common errors have been observed. Enumerations of known software weaknesses and vulnerabilities have been compiled and published as the **Common Weakness Enumeration (CWE)** and **Common Vulnerabilities and Exposures (CVE)** by the Mitre Corporation. These enumerations have enabled significant advancement in the development of methods to reduce code vulnerabilities. The CVE and CWE are vendor- and language-neutral methods of describing errors. These enumerations allow a common vocabulary for communication about weaknesses and vulnerabilities. This common vocabulary has also led to the development of automated tools to manage the tracking of these issues.

There are several ways to go about searching for coding errors that lead to vulnerabilities in software. One method is by manual code inspection. Developers can be trained to "not make mistakes," but this approach has not proven successful. This has led to the development of a class of tools designed to analyze code for potential defects.

Static code-analysis tools are a type of tool that can be used to analyze software for coding errors that can lead to known types of vulnerabilities and weaknesses. Sophisticated static code analyzers can examine codebases to find function calls of unsafe libraries, potential buffer overflow conditions, and numerous other conditions. Currently, the CWE describes more than 750 different weaknesses, far too many for developer memory and direct knowledge. In light of this, and due to the fact that some weaknesses are more prevalent than others, Mitre has collaborated with SANS to develop the **CWE/SANS Top 25 Most Dangerous Programming Errors** list. One of the ideas behind the **Top 25 list** is that it can be updated periodically as the threat landscape changes. Explore the current listing at http://cwe.mitre .org/top25/.

The current Top 25 list is divided into three high-level categories: Insecure Interactions Between Components, Risky Resource Management, and Porous Defenses. Although complete coverage of all 25 of the most dangerous programming errors is beyond the scope of this chapter, the following sections highlight some of the bad actors. The Top 25 list covers a wide range of programs, from software application programs to web applications, and across a wide range of programming skill levels. One of the more interesting finds is that, looking at current issues rather than the past issues, items such as improper input handling appear to be much more important than buffer overflows, the former #1 nemesis of coders. One of the important aspects of the list is its focus on risks from current coding practices rather than older historical data.

August 2009 Top 25 Most Dangerous Programming Errors

Insecure Interactions Between Components

- *Improper Input Validation*
- *Improper Encoding or Escaping of Output*
- *Cleartext Transmission of Sensitive Information*
- *SQL Injection*
- *OS Command Injection*
- *Cross-Site Scripting (XSS)*
- *Cross-Site Request Forgery (CSRF)*
- *Race Condition*
- *Error Message Information Leak*

Risky Resource Management

- *Buffer Overflow*
- *Code Injection*
- *External Control of Critical State Data*
- *External Control of File Name or Path*
- *Untrusted Search Path*
- *Arithmetic Overflow/Incorrect Calculation*
- *Download of Code Without Integrity Check*
- *Improper Resource Shutdown or Release*
- *Improper Initialization*

Porous Defenses

- *Improper Access Control (Authorization)*
- *Broken or Unproven Cryptographic Algorithm*
- *Hard-Coded Password*
- *Insecure Permission Assignment for Critical Resource*
- *Use of Insufficiently Random Values*
- *Execution with Unnecessary Privileges (Least Privilege)*
- *Client-Side Enforcement of Server-Side Security*

Buffer Overflows If there's one item that could be labeled as the "Most Wanted" in coding security, it would be the **buffer overflow**. The CERT/CC at Carnegie Mellon University estimates that nearly half of all exploits of computer programs stem historically from some form of buffer overflow. Finding a vaccine to buffer overflows would stamp out half of these security-related incidents, by type, and probably 90 percent by volume. The Morris finger worm in 1988 was an exploit of an overflow, as were recent big-name events such as Code Red and Slammer. The generic classification of buffer overflows includes many variants, such as static buffer overruns, indexing errors, format string bugs, Unicode and ANSI buffer size mismatches, and heap overruns.

The concept behind these vulnerabilities is relatively simple. The input buffer that is used to hold program input is overwritten with data that is larger than the buffer can hold. The root cause of this vulnerability is a mixture of two things: poor programming practice and programming language weaknesses. Programming languages such as C were designed for space and performance constraints. Many functions in C, like **gets()**, are unsafe in that they will permit unsafe operations, such as unbounded string manipulation into fixed buffer locations. The C language also permits direct memory access via pointers, a functionality that provides a lot of programming power, but carries with it the burden of proper safeguards being provided by the programmer.

The first line of defense is to write solid code. Regardless of the language used, or the source of outside input, prudent programming practice is to treat all input from outside a function as hostile. Validate all inputs as if they were hostile and an attempt to force a buffer overflow. Accept the notion that although during development, everyone may be on the same team, be conscientious, and be compliant with design rules, future maintainers may not be as robust. Designing prevention into functions is a foundational defense against this type of vulnerability. There is good news in the buffer-overflow category—significant attention has been paid to this type of vulnerability, and although it is the largest contributor to past vulnerabilities, its presence is significantly reduced in newly discovered vulnerabilities. This is one shining ray of light that shows that secure coding can be effective.

Improper Input Handling   If the bad actor from history is buffer overflow, the new leader in software vulnerabilities is improper input handling. With the move to web-based applications, the errors have shifted from buffer overflows to input-handling issues. Users have the ability to manipulate input so it is up to the programmer to handle the input appropriately to prevent malicious entries from having an effect. Buffer overflows could be considered a class of improper input, but newer attacks include canonicalization attacks and arithmetic attacks.

In today's computing environment, a wide range of character sets is used. Unicode allows multilanguage support. Character codesets allow multilanguage capability. Various encoding schemes, such as hex encoding, are supported to allow diverse inputs. The net result of all these input methods is that there are numerous ways to create the same input to a program. *Canonicalization* is the process by which application programs manipulate strings to a base form, creating a foundational representation of the input. **Canonicalization errors** arise from the fact that inputs to a web application may be processed by multiple applications, such as the web server, application server, and database server, each with its own parsers to resolve appropriate canonicalization issues. Where this is an issue relates to the form of the input string at the time of error checking. If the error checking routine occurs prior to resolution to canonical form, then issues may be missed. The string representing /../, used in directory traversal attacks, can be obscured by encoding and hence missed by a character string match before an application parser manipulates it to canonical form.

Tech Tip

A Rose Is a Rose Is a r%6fse

Canonical form *refers to simplest form, and, due to the many encoding schemes in use, can be a complex issue. Characters can be encoded in ASCII, Unicode, Hex, UTF-8, or even combinations of these. So, if the attacker desires to obfuscate his response, then several things can happen.*

By URL hex encoding URL strings, it may be possible to circumvent filter security systems and IDS:

```
http://www.myweb.com/cgi?file=/etc/passwd
```

can become

```
http://www.myweb.com/cgi?file=/
%2F%65%74%63%2F%70%61%73%73%77%64
```

Double encoding can complicate the matter even further:
Round 1 Decoding:

```
scripts/..%255c../winnt
```

becomes

```
scripts/..%5c../winnt
(%25 = "%" Character)
```

Round 2 Decoding:

```
scripts/..%5c../winnt
```

becomes

```
scripts/..\../winnt
```

The bottom line is simple: Know that encoding can be used, and plan for it when designing input verification mechanisms. Expect encoded transmissions to be used to attempt to bypass security mechanisms.

Improper Output Handling A second, and equally important, line of defense is proper string handling. String handling is a common event in programs, and string-handling functions are the source of a large number of known buffer-overflow vulnerabilities. Using **strncpy()** in place of **strcpy()** is a possible method of improving security because **strncpy()** requires an input length for the number of characters to be copied. This simple function call replacement can ultimately fail, however, because Unicode and other encoding methods can make character counts meaningless. To resolve this issue requires new library calls, and much closer attention to how input strings, and subsequently output strings, can be abused. Proper use of functions to achieve program objectives is essential to prevent unintended effects such as buffer overflows. Use of the **gets()** function can probably never be totally safe since it reads from the *stdin* stream until a linefeed or carriage return. In most cases, there is no way to predetermine whether the input is going to overflow the buffer. A better solution is to use a C++ stream object or the **fgets()** function. The function **fgets()** requires an input buffer length, and hence avoids the overflow. Simply replace

```
{
    char buf[512];
    gets( buf );    if buf is > 512 bytes, overflow will occur
/* ... The rest of your code ... */
}
```

with

```
{
    char buf[512];
    fgets( buf, sizeof(buf), stdin );
    /*  ... the rest of your code ... */
}
```

Injections Use of input to a function without validation has already been shown to be risky behavior. Another issue with unvalidated input is the case of **code injection**. Rather than the input being appropriate for the function, this code injection changes the function in an unintended way. A **SQL injection** attack is a form of code injection aimed at any Structured Query Language (SQL)–based database, regardless of vendor. An example of this type of attack is where the function takes the user-provided inputs for username and password and substitutes them into a *where* clause of a SQL statement with the express purpose of changing the *where* clause into one that gives a false answer to the query.

Assume the desired SQL statement is

```
select count(*) from users_table where username = 'JDoe' and
password = 'newpass'
```

The values JDoe and newpass are provided from the user and simply inserted into the string sequence. Though seemingly safe functionally, this can be easily corrupted by using the sequence

```
' or 1=1 --
```

since this changes the *where* clause to one that returns all records:

```
select count(*) from users_table where username = 'JDoe' and
password = '' or 1=1 --'
```

The addition of the *or* clause, with an always true statement and the beginning of a comment line to block the trailing single quote, alters the SQL statement to one in which the *where* clause is rendered inoperable.

The primary method of defense against this type of vulnerability is similar to that for buffer overflows: validate all inputs. But rather than validating toward just length, you need to validate inputs for content. Imagine a web page that asks for user input, and then uses that input in the building of a subsequent page. Now imagine that the user puts the text for a JavaScript function in the middle of their input sequence, along with a call to the script. Now, the generated web page has an added JavaScript function that is called when displayed. Passing the user input through an **HTMLencode** function before use can prevent such attacks.

Tech Tip

Testing for SQL Injection Vulnerability

There are two main steps associated with testing for SQL injection vulnerability. First one needs to confirm that the system is at all vulnerable. This can be done using various inputs to test whether an input variable can be used to manipulate the SQL command. The following are common test vectors used:

- `' or 1=1--`
- `" or 1=1--`
- `or 1=1--`
- `' or 'a'='a`
- `" or "a"="a`
- `') or ('a'='a`

Note that the use of single or double quotes is SQL implementation dependent, as there are syntactic differences between the major database engines.

The second step is to use the error message information to attempt to perform an actual exploit against the database.

Again, good programming practice goes a long way toward preventing these types of vulnerabilities. This places the burden not just on the programmers, but also on the process of training programmers, the software engineering process that reviews code, and the testing process to catch programming errors. This is much more than a single-person responsibility; everyone involved in the software development process needs to be aware of the types and causes of these errors, and safeguards need to be in place to prevent their propagation.

Least Privilege   One of the central paradigms of security is the notion of running a process with the least required privilege. **Least privilege** requires that the developer understand what privileges are needed specifically for an application to execute and access all its necessary resources. Obviously, from a developer point of view, it would be easier to use administrative-level permission for all tasks, which removes access controls from the equation, but this also removes the very protections that access-level controls are designed to provide. The other end of the spectrum is software designed for operating systems without any built-in security, such as early versions of Windows and some mainframe OSs, where security comes in the form of an application package. When migrating these applications to platforms, the issue of access controls arises.

As developers move from developing where there is no security to an operating system with built-in security, the natural tendency is to code around this "new" security requirement, developing in the same fashion as before, as if security is not an issue. This is commonly manifested as a program that runs only under an administrative-level account, or runs as a service utilizing the SYSTEM account for permissions in Windows. Both of these practices are bad practices that reduce security, introduce hard-to-fix errors, and produce code that is harder to maintain and extend.

The key principle in designing and coding software with respect to access-level controls is to plan and understand the nature of the software's interaction with the operating system and system resources. Whenever the software accesses a file, a system component, or another program, the issue of appropriate access control needs to be addressed. And although the simple practice of just giving everything root or administrative access may solve this immediate problem, it creates much bigger security issues that will be much less apparent in the future. An example is when a program runs correctly when initiated from an administrator account but fails when run under normal user privileges. The actual failure may stem from a privilege issue, but the actual point of failure in the code may be many procedures away, and diagnosing these types of failures is a difficult and time-consuming operation.

The bottom line is actually simple. Determine what needs to be accessed and what the appropriate level of permission is, then use that level in design and implementation. Repeat this for every item accessed. In the end, it is rare that administrative access is needed for many functions. Once the application is designed, the whole process will need to be repeated with the installation procedure, because frequently, installing software will need a higher level of access than needed for executing the software. Design and implementation details must be determined with respect to required

Developers who do development and testing on an integrated environment on their own PC—that is, they have a web server and/or database engine on their PC—can produce code that works fine on their machine, where unified account permissions exist (and are frequently administrator). When this code is transitioned to a distributed environment, permissions can become an issue. The proper method is to manage permissions appropriately on the developer box from the beginning.

When software fails due to an exploited vulnerability, the hacker typically achieves whatever level of privilege that the application had prior to the exploit occurrence. If an application always operates with root-level privilege, this will pass on to the hacker as well.

permission levels, not to a higher level such as administrative root access just for convenience.

The cost of failure to heed the principle of least privilege can be twofold. First, you have expensive, time-consuming access-violation errors that are hard to track down and correct. The second problem is when an exploit is found that allows some other program to use portions of your code in an un-authorized fashion. A prime example is the sendmail exploit in the UNIX environment. Because sendmail requires root-level access for some functions, the sendmail exploit inserts foreign code into the process stream, thereupon executing its code at root-level access because the sendmail process thread itself has root-level access. In this case, sendmail needs the root-level access, but this exploit illustrates that the risk is real and will be exploited once found. Proper design can, in many cases, eliminate the need for such high access privilege levels.

Cryptographic Failures   Hailed as a solution for all problems, cryptography has as much chance of being the ultimate cure-all as did the tonics sold by traveling salesmen of a different era. There is no such thing as a universal solution, yet there are some very versatile tools that provide a wide range of protections. Cryptography falls into this "very useful tool" category. Proper use of cryptography can provide a wealth of programmatic functionality, from authentication and confidentiality to integrity and nonrepudiation. These are valuable tools, and many programs rely on proper cryptographic function for important functionality. The need for this functionality in an application tempts programmers to roll their own cryptographic functions. This is a task fraught with opportunity for catastrophic error.

Cryptographic errors come from several common causes. One typical mistake is choosing to develop your own cryptographic algorithm. Development of a secure cryptographic algorithm is far from an easy task, and even when done by experts, weaknesses can occur that make them unusable. Cryptographic algorithms become trusted after years of scrutiny and attacks, and any new algorithms would take years to join the trusted set. If you instead decide to rest on secrecy, be warned that secret or proprietary algorithms have never provided the desired level of protection. One of the axioms of cryptography is that there is no security through obscurity.

Deciding to use a trusted algorithm is a proper start, but there still are several major errors that can occur. The first is an error in instantiating the algorithm. An easy way to avoid this type of error is to use a library function that has already been properly tested. Sources of these library functions abound, and provide an economical solution to this functionality's needs. Once you have an algorithm, and have chosen a particular instantiation, the next item needed is the random number to generate a random key. Cryptographic functions use an algorithm and a key, the latter being a digital number.

The generation of a real random number is not a trivial task. Computers are machines that are renowned for reproducing the same output when given the same input, so generating a pure, nonreproducible random number is a challenge. There are functions for producing random numbers built into the libraries of most programming languages, but these are pseudo-random number generators, and although the distribution of output numbers appears random, it generates a reproducible sequence. Given the same

Tech Tip

Only Use Approved Cryptographic Functions
Always use vetted and approved libraries for all cryptographic work. Never create your own cryptographic functions, even when using known algorithms. For example, the .NET framework has a number of cryptography classes that developers can call upon to perform encryption services.

input, a second run of the function will produce the same sequence of "random" numbers. Determining the seed and random sequence and using this knowledge to "break" a cryptographic function has been used more than once to bypass the security. This method was used to subvert an early version of Netscape's SSL implementation. Using a number that is **cryptographically random**—suitable for an encryption function—resolves this problem, and again the use of trusted library functions designed and tested for generating such numbers is the proper methodology.

Now you have a good algorithm and a good random number—so where can you go wrong? Well, storing private keys in areas where they can be recovered by an unauthorized person is the next worry. Poor key management has failed many a cryptographic implementation. A famous exploit of getting cryptographic keys from an executable and using them to break a cryptographic scheme is the case of hackers using this exploit to break DVD encryption and develop the DeCSS program. Tools have been developed that can search code for "random" keys and extract the key from the code or running process. The bottom line is simple: do not hard-code secret keys in your code. They can, and will, be discovered. Keys should be generated, and then passed by reference, minimizing the travel of copies across a network or application. Storing them in memory in a noncontiguous fashion is also important, to prevent external detection. Again, trusted cryptographic library functions come to the rescue.

You might have deduced by this point that the term "library function" has become synonymous with this section. This is not an accident. In fact, this is probably one of the best pieces of advice from this chapter: use commercially proven functions for cryptographic functionality.

Language-Specific Failures Modern programming languages are built around libraries that permit reuse and speed the development process. The development of many library calls and functions was done without regard to secure coding implications, and this has led to issues related to specific library functions. As mentioned previously, **strcpy()** has had its fair share of involvement in buffer overflows and should be avoided. Developing and maintaining a series of **deprecated functions** and prohibiting their use in new code, while removing them from old code when possible, is a proven path toward more secure code.

Banned functions are easily handled via automated code reviews during the check-in process. The challenge is in garnering the developer awareness as to the potential dangers and the value of safer coding practices.

Testing Phase

If the requirements phase marks the beginning of the generation of security in code, then the **testing phase** marks the other boundary. Although there are additional functions after testing, no one wants a user to validate errors in code. And errors discovered after the code has shipped are the most expensive to fix, regardless of the severity. Employing **use cases** to compare program responses to known inputs and then comparing the output to the desired output is a proven method of testing software. The design of use cases to test specific functional requirements occurs based on the requirements determined in the requirements phase. Providing additional

---

Never hard-code secrets into code bases. Hackers can use disassemblers and various code differential tools to dissect your code and find static information.

Tech Tip

Microsoft Recommended Deprecated C Functions

Function families to deprecate/ remove:

- *strcpy() and strncpy()*
- *strcat() and strncat()*
- *scanf()*
- *sprint()*
- *gets()*
- *memcpy(), CopyMemory(), and RtlCopyMemory()*

security-related use cases is the process-driven way of ensuring that security specifics are also tested.

The testing phase is the last opportunity to determine that the software performs properly before the end user experiences problems. Errors found in testing are late in the development process, but at least they are still learned about internally, before the end customer suffers. Testing can occur at each level of development: module, subsystem, system, and completed application. The sooner errors are discovered and corrected, the lower the cost and the lesser the impact will be to project schedules. This makes testing an essential step in the process of developing good programs.

One of the most powerful tools that can be used in testing is **fuzzing**, the systematic application of a series of malformed inputs to test how the program responds. Fuzzing has been used by hackers for years to find potentially exploitable buffer overflows, without any specific knowledge of the coding.

A tester can use a fuzzing framework to automate numerous input sequences. In examining whether a function can fall prey to a buffer overflow, numerous inputs can be run, testing lengths and ultimate payload-delivery options. If a particular input string results in a crash that can be exploited, this input would then be examined in detail.

Fuzzing is new to the development scene but is rapidly maturing and will soon be on nearly equal footing with other automated code-checking tools.

Chapter 18 Review

■ For More Information

- **SAFECode** www.safecode.org
- **DHS Build Security In** https://buildsecurityin.us-cert.gov/daisy/bsi/home.html
- **Microsoft SDL** www.microsoft.com/sdl
- **CVE** http://cve.mitre.org
- **CWE** http://cwe.mitre.org
- **CWE/SANS Top 25** http://cwe.mitre.org/top25/index.html

■ Chapter Summary

After reading this chapter and completing the exercises, you should understand the following about security issues related to software development.

Describe how secure coding can be incorporated into the software development process

- The requirements phase is the most important part of the software engineering process since it outlines the project's future requirements, thus defining its scope and limitations.
- The use of an enhanced lifecycle development process to include security elements will build security into the product.

List the major types of coding errors and their root causes

- The commonest coding error is a buffer-overflow condition.
- Code injection errors can result in undesired code execution as defined by the end user.

- Input validation is the best method of insuring against buffer overflows and code injection errors.

Describe good software development practices and explain how they impact application security

- Early testing helps resolve errors at an earlier stage and results in cleaner code.
- Security-related use cases can be used to test for specific security requirements.
- Fuzz testing can find a wide range of errors.

Describe how using a software development process enforces security inclusion in a project

- Security is built into the software by including security concerns and reviews throughout the software development process.
- Regardless of the specific software engineering process model used, security can be included in the normal process by being input as requirements.

■ Key Terms

agile model *(475)*
buffer overflow *(480)*
canonicalization errors *(481)*
code injection *(483)*
Common Vulnerabilities and Exposures (CVE) *(479)*
Common Weakness Enumeration (CWE) *(479)*
CWE SANS Top 25 Most Dangerous Programming Errors *(479)*
cryptographically random *(486)*
deprecated functions *(486)*
evolutionary model *(476)*

fuzzing *(487)*
least privilege *(484)*
requirements phase *(476)*
secure development lifecycle (SDL) model *(476)*
spiral model *(475)*
SQL injection *(483)*
testing phase *(486)*
Top 25 List *(479)*
use cases *(486)*
waterfall model *(475)*

Key Terms Quiz

Use terms from the Key Terms list to complete the sentences that follow. Don't use the same term more than once. Not all terms will be used.

1. The _____ is a linear software engineering model with no repeating steps.

2. _____ cause an application to malfunction due to a misrepresented name for a resource.

3. CWE-20: Improper Input Validation refers to a(n) _____.

4. Using a series of malformed input to test for conditions such as buffer overflows is called _____.

5. Modifying a SQL statement through false input to a function is an example of _____.

6. Using an administrator-level account for all functions is a violation of the principle of _____.

7. The _____ is the first opportunity to address security functionality during a project.

8. The banning of _____ helps improve code quality by using safer library calls.

9. A(n) _____ is a defined set of validated inputs and outputs used to test a module for correct functionality.

10. A number that is suitable for an encryption function is called _____.

Multiple-Choice Quiz

1. Which of the following is not related to a buffer overflow?
   A. Static buffer overflow
   B. Index error
   C. Canonicalization error
   D. Heap overflow

2. Which of the following is not involved with a code injection error?
   A. SQL statement building
   B. Input validation
   C. JavaScript
   D. A pointer in the C language

3. Input validation is important to prevent what?
   A. Buffer overflow
   B. Index sequence error
   C. Operator overload error
   D. Unhandled exception

4. The term waterfall is associated with which of the following?
   A. Buffer overflow
   B. A software engineering process model
   C. Canonicalization error
   D. Code injection

5. It's most important to define security requirements during:
   A. Testing
   B. Use case development
   C. Code walkthroughs
   D. The requirements phase of the project

6. The largest class of errors in software engineering can be attributed to:
   A. Poor testing
   B. Privilege violations
   C. Improper input validation
   D. Canonicalization errors

7. The Morris worm exploited:
   A. A buffer overflow in Windows
   B. A buffer overflow in UNIX
   C. A code injection in both Windows and UNIX
   D. A canonicalization error in UNIX

8. Least privilege applies to:
   A. Only the application code
   B. Only to calls to operating system objects
   C. All resource requests from applications to other entities
   D. Applications under named user accounts

9. Common cryptographic failures include which of the following?

    A. Use of cryptographically random numbers

    B. Cryptographic sequence failures

    C. Poor encryption protocols

    D. Canonicalization errors

10. A cryptographically random number sequence is characterized by:

    A. Large value changes between successive numbers

    B. Normal probability distribution

    C. Intersequence randomness

    D. Pseudo

11. When is testing best accomplished?

    A. After all code is finished

    B. As early as possible in the process

    C. Using cryptographically random elements

    D. Using third-party testing software

12. Security requirements are best defined in:

    A. The requirements phase

    B. The coding phase

    C. The testing phase

    D. During architectural review of the system

13. Code review by a second party is helpful to do what?

    A. Increase creativity of the junior programmer

    B. Reduce cost—making for a better, cheaper method of testing

    C. Catch errors early in the programming process

    D. Ensure all modules work together

14. Virus and worm propagation can be achieved through exploiting:

    A. Buffer overflows

    B. Cryptographically random number failures

    C. The HTMLencode function

    D. Recursive functions

15. One of the most fundamental rules to good coding practice is:

    A. Code once, test twice.

    B. Validate all inputs.

    C. Don't use pointers.

    D. Use obscure coding practices so viruses cannot live in the code.

■ Essay Quiz

1. Describe the relationship of the requirements phase, testing phase, and use cases with respect to software engineering development and secure code.

2. Develop a list of five security-related issues to be put into a requirements document as part of a secure coding initiative.

3. Choose two requirements from the previous question and describe use cases that would validate them in the testing phase.

4. As the new programmer in a small firm that uses the C language, you have been asked to bring some security lessons learned from your university to the department's brown bag session. You choose to speak on buffer overflows. Explain how to detect buffer overflow errors and how to eliminate common sources for the errors from your coding practices.

5. You have been asked by your manager to develop a worksheet for code walkthroughs, another name for structured code reviews. This worksheet should include a list of common errors to look for during the examination, acting as a memory aid. You want to leave a lasting impression on the team as a new college grad. Outline what you would include on the worksheet related to security.

Lab Projects

• Lab Project 18.1

Learn the specific software engineering process model used at a local firm (or you may be able to research a company online or find one in a software engineering textbook at a library). Examine where security is built, or could be built, into the model. Provide an overview of the strengths and opportunities of the model with respect to designing secure code.

• Lab Project 18.2

Develop an example of a SQL injection statement for a web page inquiry. List the web page inputs, what the projected back-end SQL is, and how it can be changed.

Disaster Recovery, Business Continuity, and Organizational Policies

The superior man, when resting in safety, does not forget that danger may come. When in a state of security he does not forget the possibility of ruin. When all is orderly, he does not forget disorder may come. Thus his person is not endangered and his States and all their clans are preserved.

—CONFUCIUS

In this chapter, you will learn how to

- **Describe the various ways backups are conducted and stored**
- **Explain different strategies for alternative site processing**
- **Describe the various components of a business continuity plan**
- **Explain how policies and procedures play a daily role in addressing the security needs of an organization**

Much of this book focuses on avoiding the loss of confidentiality or integrity due to a security breach. The issue of availability is also discussed in terms of specific events, such as denial-of-service and distributed DoS attacks. In reality, however, there are many things that can disrupt the operations of your organization. From the standpoint of your clients and employees, whether your organization's web site is unavailable because of a storm or because of an intruder makes little difference—the site is still unavailable. In this chapter, we'll discuss what do to when a situation arises that results in the disruption of services. This discussion includes both disaster recovery and business continuity. Organizational policies will also be discussed as those policies set the tone for security on a daily basis.

Disaster Recovery

Many types of disasters, whether natural or caused by people, can disrupt your organization's operations for some length of time. Such disasters are unlike threats that intentionally target your computer systems and networks, such as industrial espionage, hacking, attacks from disgruntled employees, and insider threats, because the events that cause the disruption are not specifically aimed at your organization. Although both disasters and intentional threats must be considered important in planning for disaster recovery, the purpose of this section is to focus on recovering from disasters.

How long your organization's operations are disrupted depends in part on how prepared it is for a disaster and what plans are in place to mitigate the effects of a disaster. Any of the following events could cause a disruption in operations:

fire	flood	tornado	hurricane
electrical storm	earthquake	political unrest/riot	blizzard
gas leak/explosion	chemical spill	terrorism	war

Fortunately these types of events do not happen frequently in any one location. It is more likely that business operations will be interrupted due to employee error (such as accidental corruption of a database, or unplugging a system to plug in a vacuum cleaner—an event that has occurred at more than one organization). A good disaster recovery plan will prepare your organization for any type of organizational disruption.

Disaster Recovery Plans/Process

No matter what event you are worried about—whether natural or not, targeted at your organization or not—you can make preparations to lessen the impact on your organization and the length of time that your organization will be out of operation. A **disaster recovery plan (DRP)** is critical for effective disaster recovery efforts. A DRP defines the data and resources necessary and the steps required to restore critical organizational processes.

Consider what your organization needs to perform its mission. This information provides the beginning of a DRP, since it tells you what needs to be quickly restored. When considering resources, don't forget to include both the *physical resources* (such as computer hardware and software) and the *personnel* (the people who know how to run the systems that process your critical data).

To begin creating your DRP, first identify all critical functions for your organization, and then answer the following questions for each of these critical functions:

- Who is responsible for the operation of this function?
- What do these individuals need to perform the function?
- When should this function be accomplished relative to other functions?
- Where will this function be performed?

Disasters can be caused by nature (such as fires, earthquakes, and floods) or can be the result of some manmade event (such as war or a terrorist attack). The plans an organization develops to address a disaster need to recognize both of these possibilities. While many of the elements in a disaster recovery plan will be similar for both natural and manmade events, some differences might exist. For example, recovering data from backup tapes after a natural disaster can use the most recent backup available. If, on the other hand, the event was a loss of all data as a result of a computer virus that wiped your system, restoring from the most recent backup tapes might result in the reinfection of your system if the virus had been dormant for a planned period of time. In this case recovery might entail restoring some files from earlier backups.

- How is this function performed (what is the process)?
- Why is this function so important or critical to the organization?

Conducting a BIA is a critical part of developing your DRP. This assessment will allow you to focus on the most critical elements of your organization. These critical elements are the ones that you want to ensure are recovered first, and this priority should be reflected in your DRP.

By answering these questions, you can create an initial draft of your organization's DRP. The name often used to describe the document created by addressing these questions is a **business impact assessment (BIA)**. The DRP, of course, will need to be approved by management, and it is essential that they buy into the plan—otherwise your efforts will more than likely fail. The old adage "Those who fail to plan, plan to fail" certainly applies in this situation.

A good DRP must include the processes and procedures needed to restore your organization to proper functioning and to ensure continued operation. What specific steps will be required to restore operations? These processes should be documented and, where possible and feasible, reviewed and exercised on a periodic basis. Having a plan with step-by-step procedures that nobody knows how to follow does nothing to ensure the continued operation of the organization. Exercising your disaster recovery plans and processes before a disaster occurs provides you with the opportunity to discover flaws or weaknesses in the plan when there is still time to modify and correct them. It also provides an opportunity for key figures in the plan to practice what they will be expected to accomplish.

It is often very informative to determine what category your various business functions fall into. You may find that certain functions currently being conducted are not essential to your operations and could be eliminated. In this way, preparing for a security event may actually help you streamline your operational processes.

Categories of Business Functions

In developing your BIA and DRP, you may find it useful to categorize the various functions your organization performs, such as shown in Table 19.1. This categorization is based on how critical or important the function is to your business operation and how long your organization can last without the function. Those functions that are the most critical will be restored first, and your DRP should reflect this. If the function doesn't fall into any of the first four categories, then it is not really needed and the organization should seriously consider whether it can be eliminated altogether.

Table 19.1	DRP Considerations	
Category	**Level of the Function's Need**	**How Long Can the Organization Last Without the Function**
Critical	Absolutely essential for operations. Without the function, the basic mission of the organization cannot occur.	The function is needed immediately. The organization cannot function without it.
Necessary for normal processing	Required for normal processing, but the organization can live without it for a short period of time.	Can live without it for at most 30 days before your organization is severely impacted.
Desirable	Not needed for normal processing but enhances the organization's ability to conduct its mission efficiently.	Can live without the function for more than 30 days, but it is a function that will eventually need to be accomplished when normal operations are restored.
Optional	Nice to have but does not affect the operation of the organization.	Not essential, and no subsequent processing will be required to restore this function.
Consider eliminating	No discernable purpose for the function.	No impact to the organization; the function is not needed for any organizational purpose.

Business Continuity Plans

Another term that is often used when discussing the issue of continued organizational operations is **business continuity plan (BCP)**. You might wonder what the difference is between a DRP and a BCP—after all, isn't the purpose of the DRP the continued operation of the organization or business? In reality, these two terms are sometimes used synonymously, and for many organizations there may be no major difference in the two. There are, however, differences between a BCP and a DRP, one of which is the *focus*.

The focus of a BCP is the continued operation of the business or organization. The focus of a DRP is on the recovery and rebuilding of the organization after a disaster has occurred. The DRP is part of the larger BCP because business continuity is always an issue. A major focus of the DRP is the protection of human life. Evacuation plans and system shutdown procedures should be addressed. The safety of employees should be a theme throughout a DRP. In a BCP, you will see a more significant emphasis placed on the critical systems the organization needs to operate. The BCP will describe the functions that are most critical, based on a previously conducted BIA, and will describe the order in which functions should be returned to operation. The BCP describes what is needed in order for the business to continue to operate. In this situation, the two documents can be considered companion documents.

The difference between a DRP and BCP is that the BCP will be used to ensure that your operations continue in the face of whatever event has occurred that has caused a disruption in operations. If a disaster has occurred and has destroyed all or part of your facility, the DRP portion of the BCP will address the building or acquisition of a new facility. The DRP can also include details related to the long-term recovery of the organization.

However you view these two plans, an organization that is not able to quickly restore business functions after an operational interruption is an organization that will most likely suffer an unrecoverable loss and may cease to exist.

Tech Tip

DRP vs. BCP

Although the terms DRP and BCP may be used synonymously in small firms, in large firms, there is a difference in focus between the two plans. The focus of the BCP is on continued operation of a business, albeit at a reduced level or through different means during some period of time. The DRP is focused specifically on recovering from a disaster. In many cases, both of these functions happen at the same time, hence they are frequently combined in small firms and in many discussions. In large, complex entities, they are separate plans used to provide management options for a range of situations. In this case, the DRP is part of the larger BCP.

Backups

A key element in any BCP or BRP is the availability of backups. This is true not only because of the possibility of a disaster but also because hardware and storage media will periodically fail, resulting in loss or corruption of critical data. An organization might also find backups critical when security measures have failed and an individual has gained access to important information that may have become corrupted or at the very least can't be trusted. Data backup is thus a critical element in these plans, as well as in normal operation. There are several factors to consider in an organization's data backup strategy:

- How frequently should backups be conducted?
- How extensive do the backups need to be?
- What is the process for conducting backups?
- Who is responsible for ensuring backups are created?
- Where will the backups be stored?

- How long will backups be kept?
- How many copies will be maintained?

Keep in mind that the purpose of a backup is to provide valid, uncorrupted data in the event of corruption or loss of the original file or the media where the data was stored. Depending on the type of organization, legal requirements for conducting backups can also affect how it is accomplished.

What Needs to Be Backed Up

Backups commonly comprise the data that an organization relies on to conduct its daily operations. While this is certainly essential, a good backup plan will consider more than just the data; it will include any application programs needed to process the data and the operating system and utilities that the hardware platform requires to run the applications. Obviously, the application programs and operating system will change much less frequently than the data itself, so the frequency with which these items need to be backed up is considerably different. This should be reflected in the organization's backup plan and strategy.

The BCP should also address other items related to backups. Personnel, equipment, and electrical power must also be part of the plan. Somebody needs to understand the operation of the critical hardware and software used by the organization. If the disaster that destroyed the original copy of the data and the original systems also results in the loss of the only personnel that know how to process the data, having backup data will not be enough to restore normal operations for the organization. Similarly, if the data requires specific software to be run on a very specific hardware platform, then having the data without the application program or required hardware will also not be sufficient. As you can see, a BCP is an involved document that must consider many different factors and take into account many different possibilities.

Strategies for Backups

The process for creating a backup copy of data and software requires more thought than simply stating "copy all required files." The size of the resulting backup must be considered, as well as the time required to conduct the backup. Both of these will affect details such as how frequently the backup will occur and the type of storage media that will be used for the backup. Other considerations include who will be responsible for conducting the backup, where the backups will be stored, and how long they should be maintained. Short-term storage for accidentally deleted files that users need to have restored should probably be close at hand. Longer-term storage for backups that may be several months or even years old should occur in a different facility. It should be evident by now that even something that sounds as simple as maintaining backup copies of essential data requires careful consideration and planning.

Types of Backups The amount of data that will be backed up, and the time it takes to accomplish this, has a direct bearing on the type of backup that should be performed. Table 19.2 outlines the four basic types of backups that can be conducted, the amount of space required for each, and the ease of restoration using each strategy.

Table 19.2	Characteristics of Different Backup Types			
	Full	**Differential**	**Incremental**	**Delta**
Amount of Space	Large	Medium	Medium	Small
Restoration	Simple	Simple	Involved	Complex

The values for each of the strategies in Table 19.2 are highly variable depending on your specific environment. The more frequently files are changed between backups, the more these strategies will look alike. What each strategy entails bears further explanation.

The easiest type of backup to understand is the **full backup**. In a full backup, all files and software are copied onto the storage media. Restoration from a full backup is similarly straightforward—you must copy all the files back onto the system. This process can take a considerable amount of time. Consider the size of even the average home PC today, for which storage is measured in tens and hundreds of gigabytes. Copying this amount of data takes time. In a full backup, the archive bit is cleared.

In a **differential backup**, only the files and software that have changed since the last full backup was completed are backed up. This also implies that periodically a full backup needs to be accomplished. The frequency of the full backup versus the interim differential backups depends on your organization and needs to be part of your defined strategy. Restoration from a differential backup requires two steps: the last full backup first needs to be loaded, and then the differential backup can be applied to update the files that have been changed since the full backup was conducted. Again, this is not a difficult process, but it does take some time. The amount of time to accomplish the periodic differential backup, however, is much less than that for a full backup, and this is one of the advantages of this method. Obviously, if a lot of time has passed between differential backups, or if most files in your environment change frequently, then the differential backup does not differ much from a full backup. It should also be obvious that to accomplish the differential backup, the system has to have a method to determine which files have been changed since some given point in time. The archive bit is not cleared in a differential backup since the key for a differential is to back up all files that have changed since the last full backup.

With incremental backups, even less information will be stored in each backup. The **incremental backup** is a variation on a differential backup, with the difference being that instead of copying all files that have changed since the last full backup, the incremental backup backs up only files that have changed since the last full *or* incremental backup occurred, thus requiring fewer files to be backed up. Just as in the case of the differential backup, the incremental backup relies on the occasional full backup being accomplished. After that, you back up only files that have changed since the last backup of any sort was conducted. To restore a system using this type of backup method requires quite a bit more work. You first need to go back to the last full backup and reload the system with this data. Then you have to update the system with every incremental backup that has occurred since the full backup. The advantage of this type of backup is that it requires less storage and time to accomplish. The disadvantage is that the restoration process is more involved. Assuming that you don't frequently have to conduct a

Tech Tip

Archive Bits
The archive bit is used to indicate whether a file has (1) or has not (0) changed since the last backup. The bit is set (changed to a 1) if the file is modified, or in some cases, if the file is copied, the new copy of the file has its archive bit set. The bit is reset (changed to a 0) when the file is backed up. The archive bit can be used to determine which files need to be backed up when using methods such as the differential backup method.

complete restoration of your system, however, the incremental backup is a valid technique. An incremental backup will clear the archive bit.

Finally, the goal of the **delta backup** is to back up as little information as possible each time you perform a backup. As with the other strategies, an occasional full backup must be accomplished. After that, when a delta backup is conducted at specific intervals, only the portions of the files that have been changed will be stored. The advantage of this is easy to illustrate. If your organization maintains a large database with thousands of records comprising several hundred megabytes of data, the entire database would be copied in the previous backup types even if only one record has changed. For a delta backup, only the actual record that changed would be stored. The disadvantage of this method is that restoration is a complex process, because it requires more than just loading a file (or several files). It requires that application software be run to update the records in the files that have been changed.

Each type of backup has advantages and disadvantages. Which type is best for your organization depends on the amount of data you routinely process and store, how frequently the data changes, how often you expect to have to restore from a backup, and a number of other factors. The type you select will greatly affect your overall backup strategy, plans, and processes.

Backup Frequency and Retention   The type of backup strategy an organization employs is often affected by how frequently the organization conducts the backup activity. The usefulness of a backup is directly related to how many changes have occurred since the backup was created, and this is obviously affected by how often backups are created. The longer it has been since the backup was created, the more changes that will likely have occurred. There is no easy answer, however, to how frequently an organization should perform backups. Every organization should consider how long it can survive without current data from which to operate. It can then determine how long it will take to restore from backups, using various methods, and decide how frequently backups need to occur. This sounds simple, but it is a serious, complex decision to make.

Related to the frequency question is the issue of how long backups should be maintained. Is it sufficient to simply maintain a single backup from which to restore data? Security professionals will tell you no; multiple backups should be maintained, for a variety of reasons. If the reason for restoring from the backup is the discovery of an intruder in the system, it is important to restore the system to its pre-intrusion state. If the intruder has been in the system for several months before being discovered, and backups are taken weekly, it will not be possible to restore to a pre-intrusion state if only one backup is maintained. This would mean that all data and system files would be suspect and may not be reliable. If multiple backups were maintained, at various intervals, then it is easier to return to a point before the intrusion (or before the security or operational event that is necessitating the restoration) occurred.

There are several strategies or approaches to backup retention. One common and easy-to-remember strategy is the "rule of three," in which the three most recent backups are kept. When a new backup is created, the oldest backup is overwritten. Another strategy is to keep the most recent copy of backups for various time intervals. For example, you might keep the

Exam Tip: Backup strategies are such a critical element of security that you need to make sure you understand the different types of backups and their advantages and disadvantages.

Tech Tip

Determining How Long to Maintain Backups

Determining the length of time that you retain your backups should not be based on the frequency of your backups. The more often you conduct backup operations, the more data you will have. You might be tempted to trim the number of backups retained to keep storage costs down, but you need to evaluate how long you need to retain backups based on your operational environment and then keep the appropriate number of backups.

latest daily, weekly, monthly, quarterly, and yearly backups. Note that in certain environments, regulatory issues may prescribe a specific frequency and retention period, so it is important to know your organization's requirements when determining how often you will create a backup and how long you will keep it.

If you are not in an environment for which regulatory issues dictate the frequency and retention for backups, your goal will be to optimize the frequency. In determining the optimal backup frequency, two major costs need to be considered: the cost of the backup strategy you choose and the cost of recovery if you do not implement this backup strategy (that is, if no backups were created). You must also factor into this equation the probability that the backup will be needed on any given day. The two figures to consider then are

(probability the backup is needed) × *(cost of restoring with no backup)*

(probability the backup isn't needed) × *(cost of the backup strategy)*

The first of these two figures can be considered the probable loss you can expect if your organization has no backup. The second figure can be considered the amount you are willing to spend to ensure that you can restore, should a problem occur (think of this as backup insurance—the cost of an insurance policy that may never be used but that you are willing to pay for, just in case). For example, if the probability of a backup being needed is 10 percent, and the cost of restoring with no backup is $100,000, then the first equation would yield a figure of $10,000. This can be compared with the alternative, which would be a 90 percent chance the backup is not needed multiplied by the cost of implementing your backup strategy (of taking and maintaining the backups), which is, say, $10,000 annually. The second equation yields a figure of $9000. In this example, the cost of maintaining the backup is less than the cost of not having backups, so the former would be the better choice. While conceptually this is an easy tradeoff to understand, in reality it is often difficult to accurately determine the probability of a backup being needed. Fortunately, the figures for the potential loss if there is no backup is generally so much greater than the cost of maintaining a backup that a mistake in judging the probability will not matter—it just makes too much sense to maintain backups. This example also uses a straight comparison based solely on the cost of the process of restoring with and without a backup strategy. What needs to be included in the cost of both of these is the loss that occurs while the asset is not available because it is being restored—in essence, a measurement of the value of the asset itself.

To optimize your backup strategy, you need to determine the correct balance between these two figures. Obviously, you do not want to spend more in your backup strategy than you face losing should you not have a backup plan at all. When working with these two calculations, you have to remember that this is a cost-avoidance exercise. The organization is not going to increase revenues with its backup strategy. The goal is to minimize the potential loss due to some catastrophic event by creating a backup strategy that will address your organization's needs.

When you're calculating the cost of the backup strategy, consider the following:

- The cost of the backup media required for a single backup
- The storage costs for the backup media based on the retention policy
- The labor costs associated with performing a single backup
- The frequency with which backups are created

All of these considerations can be used to arrive at an annual cost for implementing your chosen backup strategy, and this figure can then be used as previously described.

Storage of Backups   An important element to factor into the cost of the backup strategy is the expense of storing the backups. A simple strategy might be to store all your backups together for quick and easy recovery actions. This is not, however, a good idea. Suppose the catastrophic event that necessitated the restoration of backed-up data was a fire that destroyed the computer system the data was processed on. In this case, any backups that were stored in the same facility might also be lost in the same fire.

The solution is to keep copies of backups in separate locations. The most recent copy can be stored locally, as it is the most likely to be needed, while other copies can be kept at other locations. Depending on the level of security your organization desires, the storage facility itself could be reinforced against possible threats in your area (such as tornados or floods). A more recent advance is online backup services. A number of third-party companies offer high-speed connections for storing data in a separate facility on a frequent basis. Transmitting the backup data via network connections alleviates some other concerns with physical movement of more traditional storage media, such as the care during transportation (tapes do not fare well in direct sunlight, for example) or the time that it takes to transport the tape data.

Issues with Long-Term Storage of Backups   Depending on the media used for an organization's backups, degradation of the media is a distinct possibility and needs to be considered. Magnetic media degrades over time (measured in years). In addition, tapes can be used a limited number of times before the surface begins to flake off. Magnetic media should thus be rotated and tested to ensure that it is still usable.

Another consideration is advances in technology. The media you used to store your data two years ago may now be considered obsolete (5.25-inch floppy disks, for example). Software applications also evolve, and the media may be present but may not be compatible with current versions of the software. This may mean that you need to maintain backup copies of both hardware and software in order to recover from older backup media.

Another issue is security related. If the file you stored was encrypted for security purposes, does anybody in the company remember the password to decrypt the file to restore the data? More than one employee in the company should know the key to decrypt the files, and this information should be passed along to another person when a critical employee with that information leaves, is terminated, or dies.

Tech Tip

Onsite Backup Storage

One of the most frequent errors committed with backups is to store all backups onsite. While this greatly simplifies the process, it means that all data is stored in the same facility. Should a natural disaster occur (such as a fire or hurricane), you could lose not only your primary data storage devices but your backups as well. You need to use an offsite location to store at least some of your backups.

Tech Tip

Long-Term Backup Storage

An easy factor to overlook when upgrading systems is whether long-term backups will still be usable. You need to ensure that the type of media utilized for your long-term storage is compatible with the hardware that you are upgrading to. Otherwise, you may find yourself in a situation in which you need to restore data, and you have the data, but you don't have any way to restore it.

Alternative Sites An issue related to the location of backup storage is where the restoration services will be conducted. Determination of when or if an alternative site is needed should be included in recovery and continuity plans. If the organization has suffered physical damage to a facility, having offsite storage of data is only part of the solution. This data will need to be processed somewhere, which means that computing facilities similar to those used in normal operations are required. There are a number of ways to approach this problem, including hot sites, warm sites, cold sites, and mobile backup sites.

A **hot site** is a fully configured environment that is similar to the normal operating environment and that can be operational immediately or within a few hours depending on its configuration and the needs of the organization. A **warm site** is partially configured, usually having the peripherals and software but perhaps not the more expensive main processing computer. It is designed to be operational within a few days. A **cold site** has the basic environmental controls necessary to operate but has few of the computing components necessary for processing. Getting a cold site operational may take weeks. A mobile backup site generally is a trailer with the required computers and electrical power that can be driven to a location within hours of a disaster and set up to commence processing immediately.

Shared alternate sites may also be considered. These sites can be designed to handle the needs of different organizations in the event of an emergency. The hope is that the disaster will affect only one organization at a time. The benefit of this method is that the cost of the site can be shared among organizations. Two similar organizations located close to each should not share the same alternate site as there is a greater chance that they would both need it at the same time.

Try This

Research Alternative Processing Sites
There is an industry built upon providing alternative processing sites in case of a disaster of some sort. Using the Internet or other resources, determine what resources are available in your area for hot, warm, and cold sites. Do you live in an area in which a lot of these services are offered? Do other areas of the country have more alternative processing sites available? What makes where you live a better or worse place for alternative sites?

All of these options can come with a considerable price tag, which makes another option, mutual aid agreements, a possible alternative. With a **mutual aid agreement**, similar organizations agree to assume the processing for the other party in the event a disaster occurs. The obvious assumption here is that both organizations will not be hit by the same disaster and that both have similar processing environments. If these two assumptions are correct, then a mutual aid agreement should be considered. Such an arrangement may not be legally enforceable, even if it is in writing, and organizations must consider this when developing their disaster plans. In addition, if the organization that the mutual aid agreement is made with also is hit by the same disaster, then both organizations will be in trouble. Additional contingencies need to be planned for even if a mutual aid agreement is made with another organization. There are also the obvious security concerns that must be considered when having another organization assume your organization's processing.

Exam Tip: Understanding the differences between hot, warm, and cold sites is fundamental to understanding different business continuity strategies. Make sure that you understand the simple differences between these sites, the primary of which is how soon the alternative site can begin processing your organization's work.

Utilities

The interruption of power is a common issue during a disaster. Computers and networks obviously require power to operate, so emergency power must be available in the event of any disruption of operations. For short-term interruptions, such as what might occur as the result of an electrical storm, uninterruptible power supplies (UPSs) may suffice. These devices contain a battery that provides steady power for short periods of time—enough to keep a system running should power only be lost for a few minutes, or enough to allow administrators to gracefully halt the system or network. For continued operations that extend beyond a few minutes, another source of power will be required. Generally this is provided by a backup emergency generator.

While backup generators are frequently used to provide power during an emergency, they are not a simple, maintenance-free solution. Generators need to be tested on a regular basis, and they can easily become strained if they are required to power too much equipment. If your organization is going to rely on an emergency generator for backup power, you must ensure that the system has reserve capacity beyond the anticipated load for the unanticipated loads that will undoubtedly be placed on it.

Generators also take time to start up, so power to your organization will most likely be lost, even if only briefly, until the generators kick in. This means that you should also use a UPS to allow for a smooth transition to backup power. Generators are also expensive and require fuel—when looking for a place to locate your generator, don't forget the need to deliver fuel to it or you may find yourself hauling cans of fuel up a number of stairs.

When determining the need for backup power, don't forget to factor in environmental conditions. Running computer systems in a room with no air conditioning in the middle of the summer in the Southwest will result in an extremely uncomfortable environment for all to work in. Mobile backup sites, generally using trailers, often rely on generators for their power but also factor in the requirement for environmental controls.

Power is not the only essential utility for operations. Depending on the type of disaster that has occurred, telephone and Internet communication may also be lost, and wireless services may not be available. Planning for redundant means of communication (such as using both land lines and wireless) can help with most outages, but for large disasters, your backup plans should include the option to continue operations from a completely different location while waiting for communications in your area to be restored. Telecommunication carriers have their own emergency equipment and are fairly efficient at restoring communications, but it may take a few days.

Secure Recovery

Several companies offer recovery services, including power, communications, and technical support that your organization may need if its operations are disrupted. These companies advertise secure recovery sites or offices from which your organization can again begin to operate in a secure environment. Secure recovery is also advertised by other organizations that provide services that can remotely (over the Internet, for example) provide restoration services for critical files and data.

In both cases—the actual physical suites and the remote service—security is an important element. During a disaster, your data does not become any less important, and you will want to make sure that you maintain the security (in terms of confidentiality and integrity, for example) of your data. As in other aspects of security, the decision to employ these services should be made based on a calculation of the benefits weighed against the potential loss if alternative means are used.

Cloud Computing

One of the newer innovations coming to computing via the Internet is the concept of cloud computing. Instead of owning and operating a dedicated set of servers for common business functions such as database services, file storage, e-mail services, and so forth, an organization can contract with third parties to provide these services over the Internet from their server farms. The concept is that operations and maintenance is an activity that has become a commodity, and the Internet provides a reliable mechanism to access this more economical form of operational computing.

Pushing computing into the cloud may make good business sense from a cost perspective, but doing so does not change the fact that your organization is still responsible for ensuring that all the appropriate security measures are properly in place. How are backups being performed? What plan is in place for disaster recovery? How frequently are systems patched? What is the service-level agreement (SLA) associated with the systems? It is easy to ignore the details when outsourcing these critical yet costly elements, but when something bad occurs, you must have confidence that the appropriate level of protections has been applied. These are the serious questions and difficult issues to resolve when moving computing into the cloud—location may change, but responsibility and technical issues are still there and form the risk of the solution.

High Availability and Fault Tolerance

Some other terms that may be used in discussions of continuity of operations in the face of a disruption of some sort are high availability and fault tolerance.

One of the objectives of security is the availability of data and processing power when an authorized user desires it. **High availability** refers to the ability to maintain availability of data and operational processing despite a disrupting event. Generally this requires redundant systems, in terms of both power and processing, so that should one system fail, the other can take over operations without any break in service. High availability is more than data redundancy; it requires that both data and services be available.

Fault tolerance basically has the same goal as high availability—the uninterrupted access to data and services—and is accomplished by the mirroring of data and systems. Should a "fault" occur, causing disruption in a device such as a disk controller, the mirrored system provides the requested data with no apparent interruption in service to the user. High availability clustering is another method used to provide redundancy in critical situations. These clusters consist of additional computers upon which a critical

Tech Tip

The Sidekick Failure of 2009

In October 2009, many T-Mobile Sidekick users discovered that their contacts, calendars, to-do lists, and photos were lost when cloud-based servers lost their data. Not all users were affected by the server failure, but for those that were, the loss was complete. T-Mobile quickly pointed the finger at Microsoft, who had acquired in February 2008 the small startup company, Danger, that built the cloud-based system for T-Mobile. To end users, this transaction was completely transparent. In the end, a lot of users lost their data, and were offered $100 credit by T-Mobile against their bill. Regardless of where the blame lands, the affected end user must still face a simple question: did they consider the importance of backup? If the information on their phone was critical, did they perform a local backup? Or did they assume that the cloud and large corporations they contracted with did it for them?

Your business impact assessment can be very useful in determining whether you have a requirement for high availability. Only the most critical functions should be considered for categorization as high availability functions.

process can be started if the cluster detects that there has been a hardware or software problem on the main system.

Obviously, providing redundant systems and equipment comes with a price, and the need to provide this level of continuous, uninterrupted operation needs to be carefully evaluated.

Single Point of Failure

Related to the topic of high availability is the concept of a *single point of failure*. A single point of failure is a critical operation in the organization upon which many other operations rely and which itself relies on a single item that, if lost, would halt this critical operation. A single point of failure can be a special piece of hardware, a process, a specific piece of data, or even an essential utility. Single points of failure need to be identified if high availability is required because they are potentially the "weak links" in the chain that can cause disruption of the organization's operations. Generally, the solution to a single point of failure is to modify the critical operation so that it does not rely on this single element or to build redundant components into the critical operation to take over the process should one of these points fail.

RAID

A relatively new approach to increasing reliability in disk storage is *Redundant Array of Inexpensive Disks*, now known as *Redundant Array of Independent Disks (RAID)*. RAID takes data that is normally stored on a single disk and spreads it out among several others. If any single disk is lost, the data can be recovered from the other disks where the data also resides. With the price of disk storage decreasing, this approach has become increasingly popular to the point that many individual users even have RAID arrays for their home systems. RAID can also increase the speed of data recovery as multiple drives can be busy retrieving requested data at the same time instead of relying on just one disk to do the work. There are several varieties of RAID with RAID 0 spreading data out to speed access but with no redundancy to improve reliability and RAID 1 implementing exact copies of disks so that all data is mirrored on another drive providing complete redundancy. Since RAID 1 is extremely expensive (doubling all hardware requirements), other variations of RAID have been developed to provide both reliability and increased speed. RAID 5, for example, spreads data across disks and adds parity in a manner such that the loss of any single disk in the array will not result in the loss of any data.

Spare Parts and Redundancy

RAID increases reliability through the use of *redundancy*. When developing plans for ensuring that an organization has what it needs to keep operating, even if hardware or software fails or if security is breached, you should consider other measures involving redundancy and spare parts. Some common applications of redundancy include the use of redundant servers, redundant connections, and redundant ISPs. The need for redundant servers and connections may be fairly obvious, but the need for redundant ISPs may not be so, at least initially. Many ISPs already have multiple accesses to the Internet on their own, but by having additional ISP connections, an organization can reduce the chance that an interruption of one ISP will negatively impact the organization. Ensuring uninterrupted access to the Internet by employees or access to the organization's e-commerce site for customers is becoming increasingly important.

Many organizations don't see the need for maintaining a supply of spare parts. After all, with the price of storage dropping and the speed of processors increasing, why replace a broken part with older technology? However, a ready supply of spare parts can ease the process of bringing the system back online. Replacing hardware and software with newer versions can sometimes lead to problems with compatibility. An older version of some piece of critical software may not work with newer hardware, which may be more capable in a variety of ways. Having critical hardware (or software) spares for critical functions in the organization can greatly facilitate maintaining business continuity in the event of software or hardware failures.

 An interesting historical note is that RAID originally stood for Redundant Array of *Inexpensive* Disks but the name was changed to the currently accepted Redundant Array of *Independent* Disks as a result of industry influence.

Computer Incident Response Teams

Many of the issues discussed in this chapter illustrate the point that "if you fail to plan, you plan to fail." One of the steps that should be taken to establish a plan to handle business interruptions as a result of a cyber event of some sort is the establishment of a Computer Incident Response Team (CIRT) or a Computer Emergency Response Team (CERT). This subject is covered in greater detail in Chapter 23 when the subject of incident response and forensics is covered. Not all computer incidents will threaten the organization's business operations, and the level of response to computer incidents will not usually include activation of the BCP or DRP, but it could. At the very least, the organization's procedures to recover data from backup files may have to be exercised if a computer intrusion results in modified files or data. The organization's CIRT will conduct the investigation into the incident and make the recommendations on how to proceed. The CIRT should consist of not only permanent but also ad hoc members who may be called upon to address special needs depending on the nature of the incident. In addition to individuals with a technical background, the CIRT should include nontechnical personnel to provide guidance on ways to handle media attention, legal issues that may arise, and management issues regarding the continued operation of the organization. The CIRT should be created and team members notified before an incident occurs. Policies and procedures for conducting an investigation should also be worked out in advance of an incident occurring. It is also advisable to have the team periodically meet to review these procedures.

 Tech Tip

Incident Response Capability
Every organization, regardless of size, needs to consider what it will do (and have plans and processes established beforehand) if a security event occurs. Small organizations may not have enough personnel to warrant a dedicated response team but they should at least identify who will be responsible for responding to an event as an additional duty.

Test, Exercise, and Rehearse

An organization should practice its DRP periodically. The time to find out whether it has flaws is not when an actual event occurs and the recovery of data and information means the continued existence of the organization. The DRP should be tested to ensure that it is sufficient and that all key individuals know their role in the specific plan. The security plan determines if the organization's plan and the individuals involved perform as they should during a simulated security incident.

A test implies a "grade" will be applied to the outcome. Did the organization's plan and the individuals involved perform as they should? Was the organization able to recover and continue to operate within the predefined tolerances set by management? If the answer is no, then during the follow-up evaluation of the exercise, the failures should be identified and addressed. Was it simply a matter of untrained or uninformed individuals or was there a technological failure that necessitates a change in hardware, software, and procedures?

Whereas a test implies a "grade," an exercise can be conducted without the stigma of a pass/fail grade being attached. *Security exercises* are conducted to provide the opportunity for all parties to practice the procedures that have been established to respond to a security incident. It is important to perform as many of the recovery functions as possible, without impacting ongoing operations, to ensure that the procedures and technology will work in a real incident. You may want to periodically rehearse portions of the recovery plan, particularly those aspects that are either potentially more disruptive to actual operations or that require more frequent practice because of their importance or degree of difficulty.

Additionally, there are different formats for exercises with varying degrees of impact on the organization. The most basic is a checklist walkthrough in which individuals go through a recovery checklist to ensure that they understand what to do should the plan be invoked and that all necessary equipment (hardware and software) is available. This type of exercise normally does not divulge "holes" in a plan but will show where discrepancies exist in the preparation for the plan. To examine the completeness of a plan, a different type of exercise needs to be conducted. The simplest is a tabletop exercise in which participants sit around a table with a facilitator who supplies information related to the "incident" and processes that are being examined. No actual processes or procedures are invoked, they are just discussed. This may result in the realization that a certain type of incident is not currently covered in existing plans. Another type of exercise is a functional test in which certain aspects of a plan are tested to see how well they work (and how well prepared personnel are). At the most extreme are full operational exercises designed to actually interrupt services in order to verify that all aspects of a plan are in place and sufficient to respond to the type of incident that is being simulated.

■ Policies and Procedures

Whereas DRPs and BCPs are designed to address the needs of an organization in the event of a disruption of operations, polices and procedures govern the organization's operations on a daily basis. **Policies** are high-level, broad statements of what the organization wants to accomplish. They are made by management when laying out the organization's position on some issue. Policies are mandatory but are not specific in their details. Policies are focused on the result, not the methods for achieving that result.

Standards are mandatory elements regarding the implementation of a policy. They are accepted specifications that provide specific details on how a policy is to be enforced. **Procedures** are generally step-by-step instructions on how to implement policies in the organization. They describe exactly how employees are expected to act in a given situation or to accomplish a

Exam Tip: Exercises are an often overlooked aspect of security. Many organizations do not believe that they have the time to spend on such events, but the question to ask is whether they can afford to not conduct these exercises as they ensure the organization has a viable plan to recover from disasters and that operations can continue. Make sure you understand what is involved in these critical tests of your organization's plans.

specific task. Although standard policies can be described in general terms that are applicable to all organizations, standards and procedures are often organization-specific and driven by specific organizational policies. This section therefore concentrates on the higher-level general policy statements that apply to all organizations and does not attempt to cover the variety of specific implementations individual organizations may choose.

Regarding security, every organization should have several common policies in place. These policies include acceptable use policies, due care, separation of duties, password management, change management, classification of information, and policies governing the protection of *personally identifiable information* (PII). Other important policy-related issues include privacy, service level agreements, human resources policies, codes of ethics, and policies governing incident response.

Security Policies

In keeping with the high-level nature of policies, the *security policy* is a high-level statement produced by senior management that outlines what security means to the organization and what the organization's goals are for security. The main security policy can then be broken down into additional policies that cover specific topics. Statements such as "this organization will exercise the principle of least privilege in its handling of client information" would be an example of a security policy. The security policy can also describe how security is to be handled from an organizational point of view (such as describing which office and corporate officer or manager oversees the organization's security program).

The organization's security policy should also include the specific policies described in the following sections. All policies should be reviewed on a regular basis and updated as needed. Generally, policies need to be updated less frequently than the procedures that implement them, since the high-level goals will not change as often as the environment in which they must be implemented. All policies should be reviewed by the organization's legal counsel, and a plan should be outlined describing how the organization will ensure that employees will be made aware of the policies. Policies can also be made stronger by including references to the authority who made the policy (for example, whether the policy comes from the CEO or is a department-level policy) and also refer to any laws or regulations that are applicable to the specific policy and environment.

Acceptable Use

An **acceptable use policy (AUP)** outlines what the organization considers to be the appropriate use of company resources, such as computer systems, e-mail, telephones, Internet access, and networks. Organizations should be concerned with the personal uses of organizational assets that do not benefit the company.

The goal of the AUP is to ensure employee productivity while limiting organizational liability due to inappropriate use of the organization's assets. The policy should clearly delineate what activities are not allowed. Issues that the policy should address include such things as the use of resources to conduct personal business, installation of hardware or software, remote

In today's highly connected environment, every organization should have an AUP that spells out to all employees what the organization considers appropriate and inappropriate use of its computing and networks resources. Having this policy may be critical should the organization need to take disciplinary actions based on an abuse of its resources.

access to systems and networks, the copying of company-owned software, and the responsibility of users to protect company assets, including data, software, and hardware. Statements regarding possible penalties (such as termination) for violating or ignoring any of the policies should be included. Organizations should be careful, however, to make sure the penalty doesn't outweigh the offense.

Related to appropriate use of the organization's computer systems and networks by employees is the appropriate use by the organization. The most important of such issues is whether the organization considers it appropriate to monitor the employee's use of the systems and network. If monitoring is considered appropriate, the organization should include a statement to this effect in the banner that users see at login. This repeatedly warns employees, and possible intruders, that their actions are subject to monitoring and that any misuse of the system will not be tolerated. Should the organization need to use any information gathered during monitoring in a civil or criminal case, the issue of whether the employee had an expectation of privacy, or whether it was even legal for the organization to be monitoring, is simplified if the organization can point to a statement that is always displayed that notifies employees use of the system constitutes consent to monitoring. Before any monitoring is conducted, or the actual wording on the warning message is created, the organization's legal counsel should be consulted to determine the appropriate way to address this issue in the particular location.

Internet Usage Policy In today's highly connected environment, employee use of access to the Internet is of particular concern. The goal for the *Internet usage policy* is to ensure maximum employee productivity and to limit potential liability to the organization from inappropriate use of the Internet in a workplace. The Internet provides a tremendous temptation for employees to waste hours as they surf the Web for the scores of the important games from the previous night, conduct some quick online stock transactions, or read the review of the latest blockbuster movie everyone is talking about. Obviously, every minute they spend conducting this sort of activity is time they are not productively engaged in the organization's business and their jobs. In addition, allowing employees to visit sites that may be considered offensive to others (such as pornographic or hate sites) can expose the company to accusations of condoning a hostile work environment and result in legal liability.

The Internet usage policy needs to address what sites employees are allowed to visit and what sites they are prohibited from visiting. If the company allows employees to surf the Web during non-work hours, the policy needs to clearly spell out the acceptable parameters, in terms of when they are allowed to do this and what sites they are still prohibited from visiting (such as potentially offensive sites). The policy should also describe under

Try This

Policies for Internet Usage

Some organizations may include an Internet usage policy as part of the AUP. With the amount of time individuals spend online today, however, organizations should consider having a separate policy just for Internet usage that more completely defines what is considered acceptable and what is not. Check to see what type of acceptable use policy your organization has. What does it cover? Does your organization have a single policy or multiple policies covering different things such as a separate Internet usage policy? Compare your organization's policy or policies with any others that you can find on the Internet.

Principles of Computer Security: CompTIA Security+ and Beyond

what circumstances an employee is allowed to post something from the organization's network on the Web (on a blog, for example). A necessary addition to this policy would be the procedure for an employee to follow to obtain permission to post the object or message.

E-Mail Usage Policy   Related to the Internet usage policy is the *e-mail usage policy*, which addresses what the company will allow employees to send in terms of e-mail. This policy should spell out whether non-work e-mail traffic is allowed at all or is at least severely restricted. It needs to cover the type of message that would be considered inappropriate to send to other employees (for example, no offensive language, no sex-related or ethnic jokes, no harassment, and so on). The policy should also specify any disclaimers that must be attached to an employee's message sent to an individual outside the company.

Due Care and Due Diligence

Due care and **due diligence** are terms used in the legal and business community to address issues where one party's actions might have caused loss or injury to another party. Basically, the law recognizes the responsibility of an individual or organization to act reasonably (exercise due care and due diligence) relative to another. The organization needs to take reasonable precautions that indicate it is being responsible. In terms of security, organizations are expected to take reasonable precautions to protect the information that it maintains on other individuals. Should a person suffer a loss as a result of negligence on the part of an organization in terms of its security, that person can take legal action against the organization. Due care policies detail how employees are expected to treat equipment and data. Due diligence is the process that an organization goes through to ensure that all options were considered in development of security policies and procedures related to due care directives.

The standard applied—reasonableness—is extremely subjective and often is determined by a jury. The organization will need to show that it had taken reasonable precautions to protect the information and, despite these precautions, an unforeseen security event occurred that caused the injury to the other party. Since this is so subjective, it is hard to describe what would be considered reasonable, but many sectors have "security best practices" for their industry, which provides a basis for organizations in that sector to start from. If the organization decides to not follow any of the best practices accepted by the industry, it needs to be prepared to justify its reasons in court should an incident occur. If the sector the organization is in has regulatory requirements, explanations on why the mandated security practices were not followed will be much more difficult (and possibly impossible) to justify.

Another element that can help establish due care from a security standpoint is developing and implementing the security policies discussed in this chapter. As the policies outlined become more generally accepted, the level of diligence and care that an organization will be expected to maintain will increase.

Separation of Duties

Separation of duties is a principle employed in many organizations to ensure that no single individual has the ability to conduct transactions alone. This

Tech Tip

Prudent Person Principle
The concepts of due care and due diligence are connected. Due care addresses whether the organization has a minimal set of policies that provides reasonable assurance of success in maintaining security. Due diligence requires that management actually do something to ensure security, such as implement procedures for testing and review of audit records, internal security controls, and personnel behavior. The standard applied is one of a "prudent person"; would a prudent person find the actions appropriate and sincere? To apply this standard, all one has to do is ask the question "What would a prudent person do to protect and ensure that the security features and procedures are working or adequate?" for the issue under consideration. Failure of a security feature or procedure doesn't necessarily mean the person acted imprudently.

means that the level of trust in any one individual is lessened, and the ability for any individual to cause catastrophic damage to the organization is also lessened. An example might be an organization in which one person has the ability to order equipment, but another individual must make the payment. Thus, an individual who wants to make an unauthorized purchase for his own personal gain would have to convince another person to go along with the transaction.

Separating duties as a security tool is a good practice, but it is possible to go overboard and break transactions up into too many pieces or require too much oversight. This results in inefficiency and can actually be less secure, since individuals may not scrutinize transactions as thoroughly, knowing that others will also be reviewing them. The temptation is to hurry something along and assume that somebody else will examine or has examined it.

Another aspect of the separation of duties principle is that it spreads responsibilities out over an organization so no single individual becomes the indispensable individual with all of the "keys to the kingdom" or unique knowledge about how to make everything work. If enough tasks have been distributed, assigning a primary and a backup person for each task will ensure that the loss of any one individual will not have a disastrous impact on the organization.

Need to Know and Least Privilege

Two other common security principles are that of *need to know* and *least privilege*. The guiding factor here is that each individual in the organization is supplied with only the absolute minimum amount of information and privileges she needs to perform her work tasks. To obtain access to any piece of information, the individual must have a justified need to know. **Least privilege** means the individual will be granted only the bare minimum number of privileges needed to perform her job.

A policy spelling out these two principles as guiding philosophies for the organization should be created. The policy should also address who in the organization can grant access to information or assign privileges to employees.

Password Management

Since passwords are the most common authentication mechanism, it is imperative that organizations have a policy addressing them. The *password management policy* should address the procedures used for selecting user passwords (specifying what is considered an acceptable password in the organization in terms of the character set and length, for example), the frequency with which they must be changed, and how they will be distributed. Procedures for creating new passwords should an employee forget her old password also need to be addressed, as well as the acceptable handling of passwords (for example, they should not be

Cross Check

Password Selection Rules

Recall from Chapter 4 the rules governing password selection. Organizations should also have policies that address other issues such as the distribution of passwords, how passwords can be changed and by whom, and how frequently users will be required to change their passwords. Examine your own personal password policies as you have put them into practice on the many sites for which you have chosen a password. Do you use a dictionary word? A word with a number? Do you repeat passwords across different sites? When would this be a problem?

Principles of Computer Security: CompTIA Security+ and Beyond

shared with anybody else, they should not be written down, and so on). It might also be useful to have the policy address the issue of password cracking by administrators, to discover weak passwords selected by employees.

Note that the developer of the password management policy and associated procedures can go overboard and create an environment that negatively impacts employee productivity and leads to poorer security, not better. If, for example, the frequency with which passwords are changed is too great, users might write them down or forget them. Neither of these is a desirable outcome, as the one makes it possible for an intruder to find a password and gain access to the system, and the other leads to too many people losing productivity as they have to wait for a new password to be created to allow them access again.

Disposal and Destruction

Many potential intruders have learned the value of "dumpster diving," rummaging through the target organization's trash in an attempt to find valuable information that can be used to penetrate the organization's security. An organization should be concerned with not only paper trash and discarded objects, but also the information stored on discarded objects such as computers. Several government organizations have been embarrassed when old computers sold to salvagers proved to still contain sensitive documents on their hard drives. Other dumpster diving successes have found e-mail messages or yellow sticky notes that contained passwords and user IDs. It is critical for every organization to have a strong *disposal and destruction policy* and related procedures.

Important papers should be shredded, and *important* in this case means anything that might be useful to a potential intruder. It is amazing what intruders can do with what appear to be the most innocent pieces of information.

Magnetic storage media discarded in the trash (such as disks or tapes) or sold for salvage should first have all files deleted, and then the media should be overwritten at least three times with all 1's, all 0's, and then random characters. Commercial products are available to destroy files using this process. It is not sufficient to simply delete all files and leave it at that, since the deletion process affects only the pointers to where the files are stored and doesn't actually get rid of all of the bits in the file. This is why it is possible to "undelete" files and recover them after they have been deleted.

 Cross Check

Privacy and Disposal Policies

Securely disposing of information is a key element in information security. Once properly disposed of, information is no longer available to be part of any future security incident. This concept is important enough that the FTC has imposed rules associated with destruction of personally identifiable information and other privacy-related data. Details about this are in Chapter 25. What actions do you take personally to destroy important information? At work, do you put it in the trash and assume it is taken care of by some company process? At home, what do you do with sensitive information such as medical bills and bank statements? Policies and procedures are designed to direct personal actions. Grade yourself on how well you perform with regard to destruction of sensitive information when it is no longer needed.

A safer method for destroying files on a storage device is to destroy the data magnetically by using a strong magnetic field to *degauss* the media. This effectively destroys all data on the media. Several commercial degaussers can be purchased for this purpose. Another method that you can use on hard drives is to use a file on them (the sort of file you'd find in a hardware store) and actually file off the magnetic material from the surface of the platter. Shredding floppy media is normally sufficient, but simply cutting a floppy into a few pieces is not enough—data has been successfully recovered from floppies that were cut into only a couple of pieces. CDs and DVDs also need to be disposed of appropriately. Many paper shredders now have the ability to shred these forms of storage media. In some highly secure environments, the only acceptable method of disposing of hard drives and other storage devices is the actual physical destruction of the devices.

Change Management Policy

The purpose of *change management* is to ensure proper procedures are followed when modifications to the IT infrastructure are made. These modifications can be prompted by a number of different events, including new legislation, updated versions of software or hardware, implementation of new software or hardware, or improvements to the infrastructure. The term "management" implies that this process should be controlled in some systematic way, and that is indeed the purpose. Changes to the infrastructure might have a detrimental impact on operations. New versions of operating systems or application software might be incompatible with other software or hardware the organization is using. Without a process to manage the change, an organization might suddenly find itself unable to conduct business. A change management process should include various stages, including a method to request a change to the infrastructure, a review and approval process for the request, an examination of the consequences of the change, resolution (or mitigation) of any detrimental effects the change might incur, implementation of the change, and documentation of the process as it relates to the change.

Classification of Information

A key component of IT security is the protection of the information processed and stored on the computer systems and network. Organizations deal with many different types of information, and they need to recognize that not all information is of equal importance or sensitivity. This requires classification of information into various categories, each with its own requirements for its handling. Factors that affect the classification of specific information include its value to the organization (what will be the impact to the organization if it loses this information?), its age, and laws or regulations that govern its protection. The most widely known system of classification of information is that implemented by the U.S. government (including the military), which classifies information into categories such as *Confidential, Secret,* and *Top Secret.* Businesses have similar desires to protect information and often use categories such as *Publicly Releasable, Proprietary, Company Confidential,* and *For Internal Use Only.* Each policy for the classification of information should describe how it should be protected, who may have access to it, who has the authority to release it and how, and how it should be destroyed. All employees of the organization should be trained in the procedures for handling the information that they are authorized to access. Discretionary and mandatory access control techniques use classifications as a method to identify who may have access to what resources.

Privacy

Customers place an enormous amount of trust in organizations to which they provide personal information. These customers expect their information to be kept secure so that unauthorized individuals will not gain access to it and so that authorized users will not use the information in unintended ways. Organizations should have a *privacy policy* that explains what their guiding principles will be in guarding personal data to which they are given access. In many locations, customers have a legal right to expect that their information is kept private, and organizations that violate this trust may find themselves involved in a lawsuit. In certain sectors, such as health care, federal regulations have been created that prescribe stringent security controls on private information.

It is a general practice in most organizations to have a policy that describes explicitly how information provided to the organization will be used (for example, it will not be sold to other organizations). Watchdog organizations monitor the use of individual information by organizations, and businesses can subscribe to services that will vouch for the organization to consumers, stating that the company has agreed to protect and keep private any information supplied to it. The organization is then granted permission to display a seal or certification on its web site so that customers can see it. Organizations that misuse the information they promised to protect will find themselves subject to penalties from the watchdog organization. A special category of private information that is becoming increasingly important today is personally identifiable information (PII). This category of information includes any data that can be used to uniquely identify an individual. This would include an individual's name, address, driver's license number, and other details. With the proliferation of e-commerce on the Internet, this information is used extensively and its protection has become increasingly important. You would not have to look far to find reports in the media of data compromises that have resulted in the loss of information that has led to issues such as identity theft. An organization that collects PII on its employees and customers must make sure that it takes all necessary measures to protect the data from compromise.

 The issue of individual privacy has become increasingly important in the past decade. Several laws (with appropriate penalties for failure to follow them) have been created to help ensure that the privacy of personally identifiable information is maintained. Some sectors, such as the health care sector, have laws that mandate that they tell customers (patients) how their information will be used and protected. Even in sectors that are not covered by state or federal regulations, a privacy policy should be developed describing how both employee and customer information will be handled.

Service Level Agreements

A **service level agreement (SLA)** is a contractual agreement between entities describing specified levels of service that the servicing entity agrees to guarantee for the customer. These agreements not only clearly lay out expectations in terms of the service provided and support expected, but also generally include penalties should the described level of service or support not be provided. An organization contracting with a service provider should include in the agreement a section describing the service provider's responsibility in terms of business continuity and disaster recovery. The provider's backup plans and processes for restoring lost data should also be clearly described.

Human Resources Policies

It has been said that the weakest links in the security chain are the humans. Consequently, it is important for organizations to have policies in place in relation to its employees. Policies that relate to the hiring of individuals are primarily important. The organization needs to make sure that it hires individuals who can be trusted with the organization's data and that of its clients. Once employees are hired, they should be kept from slipping into the category of "disgruntled employee." Finally, policies must be developed to address the inevitable point in the future when an employee leaves the organization—either on her own or with the "encouragement" of the organization itself. Security issues must be considered at each of these points.

Employee Hiring and Promotions

It is becoming common for organizations to run background checks on prospective employees and check the references they supply. Drug tests, records of any past criminal activity, claimed educational background, and reported work history are all frequently checked today. For highly sensitive environments, security background checks are also typically required. Make sure that your organization hires the most capable and trustworthy employees, and that your policies are designed to ensure this.

After an individual has been hired, your organization needs to minimize the risk that the employee will ignore company rules that could affect security. Periodic reviews by supervisory personnel, additional drug checks, and monitoring of activity during work may all be considered by the organization. If the organization chooses to implement any of these reviews, this must be specified in the organization's policies, and prospective employees should be made aware of these policies before being hired. What an organization can do in terms of monitoring and requiring drug tests, for example, can be severely restricted if not spelled out in advance as terms of employment. New hires should be made aware of all pertinent policies, especially those applying to security, and they should be asked to sign documents indicating that they have read and understand them.

Occasionally an employee's status will change within the company. If the change can be construed as a negative personnel action (such as a demotion), supervisors should be alerted to watch for changes in behavior that might indicate the employee is contemplating or conducting unauthorized activity. The employee likely will be upset, and the possibility that he will act on this to the detriment of the company is something that needs to be guarded against. In the case of a demotion, the individual may also lose certain privileges or access rights, and these changes should be made quickly so as to lessen the likelihood that the employee will destroy previously accessible data if he becomes disgruntled and decides to take revenge on the organization. On the other hand, if the employee is promoted, privileges may still change, but the need to make the change to access privileges may not be as urgent, though it should still be accomplished as quickly as possible. If the move is a lateral one, changes may also need to take place, and again they should be accomplished as quickly as possible. The organization's goals in terms of making changes to access privileges should be clearly spelled out in its policies.

Retirement, Separation, or Termination of an Employee

An employee leaving an organization can be either a positive or a negative action. Employees who are retiring by their own choice may announce their

Tech Tip

Hiring Hackers
While hiring a skilled hacker may make sense from a technical skills point of view, an organization also has to consider the broader ethical and business consequences and associated risks. Is the hacker completely reformed or not? How much time is needed to determine this? The real question is not "Would you hire a hacker?" but rather "Can you fire a hacker once he has had access to your systems?" Trust is an important issue with employees who have system administrator access, and the long-term ramifications need to be considered.

Many organizations overlook the security implications that decisions by human resources may have. Human resources personnel and security personnel should have a close working relationship. Decisions on the hiring and firing of personnel have direct security implications for the organization. As a result, procedures should be in place that specify which actions must be taken when an employee is hired, is terminated, or retires.

planned retirement weeks or months in advance. Limiting their access to sensitive documents the moment they announce their intention may be the safest thing to do, but it might not be necessary. Each situation should be evaluated individually. If the situation is a forced retirement, the organization must determine the risk to its data if the employee becomes disgruntled as a result of the action. In this situation, the wisest choice might be to cut off their access quickly and provide them with some additional vacation time. This might seem like an expensive proposition, but the danger to the company of having a disgruntled employee can justify it. Again, each case should be evaluated individually.

When an employee decides to leave a company, generally as a result of a new job offer, the organization should carefully consider her continued access to sensitive information. If the employee is leaving as a result of hard feelings for the company, the wise choice might be to revoke her access privileges quickly. If she is leaving as a result of a better job offer, you may decide to allow her to transfer her projects gracefully to other employees, but the decision should be considered very carefully, especially if the new company is a competitor.

If the employee is leaving the organization because she is being terminated, you should plan on her becoming disgruntled. While it may not seem the friendliest thing to do, an employee in this situation should immediately have her access privileges to sensitive information and facilities revoked. Access cards, keys, and badges should be collected; the employee should be escorted to her desk and watched as she packs her personal belongings; and then she should be escorted from the building. Combinations should also be quickly changed. Giving somebody several weeks of paid vacation is better than having a disgruntled employee trash sensitive files they have access to.

 Exam Tip: It is not uncommon for organizations to neglect having a policy that covers the removal of an individual's computer access upon termination. This policy should also include the procedures to reclaim and "clean" a terminated employee's computer system and accounts.

No matter what the situation, the organization should have policies that describe the intended goals, and should have procedures that detail the process to be followed for each of the described situations.

Mandatory Vacations

Organizations have provided vacation time to their employees for many years. Few, however, force employees to take this time if they don't want to. At some companies, employees are given the choice to either "use or lose" their vacation time; if they do not take all of their vacation time, they lose at least a portion of it. From a security standpoint, an employee who never takes time off might be involved in nefarious activity, such as fraud or embezzlement, and might be afraid that if they leave on vacation, the organization will discover their illicit activities. As a result, requiring employees to use their vacation time through a policy of mandatory vacations can be a security protection mechanism.

Code of Ethics

Numerous professional organizations have established codes of ethics for their members. Each of these describes the expected behavior of their members from a high-level standpoint. Organizations can adopt this idea as well. For organizations, a code of ethics can set the tone for how employees will be expected to act and to conduct business. The code should demand honesty from employees and require that they perform all activities in a professional manner. The code could also address principles of privacy and confidentiality and state how employees should treat client and organizational data. Conflicts of interest can often cause problems, so this could also be covered in the code of ethics.

By outlining a code of ethics, the organization can encourage an environment that is conducive to integrity and high ethical standards. For additional ideas on possible codes of ethics, check professional organizations such as the Institute for Electrical and Electronics Engineers (IEEE), the Association for Computing Machinery (ACM), or the Information Systems Security Association (ISSA).

Incident Response Policies and Procedures

No matter how careful an organization is, eventually a security incident of some sort will occur. When it happens, how effectively the organization responds to it will depend greatly on how prepared it is to handle incidents. An **incident response policy** and associated procedures should be developed to outline how the organization will prepare for security incidents and respond to them when they occur. Waiting until an incident happens is not the right time to establish your policies—they need to be designed in advance. The incident response policy should cover five phases: preparation, detection, containment and eradication, recovery, and follow-up actions.

Preparation

Preparing for an incident is the first phase. The organization needs to establish the steps to be taken when an incident is discovered (or suspected); determine points of contact; train all employees and security professionals so they understand the steps to take and who to call; establish an incident response team; acquire the equipment necessary to detect, contain, and recover from an incident; establish the procedures and guidelines for the use of the equipment obtained; and train those who will use the equipment. During this phase, any additional specialized training in areas such as computer forensics that is determined to be necessary should also be accomplished as well as general user training in areas such as social engineering.

The incident response team is a critical part of the incident response plan. Team membership will vary depending on the type of incident or suspected incident, but may include the following members:

- Team lead
- Network/security analyst
- Internal and/or external subject matter experts
- Legal counsel
- Public affairs officer
- Security office contact

In determining the specific makeup of the team for a specific incident, there are some general points to think about. The team needs a leader, preferably a higher-level manager who has the ability to obtain cooperation from employees as needed. It also needs a computer or network security analyst, since the assumption is that the team will be responding to a computer security incident. Specialists may be added to the team for specific hardware or software platforms as needed. The organization's legal counsel should be part of the team on at least a part-time or as-needed basis. The public affairs office should also be available on an as-needed basis, because it is responsible for formulating the public response should a security incident become public. The organization's security office should also be kept informed. It should designate a point of contact for the team in case criminal activity is suspected. In this case, care must be taken to preserve evidence, should the organization decide to push for prosecution of the individual.

This is by no means a complete list, as each organization is different and needs to evaluate what the best mixture is for its own response team. Whatever the decision, the composition of the team, and how and when it will be formed, needs to be clearly addressed in the preparation phase of the incident response policy.

Detection

Of course, an incident response team can't begin an investigation until a suspected incident has been detected. At that point, the detection phase of the incident response policy kicks in. One of the first jobs of the incident response team is to determine whether an actual security incident has occurred. Many things can be misinterpreted as a possible security incident. For example, a software bug in an application may cause a user to lose a file, and the user may blame this on a virus or similar malicious software. The incident response team must investigate each reported incident and treat it as a possible security incident until it can determine whether it is or isn't. This means that your organization will want to respond initially with a limited response team before wasting a lot of time having the full team respond. This is the initial step to take when a report is received that a possible incident has been detected.

Security incidents can take a variety of forms, and who discovers the incident will vary as well. One of the groups most likely to discover an incident is the team of network and security administrators who run devices such as the organization's firewalls and intrusion detection systems. To ensure that discovering incidents is not an ad hoc, hit-or-miss proposition, the organization needs to establish procedures that describe the process administrators must follow to monitor for possible security events. The tools for accomplishing this need to be identified during the preparation phase, as well as any required training to operate the equipment. The procedures governing the monitoring tools used should be established as part of the specific guidelines governing the use of the tools but should include references to the incident response policy.

Another common incident is a virus. Several packages are available that can help an organization discover potential virus activity or other malicious code. Administrators will often be the ones to notice something is amiss, but so might an average user who has been hit by the virus. Again, the appropriate hardware, software, and training needs to be acquired during the preparation phase.

Social engineering is a common technique used by potential intruders to acquire information that may be useful in gaining access to computer systems, networks, or the physical facilities that house them. Anybody in the

Detecting that a security event is occurring or has occurred is not necessarily an easy matter. In certain situations, such as the activation of a malicious payload for a virus or worm that deletes critical files, it will be obvious that an event has occurred. In other situations, such as where an individual has penetrated your system and has been slowly copying critical files without changing or destroying anything, the event may take a lot longer to detect. Often, the first indication that a security event has occurred might be a user or administrator noticing that something is "funny" about the system or its response.

organization can be the target of a social engineering attack, so all employees need to know what to be looking for regarding this type of attack. In fact, the target might not even be one of your organization's employees—it could be a contractor, such as somebody on the custodial staff or nighttime security staff. To thwart social engineering attacks, training is essential, and the organization should have a policy on who will be required to receive this type of training and how frequently they should receive it.

Whatever the type of security incident suspected, and no matter who suspects it, a reporting procedure needs to be in place for the employees to use when an incident is detected. Everybody needs to know who to call should they suspect something, and everybody needs to know what to do. A common technique is to develop a reporting template that can be supplied to an individual who suspects an incident, so that the necessary information is gathered in a timely manner.

Containment and Eradication

Once the incident response team has determined that an incident most likely has occurred, it must attempt to quickly contain the problem. At this point, or very soon after containment begins, depending on the severity of the incident, management needs to decide whether the organization intends to prosecute the individual who has caused the incident, in which case collection and preservation of evidence is necessary, or simply wants to restore operations as quickly as possible without regard to possibly destroying evidence. In certain circumstances, management might not have a choice, such as if specific regulations or laws require it to report incidents. If management makes the decision to prosecute, specific procedures need to be followed in handling potential evidence. Individuals trained in forensics should be used in this case.

The incident response team must decide how to address containment as soon as it has determined that an actual incident has occurred. If an intruder is still connected to the organization's system, one response is to disconnect from the Internet until the system can be restored and vulnerabilities can be patched. This, however, means that your organization is not accessible to customers over the Internet during that time, which may result in lost revenue. Another response might be to stay connected and attempt to determine the origin of the intruder. A decision will need to be made as to which is more important for your organization. Your incident response policy should identify who is authorized to make this decision.

Other possible containment activities might include adding filtering rules or modifying existing rules on firewalls, routers, and intrusion detection systems, updating antivirus software, and removing specific pieces of hardware or halting specific software applications. If an intruder has gained access through a specific account, disabling or removing that account may also be necessary.

Once the immediate problems have been contained, the incident response team needs to address the cause of the incident. If the incident is the result of a vulnerability that was not patched, the patch must be obtained, tested, and applied. Accounts may need to be deleted or passwords may need to be changed. Completely reloading the entire operating system might be necessary if the intruder has been in the system for an unknown length of time or has modified system files. Determining when an intruder first gained access to your system or network is critical in determining how far back to go in restoring the system or network.

Recovery

The major thrust of this chapter has been on business continuity and the quick recovery of operations. After the incident has been contained and any malicious software or vulnerabilities have been taken care of, it may be necessary to implement your BCP should the incident result in a disruption to your operations. Again, the goal here is to restore the organization quickly to normal processing. An important first step before this can occur is the determination of what actually happened. What files have been modified or deleted? What processes were disrupted? What files or programs were created and what unauthorized e-mail may have been sent out? Answering these questions will enable the organization to focus its recovery processes on the most critical aspects.

Follow-Up Actions

Once the excitement of the incident is over and operations have been restored to their pre-incident state, it is time to take care of a few last items. Senior-level management must be informed about what occurred and what was done to address it. An after-action report should be created to outline what happened and how it was addressed. Recommendations for improving processes and policies should be incorporated so that a repeat incident will not occur. If prosecution of the individual responsible is desired, additional time will be spent helping law enforcement agencies and possibly testifying in court. Training material may also need to be developed or modified as part of the new, modified policies and procedures.

■ Chapter Summary

After reading this chapter and completing the exercises, you should understand the following regarding disaster recovery, business continuity, and organizational policies.

Describe the various ways backups are conducted and stored

■ Backups should include not only the organization's critical data but critical software as well.

■ Backups may be conducted by backing up all files (full backup), only the files that have changed since the last full backup (differential backup), only the files that have changed since the last full or differential backup (incremental backup), or only the portion of the files that has changed since the last delta or full backup (delta backup).

■ Backups should be stored both onsite for quick access if needed as well as offsite in case a disaster destroys the primary facility, its processing equipment, and the backups that are stored onsite.

Explain different strategies for alternative site processing

■ Plans should be created to continue operations at an alternative site if a disaster damages or destroys a facility.

■ Possibilities for an alternative site include hot, warm, and cold sites.

■ Developing a mutual aid agreement with a similar organization that could host your operations for a brief period of time after a disaster is another alternative.

Describe the various components of a business continuity plan

■ A business continuity plan should contemplate the many types of disasters that can cause a disruption to an organization.

■ A business impact assessment (BIA) can be conducted to identify the most critical functions for an organization.

■ A disaster recovery plan outlines an organization's plans to recover in the event a disaster strikes.

■ A business continuity plan is created to outline the order in which business functions will be restored so that the most critical functions are restored first.

■ One of the most critical elements of any disaster recovery plan is the availability of system backups.

Explain how policies and procedures play a daily role in addressing the security needs of an organization

■ Policies are high-level, broad statements of what the organization wants to accomplish. They are made by management when laying out the organization's position on some issue.

■ Standard policies that most organizations create include acceptable use, Internet usage, and e-mail usage policies.

■ Human resources policies are important to ensure that an employee who is being terminated or otherwise leaving the company does not pose an unacceptable risk to the organization.

■ Incident response policies are critical to outline, in advance, the steps the organization will take to respond to a security incident.

■ Drills and exercises play an important role because they allow personnel to practice the procedures the organization has established to respond to a security incident.

■ Key Terms

acceptable use policy (AUP) *(507)*
business continuity plan (BCP) *(495)*
business impact assessment (BIA) *(494)*

cold site *(501)*
delta backup *(498)*
differential backup *(497)*

disater recovery plan (DRP) *(493)*
due care *(509)*
due diligence *(509)*
fault tolerance *(503)*
full backup *(497)*
high availability *(503)*
hot site *(501)*
incident response policy *(516)*
incremental backup *(497)*

least privilege *(510)*
mutual aid agreement *(501)*
policies *(506)*
procedures *(506)*
separation of duties *(509)*
service level agreement (SLA) *(513)*
standards *(506)*
warm site *(501)*

■ Key Terms Quiz

Use terms from the Key Terms list to complete the sentences that follow. Don't use the same term more than once. Not all terms will be used.

1. Instructions that describe exactly how employees are expected to act in a given situation or to accomplish a specific task are known as _____.

2. A(n) _____ is a partially configured backup processing facility that usually has the peripherals and software but perhaps not the more expensive main processing computer.

3. A backup that includes only the files that have changed since the last full backup was completed is called a(n) _____.

4. A(n) _____ is an evaluation of the impact that a loss of critical functions will have on the organization.

5. A rule used in many organizations to ensure that no single individual has the ability to conduct transactions alone is _____.

6. _____ are accepted specifications that provide specific details on how a policy is to be enforced.

7. An agreement in which similar organizations agree to assume the processing for the other in the event a disaster occurs is known as a(n) _____.

8. The principle that states each individual will be granted only the bare minimum number of privileges needed to perform her job is called _____.

9. A(n) _____ is a fully configured backup environment that is similar to the normal operating environment and that can be operational within a few hours.

10. _____ is a method to ensure high availability that is accomplished by the mirroring of data and systems. Should an event occur that causes disruption in a device, the mirrored system provides the requested data, with no apparent interruption in service.

■ Multiple-Choice Quiz

1. Why is it important that security exercises be conducted?
   A. To provide the opportunity for all parties to practice the procedures that have been established to respond to a security incident.
   B. To determine if the organization's plan and the individuals involved perform as they should during a simulated security incident.
   C. To determine if processes developed to handle security incidents are sufficient for the organization.
   D. All of the above.

2. A good backup plan will include which of the following?
   A. The critical data needed for the organization to operate
   B. Any software that is required to process the organization's data

C. Specific hardware to run the software or to process the data

D. All of the above

3. In which backup strategy are only those portions of the files and software that have changed since the last backup backed up?

A. Full

B. Differential

C. Incremental

D. Delta

4. Which of the following is a consideration in calculating the cost of a backup strategy?

A. The cost of the backup media

B. The storage costs for the backup media

C. The frequency with which backups are created

D. All of the above

5. Which of the following is the name for a partially configured environment that has the peripherals and software that the normal processing facility contains and that can be operational within a few days?

A. Hot site

B. Warm site

C. Online storage system

D. Backup storage facility

6. Which of the following is considered an issue with long-term storage of magnetic media, as discussed in the chapter?

A. Tape media can be used a limited number of times before it degrades.

B. Software and hardware evolve, and the media stored may no longer be compatible with current technology.

C. Both A and B.

D. None of the above.

7. What is the first phase in an incident response policy?

A. Detection of an incident

B. Containment and eradication

C. Preparation

D. Recovery

8. What common utility or infrastructure is important to consider when developing your recovery plans?

A. Transportation

B. Oil and gas

C. Communications

D. Television/cable

9. Standards are:

A. High-level statements made by management

B. Statements that lay out the organization's position on some issue

C. Mandatory but not specific in their details

D. All of the above

E. None of the above

10. For organizations that draw a distinction between a BCP and a DRP, which of the following is true?

A. The BCP details the functions that are most critical and outlines the order in which critical functions should be returned to service to maintain business operations.

B. The BCP is a subset of the DRP.

C. The DRP outlines the minimum set of business functions required for the organization to continue functioning.

D. The DRP is always developed first and the BCP normally is an attachment to this document.

11. A business impact assessment (BIA) is conducted to

A. Outline the order in which critical functions should be returned to service to maintain business operations

B. Identify the most critical functions for an organization

C. Identify the critical employees who must be onsite to implement the BCP

D. Establish the policies governing the organization's backup policy

12. What is one of the first tasks that an incident response team must accomplish when an incident is suspected?

   A. Notify the head of the organization that an incident has occurred and that the incident response team has been activated.

   B. Determine whether an incident has occurred.

   C. Contact the applicable local, state, or federal law enforcement agency.

   D. Secure all systems and disconnect affected systems from the Internet.

■ Essay Quiz

1. Write a paragraph outlining the differences between a disaster recovery plan and a business continuity plan. Is one more important than the other?

2. Write a brief description of the different backup strategies. Be sure to include a discussion of which of these strategies requires the greatest amount of storage space to conduct and which of the strategies involves the most complicated restoration scheme.

3. Your boss recently attended a seminar in which the importance of creating and maintaining a backup of critical data was discussed. He suggested to you that you immediately make a tape backup of all data, place it in a metal box, lock it, and bury it in your backyard. You don't agree with this specific method, but you need to develop a plan that he will understand and find persuasive. Write a proposal describing your recommendations, making sure to include the issues involved with the long-term storage of backups.

4. Describe the difference in procedures an organization might use in the case of an employee retiring, an employing leaving to go to work with another organization, and an employee who is being terminated for poor performance. Using the Internet, research an example of a real-world instance in which an employee or ex-employee caused damage to a company. Summarize your findings.

5. Write a brief essay outlining the steps an organization might take when responding to a computer security incident.

Lab Projects

• Lab Project 19.1

The Windows XP, Vista, and 7 operating systems provide administrators with the ability to set a number of security policies. Identify some of the more common security settings for the Windows environment. How do you set these policies in Windows XP, Vista, and 7?

• Lab Project 19.2

Obtain copies of the acceptable use, e-mail, and Internet policies for your school or organization as well as its privacy policy (you may be able to find them on the school's or organization's web site). Compare the contents of the polices with what you have learned in this chapter should be included. Do you consider the policies sufficient for your environment? If not, what suggestions might you have to improve them?

Risk Management

A ship is safe in harbor, but that's not what ships are for.

—WILLIAM SHEDD

In this chapter, you will learn how to

- **Use risk management tools and principles to manage risk effectively**
- **Explain the differences between qualitative and quantitative risk assessment**
- **Describe essential risk management tools**

Risk management can best be described as a decision-making process. In the simplest terms, when you manage risk, you determine what could happen to your business, you assess the impact if it were to happen, and you decide what you could do to control that impact as much as you or your management deems necessary. You then decide to act or not to act, and, finally, you evaluate the results of your decision. The process may be iterative, as industry best practices clearly indicate that an important aspect of effectively managing risk is to consider it an ongoing process.

Cross Check

Change Management and Risk Management Are Critical Management Tools

Risk management is one of the reasons behind change management. Change management is a process designed to enable management efforts to understand implications of changes prior to incorporation in production systems. When someone requests a change to production, do they have answers to questions such as these:

1. What are the security implications of this change?

2. What is the back-out plan in the event the change causes unintentional problems?

For more detail, the reader is directed to Chapter 21, which explains details of change management as a critical management tool.

An Overview of Risk Management

Risk management is an essential element of management from the enterprise level down to the individual project. Risk management encompasses all the actions taken to reduce complexity, increase objectivity, and identify important decision factors. There has been, and will continue to be, discussion about the complexity of risk management and whether or not it is worth the effort. Businesses must take risks to retain their competitive edge, however, and as a result, risk management must occur as part of managing any business, program, or project.

Risk management is both a skill and a task that is performed by all managers, either deliberately or intuitively. It can be simple or complex, depending on the size of the project or business and the amount of risk inherent in an activity. Every manager, at all levels, must learn to manage risk. The required skills can be learned.

> Risk management is about making a business profitable—not about buying insurance.

> **Exam Tip:** This chapter contains several bulleted lists. These are designed for easy memorization in preparation for taking the Security+ exam.

Example of Risk Management at the International Banking Level

The Basel Committee on Banking Supervision comprises government central-bank governors from around the world. This body created a basic, global risk management framework for market and credit risk. It implemented internationally a flat 8 percent capital charge to banks to manage bank risks. In layman's terms, this means that for every $100 a bank makes in loans, it must possess $8 in reserve to be used in the event of financial difficulties. However, if banks can show they have very strong risk mitigation procedures and controls in place, that capital charge can be reduced to as low as $0.37 (0.37 percent). If a bank has poor procedures and controls, that capital charge can be as high as $45 (45 percent) for every $100 the bank makes. See www.bis.org/bcbs/ for source documentation regarding the Basel Committee.

This example shows that risk management can be and is used at very high levels—the remainder of this chapter focuses on smaller implementations and demonstrates that risk management is used in many aspects of business conduct.

Risk Management Vocabulary

You need to understand a number of key terms to manage risk successfully. Some of these terms are defined here because they are used throughout the chapter. This list is somewhat ordered according to the organization of this chapter. More comprehensive definitions and other pertinent terms are listed alphabetically in the glossary at the end of this book.

Risk Risk is the possibility of suffering harm or loss.

Risk management Risk management is the overall decision-making process of identifying threats and vulnerabilities and their potential impacts, determining the costs to mitigate such events, and deciding what actions are cost effective for controlling these risks.

Risk assessment Risk assessment is the process of analyzing an environment to identify the risks (threats and vulnerabilities) and mitigating actions to determine (either quantitatively or qualitatively) the impact of an event that would affect a project, program, or business. Also referred to as risk analysis.

Asset An asset is any resource or information an organization needs to conduct its business.

Threat A threat is any circumstance or event with the potential to cause harm to an asset. For example, a malicious hacker might choose to hack your system by using readily available hacking tools.

Vulnerability A vulnerability is any characteristic of an asset that can be exploited by a threat to cause harm. Your system has a security vulnerability, for example, if you have not installed patches to fix a cross-site scripting (XSS) error on your web site.

Impact Impact is the loss resulting when a threat exploits a vulnerability. A malicious hacker (the threat) uses an XSS tool to hack your unpatched web site (the vulnerability), stealing credit card information that is used fraudulently. The credit card company pursues legal recourse against your company to recover the losses from the credit card fraud (the impact).

Control A control is a measure taken to detect, prevent, or mitigate the risk associated with a threat. Also called countermeasure or safeguard.

Qualitative risk assessment Qualitative risk assessment is the process of subjectively determining the impact of an event that affects a project, program, or business. Completing the assessment usually involves the use of expert judgment, experience, or group consensus.

Tech Tip

Types of Controls

Controls can be classified based on the types of actions they perform. Three classes of controls exist:

- *Administrative*
- *Technical*
- *Physical*

For each of these classes, there are four types of controls:

- *Preventive (Deterrent)*
- *Detective*
- *Corrective (recovery)*
- *Compensating*

Quantitative risk assessment **Quantitative risk assessment** is the process of objectively determining the impact of an event that affects a project, program, or business. Completing the assessment usually involves the use of metrics and models.

Mitigate The term **mitigate** refers to taking action to reduce the likelihood of a threat occurring.

Single loss expectancy (SLE) The **single loss expectancy (SLE)** is the monetary loss or impact of each occurrence of a threat.

Exposure factor **Exposure factor** is a measure of the magnitude of loss of an asset. Used in the calculation of single loss expectancy.

Annualized rate of occurrence (ARO) **Annualized rate of occurrence (ARO)** is the frequency with which an event is expected to occur on an annualized basis.

Annualized loss expectancy (ALE) **Annualized loss expectancy (ALE)** is how much an event is expected to cost per year.

The distinction between qualitative and quantitative risk assessment will be more apparent as you read the section "Qualitative vs. Quantitative Risk Assessment" later in the chapter.

Exam Tip: These terms are important, and you should completely memorize their meanings before taking the Security+ exam.

■ What Is Risk Management?

Three definitions relating to risk management reveal why it is sometimes considered difficult to understand:

- The dictionary defines *risk* as the possibility of suffering harm or loss.

- Carnegie Mellon University's Software Engineering Institute (SEI) defines *continuous risk management* as "processes, methods, and tools for managing risks in a project. It provides a disciplined environment for proactive decision-making to 1) assess continuously what could go wrong (risks); 2) determine which risks are important to deal with; and 3) implement strategies to deal with those risks" (SEI, *Continuous Risk Management Guidebook* [Pittsburgh, PA: Carnegie Mellon University, 1996], 22).

- The Information Systems Audit and Control Association (ISACA) says, "In modern business terms, risk management is the process of identifying vulnerabilities and threats to an organization's resources and assets and deciding what countermeasures, if any, to take to reduce the level of risk to an acceptable level based on the value of the asset to the organization" (ISACA, *Certified Information Systems Auditor (CISA) Review Manual, 2002* [Rolling Meadows, IL: ISACA, 2002], 344).

These three definitions show that risk management is based on what can go wrong and what action should be taken, if any. Figure 20.1 provides a macro-level view of how to manage risk.

Tech Tip

Risk Management Applies to All Business Processes
Even Human Resource Management relies on risk management. For example, risk management used to say that older workers could create liabilities. Recent studies have shown that as the workforce ages, it has become apparent that older workers have lower absenteeism, are more productive, and have higher levels of job satisfaction. Their greatest risk is longer recovery time from accidents—companies are finding ways to prevent accidents to manage that risk.

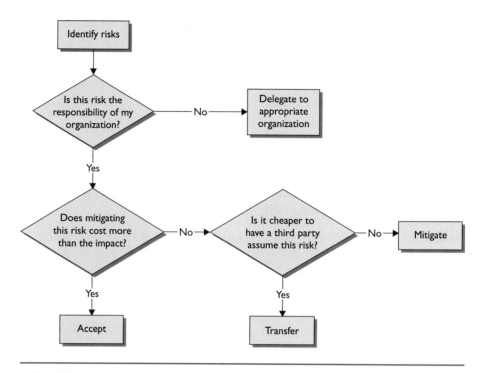

● **Figure 20.1** A planning decision flowchart for risk management

▰ Business Risks

No comprehensive identification of all risks in a business environment is possible. In today's technology-dependent business environment, risk is often simplistically divided into two areas: business risk and, a major subset, technology risk.

Examples of Business Risks

Following are some of the most common business risks:

- **Treasury management**   Management of company holdings in bonds, futures, currencies, and so on.

- **Revenue management**   Management of consumer behavior and the generation of revenue.

- **Contract management**   Management of contracts with customers, vendors, partners, and so on.

- **Fraud**   Deliberate deception made for personal gain, to obtain property or services, and so on.

- **Environmental risk management**   Management of risks associated with factors that affect the environment.

- **Regulatory risk management**   Management of risks arising from new or existing regulations.

- **Business continuity management**   Management of risks associated with recovering and restoring business functions after a disaster or major disruption occurs.
- **Technology**   Management of risks associated with technology in its many forms.

Examples of Technology Risks

Following are some of the most common technology risks:

- **Security and privacy**   The risks associated with protecting personal, private, or confidential information.
- **Information technology operations**   The risks associated with the day-to-day operation of information technology systems.
- **Business systems control and effectiveness**   The risks associated with manual and automated controls that safeguard company assets and resources.
- **Business continuity management**   The risks associated with the technology and processes to be used in event of a disaster or major disruption.
- **Information systems testing**   The risks associated with testing processes and procedures of information systems.
- **Reliability and performance management**   The risks associated with meeting reliability and performance agreements and measures.
- **Information technology asset management**   The risks associated with safeguarding information technology physical assets.
- **Project risk management**   The risks associated with managing information technology projects.
- **Change management**   The risks associated with managing configurations and changes (see Chapter 21).

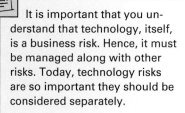

It is important that you understand that technology, itself, is a business risk. Hence, it must be managed along with other risks. Today, technology risks are so important they should be considered separately.

Tech Tip

Risk According to the Basel Committee
The Basel Committee referenced earlier in the chapter has defined three types of risk specifically to address international banking:

- *Market risk*   *Risk of losses due to fluctuation of market prices*
- *Credit risk*   *Risk of default of outstanding loans*
- *Operational risk*   *Risk from disruption by people, systems, processes, or disasters*

Risk Management Models

Risk management concepts are fundamentally the same despite their definitions, and they require similar skills, tools, and methodologies. Several models can be used for managing risk through its various phases. Two models are presented here: the first can be applied to managing risks in general, and the second is tailored for managing risk in software projects.

General Risk Management Model

The following five steps can be used in virtually any risk management process. Following these steps will lead to an orderly process of analyzing and mitigating risks.

Key Performance Indicators (KPIs)

The development of KPIs to monitor performance of systems and processes is critical to effective risk management. If you can't measure it, you have to rely on more subjective measures. Examples of KPIs for an enterprise resource planning (ERP) system such as Oracle E-Business Suite or SAP Business Suite could include:

Business KPI	Measures Growth of the Number of...
GL Business Unit growth	General Ledger (GL) Business Units (BUs) over time
AP Business Unit growth	Accounts Payable (AP) BUs over time
Purchasing Business Unit growth	Purchasing BUs over time
Project Costing Business Unit growth	Project Costing BUs over time
Asset Mgt Business Unit growth	Asset Mgt BUs over time
GL Transaction growth	GL Transactions in major tables over time
GL Journal Header growth	GL Journal Header entries over time
GL Journal Line growth	Journal Line entries over time
AP Voucher Header growth	AP Voucher Header entries over time
AP Voucher Line growth	AP Voucher Line entries over time
PO Transaction growth	Purchase Order (PO) Transactions over time
PO Line Transaction growth	PO Line Transactions over time
Asset Mgt Transaction growth	Asset Mgt Transactions over time

Step 1. Asset Identification

Identify and classify the assets, systems, and processes that need protection because they are vulnerable to threats. Use a classification that fits your business. This classification leads to the ability to prioritize assets, systems, and processes and to evaluate the costs of addressing the associated risks. Assets can include

- Inventory
- Buildings
- Cash
- Information and data
- Hardware
- Software
- Services
- Documents
- Personnel
- Brand recognition
- Organization reputation
- Goodwill

Step 2: Threat Assessment

After identifying the assets, you identify both the possible threats and the possible vulnerabilities associated with each asset and the likelihood of their occurrence. Threats can be defined as any circumstance or event with the potential to cause harm to an asset. Common classes of threats include (with examples):

- **Natural disasters**   Hurricane, earthquake, lightning, and so on.
- **Man-made disasters**   Earthen dam failure, such as the 1976 Teton Dam failure in Idaho; car accident that destroys a municipal power distribution transformer; the 1973 explosion of a railcar containing propane gas in Kingman, Arizona.
- **Terrorism**   The 2001 destruction of the World Trade Center, the 1995 gas attack on the Shinjuku train station in Tokyo.
- **Errors**   Employee not following safety or configuration management procedures.
- **Malicious damage or attacks**   A disgruntled employee purposely corrupting data files.
- **Fraud**   An employee falsifying travel expenses or vendor invoices and payments.
- **Theft**   An employee stealing from the loading dock a laptop computer after it has been inventoried but not properly secured.
- **Equipment or software failure**   An error in the calculation of a company-wide bonus overpaying employees.

Vulnerabilities are characteristics of resources that can be exploited by a threat to cause harm. Common classes of vulnerabilities include (with examples):

- **Unprotected facilities**   Company offices with no security officer present or no card-entry system.
- **Unprotected computer systems**   A server temporarily connected to the network before being properly configured/secured.
- **Unprotected data**   Not installing critical security patches to eliminate application security vulnerabilities.
- **Insufficient procedures and controls**   Allowing an accounts payable clerk to create vendors in the accounting system, enter invoices, and authorize check payments.
- **Insufficient or unqualified personnel**   A junior employee not sufficiently securing a server due to a lack of training.

Step 3: Impact Determination and Quantification

An impact is the loss created when a threat exploits a vulnerability. When a threat is realized, it turns risk into impact. Impacts can be either tangible or intangible. A **tangible impact** results in financial loss or physical damage. For an **intangible impact**, assigning a financial value of the impact can be difficult. For example, in a manufacturing facility, storing and using flammable chemicals creates a risk of fire to the facility. The vulnerability is that flammable chemicals are stored there. The threat would be that a person could cause a fire by mishandling the chemicals (either intentionally or unintentionally). A tangible impact would be the loss incurred (say $500,000) if a person ignites the chemicals and fire then destroys part of the facility. An example of an intangible impact would be the loss of goodwill or brand damage caused by the impression that the company doesn't safely protect its employees or the surrounding geographic area.

Tangible impacts include

- Direct loss of money
- Endangerment of staff or customers
- Loss of business opportunity
- Reduction in operational efficiency or performance
- Interruption of a business activity

Intangible impacts include

- Breach of legislation or regulatory requirements
- Loss of reputation or goodwill (brand damage)
- Breach of confidence

Step 4: Control Design and Evaluation

In this step, you determine which controls to put in place to mitigate the risks. Controls (also called countermeasures or safeguards) are designed to control risk by reducing vulnerabilities to an acceptable level. (For use in this text, the terms *control*, *countermeasure*, and *safeguard* are considered synonymous and are used interchangeably.)

Controls can be actions, devices, or procedures. They can be preventive or detective. *Preventive controls* are designed to prevent the vulnerability from causing an impact. *Detective controls* are those that detect a vulnerability that has been exploited so that action can be taken.

Step 5: Residual Risk Management

Understand that risk cannot be completely eliminated. A risk that remains after implementing controls is termed a **residual risk**. In this step, you further evaluate residual risks to identify where additional controls are required to reduce risk even more. This leads us to the earlier statement that the risk management process is iterative.

Software Engineering Institute Model

In an approach tailored for managing risk in software projects, SEI uses the following paradigm (SEI, *Continuous Risk Management Guidebook* [Pittsburgh, PA: Carnegie Mellon University, 1996], 23). Although the terminology varies slightly from the previous model, the relationships are apparent, and either model can be applied wherever risk management is used.

1. **Identify**—Look for risks before they become problems.
2. **Analyze**—Convert the data gathered into information that can be used to make decisions. Evaluate the impact, probability, and timeframe of the risks. Classify and prioritize each of the risks.
3. **Plan**—Review and evaluate the risks and decide what actions to take to mitigate them. Implement those mitigating actions.
4. **Track**—Monitor the risks and the mitigation plans. Trends may provide information to activate plans and contingencies. Review periodically to measure progress and identify new risks.
5. **Control**—Make corrections for deviations from the risk mitigation plans. Correct products and processes as required. Changes in business procedures may require adjustments in plans or actions, as do faulty plans and risks that become problems.

Tech Tip

Can All Risks Be Identified?

It is important to note that not all risks need to be mitigated or controlled; however, as many risks as possible should be identified and reviewed. Those deemed to have potential impact should be mitigated by countermeasures.

Model Application

The two model examples define steps that can be used in any general or software risk management process. These risk management principles can be applied to any project, program, or business activity, no matter how simple or complex. Figure 20.2 shows how risk management can be applied across the continuum and that the complexity of risk management generally increases with the size of the project, program, or business to be managed.

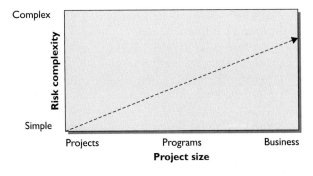

• **Figure 20.2** Risk complexity versus project size

Qualitatively Assessing Risk

Qualitative risk analysis allows expert judgment and experience to assume a prominent role. To assess risk qualitatively, you compare the impact of the threat with the probability of occurrence and assign an impact level and probability level to the risk. For example, if a threat has a high impact and a high probability of occurring, the risk exposure is high and probably requires some action to reduce this threat (pale green box in Figure 20.3). Conversely, if the impact is low with a low probability, the risk exposure is low and no action may be required to reduce this threat (white box in Figure 20.3). Figure 20.3 shows an example of a *binary assessment*, where only two outcomes are possible each for impact and probability. Either it will have an impact or it will not (or it will have a low or high impact), and it will occur or it won't (or it will have a high probability of occurring or a low probability of occurring).

In reality, a few threats can usually be identified as presenting high-risk exposure and a few threats present low-risk exposure. The threats that fall somewhere between (pale blue boxes in Figure 20.3) will have to be evaluated by judgment and management experience.

Impact		
	High impact/Low probability	High impact/High probability
	Low impact/Low probability	Low impact/High probability
	Probability	

• **Figure 20.3** Binary assessment

Tech Tip

System/Infrastructure KPIs

Typical KPIs for system performance include:

System KPI	Definition
CPU Utilization Percentage	The percentage of CPU resources used by all the processes
Memory Utilization Percentage	The percentage of memory resources used by all the processes
Busy Rate on Swap Disk	Amount of swapping
Daily, Weekly, and Monthly Peak Processing Times	Periods when CPU utilization, memory utilization, and busy rate are highest
Max, Min, and Median Run Length of Jobs	Fastest jobs, longest-running jobs, and calculated median run length of all jobs
Number and Name of Long-Running Jobs	Jobs running longer than the median
Average User Response Time	Period of time user waits for a response after pressing the ENTER key or equivalent

If the analysis is more complex, requiring three levels of analysis, such as low-medium-high or red-green-yellow, nine combinations are possible, as shown in Figure 20.4. Again, the pale green boxes probably require action, the white boxes may or may not require action, and the pale blue boxes require judgment. (Note that for brevity, in Figures 20.4 and 20.5, the first term in each box refers to the magnitude of the impact, and the second term refers to the probability of the threat occurring.)

Other levels of complexity are possible. With five levels of analysis, 25 values of risk exposure are possible. In this case, the possible values of impact and probability could take on the values: very low, low, medium, high, or very high. Also, note that the matrix does not have to be symmetrical. For example, if the probability is assessed with three values (low, medium, high) and the impact has five values (very low, low, medium, high, very high), the analysis would be as shown in Figure 20.5. (Again, note that the first term in each box refers to the impact, and the second term in each box refers to the probability of occurrence.)

So far, the examples have focused on assessing probability versus impact. Qualitative risk assessment can be adapted to a variety of attributes and situations in combination with each other. For example, Figure 20.6 shows the

Impact						
High	Low	High	Medium	High	High
Medium	Low	Medium	Medium	Medium	High
Low	Low	Low	Medium	Low	High

Probability

• **Figure 20.4**   Three levels of analysis

Impact						
Very high	Low	Very high	Medium	Very high	High
High	Low	High	Medium	High	High
Medium	Low	Medium	Medium	Medium	High
Low	Low	Low	Medium	Low	High
Very low	Low	Very low	Medium	Very low	High

Probability

• **Figure 20.5**   A 3-by-5 level analysis

comparison of some specific risks that have been identified during a security assessment. The assessment identified the risk areas listed in the first column (weak intranet security, high number of modems, Internet attack vulnerabilities, and weak incident detection and response mechanisms). The assessment also identified various potential impacts listed across the top (business impact, probability of attack, cost to fix, and difficulty to fix). Each of the impacts has been assessed as low, moderate, or high—depicted using green, yellow, and red, respectively. Each of the risk areas has been assessed with respect to each of the potential impacts, and an overall risk assessment has been determined in the last column.

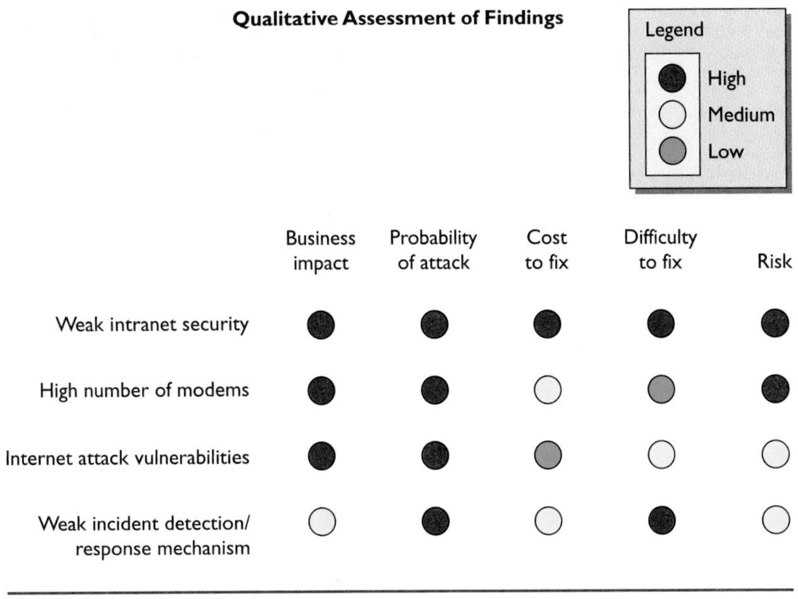

Qualitative Assessment of Findings

	Business impact	Probability of attack	Cost to fix	Difficulty to fix	Risk
Weak intranet security	●	●	●	●	●
High number of modems	●	●	○	◐	●
Internet attack vulnerabilities	●	●	◐	○	○
Weak incident detection/ response mechanism	○	●	○	●	○

Legend
● High
○ Medium
◐ Low

• **Figure 20.6**   Example of a combination assessment

Quantitatively Assessing Risk

Whereas qualitative risk assessment relies on judgment and experience, quantitative risk assessment applies historical information and trends to attempt to predict future performance. This type of risk assessment is highly dependent on historical data, and gathering such data can be difficult. Quantitative risk assessment can also rely heavily on models that provide decision-making information in the form of quantitative metrics, which attempt to measure risk levels across a common scale.

It is important to understand that key assumptions underlie any model, and different models will produce different results even when given the same input data. Although significant research and development have been invested in improving and refining the various risk analysis models, expert judgment and experience must still be considered an essential part of any risk-assessment process. Models can never replace judgment and experience, but they can significantly enhance the decision-making process.

Adding Objectivity to a Qualitative Assessment

It is possible to move a qualitative assessment toward being more quantitative. Making a qualitative assessment more objective can be as simple as assigning numeric values to one of the tables shown in Figures 20.3 through 20.6. For example, the impacts listed in Figure 20.6 can be prioritized from highest to lowest and then weighted, as shown in Table 20.1, with business impact weighted the most and difficulty to fix weighted least.

Next, values can be assigned to reflect how each risk was assessed. Figure 20.6 can thus be made more objective by assigning a value to each color that represents an assessment. For example, a red assessment indicates

Table 20.1	Adding Weights and Definitions to the Potential Impacts	
Impact	Explanation	Weight
Business impact	If exploited, would this have a material business impact?	4
Probability of attack	How likely is a potential attacker to try this technique or attack?	3
Cost to fix	How much will it cost in dollars and resources to correct this vulnerability?	2
Difficulty to fix	How hard is this to fix from a technical standpoint?	1

Table 20.2	Adding Values to Assessments	
Assessment	Explanation	Value
Red	Many critical, unresolved issues	3
Yellow	Some critical, unresolved issues	2
Green	Few unresolved issues	1

many critical, unresolved issues, and this will be given an assessment value of 3. Green means few issues are unresolved, so it is given a value of 1. Table 20.2 shows values that can be assigned for an assessment using red, yellow, and green.

The last step is to calculate an overall risk value for each risk area (each row in Figure 20.6) by multiplying the weights depicted in Table 20.1 times the assessed values from Table 20.2 and summing the products:

$$Risk = W_1 * V_1 + W_2 * V_2 + ...W_4 * V_4$$

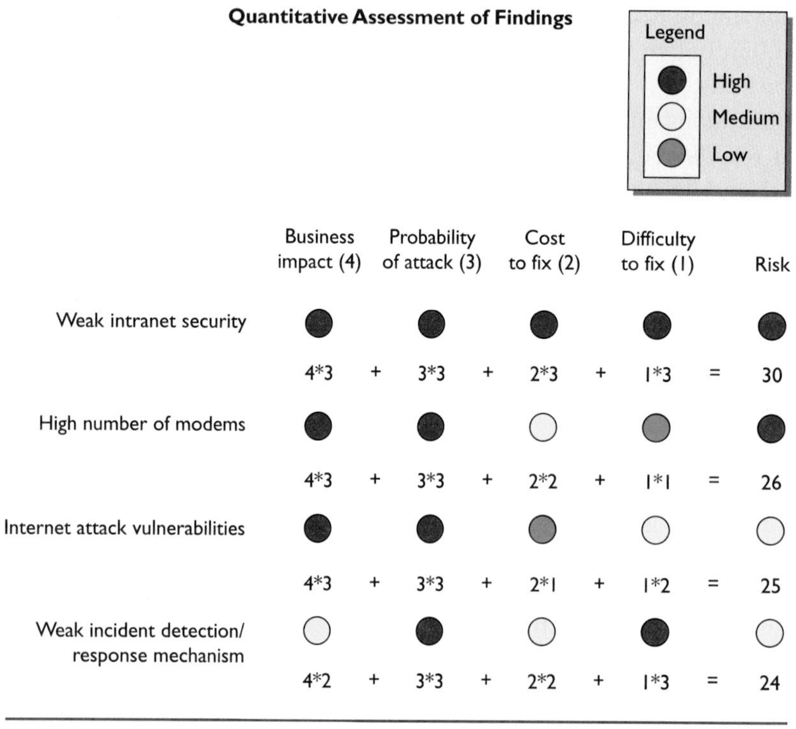

The risk calculation and final risk value for each risk area listed in Figure 20.6 have been incorporated into Figure 20.7. The assessed areas can then be ordered from highest to lowest based on the calculated risk value to aid management in focusing on the risk areas with the greatest potential impact.

A Common Objective Approach

More complex models permit a variety of analyses based on statistical and mathematical models. A common method of quantitative assessment is the calculation of the annualized loss expectancy (ALE). This calculation begins by calculating a single loss expectancy (SLE) with the following formula:

SLE = *asset value * exposure factor*

Quantitative Assessment of Findings

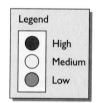

Legend
● High
○ Medium
◐ Low

	Business impact (4)	Probability of attack (3)	Cost to fix (2)	Difficulty to fix (1)	Risk
Weak intranet security	●	●	●	●	●
	4*3 +	3*3 +	2*3 +	1*3 =	30
High number of modems	●	●	○	◐	●
	4*3 +	3*3 +	2*2 +	1*1 =	26
Internet attack vulnerabilities	●	●	◐	○	○
	4*3 +	3*3 +	2*1 +	1*2 =	25
Weak incident detection/ response mechanism	○	●	○	●	○
	4*2 +	3*3 +	2*2 +	1*3 =	24

• **Figure 20.7**   Final quantitative assessment of the findings

By example, to calculate the exposure factor, assume the asset value of a small office building and its contents is $2 million. Also assume that this building houses the call center for a business, and the complete loss of the center would take away about half of the capability of the company. Therefore, the exposure factor is 50 percent. The SLE is

$2 million * 0.5 = $1 million

The ALE is then calculated simply by multiplying the SLE by the number of times the event is expected to occur in a year, which is called the annualized rate of occurrence (ARO):

ALE = SLE * ARO

If the event is expected to occur once in 20 years, then the ARO is 1/20. Typically the ARO is defined by historical data, either from a company's own experience or from industry surveys. Continuing our example, assume that a fire at this business's location is expected to occur about once in 20 years. Given this information, the ALE is

$1 million * 1/20 = $50,000

The ALE determines a threshold for evaluating the cost/benefit ratio of a given countermeasure. Therefore, a countermeasure to protect this business adequately should cost no more than the calculated ALE of $50,000 per year.

The examples in this chapter have been simplistic, but they demonstrate the concepts of both qualitative and quantitative risk analysis. More complex algorithms and software packages are available for accomplishing risk analyses, but these examples suffice for the purposes of this text.

Try This

Calculate SLE, ARO, and ALE

A company owns five warehouses throughout the United States, each of which is valued at $1 million and contributes equally to the company's capacity. Try calculating the SLE, ARO, and ALE for its warehouse located in the Mountain West, where the probability of an earthquake is once every 500 years. The solution is given in the footnote immediately below.[1]

---

[1] SLE = $1 million * 1.0; ARO = 1/500; ALE = $1 million/500, or $2000.

Exam Tip: It is always advisable to memorize these fundamental equations for certifications such as Security+.

■ Qualitative vs. Quantitative Risk Assessment

It is recognized throughout industry that it is *impossible* to conduct risk management that is purely *quantitative*. Usually risk management includes both qualitative and quantitative elements, requiring both analysis and judgment or experience. In contrast to quantitative assessment, it is *possible* to accomplish *purely qualitative* risk management. It is easy to see that it is impossible to define and quantitatively measure all factors that exist in a given risk assessment. It is also easy to see that a risk assessment that measures no factors quantitatively but measures them all qualitatively is possible.

The decision of whether to use qualitative versus quantitative risk management depends on the criticality of the project, the resources available, and the management style. The decision will be influenced by the degree to which the fundamental risk management metrics, such as asset value, exposure factor, and threat frequency, can be quantitatively defined.

Tech Tip

Accepting Risk

In addition to mitigating risk or transferring risk, it may be acceptable for a manager to accept risk in that despite the potential cost of a given risk and its associated probability, the manager of the organization will accept responsibility for the risk if it does happen. For example, a manager may choose to allow a programmer to make "emergency" changes to a production system (in violation of good segregation of duties) because the system cannot go down during a given period of time. The manager accepts the risk that the programmer could possibly make unauthorized changes because of the high-availability requirement of that system. However, there should always be some additional controls such as a management review or a standardized approval process to ensure the assumed risk is adequately managed.

Tech Tip

Risks Really Don't Change, But They Can Be Mitigated

One final thought to keep in mind is that the risk itself doesn't really change, no matter what actions are taken to mitigate that risk. A high risk will always be a high risk. However, actions can be taken to reduce the impact of that risk if it occurs.

■ Tools

Many tools can be used to enhance the risk management process. The following tools can be used during the various phases of risk assessment to add objectivity and structure to the process. Understanding the details of each of these tools is not necessary for the Security+ exam, but understanding what they can be used for is important. More information on these tools can be found in any good project-management text.

- **Affinity grouping** A method of identifying items that are related and then identifying the principle that ties them together.

- **Baseline identification and analysis** The process of establishing a baseline set of risks. It produces a "snapshot" of all the identified risks at a given point in time.

- **Cause and effect analysis** Identifying relationships between a risk and the factors that can cause it. This is usually accomplished using *fishbone diagrams* developed by Dr. Kaoru Ishikawa, former professor of engineering at the Science University of Tokyo.

- **Cost/benefit analysis** A straightforward method for comparing cost estimates with the benefits of a mitigation strategy.

- **Gantt charts** A management tool for diagramming schedules, events, and activity duration.

- **Interrelationship digraphs** A method for identifying cause-and-effect relationships by clearly defining the problem to be solved, identifying the key elements of the problem, and then describing the relationships between each of the key elements.

- **Pareto charts** A histogram that ranks the categories in a chart from most frequent to least frequent, thus facilitating risk prioritization.

- **PERT (program evaluation and review technique) charts** A diagram depicting interdependencies between project activities, showing the sequence and duration of each activity. When complete, the chart shows the time necessary to complete the project and the activities that determine that time (the critical path). The earliest and latest start and stop times for each activity and available slack times can also be shown.

- **Risk management plan** A comprehensive plan documenting how risks will be managed on a given project. It contains processes, activities, milestones, organizations, responsibilities, and details of each major risk management activity and how it is to be accomplished. It is an integral part of the project management plan.

Chapter 20 Review

■ Chapter Summary

After reading this chapter and completing the exercises, you should understand the following about risk management.

Use risk management tools and principles to manage risk effectively

- Risk management is a key management process that must be used at every level, whether managing a project, a program, or an enterprise.

- Risk management is also a strategic tool to more effectively manage increasingly sophisticated, diverse, and geographically expansive business opportunities.

- Managing risk is key to keeping a business competitive and must be done by managers at all levels.

- Common business risks include fraud and management of treasury, revenue, contracts, environment, regulatory issues, business continuity, and technology.

- Technology is a business risk that is so important it must be specifically managed.

- Technology risks include security and privacy, information technology operations, business systems control and effectiveness, information systems testing, and management of business continuity, reliability and performance, information technology assets, project risk, and change.

- A general model for managing risk includes asset identification, threat assessment, impact definition and quantification, control design and evaluation, and residual risk management.

- The SEI model for managing risk includes these steps: identify, analyze, plan, track, and control.

Explain the differences between qualitative and quantitative risk assessment

- Both qualitative and quantitative risk assessment approaches must be used to manage risk effectively, and a number of approaches were presented in this chapter.

- Qualitative risk assessment relies on expert judgment and experience by comparing the impact of a threat with the probability of it occurring.

- Qualitative risk assessment can be a simple binary assessment weighing high or low impact against high or low probability. Additional levels can be used to increase the comprehensiveness of the analysis. The well-known red-yellow-green stoplight mechanism is qualitative in nature and is easily understood.

- Quantitative risk assessment applies historical information and trends to assess risk. Models are often used to provide information to decision-makers.

- A common quantitative approach calculates the annualized loss expectancy from the single loss expectancy and the annualized rate of occurrence (ALE = SLE * ARO).

- It is important to understand that it is impossible to conduct a purely quantitative risk assessment, but it is possible to conduct a purely qualitative risk assessment.

Describe essential risk management tools

- Numerous tools can be used to add credibility and rigor to the risk assessment process.

- Risk assessment tools help identify relationships, causes, and effects. They assist in prioritizing decisions and facilitate effective management of the risk management process.

■ Key Terms

annualized loss expectancy (ALE) *(527)*
annualized rate of occurrence (ARO) *(527)*
asset *(526)*

control *(526)*
countermeasure *(526)*
exposure factor *(527)*

impact *(526)*
intangible impact *(531)*
mitigate *(527)*
qualitative risk assessment *(526)*
quantitative risk assessment *(527)*
residual risk *(532)*
risk *(526)*
risk analysis *(526)*

risk assessment *(526)*
risk management *(526)*
safeguard *(526)*
single loss expectancy (SLE) *(527)*
tangible impact *(531)*
threat *(526)*
vulnerability *(526)*

■ Key Terms Quiz

Use terms from the Key Terms list to complete the sentences that follow. Don't use the same term more than once. Not all terms will be used.

1. Asset value * exposure factor = _____.

2. A control may also be called a(n) _____ or a(n) _____.

3. When a threat exploits a vulnerability, you experience a(n) _____.

4. Single loss expectancy * annualized rate of occurrence = _____.

5. If you reduce the likelihood of a threat occurring, you _____ a risk.

6. The _____ measures the magnitude of the loss of an asset.

7. Risk analysis is synonymous with _____.

8. Any circumstance or event with the potential to cause harm to an asset is a(n) _____.

9. A characteristic of an asset that can be exploited by a threat to cause harm is its _____.

10. _____ is the overall decision-making process of identifying threats and vulnerabilities and their potential impacts, determining the costs to mitigate such events, and deciding what cost-effective actions need to be taken to control these risks.

■ Multiple-Choice Quiz

1. Which of the following correctly defines qualitative risk management?

   A. The process of objectively determining the impact of an event that affects a project, program, or business.

   B. The process of subjectively determining the impact of an event that affects a project, program, or business.

   C. The loss that results when a vulnerability is exploited by a threat.

   D. To reduce the likelihood of a threat occurring.

2. Which of the following correctly defines risk?

   A. The risks still remaining after an iteration of risk management.

   B. The loss that results when a vulnerability is exploited by a threat.

   C. Any circumstance or event with the potential to cause harm to an asset.

   D. The possibility of suffering harm or loss.

3. Single loss expectancy (SLE) can best be defined by which of the following equations?

   A. SLE = annualized loss expectancy * annualized rate of occurrence

   B. SLE = asset value * exposure factor

   C. SLE = asset value * annualized rate of occurrence

   D. SLE = annualized loss expectancy * exposure factor

4. Which of the following correctly defines annualized rate of occurrence?

   A. How much an event is expected to cost per year

   B. A measure of the magnitude of loss of an asset

C. On an annualized basis, the frequency with which an event is expected to occur

D. The resources or information an organization needs to conduct its business

5. Which of the following is a technology risk?

A. Business continuity management

B. Fraud

C. Contract management

D. Treasury management

6. The Basel Committee defines operational risk as which of the following?

A. Risk from disruption by people, systems, processes, or disasters

B. Risk of default of outstanding loans

C. Risk of losses due to fluctuations of market prices

D. The possibility of suffering harm or loss

7. Which of the following is *not* an asset?

A. Equipment failure

B. Hardware

C. Inventory

D. Cash

For questions 8 and 9, assume the following: The asset value of a small distribution warehouse is $5 million, and this warehouse serves as a backup facility. Its complete destruction by a disaster would take away about 1/5 of the capability of the business. Also assume that this sort of disaster is expected to occur about once every 50 years.

8. Which of the following is the calculated single loss expectancy (SLE)?

A. SLE = $25 million

B. SLE = $1 million

C. SLE = $2.5 million

D. SLE = $5 million

9. Which of the following is the calculated annualized loss expectancy (ALE)?

A. ALE = $50,000

B. ALE = $1 million

C. ALE = $20,000

D. ALE = $50 million

10. When discussing qualitative risk assessment versus quantitative risk assessment, which of the following is true?

A. It is impossible to conduct a purely quantitative risk assessment, and it is impossible to conduct a purely qualitative risk assessment.

B. It is possible to conduct a purely quantitative risk assessment, but it is impossible to conduct a purely qualitative risk assessment.

C. It is impossible to conduct a purely quantitative risk assessment, but it is possible to conduct a purely qualitative risk assessment.

D. It is possible to conduct a purely quantitative risk assessment, and it is possible to conduct a purely qualitative risk assessment.

11. Which of the following correctly defines residual risk?

A. The risks still remaining after an iteration of risk management

B. The possibility of suffering a loss

C. The result of a vulnerability being exploited by a threat that results in a loss

D. Characteristics of an asset that can be exploited by a threat to cause harm

12. Which of the following is a business risk?

A. Change management

B. Security and privacy

C. Environmental risk management

D. Business continuity management

13. Which of the following statements about risk is true?

A. A manager can accept the risk, which will reduce the risk.

B. The risk itself doesn't really change. However, actions can be taken to reduce the impact of the risk.

C. A manager can transfer the risk, which will reduce the risk.

D. A manager can take steps to increase the risk.

14. Which of the following correctly defines a Gantt chart?

A. A method of identifying items that are related and then identifying the principle that ties them together into a group

B. A management tool for diagramming schedules, events, and activity duration

C. A single-page form used to document new risks as they occur

D. A diagram depicting interdependencies between project activities, showing the sequence and duration of each activity

15. Which of the following is *not* a viable option when dealing with risk?

A. A manager can take action to mitigate risk.

B. A manager can take action to transfer risk.

C. A manager can take action to increase risk.

D. A manager can take action to accept risk.

■ Essay Quiz

1. You are drafting an e-mail to your risk management team members to explain the difference between tangible assets and intangible assets. Relate to tangible and intangible impacts. Write a one- or two-sentence paragraph that explains the difference and include two examples of each.

2. You have been tasked to initiate a risk management program for your company. The CEO has just asked you to succinctly explain the relationship between impact, threat, and vulnerability. Think quick on your feet and state a single sentence that explains the relationship.

3. Your CEO now says, "You mentioned that risks always exist. If I take enough measures, can't I eliminate the risk?" Explain why risks always exist.

4. You are explaining your risk management plan to a new team member just brought on as part of a college internship program. The intern asks, "With respect to impact, what does a threat do to a risk?" How would you answer?

5. The intern mentioned in Question 4 now asks you to compare and contrast accepting risk, transferring risk, and mitigating risk. What's your response?

Lab Projects

• Lab Project 20.1

The asset value of a distribution center (located in the midwestern United States) and its inventory is $10 million. It is one of two identical facilities (the other is in the southwestern United States). Its complete destruction by a disaster would thus take away half of the capability of the business. Also assume that this sort of disaster is expected to occur about once every 100 years. From this, calculate the annualized loss expectancy.

• Lab Project 20.2

You have just completed a qualitative threat assessment of the computer security of your organization, with the impacts and probabilities of occurrence listed in the table that follows. Properly place the threats in a 3-by-3 table similar to that in Figure 20.4. Which of the threats should you take action on, which should you monitor, and which ones may not need your immediate attention?

Threat	Impact	Probability of Occurrence
Virus attacks	High	High
Internet hacks	Medium	High
Wireless hacks	Low	High
Disgruntled employee hacks	High	Medium
Weak incidence response mechanisms	Medium	Medium
Theft of information by a trusted third-party contractor	Low	Medium
Competitor hacks	High	Low
Dial-up hacks	Medium	Low
Inadvertent release of noncritical information	Low	Low

Change Management

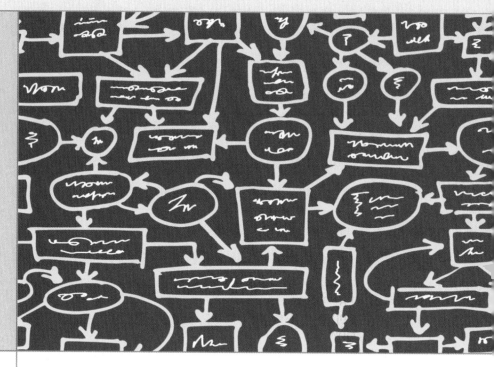

In this chapter, you will learn how to

■ **Use change management as an important enterprise management tool**

■ **Institute the key concept of separation of duties**

■ **Identify the essential elements of change management**

■ **Implement change management**

■ **Use the concepts of the Capability Maturity Model Integration**

It is well recognized that today's computer systems are extremely complex, and it is obvious that inventory management systems for large international enterprises such as Wal-Mart and Home Depot are probably as complex as an aircraft or skyscraper. Prominent operating systems such as Windows or UNIX are also very complex, as are computer processors on a chip. Many of today's web-based applications are extremely complex as well. For example, today's web-based applications typically consist of flash content on web sites interacting with remote databases through a variety of services or service-oriented architectures hosted on web servers located anywhere in the world.

You wouldn't think of constructing an aircraft, large building, computer chip, or automobile in the informal manner sometimes used to develop and operate computer systems of equal complexity. Computer systems have grown to be so complex and mission-critical that enterprises cannot afford to develop and maintain them in an ad hoc manner.

Change management procedures can add structure and control to the development and management of large software systems as they move from development to operation and during operation. In this chapter, **change management** refers to a standard methodology for performing and recording changes during software development and system operation. The methodology defines steps that ensure that system changes are required by the organization and are properly authorized, documented, tested, and approved by management. In many conversations, the term **configuration management** is considered synonymous with change management and, in a more limited manner, *version control* or *release control*.

The term change management is often applied to the management of changes in the business environment, typically as a result of business process reengineering or quality enhancement efforts. The term change management as used in this chapter is directly related to managing and controlling software development, maintenance, and system operation. Configuration management is the application of change management principles to configuration of both software and hardware.

Why Change Management?

To manage the system development and maintenance processes effectively, you need discipline and structure to help conserve resources and enhance effectiveness. Change management, like risk management, is often considered expensive, nonproductive, unnecessary, and confusing—an impediment to progress. However, like risk management, change management can be scaled to control and manage the development and maintenance of systems effectively.

Change management should be used in all phases of a system's life: development, testing, quality assurance (QA), and production. Short development cycles have not changed the need for an appropriate amount of management control over software development, maintenance, and operation. In fact, short turnaround times make change management more necessary, because once a system goes active in today's services-based en-

Cross Check

Risk Management and Change Management Are Essential Business Processes
Chapter 20 presented risk management as an essential decision-making process. In much the same way, change management is an essential practice for managing a system during its entire lifecycle, from development through deployment and operation, until it is taken out of service. What security-specific risk-based questions should be asked during change management reviews?

vironments, it often cannot be taken offline to correct errors—it must stay up and online or business will be lost and brand recognition damaged. In today's volatile stock market, for example, even small indicators of lagging performance can have dramatic impacts on a company's stock value.

The following scenarios exemplify the need for appropriate change management policy and for procedures over software, hardware, and data:

- *The developers can't find the latest version of the production source code.* Change management practices support versioning of software changes.

- *A bug corrected a few months ago mysteriously reappears.* Proper change management ensures developers always use the most-recently changed source code.

- *Fielded software was working fine yesterday but does not work properly today.* Good change management controls access to previously modified modules so that previously corrected errors aren't reintroduced into the system.

- *Development team members overwrote each other's changes.* Today's change management tools support collaborative development.

- *A programmer spent several hours changing the wrong version of the software.* Change management tools support viable management of previous software versions.

- *A customer record corrected by the call center yesterday shows the old, incorrect information today.* Good change management applies to databases as well and ensures recent changes are not lost.

- *New tax rates stored in a table have been overwritten with last year's tax rates.* Change control prevents inadvertent overwriting of critical reference data.

- *An application runs fine at some overseas locations but not at other locations.* Change management can simplify localization efforts.

- *A network administrator inadvertently brings down a server as he incorrectly punched down the wrong wires.* Just like a blueprint shows key electrical paths, data center connection paths can be version-controlled.

- *A newly installed server is hacked soon after installation because it is improperly configured.* Network and system administrators use change management to ensure configurations consistently meet security standards.

Tech Tip

Types of Changes

The Information Technology Infrastructure Library's ITIL v3 Glossary of Terms, Definitions and Acronyms (www.itil-campus.com/moodle/mod/glossary/view.php?id=166?) defines the following types of changes (with examples added in parentheses):

- ***Change*** *The addition, modification or removal of anything that could have an effect on IT Services. (For example, the modification to a module to implement a new capability.)*

- ***Standard Change*** *A pre-approved change that is low risk, relatively common and follows a procedure or work instruction. (For example, each month finance must make a small rounding adjustment to reconcile the General Ledger to account for foreign currency calculations.)*

- ***Emergency Change*** *A change that must be introduced as soon as possible. (For example, to resolve a major incident or implement a security patch. The change management process will normally have a specific procedure for handling emergency changes.)*

See www.itil-officialsite.com/home/home.asp for more information.

Try This

Scope of Change Management

See if you can explain why each of the following should be placed under an appropriate change management process:

- Web pages
- Service packs
- Security patches
- Third-party software releases
- Test data and test scripts
- Parameter files
- Scripts, stored procedures, or job control language–type programs
- Customized vendor code
- Source code of any kind
- Applications

Just about anyone with more than a year's experience in software development or system operations can relate to at least one of the preceding scenarios. However, each of these scenarios can be controlled, and impacts mitigated, through proper change management procedures.

The Sarbanes-Oxley Act of 2002, officially entitled the Public Company Accounting Reform and Investor Protection Act of 2002, was enacted July 30, 2002 to help ensure management establishes viable governance environments and control structures to ensure accuracy of financial reporting. Section 404 outlines the requirements most applicable to information technology. Change management is an essential part of creating a viable governance and control structure and critical to compliance with the Sarbanes-Oxley Act.

◼ The Key Concept: Separation of Duties

A foundation for change management is the recognition that involving more than one individual in a process can reduce risk. Good business control practices require that duties be assigned to individuals in such a way that no one individual can control all phases of a process or the processing and recording of a transaction. This is called **separation of duties** (also called *segregation of duties*). It is an important means by which errors and fraudulent or malicious acts can be discouraged and prevented. Separation of duties can be applied in many organizational scenarios because it establishes a basis for accountability and control. Proper separation of duties can safeguard enterprise assets and protect against risks. They should be documented, monitored, and enforced.

A well-understood business example of separation of duties is in the management and payment of vendor invoices. If a person can create a vendor in the finance system, enter invoices for payment, and then authorize a payment check to be written, it is apparent that fraud could be perpetrated because the person could write a check to himself for services never performed. Separating duties by requiring one person to create the vendors and another person to enter invoices and write checks makes it more difficult for someone to defraud an employer.

Information technology (IT) organizations should design, implement, monitor, and enforce appropriate separation of duties for the enterprise's information systems and processes. Today's computer systems are rapidly evolving into an increasingly decentralized and networked computer infrastructure. In the absence of adequate IT controls, such rapid growth may allow exploitation of large amounts of enterprise information in a short time. Further, the knowledge of computer operations held by IT staff is significantly greater than that of an average user, and this knowledge could be abused for malicious purposes.

Some of the best practices for ensuring proper separation of duties in an IT organization are as follows:

- ◼ Separation of duties between development, testing, QA, and production should be documented in written procedures and implemented by software or manual processes.

- Program developers' and program testers' activities should be conducted on "test" data only. They should be restricted from accessing "live" production data. This will assist in ensuring an independent and objective testing environment without jeopardizing the confidentiality and integrity of production data.

- End users or computer operations personnel should not have direct access to program source code. This control helps lessen the opportunity of exploiting software weaknesses or introducing malicious code (or code that has not been properly tested) into the production environment either intentionally or unintentionally.

- Functions of creating, installing, and administrating software programs should be assigned to different individuals. For example, since developers create and enhance programs, they should not be able to install it on the production system. Likewise, database administrators should not be program developers on database systems they administer.

- All accesses and privileges to systems, software, or data should be granted based on the principle of least privilege, which gives users no more privileges than are necessary to perform their jobs. Access privileges should be reviewed regularly to ensure that individuals who no longer require access have had their privileges removed.

- Formal change management policy and procedures should be enforced throughout the enterprise. Any changes in hardware and software components (including emergency changes) that are implemented after the system has been placed into production must go through the approved formal change management mechanism.

Tech Tip

Steps to Implement Separation of Duties

1. *Identify an indispensable function that is potentially subject to abuse.*

2. *Divide the function into separate steps, each containing the power that enables the function to be abused.*

3. *Assign each step to a different person or organization.*

Managers at all levels should review existing and planned processes and systems to ensure proper separation of duties. Smaller business entities may not have the resources to implement all of the preceding practices fully, but other control mechanisms, including hiring qualified personnel, bonding contractors, and using training, monitoring, and evaluation practices, can reduce any organization's exposure to risk. The establishment of such practices can ensure that enterprise assets are properly safeguarded and can also greatly reduce error and the potential for fraudulent or malicious activities.

Change management practices implement and enforce separation of duties by adding structure and management oversight to the software development and system operation processes. Change management techniques can ensure that only correct and authorized changes, as approved by management or other authorities, are allowed to be made, following a defined process.

■ Elements of Change Management

Change management has its roots in system engineering, where it is commonly referred to as *configuration management*. Most of today's software and hardware change management practices derive from long-standing system engineering configuration management practices. For example, automakers know that a certain amount of configuration management is necessary to build safe cars efficiently and effectively. Bolts and screws with proper strengths and qualities are used on every car, in specific places—employees don't just reach into a barrel of bolts, pull one out that looks about right, and bolt it on. The same applies to aircraft—for an aircraft to fly safely, it must be built of parts of the right size, shape, strength, and so on. Computer hardware and software development have also evolved to the point that proper management structure and controls must exist to ensure the products operate as planned.

Change management and configuration management use different terms for their various phases, but they all fit into the four general phases defined under configuration management:

- Configuration identification
- Configuration control
- Configuration status accounting
- Configuration auditing

Configuration identification is the process of identifying which assets need to be managed and controlled. These assets could be software modules, test cases or scripts, table or parameter values, servers, major subsystems, or entire systems. The idea is that, depending on the size and complexity of the system, an appropriate set of data and software (or other assets) must be identified and properly managed. These identified assets are called **configuration items** or **computer software configuration items**.

Related to configuration identification, and the result of it, is the definition of a baseline. A **baseline** serves as a foundation for comparison or measurement. It provides the necessary visibility to control change. For example, a software baseline defines the software system as it is built and running at a point in time. As another example, network security best practices clearly state that any large organization should build its servers to a standard build configuration to enhance overall network security. The servers are the configuration items, and the standard build is the server baseline.

Configuration control is the process of controlling changes to items that have been baselined. Configuration control ensures that only approved changes to a baseline are allowed to be implemented. It is easy to understand why a software system, such as a web-based order entry system, should not be changed without proper testing and control—otherwise, the system might stop functioning at a critical time. Configuration control is a key step that provides valuable insight to managers. If a system is being changed, and configuration control is being observed, managers and others concerned will be better informed. This ensures proper use of assets and avoids unnecessary downtime due to the installation of unapproved changes.

Configuration status accounting consists of the procedures for tracking and maintaining data relative to each configuration item in the baseline. It is closely related to configuration control. Status accounting involves gathering and maintaining information relative to each configuration item. For example, it documents what changes have been requested; what changes have been made, when, and for what reason; who authorized the change; who

Tech Tip

Change Management

The ITIL v3 Glossary *defines change managements as "The process responsible for controlling the lifecycle of all changes. The primary objective of change management is to enable beneficial changes to be made, with minimum disruption to IT services." See www.itil-campus .com/moodle/mod/glossary/ view.php?id=166?.*

Large enterprise application systems require viable change management systems. For example, SAP has its own change management system called the Transport Management System (TMS). Third-party software such as Phire Architect (www .phire-soft. com) and Quest Stat (www.quest.com) provide change management applications for Oracle's PeopleSoft or E-Business Suite.

It is important that you understand that even though all servers may be initially configured to the same baseline, individual applications might require a system-specific configuration to run properly. Change management actually facilitates system-specific configuration in that all exceptions from the standard configuration are documented. All people involved in managing and operating these systems will have documentation to help them quickly understand why a particular system is configured in a unique way.

performed the change; and what other configuration items or systems were affected by the change.

Returning to our example of servers being baselined, if the operating system of those servers is found to have a security flaw, then the baseline can be consulted to determine which servers are vulnerable to this particular security flaw. Those systems with this weakness can be updated (and only those that need to be updated). Configuration control and configuration status accounting help ensure that systems are more consistently managed and, ultimately in this case, the organization's network security is maintained. It is easy to imagine the state of an organization that has not built all servers to a common baseline and has not properly controlled its systems' configurations. It would be very difficult to know the configuration of individual servers, and security could quickly become weak.

Configuration auditing is the process of verifying that the configuration items are built and maintained according to the requirements, standards, or contractual agreements. It is similar to how audits in the financial world are used to ensure that generally accepted accounting principles and practices are adhered to and that financial statements properly reflect the financial status of the enterprise. Configuration audits ensure that policies and procedures are being followed, that all configuration items (including hardware and software) are being properly maintained, and that existing documentation accurately reflects the status of the systems in operation.

Configuration auditing takes on two forms: functional and physical. A *functional configuration audit* verifies that the configuration item performs as defined by the documentation of the system requirements. A *physical configuration audit* confirms that all configuration items to be included in a release, install, change, or upgrade are actually included, and that no additional items are included—no more, no less.

■ Implementing Change Management

Change management requires some structure and discipline in order to be effective. The change management function is scalable from small to enterprise-level projects. Figure 21.1 illustrates a sample software change management flow appropriate for medium to large projects. It can be adapted to small organizations by having the developer perform work only on her workstation (never on the production system) and having the system administrator serve in the buildmaster function. The buildmaster is usually an independent person responsible for compiling and incorporating changed software into an executable image.

Figure 21.1 shows that developers never have access to the production system or data. It also demonstrates proper separation of duties between developers, QA and test personnel, and production. It implies that a distinct separation exists between development, testing and QA, and production environments. This workflow is for changes that have a major impact on production or the customer's business process. For minor changes that have

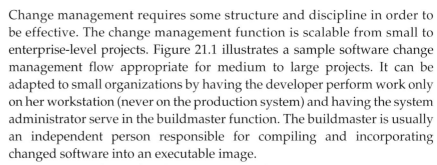

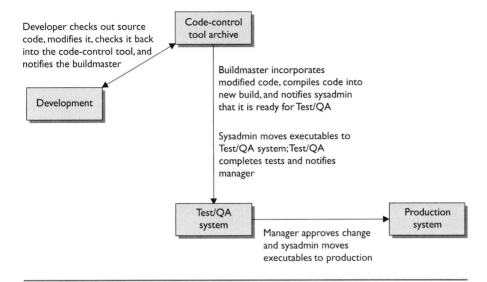

Developer checks out source code, modifies it, checks it back into the code-control tool, and notifies the buildmaster

Code-control tool archive

Development

Buildmaster incorporates modified code, compiles code into new build, and notifies sysadmin that it is ready for Test/QA

Sysadmin moves executables to Test/QA system; Test/QA completes tests and notifies manager

Test/QA system

Production system

Manager approves change and sysadmin moves executables to production

• **Figure 21.1** Software change control workflow

minimal risk or impact on business processes, some of the steps may be omitted.

The change management workflow proceeds as follows:

1. The developer checks out source code from the code-control tool archive to the development system.

2. The developer modifies the code and conducts unit testing of the changed modules.

3. The developer checks the modified code into the code-control tool archive.

4. The developer notifies the buildmaster that changes are ready for a new build and testing/QA.

5. The buildmaster creates a build incorporating the modified code and compiles the code.

6. The buildmaster notifies the system administrator that the executable image is ready for testing/QA.

7. The system administrator moves the executables to the test/QA system.

8. QA tests the new executables. If tests are passed, test/QA notifies the manager. If tests fail, the process starts over.

9. Upon manager approval, the system administrator moves the executable to the production system.

The Purpose of a Change Control Board

To oversee the change management process, most organizations establish a **change control board (CCB)**. In practice, a CCB not only facilitates adequate management oversight, but also facilitates better coordination between projects. The CCB convenes on a regular basis, usually weekly or monthly, and can be convened on an emergency or as-needed basis as well. Figure 21.2

Tech Tip

Identifying Separation of Duties

Using Figure 21-1, observe the separation of duties between development, test/QA, and production. The functions of creating, installing, and administrating are assigned to different individuals. Note also appropriate management review and approval. This implementation also ensures that no compiler is necessary on the production system. Indeed, compilers should not be allowed to exist on the production system.

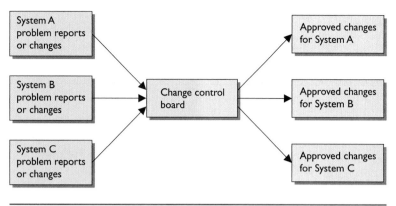

• **Figure 21.2** Change control board process

shows the process for implementing and properly controlling hardware or software during changes.

The CCB's membership should consist of development project managers, network administrators, system administrators, test/QA managers, an information security manager, an operations center manager, and a help desk manager. Others can be added as necessary, depending on the size and complexity of the organization.

A **system problem report (SPR)** is used to track changes through the CCB. The SPR documents changes or corrections to a system. It reflects who requested the change and why, what analysis must be done and by whom, and how the change was corrected or implemented. Figure 21.3 shows a sample SPR. Most large enterprises cannot rely on a paper-based SPR process and instead use one of the many software systems

> **Tech Tip**
>
> **Incident Management**
>
> *The* ITIL v3 Glossary *defines incident management as "The process responsible for managing the lifecycle of all incidents. The primary objective of incident management is to return the IT service to users as quickly as possible."*

SYSTEM PROBLEM REPORT (SPR)

❑ Error SPR Number:________

❑ Improvement Originator:________

------------------------------ **Problem** ------------------------------

System Affected: ________

Related Systems: ________

Classification: Problem Description:________

❑ Software

❑ Hardware

❑ Documentation

❑ Comment

Analysis Assigned to: ________

------------------------------ **Analysis** ------------------------------

(Prepared by responsible software design organization) Date Received:________

Classification: Explanation:

❑ Design

❑ Coding

❑ Documentation

❑ Environment

Signatures

Analyst: ______ Date:______ Originator:______ Date:______

------------------------------ **Correction** ------------------------------

Brief Description of Work and List of Modules Changed:

Documentation Changed:

Signatures

Developer:______ Date:______ Manager:______ Date:______

• **Figure 21.3** Sample system problem report

available to perform change management functions. While this example shows a paper-based SPR, it contains all the elements of change management: it describes the problem and who reported it, it outlines resolution of the problem, and it documents approval of the change.

Figure 21.4 shows the entire change management process and its relationship to incident management and release management.

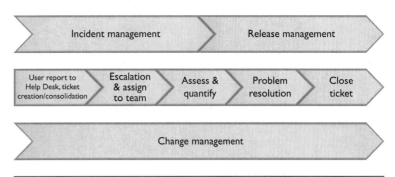

• **Figure 21.4**   Change, incident, and release management

Code Integrity

One key benefit of adequate change management is the assurance of code consistency and integrity. Whenever a modified program is moved to the production source-code library, the executable version should also be moved to the production system. Automated change management systems greatly simplify this process and are therefore better controls for ensuring executable and source-code integrity. Remember that at no time should the user or application developer have access to production source and executable code libraries in the production environment.

Finally, in today's networked environment, the integrity of the executable code is critical. A common hacking technique is to replace key system executable code with modified code that contains backdoors, allowing unauthorized access or functions to be performed. Executable code integrity can be verified using host-based intrusion detection systems. These systems create and maintain a database of the size and content of executable modules. Conceptually, this is usually done by performing some kind of hashing or sophisticated checksum operation on the executable modules and storing the results in a database. The operation is performed on a regular schedule against the executable modules, and the results are compared to the database to identify any unauthorized changes that may have occurred to the executable modules.

■ The Capability Maturity Model Integration

One area that is likely to be covered on the Security+ test is the **Capability Maturity Model Integration (CMMI)** developed at Carnegie Mellon University's Software Engineering Institute (SEI). The CMMI replaces the older Capability Maturity Model (CMM). Configuration or change management is one of the fundamental concepts of CMMI, which provides organizations with the ability to improve their software and other processes by following an evolutionary path from ad hoc processes to disciplined management processes.

The SEI's web page defines six capability levels:

- ■ **Level 0: Incomplete**   The software process is partially performed or not performed.

- **Level 1: Performed**   The process satisfies the goals of the process area but may not be sustainable because it is not institutionalized.

- **Level 2: Managed**   The process is a performed process (as defined in level 1) and has a supporting infrastructure in place, such as policies and qualified personnel, and it is monitored, controlled, reviewed, and evaluated. Most important, the processes are disciplined enough to remain intact during times of stress.

- **Level 3: Defined**   The process is managed (as defined in level 2) but is tailored from the organization's standard set of processes, according to the organization's tailoring guidelines.

- **Level 4: Quantitatively Managed**   The process is a defined process (see level 3) and uses statistical evaluation and quantitative objectives to control and manage the process.

- **Level 5: Optimizing**   Key business processes are quantitatively managed (as defined in level 4) and improved by understanding root causes of variation. Improvements can be both incremental and innovative.

Change management is a key process to implementing the CMMI in an organization. For example, if an organization is at CMMI level 0, it probably has no formal change management processes in place. At level 3, an organization has a defined change management process that is followed and tailored to the specific project needs. At level 5, the change management process is a routine, quantitatively evaluated part of improving software products and implementing innovative ideas. In order for an organization to effectively manage software development, operation, and maintenance, it should have effective change management processes in place.

Exam Tip: To complete your preparations for the Security+ exam, it is recommended that you consult SEI's web site (www.sei.cmu.edu/cmmi) for specific CMMI definitions. Be sure that you understand the differences between capability levels and maturity levels as defined in CMMI.

Chapter 21 Review

■ Chapter Summary

After reading this chapter and completing the exercises, you should understand the following about change management.

Use change management as an important enterprise management tool

- Change management should be used in all phases of the software lifecycle.
- Change management can be scaled to effectively control and manage software development and maintenance.
- Change management can prevent some of the most common software development and maintenance problems.

Institute the key concept of separation of duties

- Separation of duties ensures that no single individual or organization possesses too much control in a process.
- Separation of duties helps prevent errors and fraudulent or malicious acts.
- Separation of duties establishes a basis for accountability and control.
- Separation of duties can help safeguard enterprise assets and protect against risks.

Identify the essential elements of change management

- Configuration identification identifies assets that need to be controlled.

- Configuration control keeps track of changes to configuration items that have been baselined.
- Configuration status accounting tracks each configuration item in the baseline.
- Configuration auditing verifies the configuration items are built and maintained appropriately.

Implement change management

- A standardized process and a change control board provide management with proper oversight and control of the software development lifecycle.
- A good change management process will exhibit good separation of duties and have clearly defined roles, responsibilities, and approvals.
- An effective change control board facilitates good management oversight and coordination between projects.

Use the concepts of the Capability Maturity Model Integration

- Once proper management oversight exists, the company will be able to use CMMI to help the organization move from ad hoc activities to a disciplined software management process.
- CMMI relies heavily on change management to provide organizations with the capability to improve their software processes.

■ Key Terms

baseline *(549)*
Capability Maturity Model Integration (CMMI) *(553)*
change management *(545)*
change control board (CCB) *(551)*
computer software configuration items *(549)*
configuration auditing *(550)*
configuration control *(549)*

configuration identification *(549)*
configuration items *(549)*
configuration management *(545)*
configuration status accounting *(549)*
separation of duties *(547)*
system problem report (SPR) *(552)*

Key Terms Quiz

Use terms from the Key Terms list to complete the sentences that follow. Don't use the same term more than once. Not all terms will be used.

1. The _____ is the body that provides oversight to the change management process.

2. _____ is a standard methodology for performing and recording changes during software development and operation.

3. _____ is the process of assigning responsibilities to different individuals such that no single individual can commit fraudulent or malicious actions.

4. Procedures for tracking and maintaining data relative to each configuration item in the baseline are _____.

5. A _____ describes a system as it is built and functioning at a point in time.

6. A structured methodology that provides an evolutionary path from ad hoc processes to disciplined software management is the _____.

7. The process of verifying that configuration items are built and maintained according to requirements, standards, or contractual agreements is _____.

8. The document used by the change control board to track changes to software is called a _____.

9. When you identify which assets need to be managed and controlled, you are performing _____.

10. _____ is the process of controlling changes to items that have been baselined.

Multiple-Choice Quiz

1. The original developer of a web-based system has left the company, and the new developer assigned has been unable to find the latest source code for that system. This type of problem could have been prevented by:

   A. The system administrator making the changes instead of the developer

   B. Proper change management procedures over the object (compiled) code

   C. The use of an object-oriented design approach rather than a rapid prototyping design approach

   D. Proper change management procedures over the source code

2. Why should developers and testers avoid using "live" production data to perform various testing activities?

   A. The use of "live" production data ensures a full and realistic test database.

   B. The use of "live" production data can jeopardize the confidentiality and integrity of the production data.

   C. The use of "live" production data ensures an independent and objective test environment.

   D. Developers and testers should be allowed to use "live" production data.

3. Software change management procedures are established to:

   A. Ensure continuity of business operations in the event of a natural disaster

   B. Add structure and control to the development of software systems

   C. Ensure changes in business operations caused by a management restructuring are properly controlled

   D. Identify threats, vulnerabilities, and mitigating actions that could impact an enterprise

4. Which of the following correctly defines the principle of least privilege?

   A. Access privileges are reviewed regularly to ensure that individuals who no longer require access have had their privileges removed.

B. Authorization of a subject's access to an object depends on sensitivity labels.

C. The administrator determines which subjects can have access to certain objects based on organizational security policy.

D. Users have no more privileges than are necessary to perform their jobs.

5. Which of the following does *not* adhere to the principles of separation of duties?

   A. Software development, testing, quality assurance, and production should be assigned to the same individuals.

   B. Software developers should not have access to production data and source-code files.

   C. Software developers and testers should be restricted from accessing "live" production data.

   D. The functions of creating, installing, and administrating software programs should be assigned to different individuals.

6. Configuration auditing is:

   A. The process of controlling changes to items that have been baselined

   B. The process of identifying which assets need to be managed and controlled

   C. The process of verifying that the configuration items are built and maintained properly

   D. The procedures for tracking and maintaining data relative to each configuration item in the baseline

7. Why should end users not be given access to program source codes?

   A. It could allow an end user to identify weaknesses or errors in the source code.

   B. It ensures that testing and quality assurance perform their proper functions.

   C. It assists in ensuring an independent and objective testing environment.

   D. It could allow an end user to execute the source code.

8. Which position is responsible for modifying code in the system?

   A. System administrator

   B. Developer

   C. Manager

   D. Quality assurance

9. Configuration control is:

   A. The process of controlling changes to items that have been baselined

   B. The process of identifying which assets need to be managed and controlled

   C. The process of verifying that the configuration items are built and maintained properly

   D. The procedures for tracking and maintaining data relative to each configuration item in the baseline

10. Configuration identification is:

   A. The process of verifying that the configuration items are built and maintained properly

   B. The procedures for tracking and maintaining data relative to each configuration item in the baseline

   C. The process of controlling changes to items that have been baselined

   D. The process of identifying which assets need to be managed and controlled

11. Which position is responsible for approving the movement of executable code to the production system?

   A. System administrator

   B. Developer

   C. Manager

   D. Quality assurance

12. The purpose of a change control board (CCB) is to:

   A. Facilitate management oversight and better project coordination

   B. Identify which assets need to be managed and controlled

C. Establish software processes that are structured enough that success with one project can be repeated for another similar project

D. Track and maintain data relative to each configuration item in the baseline

13. Which computer security technology is used to ensure the integrity of executable code?

   A. Network-based intrusion detection systems

   B. Switches

   C. Routers

   D. Host-based intrusion detection systems

14. In the Software Engineering Institute's Capability Maturity Model Integration (CMMI), which of the following correctly defines level 1, Performed?

   A. The process is a performed process and has a supporting infrastructure in place.

   B. Key business processes are quantitatively managed and improved by understanding root causes of variation.

   C. The process is tailored from the organization's standard set of processes, according to the organization's tailoring guidelines.

   D. The process satisfies the goals of the process area but may not be sustainable because it is not institutionalized.

15. In the Software Engineering Institute's Capability Maturity Model Integration (CMMI), which of the following correctly defines level 5, Optimizing?

   A. The process is a performed process and has a supporting infrastructure in place.

   B. Key business processes are quantitatively managed and improved by understanding root causes of variation.

   C. The process is tailored from the organization's standard set of processes, according to the organization's tailoring guidelines.

   D. The process satisfies the goals of the process area but may not be sustainable because it is not institutionalized.

■ Essay Quiz

1. You are the project manager for a new web-based online shopping system. Due to market competition, your management has directed you to go live with your systems one week earlier than originally scheduled. One of your development team is a sharp, smart programmer with less than one year of experience. He asks you why your team is required to follow what he calls cumbersome, out-of-date change management procedures. What would you tell him?

2. Explain why the change management principles discussed in this chapter should be used when managing operating system patches.

3. Explain why a database administrator (DBA) should not be allowed to develop programs on the systems they administer.

4. Your company has just decided to follow the Capability Maturity Model Integration. You manage a development shop of 15 programmers with four team leaders. You and your team have determined that you are currently at CMMI level 1, Performed. Describe the actions you might take to move your shop to level 3, the Defined maturity level.

5. You have just been made Director of E-commerce Applications, responsible for over 30 programmers and ten major software projects. Your projects include multiple web pages on ten different production servers, system security for those servers, three development servers, three test/QA servers, and some third-party software. Which of those resources would you place under change management practices and why?

Lab Projects

• Lab Project 21.1

Using a typical IT organization from a medium-sized company (100 developers, managers, and support personnel), describe the purpose, organization, and responsibilities of a change control board appropriate for this organization.

• Lab Project 21.2

You are the IT staff auditor for the company mentioned in the first lab project. You have reviewed the change control board processes and found they have instituted the following change management process. Describe two major control weaknesses in this particular change management process. What would you do to correct these control weaknesses?

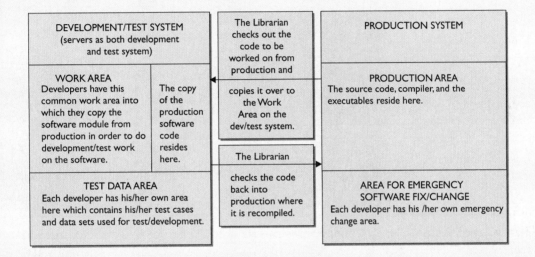

Privilege Management

Ability is what you're capable of doing. Motivation determines what you do. Attitude determines how well you do it.
—LOU HOLTZ

In this chapter, you will learn how to

- Identify the differences among user, group, and role management

- Implement password and domain password policies

- Describe methods of account management (SSO, time of day, logical token, account expiration)

- Describe methods of access management (MAC, DAC, and RBAC)

Computer systems are in such wide use now that they touch almost every facet of our lives: they process credit card transactions, handle airline reservations, store a vast amount of personal information, and manage car engines to ensure optimal fuel efficiency. Most of the time, computers— particularly the more complicated systems, such as PCs, servers, and mainframes—require interaction from a human user. The user interacts with the applications and operating system to complete tasks and perform specific functions.

On single-user systems such as PCs, the individual user typically has access to most of the system's resources, processing capability, and stored data. On multiuser systems, such as servers and mainframes, an individual user typically has very limited access to the system and the data stored on that system. An administrator responsible for managing and maintaining the multiuser system has much greater access. So how does the computer system know which users should have access to what data? How does the operating system know what applications a user is allowed to use?

On early computer systems, anyone with physical access had fairly significant rights to the system and could typically access any file or execute any application. As computers became more popular and it became obvious that some way of separating and restricting users was needed, the concepts of users, groups, and privileges came into being (**privileges** mean you have the ability to "do something" on a computer system such as create a directory, delete a file, or run a program). These concepts continue to be developed and refined and are now part of what we call *privilege management*.

Though privilege management has become a crucial part of modern operating systems and computer operations, it's really quite a simple concept. **Privilege management** is the process of restricting a user's ability to interact with the computer system. A user's interaction with a computer system covers a fairly broad area and includes viewing, modifying, and deleting data; running applications; stopping and starting processes; and controlling computer resources. Essentially, everything a user can do to or with a computer system falls into the realm of privilege management.

Privilege management occurs at many different points within an operating system or even within applications running on a particular operating system. While UNIX and Windows operating systems have a slightly different approach to privilege management, they share some similar approaches and concepts that are covered in this chapter.

■ User, Group, and Role Management

To manage the privileges of many different people effectively on the same system, a mechanism for separating people into distinct entities (*users*) is required, so you can control access on an individual level. At the same time, it's convenient and efficient to be able to lump users together when granting many different people (*groups*) access to a resource at the same time. At other times, it's useful to be able to grant or restrict access based on a person's job or function within the organization (*role*). While you can manage privileges on the basis of users alone, managing user, group, and role assignments together is far more convenient and efficient.

User

The term **user** generally applies to any person accessing a computer system. In privilege management, a user is a single individual, such as "John Forthright" or "Sally Jenkins." This is generally the lowest level addressed by privilege management and the most common area for addressing access, rights, and capabilities. When accessing a computer system, each user is generally given a **username**—a unique alphanumeric identifier he or she will use to identify himself or herself when logging into or accessing the system. Usernames are sometimes based on some combination of the user's first, middle, and last name and often include numbers as well. In other cases, usernames are based on a series of characters from a semi-random selection process that is designed to deter attacks based on easily guessing valid

Tech Tip

User ID vs. Username
The terms "user ID" and "username" are sometimes used interchangeably, but traditionally the term user ID is more often associated with UNIX operating systems. In UNIX operating systems, each user is identified by an unsigned integer called a user identifier, *often shortened to user ID.*

usernames. When developing a scheme for selecting usernames, you should keep in mind that usernames must be unique to each user, but they must also be fairly easy for the user to remember and use.

With some notable exceptions, in general a user who wants to access a computer system must first have a username created for him on the system he wishes to use. This is usually done by a system administrator, security administrator, or other privileged user, and this is the first step in privilege management—a user should not be allowed to create their own account.

Once the account is created and a username is selected, the administrator can assign specific permissions to that user. **Permissions** control what the user is allowed to do with objects on the system—which files he may access, which programs he may execute, and so on. While PCs typically have only one or two user accounts, larger systems such as servers and mainframes can have hundreds of accounts on the same system. Figure 22.1 shows the Users management tab from the Computer Management utility on a Windows Server 2008 system. Note that several user accounts have been created on this system, each identified by a unique username.

A few "special" user accounts don't typically match up one-to-one with a real person. These accounts are reserved for special functions and typically have much more access and control over the computer system than the average user account. Two such accounts are the **administrator** account under Windows and the **root** account under UNIX. Each of these accounts is also known as the **superuser**—if something can be done on the system, the superuser has the power to do it. These accounts are not typically assigned to a specific individual and are often shared, accessed only when the full capabilities of that account are required.

Due to the power possessed by these accounts, and the few, if any, restrictions placed on them, they must be protected with strong passwords that are not easily guessed or obtained. These accounts are also the most common targets of attackers—if the attacker can gain root access or assume the privilege level associated with the root account, she can bypass most access controls and accomplish anything she wants on that system.

Another account that falls into the "special" category is the system account used by Windows operating systems. The system account has the same file privileges as the administrator account and is used by the

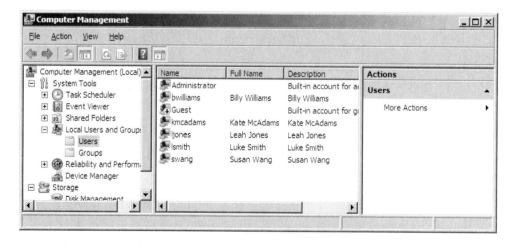

• Figure 22.1   Users tab on a Windows Server 2008 system

operating system and by services that run under Windows. By default, the system account is granted full control to all files on an NTFS volume. Services and processes that need the capability to log on internally within Windows will use the system account—for example, the DNS Server and DHCP Server services in Windows Server 2008 use the Local System account. There are some restrictions associated with system accounts, though—they do not show up in User Manager, cannot be added to any groups, and cannot have user rights assigned to them.

Group

Under privilege management, a **group** is a collection of users with some common criteria, such as a need for access to a particular dataset or group of applications. A group can consist of one user or hundreds of users, and each user can belong to one or more groups. Figure 22.2 shows a common approach to grouping users—building groups based on job function.

By assigning membership in a specific group to a user, you make it much easier to control that user's access and privileges. For example, if every member of the engineering department needs access to product development documents, administrators can place all the users in the engineering department in a single group and allow that group to access the necessary documents. Once a group is assigned permissions to access a particular resource, adding a new user to that group will automatically allow that user to access that resource. In effect, the user "inherits" the permissions of the group as soon as she is placed in that group. As Figure 22.3 shows, a computer system can have many different groups, each with its own rights and permissions.

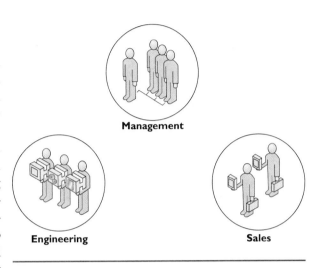

Management

Engineering

Sales

• **Figure 22.2** Logical representation of groups

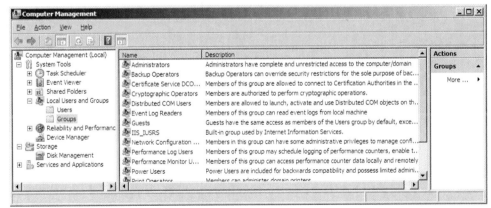

• **Figure 22.3** Group management screen from a Windows Server 2008 system

As you can see from the description for the Administrators group in Figure 22.3, this group has complete and unrestricted access to the system. This includes access to all files, applications, and datasets. Anyone who belongs to the Administrators group or is placed in this group will have a great deal of access and control over the system.

Some operating systems, such as Windows, have built-in groups—groups that are already defined within the operating system, such as Administrators, Power Users, and Everyone. The whole concept of groups revolves around making the tasks of assigning and managing permissions easier, and built-in groups certainly help to make these tasks easier.

Individual users accounts can be added to built-in groups, allowing administrators to grant permission sets to users quickly and easily without having to specify permissions manually. For example, adding a user account named "bjones" to the Power Users group gives bjones all the permissions assigned to the built-in Power Users group, such as installing drivers, modifying settings, and installing software.

Role

Another common method of managing access and privileges is by roles. A **role** is usually synonymous with a job or set of functions. For example, the role of securityadmin in Microsoft SQL Server may be applied to someone who is responsible for creating and managing logins, reading error logs, and auditing the application. Securityadmins need to accomplish specific functions and need access to certain resources that other users do not—for example, they need to be able to create and delete logins, open and read error logs, and so on. In general, anyone serving in the role of securityadmin needs the same rights and privileges as every other securityadmin. For simplicity and efficiency, rights and privileges can be assigned to the role securityadmin, and anyone assigned to fulfill that role automatically has the correct rights and privileges to perform the required tasks.

■ Password Policies

The username/password combination is by far the most common means of controlling access to applications, web sites, and computer systems. The average user may have a dozen or more username and password combinations between school, work, and personal use. To help users select a good, difficult-to-guess password, most organizations implement and enforce a **password policy**, which typically has the following components:

- **Password construction** How many characters a password should have; the use of capitalization, numbers, and special characters; not basing the password on a dictionary word or personal information; not making the password a slight modification of an existing password; and so on

- **Reuse restrictions** Whether or not passwords can be reused, and, if so, with what frequency (how many different passwords must you use before you can use one you've used before)

- **Duration** The minimum and maximum number of days a password can be used before it can be changed or must be changed

- **Protection of passwords** Not writing down passwords where others can find them, not saving passwords and not allowing automated logins, not sharing passwords with other users, and so on

- **Consequences** Consequences associated with violation of or noncompliance with the policy

The SANS Institute offers several examples of password policies (along with many other common information security policies) on its web site (www.sans.org—type **password policy** into the search box at the top of the SANS web site). Ideally, the password policy is defined within an organization's security policy. The overall guidance established by the organization's security policy should be refined into specific guidance that administrators can enforce at the operating system level.

Cross Check

Passwords on a UNIX System

In Chapter 14 we discussed changing passwords from the command line in a UNIX environment. What is the command used to change UNIX passwords from the command line in a UNIX environment? How are passwords typically stored on UNIX systems? In what files?

Domain Password Policy

A **domain password policy** is a password policy for a specific domain. As these policies are usually associated with the Windows operating system, a domain password policy is implemented and enforced on the **domain controller**, which is a computer that responds to security authentication requests, such as logging in to a computer, for a Windows domain. The domain password policy usually falls under a **group policy object** and has the following elements (see Figure 22.4):

Exam Tip: A *password policy* is a set of rules designed to enhance computer security by requiring users to employ and maintain strong passwords. A *domain password policy* is a password policy that applies to a specific domain.

- **Enforce password history** Tells the system how many passwords to remember and does not allow a user to reuse an old password

- **Maximum password age** Specifies the number of days a password may be used before it must be changed

- **Minimum password age** Specifies the number of days a password must be used before it can be changed again

- **Minimum password length** Specifies the minimum number of characters that must be used in a password

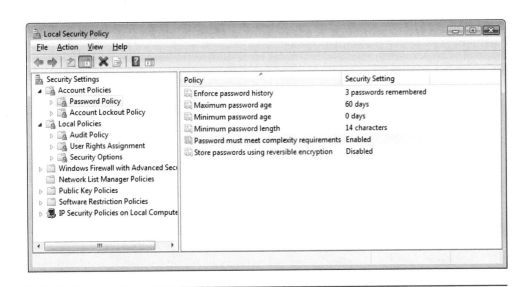

• **Figure 22.4** Password policy options in Windows Local Security Policy

- **Password must meet complexity requirements** Specifies that the password must meet the minimum length requirement and have characters from at least three of the following four groups: English uppercase characters (A through Z), English lowercase characters (a through z), numerals (0 through 9), and nonalphabetic characters (such as !, $, #, %)

- **Store passwords using reversible encryption** Reversible encryption is a form of encryption that can easily be decrypted and is essentially the same as storing a plaintext version of the password (because it's so easy to reverse the encryption and get the password). This should be used only when applications use protocols that require the user's password for authentication (such as Challenge-Handshake Authentication Protocol, or CHAP).

Try This

Calculating Unique Password Combinations

One of the primary reasons administrators require users to have longer passwords that use upper- and lowercase letters, numbers, and at least one "special" character is to help deter password-guessing attacks. One popular password-guessing technique, called a *brute-force attack*, uses software to guess every possible password until one matches a user's password. Essentially, a brute force-attack tries *a*, then *aa*, then *aaa*, and so on until it runs out of combinations or gets a password match. Increasing both the pool of possible characters that can be used in the password and the number of characters required in the password can exponentially increase the number of "guesses" a brute-force program needs to perform before it runs out of possibilities. For example, if our password policy requires a three-character password that uses only lowercase letters, there are only 17,576 possible passwords (26 possible characters, 3 characters long is 26^3 combinations). Requiring a six-character password increases that number to 308,915,776 possible passwords (26^6). See if you can calculate how many possible combinations there are in these password sets (the answers are given in the footnote at the bottom of the page*):

- A six-character password that uses both upper- and lowercase letters

- An eight-character password that uses numbers (0–9) and lowercase letters

- A ten-character password that uses numbers and upper- and lowercase letters

---

Domains are logical groups of computers that share a central directory database, known as the Active Directory database for the more recent Windows operating systems. The database contains information about the user accounts and security information for all resources identified within the domain. Each user within the domain is assigned her own unique account (that is, a domain is not a single account shared by multiple users), which is then assigned access to specific resources within the domain. In operating systems that provide domain capabilities, the password policy is set in the root container for the domain and applies to all users within that domain. Setting a password policy for a domain is similar to setting other password policies in that the same critical elements need to be considered (password length, complexity, life, and so on). If a change to one of these elements is desired for a group of users, a new domain needs to be created because the domain is considered a security boundary. In a Microsoft Windows operating system that employs Active Directory, the domain password policy can be set in the Active Directory Users and Computers menu in the Administrative Tools section of the Control Panel.

*Answers: 19,770,609,664 (52^6), 2,821,109,907,456 (36^8), 1,568,336,880,910,795,776 (62^{10})

Single Sign-On

To use a system, users must be able to access it, which they usually do by supplying their user IDs (or usernames) and corresponding passwords. As any security administrator knows, the more systems a particular user has access to, the more passwords that user must have and remember. The natural tendency for users is to select passwords that are easy to remember, or even the same password for use on the multiple systems they access. Invariably, users will forget the passwords they chose for infrequently accessed systems, which creates more work for system administrators who must assist users with password changes or password recovery efforts. Wouldn't it be easier for the user simply to log in once and have to remember only a single, good password? This is made possible with a technology called single sign-on.

Single sign-on (SSO) is an authentication process in which the user can enter a single username and password and then be able to move from application to application or resource to resource without having to supply further authentication information. Put simply, you supply the right username and password once and you have access to all the applications and data you need, without having to log in multiple times and remember many different passwords. From a user standpoint, SSO means you need to remember only one username and one password. From an administration standpoint, SSO can be easier to manage and maintain. From a security standpoint, SSO can be even more secure, as users who need to remember only one password are less likely to choose something too simple or something so complex they need to write it down. Figure 22.5 shows a logical depiction of the SSO process:

1. The user signs in once, providing a username and password to the SSO server.

2. The SSO server provides authentication information to any resource the user accesses during that session. The server interfaces with the other applications and systems—the user does not need to log into each system individually.

> **Exam Tip:** The Security+ exam will very likely contain questions regarding single sign-on because it is such a prevalent topic and a very common approach to multisystem authentication.

In reality, SSO is usually a little more difficult to implement than vendors would lead you to believe. To be effective and useful, all your applications need to be able to access and use the authentication provided by the SSO process. The more diverse your network, the less likely this is to be the case. If your network, like most, contains different operating systems, custom applications, and a diverse user base, SSO may not even be a viable option.

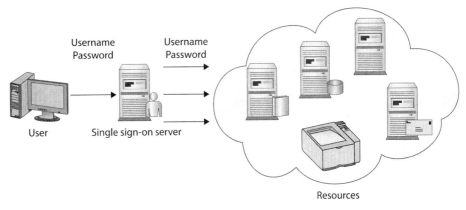

• **Figure 22.5**   Single sign-on process

Time of Day Restrictions

Some organizations need to tightly control certain users, groups, or even roles and limit access to certain resources to specific days and times. Most server-class operating systems enable administrators to implement time of day restrictions that limit when a user can log in, when certain resources can be accessed, and so on. Time of day restrictions are usually specified for individual accounts, as shown in Figure 22.6. This type of capability might be used by a bank, for example. The administrator may implement time of day restrictions on the accounts of bank tellers so that they may be logged in only from 8 A.M. to 6 P.M. Monday through Saturday. If a teller attempts to log in outside the allowed hours, he is denied access even if he supplies the proper authentication credentials. If a teller is logged in when his allowable login time expires, the system can be configured to forcibly disconnect the teller or just warn the teller that his login hours have past but still allow them to remain logged in.

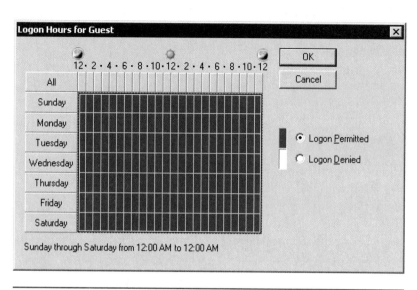

• **Figure 22.6**   Logon hours for Guest account

From a security perspective, time of day restrictions can be very useful. If a user normally accesses certain resources during normal business hours, an attempt to access these resources outside this time period (either at night or on the weekend) might indicate an attacker has gained access to or is trying to gain access to that account. Specifying time of day restrictions can also serve as a mechanism to enforce internal controls of critical or sensitive resources. Obviously, a drawback to enforcing time of day restrictions is that it means that a user can't go to work outside of normal hours to "catch up" with work tasks. As with all security policies, usability and security must be balanced in this policy decision.

⚠️ Be careful implementing time of day restrictions. Some operating systems give you the option of disconnecting users as soon as their "allowed login time" expires regardless of what the user is doing at the time. The more commonly used approach is to allow currently logged-in users to stay connected but reject any login attempts that occur outside of allowed hours.

Tokens

While the username/password combination has and continues to be the cheapest and most popular method of controlling access to resources, many organizations look for a more secure and tamper-resistant form of authentication. Usernames and passwords are "something you know" (which can be used by anyone else that knows or discovers the information). A more secure method of authentication is to combine the "something you know" with "something you have." A **token** is an authentication factor that typically takes the form of a physical or logical entity that the user must be in possession of to access their account or certain resources.

Most tokens are physical tokens that display a series of numbers that changes every 30 to 90 seconds, such as the token pictured in Figure 22.7 from Blizzard Entertainment. This sequence of numbers must be entered when the user is attempting to log in or access certain resources. The ever-changing sequence of numbers is synchronized to a remote server such that when the user enters the correct username, password, and matching sequence of numbers, she is are allowed to log in. Even if an attacker obtains the username and password, the attacker cannot log in without the matching sequence of numbers. Other physical tokens include Common Access Cards (CACs), USB tokens, smart cards, and PC cards.

Tokens may also be implemented in software. Software tokens still provide two-factor authentication but don't require the user to have a physical device on hand.

• **Figure 22.7**   Token authenticator from Blizzard Entertainment

Some tokens require software clients that store a symmetric key (sometimes called a seed record) in a secured location on the user's device (laptop, desktop, PDA, and so on). Other software tokens use public key cryptography. Asymmetric cryptography solutions, such as public key cryptography, often associate a PIN with a specific user's token. To log in or access critical resources, the user must supply the correct PIN. The PIN is stored on a remote server and used during the authentication process so that if a user presents the right token, but not the right PIN, the user's access can be denied. This helps prevent an attacker from gaining access if he gets a copy of or gains access to the software token.

 Cross Check

Symmetric and Asymmetric Cryptography

You learned about symmetric and asymmetric cryptography in Chapter 5. What is the difference between the two methods? Which one uses public keys?

Account and Password Expiration

Another common restriction that can be enforced in many access control mechanisms is either (or both) an account expiration or password expiration feature. This allows administrators to specify a period of time for which a password or an account will be active. For password expiration, when the expiration date is reached, the user generally is asked to create a new password. This means that if the password (and thus the account) has been compromised when the expiration date is reached and a new password is set, the attacker will again (hopefully) be locked out of the system. The attacker can't change the password himself, since the user would then be locked out and would contact an administrator to have the password reset, thus again locking out the attacker.

Another attack option would involve the attacker setting a new password on the compromised account and then attempting to reset the account back to the original, compromised password. If the attacker is successful, a new expiration time would be set for the account but the old password would still be used and the user would not be locked out of their account; in most cases, the user wouldn't notice anything had happened at all as their old password would continue to work. This is one reason why a *password history* mechanism should be used. The history is used to keep track of previously used passwords so that they cannot be reused. Account expiration is similar, except that it is generally put in place because a specific account is intended for a specific purpose of limited duration. When an account has expired, it cannot be used unless the expiration deadline is extended.

 Tech Tip

Best Practice: Password Expiration

One of the best practices an organization can implement is to attach an expiration date to user passwords. This helps ensure that if a password is compromised, the period that the account remains compromised is limited. In most environments and operating systems, this is expressed in terms of the number of days before the password expires and is no longer valid. For example, a maximum password age of 90 days means that a particular password will expire 90 days after that password was initially set to its current value.

■ Security Controls and Permissions

If multiple users share a computer system, the system administrator likely needs to control who is allowed to do what when it comes to viewing, using, or changing system resources. While operating systems vary in how they implement these types of controls, most operating systems use the concepts of permissions and rights to control and safeguard access to resources. As we discussed earlier, permissions control what a user is allowed to do with objects on a system and rights define the actions a user can perform on the system itself. Let's examine how the Windows operating systems implement this concept.

The Windows operating systems use the concepts of permissions and rights to control access to files, folders, and information resources. When using the NTFS file system, administrators can grant users and groups permission to perform certain tasks as they relate to files, folders, and Registry keys. The basic categories of NTFS permissions are as follows:

Try This

Folder Permissions

On a Windows XP or Vista system, right-click any folder and select Properties. Then, in the window that pops up, select the Security tab. What users or groups have Full Control permissions? Do any users or groups have only Read permissions? Now open a command prompt on the same system (you need administrator privileges). Type **icacls C:\windows** and press ENTER. This command displays group and user permissions in a text format. Look at the permissions on the folder you chose at the beginning of this exercise—is it easier to read permissions using the GUI or the command line?

- ■ **Full Control** A user/group can change permissions on the folder/file, take ownership if someone else owns the folder/file, delete subfolders and files, and perform actions permitted by all other NTFS folder permissions.

- ■ **Modify** Users/groups can view and modify files/folders and their properties, can delete and add files/folders, and can delete or add properties to a file/folder.

- ■ **Read & Execute** Users/groups can view the file/folder and can execute scripts and executables but cannot make any changes (files/folders are read-only).

- ■ **List Folder Contents** A user/group can list only what is inside the folder (applies to folders only).

- ■ **Read** Users/groups can view the contents of the file/folder and the file/folder properties.

- ■ **Write** Users/groups can write to the file or folder.

Exam Tip: *Permissions* can be applied to specific users or groups to control that user's or group's ability to view, modify, access, use, or delete resources such as folders and files.

Figure 22.8 shows the permissions on a folder called Data from a Windows Server 2008 system. In the top half of the Permissions window are the users and groups that have permissions for this folder. In the bottom half of the window are the permissions assigned to the highlighted user or group.

The Windows operating system also uses user rights or privileges to determine what actions a user or group is allowed to perform or access. These user rights are typically assigned to groups, as it is easier to deal with a few groups than to assign rights to individual users, and they are usually defined in either a group or a local security policy. The list of user rights is quite extensive but a few examples of user rights are

- **Log on locally**   Users/groups can attempt to log onto the local system itself.

- **Access this computer from the network**   Users/groups can attempt to access this system through the network connection.

- **Manage auditing and security log**   Users/groups can view, modify, and delete auditing and security log information.

Rights tend to be actions that deal with accessing the system itself, process control, logging, and so on. Figure 22.9 shows the user rights contained in the local security policy on a Windows Vista system. The user rights within Windows XP, 2003, Vista, and 2008 are very similar.

Folders and files are not the only things that can be safeguarded or controlled using permissions. Even access and use of peripherals, such as printers, can be controlled using permissions. Figure 22.10 shows the Security tab from a printer attached to a Windows Vista system. Permissions can be assigned to control who can print to the printer, who can manage documents and print jobs sent to the printer, and who can manage the printer itself. With this type of granular control, administrators have a great deal of control over how system resources are used and who uses them.

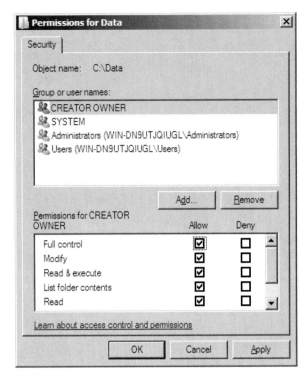

• **Figure 22.8**   Permissions for the Data folder

Access Control Lists

The term **access control list (ACL)** is used in more than one manner in the field of computer security. When discussing routers and firewalls, an ACL is a set of rules used to control traffic flow into or out of an interface or network. When discussing system resources, such as files and folders, an ACL lists permissions attached to an object—who is allowed to view, modify, move, or delete that object.

To illustrate this concept, consider an example.

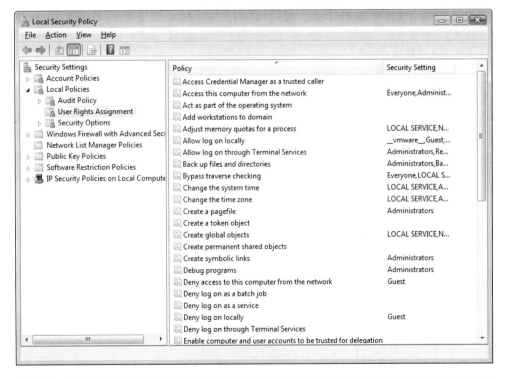

• **Figure 22.9**   User Rights Assignment options from Windows Local Security Policy

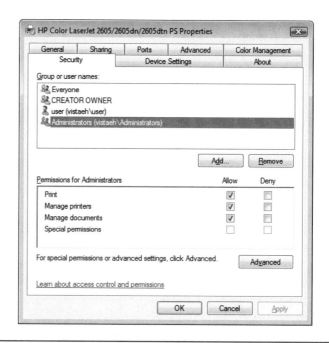

• **Figure 22.10**   Security tab showing printer permissions under Windows Vista

Figure 22.11 shows the access control list (permissions) for the Data folder. The user identified as Billy Williams has Read & Execute, List Folder Contents, and Read permissions, meaning this user can open the folder, see what's in the folder, and so on. Figure 22.12 shows the permissions for a user identified as Leah Jones, who has only Read permissions on the same folder.

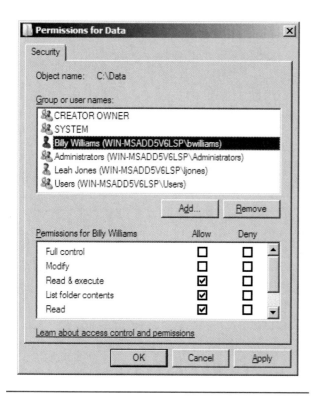

• **Figure 22.11**   Permissions for Billy Williams on the Data folder

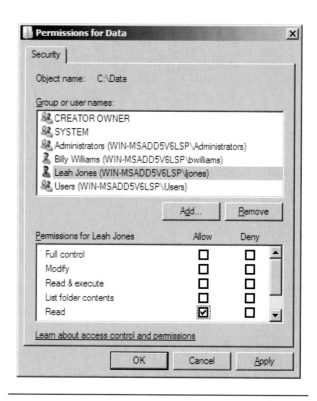

• **Figure 22.12**   Permissions for Leah Jones on the Data folder

Handling Access Control (MAC, DAC, and RBAC)

The last area of privilege management we will discuss deals with four methods for handling access control:

- **MAC**   Mandatory access control
- **DAC**   Discretionary access control
- **RBAC**   Role-based access control
- **RBAC**   Rule-based access control

Mandatory Access Control (MAC)

Mandatory access control (MAC) is the process of controlling access to information based on the sensitivity of that information and whether or not the user is operating at the appropriate sensitivity level and has the authority to access that information. Under a MAC system, each piece of information and every system resource (files, devices, networks, and so on) is labeled with its sensitivity level (such as Public, Engineering Private, Jones Secret). Users are assigned a clearance level that sets the upper boundary of the information and devices that they are allowed to access. For example, if the administrator defines a file as having an Engineering Private sensitivity level, only the members of the Engineering group with access to private information currently operating at a Private sensitivity level can access that file and its contents. A file with a Public sensitivity label would be available to anyone on the system.

The access control and sensitivity labels are required in a MAC system. Labels are defined and then assigned to users and resources. Users must then operate within their assigned sensitivity and clearance levels—they don't have the option to modify their own sensitivity levels or the levels of the information resources they create. Due to the complexity involved, MAC is typically run only on systems and operating systems such as Trusted Solaris and OpenBSD where security is a top priority.

Figure 22.13 illustrates MAC in operation. The information resource on the left has been labeled "Engineering Secret," meaning only users in the Engineering group operating at the Secret sensitivity level or above can access that resource. The top user is operating at the Secret level but is not a member of Engineering and is denied access to the resource. The middle user is a member of Engineering but is operating at a Public sensitivity level and is therefore denied access to the resource. The bottom user is a member of Engineering, is operating at a Secret sensitivity level, and is allowed to access the information resource.

In the U.S. government, the following security labels are used to classify information and information resources for MAC systems:

- **Top Secret**   The highest security level that is publicly disclosed and is defined as information that would cause "exceptionally grave damage" to national security if disclosed to the public.

 Exam Tip: Mandatory access control restricts access based on the sensitivity of the information and whether or not the user has the authority to access that information.

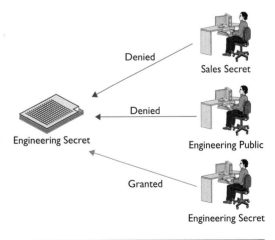

Denied — Sales Secret

Denied — Engineering Public

Granted — Engineering Secret

Engineering Secret

• **Figure 22.13**   Logical representation of mandatory access control

- **Secret** The second highest level and is defined as information that would cause "serious damage" to national security if disclosed to the public.

- **Confidential** The lowest level of classified information and is defined as information that would "damage" national security if disclosed.

- **Unclassified** Any of this information can be released to individuals without a clearance.

The labels work in a top-down fashion so that an individual holding a Secret clearance would have access to information at the Secret, Confidential, and Unclassified levels. An individual with a Secret clearance would not have access to Top Secret resources, as that label is above the highest level of the individual's clearance.

Discretionary Access Control (DAC)

Discretionary access control (DAC) is the process of using file permissions and optional ACLs to restrict access to information based on a user's identity or group membership. DAC is the most common access control system and is commonly used in both UNIX and Windows operating systems. The "discretionary" part of DAC means that a file or resource owner has the ability to change the permissions on that file or resource.

Under UNIX operating systems, file permissions consist of three distinct parts:

- **Owner permissions (read, write, and execute)** The owner of the file

- **Group permissions (read, write, and execute)** The group to which the owner of the file belongs

- **World permissions (read, write, and execute)** Anyone else who is not the owner and does not belong to the group to which the owner of the file belongs

For example, suppose a file called *secretdata* has been created by the owner of the file, Luke, who is part of the Engineering group. The owner permissions on the file would reflect Luke's access to the file (as the owner). The group permissions would reflect the access granted to anyone who is part of the Engineering group. The world permissions would represent the access granted to anyone who is not Luke and is not part of the Engineering group.

In a simplified view, a file's permissions are usually displayed as a series of nine characters, with the first three characters representing the owner's permissions, the second three characters representing the group permissions, and the last three characters representing the permissions for everyone else, or for the world. This concept is illustrated in Figure 22.14.

Suppose the file secretdata is owned by Luke with group permissions for Engineering (because Luke is part of the Engineering

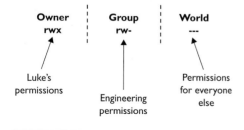

• **Figure 22.14** Discretionary file permissions in the UNIX environment

group), and the permissions on that file are rwx, rw-, and ---, as shown in Figure 22.14. This would mean that:

- Luke can read, write, and execute the file (rwx).

- Members of the Engineering group can read and write the file but not execute it (rw-).

- The world has no access to the file and can't read, write, or execute it (---).

Remember that under the discretionary model, the file's owner, Luke, can change the file's permissions any time he wants.

Role-Based Access Control (RBAC)

Role-based access control (RBAC) is the process of managing access and privileges based on the user's assigned roles. RBAC is the access control model that most closely resembles an organization's structure. Under RBAC, you must first determine the activities that must be performed and the resources that must be accessed by specific roles. For example, the role of "securityadmin" in Microsoft SQL Server must be able to create and manage logins, read error logs, and audit the application. Once all the roles are created and the rights and privileges associated with those roles are determined, users can then be assigned one or more roles based on their job functions. When a role is assigned to a specific user, the user gets all the rights and privileges assigned to that role.

 Exam Tip: Role-based and rule-based access control are both abbreviated as RBAC, so don't get the two confused. *Role*-based focuses on the user's role (administrator, backup operator, and so on). *Rule*-based focuses on predefined criteria such as time of day (users can only log in between 8 A.M. and 6 P.M.) or type of network traffic (web traffic is allowed to leave the organization).

Rule-Based Access Control (RBAC)

Rule-based access control (RBAC) is yet another method of managing access and privileges (and unfortunately shares the same acronym as role-based). In this method, access is either allowed or denied based on a set of predefined rules. Each object has an associated ACL (much like DAC), and when a particular user or group attempts to access the object, the appropriate rule is applied.

A good example is permitted logon hours. Many operating systems give administrators the ability to control the hours during which users can log in. For example, a bank may allow its employees to log in only between the hours of 8 A.M. and 6 P.M. Monday through Saturday. If a user attempts to log in during these hours, the rule will allow the user to attempt the login. If a user attempts to log in outside of these hours, 3 A.M. on Sunday for example, then the rule will reject the login attempt whether or not the user supplies valid login credentials.

Another good example of RBAC would be an ACL on a router. The ACL defines what traffic is allowed to pass through the router based on the rules established and maintained by the administrator—users cannot change access rules.

Exam Tip: The Security+ exam will very likely expect you to be able to differentiate between the four major forms of access control discussed here: mandatory access control, discretionary access control, role-based access control, and rule-based access control.

Chapter 22 Review

■ For More Information

- **Microsoft's TechNet Group Policy Page** http:// technet.microsoft .com/en-us/windowsserver/ grouppolicy/default.aspx

- **SANS Reading Room – Password Policy** www.sans.org/resources/policies/ Password_Policy.pdf

■ Chapter Summary

After reading this chapter and completing the exercises, you should understand the following about privilege management.

Identify the differences among user, group, and role management

- Privilege management is the process of restricting a user's ability to interact with the computer system.

- Privilege management can be based on an individual user basis, on membership in a specific group or groups, or on a function/role.

- Key concepts in privilege management are the ability to restrict and control access to information and information systems.

- One of the methods used to simplify privilege management is single sign-on, which requires a user to authenticate successfully once. The validated credentials and associated rights and privileges are then automatically carried forward when the user accesses other systems or applications.

Implement password and domain password policies

- Password policies are sets of rules that help users select, employ, and store strong passwords. Tokens combine "something you have" with "something you know," such as a password or PIN, and can be hardware or software based.

- Passwords should have a limited span and should expire on a scheduled basis.

Describe methods of account management (SSO, time of day, logical token, account expiration)

- Administrators have many different tools at their disposal to control access to computer resources.

- Users can be limited in the hours during which they can access resources.

- Resources such as files, folders, and printers can be controlled through permissions or access control lists.

- Permissions can be assigned based on a user's identity or their membership in one or more groups.

Describe methods of access management (MAC, DAC, and RBAC)

- Mandatory access control is based on the sensitivity of the information or process itself.

- Discretionary access control uses file permissions and ACLs to restrict access based on a user's identity or group membership.

- Role-based access control restricts access based on the user's assigned role or roles.

- Rule-based access control restricts access based on a defined set of rules established by the administrator.

■ Key Terms

administrator *(562)*
access control list (ACL) *(571)*
discretionary access control (DAC) *(574)*
domain controller *(565)*

domain password policy *(565)*
group *(563)*
group policy object *(565)*
mandatory access control (MAC) *(573)*

password policy *(564)*

permissions *(562)*

privilege management *(561)*

privileges *(561)*

rights *(562)*

role *(564)*

role-based access control (RBAC) *(575)*

root *(562)*

rule-based access control (RBAC) *(575)*

single sign-on (SSO) *(567)*

superuser *(562)*

token *(568)*

user *(561)*

username *(561)*

■ Key Term Quiz

Use terms from the Key Terms list to complete the sentences that follow. Don't use the same term more than once. Not all terms will be used.

1. In user authentication methods, a(n) _____ is used as "something you have."

2. The administrator account in Windows is also known as a(n) _____ account.

3. A(n) _____ is a user's job or job function such as "backup operator" or "administrator."

4. _____ is an authentication process where the user can enter their user ID (or username) and password and then be able to move from application to application or resource to resource without having to supply further authentication information.

5. On UNIX systems the account with the highest level of access is known as _____.

6. A(n) _____ is a set of rules designed to help users select a secure and appropriate password.

7. An access control mechanism in which the owner of an object can decide which other subjects may have access to the object and what access they may have is called _____.

8. A(n) _____ is a Windows system that responds to authentication requests and can be used to enforce password policies.

9. _____ is an access control mechanism in which the security mechanism controls access to all objects (files), and individual subjects (processes or users) cannot change that access.

10. A(n) _____ is a unique alphanumeric identifier that identifies individuals when logging into or accessing a system.

■ Multiple-Choice Quiz

1. When Bob is selecting a new password, which of the following is the best choice for Bob?

   A. Bob

   B. kitty

   C. Bob123

   D. 1c4brts9E#

2. If a user only has to provide her credentials once (user ID and password) and can then access multiple resources and applications without having to authenticate again, this is known as:

   A. Privilege management

   B. Centralized user accounts

   C. Single sign-on

   D. Access control

3. The access control model in which object owners can change the permissions of their own files is called:

   A. Mandatory access control

   B. Discretionary access control

   C. Distributed access control

   D. Dynamic access control

4. When discussing privilege management, MAC stands for:

   A. Media access control

   B. Mandatory access control

   C. Mandatory availability criteria

   D. Modified access credentials

5. Privilege management applies to:

    A. Users, physical locations, and resources

    B. Users, physical locations, and processes

    C. Files, resources, and users

    D. Applications, systems, and security

6. Under the UNIX operating system, file permissions consist of what three parts?

    A. Open, run, modify

    B. Change, delete, execute

    C. Run, write, delete

    D. Read, write, execute

7. A unique, alphanumeric identifier assigned to each user is called what?

    A. Username

    B. Privilege

    C. Single sign-on

    D. Nickname

8. To assign and manage privileges by job function, you might use what?

    A. Role-based access control

    B. Mandatory access control

    C. Process-based access control

    D. Discretionary access control

9. Under which access control system is each piece of information and every system resource (files, devices, networks, and so on) labeled with its sensitivity level?

    A. Discretionary access control

    B. Resource access control

    C. Mandatory access control

    D. Media access control

10. The process of restricting a user's ability to interact with the computer system is called what?

    A. Privilege management

    B. Audit control

    C. Access restriction

    D. User management

11. When used in authentication mechanisms, a token can be:

    A. Software based only

    B. Software or hardware based

    C. Hardware based only

    D. The same for all users

12. If a user on a Windows system only has Read & Execute permissions to a folder, that user can:

    A. Delete the folder

    B. Modify any file in that folder

    C. Only read files in that folder

    D. Execute files in that folder

13. In this chapter a password history could be used to

    A. Allow a user to re-use old passwords.

    B. Stop attackers from scanning a system.

    C. Prevent users from re-using previously used passwords.

    D. Implement role-based access control.

14. Which of the following is usually implemented and enforced on a domain controller in Windows operating systems:

    A. Privilege management

    B. Domain password policy

    C. Single sign-on

    D. Access control

15. If an administrator wants users to be able to log in only from 8 A.M. to 6 P.M., the administrator might use:

    A. Time of day restrictions

    B. Global policy objects

    C. Account expiration

    D. Role-based access control

Essay Quiz

1. Your boss just read an article about single sign-on technologies and wants to know how something like that would benefit an organization like yours. Summarize the benefits of single sign-on technologies and discuss how each benefit would affect your organization.

2. A training manager needs your help developing some new course material and wants to know if you can come up with a good discussion for how mandatory access control systems work.

3. A co-worker with a strong Windows background is having difficulty understanding UNIX file permissions. Describe UNIX file permissions for him. Compare UNIX file permissions to Windows file permissions.

Lab Projects

• Lab Project 22.1

Use the Internet to research RSA's SecurID system and Alladin's eToken system. Explain how each system works and discuss the differences between them.

• Lab Project 22.2

On a Windows XP or Vista system, log in with administrator-level permissions and create a user called **test** with a password of **Abk23p7Np#**. Now open Local Security Policy (look under Control Panel and then Computer Management). Open Account Policies and then Account Lockout Policy. Find Account Lockout Duration and set it to three minutes. Find Account Lockout Threshold and set it to three invalid login attempts. Find Reset Account Lockout Counter After and set it to three minutes. Log off as administrator. Attempt to log in as the test account (you previously created) three times as quickly as you can using the wrong password. On the fourth attempt, use the correct password. Were you able to log in? Why or why not? Wait four minutes and attempt to log in as the test account again, this time using the correct password. Were you able to log in? Why or why not?

• Lab Project 22.3

On a Windows XP or Vista system, log in with administrator-level permissions and open Local Security Policy (look under Control Panel and then Computer Management). Open Password Policy under Account Policies. Create a password policy for your local system by setting values for each of the policy settings under Password Policy. Explain why you chose those settings and how they help to ensure that your system is secure.

Computer Forensics

"How often have I said to you that when you have eliminated the impossible, whatever remains, however improbable, must be the truth?"

—Sir Arthur Conan Doyle

In this chapter, you will learn how to

- **Identify the rules and types of evidence**
- **Collect evidence**
- **Preserve evidence**
- **Maintain a viable chain of custody**
- **Investigate a computer crime or policy violation**

Computer forensics is certainly a popular buzzword in computer security. This chapter addresses the key aspects of computer forensics in preparation for the Security+ certification exam. It is not intended to be a legal tutorial regarding the presentation of evidence in a court of law. These principles are of value in conducting any investigative processes, including internal or external audit procedures, but many nuances of handling legal cases are far beyond the scope of this text.

The term **forensics** relates to the application of scientific knowledge to legal problems. Specifically, computer forensics involves the preservation, identification, documentation, and interpretation of computer data, as explained in *Hacking Exposed: Computer Forensics, Second Edition* (McGraw Hill, 2009). In today's practice, computer forensics can be performed for three purposes:

- Investigating and analyzing computer systems as related to a violation of laws

- Investigating and analyzing computer systems for compliance with an organization's policies

- Investigating computer systems that have been remotely attacked

This last point is often referred to as *incident response* and can be a subset of the first two points. If an unauthorized person is remotely attacking a system, laws may indeed have been violated. However, a company employee performing similar acts may or may not violate laws and corporate policies. Any of these three purposes could ultimately result in legal actions and may require legal disclosure. Therefore, it is important to note that computer forensics actions may, at some point in time, deal with legal violations, and investigations could go to court proceedings. As a potential first responder, you should always seek legal counsel. Also seek legal counsel ahead of time as you develop and implement corporate policies and procedures. It is extremely important to understand that even minor procedural missteps can have significant legal consequences.

The incident response cycle is a quick way to remember the key steps in computer forensics. Figure 23.1 graphically conveys the incident response cycle. There are five key steps:

1. **Discover and report**—Organizations should administer an incident reporting process to make sure that potential security breaches as well as routine application problems are reported and resolved as quickly as possible. Employees should be trained on how to report system problems.

2. **Confirm**—Specialists or a response team member should review the incident report to confirm whether or not a security incident has occurred. Detailed notes should be taken and retained as they could be critically valuable for later investigation.

3. **Investigate**—A response team composed of network, system, and application specialists should investigate the incident in detail to determine the extent of the incident and to devise a recovery plan.

4. **Recover**—The investigation is complete and documented at this point in time. Steps are taken to return the systems and applications to operational status.

5. **Lessons learned**—A post-mortem session should collect lessons learned and assign action items to correct weaknesses and to suggest ways to improve.

• **Figure 23.1**   Incident response cycle

■ Evidence

Evidence consists of the documents, verbal statements, and material objects that are admissible in a court of law. Evidence is critical to convincing management, juries, judges, or other authorities that some kind of violation has occurred. The submission of evidence is challenging, but it is even more challenging when computers are used because the people involved may not be technically educated and thus may not fully understand what's happened.

Computer evidence presents yet more challenges because the data itself cannot be sensed with the physical senses—that is, you can see printed characters, but you can't see the bits where that data is stored. Bits of data are merely magnetic pulses on a disk or some other storage technology. Therefore, data must always be evaluated through some kind of "filter" rather than sensed directly by human senses. This is often of concern to auditors, because good auditing techniques recommend accessing the original data or a version that is as close as possible to the original data.

Standards for Evidence

To be credible, especially if evidence will be used in court proceedings or in corporate disciplinary actions that could be challenged legally, evidence must meet three standards:

- **Sufficient evidence** It must be convincing or measure up without question.

- **Competent evidence** It must be legally qualified and reliable.

- **Relevant evidence** It must be material to the case or have a bearing on the matter at hand.

Types of Evidence

All evidence is not created equal. Some evidence is stronger and better than other, weaker evidence. Several types of evidence can be germane:

- **Direct evidence** Oral testimony that proves a specific fact (such as an eyewitness's statement). The knowledge of the facts is obtained through the five senses of the witness, with no inferences or presumptions.

- **Real evidence** Also known as associative or physical evidence, this includes tangible objects that prove or disprove a fact. Physical evidence links the suspect to the scene of a crime.

- **Documentary evidence** Evidence in the form of business records, printouts, manuals, and the like. Much of the evidence relating to computer crimes is documentary evidence.

- **Demonstrative evidence** Used to aid the jury and can be in the form of a model, experiment, chart, and so on, offered to prove that an event occurred.

Three Rules Regarding Evidence

An item can become evidence when it is admitted by a judge in a case. Three rules guide the use of evidence, with regard to its use in court proceedings:

- **Best evidence rule**   Courts prefer original evidence rather than a copy to ensure that no alteration of the evidence (whether intentional or unintentional) has occurred. In some instances, an evidence duplicate can be accepted, such as when the original is lost or destroyed by acts of God or in the normal course of business. A duplicate is also acceptable when a third party beyond the court's subpoena power possesses the original.

- **Exclusionary rule**   The Fourth Amendment to the U.S. Constitution precludes illegal search and seizure. Therefore, any evidence collected in violation of the Fourth Amendment is not admissible as evidence. Additionally, if evidence is collected in violation of the Electronic Communications Privacy Act (ECPA) or other related violations of the U.S. Code, it may not be admissible to a court. For example, if no policy exists regarding the company's intent to monitor network traffic or systems electronically, and the employee has not acknowledged this policy by signing an agreement, sniffing network traffic could be a violation of the ECPA.

- **Hearsay rule**   Hearsay is second-hand evidence—evidence offered by the witness that is not based on the personal knowledge of the witness but is being offered to prove the truth of the matter asserted.. Typically, computer-generated evidence is considered hearsay evidence, as the maker of the evidence (the computer) cannot be interrogated. There are exceptions being made where items such as logs and headers (computer-generated materials) are being accepted in court.

 The laws mentioned here are U.S. laws. Other countries and jurisdictions may have similar laws that would need to be considered in a similar manner.

■ Collecting Evidence

When information or objects are presented to management or admitted to court to support a claim, that information or those objects can be considered as evidence or documentation supporting your investigative efforts. Senior management will always ask a lot of questions—second- and third-order questions that you need to be able to answer quickly. Likewise, in a court, credibility is critical. Therefore, evidence must be properly acquired, identified, protected against tampering, transported, and stored.

Acquiring Evidence

When an incident occurs, you will need to collect data and information to facilitate your investigation. If someone is committing a crime or intentionally violating a company policy, she will likely try to hide her tracks. Therefore, you should collect as much information as soon as you can. In today's highly networked world, evidence can be found not only on the workstation

Tech Tip

Data Volatility

From the most volatile to the most persistent:

1. *CPU storage (registers/cache)*

2. *System storage (RAM)*

3. *Kernel tables*

4. *Fixed media*

5. *Removable media*

6. *Output/hardcopy*

Exam Tip: For Security+ testing purposes, remember this: the memory should be dumped, the system should be powered down cleanly, and an image should be made and used as you work.

or laptop computer, but also on company-owned file servers, security appliances, and servers located with the Internet service provider (ISP).

A first responder must do as much as possible to control damage or loss of evidence. Obviously, as time passes, evidence can be tampered with or destroyed. Look around on the desk, on the Rolodex, under the keyboard, in desktop storage areas, and on cubicle bulletin boards for any information that might be relevant. Secure floppy disks, CDs, flash memory cards, USB drives, tapes, and other removable media. Request copies of logs as soon as possible. Most ISPs protect logs that could be subpoenaed. Take photos (some localities require use of Polaroid photos, as they are more difficult to modify without obvious tampering) or video tapes. Include photos of operating computer screens and hardware components from multiple angles. Be sure to photograph internal components before removing them for analysis.

When an incident occurs and the computer being used is going to be secured, you must consider two questions: should it be turned off, and should it be disconnected from the network? Forensics professionals debate the reasons for turning a computer on or turning it off. Some state that the plug should be pulled in order to freeze the current state of the computer. However, this results in the loss of any data associated with an attack in progress from the machine. Any data in RAM will also be lost. Further, it may corrupt the computer's file system and could call into question the validity of your findings.

Imaging or dumping the physical memory of a computer system can help identify evidence not available on a hard drive. This is especially appropriate for rootkits, for which evidence on the hard drive is hard to find. Once the memory is imaged, you can use a hex editor to analyze the image offline on another system. (Memory-dumping tools and hex editors are available on the Internet.) Note that dumping memory is more applicable for investigative work where court proceedings will not be pursued. If a case is likely to end up in court, do not dump memory without first seeking legal advice to confirm that live analysis of the memory is acceptable; otherwise, the defendant will be able to dispute easily the claim that evidence was not tampered with.

On the other hand, it is possible for the computer criminal to leave behind a software bomb that you don't know about, and any commands you execute, including shutting down or restarting the system, could destroy or modify files, information, or evidence. The criminal may have anticipated such an investigation and altered some of the system's binary files. While teaching at the University of Texas, Austin, Dr. Larry Leibrock led a research project to quantify how many files are changed when turning off and on a Windows workstation. The research documents that approximately 0.6 percent of the operating system files are changed each time a Windows XP system is shut down and restarted.

Further, if the computer being analyzed is a server, it is unlikely management will support taking it offline and shutting it down for investigation. So, from an investigative perspective, either course may be correct or incorrect, depending on the circumstances surrounding the incident. What is most important is that you are deliberate in your work, you document your actions, and you can explain why you took the actions you did.

Many investigative methods are used. Figure 23.2 shows the continuum of investigative methods from simple to more rigorous.

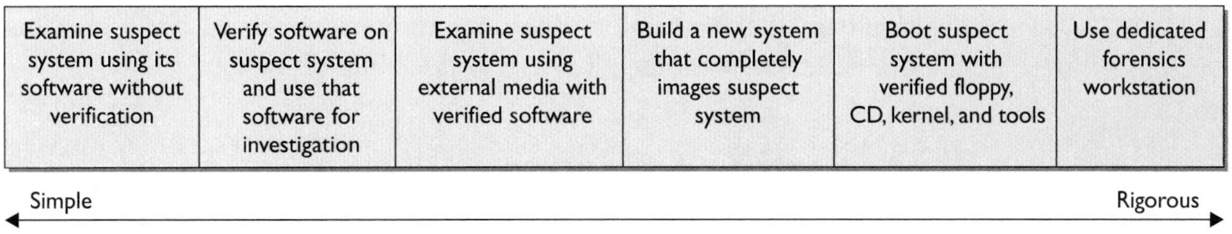

Examine suspect system using its software without verification	Verify software on suspect system and use that software for investigation	Examine suspect system using external media with verified software	Build a new system that completely images suspect system	Boot suspect system with verified floppy, CD, kernel, and tools	Use dedicated forensics workstation

Simple   Rigorous

• **Figure 23.2**   Investigative method rigor

Figure 23.3 shows the relationship between the complexity of your investigation and both the reliability of your forensic data and the difficulty of investigation.

Identifying Evidence

Evidence must be properly marked as it is collected so that it can be identified as a particular piece of evidence gathered at the scene. Properly label and store evidence, and make sure the labels can't be easily removed. Keep a log book identifying each piece of evidence (in case the label is removed); the persons who discovered it; the case number; the date, time, and location of the discovery; and the reason for collection. This information should be specific enough for recollection later in court. It is important to log other identifying marks, such as device make, model, serial number, cable configuration or type, and so on. Note any type of damage to the piece of evidence.

Being methodical is extremely important while identifying evidence. Do not collect evidence by yourself—have a second person who can serve as a witness to your actions. Keep logs of your actions during both seizure and during analysis and storage. A sample log is shown here:

Item Description	Investigator	Case #	Date	Time	Location	Reason
Dell Latitude laptop computer, D630, serial number 6RKC1G0	Smith	C-25	30 Jan 2008	1325 MST	Room 312 safe	Safekeeping

Protecting Evidence

Protect evidence from electromagnetic or mechanical damage. Ensure that evidence is not tampered with, damaged, or compromised by the procedures used during the investigation. Be careful not to damage the evidence, to avoid potential liability problems later. Protect evidence from extremes in heat and cold, humidity, water, magnetic fields, and vibration. Use static-free evidence-protection gloves as opposed to standard latex gloves. Seal the evidence in a proper container with evidence tape, and mark it with your initials, date, and case number. For example, if a mobile phone with advanced capabilities is seized, it should be properly secured in a hard container designed to prevent accidentally pressing the keys during transit and storage. If the phone is to remain turned on for analysis, radio frequency

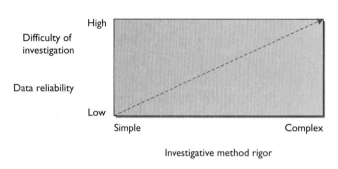

• **Figure 23.3**   Required rigor of the investigative method versus both data reliability and the difficulty of investigation

You should never examine a system with the utilities provided by that system. You should always use utilities that have been verified as correct and uncorrupted. Even better, use a *forensics workstation*, a computer system specifically designed to perform computer forensics activities. Do not open any files or start any applications. If possible, document the current memory and swap files, running processes, and open files. Disconnect the system from the network and immediately contact senior management. If your organization has Computer Incidence Response Team (CIRT) procedures, follow them. Capture and secure e-mail, Domain Name Service (DNS), and other network service logs on supporting hosts. Unless you have appropriate forensic training and experience, consider calling in a professional.

isolation bags that attenuate the device's radio signal should be used. This will prevent remote wiping, locking, or disabling of the device.

Transporting Evidence

Properly log all evidence in and out of controlled storage. Use proper packing techniques, such as placing components in static-free bags, using foam packing material, and using cardboard boxes. Be especially cautious during transport of evidence to ensure custody of evidence is maintained and the evidence isn't damaged or tampered with.

Storing Evidence

Store the evidence in an evidence room that has low traffic, restricted access, camera monitoring, and entry logging capabilities. Store components in static-free bags, foam packing material, and cardboard boxes.

Conducting the Investigation

When analyzing computer storage components, you must use extreme caution. A copy of the system should be analyzed—never the original system, as that will have to serve as evidence. A system specially designed for forensics examination, known as a forensics workstation, should be used. Forensics workstations typically contain hard drive bays, write blockers, analysis software, and other devices to safely image and protect computer forensic data. Conduct analysis in a controlled environment with strong physical security, minimal traffic, controlled access, and so on.

Remember that witness credibility is extremely important. It is easy to imagine how quickly credibility can be damaged if the witness is asked, "Did you lock the file system?" and can't answer affirmatively. Or, when asked "When you imaged this disk drive, did you use a new system?" the witness can't answer that the destination disk was new or had been completely formatted using a low-level format before data was copied to it.

Unless you have tools specifically designed to take forensic images under Windows, your imaging process should use a LiveCD that executes upon booting the system without installing anything to the hard drive. Only the minimal amount of software should be installed, to preclude propagation of a virus or the inadvertent execution of a Trojan horse or other malicious program. Windows can then be used when examining copies of the system. The Helix LiveCD contains many forensic tools, such as a tool to make a forensic image of internal devices and physical memory, a file browser that gives myriad details about files, including the MD5 hash, and tools to analyze graphic files and documents.

Although each investigation will be different, the following image backup process is a good example of a comprehensive investigation:

1. Remove and analyze/image only one component at a time to avoid corrupting data or inadvertently contaminating evidence by dealing with too many aspects of the investigation at one time. Imaging in the forensics workstation is the recommended approach.

Exam Tip: Never analyze the seized system directly. Always make multiple images of the device and analyze a copy.

Tech Tip

Tools of the Trade

- **Disk wipe utilities** *Tools to completely delete files and overwrite contents*

- **File viewers** *Text and image viewers*

- **Forensic programs** *Tools to analyze disk space, file content, system configuration, and so on*

- **Forensic workstations** *Specialized workstations containing hardware, software, and component interface capabilities to perform computer forensics activities*

- **Hard drive tools** *Partition viewing utilities, bootable CDs*

- **Unerase tools** *Tools to reverse file deletions*

2. Remove the hard disk and label it. Be sure to use an antistatic or static-dissipative wristband and mat before conducting forensic analysis.

3. Identify the disk type (IDE, SCSI, or other type). Log the disk capacity, cylinders, heads, and sectors.

4. Image the disk by using a bit-level copy, sector by sector. This will retain deleted files, unallocated clusters, and free and slack space.

5. Make either three or four copies of the drive: one replaces the drive removed if the system is to be returned to its owner and you don't want to divulge that the drive has been exchanged; a second is marked, sealed, logged, and stored with the original, unmodified disk as evidence; a third will be used for file authentication; and the last is for analysis.

6. Check the disk image to make sure no errors occurred during the imaging process by reviewing the imaging results and logs.

7. Before analyzing the suspect disk, generate a message digest for all system directories, files, disk sectors, and partitions. MD5 and SHA are suitable and are superior to the older CRC32 or weaker hashing algorithms. Remember that even creating the message digest can change file access times, so it is important that you lock the files and use the image, not the original evidence. Keep a good log of the hash values.

8. Inventory all files on the system.

9. Document the system date and time so you have a reference point for your investigation.

 Although this text describes the image backup process and provides specific steps to be performed, use the steps as guidelines. Any notes or record of results you make can end up being evidence in a court. Therefore, using a checklist and making notes on it could result in those lists and notes becoming evidence. Your credibility could be damaged if you create specific checklists and skip a step or two because they aren't applicable—remember that you may need to explain why you skipped certain steps. While following the checklist, keep a log of all commands you issued on the system between the time you identified the incident and the time you imaged the disk. That way, if you are questioned in court about whether you changed anything on the disk, you can say, in effect, "Yes, but here is exactly what I did and here is how it would have changed things."

Chain of Custody

Evidence, once collected, must be properly controlled to prevent tampering. The chain of custody accounts for all persons who handled or had access to the evidence. The chain of custody shows who obtained the evidence, when and where it was obtained, where it was stored, and who had control or possession of the evidence for the entire time since the evidence was obtained.

The following shows critical steps in a chain of custody:

1. Record each item collected as evidence.

2. Record who collected the evidence along with the date and time it was collected or recorded.

3. Write a description of the evidence in the documentation.

4. Put the evidence in containers and tag the containers with the case number, the name of the person who collected it, and the date and time it was collected or put in the container.

5. Record all message digest (hash) values in the documentation.

6. Securely transport the evidence to a protected storage facility.

7. Obtain a signature from the person who accepts the evidence at this storage facility.

8. Provide controls to prevent access to and compromise of the evidence while it is being stored.

9. Securely transport the evidence to court for proceedings.

■ Free Space vs. Slack Space

When a user deletes a file, the file is not actually deleted. Instead, a pointer in a file allocation table is deleted. This pointer was used by the operating system to track down the file when it was referenced, and the act of "deleting" the file merely removes the pointer and marks the cluster(s) holding the file as available for the operating system to use. The actual data originally stored on the disk remains on the disk (until that space is used again); it just isn't recognized as a coherent file by the operating system.

Free Space

Since a deleted file is not actually completely erased or overwritten, it sits on the hard disk until the operating system needs to use that space for another file or application. Sometimes the second file that is saved in the same area does not occupy as many clusters as the first file, so a fragment of the original file is left over.

The cluster that holds the fragment of the original file is referred to as **free space** because the operating system has marked it as usable when needed. As soon as the operating system stores something else in this cluster, it is considered *allocated*. The unallocated clusters still contain the original data until the operating system overwrites them. Looking at the free space might reveal information left over from files the user thought were deleted from the drive.

Slack Space

Another place that should be reviewed is **slack space**, which is different from free space. When a file is saved to a storage media, such as a hard drive, the operating system allocates space in blocks of a predefined size, called *clusters*. Even if your file contains only ten characters, the operating system will allocate a full cluster—with space left over in the cluster. This is slack space.

It is possible for a user to hide malicious code, tools, or clues in slack space, as well as in the free space. You may also find information in slack space from files that previously occupied that same cluster. Therefore, an investigator should review slack space using utilities that can display the information stored in these areas.

■ Message Digest and Hash

If files, logs, and other information are going to be captured and used for evidence, you need to ensure that the data isn't modified. In most cases, a tool that implements a hashing algorithm to create message digests is used.

Cross Check

Hash Algorithms and Forensics

Hash algorithms offer digital forensics the ability to "bag and tag" evidence. Although it does not protect the evidence from tampering, it provides clear proof of whether or not data has been changed. This is a very important issue to resolve, given how easy it is to change digital data and that typically no trace is left of the change. A complete review of hashing algorithms is found in Chapter 5. The important question regarding hashes and forensics is this: how and where do you record hash values to protect their integrity as part of the investigative process?

A *hashing algorithm* performs a function similar to the familiar parity bits, checksum, or cyclical redundancy check (CRC). It applies mathematical operations to a data stream (or file) to calculate some number that is unique based on the information contained in the data stream (or file). If a subsequent hash created on the same data stream results in a different hash value, it usually means that the data stream was changed.

The hash tool is applied to each file or log, and the message digest value is noted in the investigation documentation. It is a good practice to write the logs to a write-once media such as CD-ROM. When the case actually goes to trial, the investigator may need to run the tool on the files or logs again to show that they have not been altered in any way since being obtained.

■ Analysis

After successfully imaging the drives to be analyzed and calculating and storing the message digests, the investigator can begin the analysis. The details of the investigation will depend on the particulars of the incident being investigated. However, in general, the following steps will be involved:

1. Check the Recycle Bin for deleted files.

2. Check the web browser history files and address bar histories.

3. Check the web browser cookie files. Each web browser stores cookies in different places. Browsers not listed here will require individual research.

    a. Internet Explorer stores cookies in two places on Windows machines (a handy tool for viewing IE cookies is IECookiesView, which you can find at CNET Download.com):

        ■ In the Temporary Internet Files folder on Windows XP/2000, C:\Documents and Settings\<user name>\Local Settings\Temporary Internet Files; on Windows Vista, C:\Users\<user name>\AppData\Local\Microsoft\Windows\Temporary Internet Files

The mathematics behind hashing algorithms has been researched extensively, and although it is possible that two different data streams could produce the same message digest, it is very improbable. This is an area of cryptography that has been rigorously reviewed, and the mathematics behind Message Digest 5 (MD5) and Secure Hash Algorithm (SHA) is very sound. In 2005, weaknesses were discovered in the MD5 and SHA algorithms, leading the National Institute of Standards and Technology (NIST) to announce (in November 2007) a competition to find a new cryptographic hashing algorithm to be named SHA-3 (entries were due October 2008; proclamation of a winner and publication of the standard are scheduled to take place in 2012). These algorithms are still strong and are the best available—the discovered weaknesses show they aren't as strong as originally calculated. (For more information about hashing and algorithms, see Chapter 5.)

The number of files stored on today's hard drives can be very large, literally hundreds of thousands of files. Obviously this is far too many for the investigator to analyze. However, by matching the message digests for files installed by the most popular software products to the message digests of files on the drive being analyzed, the investigator can avoid analyzing approximately 90 percent of the files because he can assume they are unmodified. The National Software Reference Library (NSRL) collects software from various sources and incorporates file profiles into a Reference Data Set available for download as a service. See www.nsrl.nist.gov.

- In the Cookies folder on Windows XP/2000, C:\Documents and Settings\<user name>\Cookies; on Windows Vista, C:\Users\<user name>\AppData\Roaming\Microsoft\Windows\Cookies and C:\Users\<user name>\AppData\Roaming\Microsoft\Windows\Cookies\low

b. In Netscape for Mac, click the hard drive icon and open the System folder. Double-click Preferences | Netscape Users Folder | Your Profile Folder.

c. Netscape for UNIX stores cookies in $HOME/netscape.

4. Check the Temporary Internet Files folders. Usually these are found in the Windows directory C:\Documents and Settings\<username>\Local Settings\Temporary Internet Files. This location can be changed, so be sure to check where Internet Explorer is storing those files. In Internet Explorer, choose Tools | Internet Options | General | Browsing History | Settings. The current location will be indicated on that screen.

5. Search files for suspect character strings. To conserve valuable time, be wise in the choice of words you search for, choosing "confidential," "sensitive," "sex," or other explicit words and phrases related to your investigation.

6. Search the slack and free space for suspect character strings as described previously.

The Helix LiveCD and Knoppix Live Linux CD are just two examples of the many tools you can use to perform computer forensics activities.

Tech Tip

Cleanup: Possible Remediation Actions After an Attack

These are things you'll need to do to restore your system after you've responded to an incident and completed your initial investigation:

1. *Place the system behind a firewall.*

2. *Reload the OS.*

3. *Run scanners.*

4. *Install security software.*

5. *Remove unneeded services and applications.*

6. *Apply patches.*

7. *Restore the system from backup.*

Chapter 23 Review

■ Chapter Summary

After reading this chapter and completing the exercises, you should understand the following about incident response and forensics.

Identify the rules and types of evidence

■ Evidence must meet the three standards of being sufficient, competent, and relevant if it is to be used in legal proceedings.

■ There are four different types of evidence: direct, real, documentary, and demonstrative.

■ There are three rules regarding evidence: the best evidence rule, the exclusionary rule, and the hearsay rule.

Collect evidence

■ Evidence must be properly collected, protected, and controlled to be of value during court or disciplinary activities.

■ When acquiring evidence, one must be deliberate to ensure evidence is not damaged and operations are not negatively impacted.

Preserve evidence

■ Evidence must be properly marked so that it can be readily identified as that particular piece of evidence gathered at the scene.

■ Evidence must be protected so that it is not tampered with, damaged, or compromised.

■ Evidence should be transported cautiously to ensure custody of the evidence is maintained and the evidence itself is not tampered with or damaged.

■ Evidence should be stored in properly controlled areas and conditions.

■ When conducting an investigation on computer components, one must be deliberate and cautious to ensure evidence is not damaged.

Maintain a viable chain of custody

■ A chain of custody that accounts for all persons who handled or have access to the evidence must be maintained to prevent evidence tampering or damage.

Investigate a computer crime or policy violation

■ Information can be recorded and possibly hidden in various ways on a computer. Sometimes information will be hidden in either the free space or the slack space of the computer's disk drive.

■ Free space is the space (clusters) on a storage medium that is available for the operating system to use.

■ Slack space is the unused space on a disk drive created when a file is smaller than the allocated unit of storage, such as a cluster.

■ The use of a message digest or hashing algorithm is essential to ensure that information stored on a computer's disk drives has not been changed.

■ A hashing algorithm applies mathematical operations to a data stream or file to calculate a number that is unique, based on the information contained in the data stream or file.

■ A message digest is the result of applying the hash function to data. It is also known as a hash value.

■ If the information in the data stream or file is changed, a different message digest will result, indicating the file has been tampered with.

■ Forensic analysis of data stored on a hard drive can begin once the drive has been imaged and message digests of important files have been calculated and stored.

■ Analysis typically involves investigating the Recycle Bin, web browser and address bar history files, cookie files, temporary Internet file folders, suspect files, and free space and slack space.

■ Experience and knowledge are your most valuable tools available when performing computer forensic activities.

Key Terms

best evidence rule *(583)*
competent evidence *(582)*
demonstrative evidence *(582)*
direct evidence *(582)*
documentary evidence *(582)*
evidence *(582)*
exclusionary rule *(583)*

forensics *(581)*
free space *(588)*
hearsay rule *(583)*
real evidence *(582)*
relevant evidence *(582)*
slack space *(588)*
sufficient evidence *(582)*

Key Terms Quiz

Use terms from the Key Terms list to complete the sentences that follow. Don't use the same term more than once. Not all terms will be used.

1. Evidence collected in violation of the Fourth Amendment of the U.S. Constitution, the Electronic Communications Privacy Act (ECPA), or other aspects of the U.S. Code may not be admissible to a court under the terms of the _____.

2. Evidence that is legally qualified and reliable is _____.

3. Documents, verbal statements, and material objects admissible in a court of law are called _____.

4. The rule whereby courts prefer original evidence rather than a copy to ensure that no alteration of the evidence (whether intentional or unintentional) has occurred is termed the _____.

5. Evidence that is convincing or measures up without question is _____.

6. _____ is the preservation, identification, documentation, and interpretation of computer data to be used in legal proceedings.

7. _____ is evidence that is material to the case or has a bearing on the matter at hand.

8. _____ is the unused space on a disk drive when a file is smaller than the allocated unit of storage.

9. _____ is oral testimony or other evidence that proves a specific fact (such as an eyewitness's statement, fingerprint, photo, and so on). The knowledge of the facts is obtained through the five senses of the witness. There are no inferences or presumptions.

10. _____ is the remaining sectors of a previously allocated file that are available for the operating system to use.

Multiple-Choice Quiz

1. Which of the following correctly defines evidence as being competent?

    A. The evidence is material to the case or has a bearing on the matter at hand.

    B. The evidence is presented in the form of business records, printouts, or other items.

    C. The evidence is convincing or measures up without question.

    D. The evidence is legally qualified and reliable.

2. Which of the following correctly defines evidence as being relevant?

    A. The evidence is material to the case or has a bearing on the matter at hand.

    B. The evidence is presented in the form of business records, printouts, or other items.

    C. The evidence is convincing or measures up without question.

    D. The evidence is legally qualified and reliable.

3. Which of the following correctly defines documentary evidence?

    A. The evidence is in the form of business records, printouts, manuals, and other items.

B. The knowledge of the facts is obtained through the five senses of the witness.

C. The evidence is used to aid the jury and may be in the form of a model, experiment, chart, or other item and be offered to prove an event occurred.

D. Physical evidence that links the suspect to the scene of a crime.

4. Which of the following correctly defines real evidence?

A. The evidence is convincing or measures up without question.

B. The evidence is material to the case or has a bearing on the matter at hand.

C. The evidence is used to aid the jury and may be in the form of a model, experiment, chart, or other item and be offered to prove an event occurred.

D. Tangible objects that prove or disprove a fact.

5. Which of the following correctly defines the hearsay rule?

A. The evidence is legally qualified and reliable.

B. Tangible objects that prove or disprove a fact.

C. Evidence not from the personal knowledge of a witness.

D. Evidence in the form of business records, printouts, manuals, or other items.

6. Which of the following is the least rigorous investigative method?

A. Using a dedicated forensics workstation

B. Verifying software on suspect system and using that software for the investigation

C. Examining the suspect system using its software without verification

D. Booting the suspect system with verified floppy, CD, kernel, and tools

7. Which of the following correctly defines slack space?

A. The space on a disk drive that is occupied by the boot sector

B. The space located at the beginning of a partition

C. The remaining sectors of a previously allocated file that are available for the operating system to use

D. The unused space on a disk drive when a file is smaller than the allocated unit of storage

8. Which of the following correctly describes the minimum contents of an evidence control log book?

A. Description, Investigator, Case #, Date, Time, Location, Reason

B. Description, Investigator, Case #, Date, Location, Reason

C. Description, Case #, Date, Time, Location, Reason

D. Description, Coroner, Case #, Date, Time, Location, Reason

9. Which of the following correctly describes a message digest?

A. An algorithm that applies mathematical operations to a data stream to calculate a unique number based on the information contained in the data stream

B. A method of verifying that data has been completely deleted from a disk

C. A method of overwriting data with a specified pattern of 1's and 0's on a disk

D. A method used to keep an index of all files on a disk

10. Which of the following correctly describes the chain of custody for evidence?

A. The evidence is convincing or measures up without question.

B. Accounts for all persons who handled or had access to a specific item of evidence.

C. Description, Investigator, Case #, Date, Time, Location, Reason.

D. The evidence is legally qualified and reliable.

11. Which of the following correctly defines evidence as being sufficient?

A. The evidence is convincing or measures up without question.

B. The evidence is presented in the form of business records, printouts, and so on.

C. The evidence is material to the case or has a bearing on the matter at hand.

D. The evidence is legally qualified and reliable.

12. Which of the following correctly defines the exclusionary rule?

   A. Any evidence collected in violation of the Fourth Amendment is not admissible as evidence.

   B. The evidence consists of tangible objects that prove or disprove a fact.

   C. The knowledge of the facts is obtained through the five senses of the witness.

   D. The evidence is used to aid the jury and may be in the form of a model, experiment, chart, or the like, offered to prove an event occurred.

13. Which of the following correctly defines free space?

   A. The unused space on a disk drive when a file is smaller than the allocated unit of storage (such as a sector)

   B. The space on a disk drive that is occupied by the boot sector

   C. The space located at the beginning of a partition

   D. The remaining sectors of a previously allocated file that are available for the operating system to use

14. If you are investigating a computer incident and need to remove the disk drive from a computer and replace it with a copy so the user doesn't know it has been exchanged, how many copies of the disk should you make, and how should they be used?

   A. Five copies: one is to replace the drive that will be removed; one is marked, sealed, logged, and stored with the original, unmodified disk as evidence; one is for file authentication; one is for analysis; and one is for holding message digests.

   B. Three copies: one is to replace the drive that will be removed; one is to be used for file authentication; and one is for analysis.

   C. Four copies: one is to replace the drive that will be removed; one is marked, sealed, logged, and stored with the original, unmodified disk as evidence; one is for file authentication; and one is for holding message digests.

   D. Four copies: one is to replace the removed drive; one is marked, sealed, logged, and stored with the original, unmodified disk as evidence; one is for file authentication; and one is for analysis.

15. Which of the following correctly defines the process of acquiring evidence?

   A. Power down the system, dump the memory, create an image of the system, and analyze the image.

   B. Create an image of the system, analyze the image, dump the memory, and power down the system.

   C. Dump the memory, power down the system, create an image of the system, and analyze the image.

   D. Dump the memory, analyze the image, power down the system, and create an image of the system.

■ Essay Quiz

1. A supervisor has brought to your office a confiscated computer that was allegedly used to view inappropriate material. He has asked you to look for evidence to support this allegation. Because you work for a small company, you do not have an extra computer you can dedicate to your analysis. How would you boot the system and begin forensic analysis? Provide a reason for your method.

2. Explain why you should always search the free space and slack space if you suspect a person has deliberately deleted files or information on a workstation that you are analyzing.

3. You are a member of your company's Computer Incident Response Team and have been called in after hours to investigate an attack in progress. The network engineers have identified the attack as coming from a workstation in an office area of your company. The attack is still in progress and needs to be terminated. You are in the office where the workstation is located and the computer is on with the hard disk light flashing occasionally. What steps would you take to terminate the attack and secure the computer for later forensic analysis?

4. Due to some suspected illegal activities involving a company employee and her company computer, a senior manager directed the company's workstation support personnel to remove the hard disk from the workstation, copy the disk, and replace the hard disk with the copy. The workstation support person entered the office after hours, removed the hard disk, took it to his lab (which he shares with another person), imaged the old drive onto a new drive, replaced the drive, and then placed the original hard disk in his desk drawer. He then locked the lab and went home for the night. How will this evidence stand up in a court of law?

5. You have been asked by management to secure the laptop computer of an individual who was just dismissed from the company under unfavorable circumstances. Pretend that your own computer is the laptop that has been secured. Make the first entry in your log book and describe how you would start this incident off correctly by properly protecting and securing the evidence.

Lab Projects

• Lab Project 23.1

Use an MD5 or SHA-1 algorithm to obtain the hash value for a file of your choice. Record the hash value. Change the file with a word processor or text editor.

Obtain the hash value for the modified file. Compare the result.

• Lab Project 23.2

To understand what information is stored on your computer, examine the contents of the Temporary Internet Files folders on your own computer as described in the text. Review the filenames and

examine the contents of a few of the files. Describe how this information could be used as evidence of a crime.

• Lab Project 23.3

Visit www.ietf.org/rfc/rfc1321.txt and compile the MD5 algorithm from the information contained in Appendix A, "Reference Implementation," from

the web site. Verify your results with another version of MD5.

Legal Issues and Ethics

**In this chapter, you will learn
how to**

- Explain the laws and rules
  concerning importing and
  exporting encryption software
- Identify the laws that govern
  computer access and trespass
- Identify the laws that govern
  encryption and digital rights
  management
- Describe the laws that govern
  digital signatures
- Explore ethical issues associated
  with information security

Computer security is no different from any other subject in our society; as it
changes our lives, laws are enacted to enable desired behaviors and
prohibit undesired behaviors. The one substantial difference between this aspect
of our society and others is that the speed of advancement in the information
systems world as driven by business, computer network connectivity, and the
Internet is much greater than in the legal system of compromise and law-
making. In some cases, laws have been overly restrictive, limiting business
options, such as in the area of importing and exporting encryption technology.
In other cases, legislation has been slow in coming and this fact has stymied
business initiatives, such as in digital signatures. And in some areas, legislation
has been both too fast and too slow, as in the case of privacy laws. One thing is
certain: you will never satisfy everyone with a law, but it does delineate the
rules of the game.

The cyber-law environment has not been fully defined by the courts. Laws have been enacted, but until they have been fully tested and explored by cases in court, the exact limits are somewhat unknown. This makes some aspects of interpretation more challenging, but the vast majority of the legal environment is known well enough that effective policies can be enacted to navigate this environment properly. Policies and procedures are tools you use to ensure understanding and compliance with laws and regulations affecting cyberspace.

Cybercrime

One of the many ways to examine cybercrime is to study how the computer is involved in the criminal act. Three types of computer crimes commonly occur: computer-assisted crime, computer-targeted crime, and computer-incidental crime. The differentiating factor is in how the computer is specifically involved from the criminal's point of view. Just as crime is not a new phenomenon, neither is the use of computers, and cybercrime has a history of several decades.

What is new is how computers are involved in criminal activities. The days of simple teenage hacking activities from a bedroom have been replaced by organized crime–controlled botnets (groups of computers commandeered by a malicious hacker) and acts designed to attack specific targets. The legal system has been slow to react, and law enforcement has been hampered by their own challenges in responding to the new threats posed by high-tech crime.

What comes to mind when most people think about cybercrime is a computer that is targeted and attacked by an intruder. The criminal attempts to benefit from some form of unauthorized activity associated with a computer. In the 1980s and '90s, cybercrime was mainly virus and worm attacks, each exacting some form of damage, yet the gain for the criminal was usually negligible. Enter the 21st century, with new forms of malware, rootkits, and targeted attacks; criminals can now target individual users and their bank accounts. In the current environment it is easy to predict where this form of attack will occur—if money is involved, a criminal will attempt to obtain a cut. A common method of criminal activity is computer-based fraud. Advertising on the Internet is big business, and hence the "new" crime of **click fraud** is now a concern. Click fraud involves a piece of malware that defrauds the advertising revenue counter engine through fraudulent user clicks.

eBay, the leader in the Internet auction space, and its subsidiary, PayPal, are frequent targets of fraud. Whether the fraud occurs by fraudulent listing, fraudulent bidding, or outright stealing of merchandise, the results are the same: a crime is committed. As users move toward online banking and stock trading, so moves the criminal element. Malware designed to install a keystroke logger and then watch for bank/brokerage logins is already making the rounds of the Internet. Once the attacker finds the targets, he can begin looting accounts. His risk of getting caught and prosecuted is exceedingly low. Walk into a bank in the United States and rob it, and the odds are better than 95 percent that you will be doing time in federal prison

Tech Tip

Types of Cybercrime

There are three forms of computer involvement in criminal activity:

- *The computer as a tool of the crime*
- *The computer as a victim of a crime*
- *The computer that is incidental to a crime*

after the FBI hunts you down and slaps the cuffs on your wrists. Do the same crime via a computer, and the odds are even better than the opposite: less than 1 percent of these attackers are caught and prosecuted.

The low risk of being caught is one of the reasons that criminals are turning to computer crime. Just as computers have become easy for ordinary people to use, the trend continues for the criminal element. Today's cyber criminals use computers as tools to steal intellectual property or other valuable data and then subsequently market these material through underground online forums. Using the computer to physically isolate the criminal from the direct event of the crime has made the investigation and prosecution of these crimes much more challenging for authorities.

The last way computers are involved with criminal activities is through incidental involvement. Back in 1931, the U.S. government used accounting records and tax laws to convict Al Capone of tax evasion. Today, similar records are kept on computers. Computers are also used to traffic child pornography and engage in other illicit activities—these computers act more as storage devices than as actual tools to enable the crime. Because child pornography existed before computers made its distribution easier, the computer is actually incidental to the crime itself.

With the three forms of computer involvement in criminal activities, multiplied by the myriad of ways a criminal can use a computer to steal or defraud, added to the indirect connection mediated by the computer and the Internet, computer crime of the 21st century is a complex problem indeed. Technical issues are associated with all the protocols and architectures. A major legal issue is the education of the entire legal system as to the serious nature of computer crimes. All these factors are further complicated by the use of the Internet to separate the criminal and his victim geographically. Imagine this defense:

Tech Tip

FBI Priorities

In the post-9/11 environment, federal law enforcement priorities shifted toward terrorism. During the reassessment of national law enforcement priorities, cyber-related crimes increased in importance, moving to number three on the FBI priority list. In 2009, the priorities for the FBI are (www.fbi.gov/quickfacts.htm) as follows:

1. *Protect the United States from terrorist attack.*

2. *Protect the United States against foreign intelligence operations and espionage.*

3. *Protect the United States against cyber-based attacks and high-technology crimes.*

4. *Combat public corruption at all levels.*

5. *Protect civil rights.*

6. *Combat transnational and national criminal organizations and enterprises.*

7. *Combat major white-collar crime.*

8. *Combat significant violent crime.*

9. *Support federal, state, county, municipal, and international partners.*

10. *Upgrade technology to successfully perform the FBI's mission.*

"Your honor, as shown by my client's electronic monitoring bracelet, he was in his apartment in California when this crime occurred. The victim claims that the money was removed from his local bank in New York City. Now, last time I checked, New York City was a long way from Los Angeles, so how could my client have robbed the bank?"

Common Internet Crime Schemes

To find crime, just follow the money. In the United States, the FBI and the National White Collar Crime Center (NW3C) have joined forces in developing the Internet Crime Complaint Center (IC3), an online clearinghouse that communicates issues associated with cybercrime. One of the items provided to the online community is a list of common Internet crimes and explanations of each (www.ic3.gov/crimeschemes.aspx). A separate list offers advice on how to prevent these crimes through individual actions (www.ic3.gov/preventiontips.aspx).

Exam Tip: Computers are involved in three forms of criminal activity: the computer as a tool of the crime, the computer as a victim of a crime, and the computer that is incidental to a crime.

Tech Tip

Common Internet Crimes Identified by IC3

Here's a list of common Internet crimes from the Internet Crime Complaint Center:

- *Auction Fraud*
- *Auction Fraud—Romania*
- *Counterfeit Cashier's Check*
- *Credit Card Fraud*
- *Debt Elimination*
- *Parcel Courier Email Scheme*
- *Employment/Business Opportunities*
- *Escrow Services Fraud*
- *Identity Theft*
- *Internet Extortion*
- *Investment Fraud*
- *Lotteries*
- *Nigerian Letter or "419"*
- *Phishing/Spoofing*
- *Ponzi/Pyramid*
- *Reshipping*
- *Spam*
- *Third Party Receiver of Funds*

Sources of Laws

In the United States, three primary sources of laws and regulations affect our lives and govern actions. A **statutory law** is passed by a legislative branch of government, be it the U.S. Congress or a local city council. Another source of laws and regulations are administrative bodies given power by other legislation. The power of government-sponsored agencies, such as the Environmental Protection Agency (EPA), the Federal Aviation Administration (FAA), the Federal Communication Commission (FCC), and others, lies in this powerful ability to enforce behaviors through administrative rule making, or **administrative law**. The last source of law in the United States is **common law**, which is based on previous events or precedent. This source of law comes from the judicial branch of government: judges decide on the applicability of laws and regulations.

All three sources have an involvement in computer security. Specific statutory laws, such as the Computer Fraud and Abuse Act (CFAA), govern behavior. The CFAA is designed to deal with cases of interstate computer fraud, or accessing national security information. The law has been amended several times to keep pace with technology. The primary charge from CFAA is typically one of accessing without authority, or exceeding authority on, a system involved with interstate commerce or national security. Administratively, the FCC and Federal Trade Commission (FTC) have made their presence felt in the Internet arena with respect to issues such as intellectual property theft and fraud. Common law cases are now working their ways through the judicial system, cementing the issues of computers and crimes into the system of precedents and constitutional basis of laws.

> **Exam Tip:** Three types of laws are commonly associated with cybercrime: statutory law, administrative law, and common law.

Computer Trespass

With the advent of global network connections and the rise of the Internet as a method of connecting computers between homes, businesses, and governments across the globe, a new type of criminal trespass can now be committed. **Computer trespass** is the unauthorized entry into a computer system via any means, including remote network connections. These crimes have introduced a new area of law that has both national and international consequences. For crimes that are committed within a country's borders, national laws apply. For cross-border crimes, international laws and international treaties are the norm. Computer-based trespass can occur even if countries do not share a physical border.

Computer trespass is treated as a crime in many countries. National laws exist in many countries, including Canada, the United States, and the member states of the European Union (EU). These laws vary by country, but they all have similar provisions defining the unauthorized entry into and use of computer resources for criminal activities. Whether called *computer mischief* as in Canada or *computer trespass* as in the United States, unauthorized entry and use of computer resources is treated as a crime with significant punishments. With the globalization of the computer network infrastructure, or Internet, issues that cross national boundaries have arisen and will continue to grow in prominence. Some of these issues are dealt

> Computer trespass is a convenient catchall law that can be used to prosecute cyber criminals when evidence of other criminal behavior, such as online fraud, identity theft, and so forth, is too weak to achieve a conviction.

with through the application of national laws upon request of another government. In the future, an international treaty may pave the way for closer cooperation.

Convention on Cybercrime

The Convention on Cybercrime is the first international treaty on crimes committed via the Internet and other computer networks. The Convention is the product of four years of work by the Council of Europe (CoE), but also by the United States, Canada, Japan, and other non-CoE countries. The convention has been ratified and came into force in July 2004, and by September 2006, 15 member nations had also ratified it. The United States ratified it in the summer of 2006, with it entering into force in the U.S. in January 2007.

One of the main objectives of the Convention, set out in the preamble, is "to pursue, as a matter of priority, a common criminal policy aimed at the protection of society against cybercrime, *inter alia*, by adopting appropriate legislation and fostering international cooperation." This has become an important issue with the globalization of network communication. The ability to create a virus anywhere in the world and escape prosecution because of lack of local laws has become a global concern.

The convention deals particularly with infringements of copyright, computer-related fraud, child pornography, and violations of network security. It also contains a series of powers and procedures covering, for instance, searches of computer networks and interception. It has been supplemented by an additional protocol making any publication of racist and xenophobic propaganda via computer networks a criminal offense. This supplemental addition is in the process of separate ratification.

One of the challenges of enacting elements such as this convention is the varying legal and constitutional structures from country to country. Simple statements such as a ban on child pornography, although clearly desirable, can run into unlikely issues such as constitutional protections of free speech in the United States. Because of such issues, this well-intended joint agreement will have variations across the political boundaries of the world.

Significant U.S. Laws

The United States has been a leader in the development and use of computer technology. As such, it has a longer history associated with computers, and with cybercrime. Because legal systems tend to be reactive and move slowly, this leadership position has translated into a leadership position from a legal perspective as well. The one advantage of this legal leadership position is the concept that once an item is identified and handled by the legal system in one jurisdiction, subsequent adoption in other jurisdictions is typically quicker.

Electronic Communications Privacy Act (ECPA)

The **Electronic Communications Privacy Act (ECPA)** of 1986 was passed by Congress and signed by President Reagan to address a myriad of legal privacy issues that resulted from the increasing use of computers and other technology specific to telecommunications. Sections of this law address e-mail, cellular communications, workplace privacy, and a host of other issues related to communicating electronically. Section I was designed to modify federal wiretap statutes to include electronic communications. Section II, known as the **Stored Communications Act (SCA)**, was designed to establish criminal provisions for access to stored electronic records and communications. Section III covers pen registers and tap and trace issues.

A major provision of ECPA was the prohibition against an employer's monitoring an employee's computer usage, including e-mail, unless consent is obtained (for example, clicking Yes on a banner warning is considered consent). Other legal provisions protect electronic communications from wiretap and outside eavesdropping, as users are assumed to have a reasonable expectation of privacy and afforded protection under the Fourth Amendment to the Constitution.

 Cross Check

Cybercrime and Privacy

Cybercrime and privacy are concepts that are frequently interconnected. Identity theft is one of the fastest-rising crimes. How does a personal computer and the things you do online increase your risk in today's world? Can you actually list a dozen specific risks you are personally exposed to? Privacy issues, being a significant topic in their own right, are covered in Chapter 25.

A common practice with respect to computer access today is the use of a warning banner. These banners are typically displayed whenever a network connection occurs and serve four main purposes. First, from a legal standpoint, they establish the level of expected privacy (usually none on a business system). Second, they serve notice to end users of the intent to conduct real-time monitoring from a business standpoint. Real-time monitoring can be conducted for security reasons, business reasons, or technical network performance reasons. Third, they obtain the user's consent to monitoring. The key is that the banner tells users that their connection to the network signals their consent to monitoring. Consent can also be obtained to look at files and records. In the case of government systems, consent is needed to prevent direct application of the Fourth Amendment. And the last reason is that the warning banner can establish the system or network administrator's common authority to consent to a law enforcement search.

Computer Fraud and Abuse Act (1986)

The **Computer Fraud and Abuse Act (CFAA)** of 1986, amended in 1994, 1996, 2001 by the USA Patriot Act, and in 2008 by the Identity Theft Enforcement and Restitution Act, serves as the current foundation for criminalizing unauthorized access to computer systems. CFAA makes it a crime to knowingly access a computer that is either considered a government computer or used in interstate commerce, or to use a computer in a crime that is interstate in nature, which in today's Internet-connected age can be almost any machine. The act sets financial thresholds, which were lowered by the Patriot Act, but in light of today's investigation costs, these are easily met. The act also makes it a crime to knowingly transmit a program, code, or command that results in damage. Trafficking in passwords or similar access information is also criminalized. This is a wide-sweeping act, but the challenge of proving a case still exists.

Controlling the Assault of Non-Solicited Pornography And Marketing Act of 2003 (CAN-SPAM)

The CAN-SPAM Act was an attempt by the U.S. government to regulate commercial e-mail by establishing national guidelines and giving the FTC enforcement powers. The objective of the legislation was to curb unsolicited commercial e-mail, or *spam*. The act has applicability to mobile phones as well. Heralded as action to curb the rise of spam, since its enactment, the act has a very poor record.

CAN-SPAM allows unsolicited commercial e-mail as long as it adheres to three rules of compliance: unsubscribe, content, and sending behavior compliance. The act requires an obvious opt-out provision to allow users to unsubscribe, with these requests being honored within ten days. The content provisions state that the content must be clear and not deceptive. Adult content must be clearly labeled, and subject lines must be clear and accurate. Sending behavior rules include not using harvested e-mail addresses, not falsifying headers, and not using open relays.

CAN-SPAM makes specific exemptions for e-mail pertaining to religious messages, political messages, and national security messages. The law also blocks people who receive spam from suing spammers and restricts states from enacting and enforcing stronger antispam statutes. The law does permit ISPs to sue spammers, and this has been used by some major ISPs to pursue cases against large-scale spam operations. Major firms such as AOL have considered the law useful in their battle against spam. Regarded largely as ineffective, statistics have shown that very few prosecutions have been pursued by the FTC. The act permits both criminal charges against individuals and civil charges against entities involved in suspected spamming operations. In the FTC's 2007 report to Congress ("Spam Summit: The Next Generation of Threats and Solutions"), it lauds ISP filtering activities as a major element in the war on spam, specifically citing this action as significant in reducing spam to user inboxes.

USA Patriot Act

The USA Patriot Act of 2001, passed in response to the September 11 terrorist attacks on the World Trade Center buildings in New York and the Pentagon building in Arlington, Virginia, substantially changed the levels of checks and balances in laws related to privacy in the United States. This law extends the tap and trace provisions of existing wiretap statutes to the Internet and mandates certain technological modifications at ISPs to facilitate electronic wiretaps on the Internet. The act also permits the Justice Department to proceed with its rollout of the Carnivore program, an eavesdropping program for the Internet. Much controversy exists over Carnivore, but until it's changed, the Patriot Act mandates that ISPs cooperate and facilitate monitoring. In recent actions, the name Carnivore has been retired, but the right of the government to eavesdrop and monitor communications continues to be a hot topic and one where actions continue. The Patriot Act also permits federal law enforcement personnel to investigate computer trespass (intrusions) and enacts civil penalties for trespassers.

Tech Tip

Header Manipulation

Falsifying header information is a serious violation of the CAN-SPAM Act. This can be considered an indicator of criminal or malicious intent and can bring the attention of other law enforcement agencies besides the FTC.

Tech Tip

Computer Misuse

Two major laws, ECPA and CFAA (as amended), provide wide-sweeping tools for law enforcement to convict people who hack into computers or use them to steal information. Both laws have been strengthened and provide significant federal penalties. These laws are commonly used to convict criminals of computer misuse, even when other charges may have applied.

Gramm-Leach-Bliley Act (GLBA)

In November 1999, President Clinton signed the **Gramm-Leach-Bliley Act (GLBA)**, a major piece of legislation affecting the financial industry that includes significant privacy provisions for individuals. The key privacy tenets enacted in GLBA include the establishment of an opt-out method for individuals to maintain some control over the use of the information provided in a business transaction with a member of the financial community. GLBA is enacted through a series of rules governed by state law, federal law, securities law, and federal rules. These rules cover a wider range of financial institutions, from banks and thrifts, to insurance companies, to securities dealers. Some internal information sharing is required under the Fair Credit Reporting Act (FCRA) between affiliated companies, but GLBA ended sharing to external third-party firms.

Sarbanes-Oxley Act (SOX)

In the wake of several high-profile corporate accounting/financial scandals in the United States, the federal government in 2002 passed sweeping legislation, the **Sarbanes-Oxley Act (SOX)**, overhauling the financial accounting standards for publicly traded firms in the United States. These changes were comprehensive, touching most aspects of business in one way or another. With respect to information security, one of the most prominent changes is **Section 404** controls, which specify that all processes associated with the financial reporting of a firm must be controlled and audited on a regular basis. Since the majority of firms use computerized systems, this placed internal auditors into the IT shops, verifying that the systems had adequate controls to ensure the integrity and accuracy of financial reporting. These controls have resulted in controversy over the cost of maintaining these controls versus the risk of not using them.

Section 404 requires firms to establish a control-based framework designed to detect or prevent fraud that would result in misstatement of financials. In simple terms, these controls should detect insider activity that would defraud the firm. This has significant impacts on the internal security controls, because a system administrator with root-level access could perform many if not all tasks associated with fraud and would have the ability to alter logs and cover his tracks. Likewise, certain levels of power users of financial accounting programs would also have significant capability to alter records.

Payment Card Industry Data Security Standard (PCI DSS)

The payment card industry, including the powerhouses of MasterCard and Visa, through its PCI Security Standards Council designed a private sector initiative to protect payment card information between banks and merchants. The **Payment Card Industry Data Security Standard (PCI DSS)** is a set of contractual rules governing how credit card data is to be protected (see the Tech Tip sidebar, "PCI DSS Objectives and Requirements"). This is a voluntary, private sector initiative that is proscriptive in its security guidance. Merchants and vendors can choose not to adopt these measures, but the standard has a steep price for noncompliance; the transaction fee for

PCI DSS Objectives and Requirements

PCI DSS includes six control objectives containing a total of 12 requirements:

1. *Build and Maintain a Secure Network*

   - ***Requirement 1*** *Install and maintain a firewall configuration to protect cardholder data*

   - ***Requirement 2*** *Do not use vendor-supplied defaults for system passwords and other security parameters*

2. *Protect Cardholder Data*

   - ***Requirement 3*** *Protect stored cardholder data*

   - ***Requirement 4*** *Encrypt transmission of cardholder data across open, public networks*

3. *Maintain a Vulnerability Management Program*

   - ***Requirement 5*** *Use and regularly update anti-virus software*

   - ***Requirement 6*** *Develop and maintain secure systems and applications*

4. *Implement Strong Access Control Measures*

   - ***Requirement 7*** *Restrict access to cardholder data by business need-to-know*

   - ***Requirement 8*** *Assign a unique ID to each person with computer access*

   - ***Requirement 9*** *Restrict physical access to cardholder data*

5. *Regularly Monitor and Test Networks*

   - ***Requirement 10*** *Track and monitor all access to network resources and cardholder data*

   - ***Requirement 11*** *Regularly test security systems and processes*

6. *Maintain an Information Security Policy*

   - ***Requirement 12*** *Maintain a policy that addresses information security for all employees and contractors*

noncompliant vendors can be significantly higher, fines up to $500,000 can be levied, and in extreme cases the ability to process credit cards can be revoked.

Import/Export Encryption Restrictions

Encryption technology has been controlled by governments for a variety of reasons. The level of control varies from outright banning to little or no regulation. The reasons behind the control vary as well, and control over import and export is a vital method of maintaining a level of control over encryption technology in general. The majority of the laws and restrictions are centered on the use of cryptography, which was until recently used mainly for military purposes. The advent of commercial transactions and network communications over public networks such as the Internet has expanded the use of cryptographic methods to include securing of network communications. As is the case in most rapidly changing technologies, the practice moves faster than law. Many countries still have laws that are outmoded in terms of e-commerce and the Internet. Over time, these laws will be changed to serve these new uses in a way consistent with each country's needs.

U.S. Law

Export controls on commercial encryption products are administered by the Bureau of Industry and Security (BIS) in the U.S. Department of Commerce. The responsibility for export control and jurisdiction was transferred from the State Department to the Commerce Department in 1996 and updated on June 6, 2002. Rules governing exports of encryption are found in the Export Administration Regulations (EAR), 15 C.F.R. Parts 730–774. Sections 740.13, 740.17, and 742.15 are the principal references for the export of encryption items.

Violation of encryption export regulations is a serious matter and is not an issue to take lightly. Until recently, encryption protection was accorded the same level of attention as the export of weapons for war. With the rise of the Internet, widespread personal computing, and the need for secure connections for e-commerce, this position has relaxed somewhat.

The U.S. encryption export control policy continues to rest on three principles: review of encryption products prior to sale, streamlined post-export reporting, and license review of certain exports of strong encryption to foreign government end users. The current set of U.S. rules requires notification to the BIS for export in all cases, but the restrictions are significantly lessened for mass-market products, as defined by all of the following:

- They are generally available to the public by being sold, without restriction, from stock at retail selling points by any of these means:
  - Over-the-counter transactions
  - Mail-order transactions
  - Electronic transactions
  - Telephone call transactions
- The cryptographic functionality cannot easily be changed by the user.
- They are designed for installation by the user without further substantial support by the supplier.
- When necessary, details of the items are accessible and will be provided, upon request, to the appropriate authority in the exporter's country in order to ascertain compliance with export regulations.

As you can see, this is a very technical area, with significant rules and significant penalties for infractions. The best rule is that whenever you are faced with a situation involving the export of encryption-containing software, first consult an expert and get the appropriate permission, or a statement that permission is not required. This is one case where it is better to be safe than sorry.

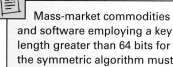

Non-U.S. Laws

Export control rules for encryption technologies fall under the Wassenaar Arrangement, an international arrangement on export controls for conventional arms and dual-use goods and technologies (see the Tech Tip sidebar, "Wassenaar Arrangement"). The Wassenaar Arrangement was established to contribute to regional and international security and stability, by promoting transparency and greater responsibility in transfers of conventional arms and dual-use goods and technologies, thus preventing destabilizing accumulations. Participating states, of which the United States is one of 41, will seek, through their own national policies and laws, to ensure that transfers of these items do not contribute to the development or enhancement of military capabilities that undermine these goals, and are not diverted to support such capabilities.

Many nations have more restrictive policies than those agreed upon as part of the Wassenaar Arrangement. Australia, New Zealand, United States, France, and Russia go further than is required under Wassenaar and restrict general-purpose cryptographic software as dual-use goods through national laws. The Wassenaar Arrangement has had a significant impact on cryptography export controls, and there seems little doubt that some of the nations represented will seek to use the next round to move toward a more repressive cryptography export control regime based on their own national laws. There are ongoing campaigns to attempt to influence other members of the agreement toward less restrictive rules or, in some cases, no rules. These lobbying efforts are based on e-commerce and privacy arguments.

Digital rights management, secure USB solutions, digital signatures, and Secure Sockets Layer (SSL)–secured connections are examples of common behind-the-scenes use of cryptographic technologies. In 2007, the United Kingdom passed a new law mandating that when requested by UK authorities, either police or military, encryption keys must be provided to permit decryption of information associated with terror or criminal investigation. Failure to deliver either the keys or decrypted data can result in an automatic prison sentence of two to five years. Although this seems reasonable, it has been argued that such actions will drive certain financial entities offshore, as the rule applies only to data housed in the United Kingdom. As for deterrence, the two-year sentence may be lighter than a conviction for trafficking in child pornography; hence the law seems not to be as useful as it seems at first glance.

Tech Tip

Cryptographic Use Restrictions

In addition to the export controls on cryptography, significant laws prohibit the use and possession of cryptographic technology. In China, a license from the state is required for cryptographic use. In some other countries, including Russia, Pakistan, Venezuela, and Singapore, tight restrictions apply to cryptographic uses. France relinquished tight state control over the possession of the technology in 1999. One of the driving points behind France's action is the fact that more and more of the Internet technologies have built-in cryptography.

Digital Signature Laws

Whether a ring and wax seal, a stamp, or a scrawl indicating a name, signatures have been used to affix a sign of one's approval for centuries. As communications have moved into the digital realm, signatures need to evolve with the new medium, and hence digital signatures were invented. Using elements of cryptography to establish integrity and nonrepudiation, digital signature schemes can actually offer more functionality than their predecessors in the paper-based world.

U.S. Digital Signature Laws

On October 1, 2000, the Electronic Signatures in Global and National Commerce Act (commonly called the E-Sign law) went into effect in the United States. This law implements a simple principle: a signature, contract, or other record may not be denied legal effect, validity, or enforceability solely because it is in electronic form. Another source of law on digital signatures is the Uniform Electronic Transactions Act (UETA), which was developed by the National Conference of Commissioners on Uniform State Laws (NCCUSL) and has been adopted in all but four states, Georgia, Illinois, New York and Washington, which have adopted a nonuniform version of UETA. The precise relationship between the federal E-Sign law and UETA has yet to be resolved and will most likely be worked out through litigation in the courts over complex technical issues.

Many states have adopted digital signature laws, the first being Utah in 1995. The Utah law, which has been used as a model by several other states, confirms the legal status of digital signatures as valid signatures, provides for use of state-licensed certification authorities, endorses the use of public key encryption technology, and authorizes online databases called repositories, where public keys would be available. The Utah act specifies a negligence standard regarding private encryption keys and places no limit on liability. Thus, if a criminal uses a consumer's private key to commit fraud, the consumer is financially responsible for that fraud, unless the consumer can prove that he or she used reasonable care in safeguarding the private key. Consumers assume a duty of care when they adopt the use of digital signatures for their transactions, not unlike the care required for PINs on debit cards.

From a practical standpoint, the existence of the E-Sign law and UETA has enabled e-commerce transactions to proceed, and the resolution of the technical details via court actions will probably have little effect on consumers. It is worth noting that consumers will have to exercise reasonable care over their signature keys, much as they must over PINs and other private numbers. For the most part, software will handle these issues for the typical user.

Try This

Digital Signature Agreements

Digital signatures are becoming more common in everyday use. When a person signs up with a bank for electronic banking services, or with a brokerage account for online trading, that person typically agrees to electronic signatures. Using your bank or brokerage account—or if you don't have one, there are free online financial service firms you can sign up for—review the online agreement for electronic signature provisions.

UN Digital Signature Laws

The United Nations has a mandate to further harmonize international trade. With this in mind, the UN General Assembly adopted in 1996 the United Nations Commission on International Trade Law (UNCITRAL) Model Law on Electronic Commerce. To implement specific technical aspects of this model law, more work on electronic signatures was needed. The General Assembly then adopted in 2001 the UNCITRAL Model Law on Electronic Signatures. These model laws have become the basis for many national and international efforts in this area.

Canadian Digital Signature Laws

Canada was an early leader in the use of digital signatures. Singapore, Canada, and the U.S. state of Pennsylvania were the first governments to have digitally signed an interstate contract. This contract, digitally signed in 1998, concerned the establishment of a Global Learning Consortium between the three governments (source: *Krypto-Digest* Vol. 1 No. 749, June 11, 1998). Canada went on to adopt a national model bill for electronic signatures to promote e-commerce. This bill, the Uniform Electronic Commerce Act (UECA), allows the use of electronic signatures in communications with the government. The law contains general provisions for the equivalence between traditional and electronic signatures (source: *BNA ECLR*, May 27, 1998, p. 700) and is modeled after the UNCITRAL Model Law on E-Commerce (source: *BNA ECLR*, September 13, 2000, p. 918). The UECA is similar to Bill C-54, Personal Information Protection and Electronic Documents Act (PIPEDA), in authorizing governments to use electronic technology to deliver services and communicate with citizens.

Individual Canadian provinces have passed similar legislation defining digital signature provisions for e-commerce and government use. These laws are modeled after the UNCITRAL Model Law on E-Commerce to enable widespread use of e-commerce transactions. These laws have also modified the methods of interactions between the citizens and the government, enabling electronic communication in addition to previous forms.

European Laws

The European Commission adopted a Communication on Digital Signatures and Encryption: "Ensuring Security and Trust in Electronic Communication— Towards a European Framework for Digital Signatures and Encryption." This communication states that a common framework at the EU level is urgently needed to stimulate "the free circulation of digital signature related products and services within the Internal market" and "the development of new economic activities linked to electronic commerce" as well as "to facilitate the use of digital signatures across national borders." Community legislation should address common legal requirements for certificate authorities, legal recognition of digital signatures, and international cooperation. This communication was debated, and a common position was presented to the member nations for incorporation into national laws.

On May 4, 2000, the European Parliament and Council approved the common position adopted by the council. In June 2000, the final version, the Electronic Commerce Directive (2000/31/EC), was adopted. The directive has been implemented by member states. To implement the articles contained in the directive, member states had to remove barriers, such as legal form requirements, to electronic contracting, leading to uniform digital signature laws across the EU.

Digital Rights Management

The ability to make flawless copies of digital media has led to another "new" legal issue. For years, the music and video industry has relied on technology to protect its rights with respect to intellectual property. It has been illegal for decades to copy information, such as music and videos, protected by copyright. Even with the law, people have for years made copies of music and videos to share, violating the law. This has not had a significant economic impact in the eyes of the industry, as the copies were of lesser quality and people would pay for original quality in sufficient numbers to keep the economics of the industry healthy. As such, legal action against piracy was typically limited to large-scale duplication and sale efforts, commonly performed overseas and subsequently shipped to the United States as counterfeit items.

The primary statute enacted in the United States to bring copyright legal concerns up-to-date with the digital world is the **Digital Millennium Copyright Act (DMCA).** The DMCA states its purpose as follows: "To amend title 17, United States Code, to implement the World Intellectual Property Organization Copyright Treaty and Performances and Phonograms Treaty, and for other purposes." The majority of this law was well crafted, but one section has drawn considerable comment and criticism. A section of the law makes it illegal to develop, produce, and trade any device or mechanism designed to circumvent technological controls used in copy protection.

Although, on the surface, this seems a reasonable requirement, the methods used in most cases are cryptographic in nature, and this provision had the ability to eliminate and/or severely limit research into encryption and the strengths and weaknesses of specific methods. A DMCA provision, Section 1201(g), was included to provide for specific relief and allow exemptions for legitimate research (see the Tech Tip sidebar, "DMCA Research Exemption Requirements"). With this section, the law garnered industry support from several organizations such as the Software & Information Industry Association (SIIA), Recording Industry Association of America (RIAA), and Motion Picture Association of America (MPAA). Based on these inputs, the U. S. Copyright Office issued a report supporting the DMCA in a required report to the U.S. Congress. This seemed to settle the issues until the RIAA threatened to sue an academic research team headed by Professor Edward Felten from Princeton University. The issue behind the suit was the potential publication of results demonstrating that several copy protection methods were flawed in their application. This research came in response to an industry-sponsored challenge to break the methods. After breaking the methods developed and published by the industry, Felten and his team prepared to publish their findings. The RIAA objected and threatened a suit under provisions of DMCA. After several years of litigation and support of Felten by the Electronic Freedom Foundation (EFF), the case was eventually resolved in the academic team's favor, although no case law to prevent further industry-led threats was developed.

This might seem a remote issue, but industries have been subsequently using the DMCA to protect their technologically inspired copy-protection schemes for such products as laser-toner cartridges and garage-door openers. It is doubtful that the U.S. Congress intended the law to have such effects, yet until these issues are resolved in court, the DMCA may have wide-reaching implications.

Exemptions are scattered through the DMCA, although many were created during various deliberations on the act and do not make sense when the act is viewed in whole. The effect of these exemptions upon people in the software and technology industry is not clear, and until restrained by case law, the DMCA gives large firms with deep legal pockets a potent weapon to use against parties who disclose flaws in encryption technologies used in various products. Actions have already been initiated against individuals and organizations who have reported security holes in products. This will be an active area of legal contention as the real issues behind digital rights management have yet to be truly resolved.

Ethics

Ethics has been a subject of study by philosophers for centuries. It might be surprising to note that ethics associated with computer systems has a history dating back to the beginning of the computing age. The first examination of cybercrime occurred in the late 1960s, when the professional conduct of computer professionals was examined with respect to their activities in the workplace. If we consider ethical behavior to be consistent with that of existing social norms, it can be fairly easy to see what is considered right and wrong. But with the globalization of commerce, and the globalization of communications via the Internet, questions are raised on what is the *appropriate* social norm. Cultural issues can have wide-ranging effects on this, and although the idea of an appropriate code of conduct for the world is appealing, it is as yet an unachieved objective.

The issue of globalization has significant local effects. If a user wishes to express free speech via the Internet, is this protected behavior or criminal behavior? Different locales have different sets of laws to deal with items such as free speech, with some recognizing the right, while others prohibit it. With the globalization of business, what are the appropriate controls for intellectual property when some regions support this right, while others do not even recognize intellectual property as something of value, but rather something owned by the collective of society? The challenge in today's business environment is to establish and communicate a code of ethics so that everyone associated with an enterprise can understand the standards of expected performance.

A great source of background information on all things associated with computer security, the SANS Institute, published a set of IT ethical guidelines ("IT Code of Ethics") in April 2004: see www.sans.org/resources/ethics.php?ref=3781.

SANS Institute IT Code of Ethics[1]

Version 1.0 – April 24, 2004

The SANS Institute

I will strive to know myself and be honest about my capability.

- *I will strive for technical excellence in the IT profession by maintaining and enhancing my own knowledge and skills. I acknowledge that there are many free resources available on the Internet and affordable books and that the lack of my employer's training budget is not an excuse nor limits my ability to stay current in IT.*

- *When possible I will demonstrate my performance capability with my skills via projects, leadership, and/or accredited educational programs and will encourage others to do so as well.*

- *I will not hesitate to seek assistance or guidance when faced with a task beyond my abilities or experience. I will embrace other professionals' advice and learn from their experiences and mistakes. I will treat this as an opportunity to learn new techniques and approaches. When the situation arises that my assistance is called upon, I will respond willingly to share my knowledge with others.*

- *I will strive to convey any knowledge (specialist or otherwise) that I have gained to others so everyone gains the benefit of each other's knowledge.*

- *I will teach the willing and empower others with Industry Best Practices (IBP). I will offer my knowledge to show others how to become security professionals in their own right. I will strive to be perceived as and be an honest and trustworthy employee.*

- *I will not advance private interests at the expense of end users, colleagues, or my employer.*

- *I will not abuse my power. I will use my technical knowledge, user rights, and permissions only to fulfill my responsibilities to my employer.*

- *I will avoid and be alert to any circumstances or actions that might lead to conflicts of interest or the perception of conflicts of interest. If such circumstance occurs, I will notify my employer or business partners.*

- *I will not steal property, time or resources.*

- *I will reject bribery or kickbacks and will report such illegal activity.*

- *I will report on the illegal activities of myself and others without respect to the punishments involved. I will not tolerate those who lie, steal, or cheat as a means of success in IT.*

(continued)

Tech Tip

I will conduct my business in a manner that assures the IT profession is considered one of integrity and professionalism.

- *I will not injure others, their property, reputation, or employment by false or malicious action.*

- *I will not use availability and access to information for personal gains through corporate espionage.*

- *I distinguish between advocacy and engineering. I will not present analysis and opinion as fact.*

- *I will adhere to Industry Best Practices (IBP) for system design, rollout, hardening and testing.*

- *I am obligated to report all system vulnerabilities that might result in significant damage.*

- *I respect intellectual property and will be careful to give credit for other's work. I will never steal or misuse copyrighted, patented material, trade secrets or any other intangible asset.*

- *I will accurately document my setup procedures and any modifications I have done to equipment. This will ensure that others will be informed of procedures and changes I've made.*

I respect privacy and confidentiality.

- *I respect the privacy of my co-workers' information. I will not peruse or examine their information including data, files, records, or network traffic except as defined by the appointed roles, the organization's acceptable use policy, as approved by Human Resources, and without the permission of the end user.*

- *I will obtain permission before probing systems on a network for vulnerabilities.*

- *I respect the right to confidentiality with my employers, clients, and users except as dictated by applicable law. I respect human dignity.*

- *I treasure and will defend equality, justice and respect for others.*

- *I will not participate in any form of discrimination, whether due to race, color, national origin, ancestry, sex, sexual orientation, gender/sexual identity or expression, marital status, creed, religion, age, disability, veteran's status, or political ideology.*

Chapter 24 Review

■ Chapter Summary

After reading this chapter and completing the exercises, you should understand the following regarding the basics of legal and ethical considerations associated with information security.

Explain the laws and rules concerning importing and exporting encryption software

- Import and export of high-strength cryptographic software is controlled in many countries, including the United States.

- Possession of encryption programs or encrypted data can be a crime in many countries.

- The Wassenaar Arrangement is an international agreement between countries concerning the import/export of cryptographic software and has enabled mass-marketed products to generally flow across borders.

Identify the laws that govern computer access and trespass

- Gaining unauthorized access, by whatever means, including using someone else's credentials, is computer trespass.

- Exceeding granted authority is also computer trespass.

- Many nations have versions of computer trespass or misuse statutes, although the terminology varies greatly among countries.

Identify the laws that govern encryption and digital rights management

- Encryption technology is used to protect digital rights management and prevent unauthorized use.

- Circumventing technological controls used to protect intellectual property is a violation of the DMCA.

- In some countries, carrying encrypted data can result in authorities demanding the keys or threatening prosecution for failure to disclose the keys.

Describe the laws that govern digital signatures

- Digital signatures have the same legal status as written signatures.

- Digital signatures use PINs or other "secrets" that require end-user protection to be protected from fraud.

Explore ethical issues associated with information security

- Ethics is the social–moral environment in which a person makes decisions.

- Ethics can vary by socio-cultural factors and groups.

■ Key Terms

administrative law *(600)*
click fraud *(597)*
common law *(600)*
Computer Fraud and Abuse Act (CFAA) *(602)*
computer trespass *(600)*
Digital Millennium Copyright Act (DMCA) *(610)*
Electronic Communications Privacy Act (ECPA) *(601)*
Gramm-Leach-Bliley Act (GLBA) *(604)*

Payment Card Industry Data Security Standard (PCI DSS) *(604)*
Sarbanes-Oxley Act (SOX) *(604)*
Section 404 *(604)*
statutory law *(600)*
Stored Communications Act (SCA) *(602)*
Wassenaar Arrangement *(606)*

Key Terms Quiz

1. IT controls were mandated in public companies by _____, part of the Sarbanes-Oxley Act.

2. The contractual set of rules governing credit card security is the _____.

3. A catchall law to prosecute hackers is the statute on _____.

4. The _____ is the primary U.S. federal law on computer intrusion and misuse.

5. The power of government-sponsored agencies lies in _____.

6. A(n) _____ is passed by a legislative branch of government.

7. _____ comes from the judicial branch of government.

Multiple-Choice Quiz

1. The VP of IS wants to monitor user actions on the company's intranet. What is the best method of obtaining the proper permissions?

   A. A consent banner displayed upon login

   B. Written permission from a company officer

   C. Nothing, because the system belongs to the company

   D. Written permission from the user

2. Your Social Security number and other associated facts kept by your bank are protected by what law against disclosure?

   A. The Social Security Act of 1934

   B. The USA Patriot Act of 2001

   C. The Gramm-Leach-Bliley Act

   D. HIPAA

3. Breaking into another computer system in the United States, even if you do not cause any damage, is regulated by what laws?

   A. State law, as the damage is minimal

   B. Federal law under the Identity Theft and Assumption Deterrence Act

   C. Federal law under the Electronic Communications Privacy Act (ECPA) of 1986

   D. Federal law under the USA Patriot Act of 2001

4. Export of encryption programs is regulated by which entity?

   A. U.S. State Department

   B. U.S. Commerce Department

   C. U.S. Department of Defense

   D. National Security Agency

5. For the FBI to install and operate Carnivore on an ISP's network, what is required?

   A. A court order specifying specific items being searched for

   B. An official request from the FBI

   C. An impact statement to assess recoverable costs to the ISP

   D. A written request from an ISP to investigate a computer trespass incident

6. True or false: Digital signatures are equivalent to notarized signatures for all transactions in the United States.

   A. True for all transactions in which both parties agree to use digital signatures

   B. True only for non–real property transactions

   C. True only where governed by specific state statute

   D. False, as the necessary laws have not yet passed

7. Is a sysadmin who is reading employee e-mail to look for evidence of someone stealing company passwords protected by the company-owned equipment exemption on eavesdropping:

   A. False, there is no "company-owned exemption."

   B. True, provided he or she has his or her manager's approval.

   C. True, provided he or she has senior management permission in writing,

   D. True, if it is in his or her job description.

8. True or false: Writing viruses and releasing them across the Internet is a violation of law.

   A. Always true. All countries have reciprocal agreements under international law.

   B. Partially true. Depends on the laws in the country of origin.

   C. False. Computer security laws do not cross international boundaries.

   D. Partially true. Depends on the specific countries involved, of the virus author and the recipient.

9. Publication of flaws in encryption used for copy protection is a potential violation of:

   A. HIPAA

   B. U.S. Commerce Department regulations

   C. DMCA

   D. National Security Agency regulations

10. Violation of DMCA can result in:

    A. Civil fine

    B. Jail time

    C. Activity subject to legal injunctions

    D. All of the above

11. PCI DSS requires all of the following except:

    A. Install and maintain firewall.

    B. Install and use antivirus software.

    C. Install and use intrusion detection systems.

    D. Use Unique UserIDs.

12. Circumventing technological controls to prevent reverse-engineering is a violation of:

    A. HIPAA

    B. DMCA

    C. ECPA

    D. All of the above

13. Logging in as your boss to fix your time records is:

    A. OK, if you are accurately reporting your time

    B. One of the obscure elements of DMCA

    C. A violation of the Separation of Duties Law

    D. A form of computer trespass

14. You are arrested as a result of your hacking activities and investigators find you have been breaking password files and sharing them across the Internet. Which law have you violated?

    A. CFAA

    B. ECPA

    C. DMCA

    D. HIPAA

15. A good ethics policy would include the following elements except for:

    A. **Loyalty**   Report to the boss any violations of company policy

    B. **Duty**   Do the best you can do every day, even if it exceeds what is expected of your position.

    C. **Teamwork**   Act as your fellow worker would.

    D. **Honesty**   Do not misuse or steal company resources.

■ Essay Quiz

1. You are being hired as the director of IT for a small firm that does retail trade business, and you will be the source of knowledge for all things IT, including security and legal regulations. Outline the legal elements you would want to have policy covering, and include how you would disseminate this information.

2. You have just been hired as a system administrator for a small college. Your servers are used for database storage and website serving to the university community. Describe the laws that will potentially impact your job with respect to computer security. What actions will you take to ensure compliance with laws and regulations?

3. You have joined a small doctor's group as their only system administrator. They expressed concern over HIPAA compliance at the interview process, which you obviously successfully passed. What do you do to put in place a HIPAA-compliant solution?

chapter 25

Privacy

They who would give up an essential liberty for temporary security, deserve neither liberty or security.

—BENJAMIN FRANKLIN

In this chapter, you will learn how to

- **Define privacy**
- **Identify privacy laws relative to computer security in various industries**
- **Describe issues associated with technology and privacy**
- **Explain the concept of personally identifiable information (PII)**
- **Craft a privacy policy for online records**
- **Recognize web-related privacy issues**

The advent of interconnected computer systems has enabled businesses and governments to share and integrate information. This has led to a resurgence in the importance of privacy laws worldwide. Governments in Europe and the United States have taken different approaches in attempts to control privacy via legislation. As a new generation grows up in a digital world, its view of information sharing services, such as social networking sites, has created a shift in how people view privacy. Many social and philosophical differences have led to the differing views on privacy, but as the world becomes interconnected, understanding and resolving them will be important.

Privacy can be defined as the power to control what others know about you and what they can do with that information. In the computer age, personal information forms the basis for many decisions, from credit card transactions to purchase goods, to the ability to buy an airplane ticket and fly domestically. Although it is theoretically possible to live an almost anonymous existence today, the price for doing so is high—from higher prices at the grocery store (no frequent shopper discount), to higher credit costs, to challenges with air travel, opening bank accounts, and seeking employment.

Information is an important item in today's society. From instant credit, to digital access to a wide range of information via the Internet, to electronic service portals such as e-commerce sites, e-government sites, and so on, our daily lives have become intertwined with privacy issues. Information has become a valuable entity, for it is an enabler of many functions. A few hundred years ago, if someone wanted to procure ownership of an item, he would typically trade something of tangible value (for example, coins) with the current owner of the item, and an exchange would take place. The two parties, buyer and seller, would have to meet in space and time and conduct a transaction. Or, in some cases, they would employ a third-party agent to act as a proxy and do the transaction for them. Today, one would go online, search for the best deal (information-centric), conduct business via e-commerce (use computer programs as agents), pay for the item via bankcard transaction (information exchange concerning funds availability and transfer), and, in some cases, receive delivery digitally (in the case of software, books, videos, and so forth). The creation of an information-centric economy is as dramatic a revolution as the adoption of money to act as an economic utility, simplifying bartering. This revolution and reliance on information imbues information with value, creating the need to protect it.

Privacy is the right to control information about you and what others can do with that information.

Personally Identifiable Information (PII)

When information is about a person, failure to protect it can have specific consequences. Business secrets are protected through trade secret laws, government information is protected through laws concerning national security, and privacy laws protect information associated with people. A set of elements that can lead to the specific identity of a person is referred to as **personally identifiable information (PII)**. By definition, PII can be used to identify a specific individual, even if an entire set is not disclosed.

PII is an essential element of many online transactions, but it can also be misused if disclosed to unauthorized parties. For this reason, it should be protected at all times, by all parties that possess it.

TRUSTe (www.truste.com), an independent trust authority, defines personally identifiable information as

> any information… (i) that identifies or can be used to identify, contact, or locate the person to whom such information pertains, or (ii) from which identification or contact information of an individual person can be derived. Personally Identifiable Information includes, but is not limited to: name, address, phone number, fax number, e-mail address, financial profiles, medical profile, social security number, and credit card information.

The concept of PII is used to identify which data elements require a specific level of protection. When records are used individually (not in aggregate form), then PII is the concept of connecting a set of data elements to a specific purpose. If this can be accomplished, then the information is PII and needs specific protections. The U.S. Federal Trade Commission has

As little information as the ZIP code, gender, and date of birth can resolve to a single person.

Tech Tip

Collecting PII
PII is by nature sensitive to end users. Loss or compromise of end-user PII can result in financial and other impacts borne by the end user. For this reason, collection of PII should be minimized to what is actually needed. Three great questions to ask when determining whether to collect PII are

- *Do I need each specific data element?*

- *What is my business purpose for each specific element?*

- *Will my customers/end users agree with my rationale for collecting each specific element?*

repeatedly ruled that if a firm collects PII, it is responsible for it through the entire lifecycle, from initial collection, through use, retirement, and destruction. Only after the PII is destroyed in all forms and locations, is the company's liability for its compromise abated.

Sensitive PII

Some PII is so sensitive to disclosure and resulting misuse that it requires special handling to ensure protection. Data elements such as credit card data, bank account numbers, and government identifiers (social security number, driver's license number, and so on) require extra levels of protection to prevent harm from misuse. Should these elements be lost or compromised, direct, personal financial damage may occur to the person identified by the data. These elements need special attention when planning data stores and executing business processes associated with PII data, including collection, storage, and destruction.

If the accidental disclosure of user data could cause the user harm, such as discrimination (political, racial, health related, or lifestyle), then the best course of action is to treat the information as sensitive PII.

Try This

Search for Your Own PII

Modern Internet search engines have the ability to catalog tremendous quantities of information and make wide-area searches for specific elements easy. Using your own elements of PII, try searching the Internet and see what is returned on your name, address, phone number, social security number, date of birth, and so forth. For security reasons, be sure to be anonymous when doing this—that is, log out of Google applications before using Google Search, Microsoft/Live applications before using Bing, or Yahoo applications before using Yahoo Search. This step may seem minor, but with search records being stored, the last thing you want to do is provide records that can cross-correlate data about yourself. If you find data on yourself, analyze the source and whether or not the data should be publicly accessible.

Notice, Choice, and Consent

As privacy is defined as the power to control what others know about you and what they can do with this information, and PII represents the core items that should be controlled, communication with the end user concerning privacy is paramount. Privacy policies are presented later in the chapter, but with respect to PII, three words can govern good citizenry when collecting PII. **Notice** refers to informing the customer that PII will be collected and used and/or stored. **Choice** refers to the opportunity for the end user to consent to the data collection or to opt out. **Consent** refers to the positive affirmation by a customer that she read the notice, understands her choices, and agrees to release her PII for the purposes explained to her.

■ U.S. Privacy Laws

Identity privacy and the establishment of identity theft crimes is governed by the Identity Theft and Assumption Deterrence Act, which makes it a violation of federal law to knowingly use another's identity. The collection of information necessary to do this is also governed by the Gramm-Leach-Bliley Act (GLBA), which makes it illegal for someone to gather identity information on another under false pretenses. In the education area, privacy laws have existed for years (see "Family Education Records and Privacy Act (FERPA)" later in the chapter).

One of the original privacy regulation efforts in the United States was a study in 1973, by the Department of Health, Education, and Welfare (HEW). This task force examined the impact of computerization on medical records privacy. The task force's charge was to develop policies that would allow the benefits of computerization to go forward, but at the same time provide appropriate safeguards for personal privacy. The task force developed the Code of Fair Information Practices, consisting of five clauses: openness, disclosure, secondary use, correction, and security. These main subjects continue today as the core of many privacy practices. Two major privacy initiatives followed from the U.S. government, the Privacy Act of 1974 and the Freedom of Information Act of 1996.

Privacy Act of 1974

The **Privacy Act of 1974** was an omnibus act designed to affect the entire federal information landscape. This act has many provisions that apply across the entire federal government, with only minor exceptions for national security (classified information), law enforcement, and investigative provisions. This act has been amended numerous times, and you can find current, detailed information at the Electronic Privacy Information Center (EPIC) web site, http://epic.org/privacy/laws/privacy_act.html.

Freedom of Information Act (FOIA)

The **Freedom of Information Act (FOIA)** of 1996 is one of the most widely used privacy acts in the United States, so much so that its acronym, FOIA (pronounced "foya"), has reached common use. FOIA was designed to enable public access to U.S. government records, and "public" includes the press, which purportedly acts on the public behalf and widely uses FOIA to obtain information. FOIA carries a presumption of disclosure; the burden is on the government, not the requesting party, to substantiate why information cannot be released. Upon receiving a written request, agencies of the U.S. government are required to disclose those records, unless they can be lawfully withheld from disclosure under one of nine specific exemptions in FOIA. The right of access is ultimately enforceable through the federal court system. The nine specific exemptions, listed in Section 552 of U.S. Code Title 5, fall within the following general categories:

1. National security and foreign policy information
2. Internal personnel rules and practices of an agency
3. Information specifically exempted by statute
4. Confidential business information
5. Inter- or intra-agency communication that is subject to deliberative process, litigation, and other privileges
6. Information that, if disclosed, would constitute a clearly unwarranted invasion of personal privacy

Tech Tip

Major Elements of the Privacy Act

The Privacy Act has numerous required elements and definitions. Among other things, the major elements require federal agencies to

- *Publish in the Federal Register a notice of each system of records that it maintains, including information about the type of records maintained, the purposes for which they are used, and the categories of individuals on whom they are maintained.*

- *Maintain only such information about an individual as required by law, or is needed to perform a statutory duty.*

- *Maintain information in a timely, accurate, relevant, secure, and complete form.*

- *Inform individuals about access to PII upon inquiry.*

- *Notify individuals from whom it requests information, what authorizes it to request the information; whether disclosure is mandatory or voluntary; the purpose for which the information may be used; and penalties for not providing the requested information.*

- *Establish appropriate physical, technical, and administrative safeguards for the information that is collected and used.*

Additional elements can be found by examining provisions of the act itself, although it is drafted in legislative form and requires extensive cross-referencing and interpretation.

7. Law enforcement records that implicate one of a set of enumerated concerns

8. Agency information from financial institutions

9. Geological and geophysical information concerning wells

Record availability under FOIA is less of an issue than is the backlog of requests.

To defray some of the costs associated with record requests, and to prevent numerous trivial requests, agencies are allowed to charge for research time and duplication costs. These costs vary by agency, but are typically nominal, in the range of $8.00 to $45.00 per hour for search/review fees and $.10 to $.35 per page for duplication. Agencies are not allowed to demand a requester to make an advance payment unless the agency estimates that the fee is likely to exceed $250 or the requester previously failed to pay proper fees. For many uses, the first 100 pages are free, and under some circumstances the fees can be waived.

Family Education Records and Privacy Act (FERPA)

Student records have significant protections under the Family Education Records and Privacy Act of 1974, which includes significant restrictions on information sharing. FERPA operates on an opt-in basis, as the student must approve the disclosure of information prior to the actual disclosure. FERPA was designed to provide limited control to students over their education records. The law allows students to have access to their education records, an opportunity to seek to have the records amended, and some control over the disclosure of information from the records to third parties. For example, if the parent of a student who is 18 or older inquires about the student's schedule, grades, or other academic issues, the student has to give permission before the school can communicate with the parent, even if the parent is paying for the education.

FERPA is designed to protect privacy of student information. At the K–12 school level, students are typically too young to have legal standing associated with exercising their rights, so FERPA recognizes the parents as part of the protected party. FERPA provides parents with the right to inspect and review their children's education records, the right to seek to amend information in the records they believe to be inaccurate, misleading, or an invasion of privacy, and the right to consent to the disclosure of PII from their children's education records. When a student turns 18 years old or enters a postsecondary institution at any age, these rights under FERPA transfer from the student's parents to the student.

U.S. Computer Fraud and Abuse Act (CFAA)

The U.S. Computer Fraud and Abuse Act (as amended in 1994, 1996, 2001, and 2008) and privacy laws such as the EU Data Protection Directive have several specific objectives, but one of the main ones is to prevent unauthorized parties access to information they should not have access to. Fraudulent access, or even exceeding one's authorized access, is defined as a crime and can be punished. Although the CFAA is intended for broader purposes, it can be used to protect privacy related to computer records through its enforcement of violations of authorized access.

U.S. Children's Online Privacy Protection Act (COPPA)

Children lack the mental capacity to make responsible decisions concerning the release of PII. The U.S. Children's Online Privacy Protection Act of 1998 (COPPA) specifically addresses this privacy issue with respect to children accessing and potentially releasing information on the Internet. Any web site that collects information from children (ages 13 and under), even simple web forms to allow follow-up communications and so forth, is covered by this law. Before information can be collected and used, parental permission needs to be obtained. This act requires that sites obtain parental permission, post a privacy policy detailing specifics concerning information collected from children, and describe how the children's information will be used.

Video Privacy Protection Act (VPPA)

Considered by many privacy advocates to be the strongest U.S. privacy law, the Video Privacy Protection Act of 1988 provides civil remedies against unauthorized disclosure of personal information concerning video tape rentals and, by extension, DVDs and games as well. This is a federal statute, crafted in response to media searches of rental records associated with Judge Bork when he was nominated to the U.S. Supreme Court. Congress, upset with the liberal release of information, reacted with legislation, drafted by Senator Leahy, who noted during the floor debate that new privacy protections are necessary in "an era of interactive television cables, the growth of computer checking and check-out counters, of security systems and telephones, all lodged together in computers...." (S. Rep. No. 100-599, 100th Cong., 2d Sess. at 6 (1988)).

This statute, civil in nature, provides for civil penalties of up to $2500 per occurrence, as well as other civil remedies. The statute provides the protections by default, thus requiring a video rental company to obtain the renter's consent to opt out of the protections if the company wants to disclose personal information about rentals. Exemptions exist for issues associated with the normal course of business for the video rental company as well as for responding to warrants, subpoenas, and other legal requests. This law does not supersede state laws, of which there are several.

Many states have enacted laws providing both wider and greater protections than the federal VPPA statute. Connecticut and Maryland laws brand video rental records as confidential, and therefore not subject to sale. California, Delaware, Iowa, Louisiana, New York, and Rhode Island have state statutes providing protection of privacy with respect to video rental records. Michigan's video privacy law is as sweeping as its broad super-DMCA state statute. This state law specifically protects records of book purchases, rentals, and borrowing as well as video rentals.

Health Insurance Portability & Accountability Act (HIPAA)

Medical and health information also has privacy implications, which is why the U.S. Congress enacted the **Health Insurance Portability and Accountability Act (HIPAA)** of 1996. HIPAA calls for sweeping changes in the way health and medical data is stored, exchanged, and used. From a privacy perspective, significant restrictions of data transfers to ensure privacy are included in HIPAA, including security standards and electronic signature provisions. HIPAA security standards mandate a uniform level of protections regarding all health information that pertains to an individual and is housed or transmitted electronically. The standards mandate safeguards for physical storage, maintenance, transmission, and access to individuals' health information. HIPAA mandates that organizations that use electronic signatures have to meet standards ensuring information integrity, signer authentication, and nonrepudiation. These standards leave to industry the task of specifying the technical solutions and mandate compliance only to significant levels of protection as provided by the rules being released by industry.

HIPAA's language is built upon the concepts of Protected Health Information (PHI) and Notice of Privacy Practices (NPP). HIPAA describes "covered entities" including medical facilities, billing facilities, and insurance (third-party payer) facilities. Patients are to have access to their PHI, and an expectation of appropriate privacy and security associated with medical records. HIPAA mandates a series of administrative, technical, and physical security safeguards for information, including elements such as staff

Tech Tip

Protected Health Information (PHI)

*HIPAA regulations define **Protected Health Information (PHI)** as "any information, whether oral or recorded in any form or medium" that*

> *"[i]s created or received by a health care provider, health plan, public health authority, employer, life insurer, school or university, or health care clearinghouse"; and*
> *"[r]elates to the past, present, or future physical or mental health or condition of an individual; the provision of health care to an individual; or the past, present, or future payment for the provision of health care to an individual."*

Try This

Notice of Privacy Practices

Visit your local doctor's office, hospital, or clinic and ask for their **Notice of Privacy Practices (NPP)**. This notice to patients details what information will be collected and the uses and safeguards that are applied. These can be fairly lengthy and detailed documents, and in many cases are in a booklet form.

training and awareness, and specific levels of safeguards for PHI when in use, stored, or in transit between facilities.

In 2009, as part of the American Recovery and Reinvestment Act of 2009, the Health Information Technology for Economic and Clinical Health Act (HITECH Act) was passed into law. Although the primary purpose of the HITECH Act was to provide stimulus money for the adoption of electronic medical records (EMR) systems at all levels of the healthcare system, it also contained new security and privacy provisions to add teeth to those already in HIPAA. HIPAA protections were confined to the direct medical profession, and did not cover entities such as health information exchanges and other "business associates" engaged in the collection and use of PHI. Under HITECH, business associates will be required to implement the same security safeguards and restrictions on uses and disclosures, to protect individually identifiable health information, as covered entities under HIPAA. It also subjects business associates to the same potential civil and criminal liability for breaches as covered entities.

Gramm-Leach-Bliley Act (GLBA)

In the financial arena, GLBA introduced the U.S. consumer to privacy notices, requiring firms to disclose what they collect, how they protect the information, and with whom they will share it. Annual notices are required as well as the option for consumers to opt out of the data sharing. The primary concept behind U.S. privacy laws in the financial arena is that consumers be allowed to opt out. This was strengthened in GLBA to include specific wording and notifications as well as requiring firms to appointment a privacy officer. Most U.S. consumers have witnessed the results of GLBA, every year receiving privacy notices from their banks and credit card companies. These notices are one of the visible effects of GLBA on changing the role of privacy associated with financial information.

California Senate Bill 1386 (SB 1386)

California Senate Bill 1386 (SB 1386) was a landmark law concerning information disclosures. It mandates that Californians be notified whenever PII is lost or disclosed. Since the passage of SB 1386, numerous other states have modeled legislation on this bill, and although national legislation has been blocked by political procedural moves, it will eventually be passed. The current list of U.S. states and territories that require disclosure notices (as of summer 2009) is up to 48, with only Alabama, Mississippi, New Mexico, and South Dakota without bills. Each of these disclosure notice laws is different, making the case for a unifying federal statute compelling, but currently it is low on the priority lists of most politicians.

U.S. Banking Rules and Regulations

Banking has always had an element of PII associated with it, from who has deposits to who has loans. As the scale of operations increased, both in numbers of customers and products, the importance of information for processing grew. Checks became a utility instrument to convey information associated with funds transfer between parties. As a check was basically a promise to pay, in the form of directions to a bank, occasionally the check was not honored and a merchant had to track down the party to demand payment. Thus, it became industry practice to write additional information on a check to assist a firm in later tracking down the drafting party. This information included items such as address, work phone number, a credit card number, and so on. This led to the co-location of information about an individual, and this information was used at times to perform a crime of **identity theft**. To combat this and prevent the gathering of this type of information, a series of banking and financial regulations were issued by the U.S. government to prohibit this form of information collection. Other regulations addressed items such as credit card numbers being printed on receipts, mandating only the last five digits be exposed.

Payment Card Industry Data Security Standard (PCI DSS)

As described in Chapter 24, the major credit card firms, such as MasterCard, Visa, American Express, and Discover, designed a private sector initiative to deal with privacy issues associated with credit card transaction information. PCI DSS is a standard that provides guidance on what elements of a credit card transaction need protection and the level of expected protection. PCI DSS is not a law, but rather a contractual regulation, enforced through a series of fines and fees associated with performing business in this space. PCI DSS was a reaction to two phenomena, data disclosures and identity theft.

PCI DSS consists of a series of prescriptive steps to ensure the security of certain elements of credit card transactions. The purpose behind these steps is to prevent obvious disclosures of information that can be used in identity theft. The contractual nature of the transactional credit card business makes this form of enforcement very lucrative, as violations by a merchant or other entity can place its business at risk by losing the ability to accept credit cards for payment.

Cross Check

USA Patriot Act

The USA Patriot Act, enacted in response to September 11, 2001 and amended in 2006, has changed search and seizure notification requirements, allowing secret sneak and peak searches and warrantless evidence collection under certain circumstances. As it has not been challenged or tested in court, with respect to many of the privacy laws, the outcome of it applicability is still uncertain. Is privacy impacted by this new law? If so, in what way? More detail on the USA Patriot Act is provided in Chapter 24.

Fair Credit Reporting Act (FCRA)

The Fair Credit Reporting Act of 1999 brought significant privacy protections to the consumer credit reporting agencies (CRAs). This act requires that the agencies provide consumers notice of their rights and responsibilities. The agencies are required to perform timely investigations on inaccuracies reported by consumers. The agencies are also required to notify the other CRAs when consumers close accounts. The act also has technical issues associated with data integrity, data destruction, data retention, and consumer and third party access to data. The details of FCRA proved to be insufficient with respect to several aspects of identity theft, and in 2003, the Fair and Accurate Credit Transactions Act was passed, modifying and expanding on the privacy and security provisions of FCRA.

Fair and Accurate Credit Transactions Act (FACTA)

The Fair and Accurate Credit Transactions Act of 2003 was passed to enact stronger protections for consumer information from identity theft, errors, and omissions. FACTA amended portions of FCRA to improve the accuracy of customer records in consumer reporting agencies, to improve timely resolution of consumer complaints concerning inaccuracies, and to make businesses take reasonable steps to protect information that can lead to identity theft.

FACTA also had other "disposal rules" associated with consumer information. FACTA mandates that information that is no longer needed must be properly disposed of, either by burning, pulverizing, or shredding. Any electronic information must be irreversibly destroyed or erased. Should third-party firms be used for disposal, the rules still pertain to the original contracting party, so third parties should be selected with care and monitored for compliance. FACTA mandated that the FTC develop the appropriate disposal rules and regulations for enforcement (see the Tech Tip sidebar "FTC Disposal Rule").

FACTA put financial institutions and creditors on notice that they are responsible for developing safeguards against identify theft. Per FACTA, the FTC and other agencies created the Red

Tech Tip

FACTA and Credit Card Receipts

One of the provisions of FACTA was to compel businesses to protect credit card information on receipts. Before FACTA, it was common for receipts to have entire credit card numbers, as well as additional information. Today, receipts can display only the last five digits of the card number and cannot include the card expiration date. These rules went into effect in 2005 and merchants had one year to comply.

Tech Tip

FTC Disposal Rule

*The FTC's **Disposal Rule** applies to consumer reporting agencies as well as to any individuals and businesses that use consumer reports. The FTC lists the following as among those who must comply with the rule:*

- *Lenders*
- *Insurers*
- *Employers*
- *Landlords*
- *Government agencies*
- *Mortgage brokers*
- *Automobile dealers*
- *Attorneys and private investigators*
- *Debt collectors*
- *Individuals who obtain a credit report on prospective nannies, contractors, or tenants*
- *Entities that maintain information in consumer reports as part of their role as service providers to other organizations covered by the rule*

For more information, see the FTC web page www.ftc.gov/bcp/edu/pubs/business/alerts/alt152.shtm.

Flags rule, which requires financial institutions and creditors to make an effort to identify and respond to patterns, practices, and activities (**red flags**) that indicate identity theft is being attempted.

■ Non-Federal Privacy Concerns in the United States

Despite the wide assortment of federal statutes associated with privacy, a significant gap remains in privacy protection in the United States. Government information about its citizens is not limited to just the federal government. State and local governments also have significant information holdings associated with individuals. In fact, it is not uncommon for the quantity and detail of information to increase as proximity to individuals increases. Local governments have significant quantities of government-compiled personal information (such as property ownership, court records, voter registration, fictitious business names, vital records, and so forth). Only about half the states have similar privacy acts concerning state government agencies' handling of personal information. In California, this statute is the Information Practices Act. Each state that has such protection provisions does so under its own set of rules and regulations, creating a patchwork approach to this topic. In only a handful of states does the state's "privacy act" extend to local government, where, as already noted, exists the lion's share of information. This lack of unified treatment has placed the United States behind many other nations with respect to this issue and has created safe harbor issues that regularly require time and effort to address at the highest levels of government with a differing set of officials depending upon the source of the information. For example, if privacy concerns arise from travel issues, the Department of Homeland Security would respond; for financial transaction privacy issues, it would be the Treasury Department; and for export and import, it would be the Commerce Department. This channel-dependent responsibility complicates negotiations over issues as the U.S. party is always changing as the source of the privacy issue changes.

International Privacy Laws

Privacy is not a U.S.-centric phenomenon, but it does have strong cultural biases. Legal protections for privacy tend to follow the socio-cultural norms by geography; hence, there are different policies in European nations than in the United States. In the United States, the primary path to privacy is via **opt-out**, whereas in Europe and other countries, it is via **opt-in**. What this means is that the fundamental nature of control shifts. In the U.S., a consumer must notify a firm that they wish to block the sharing of personal information; otherwise the firm has permission by default. In the EU, sharing is blocked unless the customer specifically opts in to allow it. The Far East has significantly different cultural norms with respect to individualism vs. collectivism and this is seen in their privacy laws as well. Even in countries with common borders, distinct differences exist, such as the United States and Canada; Canadian laws and customs have strong roots to their UK history, and in many cases follow European ideals as opposed to U.S. ones. One of the primary sources of intellectual and political thought on privacy has been the Organisation for Economic Co-operation and Development (OECD). This multinational entity has for decades conducted multilateral discussions and policy formation on a wide range of topics, including privacy.

OECD Fair Information Practices

OECD Fair Information Practices are the foundational element for many worldwide privacy practices. Dating to 1980, Fair Information Practices are a set of principles and practices that set out how an information-based society may approach information handling, storage, management, and flows with a view toward maintaining fairness, privacy, and security. Members of the OECD recognized that information was a critical resource in a rapidly evolving global technology environment, and that proper handling of this resource was critical for long-term sustainability of growth.

European Laws

The EU has developed a comprehensive concept of privacy, which is administered via a set of statutes known as **data protection**. These privacy statutes cover all personal data, whether collected and used by government or by

Tech Tip

OECD's Privacy Code
OECD's privacy code was developed to help "harmonise national privacy legislation and, while upholding such human rights, [to] at the same time prevent interruptions in international flows of data. [The Guidelines] represent a consensus on basic principles which can be built into existing national legislation, or serve as a basis for legislation in those countries which do not yet have it." (Source: "OECD Guidelines on the Protection of Privacy and Transborder Flows of Personal Data," www.oecd.org/document/18/0,3343,en_2649_34255_1815186_1_1_1_1,00.html.)

private firms. These laws are administered by state and national data protection agencies in each country. With the advent of the EU, this common comprehensiveness stands in distinct contrast to the patchwork of laws in the United States.

Privacy laws in Europe are built around the concept that privacy is a fundamental human right that demands protection through government administration. When the EU was formed, many laws were harmonized across the original 15 member nations, and data privacy was among those standardized. One important aspect of this harmonization is the Data Protection Directive, adopted by EU members, which has a provision allowing the European Commission to block transfers of personal data to any country outside the EU that has been determined to lack adequate data protection policies. The impetus for the EU Directive is to establish the regulatory framework to enable the movement of personal data from one country to another, while at the same time ensuring that privacy protection is "adequate" in the country to which the data is sent. This can be seen as a direct result of early HEW task force (see "U.S. Privacy Laws" earlier in the chapter) and OECD directions. If the recipient country has not established a minimum standard of data protection, it is expected that the transfer of data will be prohibited.

The differences in approach between the U.S. and the EU with respect to data protection led to the EU issuing expressions of concern about the adequacy of data protection in the United States, a move that could have paved the way to the blocking of data transfers. After negotiation, it was determined that U.S. organizations that voluntarily joined an arrangement known as **Safe Harbor** would be considered adequate in terms of data protection. Safe Harbor is a mechanism for self-regulation that can be enforced through trade practice law via the FTC. A business joining the Safe Harbor Consortium must make commitments to abide by specific guidelines

Tech Tip

Safe Harbor Principles

Safe Harbor is built upon seven principles:

- ■ *Notice*   *A firm must give notice of what is being collected, how it will be used, and with whom it will be shared.*

- ■ *Choice*   *A firm must allow the option to opt out of transfer of PII to third parties.*

- ■ *Onward Transfer*   *All disclosures of PII must be consistent with the previous principles of Notice and Choice.*

- ■ *Security*   *PII must be secured at all times.*

- ■ *Data Integrity*   *PII must be maintained accurately and, if incorrect, the customer has the right to correct it.*

- ■ *Access*   *Individuals must have appropriate and reasonable access to PII for the purposes of verification and correction.*

- ■ *Enforcement*   *Issues with privacy and PII must have appropriate enforcement provisions to remain effective.*

See www.export.gov/safeharbor/eg_main_018236.asp for more information.

concerning privacy. Safe Harbor members also agree to be governed by certain self-enforced regulatory mechanisms, backed ultimately by FTC action.

Another major difference between U.S. and European regulation lies in where the right of control is exercised. In European directives, the right of control over privacy is balanced in such a way as to favor consumers. Rather than having to pay to opt out, as with unlisted phone numbers in the United States, consumers have such services for free. Rather than having to opt out at all, the default privacy setting is deemed to be the highest level of data privacy, and users have to opt in to share information. This default setting is a cornerstone of the European Union's Directive on Protection of Personal Data and is enforced through national laws in all member nations.

Canadian Laws

Like many European countries, Canada has a centralized form of privacy legislation that applies to every organization that collects, uses, or discloses personal information, including information about employees. These regulations stem from the **Personal Information Protection and Electronic Data Act (PIPEDA)**, which requires that personal information be collected and used only for appropriate purposes. Individuals must be notified as to why the information is requested and how it will be used. The act has safeguards associated with storage, use, reuse, and retention.

To ensure leadership in the field of privacy issues, Canada has a national-level privacy commissioner and each province has a province-level privacy commissioner. These commissioners act as advocates on behalf of individuals and have used legal actions to enforce the privacy provisions associated with PIPEDA to protect personal information.

Asian Laws

Japan has a Personal Information Protection Law that requires protection of personal information used by the Japanese government, third parties, and the public sector. The Japanese law has provisions where the government entity must specify the purpose for which information is being collected, the safeguards applied, and when permitted, discontinue use of the information upon request.

Hong Kong has an office of the Privacy Commissioner for Personal Data (PCPD), a statutory body entrusted with the task of protecting personal data privacy of individuals and to ensure compliances with the Personal Data (Privacy) Ordinance in Hong Kong. One main task of the Commissioner is public education, creating greater awareness of privacy issues and the need to comply with the Personal Data Ordinance.

China has had a long reputation of poor privacy practices. Some of this comes from the cultural bias toward collectivism, and some comes from the long-standing government tradition of surveillance. Recent news of the Chinese government eavesdropping on Skype and other Internet-related communications has heightened this concern. China's constitution has provisions for privacy protections for the citizens. Even so, issues have come in the area of enforcement and penalties, and privacy items that have been far from uniform in their judicial history.

Tech Tip

Encryption and Privacy

Encryption has long been held by governments to be a technology associated with the military. As such, different governments have regulated it in different manners. The U.S. government has greatly reduced controls over encryption in the past decade. Other countries, such as Great Britain, have enacted statutes that compel users to turn over encryption keys when asked by authorities. Countries such as France, Malaysia, and China still tightly control and license end-user use of encryption technologies. The primary driver for Phil Zimmerman to create Pretty Good Privacy (PGP) was the need for privacy in countries where the government was considered a threat to civil liberties.

Privacy-Enhancing Technologies

One principal connection between information security and privacy is that without information security, you cannot have privacy. If privacy is defined as the ability to control information about oneself, then the aspects of confidentiality, integrity, and availability from information security become critical elements of privacy. Just as technology has enabled many privacy-impacting issues, technology also offers the means in many cases to protect privacy. An application or tool that assists in such protection is called a **privacy-enhancing technology (PET)**.

Encryption is at the top of the list of PETs for protecting privacy and anonymity. As noted earlier, one of the driving factors behind Phil Zimmerman's invention of PGP was the desire to enable people living in repressive cultures to communicate safely and freely. Encryption can keep secrets secret, and is a prime choice for protecting information at any stage in its lifecycle. The development of Tor routing to permit anonymous communications coupled with high-assurance, low-cost cryptography has made many web interactions securable and safe from eavesdropping.

Other PETs include small application programs, called **cookie cutters**, that are designed to prevent the transfer of cookies between browsers and web servers. Some cookie cutters block all cookies, while others can be configured to selectively block certain cookies. Some cookie cutters also block the sending of HTTP headers that may reveal personal information but may not be necessary to access a web site, and some block banner ads, pop-up windows, animated graphics, or other unwanted web elements. Some related PET tools are designed specifically to look for invisible images that set cookies (called web beacons or web bugs).

Other PETs are available to PC users, including encryption programs that allow users to encrypt and protect their own data, even on USB keys. TrueCrypt, an open source, free program enables users to perform their own encryption on disks and devices (www.truecrypt.org). Use of these programs is not difficult and can be mastered by most PC users with a little practice.

Privacy Policies

One of the direct outcomes of the legal statutes associated with privacy has been the development of a need for corporate privacy policies associated with data collection. With a myriad of government agencies involved, each with a specific mandate to "assist" in the protection effort associated with PII, one can ask, what is the best path for an industry member? If your organization needs PII to perform its tasks, obtaining and using it is fine in most cases, but you must ensure that everyone in the organization complies with the acts, rules, and regulations associated with these government agencies. Policies and procedures are the best way to ensure uniform compliance across an organization. The development of a **privacy policy** is an essential foundational element of a company's privacy stance.

Privacy Compliance Steps

To ensure that an organization complies with the numerous privacy requirements and regulations, a structured approach to privacy planning and policies is recommended:

1. *Identify the role in the organization that will be responsible for compliance and oversight.*

2. *Document all applicable laws and regulations, industry standards, and contract requirements.*

3. *Identify any industry best practices.*

4. *Perform a privacy impact assessment (PIA) and a risk assessment.*

5. *Map the identified risks to compliance requirements.*

6. *Create a unified risk mitigation plan.*

Privacy Impact Assessment

A **privacy impact assessment (PIA)** is a structured approach to determining the gap between desired privacy performance and actual privacy performance. A PIA is an analysis of how PII is handled through business processes and an assessment of risks to the PII during storage, use, and communication. A PIA provides a means to assess the effectiveness of a process relative to compliance requirements and identify issues that need to be addressed. A PIA is structured with a series of defined steps to ensure a comprehensive review of privacy provisions.

The following steps comprise a high-level methodology and approach for conducting a PIA:

1. *Establish PIA scope.* Determine the departments involved and the appropriate representatives. Determine which applications and business processes need to be assessed. Determine applicable laws and regulations associated with the business and privacy concerns.

2. *Identify key stakeholders.* Identify all business units that use PII. Examine staff functions such as HR, Legal, IT, Purchasing, and Quality Control.

3. *Document all contact with PII:*
   - PII collection, access, use, sharing, disposal
   - Processes and procedures, policies, safeguards, data-flow diagrams, and any other risk assessment data
   - Web site policies, contracts, HR, and administrative for other PII

4. *Review legal and regulatory requirements, including any upstream contracts.* The sources are many, but some commonly overlooked issues are agreements with suppliers and customers over information sharing rights.

5. *Document gaps and potential issues between requirements and practices.* All gaps and issues should be mapped against where the issue was discovered and the basis (requirement or regulation) that the gap maps to.

6. *Review findings with key stakeholders to determine accuracy and clarify any issues.* Before the final report is written, any issues or possible miscommunications should be clarified with the appropriate stakeholders to ensure a fair and accurate report.

7. *Create final report for management.*

■ Web Privacy Issues

The Internet acts as a large information-sharing domain, and as such can be a conduit for the transference of information among many parties. The Web offers much in the form of communication between machines, people, and systems, and this same exchange of information can be associated with privacy based on the content of the information and the reason for the exchange.

Platform for Privacy Preferences Project (P3P)

The **Platform for Privacy Preferences Project (P3P)** is a privacy initiative designed to enable web sites to express their privacy policies in machine-readable form, so that user agents can gather information for end users. The automatic retrieval and interpretation of privacy policies enables user agents to adapt to and respond to designated user preferences regarding which web sites they want to visit. The P3P specification also enables user agents to generate privacy policies in human-readable format. P3P is under the auspices of the World Wide Web Consortium (W3C) and the specification is currently at version 1.1 (P3P1.1) as a Working Group Note. To use P3P1.1 on the web server design side, tools are available to translate privacy policy elements into the necessary XML structures to be transmitted to user agents. Once a privacy policy is posted in this fashion, a wide range of readers can consume this product in a formal fashion. For additional information, consult the W3C working group page, www.w3c.org/P3P/.

Cookies

Cookies are small bits of text that are stored on a user's machine and sent to specific web sites when the user visits. Cookies can store many different things, from tokens that provide a reference to a database server behind the web server to assist in maintaining state through an application, to the contents of a shopping cart. Cookies can also hold data directly, in which case there are possible privacy implications. When a cookie holds a token number that is meaningless to outsiders, but meaningful to a back-end server, then the loss of the cookie represents no loss at all. When the cookie text contains meaningful information, then the loss can result in privacy issues. For instance, when a cookie contains a long number that has no meaning except to the database server, then the number has no PII. But if the cookie contains text, such as a ship to address for an order, this can represent PII and can result in a privacy violation. It is common to encode the data in cookies, but Base64 encoding is not encryption and can be decoded by anyone, thus providing no confidentiality.

Cookies provide a useful service of allowing state to be maintained in a stateless process, web serving (see "Cookies" in Chapter 17). But because of the potential for PII leakage, many users have sworn off cookies. This leads to issues on numerous web sites, for when properly implemented, they pose no privacy danger and can greatly enhance web site usefulness. The federal government has gone through cycles of swearing off cookies and then restoring them on their sites. Cookies were used, then considered a threat to privacy and disallowed. The federal government has since recognized cookies for what they are, and now prohibits only certain types of cookies, allowance of which generally would be a bad practice anyway. The bottom line for cookies is fairly easy—done correctly, they do not represent a security or privacy issue. Done incorrectly, they can be a disaster. A simple rule solves most problems with cookies: never store data directly on a cookie; instead, store a reference to another web application that permits the correct actions to occur based on the key value.

Chapter 25 Review

■ Chapter Summary

After reading this chapter and completing the exercises, you should understand the following aspects of privacy.

Define privacy

- Privacy is the power to control what others know about you and what they can do with that information.

- The concept of privacy does not translate directly to information about a business as it is not about a person.

Identify privacy laws relative to computer security in various industries

- Numerous U.S. federal statutes have privacy provisions, including FERPA, VPPA, GLBA, HIPAA, and so on.

- The number of state and local laws that address privacy issues is limited.

- A wide array of international laws address privacy issues, including those of the EU, Canada, and other nations.

Describe issues associated with technology and privacy

- A direct relationship exists between information security and privacy—one cannot have privacy without security.

- Privacy-enhancing technologies (PETs) are used in the technological battle to preserve anonymity and privacy.

Explain the concept of personally identifiable information (PII)

- Specific constituent elements of PII need to be protected.

- Corporate responsibilities associated with PII include the need to protect PII appropriately when in storage, use, or transmission.

Craft a privacy policy for online records

- Policies drive corporate actions, and privacy policies are required by several statutes and are essential to ensure compliance with the myriad of mandated actions.

Recognize web-related privacy issues

- The Platform for Privacy Preferences Project (P3P) provides an agent-aware method of automating usage of privacy policy information.

- Cookies represent a useful tool to maintain state when surfing the Web, but if used incorrectly, they can represent a security and privacy risk.

■ Key Terms

choice *(620)*
consent *(620)*
cookie cutters *(632)*
cookies *(634)*
data protection *(629)*
Disposal Rule *(627)*
Freedom of Information Act (FOIA) *(621)*
Health Insurance Portability and Accountability Act (HIPAA) *(624)*
identity theft *(626)*

notice *(620)*
Notice of Privacy Practices (NPP) *(624)*
opt-in *(629)*
opt-out *(629)*
Personal Information Protection and Electronic Data Act (PIPEDA) *(631)*
personally identifiable information (PII) *(619)*
Platform for Privacy Preferences Project (P3P) *(634)*
privacy *(618)*
Privacy Act of 1974 *(621)*

privacy-enhancing technology (PET) *(632)*
privacy impact assessment (PIA) *(633)*
privacy policy *(632)*

Protected Health Information (PHI) *(624)*
red flags *(628)*
Safe Harbor *(630)*

■ Key Terms Quiz

1. In the United States, the standard methodology for consumers with respect to privacy is to _____, whereas in the EU it is to _____.

2. _____ is the right to control information about oneself.

3. The FTC mandates firms' use of _____ procedures to identify instances where additional privacy measures are warranted.

4. Differences between privacy rules and regulations in the United States and the EU are resolved through _____ conventions.

5. Data that can be used to identify a specific individual is referred to as _____.

6. Programs used to control the use of _____ when web browsing are referred to as _____.

7. The major U.S. privacy statutes are _____ and _____.

8. Medical information in the United States is protected via the _____.

9. Many privacy regulations have specified that firms provide an annual _____ to customers.

10. To evaluate the privacy risks in a firm a(n) _____ can be performed.

■ Multiple-Choice Quiz

1. The Freedom of Information Act applies to:

   A. All federal government documents, without restrictions

   B. All levels of government documents (federal, state, and local)

   C. Federal government documents, with a few enumerated restrictions

   D. Only federal documents containing information concerning the requester

2. HIPAA requires the following controls for medical records:

   A. Encryption of all data

   B. Technical safeguards

   C. Physical controls

   D. Administrative, technical, and physical controls

3. Which of the following is not PII?

   A. Customer name

   B. Customer ID number

   C. Customer social security number or taxpayer identification number

   D. Customer birth date

4. A privacy impact assessment:

   A. Determines the gap between a company's privacy practices and required actions

   B. Determines the damage caused by a breach of privacy

   C. Determines what companies hold information on a specific person

   D. Is a corporate procedure to safeguard PII

5. Which of the following should trigger a response under the Red Flag Rule?

   A. All credit requests for people under 25 or over 75

   B. Any new customer credit request, except for name changes due to marriage

   C. Request for credit from a customer who has a history of late payments and poor credit

   D. Request for credit from a customer with a credit freeze on his credit reporting record

6. Which of the following is an acceptable PII disposal procedure?

   A. Shredding

   B. Burning

   C. Electronic destruction per military data destruction standards

   D. All of the above

7. Safe Harbor principles include:

   A. Notice, Choice, Privacy Policy, Data Restrictions

   B. Notice, Choice, Security, Privacy, Integrity

   C. Notice, Physical Safeguards, Choice, Security, Data Integrity

   D. Notice, Choice, Onward Transfer, Enforcement, Security, Data Integrity

8. European privacy laws are built upon:

   A. EU Data Protection Directive

   B. Personal Information Protection and Electronic Data Act (PIPEDA)

   C. Safe Harbor Principles

   D. Common Law Practices

9. In the United States, company responses to data disclosures of PII are regulated by:

   A. Federal law, the Privacy Act

   B. A series of state statutes

   C. Contractual agreements with banks and credit card processors

   D. The Gramm-Leach-Bliley Act (GLBA)

10. The U.S. Privacy Act of 1974 applies to:

    A. Corporate records for U.S.-based companies

    B. Records from any company doing business in the United States

    C. Federal records containing PII

    D. All levels of government records containing PII

11. The primary factor(s) behind data-sharing compliance between U.S. and European companies is/are?

    A. Safe Harbor Provision

    B. European Data Privacy Laws

    C. U.S. FTC enforcement actions

    D. All of the above

12. Privacy is defined as:

    A. One's ability to control information about himself or herself

    B. Being able to keep your information secret

    C. Making data-sharing illegal without consumer consent

    D. Something that is outmoded in the Internet age

13. The following are items associated with privacy and health records except:

    A. Protected Health Information

    B. Personal Health Information

    C. Notice of Privacy Practices

    D. HITECH Act extension of HIPAA

14. Which of the following records is not protected from disclosure by U.S. law?

    A. A list for marketing of who has received a prescription for a new drug

    B. Class schedules for students in college

    C. Video rental records at your local video store

    D. Library loan records from your public library

15. The FTC disposal rule applies to:

    A. Small businesses using consumer reporting information

    B. Debt collectors

    C. Individuals using consumer reporting information

    D. All of the above

Essay Quiz

1. Privacy and technology often clash, especially when technology allows data collection that can have secondary uses. In the case of automotive technology, black boxes are being installed in new cars in the United States. What are the privacy implications, and what protections exist?

2. Privacy policies are found all over the Web. Pick three web sites with privacy policies and compare and contrast them. What do they include and what is missing?

Lab Project

• Lab Project 25.1

Privacy-enhancing technologies can do much to protect a user's information and/or maintain anonymity when using the Web. Research onion routing and the Tor project. What do these things do? How do they work?

Objectives Map: CompTIA Security+

Topic	Chapter(s)
1.0 Systems Security	
1.1 Differentiate among various systems security threats.	
Privilege escalation	15
Virus	15, 16
Worm	15, 16
Trojan	15, 16
Spyware	15, 16
Spam	15, 16
Adware	15, 16
Rootkits	15
Botnets	15
Logic bomb	15
1.2 Explain the security risks pertaining to system hardware and peripherals.	
BIOS	10
USB devices	10
Cell phones	10
Removable storage	10
Network attached storage	10
1.3 Implement OS hardening practices and procedures to achieve workstation and server security.	
Hotfixes	10, 14
Service packs	10, 14
Patches	10, 14
Patch management	10, 14
Group policies	14
Security templates	14
Configuration baselines	14
1.4 Carry out the appropriate procedures to establish application security.	
ActiveX	17
Java	17
Scripting	17
Browser	17
Buffer overflows	17, 18

Topic	Chapter(s)
Cookies	17
SMTP open relays	17, 18
Instant messaging	16, 17
P2P	17
Input validation	17, 18
Cross-site scripting (XSS)	17
1.5 Implement security applications.	
HIDS	13
Personal software firewalls	10, 13
Antivirus	10, 13
Anti-spam	10, 13
Popup blockers	10, 13
1.6 Explain the purpose and application of virtualization technology.	
	10
2.0 Network Infrastructure	
2.1 Differentiate between the different ports & protocols, their respective threats and mitigation techniques.	
Antiquated protocols	11
TCP/IP hijacking	11, 15
Null sessions	15
Spoofing	15
Man-in-the-middle	15
Replay	15
DOS	15
DDOS	15
Domain Name Kiting	15
DNS poisoning	15
ARP poisoning	15
2.2 Distinguish between network design elements and components.	
DMZ	9
VLAN	9
NAT	9
Network interconnections	9
NAC	10
Subnetting	9
Telephony	3, 10
2.3 Determine the appropriate use of network security tools to facilitate network security.	
NIDS	10, 13
NIPS	10, 13
Firewalls	10, 13

Topic	Chapter(s)
Proxy servers	10, 13
Honeypot	10, 13
Internet content filters	13
Protocol analyzers	10, 13
2.4 Apply the appropriate network tools to facilitate network security.	
NIDS	10, 13
Firewalls	10, 13
Proxy servers	10, 13
Internet content filters	13
Protocol analyzers	10, 13
2.5 Explain the vulnerabilities and mitigations associated with network devices.	
Privilege escalation	10
Weak passwords	10
Back doors	10
Default accounts	10
DOS	10
2.6 Explain the vulnerabilities and mitigations associated with various transmission media.	
Vampire taps	10
2.7 Explain the vulnerabilities and implement mitigations associated with wireless networking.	
Data emanation	3, 12
War driving	12
SSID broadcast	12
Blue jacking	12
Bluesnarfing	12
Rogue access points	12
Weak encryption	12
3.0 Access Control	
3.1 Identify and apply industry best practices for access control methods.	
Implicit deny	1
Least privilege	1, 18, 19
Separation of duties	1, 19
Job rotation	1
3.2 Explain common access control models and the differences between each.	
MAC	1, 11, 22
DAC	1, 11, 22
Role & Rule based access control	1, 11, 22
3.3 Organize users and computers into appropriate security groups and roles while distinguishing between appropriate rights and privileges.	
	2, 11, 22

Topic	Chapter(s)
3.4 Apply appropriate security controls to file and print resources.	
	2, 22
3.5 Compare and implement logical access control methods.	
ACL	2, 11, 22
Group policies	2, 11, 22
Password policy	2, 4, 22
Domain password policy	2, 11, 22
User names and passwords	2, 4, 22
Time of day restrictions	2, 22
Account expiration	2, 4, 22
Logical tokens	2, 11, 22
3.6 Summarize the various authentication models and identify the components of each.	
One, two and three-factor authentication	11
Single sign-on	11, 22
3.7 Deploy various authentication models and identify the components of each.	
Biometric reader	3, 11
RADIUS	11
RAS	11
LDAP	11
Remote access policies	11
Remote authentication	11
VPN	11
Kerberos	11
CHAP	11
PAP	11
Mutual	11
802.1x	11
TACACS	11
3.8 Explain the difference between identification and authentication (identity proofing).	
	11
3.9 Explain and apply physical access security methods.	
Physical access logs/lists	8
Hardware locks	8
Physical access control – ID badges	8
Door access systems	8
Man-trap	8
Physical tokens	8
Video surveillance – camera types and positioning	8
4.0 Assessments & Audits	
4.1 Conduct risk assessments and implement risk mitigation.	
	14

Topic	Chapter(s)
4.2 Carry out vulnerability assessments using common tools.	
Port scanners	14
Vulnerability scanners	14
Protocol analyzers	14
OVAL	17
Password crackers	15
Network mappers	14
4.3 Within the realm of vulnerability assessments, explain the proper use of penetration testing versus vulnerability scanning.	
	14
4.4 Use monitoring tools on systems and networks and detect security-related anomalies.	
Performance monitor	14
Systems monitor	14
Performance baseline	14
Protocol analyzers	14
4.5 Compare and contrast various types of monitoring methodologies.	
Behavior-based	13
Signature-based	13
Anomaly-based	13
4.6 Execute proper logging procedures and evaluate the results.	
Security application	14
DNS	14
System	14
Performance	14
Access	14
Firewall	13
Antivirus	14
4.7 Conduct periodic audits of system security settings.	
User access and rights review	2, 19
Storage and retention policies	19
Group policies	19
5.0 Cryptography	
5.1 Explain general cryptography concepts.	
Key management	5, 6, 7
Steganography	5
Symmetric key	5
Asymmetric key	5
Confidentiality	5
Integrity and availability	5

Topic	Chapter(s)
Non-repudiation	5
Comparative strength of algorithms	5
Digital signatures	5
Whole disk encryption	5
Trusted Platform Module (TPM)	5
Single vs. Dual sided certificates	5, 6
Use of proven technologies	5
5.2 Explain basic hashing concepts and map various algorithms to appropriate applications.	
SHA	5, 23
MD5	5, 23
LANMAN	5
NTLM	5
5.3 Explain basic encryption concepts and map various algorithms to appropriate applications.	
DES	5
3DES	5
RSA	5
PGP	5
Elliptic curve	5
AES	5
AES256	5
One time pad	5
Transmission encryption (WEP TKIP, etc.)	5, 7
5.4 Explain and implement protocols.	
SSL/TLS	5,
S/MIME	5, 7, 16
PPTP	5, 7, 11
HTTP vs. HTTPS vs. SHTTP	5, 7
L2TP	5, 11
IPSEC	5, 7, 11
SSH	5, 11
5.5 Explain core concepts of public key cryptography.	
Public Key Infrastructure (PKI)	6, 16
Recovery agent	6
Public key	6
Private keys	6
Certificate Authority (CA)	6
Registration	6
Key escrow	6
Certificate Revocation List (CRL)	6
Trust models	6

Topic	Chapter(s)
5.6 Implement PKI and certificate management.	
Public Key Infrastructure (PKI)	6, 16
Recovery agent	6
Public key	6
Private keys	6
Certificate Authority (CA)	6
Registration	6
Key escrow	6
Certificate Revocation List (CRL)	6
6.0 Organizational Security	
6.1 Explain redundancy planning and its components.	
Hot site	19
Cold site	19
Warm site	19
Backup generator	19
Single point of failure	19
RAID	19
Spare parts	19
Redundant servers	19
Redundant ISP	19
UPS	19
Redundant connections	19
6.2 Implement disaster recovery procedures.	
Planning	19
Disaster recovery exercises	19
Backup techniques and practices – storage	19
Schemes	19
Restoration	19
6.3 Differentiate between and execute appropriate incident response procedures.	
Forensics	19, 23
Chain of custody	19, 23
First responders	19, 23
Damage and loss control	19, 23
Reporting – disclosure of	19, 23
6.4 Identify and explain applicable legislation and organizational policies.	
Secure disposal of computers	2
Acceptable use policies	2, 19
Password complexity	2, 4
Change management	2, 19
Classification of information	2, 19

Topic	Chapter(s)
Mandatory vacations	2, 4, 19
Personally Identifiable Information (PII)	2, 25
Due care	2, 19
Due diligence	2, 19
Due process	2, 19
SLA	2, 19
Security-related HR policy	2, 4
User education and awareness training	2, 4
6.5 Explain the importance of environmental controls.	
Fire suppression	3, 8
HVAC	3, 8
Shielding	3, 8
6.6 Explain the concept of and how to reduce the risks of social engineering.	
Phishing	2, 4
Hoaxes	2, 4
Shoulder surfing	2, 4
Dumpster diving	2, 4
User education and awareness training	2, 4

About the CD

The CD-ROM included with this book comes complete with MasterExam, the electronic version of the book, and Session #1 of LearnKey's online training. The software is easy to install on any Windows 2000/XP/Vista computer and must be installed to access the MasterExam feature. You may, however, browse the electronic book directly from the CD without installing the software. To register for LearnKey's online training or the bonus MasterExam, simply click the Bonus MasterExam link on the main launch page and follow the directions to the free online registration.

System Requirements

Software requires Windows 2000 or higher and Internet Explorer 6.0 or above and 20MB of hard disk space for full installation. The electronic book requires Adobe Reader. To access the online training from LearnKey, you must have Windows Media Player 9 or higher and Adobe Flash Player 9 or higher.

■ LearnKey Online Training

Clicking the LearnKey Online Training link will allow you to access online training from Osborne.OnlineExpert.com. The first session of this course is provided at no charge. Additional session for this course and other courses may be purchased directly from www.LearnKey.com or by calling 800-865-0165.

The first time that you click the LearnKey Online Training link, you will be required to complete a free online registration. Follow the instructions for a first-time user. Please make sure to use a valid e-mail address.

■ Installing and Running MasterExam

If your computer CD-ROM drive is configured to autorun, the CD-ROM will automatically start up when you insert the disc. From the opening screen, you may install MasterExam by clicking the MasterExam link. This will begin the installation process and create a program group named LearnKey. To run MasterExam, select Start | All Programs | LearnKey | MasterExam. If the autorun feature did not launch your CD, browse to the CD drive and click the LaunchTraining.exe icon.

MasterExam

MasterExam provides you with a simulation of the actual exam. The number of questions, the type of questions, and the time allowed are intended to be an accurate representation of the exam environment. You have the option to take an open-book exam, including hints, references, and answers, a closed-book exam, or the timed MasterExam simulation.

When you launch MasterExam, a digital clock display will appear in the bottom-right corner of your screen. The clock will continue to count down to zero unless you choose to end the exam before the time expires.

Electronic Book

The entire contents of the textbook are provided as a PDF. Adobe Reader has been included on the CD.

Help

A help file is provided through the Help button on the main page in the lower-left corner. Individual help features are also available through MasterExam and LearnKey's online training.

Removing Installation(s)

MasterExam is installed to your hard drive. For best results removing the program, select the Start | All Programs | LearnKey | Uninstall option to remove MasterExam.

Technical Support

For questions regarding the content of the electronic book or MasterExam, please visit www.mhprofessional.com or e-mail customer.service@mcgraw-hill.com. For customers outside the 50 United States, e-mail international_cs@mcgraw-hill.com.

LearnKey Technical Support

For technical problems with the software (installation, operation, installation removal) and for questions regarding LearnKey online training content, please visit www.learnkey.com, e-mail techsupport@learnkey.com, or call toll free 800-482-8244.

GLOSSARY

*-property Pronounced "star property," this aspect of the Bell-La Padula security model is commonly referred to as the "no-write-down" rule because it doesn't allow a user to write to a file with a lower security classification, thus preserving confidentiality.

3DES Triple DES encryption—three rounds of DES encryption used to improve security.

802.11 A family of standards that describe network protocols for wireless devices.

802.1X An IEEE standard for performing authentication over networks.

AAA See authentication, authorization, and accounting.

acceptable use policy (AUP) A policy that communicates to users what specific uses of computer resources are permitted.

access A subject's ability to perform specific operations on an object, such as a file. Typical access levels include read, write, execute, and delete.

access controls Mechanisms or methods used to determine what access permissions subjects (such as users) have for specific objects (such as files).

access control list (ACL) A list associated with an object (such as a file) that identifies what level of access each subject (such as a user) has—what they can do to the object (such as read, write, or execute).

Active Directory The directory service portion of the Windows operating system that stores information about network-based entities (such as applications, files, printers, and people) and provides a structured, consistent way to name, describe, locate, access, and manage these resources.

ActiveX A Microsoft technology that facilitates rich Internet applications, and therefore extends and enhances the functionality of Microsoft Internet Explorer. Like Java, ActiveX enables the development of interactive content. When an ActiveX-aware browser encounters a web page that includes an unsupported feature, it can automatically install the appropriate application so the feature can be used.

Address Resolution Protocol (ARP) A protocol in the TCP/IP suite specification used to map an IP address to a Media Access Control (MAC) address.

adware Advertising-supported software that automatically plays, displays, or downloads advertisements after the software is installed or while the application is being used.

algorithm A step-by-step procedure—typically an established computation for solving a problem within a set number of steps.

annualized loss expectancy (ALE) How much an event is expected to cost the business per year, given the dollar cost of the loss and how often it is likely to occur. ALE = single loss expectancy * annualized rate of occurrence.

annualized rate of occurrence (ARO) The frequency with which an event is expected to occur on an annualized basis.

anomaly Something that does not fit into an expected pattern.

application A program or group of programs designed to provide specific user functions, such as a word processor or web server.

ARP *See* Address Resolution Protocol.

ARP backscatter The use of ARP scanning against a gateway device to detect the presence of a device behind the gateway or router.

ARP poisoning An attack characterized by changing entries in an ARP table to cause misdirected traffic.

asset Resources and information an organization needs to conduct its business.

asymmetric encryption Also called public key cryptography, this is a system for encrypting data that uses two mathematically derived keys to encrypt and decrypt a message—a public key, available to everyone, and a private key, available only to the owner of the key.

audit trail A set of records or events, generally organized chronologically, that records what activity has occurred on a system. These records (often computer files) are often used in an attempt to re-create what took place when a security incident occurred, and they can also be used to detect possible intruders.

auditability The property of an item that makes it available for verification upon inspection.

auditing Actions or processes used to verify the assigned privileges and rights of a user, or any capabilities used to create and maintain a record showing who accessed a particular system and what actions they performed.

authentication The process by which a subject's (such as a user's) identity is verified.

authentication, authorization, and accounting (AAA) Three common functions performed upon system login. Authentication and authorization almost always occur, with accounting being somewhat less common.

Authentication Header (AH) A portion of the IPsec security protocol that provides authentication services and replay-detection ability. AH can be used either by itself or with Encapsulating Security Payload (ESP). Refer to RFC 2402.

authorization The function of determining what is permitted for an authorized user.

availability Part of the "CIA" of security. Availability applies to hardware, software, and data, specifically meaning that each of these should be present and accessible when the subject (the user) wants to access or use them.

backdoor A hidden method used to gain access to a computer system, network, or application. Often used by software developers to ensure unrestricted access to the systems they create. Synonymous with trapdoor.

backup Refers to copying and storing data in a secondary location, separate from the original, to preserve the data in the event that the original is lost, corrupted, or destroyed.

baseline A system or software as it is built and functioning at a specific point in time. Serves as a foundation for comparison or measurement, providing the necessary visibility to control change.

Bell-La Padula security model A computer security model built around the property of confidentiality and characterized by no-read-up and no-write-down rules.

BGP *See* Border Gateway Protocol.

Biba security model An information security model built around the property of integrity and characterized by no-write-up and no-read-down rules.

biometrics Used to verify an individual's identity to the system or network using something unique about the individual, such as a fingerprint, for the verification process. Examples include fingerprints, retinal scans, hand and facial geometry, and voice analysis.

BIOS The part of the operating system that links specific hardware devices to the operating system software.

birthday attack A form of attack in which the attack needs to match not a specific item but just one of a set of items.

block cipher A cipher that operates on blocks of data.

Blowfish A free implementation of a symmetric block cipher developed by Bruce Schneier as a drop-in replacement for DES and IDEA. It has a variable bit-length scheme from 32 to 448 bits, resulting in varying levels of security.

bluebugging The use of a Bluetooth-enabled device to eavesdrop on another person's conversation using that person's Bluetooth phone as a transmitter. The bluebug application silently causes a Bluetooth device to make a phone call to another device, causing the phone to act as a transmitter and allowing the listener to eavesdrop on the victim's conversation in real time.

bluejacking The sending of unsolicited messages over Bluetooth to Bluetooth-enabled devices such as mobile phones, PDAs, or laptop computers.

bluesnarfing The unauthorized access of information from a Bluetooth-enabled device through a Bluetooth connection, often between phones, desktops, laptops, and PDAs.

Border Gateway Protocol (BGP) The interdomain routing protocol implemented in Internet Protocol (IP) networks to enable routing between autonomous systems.

botnet   A term for a collection of software robots, or bots, that runs autonomously and automatically and commonly invisibly in the background. The term is most often associated with malicious software, but it can also refer to the network of computers using distributed computing software.

bridge   A network device that separates traffic into separate collision domains at the data layer of the OSI model.

buffer overflow   A specific type of software coding error that enables user input to overflow the allocated storage area and corrupt a running program.

Bureau of Industry and Security (BIS)   In the U.S. Department of Commerce, the department responsible for export administration regulations that cover encryption technology in the United States.

bus topology   A network layout in which a common line (the bus) connects devices.

cache   The temporary storage of information before use, typically used to speed up systems. In an Internet context, refers to the storage of commonly accessed web pages, graphic files, and other content locally on a user's PC or a web server. The cache helps to minimize download time and preserve bandwidth for frequently accessed web sites, and it helps reduce the load on a web server.

Capability Maturity Model (CMM)   A structured methodology helping organizations improve the maturity of their software processes by providing an evolutionary path from ad hoc processes to disciplined software management processes. Developed at Carnegie Mellon University's Software Engineering Institute (SEI).

Capability Maturity Model Integration (CMMI)   A trademarked process improvement methodology for software engineering. Developed at Carnegie Mellon University's Software Engineering Institute (SEI).

centralized management   A type of privilege management that brings the authority and responsibility for managing and maintaining rights and privileges into a single group, location, or area.

CERT   *See* Computer Emergency Response Team.

certificate   A cryptographically signed object that contains an identity and a public key associated with

this identity. The certificate can be used to establish identity, analogous to a notarized written document.

certificate revocation list (CRL)   A digitally signed object that lists all of the current but revoked certificates issued by a given certification authority. This allows users to verify whether a certificate is currently valid even if it has not expired. CRL is analogous to a list of stolen charge card numbers that allows stores to reject bad credit cards.

certification authority (CA)   An entity responsible for issuing and revoking certificates. CAs are typically not associated with the company requiring the certificate, although they exist for internal company use as well (such as Microsoft). This term is also applied to server software that provides these services. The term *certificate authority* is used interchangeably with *certification authority*.

chain of custody   Rules for documenting, handling, and safeguarding evidence to ensure no unanticipated changes are made to the evidence.

Challenge-Handshake Authentication Protocol (CHAP)   Used to provide authentication across point-to-point links using the Point-to-Point Protocol (PPP).

change (configuration) management   A standard methodology for performing and recording changes during software development and operation.

change control board (CCB)   A body that oversees the change management process and enables management to oversee and coordinate projects.

CHAP   *See* Challenge-Handshake Authentication Protocol.

CIA of security   Refers to confidentiality, integrity, and authorization, the basic functions of any security system.

cipher   A cryptographic system that accepts plaintext input and then outputs ciphertext according to its internal algorithm and key.

ciphertext   Used to denote the output of an encryption algorithm. Ciphertext is the encrypted data.

CIRT   *See* Computer Emergency Response Team.

Clark-Wilson security model   A security model that uses transactions and a differentiation of constrained data items (CDI) and unconstrained data items (UDI).

cold site An inexpensive form of backup site that does not include a current set of data at all times. A cold site takes longer to get your operational system back up, but it is considerably less expensive than a warm or hot site.

collision attack An attack on a hash function in which a specific input is generated to produce a hash function output that matches another input.

collisions Used in the analysis of hashing cryptography, it is the property by which an algorithm will produce the same hash from two different sets of data.

Computer Emergency Response Team (CERT) Also known as a Computer Incident Response Team (CIRT), this group is responsible for investigating and responding to security breaches, viruses, and other potentially catastrophic incidents.

computer security In general terms, the methods, techniques, and tools used to ensure that a computer system is secure.

computer software configuration item See configuration item.

confidentiality Part of the CIA of security. Refers to the security principle that states that information should not be disclosed to unauthorized individuals.

configuration auditing The process of verifying that configuration items are built and maintained according to requirements, standards, or contractual agreements.

configuration control The process of controlling changes to items that have been baselined.

configuration identification The process of identifying which assets need to be managed and controlled.

configuration item Data or software (or other asset) that is identified and managed as part of the software change management process. Also known as computer software configuration item.

configuration status accounting Procedures for tracking and maintaining data relative to each configuration item in the baseline.

content protection The protection of the header and data portion of a user datagram.

context protection The protection of the header of a user datagram.

control A measure taken to detect, prevent, or mitigate the risk associated with a threat.

cookie Information stored on a user's computer by a web server to maintain the state of the connection to the web server. Used primarily so preferences or previously used information can be recalled on future requests to the server.

countermeasure See control.

cracking A term used by some to refer to malicious hacking, in which an individual attempts to gain unauthorized access to computer systems or networks. See also hacking.

critical infrastructure Infrastructure whose loss or impairment would have severe repercussions on society.

CRC See cyclic redundancy check.

CRL See certificate revocation list.

cryptanalysis The process of attempting to break a cryptographic system.

cryptography The art of secret writing that enables an individual to hide the contents of a message or file from all but the intended recipient.

cyclic redundancy check (CRC) An error detection technique that uses a series of two, 8-bit block check characters to represent an entire block of data. These block check characters are incorporated into the transmission frame and then checked at the receiving end.

DAC See discretionary access control.

data aggregation A methodology of collecting information through the aggregation of separate pieces and analyzing the effect of their collection.

Data Encryption Standard (DES) A private key encryption algorithm adopted by the government as a standard for the protection of sensitive but unclassified information. Commonly used in Triple DES (3DES), where three rounds are applied to provide greater security.

datagram A packet of data that can be transmitted over a packet-switched system in a connectionless mode.

decision tree A data structure in which each element in the structure is attached to one or more structures directly beneath it.

demilitarized zone (DMZ) A network segment that exists in a semiprotected zone between the Internet and the inner secure trusted network.

denial-of-service (DoS) attack An attack in which actions are taken to deprive authorized individuals from accessing a system, its resources, the data it stores or processes, or the network to which it is connected.

DES *See* Data Encryption Standard.

DHCP *See* Dynamic Host Configuration Protocol.

Diameter The base protocol that is intended to provide an authentication, authorization, and accounting (AAA) framework for applications such as network access or IP mobility. Diameter is a draft IETF proposal.

differential cryptanalysis A form of cryptanalysis that uses different inputs to study how outputs change in a structured manner.

Diffie-Hellman A cryptographic method of establishing a shared key over an insecure medium in a secure fashion.

digital rights management The control of user activities associated with a digital object via technological means.

digital signature A cryptography-based artifact that is a key component of a public key infrastructure (PKI) implementation. A digital signature can be used to prove identity because it is created with the private key portion of a public/private key pair. A recipient can decrypt the signature and, by doing so, receive the assurance that the data must have come from the sender and that the data has not changed.

direct-sequence spread spectrum (DSSS) A method of distributing a communication over multiple frequencies to avoid interference and detection.

disaster recovery plan (DRP) A written plan developed to address how an organization will react to a natural or manmade disaster in order to ensure business continuity. Related to the concept of a business continuity plan (BCP).

discretionary access control (DAC) An access control mechanism in which the owner of an object (such as a file) can decide which other subjects (such as other users) may have access to the object, and what access (read, write, execute) these objects can have.

distributed denial-of-service (DDoS) attack A special type of DoS attack in which the attacker elicits the generally unwilling support of other systems to launch a many-against-one attack.

diversity of defense The approach of creating dissimilar security layers so that an intruder who is able to breach one layer will be faced with an entirely different set of defenses at the next layer.

Domain Name Service (DNS) The service that translates an Internet domain name (such as www.mcgraw-hill.com) into IP addresses.

DNS kiting The use of a DNS record during the payment grace period without paying.

drive-by download attack An attack on an innocent victim machine where content is downloaded without the user's knowledge.

DRP *See* disaster recovery plan.

DSSS *See* direct-sequence spread spectrum.

dumpster diving The practice of searching through trash to discover material that has been thrown away that is sensitive, yet not destroyed or shredded.

Dynamic Host Configuration Protocol (DHCP) An Internet Engineering Task Force (IETF) Internet Protocol (IP) specification for automatically allocating IP addresses and other configuration information based on network adapter addresses. It enables address pooling and allocation and simplifies TCP/IP installation and administration.

EAP *See* Extensible Authentication Protocol.

elite hackers Hackers who have the skill level necessary to discover and exploit new vulnerabilities.

elliptic curve cryptography (ECC) A method of public-key cryptography based on the algebraic structure of elliptic curves over finite fields.

Encapsulating Security Payload (ESP) A portion of the IPsec implementation that provides for data confidentiality with optional authentication and replay detection services. ESP completely encapsulates user data in the datagram and can be used either by itself or in conjunction with Authentication Headers for varying degrees of IPsec services.

escalation auditing   The process of looking for an increase in privileges, such as when an ordinary user obtains administrator-level privileges.

evidence   The documents, verbal statements, and material objects admissible in a court of law.

exposure factor   A measure of the magnitude of loss of an asset. Used in the calculation of single loss expectancy (SLE).

Extensible Authentication Protocol (EAP)   A universal authentication framework used in wireless networks and point-to-point connections. It is defined in RFC 3748 and has been updated by RFC 5247.

false positive   Term used when a security system makes an error and incorrectly reports the existence of a searched-for object. Examples include an intrusion detection system that misidentifies benign traffic as hostile, an antivirus program that reports the existence of a virus in software that actually is not infected, or a biometric system that allows access to a system to an unauthorized individual.

FHSS   *See* frequency-hopping spread spectrum.

File Transfer Protocol (FTP)   An application-level protocol used to transfer files over a network connection.

firewall   A network device used to segregate traffic based on rules.

forensics (or computer forensics)   The preservation, identification, documentation, and interpretation of computer data for use in legal proceedings.

free space   Sectors on a storage medium that are available for the operating system to use.

frequency-hopping spread spectrum (FHSS)   A method of distributing a communication over multiple frequencies over time to avoid interference and detection.

Generic Routing Encapsulation (GRE)   A tunneling protocol designed to encapsulate a wide variety of network layer packets inside IP tunneling packets.

group policy   The mechanism that allows for centralized management and configuration of computers and remote users in a Microsoft Active Directory environment.

group policy object (GPO)   Stores the group policy settings in a Microsoft Active Directory environment.

hacking   The term used by the media to refer to the process of gaining unauthorized access to computer systems and networks. The term has also been used to refer to the process of delving deep into the code and protocols used in computer systems and networks. *See also* cracking.

hactivist   A hacker who uses his or her skills for political purposes.

hash   Form of encryption that creates a digest of the data put into the algorithm. These algorithms are referred to as one-way algorithms because there is no feasible way to decrypt what has been encrypted.

hash value   *See* message digest.

HIDS   *See* host-based intrusion detection system.

highly structured threat   A threat that is backed by the time and resources to allow virtually any form of attack.

HIPS   *See* host-based intrusion prevention system.

honeypot   A computer system or portion of a network that has been set up to attract potential intruders, in the hope that they will leave the other systems alone. Since there are no legitimate users of this system, any attempt to access it is an indication of unauthorized activity and provides an easy mechanism to spot attacks.

host-based intrusion detection system (HIDS)   A system that looks for computer intrusions by monitoring activity on one or more individual PCs or servers.

host-based intrusion prevention system (HIPS)   A system that automatically responds to computer intrusions by monitoring activity on one or more individual PCs or servers and with the response being based on a rule set.

hot site   A backup site that is fully configured with equipment and data and is ready to immediately accept transfer of operational processing in the event of failure of the operational system.

hub   A network device used to connect devices at the physical layer of the OSI model.

Hypertext Transfer Protocol (HTTP)   A protocol for transfer of material across the Internet that contains links to additional material.

ICMP   *See* Internet Control Message Protocol.

IDEA   *See* International Data Encryption Algorithm.

identification The process of determining identity as part of identity management and access control. Usually performed only once, when the user ID is assigned.

IEEE *See* Institute for Electrical and Electronics Engineers.

IETF *See* Internet Engineering Task Force.

IKE *See* Internet Key Exchange.

impact The result of a vulnerability being exploited by a threat, resulting in a loss.

implicit deny A philosophy that all actions are prohibited unless specifically authorized.

incident response The process of responding to, containing, analyzing, and recovering from a computer-related incident.

information security Often used synonymously with computer security but places the emphasis on the protection of the information that the system processes and stores, instead of on the hardware and software that constitute the system.

information warfare The use of information security techniques, both offensive and defensive, when combating an opponent.

Institute for Electrical and Electronics Engineers (IEEE) A nonprofit, technical, professional institute associated with computer research, standards, and conferences.

intangible asset An asset for which a monetary equivalent is difficult or impossible to determine. Examples are brand recognition and goodwill.

integrity Part of the CIA of security, the security principle that requires that information is not modified except by individuals authorized to do so.

International Data Encryption Algorithm (IDEA) A symmetric encryption algorithm used in a variety of systems for bulk encryption services.

Internet Assigned Numbers Authority (IANA) The central coordinator for the assignment of unique parameter values for Internet protocols. The IANA is chartered by the Internet Society (ISOC) to act as the clearinghouse to assign and coordinate the use of numerous Internet protocol parameters.

Internet Control Message Protocol (ICMP) One of the core protocols of the TCP/IP protocol suite, used for error reporting and status messages.

Internet Engineering Task Force (IETF) A large international community of network designers, operators, vendors, and researchers, open to any interested individual concerned with the evolution of the Internet architecture and the smooth operation of the Internet. The actual technical work of the IETF is done in its working groups, which are organized by topic into several areas (such as routing, transport, and security). Much of the work is handled via mailing lists, with meetings held three times per year.

Internet Key Exchange (IKE) The protocol formerly known as ISAKMP/Oakley, defined in RFC 2409. A hybrid protocol that uses part Oakley and part of Secure Key Exchange Mechanism for Internet (SKEMI) protocol suites inside the Internet Security Association and Key Management Protocol (ISAKMP) framework. IKE is used to establish a shared security policy and authenticated keys for services that require keys (such as IPsec).

Internet Message Access Protocol version 4 (IMAP4) One of two common Internet standard protocols for e-mail retrieval.

Internet Protocol (IP) The network layer protocol used by the Internet for routing packets across a network.

Internet Protocol Security (IPsec) A protocol used to secure IP packets during transmission across a network. IPsec offers authentication, integrity, and confidentiality services and uses Authentication Headers (AH) and Encapsulating Security Payload (ESP) to accomplish this functionality.

Internet Security Association and Key Management Protocol (ISAKMP) A protocol framework that defines the mechanics of implementing a key exchange protocol and negotiation of a security policy.

Internet service provider (ISP) A telecommunications firm that provides access to the Internet.

intrusion detection system (IDS) A system to identify suspicious, malicious, or undesirable activity that indicates a breach in computer security.

IPsec *See* Internet Protocol Security.

ISAKMP/Oakley *See* Internet Key Exchange.

Kerberos A network authentication protocol designed by MIT for use in client/server environments.

key In cryptography, a sequence of characters or bits used by an algorithm to encrypt or decrypt a message.

key distribution center A portion of the Kerberos authentication system.

keyspace The entire set of all possible keys for a specific encryption algorithm.

layered security The arrangement of multiple layers of defense, a form of defense in depth.

LDAP *See* Lightweight Directory Access Protocol.

least privilege A security principle in which a user is provided with the minimum set of rights and privileges that he or she needs to perform required functions. The goal is to limit the potential damage that any user can cause.

Level Two Tunneling Protocol (L2TP) A Cisco switching protocol that operates at the data link layer.

Lightweight Directory Access Protocol (LDAP) An application protocol used to access directory services across a TCP/IP network.

linear cryptanalysis The use of linear functions to approximate a cryptographic function as a means of analysis.

local area network (LAN) A grouping of computers in a network structure confined to a limited area and using specific protocols, such as Ethernet for OSI Layer 2 traffic addressing.

logic bomb A form of malicious code or software that is triggered by a specific event or condition. *See also* time bomb.

Low-Water-Mark policy An integrity-based information security model derived from the Bell-La Padula model.

MAC *See* mandatory access control or Media Access Control.

malware A class of software that is designed to cause harm.

man-in-the-middle attack Any attack that attempts to use a network node as the intermediary between two

other nodes. Each of the endpoint nodes thinks it is talking directly to the other, but each is actually talking to the intermediary.

mandatory access control (MAC) An access control mechanism in which the security mechanism controls access to all objects (files), and individual subjects (processes or users) cannot change that access.

MD5 Message Digest 5, a hashing algorithm and a specific method of producing a message digest.

Media Access Control (MAC) A protocol used in the data link layer for local network addressing.

message digest The result of applying a hash function to data. Sometimes also called a hash value. *See* hash.

metropolitan area network (MAN) A collection of networks interconnected in a metropolitan area and usually connected to the Internet.

Microsoft Challenge-Handshake Authentication Protocol (MSCHAP) A Microsoft-developed variant of the Challenge-Handshake Authentication Protocol (CHAP).

mitigate Action taken to reduce the likelihood of a threat occurring.

modem A modulator/demodulator that is designed to connect machines via telephone-based circuits.

MSCHAP *See* Microsoft Challenge-Handshake Authentication Protocol.

multiple encryption The use of multiple layers of encryption to improve encryption strength.

NAC *See* network access control or Network Admission Control.

NAP *See* Network Access Protection.

NAT *See* Network Address Translation.

network access control (NAC) An approach to endpoint security that involves monitoring and remediating endpoint security issues before allowing an object to connect to a network.

Network Access Protection (NAP) A Microsoft approach to network access control.

Network Address Translation (NAT) A method of re-addressing packets in a network at a gateway point to enable the use of local nonroutable IP addresses over a public network such as the Internet.

Network Admission Control (NAC) The Cisco technology approach for generic network access control.

network attached storage The connection of storage to a system via a network connection.

network-based intrusion detection system (NIDS) A system for examining network traffic to identify suspicious, malicious, or undesirable behavior.

network-based intrusion prevention system (NIPS) A system that examines network traffic and automatically responds to computer intrusions.

network interface card (NIC) A piece of hardware designed to connect machines at the physical layer of the OSI model.

network operating system (NOS) An operating system that includes additional functions and capabilities to assist in connecting computers and devices, such as printers, to a local area network.

NIC *See* network interface card.

nonrepudiation The ability to verify that an operation has been performed by a particular person or account. This is a system property that prevents the parties to a transaction from subsequently denying involvement in the transaction.

null session The way in which Microsoft Windows represents an unauthenticated connection.

Oakley protocol A key exchange protocol that defines how to acquire authenticated keying material based on the Diffie-Hellman key exchange algorithm.

object reuse Assignment of a previously used medium to a subject. The security implication is that before it is provided to the subject, any data present from a previous user must be cleared.

one-time pad An unbreakable encryption scheme in which a series of nonrepeating, random bits is used once as a key to encrypt a message. Since each pad is used only once, no pattern can be established and traditional cryptanalysis techniques are not effective.

open relay A mail server that receives and forwards mail from outside sources.

Open Vulnerability and Assessment Language (OVAL) An XML-based standard for the communication of security information between tools and services.

operating system (OS) The basic software that handles input, output, display, memory management, and all the other highly detailed tasks required to support the user environment and associated applications.

operational model of computer security Structuring activities into prevention, detection, and response.

Orange Book The name commonly used to refer to the now outdated Department of Defense Trusted Computer Security Evaluation Criteria (TCSEC).

OVAL *See* Open Vulnerability and Assessment Language.

P2P *See* peer-to-peer.

PAP *See* Password Authentication Protocol.

password A string of characters used to prove an individual's identity to a system or object. Used in conjunction with a user ID, it is the most common method of authentication. The password should be kept secret by the individual who owns it.

Password Authentication Protocol (PAP) A simple protocol used to authenticate a user to a network access server.

patch A replacement set of code designed to correct problems or vulnerabilities in existing software.

PBX *See* private branch exchange.

peer-to-peer (P2P) A network connection methodology involving direct connection from peer to peer.

penetration testing A security test in which an attempt is made to circumvent security controls in order to discover vulnerabilities and weaknesses. Also called a pen test.

permissions Authorized actions a subject can perform on an object. *See also* access controls.

personally identifiable information (PII) Information that can be used to identify a single person.

pharming The use of a fake web site to socially engineer someone out of credentials.

phishing   The use of social engineering to trick a user into responding to something such as an e-mail to instantiate a malware-based attack.

phreaking   Used in the media to refer to the hacking of computer systems and networks associated with the phone company. *See also* cracking.

PID   *See* process identifier.

PII   *See* personally identifiable information.

ping sweep   The use of a series of ICMP ping messages to map out a network.

plaintext   In cryptography, a piece of data that is not encrypted. It can also mean the data input into an encryption algorithm that would output ciphertext.

Point-to-Point Protocol (PPP)   The Internet standard for transmission of IP packets over a serial line, as in a dial-up connection to an ISP.

Point-to-Point Protocol Extensible Authentication Protocol (PPP EAP)   EAP is a PPP extension that provides support for additional authentication methods within PPP.

Point-to-Point Protocol Password Authentication Protocol (PPP PAP)   PAP is a PPP extension that provides support for password authentication methods over PPP.

port scan   The examination of TCP and UDP ports to determine which are open and what services are running.

Pretty Good Privacy (PGP)   A popular encryption program that has the ability to encrypt and digitally sign e-mail and files.

preventative intrusion detection   A system that detects hostile actions or network activity and prevents them from impacting information systems.

privacy   Protecting an individual's personal information from those not authorized to see it.

private branch exchange (PBX)   A telephone exchange that serves a specific business or entity.

privilege auditing   The process of checking the rights and privileges assigned to a specific account or group of accounts.

privilege management   The process of restricting a user's ability to interact with the computer system.

process identifier (PID)   A unique identifier for a process thread in the operating system kernel.

public key cryptography   *See* asymmetric encryption.

public key infrastructure (PKI)   Infrastructure for binding a public key to a known user through a trusted intermediary, typically a certificate authority.

qualitative risk assessment   The process of subjectively determining the impact of an event that affects a project, program, or business. It involves the use of expert judgment, experience, or group consensus to complete the assessment.

quantitative risk assessment   The process of objectively determining the impact of an event that affects a project, program, or business. It usually involves the use of metrics and models to complete the assessment.

RADIUS   Remote Authentication Dial-In User Service is a standard protocol for providing authentication services. It is commonly used in dial-up, wireless, and PPP environments.

RAS   *See* Remote Access Service.

RBAC   *See* rule-based access control or role-based access control.

Realtime Blackhole List (RBL)   A system that uses DNS information to detect and dump spam e-mails.

Remote Access Service (RAS)   A combination of hardware and software used to enable remote access to a network.

replay attack   An attack where data is replayed through a system to reproduce a series of transactions.

repudiation   The act of denying that a message was either sent or received.

residual risk   Risks remaining after an iteration of risk management.

risk   The possibility of suffering a loss.

risk assessment or risk analysis   The process of analyzing an environment to identify the threats, vulnerabilities, and mitigating actions to determine (either quantitatively or qualitatively) the impact of an event affecting a project, program, or business.

risk management Overall decision-making process of identifying threats and vulnerabilities and their potential impacts, determining the costs to mitigate such events, and deciding what actions are cost effective to take to control these risks.

role-based access control (RBAC) An access control mechanism in which, instead of the users being assigned specific access permissions for the objects associated with the computer system or network, a set of roles that the user may perform is assigned to each user.

router A network device that operates at the network layer of the OSI model.

rule-based access control (RBAC) An access control mechanism based on rules.

safeguard *See* control.

SAN *See* storage area network.

script kiddies Hackers with little true technical skill and hence use only scripts that someone else developed.

Secure Hash Algorithm (SHA) A hash algorithm used to hash block data. The first version is SHA1, with subsequent versions detailing hash digest length: SHA256, SHA384, and SHA512.

Secure/Multipurpose Internet Mail Extensions (S/MIME) An encrypted implementation of the MIME (Multipurpose Internet Mail Extensions) protocol specification.

Secure Shell (SSH) A set of protocols for establishing a secure remote connection to a computer. This protocol requires a client on each end of the connection and can use a variety of encryption protocols.

Secure Sockets Layer (SSL) An encrypting layer between the session and transport layer of the OSI model designed to encrypt above the transport layer, enabling secure sessions between hosts.

security association (SA) An instance of security policy and keying material applied to a specific data flow. Both IKE and IPsec use SAs, although these SAs are independent of one another. IPsec SAs are unidirectional and are unique in each security protocol, whereas IKE SAs are bidirectional. A set of SAs is needed for a protected data pipe, one SA per direction per protocol. SAs are uniquely identified by destination (IPsec endpoint) address, security protocol (AH or ESP), and security parameter index (SPI).

security baseline The end result of the process of establishing an information system's security state. It is a known good configuration resistant to attacks and information theft.

segregation or separation of duties A basic control that prevents or detects errors and irregularities by assigning responsibilities to different individuals so that no single individual can commit fraudulent or malicious actions.

sequence number A number within a TCP packet to maintain TCP connections and conversation integrity.

service set identifier (SSID) Identifies a specific 802.11 wireless network. It transmits information about the access point to which the wireless client is connecting.

signature database A collection of activity patterns that have already been identified and categorized and that typically indicate suspicious or malicious activity.

Simple Mail Transfer Protocol (SMTP) The standard Internet protocol used to transfer e-mail between hosts.

simple security rule The principle that states complexity makes security more difficult and hence values simplicity.

single loss expectancy (SLE) Monetary loss or impact of each occurrence of a threat. SLE = asset value * exposure factor.

single sign-on (SSO) An authentication process by which the user can enter a single user ID and password and then move from application to application or resource to resource without having to supply further authentication information.

slack space Unused space on a disk drive created when a file is smaller than the allocated unit of storage (such as a sector).

smurf attack An method of generating significant numbers of packets for a DoS attack.

sniffer A software or hardware device used to observe network traffic as it passes through a network on a shared broadcast media.

social engineering   The art of deceiving another person so that he or she reveals confidential information. This is often accomplished by posing as an individual who should be entitled to have access to the information.

spam   E-mail that is not requested by the recipient and is typically of a commercial nature. Also known as unsolicited commercial e-mail (UCE).

spear phishing   A form of targeted phishing where specific information is included to convince the recipient that the communication is genuine.

spoofing   Making data appear to have originated from another source so as to hide the true origin from the recipient.

storage area network (SAN)   A technology-based storage solution consisting of network attached storage.

structured threat   A threat that has reasonable financial backing and can last for a few days or more. The organizational elements allow for greater time to penetrate and attack a system.

subnet mask   The information that tells a device how to interpret the network and host portions of an IP address.

subnetting   The creation of a network within a network by manipulating how an IP address is split into network and host portions.

switch   A network device that operates at the data layer of the OSI model.

SYN flood   A method of performing DoS by exhausting TCP connection resources through partially opening connections and letting them time-out.

symmetric encryption   Encryption that needs all parties to have a copy of the key, sometimes called a shared secret. The single key is used for both encryption and decryption.

tangible asset   An asset for which a monetary equivalent can be determined. Examples are inventory, buildings, cash, hardware, software, and so on.

Tempest   The U.S. military's name for the field associated with electromagnetic eavesdropping on signals emitted by electronic equipment. *See also* van Eck phenomenon.

Temporal Key Integrity Protocol (TKIP)   A security protocol used in 802.11 wireless networks.

threat   Any circumstance or event with the potential to cause harm to an asset.

three-way handshake   A means of ensuring information transference through a three-step data exchange. Used to initiate a TCP connection.

ticket granting server (TGS)   A portion of the Kerberos authentication system.

time bomb   A form of logic bomb in which the triggering event is a date or specific time. *See also* logic bomb.

TKIP   *See* Temporal Key Integrity Protocol.

token   A hardware device that can be used in a challenge-response authentication process.

Transmission Control Protocol (TCP)   The transport layer protocol for use on the Internet that allows packet-level tracking of a conversation.

Transport Layer Security (TLS)   A newer form of SSL being proposed as an Internet standard.

trapdoor   *See* backdoor.

Trojan horse   A form of malicious code that appears to provide one service (and may indeed provide that service) but that also hides another purpose. This hidden purpose often has a malicious intent. This code may also be referred to as simply a Trojan.

trunking   The process of spanning a single VLAN across multiple switches.

Trusted Platform Module (TPM)   A hardware chip to enable trusted computing platform operations.

tunneling   The process of packaging packets so that they can traverse a network in a secure, confidential manner.

uninterruptible power supply (UPS)   A source of power (generally a battery) designed to provide uninterrupted power to a computer system in the event of a temporary loss of power.

unshielded twisted-pair (UTP)   A form of network cabling in which pairs of wires are twisted to reduce crosstalk. Commonly used in LANs.

usage auditing   The process of recording who did what and when on an information system.

User Datagram Protocol (UDP) A protocol in the TCP/IP protocol suite for the transport layer that does not sequence packets—it is "fire and forget" in nature.

user ID A unique alphanumeric identifier that identifies individuals when logging into or accessing a system.

UTP *See* unshielded twisted-pair.

vampire tap A tap that connects to a network line without cutting the connection.

Van Eck phenomenon Electromagnetic eavesdropping through the interception of electronic signals emitted by electrical equipment. *See also* Tempest.

virtual local area network (VLAN) A broadcast domain inside a switched system.

virtual private network (VPN) An encrypted network connection across another network, offering a private communication channel across a public medium.

virus A form of malicious code or software that attaches itself to other pieces of code in order to replicate. Viruses may contain a payload, which is a portion of the code that is designed to execute when a certain condition is met (such as on a certain date). This payload is often malicious in nature.

vishing Phishing over voice circuits, specifically voice over IP (VoIP).

vulnerability A weakness in an asset that can be exploited by a threat to cause harm.

WAP *See* Wireless Application Protocol.

war-dialing An attacker's attempt to gain unauthorized access to a computer system or network by discovering unprotected connections to the system through the telephone system and modems.

war-driving The attempt by an attacker to discover unprotected wireless networks by wandering (or driving) around with a wireless device, looking for available wireless access points.

WEP *See* Wired Equivalent Privacy.

wide area network (WAN) A network that spans a large geographic region.

Wi-Fi Protected Access (WPA/WPA2) A protocol to secure wireless communications using a subset of 802.11i standard.

Wired Equivalent Privacy (WEP) The encryption scheme used to attempt to provide confidentiality and data integrity on 802.11 networks.

Wireless Application Protocol (WAP) A protocol for transmitting data to small handheld devices such as cellular phones.

Wireless Transport Layer Security (WTLS) The encryption protocol used on WAP networks.

worm An independent piece of malicious code or software that self-replicates. Unlike a virus, it does not need to be attached to another piece of code. A worm replicates by breaking into another system and making a copy of itself on this new system. A worm can contain a destructive payload but does not have to.

X.509 The standard format for digital certificates.

XOR Bitwise exclusive OR, an operation commonly used in cryptography.

zombie A machine that is at least partially under the control of a botnet.

INDEX

applications
  bugs, 289
  cryptographic, 108–109
  finding vulnerabilities, 12–13
  hardening, 377–380
  malware, 597
  patches, 377–378
  permissions/privileges, 25
  Trojan horse. *See* Trojan
    horses
  upgrades, 377–378
  viruses, 407
  vulnerabilities, 412, 467–469
APs. *See* access points
archive bit, 497
ARL (authority revocation list), 131
ARP (Address Resolution Protocol),
  213–214
ARP poisoning, 234, 404
ARPANET, 320
AS (authentication server), 263
assets
  acceptable use of, 36–37,
    507–508
  change management, 549
  hiding, 29–30
  identifying, 530
  safeguarding, 548
asymmetric cryptography. *See*
  public key cryptography
asymmetric encryption, 86, 98–101
Asynchronous Transfer Mode
  (ATM), 207, 223
AT commands, 302
ATM (Asynchronous Transfer
  Mode), 207, 223
ATMs (automated teller
  machines), 70
attachments, e-mail, 424
attacks, 388–419. *See also* threats;
  vulnerabilities
  9/11 attack, 603, 626
  address system, 403–404
  application-level, 412–413
  avenues of, 11–14, 389–392
  backdoors, 74, 75, 391, 395
  birthday, 405
  brute-force, 13, 87,
    404–405, 566

buffer overflows, 5, 406,
  456–457, 480–481
covering tracks, 391
cross-site–scripting, 336
DDoS, 393–394, 425
dictionary, 404
DNS system, 403
DoS, 182–183, 212–213,
  392–395
download, 401
on encryption, 402–403
flooding. *See* flooding attacks
hacktivist, 11–14
hybrid, 405
indirect, 403
information gathering, 12–13
man-in-the-middle, 86, 115,
  308, 400
minimizing, 13–14, 391–392
null sessions, 395
password guessing, 404–405
performing, 390–391
pharming, 69–70, 401
phishing, 69–70, 401, 402
ping of death, 325, 393
planning of, 12–13
replay, 400–401
researching vulnerabilities, 390
rootkits, 410
scanning. *See* scanning
smurf, 397–398
sniffing. *See* sniffers
software exploitation, 405–406
spyware, 346, 351, 352, 409
SSL/TLS, 449–451
steps in, 12–13, 389–390
TCP/IP hijacking, 401
terrorist, 9–10, 56, 603
trapdoors, 98, 395
Trojan horses. *See* Trojan
  horses
war-dialing, 307, 413–414
war-driving, 250, 306, 307,
  413–414
Attribute Certificates (ACs), 155, 156
audit capabilities, 362
audit trails, 340
auditability, 22
auditing, 414–415, 550

AUP (acceptable use policy), 36–37,
  507–508
authentication, 261–294. *See also*
  authorization
  802.1x standard, 270–271
  AAA, 261, 271, 274
  access tokens, 195–196,
    198, 199
  basics, 195
  biometric devices/systems,
    55–56, 105, 263
  CCMP, 310–311
  certificates. *See* certificates
  challenge/response, 265,
    272, 280
  CHAP, 279–280
  described, 22, 31, 195, 261,
    262, 268
  Diameter, 271, 273–274
  digital certificates. *See* digital
    certificates
  EAP. *See* EAP
  Kerberos, 263–264
  L2TP, 277, 280–281
  lock/key systems, 263
  m of n, 136
  methods for, 30
  multiple-factor, 198–199, 266
  mutual, 267
  NTLM, 280
  one-way, 105
  overview, 31–32, 105
  PAP, 278, 280
  passwords. *See* passwords
  policies, 32–33
  PPP, 277–278
  PPTP, 172, 277, 278–279
  RADIUS, 271–274
  remote access, 261, 262–267
  servers, 263
  shared secrets, 91–92, 263
  single sign-on, 266–267,
    567–569
  TACACS+, 275–276
  three-factor, 199
  two-factor, 56, 199
  two-way, 105
  user IDs, 31
  vs. access control, 31–32, 54,
    55, 268

Cipher Block Chaining-Message Authentication Coded Protocol (CCMP), 310–311
ciphers, 82–83, 96. *See also specific ciphers*
ciphertext, 82, 87, 298, 299
CIRT (Computer Incidence Response Team), 505, 585
Cisco IOS, 373–375
Cisco NAC (network access control) system, 242
Citibank incident, 2
civil liberties, 609, 632
Clark-Wilson security model, 45
classification of information, 36, 512
clear text, 281, 282, 283, 288
clearance levels, 573–574
click fraud, 597
clients
    certificates stored on, 117
    FTP, 455, 456
    LDAP, 121
    RADIUS, 271–272, 273
client/server networks, 206
client-side extensions (CSEs), 380–381
client-to-server ticket, 264
Clipper chip, 136–137
closed circuit television (CCTV) systems, 189, 190
cloud computing, 503
clusters, 588
CMM (Capability Maturity Model), 553
CMMI (Capability Maturity Model Integration), 553–554
CMP (Certificate Management Protocol), 163–164
CMS (Cryptographic Message Syntax), 167–168
coaxial cables, 245
code. *See also* software development
    HTML, 350, 444
    integrity of, 553
    malicious, 187, 406–413, 423–427
    vulnerabilities, 455–466
code injection, 483–484
code of ethics, 515–516, 611–613

Code of Fair Information Practices, 621
Code Red II worm, 411
Code Red worm, 4–5
code signing, 460, 464–465
cold sites, 501
collision domains, 233, 234
collisions, 89, 90, 233, 234
Common Criteria (CC), 171
Common Gateway Interface (CGI), 461–462
common law, 600
Common Vulnerability and Exposures (CVE), 412, 468
communications security (COMSEC), 21
CompactFlash cards, 254
company confidential information, 36, 43
Computer Emergency Response Team (CERT), 437, 505
Computer Fraud and Abuse Act (CFAA), 600, 602, 603, 622
computer IDs, 262
Computer Incidence Response Team (CIRT), 505, 585
computer mischief, 600–601
computer misuse laws, 603
computer readers, 254
computer rooms, 189
Computer Security Institute (CSI), 11
computer software configuration items, 549
computer trespass, 600–601
computer-assisted crime, 597
computer-incidental crime, 597, 598
computers. *See also* operating systems
    destruction/disposal of, 39–40, 511–512
    disabling unnecessary services, 232
    eavesdropping on, 59–60
    as evidence, 582–586
    firewalls. *See* firewalls
    laptop. *See* laptop computers
    memory, 584
    theft of, 182, 187

    trends, 10
    zombie, 179, 230, 393, 394, 425
computer-targeted crime, 597
COMSEC (communications security), 21
Concept virus, 407
Conficker worm, 6
confidential data, 36, 42–43
confidential security level, 43, 574
confidentiality, 22, 104, 298
confidentiality, integrity, and availability (CIA), 22
confidentiality models, 42–43
configuration
    auditing, 550
    devices, 376–377
    management, 545, 548–549
    services, 376–377
configuration control, 549
configuration identification, 549
configuration items, 549
configuration status accounting, 549–550
consent, 620
Constitution, 38
constrained data items (CDI), 45
consultants, 76
contact information, 14
contactless access cards, 189
content filtering, 335, 336, 353
content protection, 284
Content Scramble System (CSS), 107
content-based signatures, 327, 328
context protection, 284
context-based signatures, 327–328
contractors, 76, 188
Controlling the Assault of Non-Solicited Pornography and Marketing (CAN-SPAM) Act, 353, 429, 603
controls, 25, 526. *See also* access control
Convention on Cybercrime, 601
cookie cutters, 632
cookies, 462–464, 589–590, 634–635
COPPA (Children's Online Privacy Protection Act of 1998), 623
copyright, 610
corporate networks, 221

privacy screens, 61
privacy-enhancing technologies (PETs), 632
private address spaces, 216
private branch exchanges (PBXs), 240
private certificate authorities, 137
private IP addresses, 217–218
private keys
  certificate authority, 135
  certificate verification, 116, 123–124
  compromised, 128
  considerations, 116
  described, 116
  destruction of, 132
  guidelines, 134–135
  key escrow, 105–106, 136–137
  PGP and, 436–437
  protection of, 134–135
  storage of, 133
privileges. *See also* permissions
  applications, 25
  described, 561
  groups, 23–24, 563–564
  least, 24–25, 484–485, 510
  managing, 560–579
  users, 23–24, 561–563
procedures
  described, 34, 51, 506–507
  developing, 52
  implementing, 52
  instruction period, 52
  keeping current, 51–52
  physical security, 53, 184–188
process identifier (PID), 365
profiling, 12
programs. *See* applications; software
promiscuous mode, 323, 337
proof of possession, 127
Proposed Encryption Cipher (PES), 97
proprietary information, 11, 43
Protected Health Information (PHI), 624
protocol analyzers, 336–338
protocols. *See also* standards
  AppleTalk, 207
  ATM, 207
  CC, 171
  CEP, 170
  CHAP, 279–280
  CMP, 162–163

DAP, 453–454
DECnet, 208
described, 207
DHCP, 240
Diameter, 271, 273–274
EAP, 279
EAPOL, 271
e-mail, 421
Ethernet, 208
FDDI, 208
FIPS, 170–171
FTP, 156
HTTP. *See HTTP entries*
HTTPS, 145, 153, 169, 452–453
ICMP, 325
IKE, 163, 286, 289
IKMP, 286
IP. *See* IP
IPsec, 99, 170, 241
IPv4, 237, 288
IPv6, 241, 288
IPX, 208
ISAKMP, 162–163, 286
L2F, 280
L2TP, 277, 280–281
LDAP, 453–454
Needham-Schroeder, 263
Oakley, 286
OCSP, 123
overview, 153–154
PAP, 278, 280
PGP, 168–169
PPP, 277–278
PPTP, 172, 277, 278–279
SKEMI, 286
SNA, 208
SNMP, 234, 242, 243
SS7, 208
SSL. *See SSL entries*
SSL/TLS, 161–162, 446–452, 455
TACACS+, 274–277
TCP/IP, 208, 210, 277, 278, 281
Telnet, 281
Token Ring, 208
VPNs, 283–284
vulnerabilities, 455
WAP, 171
web components, 445–455
WEP. *See* WEP
WTLS, 153, 171, 297, 298
X.25, 208

proxies
  anonymizing, 334
  application layer, 331, 332
  caching, 335
  content filtering, 335
  reverse, 335
  SMTP, 332
  tunneling, 334
  web, 335
proxy servers, 221, 238, 334–336
prudent person principle, 509
ps command, 365, 367
PSH flag, 211
PSTN (public switched telephone network), 53, 278
public algorithms, 84
public certificate authorities, 137–139
public IP addresses, 217–218
public key algorithm, 101
Public Key Certificate. *See* PKC
public key cryptography, 98
Public Key Cryptography Standards. *See* PKCS
public key infrastructures. *See* PKIs
public keys, 116, 120–121, 436–437
public switched telephone network (PSTN), 53, 278
publicly releasable information, 36, 43
pull model, 381

Q

QC (Qualified Certificate), 156
Qualified Certificate (QC), 156
qualitative risk analysis, 533–535
Quest Stat, 549

R

radio frequency (RF) cards/readers, 195–196
radio frequency (RF) waves, 248–249
radio waves, 207
RADIUS (Remote Authentication Dial-In User Service), 271–274
RADIUS accounting, 273–274
RADIUS authorization, 273
RADIUS clients, 271–272, 273
RADIUS servers, 271–274
RAID (Redundant Array of Inexpensive Disks), 504–505
RAs (registration authorities), 115, 116, 118–120, 154

UNCITRAL (United Nations
    Commission on International
    Trade Law), 608
unclassified security level, 43, 574
unconstrained data items (UDI), 45
unerase tools, 586
unguided media, 248–249
Uniform Electronic Commerce Act
    (UECA), 609
Uniform Electronic Transactions Act
    (UETA), 608
uniform resource locators
    (URLs), 444
uninterruptible power supplies
    (UPSs), 57, 502
United Nations Commission on
    International Trade Law
    (UNCITRAL), 608
Universal Serial Bus. *See* USB
UNIX systems
        baselines, 364–366
        discretionary access
            control, 574
        firewalls, 349, 350
        hardening, 364–373
        key stores, 119–120
        passwords, 565
        patches, 366
        removing unnecessary
            programs, 364
        root account, 562
        run levels, 365
        turning services on/off, 365
        user account names, 327
        user accounts, 365–366
unshielded twisted-pair (UTP)
    cables, 245–247
unsolicited commercial e-mail, 603
unstructured threats, 8
updates, 348, 373–376, 412
upgrades, application, 377–378
UPSs (uninterruptible power
    supplies), 57, 502
urban legends, 70, 422
URG flag, 211
URLs (uniform resource
    locators), 444
U.S. Air Force, 319
U.S. Banking Rules and Regulations,
    625–626
U.S. Department of Defense, 319
U.S. Electric Power Grid
    incident, 5–6

U.S. Federal Trade Commission,
    619–620
U.S. government
        classification of
            information, 36
        encryption controls, 631
U.S. laws
        administrative law, 600
        common law, 600
        cybercrime, 601–604
        digital signatures, 608
        encryption regulations, 606
        import/export, 606
        legislative laws, 600
        privacy, 583, 601–602, 618,
            620–628
        sources of, 600
        statutory laws, 600
USA Patriot Act, 602, 603, 626
USB boot device, 254–255
USB devices, 180, 186–187
USB drive keys, 187
USB drivers, 187
USB keys, 107
USB ports, 254
USB sticks, 254, 255
user accounts
        administrator, 562
        expired, 569
        Linux systems, 371
        Mac systems, 373
        Solaris systems, 369
        UNIX systems, 365–366
        Windows, 362
User Datagram Protocol. *See* UDP
user IDs, 262, 265–267
        as authentication
            mechanism, 30
        described, 561
        single sign-on authentication,
            567–569
        vs. usernames, 561
useradd command, 369, 371
user-defined filtering, 353
userdel command, 371
usernames, 561–562
users. *See also* employees
        chain of custody, 587–588
        described, 561
        disgruntled, 40, 41, 53
        end-entities, 154–155, 164
        guest, 568
        identity verification, 55

        implicit deny policy, 26
        job rotation, 26
        names, 561–562
        need-to-know principle,
            39, 510
        permissions, 570
        physical location, 60–61
        privileges, 23–24, 561–563
        rights, 562, 570–571
        security awareness, 76
        security responsibilities, 77
        shoulder surfing and, 61,
            70–71
        superusers, 562
        time-of-day restrictions, 568
utilities, 214
UTP (unshielded twisted-pair)
    cables, 245–247

■ V

vacations, mandatory, 42, 515
van Eck, Wim, 59–60
van Eck phenomenon, 59–60
verification, certificate authorities,
    121–124
VeriSign, 137, 170
version control, 545
version number, 124
Video Privacy Protection Act
    (VPPA), 623
video recorders, 190
video surveillance, 55
Vigenère cipher, 85–86
virtual LANs (VLANs), 206, 222–223
virtual networks, 339
virtual private networks. *See* VPNs
virtualization, 232
virus signatures, 348
viruses, 406–408. *See also* worms
        applications, 407
        boot sector, 406–407
        Concept virus, 407
        e-mail, 346–348, 421, 423–424
        encryption in, 346–347
        evolution of, 424
        on floppy disks, 423
        Good Times virus, 408
        hoaxes, 408
        ILOVEYOU, 4
        macro, 3–4, 407
        Melissa virus, 3–4
        over networks, 423–424
        overview, 7, 230